Truth About Trade

Reflections on International Trade and Law

Truth About Trade

Reflections on International Trade and Law

James Bacchus
University of Central Florida, USA

World Scientific

NEW JERSEY · LONDON · SINGAPORE · BEIJING · SHANGHAI · HONG KONG · TAIPEI · CHENNAI · TOKYO

Published by

World Scientific Publishing Co. Pte. Ltd.

5 Toh Tuck Link, Singapore 596224

USA office: 27 Warren Street, Suite 401-402, Hackensack, NJ 07601

UK office: 57 Shelton Street, Covent Garden, London WC2H 9HE

Library of Congress Cataloging-in-Publication Data
Names: Bacchus, Jim, 1949– author.
Title: Truth about trade : reflections on international trade and law /
    James Bacchus, University of Central Florida, USA.
Description: New Jersey, NJ : World scientific, [2024] | Includes bibliographical references and index.
Identifiers: LCCN 2023039675 | ISBN 9789811282102 (hardcover) |
    ISBN 9789811282119 (ebook for institutions) | ISBN 9789811282126 (ebook for individuals)
Subjects: LCSH: International trade. | International law.
Classification: LCC HF1379 .B323 2024 | DDC 382--dc23/eng/20230925
LC record available at https://lccn.loc.gov/2023039675

British Library Cataloguing-in-Publication Data
A catalogue record for this book is available from the British Library.

Copyright © 2024 by World Scientific Publishing Co. Pte. Ltd.

All rights reserved. This book, or parts thereof, may not be reproduced in any form or by any means, electronic or mechanical, including photocopying, recording or any information storage and retrieval system now known or to be invented, without written permission from the publisher.

For photocopying of material in this volume, please pay a copying fee through the Copyright Clearance Center, Inc., 222 Rosewood Drive, Danvers, MA 01923, USA. In this case permission to photocopy is not required from the publisher.

For any available supplementary material, please visit
https://www.worldscientific.com/worldscibooks/10.1142/13564#t=suppl

Desk Editors: Soundararajan Raghuraman/Yulin Jiang

Typeset by Stallion Press
Email: enquiries@stallionpress.com

Printed in Singapore

*To my brother Tom and my sisters Debby, Cindy, and Terri,
with love and fond remembrance of all our good times together*

About the Author

James Bacchus is Distinguished University Professor of Global Affairs and Director of the Center for Global Economic and Environmental Opportunity at the University of Central Florida. He was a founding judge and was twice the chairman — the chief judge — of the highest tribunal of world trade, the Appellate Body of the World Trade Organization in Geneva, Switzerland. He is a former Member of the Congress of the United States, from Florida, and a former international trade negotiator for the United States. He is the author of the books *Trade and Freedom* (Cameron May, 2004); *The Willing World: Shaping and Sharing a Sustainable Global Prosperity* (Cambridge University Press, 2018); *The Development Dimension: Special and Differential Treatment in Trade*, with co-author Inu Manak (Routledge Press, 2021); and *Trade Links: New Rules for a New World* (Cambridge University Press, 2022). He is a Senior Research Fellow of the Earth System Governance Project, Global Fellow of the Centre for International Governance Innovation, Adjunct Scholar of the Cato Institute, Distinguished Fellow of the European Institute of International Law and International Relations, Senior Fellow of the Centre for International Sustainable Development Law, Distinguished Global Fellow of the Hellenic Foundation for European and Foreign Policy, and life member of the Council on Foreign Relations. He has been a Visiting Fellow at the Lauterpacht Centre for International Law and Wolfson College of the University of Cambridge in the United Kingdom. He is a leading advocate and activist worldwide for international cooperation, international trade, the international rule of law, global democracy, and global sustainable development.

Contents

About the Author — vii

Introduction — xi

Chapter 1   Truth About Trade: Dispelling the Beltway Myths About the World Trade Organization — 1

Chapter 2   Biden and Trade at Year One: The Reign of Polite Protectionism — 23

Chapter 3   Reviving the WTO: Five Priorities for Liberalization — 73

Chapter 4   Some But Not (Yet) All: Plurilateral Agreements and the Future of the World Trade Organization — 119

Chapter 5   The High Price of Buying American: The Harms of Domestic Content Mandates — 151

Chapter 6   Democrats and Trade: A Pro-Trade Policy for the Democratic Party — 181

Chapter 7   The Black Hole of National Security: Striking the Right Balance for the National Security Exception in International Trade — 213

Chapter 8 Might Unmakes Right: The American Assault
           on the Rule of Law in World Trade   235

Chapter 9 The Digital Decide: How to Agree on WTO
           Rules for Digital Trade   287

Chapter 10 TRIPS-Past to TRIPS-Plus: Upholding the
           Balance Between Exclusivity and Access   339

Chapter 11 A Common Gauge: Harmonization and
           International Law   365

Chapter 12 Appellators: The Quest for the Meaning of And/Or   383

Chapter 13 The Garden   411

Chapter 14 Turning to Tacitus   455

Index   473

Introduction

At first, when I was asked by World Scientific Publishing if I would be interested in submitting some of my previously uncollected essays on international trade and international law for publication, I demurred. I explained that I doubted whether I had written a sufficient number of essays since leaving the Appellate Body of the World Trade Organization to comprise a collection. Then, while on a long airplane flight, I made from memory a list of, to my surprise, several dozen essays I had written and published since then that had not been included in my previous books. I chose the fourteen essays that are collected here for two reasons. First, they are broadly representative of all I have written since leaving the WTO about the need to continue lowering barriers to international trade and about the necessity of upholding trade rules and other international rules through the international rule of law. Second, although some of these essays were written some time ago, the issues they address remain current, and so do many of the points I have made in them. I continue to write as part of my way of continuing to serve the public purposes to which I have now devoted many years during a life of public service. Perhaps, in another several years, there will be another such collection of my writing. In the meantime, I offer these essays as one contribution to the ongoing global debate about the facts and the fates of international trade and international law. My favorite among them — for readers who may not always make it all the way to the end — are the final two, "The Garden" (on the unacceptability of torture) and

"Turning to Tacitus" (on the sometimes-high price of freedom). I hope you will enjoy and benefit from reading them all.

James Bacchus
Orlando, Florida
June, 2023

Chapter 1

Truth About Trade: Dispelling the Beltway Myths About the World Trade Organization*

Introduction

There are myths throughout the world about the World Trade Organization. In much of the world, the WTO is believed to be a creation of the United States, imposed on other countries — and especially poorer developing countries — through a calculated exercise of the considerable economic leverage of the United States, and intended to bring the rest of the world to heel in embracing American ways and heeding American wishes in the conduct and course of world trade. WTO rules are thought in many other countries to be mainly American rules, even though every WTO rule that applies to all WTO members has been agreed by all WTO members in successive rounds of multilateral trade negotiations. Ignoring this reality, the myth about the WTO in much of the world is that "the Americans are making us do it."

This belief beyond the borders of the United States is only myth, but it is closer to the truth about trade than the contrasting myth that prevails within the borders of the United States, and especially within the Washington Beltway, where national decisions on trade policy are made

---

*An abbreviated version of this essay was previously published by the Cato Institute as "The World Trade Organization: Myths versus Reality" (September 26, 2023).

and implemented. Within the Beltway — in the Congress, in the executive branch, in the media, and in many of the trade associations, think tanks, and NGOs that strive to influence trade policy — the WTO is increasingly believed to be, at best, a misguided mistake by the United States in foreign commercial policy, or, at worst, a conspiracy by other countries against the United States, a "globalist" creation designed to constrain the United States from freedom of action in its domestic and international commerce, and to reduce American manufacturing and other economic might with the aim of diminishing the current extent of American say and sway in international trade and in the overall world economy.

More and more, within the Beltway, the WTO as an international institution is being pushed to the periphery of trade debates, and WTO rules and rulings are being ignored in trade decision-making, with reverberating harmful repercussions throughout the WTO-based multilateral trading system as other countries suffer from unilateral US trade discrimination and as some countries begin to emulate the scofflaw practices of the United States in international trade. This is happening because the prevailing suspicion in both major US political parties is that the WTO is an international institution that has somehow been imposed on the United States and is bent on undermining the United States through the application of unfair trade rules rigged against American goods and services. This, too, is only myth, symptomatic of the short-term memory that characterizes much public policy-making; but it is a powerful myth that is politically potent, one that rationalizes the recent retreat by the United States into self-defeating trade protectionism by deceiving Americans into thinking about the WTO that "the foreigners are making us do it."

The myths about the World Trade Organization that are increasingly assumed to be facts by many within the Beltway, are numerous and too many to recount here. These myths relate to the WTO as an institution, to the ways the WTO makes rules, and to the ways it upholds rules through international trade dispute settlement. These myths are much in need of dispelling as a necessary prelude to the return to a rational US policy of expanding trade with the goal of expanding the potential for human flourishing through shared prosperity. Some of these myths deserving of dispelling follow. With each, the misconception of the myth is dispelled by the truth about trade as it relates to the WTO and to the rules the WTO makes and upholds for the purpose of adding to the flow of trade, and thus to the potential economic gains from trade, throughout the United States and throughout all the rest of the world economy.

Myth # 1 — The WTO is part of a global plot to create a world government

To anyone at all acquainted with the day-to-day reality of the World Trade Organization, the very thought of the WTO as some kind of would-be "world government" is laughable. The WTO is not a government of any kind, and no one anywhere who is involved with the WTO has even the remoted desire to make it one. The WTO is a creation and an expression of *internationalism*, which assumes and proceeds from the existence of sovereign nation-states in a system of international governance dating back to the Treaty of Westphalia in 1648. In contrast, the *globalism* that might seek a "world government" transcends the existence of nation-states and contemplates a borderless world. The irony of anti-WTO sentiment is that the more that Westphalian international institutions are undermined, the more the temptation exists to seek as an alternative another and perhaps "globalist" form of global governance.

Entirely separate from the United Nations, the WTO is an international economic organization *consisting of governments* that has been established by an international agreement *among those governments*. It is a forum where governments can agree by consensus to establish rules that can lower international barriers to trade, and it is a way for governments to ensure compliance with those rules when disputes arise between them about what they mean. As the WTO website explains, "The overall objective of the WTO is to help its members use trade as a means to raise living standards, create jobs and improve people's lives. The WTO operates the global system of trade rules and helps developing countries build their trade capacity. It also provides a forum for its members to negotiate trade agreements and to resolve the trade problems they face with each other."[1]

Myth # 2 — The United States has no choice but to be a member of the WTO

No country is compelled to sign the WTO agreement and become a member of the WTO. The WTO is a *voluntary* organization. Every member of the WTO is a member by choice. Furthermore, under the WTO agreement, every member of the WTO can withdraw from membership with six months of notice.[2] Yet, no member has ever withdrawn from the WTO for a very simple reason — every member desires the many economic benefits that come with being a WTO member. From time to time, a few members of the United States Congress introduce proposals to withdraw the United States from the WTO, but they never pass.[3] Former President Donald Trump threatened from time to time to withdraw the United States from the WTO, but he never did.[4] Even some in the Trump administration must have recognized (and maybe even had the temerity to tell Trump) that the economic price of withdrawal from WTO membership would be too high. For, in the absence of the shelter and benefits of binding WTO rules, the result would be a worldwide free-for-all of discrimination against US trade and the restoration of myriad high tariffs and other high non-tariff barriers to US exports that have been eliminated during decades of WTO multilateral trade negotiations and agreements. Other countries seem of the same mind. At present, there are 164 members of the WTO, accounting altogether for about 98 percent of all world commerce.

Myth # 3 — The WTO is a "free trade" organization

The WTO is not a "free trade" organization. Indeed, the phrase "free trade" appears nowhere in the WTO agreement. Instead, as, again, is explained on the WTO website, "The WTO provides a forum for negotiating agreements aimed at reducing obstacles to international trade and ensuring a level playing field for all, thus contributing to economic growth and development."[5] As is further specified on the WTO website, "The fundamental goal of the WTO is to improve the welfare of people around the world. The WTO's founding Marrakesh Agreement recognizes that trade should be conducted with a view to raising standards of living, ensuring full employment, increasing real income and expanding global trade in goods and services while allowing for the optimal use of the world's resources."[6] Very often, achieving this goal means freeing trade; but, in many cases, it can also mean erecting tariffs and other barriers against unfair trade where there is dumping by private companies (basically, selling in the target market at below the cost of production in the home market, with injurious results) or subsidies by governments that cause injury by distorting the marketplace. The past three-quarters of a century have largely been devoted by the members of the WTO to lowering barriers to trade by mutual agreement. The WTO has long been a multilateral means for achieving freer trade; but this has been because the members of the WTO have long wanted it to serve that purpose. There is nothing in the WTO agreement that requires countries to lower their tariffs and other trade barriers unless they have freely chosen and agreed to do so.

Myth # 4 — The WTO aims to fulfill a "neoliberal" agenda of laissez faire and "free market fundamentalism" that mandates the removal of all international barriers to trade

It is sometimes said by critics of the WTO that the purpose of the organization is to implement worldwide a "neoliberal" agenda that would eliminate all governmental restrictions and regulations on trade as part of imposing "free market fundamentalism." These critics characterize and castigate the WTO as a "neo-liberal" enterprise aimed at instilling a strict *laissez faire* — a rigid policy of hands-off that privatizes public services, rips holes in the social safety net, and shuns local governmental laws or regulations that might impede the unrestricted flow of global commerce. The truth is, there is nothing in the WTO agreement that requires this or aspires to this. The WTO agreement is replete with places in which all kinds of domestic governmental regulations are assumed. The concern in the context of the trade rules in the WTO agreement is not with *whether* governmental regulations are imposed; rather, it is with *how those regulations affect trade*. If those regulations do not affect trade, then WTO rules are not relevant, and there is no justification for the WTO to be involved. If those regulations do affect trade but do not involve trade discrimination, then there is usually no WTO concern. However, if, as written or as applied, those regulations affect trade in ways that cause discrimination against imported products, or between and among imported products, then they may be inconsistent with a member's obligations under the WTO agreement. In such a case, the WTO agreement provides that the WTO has legal jurisdiction, and the member country whose products are discriminated against, can have recourse to the legal mechanism of WTO dispute settlement.

Myth # 5 — The WTO is not a "neoliberal" free trade organization but rather an organization committed to state-directed economic outcomes through "managing trade"

Senator John Hawley of Missouri, among others, has accused the WTO of performing "the role of managing the world economy," including world trade.[7] In truth, the WTO is no more an organization committed to "managed trade" than it is one committed to "free trade." The extent to which WTO agreements and the rules contained within them either "manage" trade by limiting it or "free" trade by opening it, is a matter entirely for decision-making by the WTO members in their ongoing negotiations. For example, the members have decided that state trading enterprises — a form of managed trade — are permitted under WTO rules so long as they "act in a manner consistent with the general principles of non-discrimination" in the WTO agreement.[8] The WTO members have also decided that, so long as they follow certain standards and procedures set out in WTO rules, members will remain free to apply trade restrictions to counter what they perceive to be unfair trade practices. WTO rules are only a reflection of the collective cooperative will of the WTO members themselves. The members can decide to lower or eliminate tariffs and other obstacles to trade, or they can decide to keep them. The WTO agreement leaves it to individual countries to set their own trade and other economic policies. The WTO is simply an international legal framework for enabling the multilateral making of trade decisions by the 164 countries and other customs territories that have agreed of their own choosing to participate in the framework.

Myth # 6 — The WTO undermines the sovereignty of the United States

The WTO does not undermine the sovereignty of the United States or any other member of the WTO. The WTO is frequently called a "member-driven" organization because (in contrast to some other international institutions) it is an institution that can only act when and if and how its members choose to act. In fact, the entity called "the WTO" is really nothing more nor less than its members choosing to act as something they have chosen to describe as "the WTO." (It is politically convenient back home throughout the word to pretend, when acting pursuant to a WTO obligation or ruling, that "the WTO" is some alien and overweening Leviathan compelling such action; but this is not so.) True, there are about 620 people — mostly economists, lawyers, translators, and administrative staff — working for the WTO members in an ornate Italianate building on the shore of Lac Leman in Geneva, Switzerland, which is adorned with an ornate sign labeled "the WTO." But none of these people can take any action that binds the organization other than the most basic ministerial and administrative tasks. Only the members of the WTO acting together — usually by consensus — can take actions that affect international trade.

This is not an undermining of their sovereignty. This is an exercise of their sovereignty; for each of the 164 WTO members has made a sovereign choice that participating in the WTO is in their sovereign interest. We Americans have made this choice knowing that, as trade scholar Daniel Griswold has aptly put it, "Trade agreements do not limit our freedom as individual Americans. They are written to limit the power of governments to interfere in the peaceful commerce of their citizens. By limiting the scope of government action, trade agreements actually enhance the liberty and prosperity of the people living in the participating countries."[9]

Myth # 7 — The WTO harms the American economy

According to Donald Trump, "The WTO…was set up for the benefit for everybody but us. They have taken advantage of this country like you wouldn't believe."[10] This is the ascendant and bipartisan Beltway myth. The truth is, according to a study by the Bertelsmann Foundation in Germany, the GDP of the United States has been increased by about $87 billion since the establishment of the WTO in 1995 — *more than any other country.* Every member of the WTO has benefited from their membership in the multilateral trading system since then; but the United States has benefited more than all the rest.[11] A study done for the Business Roundtable found that international trade supports nearly 39 million American jobs. One in every five American jobs is linked to imports and exports of goods and services. In the first twenty-five years following the establishment of the WTO, trade-dependent jobs grew more than four times as fast as US jobs generally. Every one of the fifty US states realized net job gains that can be directly attributed to trade.[12]

In another trade study, economists at the Peterson Institute for International Economics estimated "that the payoff to the United States from trade expansion — stemming from policy liberalization and links to the global economy and improved transportation and communications technology — from 1950 to 2016 (was) roughly $2.1 trillion … (and) that US GDP per capita and GDP per household accordingly increased by $7,014 and $18,131, respectively."[13] Further, "disproportionate gains probably accrue(d) to poorer households."[14] The truth is, domestically, the United States has done a poor job since the turn of the century of making certain that the American people widely benefit from the considerable gains the United States has garnered overall from trade. This, however, is a failure of the politicians in both political parties in the United States. It is not the necessary economic result of freer trade or the fault of the WTO, which, quite rightly, does not make decisions about how the gains from trade are distributed domestically by WTO members. Those sovereign decisions are made, as they should be, by the WTO members themselves. Do we want the WTO deciding what the marginal tax rates should be in the United States? Of course not.

Myth # 8 — *The WTO is biased against the United States*

Because the WTO is "member-driven," the truth is, there is no entity called the "WTO" that can be biased against anyone, including the United States. Moreover, the international civil servants who work for the members on the WTO Secretariat shed their nationality as soon as they cross the threshold of the WTO. They are, by definition and in practice, unbiased and bound by a mandatory set of ethics rules that keeps them so. Therefore, what this assertion is really saying is that *other countries* are biased against the United States. All countries have their biases, some more than others. The United States itself is not universally popular with all other countries all the time. In part, this is the price of global leadership; in part, this is because of some of America's best geopolitical actions; in part, too, it must be said, this is because of some of America's recent geopolitical mistakes.

The United States also has its biases against a few other countries (with some, rightly so). Yet, 164 countries of all geopolitical views have agreed to cooperate on trade matters by signing the WTO agreement. The United States has long agreed that such cooperation is necessary. The WTO members can make trade rules that bind all members only by consensus. The United States can, if it wishes, block that consensus; it can only be bound legally by rules with which it has agreed. Dating back decades, though, the far bigger problem for the United States has been that other countries have sometimes refused to go along with the new rules that the US has sought for world trade as the world economy has evolved and changed.

One charge made by some critics is that the United States (and other developed countries) suffer because WTO rules are biased against all developed countries and are tilted toward developing countries. In his own unique and jejune style, former President Trump voiced this sentiment on Twitter in this way: "The WTO is BROKEN when the world's RICHEST countries claim to be developing countries to avoid WTO rules and get special treatment. No more!!!"[15] The assumption in this statement is that developing countries are profiting from being in the WTO while developed countries are not. The results of the Bertelsmann study refute this; so do many other economic studies based on the evidence of the facts of actual performance. Being in the WTO is an economic "win-win" for all its members.

True, the least developed countries — currently 47 countries with less than $1025 in per capita income — are generally given "special and differential treatment" that has frequently excused them from trade liberalization. This is not, in fact, in their economic interest; but, because the economies of these countries are so small, this is hardly a policy that causes economic harm to the United States.[16] Also, developing countries that have entered higher stages of development — such as China — still claim to be entitled to "special and differential treatment." Yet, this claimed status is not especially benefiting China, Brazil, India, or other larger developing countries in the WTO.[17] The whole concept of "special and differential treatment" has failed because, as my co-author Inu Manak and I concluded in our book *The Development Dimension*, "it is based on the premise that the growth of developing countries will be hastened if they postpone opening their markets to freer trade for as long as they can."[18] The opposite is true. The truth is, the entire notion of "special and differential treatment" should be revisited by the members of the WTO, for the sake of developed and developing countries alike.

Myth # 9 — Through the operation of the rules in the WTO agreement, the WTO has "police power" to impose its will on sovereign countries

The WTO cannot do anything unless its members agree to it. There are no black WTO helicopters. There are no blue WTO helmets. There is no WTO "police force." The WTO has a legal identity in international law only for the limited and practical purposes of providing office space; retaining employees; purchasing pens, paper, and computers; and keeping the cafeteria open and the windows clean. The WTO has an annual budget of about $220 million, a small sum by global standards, which is contributed by members based on their proportion of international trade each year. Because the United States has the largest proportion of international trade and thus contributes the most to the WTO budget, it chairs the WTO budget committee, which makes all financial decisions for the organization.[19]

Moreover, all members of the WTO — including the United States — can choose to ignore WTO rules and WTO rulings if they wish. That is their sovereign right. As a matter of principle, and consistently with their collective interest in the success of the enterprise of making and upholding international law, no country should exercise this right. Every country should respect — as the United States Constitution puts it — "the law of nations"[20] by complying with all international law, including the international trade law in the WTO agreement. However, if WTO members so choose, they remain free to subvert international law by ignoring WTO rules and rulings — if they are willing to accept the loss of previously granted trade concessions that is the price for making such a choice, as has been set out and agreed by all WTO members in the WTO agreement. This price can sometimes total billions of dollars of lost trade benefits annually, which has usually proven a strong incentive for WTO members to comply with the rules and the rulings.

Myth # 10 — WTO rules do not allow sovereign countries the "policy space" they need to address, health, safety, environment, and other important domestic issues

Critics of the WTO talk much about "policy space" — about the concept of a sovereign "space" reserved for domestic policymaking, a "space" that is beyond the reach of international economic rules and rulings by international institutions such as the WTO. Many of them fear that the WTO, in service to selfish and shortsighted multinational corporate interests, will overrule numerous local laws and local regulations that serve other vital, non-commercial societal values, and establish higher standards than those that avail in the rest of the world. And this, it is widely feared, will lead, if trade is allowed to trump all else, to tainted "Frankenfoods," other toxic products, diminished labor protections, shrinking public services, and a long list of harmful risks to public health, public safety, the environment, and much more. These critics fear that WTO rules and rulings will undermine local efforts to guard against these risks by overturning existing laws and by having a "chilling effect" on the enactment of needed new laws.[21]

None of this is true. The truth is, WTO rules allow considerably more local policy space than many WTO critics realize or, in some cases, will admit. National "measures" — domestic laws, regulations, and practices — are unlikely to be inconsistent with WTO rules so long as they provide an equal competitive opportunity in the domestic marketplace for all like foreign and domestic products. The basic WTO rules on trade in goods generally intrude on the reserve of the sovereign "right to regulate" only if local laws or regulations discriminate between and among like traded products, either in favor of domestic over foreign products or in favor of some foreign products over others.[22] Much the same is true in the reservation of policy space under the WTO rules on trade in services. The services rules, to cite just one instance, allow ample room for domestic regulation of financial services for "prudential reasons... to ensure the integrity and the stability of the financial system."[23]

Likewise, although intellectual property rights must be protected under the WTO rules, considerable latitude is allowed to WTO Members, if done consistently with those rules, to provide such protection "in a manner conducive to social and economic welfare," and "to promote the public interest" through domestic measures that "protect public health and nutrition" and promote "socio-economic and technological development...."[24] Moreover, the WTO rules on technical regulations generally limit local regulations only if they discriminate between and among like traded products, or if they create unnecessary obstacles to international trade or are more trade-restrictive than necessary to fulfill a legitimate objective.[25]

Similarly, the rules on "sanitary and phytosanitary" measures specify that WTO Members have the right to take measures that are necessary for the protection of human, animal, or plant life or health.[26] Such so-called "SPS" measures must, however, be based on a risk assessment and on scientific principles, and must not be maintained without sufficient scientific evidence.[27] In addition, such local health and safety measures must be applied only to the extent necessary to achieve their purposes; and they must not involve arbitrary or unjustifiable discrimination, or be applied in a manner which constitutes a disguised restriction on international trade.[28] Would we Americans, for example, want to maintain health and safety measures that are not based on a risk assessment and sufficient scientific evidence? Many of us have forgotten that it was the United States that insisted on these rules when the WTO was established.

Myth # 11 — WTO rules cause a global "race to the bottom" in environmental protection

WTO critics also maintain that WTO rules encourage a "race to the bottom" in a competition to lower environmental standards worldwide.[29] This, too, is not true. Economists have mostly concluded that international trade is, overall, beneficial for the environment. One reason they usually give for this conclusion is that, in adding to economic growth, trade adds also to the tax revenues available for paying for more effective environmental protection. In addition, there is the positive environmental payoff from the elongation of Adam Smith's division of labor and from the application of David Ricardo's concept of comparative advantage. By encouraging more specialization, freer trade increases productivity. This, in turn, enhances the ability to expand production while employing relatively fewer resources, and thus improves the efficiency of the overall allocation and use of resources, which, with the right domestic policies in place, should limit environmental harm. As the distinguished trade economist Jagdish Bhagwati has said, "Efficient policies, such as freer trade, should generally help the environment, not hurt it."[30] Furthermore, there is empirical evidence that — over time — a rising income in a country, results in rising environmental protection. Economists call this the "Environmental Kuznets Curve." At first, in the early stages of development, as incomes start to increase, environmental degradation increases as well. But then, as incomes continue to rise, "Eventually environmental degradation peaks. It then begins a steep descent as economy and incomes continue to grow."[31]

Despite this evidence, there is, however, a widespread fear in developed countries such as the United States that freeing trade and foreign direct investment leads, inevitably, to fleeing jobs as producers — in search of sanctuary from environmental regulation — shift jobs from developed countries to dirty "pollution havens" in developing countries.[32] Following from this fear is a widespread belief that lowering barriers to trade leads, unavoidably, to pressure everywhere to reduce environmental standards. The assumption is that developed countries will lower their standards to keep jobs, and that developing countries will lower their standards to get jobs. This belief inspires all the endless talk by the opponents of liberalizing trade of a so-called global "race to the bottom" in environmental protection. Especially in the United States and in the European Union, the "race to the bottom" is a staple of political stump speeches along the campaign trail. Few of those seeking or holding elected office ever bother to question it.

But it turns out that, in truth, there is "very little evidence" that we are seeing a "race to the bottom."[33] In particular, "there is actually little evidence that polluting industries relocate to jurisdictions with lower environmental standards in order to reduce compliance costs."[34] The empirical research thus far, as distilled in a study done for the World Bank, "has found little or no evidence that pollution intensive industry is systematically migrating to jurisdictions with weak environmental policy; hence maintaining a weak environmental policy regime appears to have little effect on a country's comparative advantage. Other factors such as labor productivity, capital abundance, and proximity to markets are much more important in determining firm location and output."[35]

In describing the "race to the bottom" as a "non-existent threat," the American political scientist Daniel Drezner, who has focused a good deal of his scholarship on international trade, has been blunt: "The race-to-the-bottom hypothesis appears logical. But it is wrong. Indeed, the lack of supporting evidence is startling."[36] He contends that, despite the generalized fears, "there is no indication that the reduction of controls on trade and capital flows has forced a generalized downgrading in labor or environmental conditions. If anything, the opposite has occurred."[37] Detzner observes that the countries that are the most open to trade and investment — the OECD countries — have the highest environmental standards, and that a number of developing countries have raised their environmental standards even as they have become more open to trade and investment.

Myth # 12 — The WTO offers no remedies for the trade and other commercial abuses of the "state capitalism" of China, nor does it offer any redress for unfair trade practices in many areas of the new "21st century" economy

Another prevailing myth about the WTO within the Beltway is that WTO rules are antiquated and therefore not up to the contemporary task of disciplining the trade and other commercial abuses of the state-directed version of capitalism of China. This is not true. It is true that, in a number of respects, China's economic rise poses a unique challenge to the world trading system. Yet, WTO dispute settlement has more potential to address China's practices than is understood within the Beltway or has been employed by the United States.[38] A lengthy list of legal claims could be made by the United States against an array of abusive Chinese trade practice *under existing WTO rules.*³⁹ Four promising areas of WTO complaints against China under existing WTO rules are general intellectual property protection and enforcement; trade secrets protection; forced technology transfer; and subsidies. The case is waiting to be made against by the United States or by some other country or group of countries in WTO dispute settlement; but, so far, it has not been brought to the dispute settlement system.

This is not to say that current WTO rules should not be improved or that new WTO rules should not be negotiated and agreed that could do more to help counter the challenge posed by China to the multilateral trading system. They should be. But the means of accomplishing this (admittedly difficult) end is not by ignoring the WTO and WTO rules; it is by employing those rules in dispute settlement and by giving priority to negotiating new and improved rules within the WTO. (And, by the way, it is also a myth that China routinely ignores adverse WTO rulings; in fact, given US foot-dragging all along and its recent bipartisan recalcitrance, China may have a better record of complying with adverse WTO rulings than the United States.⁴⁰)

This is also not to say that WTO rules do not need to be broadened while being modernized. Indeed, they do. The fundamental non-discrimination principles of the WTO are timeless, and most WTO rules are still mostly current and fit for purpose. However, on digital trade, trade in medical goods, trade in environmental goods and services, investment facilitation, the relationship between trade and climate change, and much more that has emerged into the forefront of the world economy since the establishment of the WTO in the last decade before the turn of the century, there is pressing need for more and better rules. As it is, for example, the WTO has no specific rules on digital trade. How, then, can the WTO expect to remain relevant, much less central, to world trade in this century? Yet, on this, too, the answer is not to set aside the WTO; the answer is to seize the opportunity once again to use it in negotiating and agreeing on the new and improved trade rules the world much needs.⁴¹

Myth # 13 — The United States has lost all its cases in WTO dispute settlement

President Trump told Americans that "we lose the lawsuits, almost all the lawsuits in the WTO," and many Americans, including many decision-makers within the Beltway, believe him.⁴² The truth is that, quite the contrary, the United States has *won* the vast majority of the cases it has brought as a complainant in WTO dispute settlement (including the overwhelming majority of the cases it has brought against China).[43] US wins in the WTO are, however, discounted politically in the American trade debate because, of course, the United States, being the United States, is, in the US view, *supposed* to win the cases it takes to the WTO. In its winning record, the United States is like other WTO members. Out of more than 600 international trade disputes so far, complaining countries have won about 90 percent of the cases they have taken to WTO dispute settlement. For the most part, this is because countries tend not to undertake the laborious task of filing a complaint against another country in WTO dispute settlement, with all the costs and geopolitical consequences that sometimes result, unless they believe they have a strong legal case that can be made.

In contrast, the United States — again like other WTO members — has *lost* most of the cases that have been brought against it in WTO dispute settlement. Many of these losses could have been avoided. Many of the cases the United States has lost have involved the expansive American use of anti-dumping duties, countervailing duties to governmental subsidies, and other trade retaliations that are generally known as "trade remedies." In these cases, the US has pushed past the legal boundaries of some of the WTO rules relating to the conditions and the procedures for applying such trade restrictions — rules which the US had much say in negotiating and with which it agreed when the WTO was established. A number of these lost trade remedies cases have involved the same legal issues and similar challenged US measures because the United States has, in an exercise of its sovereignty, chosen not to comply with these WTO trade remedies rulings, often by construing them in the narrowest possible way or by dragging its administrative feet while purporting to comply. In general, the United States seeks much broader latitude in applying trade remedies than WTO rules allow. Because of the political salience of this issue for both US political parties, namely the desire of both parties to win votes in swing states where trade protectionism is popular, these losses are the source of much of the reactive angst of the US to these outcomes in WTO dispute settlement. The existence of this angst is not, however, evidence that, in ruling against the United States in these trade remedies cases, WTO jurists have, as the US alleges, been wrong.[44]

Myth # 14 — It is always bad when the United States loses a case in the WTO

In the narrow context of the discreet dispute at issue involving a certain product and a certain group of producers, losing a WTO case may well be seen by those immediately affected by the ruling as bad. But each WTO case can be seen as two cases. One case is about the product immediately affected by the dispute. The other case is about the meaning of the WTO rules that are invoked by the legal claims made in the dispute. Over the long term, the outcome on the rule may prove to be more important than the outcome on the product. A legal ruling against the United States position in one case may well be (and frequently has been) the legal position the United States has asserted successfully in a later case. WTO rulings are not precedents. There is no law of precedent — no *stare decisis* — in public international law, including international trade law. However, the clarification of the meaning of a WTO rule in one case can have an impact on the outcome of a future case if the jurists in the future case think the reasoning by the jurists in the first case makes sense and is also appropriate to their case.[45] Not surprisingly, very often that is what they think.

Fundamental WTO rules — such as those prohibiting trade discrimination — must mean the same thing every day in world trade to ensure — as the WTO agreement seeks — "security and predictability" in the trading system.[46] Otherwise, the global flow of trade will be impeded. As the largest trading country in the world, this "security and predictability," which is furthered by consistent legal rulings by WTO jurists, should surely continue to be the goal of the United States. In addition, as an economic matter, there is also this. If, in, for instance, a trade remedies case, the United States has acted outside the bounds of WTO rules in applying a trade restriction, then the removal of that restriction in compliance with a WTO ruling will result in lower prices for American consumers of that product, both at retail and in inputs into the production of American-made goods, and thus in greater American productivity and therefore competitiveness. Economically, this is not a "loss."

Myth # 15 — WTO jurists are biased against the United States and routinely exceed their authority under the WTO agreement

In berating the WTO dispute settlement system, former President Trump told the American people, "Because we have fewer judges than other countries. It's set up as you can't win. In other words, the panels are set up so that we don't have majorities. It was set up for the benefit of taking advantage of the United States."[47] In reply, one might begin by asking: on what basis should the United States expect to have "majorities" of American jurists in a dispute settlement system that serves 164 countries and other customs territories? But, more than that, this assertion betrays a total lack of knowledge of the facts about WTO jurists. The jurists who serve the WTO do not serve any one country; they serve the multilateral trading system as a whole. Toward this end, they shed their nationality when they become WTO jurists. To ensure this, there are WTO Rules of Conduct, which states that WTO jurists "shall be independent and impartial" and "shall avoid direct or indirect conflicts of interest," among other requirements designed to safeguard "the integrity and impartiality" of the dispute settlement system.[48] In the nearly three decades since the establishment of the WTO and the adoption of these rules of conduct, the United States has brought not even one claim contending that a WTO jurist is not "independent and impartial" or has a "direct or indirect conflict of interest."

Nevertheless, the Trump administration emptied the WTO Appellate Body of jurists, which denies all members of the WTO — including the United States — of their right of appeal from the decisions of the panels selected to judge each WTO case. President Joe Biden has continued this policy of obstructionism, even calling for the formal abolition of the Appellate Body. As a result, the United States and other members that lose before WTO panels are filing appeals of legal rulings by WTO panels into the abyss of the absence of a sitting appellate tribunal, causing them to be denied their legal right to appeal and therefore preventing the WTO from adopting the panel rulings. Also, in the absence of an Appellate Body to help ensure "security and predictability" for the trading system through a consistency in legal rulings, WTO panels are showing the early signs of straying from consistency and toward an inconsistency in their legal conclusions and recommendations, which could add more and entirely unnecessary obstacles to the continued flow of world trade.

This American obstructionism has been rationalized — first by Trump and now by an echoing Biden — by a charge that the WTO jurists on the Appellate Body have routinely exceeded their authority under the WTO agreement. The Appellate Body members are said to have frequently engaged in "overreaching" and in "gap filling" that has altered and added to the obligations of the United States in the WTO agreement, which is in direct violation of their own obligations as an appellate tribunal in that agreement.[49] This, however, is not true. Like any tribunal, the Appellate Body is comprised of jurists who fall short of perfection. But, contrary to how the US has portrayed its actions, what the United States is doing is essentially accusing the Appellate Body of doing its job properly as mandated in the WTO agreement.

In the dispute settlement rules that are part of that agreement, the members of the WTO — including the United States — have instructed WTO jurists "to clarify the existing provisions of" the various trade agreements that altogether comprise the WTO agreement "in accordance with customary rules of interpretation of public international law."[50] Those customary rules require that a treaty shall be interpreted in good faith in accordance with the ordinary meaning to be given to the terms of the treaty in their context and in the light of its object and purpose.[51] Thus, the members of the Appellate Body are tasked with clarifying the meaning of the provisions in the WTO agreement in accordance with these rules. When a legal issue is raised in an appeal, they do not have the legal authority to refuse to address a legal claim and thus forgo identifying and clarifying the ordinary meaning of a treaty term. The customary rules of interpretation assume that each term in a treaty has a meaning, and, according to its instructions from the WTO members, the Appellate Body must identify and clarify it. This is not "overreaching" or "gap-filling." It is simply the Appellate Body doing what the members of the WTO have told it to do in the WTO agreement.

If, in fulfilling their mandate, the Appellate Body, as a fallible human institution, makes a mistake in doing its job by reaching the wrong result in their clarification, then there is a ready remedy. If the WTO members believe the appellate jurists gave the wrong answer to a legal issue raised on appeal, they can overrule a legal ruling by the Appellate Body by adopting their own legal interpretation, which will be binding on the Appellate Body and all other WTO jurists. This would take a vote of a "three-fourths majority of the Members."[52] Despite all its criticisms and complaints about the rulings of the Appellate Body, the United States has not, so far, sought to overturn a single Appellate Body ruling by trying to adopt a binding legal interpretation by the WTO membership. Could it be that the vast majority of the members of the WTO do not agree with the United States that the Appellate Body, whatever its imperfections, has not been doing the job they gave it to do in the right way?[53]

Conclusion

For the sake of brevity, only fifteen myths about the WTO have been addressed here. There are more. Indeed, new myths seem to emerge about the multilateral trading system almost every day. These myths are helpful to those who wish to disparage the WTO because they do not share its goals. They are not helpful to those who truly do wish to improve a system for conducting trade that is much in need of modernization. Those who seek genuine WTO reforms that would help improve the trading system to enable it better to accomplish its longstanding goals of peace and prosperity through trade, are well advised to join in dispelling these myths about the WTO as a necessary prelude to building a multilateral consensus to achieve such reforms and, in so doing, to restore the WTO to its rightful place at the center of world trade and of world trade policy and decision-making. It is long past time, in the United States especially, to tell the truth about trade.

Endnotes

[1] "Who we are," World Trade Organization, at WTO | What is the WTO? — Who we are.

[2] Article XV, WTO Agreement.

[3] Simon Lester, "Congressman DeFazio's Misinformed Arguments for Leaving the WTO," Cato at Liberty (June 29, 2020); Simon Lester, "Senator Hawley's Many Misunderstandings of the WTO," Cato at Liberty (May 5, 2020).

[4] *See, e.g.,* "Trump threatens to pull US out of World Trade Organization," *BBC News* (August 31, 2018), at Trump threatens to pull US out of World Trade Organization — BBC News. Some Members of Congress in both parties have also urged withdrawal. *See, e.g.,* Keith Johnson, "U.S. Effort to Depart WTO Gathers Momentum," *Foreign Policy* (May 27, 2020), at U.S. Frustration at WTO Boils Over, but Departure Would Be Self-Defeating (foreignpolicy.com).

[5] "Overview," World Trade Organization, at WTO | What is the WTO? — About the WTO — A statement by former Director-General Pascal Lamy.

[6] "Who we are," World Trade Organization, at WTO | What is the WTO? — Who we are.

[7] Josh Hawley, "The W.T.O. Should be Abolished," *New York Times* (May 5, 2020).

[8] Article XVII, General Agreement on Tariffs and Trade.

[9] Daniel Griswold, *Mad About Trade: Why Main Street America Should Embrace Globalization* (Washington, D.C.: Cato Institute, 2009), at 120.

[10] Robert Farley, "Trump Wrong About WTO Record," Fact Check (October 27, 2017), at Trump Wrong About WTO Record — FactCheck.org.

[11] These numbers are from 2019. Gabriel Felbermayr, Mario Larch, Yoto V. Yotove, and Erdal Yalcin, "The World Trade Organization at 25: Assessing the Economic Value of the Rules-Based Global Trading Systems," *Bertelsmann Shiftung* (November 2019), at 33.

[12] These are 2019 numbers. "Trade and American Jobs: The Impact of Trade on U.S. and State-Level Employment: 2019 Update," prepared by Trade Partnership Worldwide for Business Roundtable (March 2019), at 2.

[13] Gary Clyde Hufbauer and Zhiyao (Lucy) Lu, "The Payoff to America from Globalization: A Fresh Look with a Focus on Costs to Workers," Peterson Institute for International Economics Policy Brief 17–16 (May 2017), 1. These numbers are in 2016 dollars and reflect a household consisting of 2.64 persons.

[14] *Ibid.*

[15] Jacob M. Schlesinger and Alex Leary, "Trump Denounces Both China and WTO," *Wall Street Journal* (July 26, 2019).

[16] *See* James Bacchus and Inu Manak, *The Development Dimension: Special and Differential Treatment in Trade* (London and New York: Routledge, 2021).

[17] Emanuel Ornelas, "Special and differential treatment for developing countries reconsidered," Center for Economic Policy Research (May 14, 2016) https://voxeu.org/article/special-and-differential-treatment-developing-countries-reconsidered.

[18] James Bacchus and Inu Manak, *The Development Dimension*, at 35.

[19] "WTO Secretariat budget for 2022," World Trade Organization, at WTO | Budget for the year.

[20] Article I, Section 8, Clause 10, United States Constitution.

[21] *See* my longer discussion of the issue of "policy space" in James Bacchus, *The Willing World: Shaping and Sharing a Sustainable Global Prosperity* (Cambridge, U.K.: Cambridge University Press, 2018), 289–297.

[22] Article I and Article III, General Agreement on Tariffs and Trade.

[23] Paragraph 2, Annex on Financial Services, General Agreement on Trade in Services.

[24] Article 7 and Article 8, Agreement on Trade-related Aspects of Intellectual Property Rights.

[25] Article 2.1 and Article 2.2, Agreement on Technical Barriers to Trade.

[26] Article 2.1, Agreement on the Application of Sanitary and Phytosanitary Measures.

[27] Article 2.2 and Article 5.1, Agreement on the Application of Sanitary and Phytosanitary Measures.

[28] Article 2.3, Agreement on the Application of Sanitary and Phytosanitary Measures.

[29] *See* my longer discussion of the supposed "race to the bottom" in James Bacchus, *The Willing World: Shaping and Sharing a Sustainable Global Prosperity* (Cambridge, U.K.: Cambridge University Press, 2018), 54–57.

[30] Jagdish Bhagwati, "The Case for Free Trade," *Scientific American*, Volume 269 (November 1993), at 43.

[31] Leslie Paul Thiele, *Sustainability (Key Concepts)* (Cambridge, U.K.: Polity Press, 2013), at 162; *see also* John Antle and Gregg Heidebrink, "Environment and Development: Theory and International Evidence," *Economic Development and Cultural Change*, Volume 43 (April 1995), 603–625.

[32] Economists call this notion the "Pollution Haven Hypothesis." *See,* for example, Brian R. Copeland, "International Trade and Green Growth" (Washington, D.C.: World Bank, 2012), at 3.

[33] Edward M. Graham, Fighting the Wrong Enemy: Antiglobal Activists and Multinational Enterprises (Washington: Institute for International Economics, 2000), 141.

[34] David Collins, An Introduction to International Investment Law (Cambridge, U.K.: Cambridge University Press, 2017), 257, citing A. Harrison, "Do Polluters Head Overseas: Testing the Pollution Haven Hypothesis" ARE Update (University of California Gianni Foundation of Agricultural Economics, December 2001).

[35] *Ibid.* The World Bank does note that there is more evidence thus far from developed than from developing countries.

[36] Daniel W. Drezner, "Bottom Feeders," *Foreign Policy* (November 19, 2009).

[37] *Ibid.*

[38] My former Cato colleagues Simon Lester, Huan Zhu, and I explored this myth in depth in 2018 in James Bacchus, Simon Lester, and Huan, "Disciplining China's Trade Practices at the WTO: How WTO Complaints Can Help Make China More Market-Oriented," Cato Institute, Cato Policy Analysis Number 856 (November 15, 2018). In that paper, we provided a detailed outline of a legal case that could be brought by the United States against China in WTO dispute settlement based on current WTO rules. To date, the United States has, for whatever reason, not brought that case against China.

[39] *Ibid.* at Appendix 2.

[40] *Ibid.* at 6–7.

[41] *See* James Bacchus, "Reviving the WTO: Five Priorities for Liberalization," Cato Institute, Cato Policy Analysis Number 911 (February 23, 2021); and James Bacchus, *Trade Links. New Rules for a New World* (Cambridge, U.K.: Cambridge University Press, 2022).

[42] Robert Farley, "Trump Wrong About WTO Record," Fact Check (October 27, 2017), at Trump Wrong About WTO Record — FactCheck.org.

[43] For numbers through 2019, *see* Jeffrey J. Schott and Euijin Jung, "The United States Wins More WTO Cases Than China in US-China Trade Disputes," Peterson Institute for International Economics (November 22, 2019),

at The United States Wins More WTO Cases than China in US-China Trade Disputes | PIIE.

[44] Here it is appropriate for me to disclose to readers that, while serving as a founding member on the Appellate Body of the WTO, I was one of the WTO jurists who ruled against the United States in some of its early trade remedies cases.

[45] James Bacchus and Simon Lester, "The Rule of Precedent and the Role of the Appellate Body," *Journal of World Trade*, Volume 54, Number 2 (2020), 183–198.

[46] Article 3.2, WTO Dispute Settlement Understanding.

[47] Robert Farley, "Trump Wrong About WTO Record," Fact Check (October 27, 2017), at Trump Wrong About WTO Record — FactCheck.org.

[48] World Trade Organization, "Rules of conduct for the understanding on rules and procedures governing the settlement of disputes," WT/DSB/RC/1 (December 11, 1996), II.1, at WTO | Rules of conduct.

[49] Article 3.2, WTO Dispute Settlement Understanding.

[50] *Ibid.*

[51] These customary rules of treaty interpretation are expressed in Articles 31 and 32 of the Vienna Convention on the Law of Treaties; however, as customary rules, they exist independently of that Convention.

[52] Article IX.2, WTO Agreement.

[53] I explore the sad misdeeds of the United States in its dismantling of the WTO Appellate Body at length in James Bacchus, "Might Unmakes Right: The American Assault on the Rule of Law in World Trade," Centre for International Governance Innovation, CIGI Papers Number 173 (May 2018), at Paper no. 173.pdf (cigionline.org).

Chapter 2

Biden and Trade at Year One: The Reign of Polite Protectionism*

Introduction

Former president Donald Trump no longer presides over U.S. trade policy. Yet, under President Biden, the Trump administration's trade policy remains largely intact. As a presidential candidate, Joe Biden promised a change from the go-it-alone, my-way-or-the-highway approach to trade policy of Donald Trump. Disappointingly, during the first year of his presidency, Biden has instead largely embraced the failed Trump policy of unilateralism and protectionism in trade. He and his administration have done so politely, without Trump's bluster and bombast. Yet, the results have been mostly the same: a turn toward more trade protection and managed trade, toward a proposed industrial policy that would add more restrictions on trade, and toward a destructive unilateralism that threatens to continue undermining the multilateral trading system overseen by the World Trade Organization. If President Biden continues to pursue this misguided trade policy, American recovery and prosperity are at risk. There is still time — at least three years — for him to end this reign of polite protectionism by framing and pursuing a new trade policy that will benefit all Americans: a policy that will achieve more trade liberalization, stop managed trade, halt trade-restrictive industrial policy, renew trade

---

*This essay was previously published by the Cato Institute as James Bacchus, "Biden and Trade at Year One: The Reign of Polite Protectionism," Cato Policy Analysis no. 926 (April 26, 2022).

multilateralism, and give restored and unflinching support to the international rule of law in trade.

Polite Protectionism

There are no tweets. There are no insults. There are no sudden shifts of policy in the middle of the night. There are no threats to pull out in a pique from international institutions. There are no macho public displays of breast-beating bullying of America's allies and other trading partners, large and small. Former president Donald Trump no longer presides over U.S. trade policy. Yet, under President Joe Biden, the Trump administration's trade policy remains largely intact. Shorn of the sharpest edges of Trump's "America First" protectionism, the Biden administration's trade policy, a year on, seems increasingly to be merely a smoother and more polished version of the same turning away from the wider world, of the same myopic mercantilist view of how the United States should address trade domestically, and of how it should engage in trade and trade relations globally. So far, U.S trade policy in the Biden administration has been the reign of polite protectionism.

This quieter continuation of Trump's headlong retreat after three-quarters of a century of bipartisan support for multilateral trade liberalization was signaled in the first weeks of the new administration. During the Senate confirmation hearing for Katherine Tai, a highly skilled U.S. trade negotiator of long experience chosen by Biden to serve as the United States Trade Representative (USTR), she was asked by Sen. Patrick J. Toomey (R-PA), one of the few remaining congressional champions of free trade, whether two countries negotiating a trade agreement should share as their goal the elimination of tariffs and other barriers to trade. She replied, "Maybe if you'd asked me this question five or 10 years ago, I would have been inclined to say yes," but "I think that our trade policies need to be nuanced and need to take into account all the lessons that we have learned, many of them very painful, from our most recent history."[1]

Up until Trump's election in 2016 and the destructive four-year tenure of his protectionist chief trade negotiator, Robert Lighthizer, no presidential nominee for USTR from either the Democratic or Republican Party would have given any other answer to this question than yes. It is true that this affirmation might sometimes have been followed by a "but" and then some politically expedient qualification; however, it was generally agreed for decades by both Republican and Democratic administrations alike that, in economic principle, if not in every dicey domestic political circumstance, trade liberalization was a desirable goal for the United States. But no more. As a headline writer for the New York Times rightly put it following the Toomey-Tai exchange, "In Washington, 'Free Trade' Is No Longer Gospel."[2]

Presumably, as his appointee, Tai speaks for Biden on trade. Unlike some of Trump's cabinet members, Biden's cabinet members do not seem inclined, to date, to freelance when speaking about policy. Also, Tai has broad support on both sides of the Hill, having previously worked, often in a bipartisan way, in a key staff role for the Ways and Means Committee in the House of Representatives, and she has been — quite justly — praised by members of both political parties for her labors there. The Senate confirmed her appointment as trade representative by a vote of 98–0.[3] The sparing use of "free trade" in her vocabulary does not seem to be any hindrance to her in generating significant support for her advocacy of the White House's approach to trade from members of either party. Indeed, it may well be a political asset.

Tai's reply to Toomey has been echoed in many of her words and actions — as well as those of others in the Biden administration who are responsible for various aspects of the international economic portfolio — in the months since. Perhaps most telling was her response in December 2021, when asked at an event hosted by the U.S. Chamber of Commerce, why Biden has not enlisted the United States in the "Ottawa Group," a subset of members of the World Trade Organization led by the European Union and Canada that is trying, amid the COVID-19 pandemic, to reduce barriers to trade in medical goods. This would do much to help combat the pandemic, yet Tai answered that the Biden administration was at odds with the Ottawa Group about how far to go in removing the barriers.[4] She added, "I think we have pursued a really unfettered liberalization policy for the past many years and decades, and it is part of what has brought us to this current reality of very, very fragile supply chains."[5]

"Unfettered liberalization"? Hardly. Although trade has been significantly liberalized through successive global rounds of trade negotiations and numerous bilateral and regional trade agreements, many U.S.-imposed tariffs and other non-tariff trade barriers remain in place, including most of those that were applied unilaterally — and, thus, illegally under WTO rules — by the pro-tariff Trump administration. Furthermore, this statement overlooks an array of other obstacles that America's trading partners face in securing access to the U.S. market: ordinary tariffs in the U.S. tariff schedule; tariffs in the form of trade remedies, such as anti-dumping duties and countervailing duties to foreign governmental subsidies; Section 301 tariffs levied in retaliation for alleged unfair trade practices; Section 232 tariffs, levied in response to claimed threats to national security; "buy American" requirements; and more. As trade scholar Simon Lester has summed it up, "While there has been liberalization in the last few years and decades, there has been plenty of fetter as well."[6] Surely, with all her expertise and all her years of valuable experience, Tai must know that trade liberalization by the United States has been far from "unfettered."

She must also know the vast extent of what trade liberalization has accomplished for the people of the United States since the signing of the General Agreement on Tariffs and Trade — later transformed into the WTO — in the aftermath of the Second World War. Instead of disparaging the freeing of trade, the USTR should be reminding the American people at every opportunity of how very much they have benefited — and are benefiting every day — from the freeing of trade. International trade supports nearly 39 million American jobs.[7] Overall, "the payoff to the United States from trade expansion — stemming from policy liberalization and improved transportation and communications technology — from 1950 to 2016 (was) roughly $2.1 trillion ... US GDP per capita and GDP per household accordingly increased by $7,014 and $18,131, respectively." What is more, "disproportionate gains" probably accrued to poorer households.[8] Membership in the WTO system has boosted annual GDP by about $87 billion in the 25 years since the establishment of the WTO — more than for any other country.[9] Yet none of this has been highlighted by Tai, Biden, or anyone else in the administration.

I am a Democrat and a former Democratic member of Congress from Florida. I am a lifelong advocate of free trade. I am also a supporter of Biden and of much he is trying to accomplish nationally and internationally. I had hoped — I still hope — for a Biden trade policy that will free more trade and thereby help increase, broaden, and deepen American prosperity. Yet, at this point, after a year of dashed hopes for trade-freeing initiatives from the new president, those of us who believe in the benefits of free trade must set aside wishful thinking and realize that the Biden administration truly means all that it has been saying about trade.[10] With this unwelcome realization, other unhappy conclusions must proceed from it and from the administration's trade actions and inactions during its first year.

In the Biden administration, there is no commitment to free trade. There is no priority commitment to working with other countries to lower the barriers to trade through multilateral negotiations. There is no solid support for the WTO as a central and necessary multilateral institution. There is only the thinnest of support for the international rule of law in trade. There is a pronounced inclination to use trade increasingly for geopolitical and for other non-trade purposes, especially against perceived competitors such as China. And, not least, there is the continuation and intensification of the previous self-destructive tendency toward managed trade and industrial policy. All this adds up to an all-too-real and ever-so-polite protectionism, delivered in a soft voice and with a smile.

Biden before the White House

This trade policy is not what many of us who voted for him thought we were promised by presidential candidate Joe Biden. As a candidate, Biden criticized Trump's go-it-alone, my-way-or-the-highway approach to trade. He promised to work with American allies and other trading partners on trade issues of mutual concern. He said that the United States must "write the rules on trade" within the existing WTO-based multilateral trading system.[11] Although he promised aggressive action as president against China's alleged failures to fulfill its treaty obligations on trade, candidate Biden opposed Trump's trade war against China and described Trump's avalanche of unilateral tariffs on imports of Chinese goods as self-defeating because of their high costs for Americans. He called China the big winner in the transactional face-saving Phase One trade deal that Trump and Lighthizer concocted with China after the trade war, predictably, got out of hand. He stated also, correctly, that Trump's decision on his first day in office to withdraw from the trade-liberalizing Trans-Pacific Partnership "put China in the driver's seat."[12]

Other aspects of the Biden campaign platform were, however, disconcerting to advocates of more trade liberalization who see international trade as an essential contributor to domestic prosperity. Biden seemed to perceive trade as separate from domestic policy, despite the fact that Americans live, to a great extent, in an economically integrated world. While denouncing many of Trump's trade decisions during his campaign, Biden made it clear that he would put domestic recovery and reform first and that trade would not be an initial, or even a high priority, for his administration. He promised not to sign any new trade deals "until we've made major investments here at home, in our workers and communities."[13]

Furthermore, Biden pledged not to agree to any new trade deal that was not accompanied by such major investments and that did not include advocates for labor and the environment at the negotiating table. He stressed, too, that the United States must "write the rules of the road for the world" to ensure fair treatment for American workers and to protect the environment.[14] All this suggested a trade policy that would be secondary to other considerations, closely connected to and conditioned on domestic economic and social actions, and aimed at linking trade increasingly and innovatively to domestic labor and global environmental concerns.

Ominously missing in Biden's campaign was any full-throated advocacy of the bountiful potential advantages of opening the borders of the United States and the other countries in the world to more and freer trade. There were the usual paeans to exports. But there was no praise of imports. Omitted was any explanation of how imports provide lower-priced inputs into American manufactured goods that create and save American jobs by making those goods more competitive in domestic and world markets, or how imports lead to lower prices and to more product choices for American consumers, or how imports spur American innovation through the incentive of competition. This was disappointing, but it was not surprising. The last president of the United States to speak boldly about the overall benefits of trade was George W. Bush when he was in Shanghai a few weeks after the terrorist attacks on September 11, 2001. He explained then, clearly and eloquently, "that progress begins with trade. Trade is the engine of economic advancement. On every continent, in every culture, trade generates opportunity, enhances entrepreneur growth. And trade applies the power of markets to the needs of the poor. It has lifted countless lives."[15]

In this speech, the Republican Bush echoed many former presidents, including Democrats. Biden, however, both as a senator and as vice president, has a long history of ambivalence on trade. It is not surprising that, in a time of growing trade skepticism, he incorporated some elements of Trump's mercantilism in his successful presidential campaign. And as president, he has broken with the generations of past support of freer trade by Democratic presidents. Throughout his political career, Biden has never been known as someone motivated by a basic philosophical commitment to free trade or by the oft-neglected connection between trade and freedom.[16] He has rarely focused on trade or been in the forefront on trade, and he has often seemed ambivalent about it.

While in the Senate, Biden voted for the North American Free Trade Agreement with Canada and Mexico, the legislation implementing the Uruguay Round Trade Agreements that established the WTO, and the legislation supporting China's entry into the WTO. And, while vice president, he supported the Trans-Pacific Partnership. Along the way, however, he voted against the bilateral U.S. free trade agreements with Chile, Oman, Peru, and Singapore, and against the regional Dominican Republic–Central America Free Trade Agreement. He did this largely, he said, because in his view these agreements did too little to address legitimate labor and environmental concerns.[17] Notably, he also voted for steel import quotas and agricultural subsidies, two of the leading examples of persistent American protectionism.[18]

Nor were these Biden campaign positions surprising, given the political climate in the country as a whole and in the organizational base of the Democratic Party in particular. Trade remains broadly popular among the American people, including a growing majority of Democrats, particularly in the urban and suburban parts of the country where Democratic voting strength has been rising in recent elections.[19] But this is not so among many of the interest groups that contribute much of the money to finance political campaigns and control many of the portals to election to political office. In the Democratic Party, for instance, organized labor has great influence and, fearful of foreign competition, it is ardently opposed to freer trade. For this reason, any defense of freer trade by a Democrat is assumed nowadays to be politically perilous. Increasingly, Republicans also espouse freer trade at their political peril as the false panacea of economic nationalism spreads ever more widely among Republican voters.

Supporting freer trade is especially risky in primaries, where the activist base of voters in both parties tends to turn out and prevail, and where many of the most influential activists in both — for varying (and for mostly mistaken) reasons — largely oppose freer trade. The Democratic and Republican bases alike blame freer trade for the loss of manufacturing and other American jobs, and much of the Democratic base adds to that a belief that freer trade, and the trade rules that come with it, harm the environment and unduly limit the discretion of the United States in protecting public health and safety. The fact that these assumptions are incorrect is politically irrelevant — and will remain so for as long as American politicians who know better remain unwilling to say so publicly.[20] In politics, the truism is accurate: perception is reality.

Biden in the White House

Now that he is in the White House, Biden confronts some stark practical political realities that make it even harder for him to support trade. The long-standing historical bipartisan support for trade in the Congress no longer exists. Some Republicans still favor freer trade, but, in the aftermath of the rise of economic nationalism and the Republican Party's embrace of Trump and his policies, there are not nearly as many as before. And, amid the current polarization of the two parties, even some of those Republicans who continue to support trade may be reluctant to vote for a trade agreement if it is presented to them by Biden. Partisan pressures in this era of polarization push against giving a president from the other party a congressional success of any kind. Thus, for support on trade in the Congress, as on almost all else, Biden must depend on Democratic votes.

Democrats hold the slimmest of voting margins in the House and in the Senate (a margin they may well lose in both chambers in the forthcoming midterm elections). Although an unknown number of Republican votes remain for freer trade, and some of those Republicans may be willing to vote for trade-freeing legislation proposed by a Democratic president, a goodly majority of Democrats must vote for any proposed trade legislation for it to be enacted by the Congress. Consequently, the president must pay constant attention to the views of his fellow Democrats on the Hill on trade.

And, up on the Hill, the Democratic leadership in both the chambers is, at best, reluctant to support trade liberalization and, at worst, increasingly inclined to oppose it. On the left, self-styled "progressive" Democrats — now large in numbers in the House and led assertively by Bernie Sanders (VT) and Elizabeth Warren (MA) in the Senate — are often anything but progressive on trade; many of them are outright protectionists. Complicating matters further, the embattled moderate and centrist Democrats — shrinking in numbers, ever mindful of their demanding base, and always fearful of being "primaried" by an anti-trade opponent on their left — are likewise reluctant to cast a divisive vote for freer trade even though many of them are, in principle, for it. A vote for freer trade is, therefore, especially difficult during an election year.

All this helps explain why Biden and Tai have not proposed a renewal by the Congress of trade promotion authority (TPA), the presidential trade negotiating authority that lapsed at the end of June 2021. Congresses have repeatedly delegated this time-limited authority to presidents since 1974. One year into his term, Biden has not even asked for it.[21] In explanation, Tai has said only that she wants to rethink the objective of trade agreements before seeking TPA.[22] One would think that anyone assuming the office of USTR would have thought this objective through before becoming USTR.

The reluctance to move forward in trying to restore this executive authority poses a constitutional hurdle to the conclusion of any new international trade agreements — even if Biden changes course and decides he wants to pursue them sooner than he has previously said. Under Article I, Section 8, of the Constitution, the Congress has the authority to "lay and collect ... duties" and to "regulate Commerce with foreign Nations." Under Article I, Section 8, it has the authority also to "make all Laws which shall be necessary and proper for carrying into execution" these powers. Under Article II, Section 2, of the Constitution, the president has the "Power, by and with the Advice and Consent of the Senate, to make Treaties, provided two thirds of the Senators present concur." The Constitution, though, does not assign any specific power over international commerce and trade to the president. Thus, the Congress must specifically delegate trade negotiating authority to the president through legislation.[23]

Without this congressional delegation, the president and his trade negotiators can negotiate all they want about trade with other countries, but they cannot conclude any new trade deals, and other countries are less likely to negotiate with them if they do not have that authority. Moreover, without it, trade agreements cannot be voted up or down by the Congress without amendment, which is, practically speaking, a prerequisite for cutting new deals. It is necessary to ensure that agreements struck by U.S. trade negotiators not be amended by the Congress; another country will not give the United States its best offer in a negotiation if it thinks the Congress will amend a negotiated agreement and then demand more and deeper trade commitments. From the perspective of other countries, why make your best offer until you absolutely must do so to close a deal? Thus, without the assurance of a simple up or down vote by the Congress, the United States will never get the best bargain it could get in an international trade agreement.

Given what the president has said, presumably he will not request a renewal of TPA by the Congress unless key parts of his ambitious domestic policy agenda are enacted by the Congress and implemented by the administration. He wants improvements in American competitiveness before opening American doors wider to imports. A bipartisan version of Biden's infrastructure proposal — the Infrastructure Investment and Jobs Act — has been approved by Congress and signed into law by the president.[24] Yet, at this writing, the fate of the various parts of Biden's proposed $1.8 trillion Build Back Better bill for social spending is decidedly grim.[25] It is far from clear that all the domestic investments he has portrayed as a prerequisite to returning to negotiating international trade agreements will be made. A TPA request is not even on the horizon.

Furthermore, this Biden approach to trade betrays a lack of understanding about some of the trade-related sources of American competitiveness. Just as he did when a candidate, Biden, as president, is overlooking the need for imports to maintain and enhance the competitiveness of American businesses and American workers. Denied the spur of the additional innovation and competition provided by additional imports, domestic production in the United States will lose its competitive edge. Denied imported inputs into U.S. production, American products will be put at a competitive disadvantage in pricing, both domestically and internationally. In addition, if the United States refuses to keep its market open to imports and, moreover, if it refuses to open its market to imports even more, then the trading partners of the United States will, in turn, refrain from opening their markets further to more American exports.

Meanwhile, elsewhere in the world, other countries are continuing to conclude new free trade agreements while the United States falls behind in trade liberalization.[26] Although multilateral negotiations in the WTO remain stalled, in no small part at this juncture because of the low priority given to them by the Biden administration, bilateral and regional deals are proliferating throughout the world that do not include the United States. The latest, which took effect on the first day of 2022, is the Regional Comprehensive Economic Partnership (RCEP) among 15 Asia-Pacific countries. The RCEP is the worlds' largest regional trade agreement, accounting for 30 percent of global population and global GDP. Over time, it will eliminate more than 90 percent of the tariffs among its member countries.[27] The largest of these countries is China. It is China, not the United States, that seems most poised at this point to, in Biden's phrase, "write the rules of the road for the world" on trade.

Biden and Trade at Home

Biden's actions domestically so far demonstrate a failure to understand the necessity of freer trade as part of a successful policy for American recovery and prosperity. His intention to achieve domestic recovery and reform before attempting to negotiate any new trade agreements is founded on the mistaken belief that increasing trade has been harmful to the American economy and workforce, and on the errant notion that the American economy and workforce can be sustained and strengthened without increasing trade. Without question, many Americans today are ill-prepared to compete in today's global economy, which features increasing international trade, or to adjust to the inevitable disruptions that free market competition entails. This has happened in manufacturing and other sectors of the economy. But this is not because of freer trade. It is because of the political failure, while liberalizing trade, to provide many Americans with the enabling tax and regulatory atmosphere and the quantity and quality of education, training, and other tools they need to take best advantage of the new opportunities provided by globalization.

To remedy this failure, Biden has proposed infrastructure investments and an array of social reforms. He has also proposed a worker-centric trade policy. In explaining what this policy means in June 2021 to the union workers of the AFL-CIO, which had much to do with Biden's election, Tai spoke about this goal. She said: "The first step to achieving this goal is creating a more inclusive process.... By bringing workers from all backgrounds and experiences to the table, we will create inclusive trade policy that advances economic security and racial and gender equity. We want to lift up women, communities of color, and rural America — people that have been systematically excluded or overlooked.... We're putting foreign policy and trade together for the middle class."[28]

These are worthy — albeit tardy — objectives. Yet the methods the Biden administration has in mind for achieving them through trade policy are less than clear. The administration describes its worker-centric trade policy as "historic."[29] But of what, in the actual implementation of American trade policy, is this supposedly historic approach comprised?

The president and his administration have set out globally to combat forced labor and child labor related to trade.[30] This emphasis is long overdue. Yet, based on the totality of their trade actions during Biden's first year, it appears that, to a worrying extent, worker-centric trade is merely a new rhetorical cloak for long-familiar forms of protectionism. Although many of the new infrastructure and other domestic investments Biden has sought are surely needed in some form, they have been accompanied so far by a growing number of trade-restricting measures that demonstrate an apparent indifference to whether U.S. markets remain open to trade. Indeed, some of these measures suggest that the president, his administration, and many of his supporters in the Congress wrongly see the imposition of trade restrictions as actively enhancing the overall health of the American economy. Instead of further liberalizing trade, they seem bent — much like the Trump administration — on trying to manage trade.

Since the signing of the GATT in 1947, both Republican and Democratic administrations before Trump had proceeded from the premise that establishing the right global ground rules for trade — and upholding them — was the best way to grow American prosperity. If the rules were right, it was believed, then American businesses and workers would succeed in the world economy. The underlying bipartisan assumption was the Smithian view that more trade can be a win-win for everyone and that, within the right enabling trading system of rules-based non-discrimination, sales of American goods and services would, because of their comparative advantages, help produce that growth. This assumption inspired the leading role taken by the United States in the transformation of the GATT and the reformation of the rules-based multilateral trading system under the international institutional auspices of the WTO in 1995.

With his view of trade as zero-sum and as purely transactional, Trump discarded this long-standing bipartisan premise in favor of seeking trade wins for certain politically favored U.S.-based companies and industries by dictating specific trade outcomes. This approach, of course, only distorted what would otherwise have been market outcomes while empowering bureaucrats to pick and choose winners and losers by manipulating tariffs, tariff exemptions, antidumping and other trade remedies, and governmental subsidies. It also enabled the individuals and the interest groups that supported Trump politically and financially to influence administration decisionmaking in ways that distorted market results even more.

During his first year, Biden has embraced — and has been building on — Trump's turn toward managed trade. Examples are many. Most telling is his support for Buy American requirements, which are less-strident echoes of Trump's calls for putting America first. To begin with, in July 2021 there came new domestic-content requirements for government purchases.[31] Next, in November, were Buy American mandates in the omnibus infrastructure legislation, which require that all the iron and steel in new federal infrastructure projects be sourced in the United States.[32] These nationalistic preferences, favored by Trump, are further proliferating under Biden and congressional Democrats, with potentially economically destructive consequences and national security implications in federal defense purchases.[33] Buy American provisions, as Scott Lincicome of the Cato Institute has written, "are just another form of protectionism; they've been found, for example, to act as a barrier to entering the U.S. market and to raise domestic prices in the same way that a tariff does."[34] Such provisions impose high costs on taxpayers and deny Americans who are not favored with these preferences what would otherwise be economic opportunities, resulting in an opportunity cost for these Americans and for our country as a whole, both now and in the future.[35]

Many domestic industries that benefit from lower-cost and, sometimes, higher-quality imports in their inputs have opposed these requirements because they will add to production costs, be passed along to consumers as increased prices, and thus diminish the industries' competitiveness, both at home and abroad. But domestic-content requirements are popular with domestic steelmakers, labor unions, and other key constituencies in the pivotal political states of the Midwest that have long been advocates of protectionism. Thus, the requirements are widely supported by Democrats and Republicans alike. (It is also much easier for a member of Congress to vote for a Buy American requirement than it is to explain the counterintuitive logic of comparative advantage to a voter at a town hall meeting in their congressional district.)

These and similar endeavors to manage trade by mandating domestic content are inspiring increasing controversy with U.S. trading partners, with some suggesting that these measures may be inconsistent with U.S. treaty obligations. As one example, Biden's Build Back Better bill would provide a subsidy in the form of a $12,500 tax credit for purchases of electric vehicles (EVs), which are intended to boost production in that emerging auto sector (but, given that the market seems to be rapidly moving to EVs anyway, may not do so).[36] Attracting concern from some auto producers, as well as from some of America's most important trading partners, is that this tax credit is reduced by $4,500 if the purchase is not a union-made EV assembled in the United States. The subsidy is reduced another $500 if the battery in the EV is not American-made. Moreover, beginning in 2027, only EVs assembled in the United States would qualify for the tax credit.[37] Canada, for one, says this buy American, buy union subsidy would amount to a 34 percent tariff on vehicles assembled in Canada, and it has promised retaliation and legal action over this discriminatory provision under the United States-Mexico-Canada Agreement (USMCA) if Biden and the Congress do not relent.[38]

Also in the auto sector, Canada and Mexico are mulling joint-trade action against the United States under the USMCA over the highly restrictive way in which the Biden administration is interpreting the rules of origin for auto parts under that regional agreement.[39] Rules of origin determine whether a product can cross a border duty-free. Tightening the origin rules to require more domestic content was one of the protectionist changes sought, and proclaimed as a success, by Trump, Lighthizer, and congressional Republicans and Democrats alike, during the North American Free Trade Agreement (NAFTA) renegotiation that resulted in the USMCA.[40] Such requirements do little to create American jobs, and they raise auto prices for consumers.[41] But now, Tai and others in the Biden administration are supporting this de facto restriction of regional trade entry and trade assembly for Canadian and Mexican auto parts in the U.S. market; allegedly, they are also applying the rules so as to be even more trade-restrictive than was agreed. It was Tai, of course, who helped craft these protectionist rules while working in concert with Lighthizer during her service to the Democrats in the Congress, who supported Trump on this issue. Unlike Trump, Biden and Tai are not hurling insults against our nearest neighbors and large trading partners, Canada and Mexico; but, in this and other ways, they are, very politely, doing their best to limit the access of Canadian and Mexican products to the American market and to draw the line against further North American economic integration.

Another instance of Biden's support for managed trade is his approach to the international supply chains that are the formative links for regional and global economic integration. Assailed on all sides by outcries over supply-chain bottlenecks, the president is under pressure from "a once-in-a-lifetime shock to supply and demand" in the wake of the prolonged COVID-19 shutdowns of the past two years and the ongoing economic consequences of successive variants of the novel coronavirus.[42] Adding to this pressure are concerns borne of the pandemic about the ready and reliable availability of medicines and other medical goods.[43] If supply-chain obstructions persist, a geographical consolidation of hitherto fine-tuned shipping networks could significantly alter international trade by moving producers closer to consumers.[44] The politically expedient choice — the one that resonates most with a public that may not all remember the basic economic lessons of Adam Smith and his successors — is to shorten, or even cut, international supply chains.

We have learned during the pandemic that, with some essential products, we need more — and geographically more varied — sources of supply. We have learned, too, that we must keep larger inventories on hand in case of an emergency such as the COVID-19 pandemic. The corporate drive for efficiency must be tempered by an awareness of the necessity for ready availability. But a concerted effort to shorten or cut supply chains would be a mistake. The idea that the United States (or any other country) can be resilient, self-sufficient, and independent of all international supply chains is a fantasy. As Lincicome has rightly observed, there is "the very real risk that supply chain nationalism would make the United States less, not more, resilient," for "nationalist policies intended to boost 'essential' industries — for steel, ships, machine tools, semiconductors, and other 'essential' goods — have a long track record of high costs, high risks, failed objectives, and unintended consequences. In case after case, the protected industries did not emerge stronger or more resilient — in fact, just the opposite."[45] Protectionism already distorts supply chains, driving up prices.[46] More protectionism will not end the supply-chain crisis.[47]

Biden's evident commitment to managed trade is an international manifestation of his concomitant commitment, and that of many of the congressional members of the Democratic Party, to the seductive siren song of industrial policy, which focuses government support on "targeted and directed efforts to plan for specific future industrial outputs and outcomes."[48] In sum, industrial policy is the substitution of a government decision for a market decision pursuant to a government plan that is intended to shape the economic future toward a predetermined direction. It is usually centered on commercial manufacturing. And it is usually accompanied by nationalistic measures that are framed to keep foreign products out of the national market and to subsidize domestic production and exports in favored sectors through a variety of tariffs, non-tariff trade barriers, and governmental grants, loans, tax breaks, and other subsidies that are the antithesis of trade and market liberalization.

Inspired to varying extents by the need to recover from the economic plunge caused by the pandemic, a desire to address climate change by transitioning away from carbon as an energy source, and an apprehension over intensifying competition with the output of China's state-directed economy, many congressional Democrats (along with the growing number of economic nationalists among congressional Republicans) have turned more and more toward governmental intervention in the American marketplace. To cite one instance, in addition to the domestic-content discrimination in proposed tax credits for purchases of electric vehicles, Biden's proposed Build Back Better plan would inflate the costs and impede the innovativeness of clean energy and clean electricity projects by burdening them with Buy American requirements.[49] New subsidies abound in the Biden plan. Also, new subsidies, along with new trade restrictions, are among the shortcomings in the various versions of the America COMPETES Act, which currently awaits action by a joint conference of the House and Senate. A number of these proposed measures raise serious concerns under the rules of the WTO to which the United States has agreed in the WTO treaty.[50]

In addition to the possibility of inconsistency with U.S. international trade obligations, the problem with industrial policy is that, economically, it will not accomplish what its advocates hope to accomplish. It will undermine American competitiveness while attempting to enhance it. Targeted governmental intervention through subsidies and other means can "crowd out private investments and steer public resources into unproductive endeavors, as well as more serious problems, such as cronyism and corruption."[51] Such intervention also amounts to having the government pick winners and losers in the marketplace, which risks wasting tax dollars and sabotaging the initiative and innovation that are essential to retaining and improving the competitiveness of American production.

The appropriate response to China's state-driven industrial policy and its turn away from freer markets is not to imitate the economic shortsightedness of the Chinese government under the dictates of President Xi Jinping, which will in time come to haunt and hinder China; rather, it is to recommit to the free market foundations of liberal capitalism that have made the American economy the largest and most successful in human history. That is the path to more American competitiveness. The United States does not need to become more like China; the United States needs to become more like America.[52] Tried intermittently in the past, "industrial policy has an extensive and underwhelming history in the United States, featuring both seen and unseen high costs, failed objectives, and political manipulation."[53]

As with Trump before him, some of Biden's industrial policy proposals are simply responses to pleas for direct and indirect government handouts by politically connected companies, unions, trade associations, and other interest groups. Many of these proposals are well intended, including most that relate to addressing climate change. Yet tax credits, subsidies, and other discriminatory endeavors to sway market decisions toward preferred outcomes, however desirable, are fraught with risk. They are far from guaranteed to achieve their stated goals, and they are likely to undermine — instead of add — to the domestic and global competitiveness of American businesses and workers.[54] Tax dollars should be spent instead on significantly increasing funding for basic scientific research and development, ensuring an adequate social safety net that furthers worker mobility, and reforming and elevating every level of American education. According to the Department of Education, 54 percent of adults in the United States — about 130 million people — read and comprehend below the sixth-grade level. The low level of literacy in America alone could be costing the economy as much as $2.2 trillion a year.[55] This is not the path to improved American competitiveness, and this failure on our part cannot be blamed on China.

Biden and Tariffs

Trump proclaimed himself a "tariff man."[56] Biden would not be so brash, but he and his administration seem to share Trump's addiction to tariffs. Candidate Biden described the tariffs — the border taxes on imports — that were imposed by Trump on rivals and allies alike as "damaging," "reckless," and "disastrous."[57] His supporters can be forgiven for assuming he would remove those tariffs as soon as he was inaugurated. However, now that he is in the White House, Biden appears to be enamored of tariffs almost as much as his predecessor. So, too, it appears, is his chief trade negotiator. Tai has not only defended the Trump tariffs — and tariffs in general — she has also, to the utter bewilderment of many economists, challenged the notion that tariffs are ultimately paid by consumers. She has claimed that it is a more complicated calculation than it appears.[58] Furthermore, she has made it clear that she sees tariffs — including the Trump tariffs — as valuable negotiating leverage with China and other U.S. trading partners. She calls tariffs a "very important tool" in the administration's trade policy.[59]

Biden and Tai are ignoring the extensive harms to American businesses and workers that have been caused by these tariffs, which will continue for as long as they remain in place. Tariffs are not paid by foreign exporters; they are paid by importers. Whatever Tai may think, the costs of tariffs are passed along to domestic purchasers. They increase both the consumption and production costs of goods in the United States, and, as a result, they diminish the competitiveness of U.S. production and the economic benefits of competition, thus constraining economic growth.[60] The Trump tariffs have resulted in a peak loss of 245,000 American jobs.[61] They "currently impact over $400 billion of imports and exports and increase consumer costs by roughly $51 billion annually."[62] The cost of these tariffs has been borne almost entirely by American consumers, including both individual buyers of retail products and business buyers of intermediate goods that are inputs into U.S. production.[63]

One economic consequence of COVID-19 in the United States is inflation. With shortages of supply unable to meet rising demands amid the supply-chain constrictions of the continuing pandemic, inflation is increasing. These constrictions will be eased when supply catches up with demand, which should, in turn, help reduce inflation. Domestic inflationary pressures also could, in certain cases, be reduced by the reduction or elimination of tariffs. This, though, does not seem to be a consideration in Biden's trade policy. In casting about for culprits to blame for inflation, the Biden administration has generally not mentioned tariffs. Treasury Secretary Janet Yellen, a former chair of the Federal Reserve who fully understands the inflationary and other harmful effects of tariffs, has ventured so far as to point out that lowering tariffs would have a "disinflationary" effect.[64] But no one else in the administration seems to be listening to her.

One of the most egregious examples of the Biden administration's affection for tariffs is the recent decision of his Commerce Department to double the average tariff on imports of Canadian softwood lumber, which will add to rapidly rising building costs in a heated U.S. housing market.[65] These tariffs may yet be cut, and, to be sure, the Canadians should cut any lumber subsidies. Also, to be fair, the problematic U.S. trade remedies system existed long before Biden took office. But cheaper imported lumber means more affordable housing for Americans. Lumber prices in the United States are already three times what they were before the pandemic began. The National Association of Home Builders reports that rising lumber prices alone have added nearly $36,000 to the price of a new home.[66] These lumber tariffs are defended by the Biden administration as leverage to encourage the Canadians to discipline their lumber subsidies. But, given lumber shortages, is this really the best time to make this point, however valid and however politely, to our friends in Canada, about the trade-distorting ways in which they contort their lumber stumpage fees? It is through this tariff-tainted perspective of polite protectionism that Biden and Tai view the wider trading world.

But perhaps the worst example of Biden's affection for tariffs is his refusal to eliminate the tariffs that Trump imposed on imports of steel and aluminum. In part to forge a common trade strategy for confronting China, the Biden administration is working worldwide to try to repair the damage done to U.S. trade relations with numerous American allies and other trading partners by the steel and aluminum tariffs, among other issues. The metals tariffs are at the center of many of these discussions, but, under pressure from labor unions and trade-exposed domestic steel manufacturers, the president has mostly kept these tariffs in place. Where he has agreed to modify them, he has not removed them but merely transformed them, for the most part, into another form of trade protectionism.

In trade relations with the European Union, in particular, the president and his team have made notable progress. In June 2021, the United States and the EU settled their 17-year-long WTO dispute over large commercial aircraft subsidies.[67] In September 2021, in Pittsburgh, the United States and the EU convened the first meeting of their newly-formed United States–European Union Trade and Technology Council (TTC) to try to align and coordinate mutual approaches to technology standards, data governance, climate and clean technologies, semiconductor supply chains, and other common technology and technology-related concerns. As Jennifer Hillman and Seara Grundhoefer have written, the council offers the two sides a chance to put mutual grievances behind them and "turn the page on U.S.-EU economic relations by focusing on a limited but strategically important set of issues."[68]

Then, in October 2021, the Biden administration concluded a deal with the EU to ease the effects of American tariffs on imports of European steel and aluminum.[69] In 2018, Trump had levied tariffs of 25 percent on imports of steel and 10 percent on imports of aluminum. He did this under the authority of Section 232 of the Trade Expansion Act of 1962 based on the dubious notion that these imports were undermining American national security. As Chad P. Bown and Kadee Russ have pointed out, although these Section 232 tariffs "were motivated by combatting China, they were imposed on NATO and other alliance members, because the United States had largely stopped importing steel and aluminum from China, as a result of antidumping and countervailing duties imposed by earlier US administrations."[70] In other words, for supposed national security reasons, the United States imposed harmful trade restrictions on its own treaty allies. These reasons were spurious, to say the least, but they remained in place during Trump's term.[71]

Under intense pressure from Lighthizer and others in the Trump administration, several countries tacitly agreed to "voluntary export restraints" of their steel and aluminum. Under additional pressure, "voluntary" restrictions were later changed to quotas with South Korea, Brazil, and Argentina. Voluntary export restraints are illegal under the WTO treaty. Without qualification, Article 11.1(b) of the WTO Agreement on Safeguards states that "a Member shall not seek, take or maintain any voluntary export restraints, orderly marketing arrangement or any other similar measures on the export or the import side."[72] Indeed, much of the impetus for concluding that agreement in the Uruguay Round of multilateral trade negotiations was to discipline the rampant use — often by the United States — of voluntary export restraints, which impose invisible distortions on trade outcomes in the market and put smaller countries at the mercy of larger ones. Trump and Lighthizer (who had previously negotiated voluntary export restraints with Japan during the Reagan administration in the 1980s) blithely ignored this WTO obligation, and Biden and Tai have not mentioned it.

In response to the Trump steel and aluminum tariffs, other countries refused to buckle to U.S. pressure. The 26 member states of the European Union and 7 other WTO members chose instead to retaliate by imposing tariffs of their own. These are equally illegal under WTO rules because the retaliation has not been authorized after a finding of a treaty violation by the United States in a WTO dispute settlement. And a total of 34 WTO members initiated a total of eight legal complaints against the United States in the WTO: Canada, Mexico, Russia, Turkey, India, Switzerland, Norway, China, and the 26 member states of the European Union. Seven of these WTO cases are still pending in Geneva. The Biden administration is not looking forward to legal judgments in these pending WTO disputes.[73] The U.S. defense to these unilateral tariffs in the WTO depends on whether the United States can succeed legally in its claim of an exception based on national security.

Given the speciousness of the Trump administration's descriptions of its "national security" excuses for applying these tariffs, including on products from America's NATO and other allies, this seems unlikely. And this unlikelihood is perhaps one reason why the Biden administration continues to procrastinate on participating with other WTO members in reviving the appellate function of the WTO dispute settlement system. Like the Trump administration, the Biden administration insists that the WTO has no jurisdiction to judge a WTO member's claim of a national security excuse. But this view has already been rejected by one WTO panel chaired by distinguished former WTO Appellate Body Member Georges Abi-Saab.[74] And it begs the inevitable question: If the WTO has no jurisdiction, then why have the limited circumstances in which this excuse can be justified been spelled out in some detail in Article XXI of the GATT — and remained there without change for 75 years?[75]

The EU — hardest hit by the tariffs among all U.S. trading partners — held off for as long as it could politically, but then, under mounting domestic pressure, eventually imposed $3 billion in retaliatory tariffs on U.S. exports in other sectors of trade. Later, the EU threatened to levy an additional $4 billion in tariffs on U.S. exports. Facing the imminence of these additional tariffs, the Biden administration decided to negotiate with the Europeans and, in October 2021, concluded a deal with the EU to ease the effects of the trade restrictions that the Trump administration had imposed on imports of European steel and aluminum.[76] The deal the Biden administration concluded with the EU on the metals tariffs has been praised for freeing up transatlantic trade. To some extent, it does that. But not entirely. Although the president said that the deal "immediately removes tariffs on the European Union," in fact it substitutes new bilateral tariff-rate quotas for the tariffs. These remove the tariffs from a set amount of goods, but above that low number, the tariffs still apply.[77] Thus, the U.S.-EU deal on steel and aluminum is simply one more example of the Biden administration trying to manage trade. The fact that this continued distortion of trade has been done politely and with the, no doubt, reluctant acquiescence of the Europeans does not make it any less a distortion.

The managed trade in steel and aluminum imports has already imposed heavy costs on American businesses and workers. Like Trump, Biden is, for political reasons, giving priority to trying to protect the jobs of metals workers in the swing states of the Midwest that often determine the outcome of national elections. But jobs in U.S. industries that use steel vastly outnumber jobs in industries that make steel.[78] Thus, "ultimately, Biden must decide whether the good of the few in American manufacturing — the 137,200 or so steel and ironworkers in the country last year — outweighs the good of the many — the 6.5 million workers, by one estimate, who need steel or aluminum for the goods they make. A number of economists warn that steel tariffs could imperil more jobs than they preserve."[79] Gary Hufbauer has estimated that Trump's steel and aluminum tariffs have already cost American consumers $900,000 per year for every steel industry job that has been saved or created.[80] The latest analysis using Statistica software shows that, in the United States, the steel and aluminum tariffs have created 26,280 jobs in the steel and aluminum sector but have caused the loss of 428,725 jobs in other sectors, for a net job loss of 402,445 jobs.[81]

As part of Biden's steel and aluminum deal with the EU, the EU agreed to suspend its WTO case; however, under WTO rules, it could later be revived.[82] Moreover, all the other cases brought against the United States because of the steel and aluminum tariffs by other WTO members continue, although the WTO panels seem to be prolonging their deliberations in hopes that settlements will be reached and they will thereby be rescued from having to rule on the legitimacy of the American national security defense claim. In February 2022, the United States reached a similarly structured — and similarly injurious — deal on steel trade with Japan.[83] In March 2022, the United States struck essentially the same deal with the United Kingdom.[84] American businesses are continuing to be priced out of markets and more American workers are losing their jobs because of these steel and aluminum tariffs and the tariff-rate quotas that the Biden administration has negotiated to replace some of them.

Under any circumstances, tariffs (like entitlements) are easier to implement than to eliminate. Under the prevailing economic and political circumstances in the United States and the rest of the world, eliminating tariffs is even more difficult. The Section 232 tariffs on steel and aluminum illustrate this difficulty. Witness also the recent decision by Biden to extend for four years the safeguard tariffs imposed by Trump on imports of some solar energy products. Not only have these solar tariffs not produced the jobs promised by the domestic solar manufacturing industry that sought them; they have, in fact, caused the loss of 6,000 jobs, while the U.S. solar industry as a whole has "missed out on more than 62,000 jobs, $19 billion in private sector investment and more than 10 gigawatts of solar deployment."[85] In addition to these economic costs, it is hard to see how extending the solar tariffs, and thus making solar energy products more expensive, helps Biden achieve his goal of having solar energy produce nearly half of U.S. electricity by 2050.[86]

As Noah C. Gould has explained, "Trade wars create a deadly cycle of market distortion. Tariffs are followed by subsidies to help domestic industry harmed by tariffs. Tariffs persist long after they are implemented despite efforts to remove them."[87] Moreover, although tariffs are taxes, they are invisible taxes. For consumers, there is no separate line on a sales receipt that itemizes what tariffs add to prices. So, consumers are less likely to realize that they are paying the tariffs that Trump told them were paid by the Chinese and other foreigners.[88] To his credit, Biden has not made such specious assertions. Yet, to remove tariffs, there must first be a desire to remove them. And there is scant evidence that removing tariffs is a priority for the Biden administration.

Biden and China

The Biden trade focus is mainly on China, where there has been little progress toward bilateral trade understanding in his first year. The clear impression is that, in the Biden trade policy, much as in the Trump trade policy before it, all else is seen through the prism of how it relates to China and especially to the geopolitical dimensions of the U.S.-China relationship. This focus is understandable, given the rapid rise of China and the challenge it poses to the long-assumed economic primacy of the United States and the perpetuation of a liberal international order that has long been led by the United States. It is also understandable given the polarization of American politics. Any move made by Biden to lessen the trade tensions with the Chinese government will immediately be attacked by his Republican adversaries as incriminating evidence of his being soft on China and could, therefore, have harmful repercussions for Biden and for Democrats when Americans return to the ballot box in November. To be fair, at this point, if the political tables were turned, and if any such action were taken by a Republican president, the Democrats would likely do the same.

Foremost among the Trump tariffs still in place are, of course, the illegal unilateral tariffs that were imposed on, at their height, more than $400 billion of imports from China under Section 301 of the Trade Act of 1974. These tariffs are illegal under WTO rules because they are unilateral. The WTO treaty states that a WTO member cannot retaliate unilaterally against what it perceives to be a violation of a WTO obligation by another WTO member. The aggrieved member must act multilaterally by first engaging in WTO dispute settlement. If a determination is made that a violation has occurred, then retaliation will be authorized by the total membership of the WTO if the member found to be in violation does not eliminate that violation. Acting unilaterally without first engaging in WTO dispute settlement is a violation of the agreement in and of itself.[89] In the current trade mix of uniliteral actions and unilateral retaliations, some complainants who have responded to Trump's unilateralism with their own are reluctant to make this particular claim, but several cases challenging the unilateral actions by the Trump administration are pending in the WTO.[90]

According to Moody's Investors Service, American consumers are bearing nearly 93 percent of the costs of these tariffs on Chinese goods, and American businesses that export to China have been hurt worse by China's retaliatory tariffs (equally illegal under WTO rules) than have the Chinese exporters to the United States.[91] There has been no winner in the Trump trade war with China. Both countries are losers. And all evidence suggests that the United States has been, by far, the bigger loser.[92] Meanwhile, Trump's avalanche of tariffs has had no discernable effect on his stated and worthy objective of encouraging China to depart from its own discriminatory industrial policy of subsidies, technology transfer requirements, intellectual property piracy, and other shadowy practices that are the source of most of the legitimate concerns of the United States and many of China's other trading partners. Without question, Trump's approach has failed.[93]

And yet, despite all the evidence of this failure, and despite Biden's critical assessment while a candidate of the consequences of Trump's "tariff man" excesses, the Biden administration has, thus far, made no move whatsoever to diminish Trump's China tariffs. Quite the opposite. Tai has publicly and pointedly refused to label the Trump trade policy a failure as it relates to China. "I don't think it's fair to say that I've characterized the previous administration's efforts as 'failed,'" she responded to one questioner. "What I would say is that it hasn't gotten us to where we want to go."[94] As Eric Boehm of Reason has observed, "Most people would call that failure."[95]

Yet, in getting us to where Biden and Tai want us to go with our economic relations with China, Tai seems to have no interest in reducing, much less in eliminating, the bulk of the remaining China tariffs, despite mounting pleas from U.S. businesses desperate to get rid of them.[96] She has restored a lapsed process for seeking exemptions from some of them (through more bureaucratic industrial policy). Tai has said, however, that, in confronting China, she will build on the existing tariffs in crafting

Biden's version of an American trade policy addressed at China.⁹⁷ Meanwhile, although some of Trump's tariffs have been reduced or excluded through exemptions, they still apply to about two-thirds of U.S. imports from China.⁹⁸

Biden has inherited a mutual exercise with China in discriminatory and managed trade that is commonly known as the Phase One trade agreement between the two countries. The transactional deal is a poor substitute for the structural trade deal that Trump and Lighthizer wanted but could not get. By its terms, the Chinese agreed to import $200 billion in additional U.S. agricultural, manufacturing, energy, and services products above their purchase amounts in 2017 between the beginning of 2020 and the end of 2021 — a promised increase of 55 percent.⁹⁹ From the beginning, it has been clear that, whatever China's intent, this goal was unrealistic and unachievable. The general economic slowdown caused by the COVID-19 pandemic only made achieving this goal more problematic. Trump himself has acknowledged that he conjured some of the numerical targets in the deal out of thin air.¹⁰⁰ By year-end 2021, China had met only about 62 percent of the Phase One goal.¹⁰¹

What China did accomplish toward the Phase One goal was done through, as noted trade economist Claude Barfield has put it, "managed trade at its most naked."¹⁰² As another leading trade economist, Gary Hufbauer, explained it at the time of the deal, the only way for China to meet the goal was "to resort to Soviet-style managed trade — in other words, China promises to import a certain dollar or physical volumes of detailed goods and services, regardless of market prices or demand conditions. That's the way the old Soviet Union conducted trade with its satellites for 40 years."¹⁰³ This, of course, is precisely what the United States, traditionally a defender of free markets, has spent decades urging China not to do. This is the tacit adoption by the United States of a home-grown version of the Chinese industrial policy in the form of government-directed economic planning.

To try to fulfill its obligations under the Phase One deal, China has had to divert at least some trade from other trading partners to the United States. Especially given the overall pandemic economic plunge, there may not, so far, have been that much diversion.¹⁰⁴ However, to the extent that this has happened, imports of U.S. goods into the Chinese market have replaced imports from other countries. If this has happened in individual instances because of actions by the Chinese government, then these are violations by China of one of the most fundamental of WTO trade obligations — the most-favored-nation obligation not to discriminate between and among like traded products from other WTO members.[105] In any such violation by China of this core international trade law, the United States is, if not guilty, then clearly complicit as the beneficiary of the violation. Some other countries have threatened to challenge China on the Phase One deal in the WTO if it distorts their trade.[106]

Now that the deadline in the Phase One deal has passed, Biden must decide what to do about the deal and about the fact that China has failed to fulfill its obligations under it. Instead of discarding the deal or trying to renegotiate it in ways that might give it a grip on reality and some semblance of compliance with WTO obligations, Biden and Tai have doubled down on it. They say they will try to enforce it.[107] Tai has called Phase One "a living agreement." But she has yet to offer much enlightenment on how she would change it. For now, she is simply saying that "we are holding them responsible" under the Phase One agreement.[108] Instead of offering a new approach to trade relations between the United States and China, Biden and Tai are mainly proceeding by digging deeper into the muddy mire of the Trump trade ditch.

Without doubt, there is still a central concern in the Biden administration for the fundamental systemic issues and the discriminatory trade practices that have long been the most salient for the United States in its critique of how China treats foreign trade: trade-distorting industrial subsidies to state-owned enterprises, widespread disregard for intellectual property rights, heavy-handed technology transfer requirements, and the like. These were supposed to be the centerpiece for a promised Phase Two trade deal between a second Trump administration and China. It is unclear, though, how Biden and Tai will be able to strike a new deal with China that will require China to stop managing trade when they are spending so much of their limited political capital on insisting that China adhere to the full letter of a deal that does exactly the opposite. The specific transactional targets in the Phase One deal only reinforce state control of the Chinese economy. The United States should instead be pushing China to turn back toward the "reform and opening up" that has been increasingly discarded by Xi and that would result in a more market-oriented Chinese economy.

The obvious first move the Biden administration should have made to intensify the pressure on China to improve its trade behavior and make some of the systemic changes its trading partners desire, would have been to return the United States to the Trans-Pacific Partnership, a regional trade agreement that the Obama administration had negotiated with 11 other Pacific Rim countries. On his first day in office, Trump withdrew the United States from the partnership. Somewhat surprisingly, the 11 other countries decided to go ahead without the recalcitrant Americans and have made a success of the arrangement, which they have renamed the Comprehensive and Progressive Agreement for Trans-Pacific Partnership. Presumably, these countries would welcome the return of the United States, while probably also requiring the United States to make some additional liberalizing commitments as the price of its return. Yet, the Biden administration has made no move to rejoin the partnership.

This is not surprising. Beltway Democrats are so locked in their own unwise embrace of an abundance of false criticisms of the Trans-Pacific trade agreement that returning to it now would cause them to engage in rhetorical contortions even more twisted than those that are increasingly commonplace in the cacophony of contemporary American politics. Plus, returning to the agreement would provoke the ire of labor unions and other protectionist interests that increasingly dominate the official apparatus of the Washington wing of the Democratic Party. Such a show of political courage for the sake of the common good of the country from Biden and Tai would be most welcome, but it appears unlikely, especially in an election year.

In the meantime, the Comprehensive and Progressive Agreement for Trans-Pacific Partnership is otherwise occupied with a recent application for membership from — China. The Chinese have already seized the trade initiative in the Asia-Pacific region, which is central to hopes for future growth in U.S. trade, with the entry into force of their new Regional Comprehensive Economic Partnership with 14 other countries in the region, which is mostly a tariff-cutting exercise.[109] As my Cato colleagues have written elsewhere, the successful establishment of the RCEP has had the effect of "enhancing China's economic and geopolitical gravity in the region at the United States' expense."[110] Biden has promised to increase engagement in Asia to secure economic gains from that fastest-growing part of the global economy, repair the damage done by Trump, and counter the ever-rising Chinese influence there. Yet, on trade with Asia, the president and his administration, with their Trump-like America-first mentality, have so far done little more than utter vague musings about exploring some kind of new Indo-Pacific economic framework.[111]

To the extent the Biden administration has set out a strategy for facing China on trade, it has been that of combining with the EU, Japan, and other Chinese trading partners to challenge abusive Chinese trade practices through joint action. It is thought that, with their combined economic weight, a sizeable group of countries could do more to entice China into eliminating, or at least easing, some of the concerns they share about China's structural forms of state-directed trade discrimination. It is far from clear that this will work, but, at the same time, it has not yet been tried. Thus, instead of the unilateralism of Trump toward China, the United States would try to assemble some sort of a coalition. Biden and Tai have not been clear as to whether this hoped-for coalition would work within the WTO or without. Combined legal actions against China's alleged illegal trade actions under the WTO treaty would multiply the pressure on China to comply with an adverse ruling by the WTO by multiplying the possible legal economic sanctions on China if it did not comply. At the same time, a combined negotiating stance by China's major trading partners could move the Chinese government closer to agreeing to needed new and revised WTO rules on investment, industrial subsidies, and other key areas where WTO rules do not yet exist or are inadequate to address the commercial realities of the 21st century economy.[112]

Human Rights and Democracy

A notable priority in the Biden trade policy is an added emphasis on human rights in relation to trade. Thus far, this priority has centered primarily on worker rights. Foremost has been the focus of the Congress and the Biden administration on the forced labor and other pervasive violations by the Chinese government of the human rights of Muslim Uyghurs and members of other ethnic and religious minority groups in Xinjiang Province in northwest China. In December 2021, the president signed into law the Uyghur Forced Labor Prevention Act, which passed with overwhelming bipartisan support in the Congress.[113] This new law bans imports into the United States of products made in whole or in part in the Xinjiang region unless it can be proven that those products have not been made with forced labor.

Despite abundant evidence to the contrary,[114] the Chinese government denies that there is any forced labor in Xinjiang.[115] Also, Chinese officials say the new U.S. statute is contrary to market principles.[116] Yet those people forced into slave labor are not engaging in voluntary commerce in the market, so opposing forced labor is not inconsistent with market principles. What is more, an exception of this kind has long been permitted in both domestic and international law. All goods made with forced labor have been banned in the United States since 1930.[117] This longstanding law complies with U.S. international trade obligations, and so does the new Uyghur Forced Labor Prevention Act. Under the GATT, which is now part of the WTO treaty, an exception to what would otherwise be an obligation of non-discriminatory treatment for traded products has, since 1947, existed for products of prison labor.[118] In addition, an exception has existed since then for trade restrictions "necessary to protect public morals."[119] Forced labor has long been illegal under international law.[120] It is clearly a violation of public morals. This U.S. action should be able to withstand a challenge by China in the WTO.

A broader emerging question is: How far should WTO members go in linking trade to non-trade considerations? The Biden administration must soon respond to the fact that, increasingly, China has been injecting non-trade considerations into trade decisions where there is no exception in the WTO treaty. First, the Chinese government restricted imports of wine and barley from Australia after the Australian government was so bold as to call for an independent investigation of the origin of the COVID-19 pandemic — which started in China — and to criticize repeatedly the Chinese government's actions in Xinjiang and its crackdown on democracy in Hong Kong.[121] Pending disputes between the two countries are now before WTO panels. More recently, the Chinese government has punished Lithuania for permitting the opening there of a representative office for Taiwan by blocking imports of Lithuanian goods and of goods shipped from other countries that include Lithuanian parts.[122] This has disrupted supply chains in much of Europe. The European Union has challenged these actions in the WTO.[123]

There is urgency for attention by the entire WTO membership to this growing practice of trade coercion. Inaction would embolden China to expand those practices and entice other large countries to likewise push smaller countries around. This kind of trade bullying is a far step beyond what Trump did and is precisely the opposite of what the rule of law in the rules-based multilateral trading system is supposed to be about. Likewise, any "anti-coercion" countermeasures the injured countries may choose to take against such bullying could raise some fundamental issues in international trade law and other public international law.

These kinds of non-trade considerations have not historically entered into the trade decisions of the countries that comprise the members of the system. The underlying understanding among WTO members has always been that the members of the multilateral trading system will trade with one another independently of whatever may be their geopolitical considerations at the time, subject to the national security and other exceptions set out in the WTO treaty. The Chinese actions toward Australia and Lithuania fly in the face of this traditional understanding.

WTO action to address this emerging issue cooperatively will happen only if there is concerted leadership by the Biden administration to help make it happen. At the same time, the president must clarify the link that he and some in his administration have suggested between trade and democracy. Biden has argued that "market democracies, not China or any other country, will write the 21st-century rules around trade and technology."[124] Yet, not all the 164 members of the WTO are democracies, and some others have only the trappings but little or none of the reality of true democracy. Being a genuine democracy is not a prerequisite for membership in the WTO any more than it is for membership in the United Nations. Are the president and others in his administration saying they prefer to make any new trade rules outside the legal framework of the WTO? Are they saying they wish to give preference in trade to products from other democracies, which would violate the WTO obligation of most-favored-nation treatment? Are they saying they wish only to trade with other democracies, which would likewise be inconsistent with WTO rules? Are they saying they intend to make needed new rules for trade only with other democracies? Or are they perhaps saying they wish to agree first on needed new trade rules with other democracies before going together as a group to the other members of the WTO to try to make those new rules fully multilateral within the WTO? Even after the president's first Summit for Democracy in December 2021 — which centered on defending democracy against authoritarianism, fighting governmental corruption, and advancing respect for human rights, and did not delve much into economics — we still do not know.[125]

Biden and the World Trade Organization

There are many puzzling aspects of the Biden trade policy as it relates to the World Trade Organization. Following the scornful retreat from the WTO by Trump, it is altogether unclear how his successor sees the role of the WTO and of the United States in the organization. WTO members failed to agree on a unified statement for the customary concluding declaration at the last ministerial conference in Buenos Aires in 2017 and, for the first time, ended up with no final declaration because the Trump administration insisted on excluding language from the declaration describing the WTO as central to the multilateral trading system.[126] Like other WTO members, the United States had previously insisted on including this statement, which professes a mutual allegiance to the multilateral trading system, in ministerial declarations. Not only did Trump not see the WTO as central to world trade; evidently, he did not see a need for the WTO at all. Does Biden see the WTO as central to world trade?

Unlike Trump, Biden has not threatened to pull the United States out of the WTO and is highly unlikely to do so. Perhaps he comprehends the grave economic and geopolitical consequences for the United States if it were to be so reckless as to do so, which range from a return to astronomical tariffs on American exports to rampant discrimination against American goods and services worldwide and to an unraveling of much of what has been achieved multilaterally toward peaceful global economic governance. And while Trump's trade ambassador, Robert Lighthizer (who had been rejected by other WTO members when nominated for the WTO Appellate Body) rarely missed a chance to denigrate the WTO and made a point of never appearing at the WTO headquarters in Geneva, Tai visited Geneva in October 2021, where she spoke briefly. She stated then that she was there for the purpose of "affirming the United States' continued commitment to the WTO."[127] She added, "The Biden-Harris administration believes that trade — and the WTO — can be a force for good that encourages a race to the top and addresses global challenges as they arise."[128] However, apart from repeating — in perfectly polite terms — the essence of some of the unfounded Beltway aspersions on the Appellate Body and the rest of the WTO dispute settlement system, and making some encouraging statements about the need to conclude some of the current and tediously prolonged WTO negotiations, she had little to say about the details of what she and Biden seek as WTO action and reform.

So far, the WTO seems anything but central to the trade policy of the Biden administration. Trade itself is not an early priority, according to the president himself. And the WTO is treated by the administration as, at best, peripheral to most of what it is doing that relates to trade. WTO obligations are rarely mentioned. WTO options are largely down at the bottom of the list of the administration's trade talking points. Might their slew of Buy American and domestic-content requirements violate WTO rules? Might the Phase One trade deal with China that they inherited from Trump and are insisting on implementing do the same? Might WTO panels rule against the unilateral Trump tariffs that Biden has refused to remove? The Biden administration does not even mention these very real possibilities, much less bother to explain why, despite appearances, these and other legal transgressions are not, in their view, WTO violations. All in all, in the Biden trade policy, the WTO and its rules seem mostly an annoying afterthought.

The tacit policy of the Trump administration was to comply with WTO rules when it was expedient and ignore them when it was not. Despite some soft and reassuring words to other WTO members, there is no evidence thus far that the policy of the Biden administration is any different. Nor does the Biden administration appear to be doing much more than going through the motions in Geneva. According to former WTO director-general Pascal Lamy of France, a firm friend of the United States, "What Katherine Tai has been doing is all talk and no walk. If you look where they have moved, so far, zero concrete moves."[129] The professional career USTR trade negotiators who endured Trump and are now directed by Biden and Tai say they are "deeply engaged" in WTO deliberations, and there is no doubt a number of them are. But negotiators in Geneva can make only so much progress without strong political backing and the presence and push of political priority. And, on trade, Biden's backing is limited, and his priorities are elsewhere. Also, as is obvious to any seasoned American political observer, if the Biden administration wishes to do anything multilaterally on trade, it does not wish to do it until after the U.S. midterm elections in November.

Because of the surge of the Omicron variant of COVID-19, the long-delayed 12th Ministerial Conference of the WTO (originally planned for Kazakhstan in 2019, and, most recently, for Geneva in 2021) was postponed, yet again, until June. Sadly, this is just as well. In part because of the failure of the Biden administration in its first year to seize the initiative and make revival and reinvigoration of the WTO an American priority, an earlier conference would likely have accomplished little. Current WTO negotiations — including those aimed at ending tariffs on environmental goods, establishing new disciplines on fisheries subsidies, and agreeing on core rules on digital trade — are either in impasse or are still short of the consensus necessary for agreement. Numerous new international trade issues are not even on the WTO negotiating agenda.[130] The opportunity is still there for the Biden administration to make the modernization and continued success of the WTO a priority, but positive U.S. leadership is missing. Try as they may, other WTO members are unlikely to succeed without renewed and creative U.S. leadership.

Standing in the way of a return by the United States to an affirmative and positive role as a leader in the WTO is the misguided and misleading assault, by Congressional Democrats and Republicans alike, on the procedures and substance of WTO dispute settlement. Biden and Tai are no exceptions to this errant attack (although Tai, as an experienced WTO litigator, probably knows better but finds it impolitic to acknowledge it). Primarily, this rhetorical mugging has been inflicted on the Appellate Body, the WTO tribunal of final appeal. In the rest of the world, the Appellate Body is widely respected as a fair and impartial tribunal whose jurists have been firmly committed to upholding WTO rules and the rule of law in world trade. Within the Beltway, though, it has long since become gospel that the Appellate Body has exceeded its mandate in the WTO treaty by overreaching and inventing WTO obligations that were never agreed to in the WTO treaty.[131]

This is not true. The Appellate Body — like the Supreme Court of the United States and every other judicial tribunal in the world — is not perfect. It is comprised of human beings with all their frailties. Yes, the Appellate Body has increasingly taken longer than the treaty-allotted 90 days to render its reports. Also, departing Appellate Body members have sometimes remained much longer than originally anticipated to complete pending appeals. And yes, a few of the reports of the Appellate Body in recent years have said more than, strictly speaking, has been needed to be said to render the necessary legal rulings. The better course for the Appellate Body is always to say less rather than more. All this is fair criticism and should be addressed.

Yet the supposed sins of the Appellate Body in recent years have been wildly exaggerated by the United States — mainly for domestic political reasons.[132] Republican and Democratic administrations alike have lost a long series of antidumping and other trade remedies cases before the Appellate Body in main because they have pushed past what the outer bounds of the WTO rules permit in applying such trade restrictions. This is of great importance in American politics because those who seek restrictions on imports in the form of these remedies are mostly located in Pennsylvania, Michigan, Wisconsin, and other swing states in the Midwest that usually determine the outcomes of national elections. Thus, these interests have inordinate influence in both political parties.

American political concerns about legal limits on trade remedies — limits to which the United States agreed to in the WTO treaty — are rarely mentioned in criticisms of the Appellate Body. The largely bogus and often self-righteous rationales of both the Trump and Biden administrations for dismantling the Appellate Body by depriving it of any judges are mostly charades for their politically expedient capitulation to domestic protectionist interests.

More than two years have passed since the Trump administration completed emptying the Appellate Body of its treaty complement of seven judges by blocking a needed consensus on new appointments. This has prevented appeals from WTO panel reports — and thus precluded the WTO membership from finalizing them by adopting them. And this has returned the WTO to the pre-WTO days of the old GATT organization by effectively permitting a country that loses a dispute before a WTO panel to veto enforcement of that judgment. By all appearances, Biden and Tai, like their predecessors, prefer this resulting arrangement, which generally enables the United States to have its way against other — usually smaller — countries. If the United States wins a case before a panel and the losing party blocks the adoption of the panel report, then the United States can proceed with economic sanctions anyway, relying on its enormous economic clout to bludgeon the other country into submission. If the United States loses a case before a panel, however, it can — a as it has, hypocritically, already done — appeal the panel ruling to the now-empty Appellate Body and then correctly claim that it has been denied its right of appeal in the WTO treaty and therefore the panel report cannot be adopted. And then only the largest of the U.S. trading partner — the European Union, China, or Japan, perhaps — may have the economic clout to insist that the United States comply with the panel's rulings and recommendations. This is not the international rule of law. This is might makes right.

Perhaps because it prefers the current situation, thus far the Biden administration has refused to tell other WTO members the precise reforms it seeks in WTO dispute settlement as the price for agreeing to reconstituting the Appellate Body. Other WTO members — while largely disagreeing with almost all of the criticisms the United States has made of the Appellate Body — have bent over backward to try to accommodate the United States on this crucial issue, increasingly to the point of appeasement. Desperate to have the Americans fully engaged once again in the WTO, they seem to be slowly acquiescing to U.S. intransigence.

Unintentionally, if these members capitulate to U.S. demands, they risk the independence and impartiality of the Appellate Body and, with it, the entirety of the integrity of the WTO dispute settlement system. This must not happen. Without a system for resolving international trade disputes that upholds those rules independently and impartially, WTO rules will cease to have practical meaning and the WTO as an institution will wither away.

Unless and until this impasse is ended with the reinforcement of the rule of law in the multilateral trading system, the WTO will not be in a position diplomatically to proceed with a broader agenda of reform that would revise and update its rules to realign this essential organization and bring it more fully into the commercial and ecological world of the 21st century.[133] And, without such reforms, the WTO will become increasingly irrelevant as world trade shifts from global governance to an array of multiplying bilateral and regional blocs and trade and trade-related confrontations in which the outcomes are shaped, not by law, but by economic and potentially other forms of international intimidation. In international trade, the rule of law will slowly succumb to the rule of power.

A choice of words often reveals an underlying belief. In her remarks in Geneva, Tai declared that trade "can be a force for good."[134] Can be? Why not "has been?" Or, better yet, why not "is?" In her telling phrasing, America's trade ambassador implies, however unwittingly, that trade is not — and has not been — a force for good for the United States and for the wider world. In this, she discloses what is, at bottom, the flawed foundation of the Biden trade policy: it does not assume that trade, as trade, is inherently good, subject to the kinds of exceptions that are set out in the WTO treaty. So long as this view prevails in the Biden administration, there will be no affirmative modernization of the WTO, and thus there will be no real progress in combating and lowering the barriers to trade that are imposing obstacles to the achievement of a broader, more inclusive, and more sustainable prosperity in the United States and in the rest of the world.

Conclusion

The current Biden trade policy is the reign of polite protectionism. Trump may return to the White House after the 2024 election, but he does not live there now. For now, there is no reckless talk that "trade wars are good, and easy to win."[135] Presumably, Biden knows better. The words about trade are now in quiet and civil terms. The deeds, however, are still often protectionist, although they may parade under other, less minatory names. Many of the Trump trade restrictions remain. Many more similar restrictions have been proposed. Can this change? After a first year of going mostly in the wrong direction on trade, can Biden and his administration turn the United States away from its self-defeating inward course on trade and turn it back toward the right course of trade liberalization and multilateralism?

Doing so will require the expression of a much clearer understanding by the president and by his administration of the vast benefits of trade for Americans and the inevitable economic and other costs for Americans of curbing it. Those in the Biden administration and on Capitol Hill who advocate restraining trade would do well to reexamine some of their premises that tilt them toward old and new kinds of trade protection. Biden's trade policy does not yet reflect it, but, even amid the mire of misinformation about trade and the morass of American political polarization, an American leader with so many achievements and such long experience must surely be aware that trade has been — and is — a force of good, and that more trade is a necessary means of making more prosperity.

Doing so will also require political courage. Trade policy can never be separated from domestic politics — and certainly not in a democracy. Increasingly, too, in the complexity of an interconnected world, it is harder and harder to separate the commercial considerations of trade policy from the broader decisions of geopolitics. Trade concerns are inextricably interwoven with other concerns. Politically, the easier course by far today is the course of trade protection. Freer trade is hard to advocate at a time when there is so much popular mistrust of expertise and of elites, including elected leaders and established institutions. Yet, the essence of political leadership is finding a way to do what is right and what is most needed even when there are difficult political constraints. In trade, as in all else, this is an everyday challenge for Biden, as it is with everyone who is privileged to serve in an elected office in the representative democracy that is the United States.

Lastly, doing so will require the president and others in his administration — along with their allies in the Congress — to educate the American people anew about how much they have benefited, and are benefiting, from trade and how much more they could benefit if they were willing to support making and maintaining a more open economy as a vital part of an open society. Much of the challenge of democratic representation lies in summoning the resolve to do something other than merely raising a finger to gauge the current direction of the political wind. Democratic governance should not be simply governance by the most recent political poll. A corollary of this challenge as it relates to trade is having the courage to tell the American people the truth about trade. It is cutting through all the misconceptions many of them have about the effects of trade to impart the reality of all that trade has done and can do for them.

Rising to this challenge has never been easy in American politics. It is not easy now. As Tai has ruefully said on trade, "It's really complicated right now."[136] But this is no excuse for not doing what our chosen leaders must do: rise above the complications to end the reign of polite protectionism by framing and pursuing a new trade policy for all Americans — a policy that will achieve additional trade liberalization, stop managed trade, halt trade-restrictive industrial policy, renew trade multilateralism, and give restored and unflinching support to the international rule of law in trade.

Appendix

Biden administration's major actions on trade, January 2021–March 2022

Date	Action	Updates
January 20, 2021	Biden signs Executive Order 13990: "Protecting Public Health and the Environment and Restoring Science to Tackle the Climate Crisis," revoking the permit for the Keystone XL pipeline.	—
January 25, 2021	Biden signs Executive Order 14005: "Ensuring the Future Is Made in All of America by All of America's Workers," to tighten certain buy American regulations.	Made in America office established within the Office of Management and Budget; "Made in America" website launched; proposals to amend the Federal Acquisition Regulation and the Defense Federal Acquisition Regulation Supplement published on July 30 and August 30, 2021.

(Continued)

Table A.1. (*Continued*)

Date	Action	Updates
February 24, 2021	Biden signs Executive Order 14017: "America's Supply Chains," to review vulnerabilities in the supply chains of semiconductors, high-capacity batteries, critical minerals and other strategic materials, and pharmaceuticals and active pharmaceutical ingredients.	100-day supply chain assessments completed on June 8, 2021; established Supply Chain Disruptions Task Force in June 2021; one-year reports analyzing key weaknesses and devising multiyear strategies to address them published on February 24, 2022.
March 4, 2021	Reaches an agreement on a four-month suspension of tariffs related to the Airbus-Boeing dispute with the UK.	Agreement for a five-year suspension reached with the UK.
March 5, 2021	Reaches an agreement on a four-month suspension of tariffs related to the Airbus-Boeing dispute with the EU.	Agreement for a five-year suspension reached with the EU.
May 5, 2021	Announces support for TRIPS waiver for COVID-19 vaccines.	Negotiations ongoing at the WTO.
May 12, 2021	Invokes USMCA labor rapid-response mechanism for the first time due to concerns about denials of labor rights at a General Motors plant in Silao, Mexico.	Remediation agreed with Mexico.
May 25, 2021	Requests USMCA panel to challenge Canada's allocation of dairy tariff-rate quotas.	Prevailed in panel on January 4, 2022.
May 26, 2021	Submits proposal on addressing forced labor as part of WTO negotiations on fisheries subsidies.	Negotiations ongoing at the WTO.
June 2, 2021	Announces Section 301 tariffs on Austria, India, Italy, Spain, Turkey, and the UK, due to their digital services taxes, immediately suspending them to allow time for negotiations on international taxation at the OECD and the G20.	—

Table A.1. (*Continued*)

Date	Action	Updates
June 9, 2021	Invokes USMCA labor rapid-response mechanism due to concerns about denials of rights at an auto parts manufacturing facility in Matamoros, Mexico.	Remediation agreed with the auto parts company in Mexico.
June 15, 2021	Announces joint U.S.-EU cooperative framework for large civil aircraft. Suspends Section 301 related to Airbus-Boeing dispute for five years.	—
June 17, 2021	Announces joint U.S.-UK cooperative framework for large civil aircraft. Suspends Section 301 tariffs related to Airbus-Boeing dispute for five years.	—
July 19, 2021	Reaches an agreement with State Bank of Vietnam on addressing Vietnam's currency practices, settling Section 301 investigation on this matter.	—
July 20, 2021	Joins WTO negotiations on services domestic regulation.	Negotiations concluded on December 2, 2021.
September 27, 2021	Build Back Better Act, containing protectionist provisions such as a tax credit for union-made electric vehicles, introduced in the House of Representatives.	Passed in the House on November 19, 2021; held up in the Senate due to political disagreements.
September 28–29, 2021	Convenes inaugural U.S.-EU Trade and Technology Council meeting in Pittsburgh.	—
October 1, 2021	Reaches an agreement with Vietnam on addressing illegal timber trade, settling Section 301 investigation on this matter.	—
October 4, 2021	United States Trade Representative Katherine Tai delivers a speech outlining the Biden administration's approach to the U.S.-China trading relationship.	China has not fulfilled its purchase commitments under the Phase One deal.

(*Continued*)

Table A.1. (*Continued*)

Date	Action	Updates
October 13–25, 2021	Reaches agreements with businesses, port authorities, and labor unions to get the Port of Los Angeles/Long Beach to expand to 24/7 operations.	—
October 21, 2021	Reaches an agreement with Austria, France, Italy, Spain, and the UK to resolve Section 301 investigation on their digital services taxes in light of OECD/G20 framework announced on October 8, 2021.	—
October 31, 2021	Reaches an agreement with the EU on steel overcapacity and clean manufacturing, replacing Section 232 tariffs with tariff-rate quota system.	—
November 15, 2021	Signs Infrastructure Investment and Jobs Act into law, tightening buy America mandates for federal procurement.	—
November 22, 2021	Reaches an agreement with Turkey to resolve Section 301 investigation on its digital services taxes in light of OECD/G20 framework announced on October 8, 2021.	—
November 24, 2021	Reaches an agreement with India to resolve Section 301 investigation on its digital services taxes in light of OECD/G20 framework announced on October 8, 2021.	—
November 30, 2021	Renews trilateral partnership with Japan and the EU to address challenges posed by non-market policies and practices of third countries.	—
December 16, 2021	Announces temporary relaxation of trucking regulations to expand the amount of truckers on the road.	—

Table A.1. (*Continued*)

Date	Action	Updates
January 1, 2022	Terminates African Growth and Opportunity Act preferences for Ethiopia, Mali, and Guinea.	—
February 4, 2022	Biden extends Trump-era tariffs on imported solar cells and panels, with some changes.	—
February 7, 2022	Reaches an agreement with the EU on steel overcapacity and clean manufacturing, replacing Section 232 tariffs with tariff-rate quota system.	—
February 11, 2022	Releases Indo-Pacific Strategy.	—
February 24, 2022	Announces plan to leverage federal funds, along with the Infrastructure Investment and Jobs Act, American Rescue Plan, Buy American Act, and Defense Production Act to strengthen supply chains and expand the U.S. industrial base.	—

Sources: White House, Office of the United States Representative, and the *Federal Register*.
Note: G20 = Group of Twenty; OECD = Organisation for Economic Co-operation and Development; TRIPS = Trade-Related Aspects of Intellectual Property Rights; USMCA = United States-Mexico-Canada Agreement; WTO = World Trade Organization.

Endnotes

[1] Ana Swanson, "In Washington, 'Free Trade' Is No Longer Gospel," *New York Times*, March 17, 2021.
[2] *Ibid*.
[3] "Confirmation Process for Katherine Tai for U.S. Trade Representative," Ballotpedia, https://ballotpedia.org/Confirmation_process_for_Katherine_Tai_for_U.S._trade_representative.
[4] *See* James Bacchus, "Trade Is Good for Your Health: Freeing Trade in Medicines and Other Medical Goods during and Beyond the COVID-19 Emergency," Cato Institute Policy Analysis no. 918, June 30, 2021.
[5] Doug Palmer, "Tai Wary of Cutting Tariffs on Health Care Goods," *Politico*, December 9, 2021.

[6] Simon Lester, "Countering the 'Unfettered Liberalization' Narrative," *International Economic Law and Policy* (blog), WorldTradeLaw.net, December 9, 2021.

[7] "Trade and American Jobs: The Impact of Trade on U.S. and State-Level Employment: 2019 Update," Trade Partnership Worldwide, March 2019, p. 2.

[8] Gary Clyde Hufbauer and Zhiyao (Lucy) Lu, "The Payoff to America from Globalization: A Fresh Look with a Focus on Costs to Workers," Peterson Institute for International Economics, Policy Brief 17–16, May 2017, p. 1. These numbers are in 2016 dollars and reflect a household consisting of 2.64 persons.

[9] Gabriel Felbermayr, Yoto V. Yotov, and Erdal Yalcin, "The World Trade Organization at 25: Assessing the Economic Value of the Rules Based Global Trading System," Bertelsmann Stiftung, November 2019, p. 33.

[10] For some of these dashed hopes, *see* James Bacchus, "Democrats and Trade 2021: A Pro-Trade Policy for the Democratic Party," Cato Institute Policy Analysis no. 900, August 11, 2020.

[11] James McBride, "After Trump: What Will Biden Do on Trade?," Council on Foreign Relations, January 13, 2021.

[12] "President-Elect Biden on Foreign Policy," Council on Foreign Relations, November 7, 2020.

[13] Edward Alden, "No, Biden Will Not End Trade Wars," *Foreign Policy*, October 2, 2020.

[14] "President-Elect Biden on Foreign Policy."

[15] "Text: George Bush's Address to the APEC Summit in Shanghai," *The Guardian*, October 20, 2001.

[16] *See* James Bacchus, *Trade and Freedom* (London: Cameron May, 2004).

[17] Sean D. Ehrlich, "Opinion — How Much Will Biden's Trade Policy Differ from Trump's?," *E-International Relations*, May 5, 2021; and McBride, "After Trump: What Will Biden Do on Trade?"

[18] Daniel Griswold, "Joe Biden's So-So Record on Trade," *Cato at Liberty* (blog), Cato Institute, August 25, 2008.

[19] James Bacchus, "Democrats, Free Trade Is Your Destiny," *Wall Street Journal*, December 3, 2018.

[20] For my explanation of why these assumptions are incorrect, *see* James Bacchus, *Trade Links: New Rules for a New World* (Cambridge: Cambridge University Press, 2022), pp. 58–60, 128–132; and James Bacchus, *The Willing World: Shaping and Sharing a Sustainable Global Prosperity* (Cambridge: Cambridge University Press, 2018), pp. 83, 86–90.

[21] Eric Martin, "Biden's Fast-Track Trade Authority Is Set to Expire This Week," *Bloomberg*, June 29, 2021.

[22] Martin, "Biden's Fast-Track Trade Authority Is Set to Expire This Week."

[23] *See* Caitlan Devereaux, "Presidential Authority over Trade: Imposing Tariffs and Duties," Congressional Research Service, R44707, December 9, 2016.

24 White House, "Fact Sheet: The Bipartisan Infrastructure Deal," press release, November 6, 2021.
25 Mason Bissada, "Biden and Manchin Kept Discussing Build Back Better Bill after Manchin's Public Rejection," *Forbes*, December 31, 2021.
26 Marc L. Busch, "Biden's Muddled Trade Policy," *The Hill*, December 24, 2021.
27 Yuka Hayashi, "U.S. on Sidelines as China and Other Asia-Pacific Nations Launch Trade Pact," *Wall Street Journal*, January 1, 2022.
28 Office of the United States Trade Representative, "U.S. Trade Representative Katherine Tai Outlines Biden-Harris Administration's Historic 'Worker-Centered Trade Policy,'" press release, June 10, 2021.
29 "Tai Outlines Biden-Harris Administration's Historic 'Worker-Centered Trade Policy.'"
30 Office of the United States Trade Representative, "USTR Announces the Development of a Focused Trade Strategy to Combat Forced Labor," press release, January 25, 2022.
31 White House, "Fact Sheet: Biden-Harris Administration Issues Proposed Buy American Rules, Advancing the President's Commitment to Ensuring the Future of America Is Made in America by All of America's Workers," press release, July 28, 2021.
32 Stephen Barlas, "Domestic Iron and Steel Content Requirements Increase Sharply in Infrastructure Bill," *The Fabricator*, December 13, 2021.
33 Joe Gould, "Buy American: Biden Sees Industry Pushback as Allies Warn of Trade Consequences," *Defense News*, November 1, 2021.
34 Scott Lincicome, "Biden Rejects Open Trade at a U.S. Factory Dependent On It," *Cato at Liberty* (blog), Cato Institute, July 28, 2021.
35 Gary Clyde Hufbauer and Eujin Jung, "'Buy American' and Similar Domestic Purchase Policies Impose High Costs on Taxpayers," Peterson Institute for International Economics, August 6, 2020.
36 Chris Edwards, "No Need for Biden's Electric Vehicle Subsidies," *Cato at Liberty* (blog), Cato Institute, April 26, 2021.
37 Scott Lincicome and Ilana Blumsack, "On EV Tax Credits, What's Proponents' Real Objective?" *Cato at Liberty* (blog), Cato Institute, November 19, 2021.
38 Riley Beggin, "Canada Threatens to Impose Tariffs if EV Tax Credits Pass," *Detroit News*, December 10, 2021.
39 Stephen Wicary, "Trudeau Weighs Auto-Content Rules as Next U.S. Trade Flashpoint," *Bloomberg*, November 29, 2021.
40 *See* Simon Lester and Inu Manak, "The USMCA Is Moving Forward (Too) Quickly," *Cato at Liberty* (blog), Cato Institute, December 16, 2019; and Simon Lester and Inu Manak, "Evaluating the New USMCA," *Cato at Liberty* (blog), Cato Institute, December 11, 2019.
41 *Hearing on Implementation and Enforcement of the United States-Mexico-Canada Agreement: One Year After Entry into Force, Before the Committee on*

Finance, 117th Cong. (2021) (testimony by Inu Manak, Research Fellow at the Cato Institute), https://www.cato.org/testimony/hearing-implementation-enforcement-united-states-mexico-canada-agreement-one-year-after.

[42] Scott Lincicome, "A Reality Check on the Pandemic, Supply Chains, and Our 'April 2020 Mindset,'" *The Dispatch*, March 3, 2021.

[43] *See* James Bacchus, "Trade Is Good for Your Health."

[44] Harry Dempsey, "No End in Sight," *Financial Times*, January 10, 2022.

[45] *Ibid. See also* Scott Lincicome, "Manufactured Crisis: 'Deindustrialization,' Free Markets, and National Security," Cato Institute Policy Analysis no. 907, January 27, 2021.

[46] *See,* for example, Gabriella Beaumont-Smith, "More Regulation Will Not Improve Port Efficiency," *Cato at Liberty* (blog), Cato Institute, November 16, 2021.

[47] Scott Lincicome, "More Protectionism Won't Fix the Supply-Chain Crisis," *Barron's*, November 8, 2021.

[48] Adam Thierer, "On Defining 'Industrial Policy,'" *Technology Liberation Front* (blog), September 3, 2020.

[49] Brian Picone and David E. Bond, "House 'Build Back Better Act' Sets Stage for Trade Disputes over Green Energy," White and Case, November 19, 2021.

[50] Scott Lincicome, "Moving Fast and Breaking Things," *The Dispatch*, February 2, 2022.

[51] Adam Thierer and Connor Haaland, "Does the United States Need a More Targeted Industrial Policy for High Tech?," Mercatus Center, George Mason University, November 17, 2021.

[52] For a concurring view, *see* Tori K. Smith, "Joe Biden's China Trade Strategy Would Make U.S. More like China," Heritage Foundation, October 7, 2021.

[53] Scott Lincicome and Huan Zhu, "*Questioning Industrial Policy: Why Government Manufacturing Plans Are Ineffective and Unnecessary*," Cato Institute White Paper, September 2021, p. 48.

[54] *See generally* Daniel Ikenson, "Mercantilist Reciprocity or Free Trade: Globalization at a Crossroads," Hinrich Foundation, October 2021.

[55] Michael T. Nietzel, "Low Literacy Levels among U.S. Adults Could Be Costing the Economy $2.2 Trillion a Year," *Forbes*, September 9, 2020.

[56] Jacob Pramuk, "'I Am a Tariff Man': Trump Threatens to Restart Trade War if China Talks Fail," *CNBC*, December 4, 2018.

[57] "Biden's Hands May Be Tied on Trump's China Tariffs, Trade Experts Say," *Reuters*, September 8, 2020.

[58] Steven Overly, "U.S. Trade Chief: Biden Will Build from Trump-Era Tariffs to Confront China," *Politico*, September 30, 2021.

[59] Noah C. Gould, "Biden Continues Trump's Harmful Trade Policy," *National Review*, October 11, 2021.

[60] Andrew Chatzky and Anshu Siripurapu, "The Truth about Tariffs," Council on Foreign Relations, October 8, 2021.

61 "The US-China Economic Relationship: A Crucial Partnership at a Critical Juncture," US-China Business Council and Oxford Economics, January 2020.

62 Tom Lee and Jacqueline Varas, "The Total Cost of U.S. Tariffs," American Action Forum, November 16, 2021.

63 *See*, for example, Mary Amiti, Stephen J. Redding, and David Weinstein, "The Impact of the 2018 Trade War on U.S. Prices and Welfare," National Bureau of Economic Research Working Paper no. 25672, March 2019; Pablo D. Fajgelbaum et al., "The Return to Protectionism," National Bureau of Economic Research Working Paper no. 25638, October 2019; and Mary Amiti, Stephen J. Redding, and David E. Weinstein, "Who's Paying for the US Tariffs? A Longer-Term Perspective," National Bureau of Economic Research Working Paper no. 26610, January 2020.

64 David Wainer, "End Trump's Trade War? Easy Inflation Win Could Backfire on Biden," *Bloomberg*, November 18, 2021.

65 "Biden Joins the Lumber Trade Wars," *Wall Street Journal*, November 29, 2021.

66 "Skyrocketing Lumber Prices Add Nearly $36,000 to New Home Prices," National Association of Home Builders, April 28, 2021.

67 Silvia Amar and Leslie Josephs, "U.S. and EU Resolve 17-Year Boeing-Airbus Trade Dispute," CNBC, June 15, 2021; and see also Sylvia Pfeifer and Aime Williams, "UK and US Settle Long-Running Airbus-Boeing Trade Dispute," *Financial Times*, June 17, 2021.

68 Jennifer Hillman and Seara Grundhoefer, "Can the U.S.-EU Trade and Technology Council Succeed?," Council on Foreign Relations, October 29, 2021.

69 Seung Min Kim and Jeff Stein, "U.S. Announces Deal with European Union to Ease Steel and Aluminum Tariffs Enacted under Trump," *Washington Post*, October 30, 2022; *see also* Scott Lincicome and Inu Manak, "Protectionism or National Security? The Use and Abuse of Section 232," Cato Institute Analysis no. 912, March 9, 2021.

70 Chad P. Bown and Katheryn (Kadee) Russ, "Biden and Europe Remove Trump's Steel and Aluminum Tariffs, but It's Not Free Trade," *Trade and Investment Policy Watch* (blog), Peterson Institute for International Economics, November 11, 2021.

71 Aaron Gregg and Christian Davenport, "Trump Says Steel Imports Are a Threat to National Security. The Defense Industry Disagrees," *Washington Post*, March 5, 2018.

72 Agreement on Safeguards art. 11(b), April 15, 1994, Marrakesh Agreement Establishing the World Trade Organization, Annex 1A, 1869 U.N.T.S. 154.

73 Marc L. Busch, "The Six Trade Disputes That Could Imperil American Exports for Years to Come," *The Hill*, February 5, 2022.

74 "Russia — Measures Concerning Traffic in Transit," Report of the Panel, World Trade Organization, WT/DS512/R, April 5, 2019.

[75] General Agreement on Tariffs and Trade, art. XXI, October 30, 1947, 61 Stat. A-11, 55 U.N.T.S. 194.

[76] Kim and Stein, "U.S. Announces Deal with European Union."

[77] Bown and Russ, "Biden and Europe Remove Trump's Steel and Aluminum Tariffs."

[78] Kadee Russ and Lydia Cox, "Will Steel Tariffs Put U.S. Jobs at Risk?," *Econofact*, February 26, 2018.

[79] Steven Overly, "Why Trump's Steel Tariffs Are Now Biden's Political Headache," *Politico*, September 6, 2021.

[80] Heather Long, "Trump's Steel Tariffs Cost U.S. Consumers $900,000 for Every Job Created, Experts Say," *Washington Post*, May 7, 2019.

[81] "Projected Overall Number of Jobs Gained or Lost as a Result of Steel and Aluminum Tariffs and Subsequent Retaliations in 2018, by State," Statista, 2022, https://www.statista.com/statistics/914135/predicted-job-gains-losses-steel-aluminum-import-tariffs-state/.

[82] "U.S., EU Downgrade Metal Tariff Dispute at WTO," *Reuters*, January 21, 2022.

[83] Scott Lincicome, "This (Steel) Deal Is Getting Worse All the Time," *Cato at Liberty* (blog), Cato Institute, February 8, 2022.

[84] Andrea Shalal and David Lawder, "New U.S.-U.K. Trade Deal Cuts Tariffs on British Steel, American Motorcycles, Bourbon," *Reuters*, March 22, 2022.

[85] These numbers are according to the Solar Energy Industries Association. *See* James Bacchus and Gabriella Beaumont-Smith, "Let the Sun Set on Solar Tariffs," *Cato at Liberty* (blog), Cato Institute, January 19, 2022.

[86] Darryl Fears, "Biden Officials Trumpet How Solar Energy Can Provide Nearly Half of the Nation's Electricity by 2050," *Washington Post*, September 8, 2021; *see also* James Bacchus and Gabriella Beaumont Smith, "Solar Tariffs on the Horizon," *Cato at Liberty* (blog), Cato Institute, February 8, 2022.

[87] Noah C. Gould, "Biden Continues Trump's Harmful Trade Policy."

[88] "Who Pays Trump's Tariffs, China or U.S. Customers and Companies?," *Reuters*, May 21, 2019.

[89] Understanding on Rules and Procedures Governing the Settlement of Disputes art. 23, Marrakesh Agreement Establishing the World Trade Organization, Annex 2, 1869 U.N.T.S. 401, 33 I.L.M. 1226 (1994); and "Canada — Continued Suspension of Obligations in the EC — Hormones Dispute," Report of the Appellate Body, World Trade Organization, AB/R, WT/DS321, October 16, 2008, para. 373.

[90] *See* "United States — Tariff Measures on Certain Goods from China," Report of the Panel, World Trade Organization, WT/DS543/R, September 15, 2020, which the United States has appealed; *see also* "DS565: United States — Tariff Measures on Certain Goods from China II," Dispute Settlement, World Trade Organization, https://www.wto.org/english/tratop_e/dispu_e/cases_e/ds565_e.htm; and

"DS587: United States — Tariff Measures on Certain Goods from China III," Dispute Settlement, World Trade Organization, https://www.wto.org/english/tratop_e/dispu_e/cases_e/ds587_e.htm.

[91] Eric Boehm, "China Is Paying Less than 8 Percent of Tariff Costs. Americans Are Paying the Rest," *Reason*, May 24, 2021.

[92] Huang Tran, "Decoupling/Reshoring versus Dual Circulation: Competing Strategies for Security and Influence," Atlantic Council, April 2021.

[93] Eric Boehm, "Tariffs on Chinese Imports Have Accomplished Approximately Nothing," Reason, September 23, 2021; and Samantha Vortherms and Jiakun Jack Zhang, "Political Risk and Firm Exit: Evidence from the US–China Trade War," 21st Century China Center Research Paper no. 2021-09, September 2, 2021.

[94] "A Conversation with Ambassador Katherine Tai, U.S. Trade Representative," Center for Strategic and International Studies, October 4, 2021.

[95] Eric Boehm, "Biden's China Trade Policy Is Littered with Contradictions," *Reason*, October 4, 2021.

[96] Jacob Fromer, "Biden Administration Shrugs Off Pressure to Remove Trump-Era China Trade War Tariffs," *South China Morning Post*, August 7, 2021.

[97] Steven Overly, "Biden Will Build from Trump-Era Tariffs."

[98] Ana Swanson, "Biden's China Dilemma: How to Enforce China's Trade Pact," *New York Times*, December 15, 2021.

[99] "Economic and Trade Agreement Between the Government of the United States and the People's Republic of China," January 15, 2020.

[100] Swanson, "Biden's China Dilemma."

[101] Chad P. Bown, "US-China Phase One Tracker: China's Purchases of US Goods," Peterson Institute for International Economics, November 2021.

[102] Claude Barfield, "The Biden Administration's New (Old) China Trade Policy," American Enterprise Institute, October 8, 2021.

[103] Gary Clyde Hufbauer, "Managing Trade: Centerpiece of US-China Phase One Deal," *Trade and Investment Policy Watch* (blog), Peterson Institute for International Economics, January 16, 2020.

[104] Hunter L. Clark, "An Update on the U.S.-China Phase One Trade Deal," *Liberty Street Economics* (blog), Federal Reserve Bank of New York, October 6, 2021.

[105] General Agreement on Tariffs and Trade, art. I.

[106] *See*, for example, "EU Warns of WTO Challenge If China-US Deal Creates 'Distortions,'" *France 24*, January 17, 2020.

[107] Chad P. Bown, "Why Biden Will Try to Enforce Trump's Phase One Trade Deal with China," *Trade and Investment Policy Watch* (blog), Peterson Institute for International Economics, December 15, 2021.

[108] Swanson, "Biden's China Dilemma."

[109] Hayashi, "U.S. on Sidelines."

[110] Scott Lincicome et al., "The Cato Trade Team's 2022 Policy Wish List," *Cato at Liberty* (blog), Cato Institute, January 10, 2022.

[111] Philip Heijmans, "Biden's 'America First' Trade Policy Gives China an Opportunity," *Bloomberg*, November 9, 2021.

[112] For much more on the need for new and revised WTO rules, *see* James Bacchus, *Trade Links: New Rules for a New World.*

[113] Felicia Sonmez, "Biden Signs Uyghur Forced Labor Prevention Act into Law," *Washington Post*, December 23, 2021.

[114] *See* "Xinjiang Internment Camps," Wikipedia, February 14, 2022.

[115] "China Rejects All Accusations of Abuses in Xinjiang," *Associated Press*, April 20, 2021.

[116] "China Firmly Rejects U.S. Signing of So-Called 'Uyghur Forced Labor Prevention Act,'" *Xinhua*, December 24, 2021.

[117] Tariff Act of 1930, 19 U.S.C. § 1307.

[118] General Agreement on Tariffs and Trade, art. XX(e).

[119] General Agreement on Tariffs and Trade, art. XX(a).

[120] See, for example, "P029 — Protocol of 2014 to the Forced Labour Convention, 1930," International Labour Organization, June 11, 2014, https://www.ilo.org/dyn/normlex/en/f?p=NORMLEXPUB:12100:0::NO::P12100_INSTRUMENT_ID:3174672.

[121] "China-Australia Relations: 'Unconscionable' Trade Sanctions on Wine Warrant WTO Intervention, Scott Morrison Says," *South China Morning Post*, June 10, 2021.

[122] Elizabeth Braw, "China Takes Lithuania as an Economic Hostage," *Wall Street Journal*, January 6, 2022.

[123] Finbarr Bermingham, "Back Lithuania or Face More Coercion from China, Lawmakers Tell EU Chiefs," *South China Morning Post*, January 18, 2022; and Raf Casert and Lorne Cook, "EU Launches WTO Action against China over Lithuania Dispute," Associated Press, January 27, 2022.

[124] Joe Biden, "My Trip to Europe Is about America Rallying the World's Democracies," *Washington Post*, June 5, 2021.

[125] "Global Perspectives on Biden's Democracy Summit," Council of Councils, December 16, 2021.

[126] James Bacchus, "Was Buenos Aires the Beginning of the End or the End of the Beginning? The Future of the World Trade Organization," Cato Institute Policy Analysis no. 841, May 8, 2018.

[127] Office of the United States Trade Representative, "Ambassador Katherine Tai's Remarks as Prepared for Delivery on the World Trade Organization," press release, October 2021.

[128] "Ambassador Katherine Tai's Remarks."

[129] Sarah Anne Aarup, "'All Talk and No Walk': America Ain't Back at the WTO," *Politico*, November 23, 2021.

[130] For a lengthy list of these issues and a discussion of each, *see* James Bacchus, *Trade Links: New Rules for a New World.*

[131] Nina M. Hart and Brandon J. Murrill, "The World Trade Organization's (WTO's) Appellate Body: Key Disputes and Controversies," Congressional Research Service, R46852, July 22, 2021.

[132] *See* James Bacchus, "Might Unmakes Right: The American Assault on the Rule of Law in World Trade," Centre for International Governance Innovation, CIGI Papers no. 173, May 2018.

[133] For much more on the modernization that is needed, *see* James Bacchus, *Trade Links: New Rules for a New World.*

[134] "Ambassador Katherine Tai's Remarks."

[135] "Trump Tweets: 'Trade Wars Are Good, and Easy to Win,'" *Reuters*, March 2, 2018.

[136] Annie Lowrey, "Where Biden Agrees with Trump," *The Atlantic*, October 5, 2021.

Chapter 3

Reviving the WTO: Five Priorities for Liberalization*

Introduction

When the novel coronavirus outbreak occurred in Wuhan, China, near the end of 2019, the World Trade Organization was already in existential crisis. It had been for some time. In the quarter century since its establishment in 1995, a concatenation of circumstances had left the WTO largely paralyzed. It was already adrift amid the grumblings of growing global discord when Covid-19 arrived. The arrival of the pandemic only worsened pre-existing conditions that had long been leading to this existential crisis.

Even before the pandemic, the slow suicide of the Doha Development Round, the emerging role of developing countries, the divide over "special and differential treatment" for developing countries, the multiplication of bilateral and regional agreements outside the WTO framework, the historic resurgence of China as a global economic power, the apprehensive US reaction to China's rise, the US retreat from rule-based multilateralism in trade under a unilateralist and protectionist President, and the worldwide surge in managed and manipulated trade as part of an intensifying economic nationalism in the United States and elsewhere, had all

---

*This essay was previously published by the Cato Institute as James Bacchus, "Reviving the WTO: Five Priorities for Liberalization," Cato Policy Analysis no. 911 (February 23, 2021).

combined to call into question the centrality and the very survival of the WTO.

To be sure, WTO trade dispute settlement continues, albeit in a truncated and increasingly ineffective form because of the successful assault by a protection-minded administration in the United States on the continued functioning of the system's court of final appeal, the WTO Appellate Body. Trade monitoring continues as usual. Trade reports are still published. But the central task of the trading system — necessary trade rulemaking in timely and relevant response to the ever-changing needs of an ever-changing global economy — remains mired in impasse as the WTO trade negotiations that have not already collapsed have mostly crawled to nowhere.

The 12th Ministerial Conference of the WTO, which is currently expected to take place in Nur-Sultan, Kazakhstan, in June 2021, may be the last chance for the WTO to reclaim a central role for the WTO-based multilateral trading system in the global economy. In the worst case, failure to seize this last chance could ultimately lead to the collapse of the entire system. WTO members must prove anew not only that they can negotiate on new rules, but also that they can agree on new rules and put them into effect. To prove this, they must identify now and pursue immediately negotiations on those issues on which a consensus can be achieved at the next ministerial conference. In the countdown to Kazakhstan, they should focus above all else on five issues: free trade in medical goods, free trade in environmental goods, disciplines on fisheries subsidies, investment facilitation, and digital trade. These could be the five first pieces of WTO reform.

Free Trade in Medical Goods

As journalist Peter S. Goodman has explained, "Part of the world's vulnerability to supply chain disruption stems from the excessive embrace of the so-called just-in-time mode of manufacturing: Rather than keep warehouses stocked with needed parts, ensuring that they are on hand come what may, the modern factory uses the web to order parts as the need arises, while relying on global air and shipping networks to deliver them on a timeline synchronized with production."[1] The legitimacy of this assertion has been revealed to all the world in the fierce competition for limited supplies of medicines and other medical goods during the

Covid-19 pandemic. In the new pandemic world, as never before, the rival approaches of economic self-sufficiency and economic interdependence are on global display.

"Just-in-time" manufacturing that relies on far-flung supply chains to provide inputs and boost inventories only when needed and not until needed, is a modern business model inspired by the death of distance. In maximizing efficiencies, this business model maximizes profits, and, in turn, maximizes opportunities for more prosperity, including through the creation and operation of global value chains. This model works well when international trade goes smoothly. It works less well when trade is subject to shortages, uncertainties, and interruptions, as has often been the case with medicines and medical supplies during the pandemic. The arrival of the novel coronavirus has called this business model into question throughout the world.

Goal 3 of the United Nations Sustainable Development Goals for 2030 is to "[e]nsure healthy lives and promote well-being for all at all ages," including by combating communicable diseases and by providing access to affordable essential medicines and vaccines.[2] International trade is indispensable to meeting these goals. World imports of medical products totaled about $1.01 trillion in 2019.[3] Of these imports, about $597 billion are linked to the Covid-19 pandemic.[4] These essential products include medicines, medical supplies, medical equipment and technology, and personal protective products (PPP) such as face masks, sanitizer, and hand soaps. Medicines amount to 56 percent of these imports.[5]

Like much of trade along global value chains, this medical trade is concentrated. "The top 10 exporters (of medical products) account for almost three-quarters of world exports."[6] Germany, the United States, and Switzerland supply 35 percent of the medical products in the world."[7] The top 10 importers of medical products account for 65 percent of all imports.[8] The United States, Germany, China, and Belgium represent 40 percent of all medical imports.[9] With its vast affluent market, the United States is the single largest global importer of medical products, with 19 percent.[10]

Tariffs increase the prices of medicines and other medical products, and tariffs on some medical products remain high. For all medical products, the average "bound" tariff — the average tariff ceiling pledged by a country in its WTO concessions — is 26 percent.[11] Almost one-third of WTO members have an average bound tariff on medical goods of more than 50 percent.[12] However, the average "applied" tariff on medical products — the tariff currently in use — is considerably lower, 4.8 percent.[13] In the United States, the applied average tariff on medical goods is 0.9 percent.[14] The gap between the bound and the applied tariffs (in trade argot, the "overhang" or "water") leaves ample legal room for increasing tariffs on these products without violating WTO rules.

Generally, among international trade negotiators, a tariff of 15 percent or higher is consider a "tariff peak."[15] But some members of the WTO apply tariffs soaring as high as 65 percent on some of these essential products.[16] The average tariffs on the protective supplies used to combat Covid-19 are as high as 27 percent in some countries.[17] The average applied tariff on hand soap is 17 percent.[18] Surprisingly, only nine WTO members allow a health product as basic as soap to enter duty-free.[19] As Swiss trade economist Simon Evenett has mused, "At a time when the frequent washing of hands is recommended by the World Health Organization, policies that increase the cost of soap are particularly difficult to rationalize."[20]

The shortages of medicines and other medical goods that occurred immediately following the Covid-19 outbreak were not wholly anticipated by trading countries. In the decades leading up to the pandemic, intermittent efforts were made to free up trade in medical products. But those efforts fell far short of full liberalization. Six WTO members — Canada; the European Union; Macao, China; Switzerland; Norway; and the United States have concluded an agreement within the WTO framework establishing zero-for-zero tariff treatment on pharmaceutical products.[21] In addition to this limited accord, four members — Macao, China; Hong Kong, China; Singapore; and Iceland — have eliminated all duties on all medical products.[22] The overwhelming majority of WTO members, however, have not taken such liberalizing actions.

The chemical or other substance that produces the intended beneficial effect in a drug is called the "active pharmaceutical ingredient." Some drugs have multiple active ingredients. At one time, most pharmaceutical companies created the API, made the tablet or capsule, and packaged the final medical product. With the death of distance, major pharmaceutical firms in developed countries began to specialize in the value-added portions of the drug production process. These mostly American and European firms "began to focus on pursuing potentially lucrative, blockbuster patents rather than producing lower-margin bulk pharmaceuticals that are no longer covered by patents."[23] They started outsourcing much of the lower-end pharma work in the production of both generic drugs and APIs to factories in developing countries.

About 90 percent of the drugs taken by Americans are generic drugs for which the patents have expired.[24] It is not profitable economically to produce many of these drugs in the United States or in the European Union. Similarly, outsourcing the production of active pharmaceutical ingredients made sense because most APIs are commodity products; they are substitutable irrespective of where they originate. They are also largely tradable; they do not have to be made near to where they are consumed. All drugs contain API. Thus, for its huge domestic market, the largest in the world, "The United States sources 80 percent of its APIs from overseas, and a substantial portion of U.S. generic drug imports come either directly from China or from third countries like India that use APIs sourced from China."[25] Sourcing in these developing countries offers distinct cost advantages in labor, energy, water, and other factors of production that lower prices for U.S. pharmaceutical companies and, thus, for US medical consumers.

This shift in the low-end production of pharmaceuticals went largely unnoticed until the arrival of Covid-19. Since then, it has drawn much media attention, especially in the United States. The Center for Disease Research and Policy at the University of Minnesota has listed 156 acute critical drugs often used in the United States — "the drugs without which patients would die in hours."[26] The center's director and a co-author have explained, "All these drugs are generic; most are now made overseas; and many of them, or their active pharmaceutical ingredients, are manufactured in China or India. A pandemic that idles Asian factories or shuts down shipping routes thus threatens the already strained supply of these drugs to Western hospitals, and it doesn't matter how good a modern hospital is if the bottles and vials on the crash cart are empty.[27]

Specializing as a source of low-end manufacture for such products on global pharmaceutical value chains, China has become the second largest exporters of drugs and biologics to the United States, accounting for 13.4 percent of US imports of those products in 2018.[28] In particular, China has become a key supplier to the United States of active pharmaceutical ingredients and generic medicines for which the patents have expired. China is the world's leading supplier of active pharmaceutical ingredients, accounting for 16 percent of world exports in 2019.[29] Otherwise, though, China is not yet a major source of medical products. In 2019, China accounted for only one percent of world exports of final medical products.[30] On the other hand, with its growth, China has become the world's second-largest drug market, after the United States.[31] Thus, China is not only a source of low-end supply; increasingly, it also represents a major potential new market for US and European medical exports.

Many of the Chinese pharmaceutical products are drugs that American companies simply found it unprofitable to produce.[32] Notably, Chinese medical exports to the United States are often generic equivalents and raw materials for older medical products that are still used by many Americans. For example, China is the principal source for the United States "of the chemical and raw materials for popular blood pressure medicines and several older antibiotics that are no longer manufactured in the U.S., such as doxycycline and penicillin."[33] China is also "the only maker of key ingredients in a class of decades-old antibiotics known as cephalosporins, which treat a range of bacterial infections, including pneumonia."[34] About 70 percent of the acetaminophen used in the United States is made in China.[35]

Like China, India is one of the world's leading suppliers of drugs, and it is the world's leading supplier of generic drugs. In recent years, India has also become a significant supplier of medicines for the United States, including 40 percent of the generic drugs consumed by Americans.[36] The Indians import about 70 percent of their API from China.[37] Because of the sizeable extent of this dependence on Chinese imports, and because of the need to avoid supply chain disruptions, the Indian government has, since the start of the pandemic, established new incentives to encourage the domestic manufacture of key starting materials and active ingredients that are now sourced from China.[38]

All this is not to say, though, that China and India monopolize the global marketplace for these and other medical products. China ranked seventh among the top ten exporters of medical products in 2019, with just five percent of world exports; India ranked much lower.[39] The global statistics on API sourcing and production are sketchy; but, according to the US Food and Drug Administration, of about 2,000 manufacturing facilities in the world producing API, 13 percent are in China, 18 percent are in India, 26 percent are in the European Union, and 28 percent are in the United States. For those APIs that the World Health Organization has identified as "essential medicines," 21 percent of the manufacturing facilities are in the United States, 15 percent in China, and the rest are spread among India, Canada, and the European Union. The FDA reports that in 2019, there were 510 API facilities in the United States, and that 221 of them were supplying "essential medicines."[40] This global industry has hardly been ceded to the two largest countries in Asia. Most of the value in medical products is still added in the United States and in Europe.

Simultaneously, with the sudden outbreak of the pandemic, trade in essential medical products experienced demand shock, supply shock, and disruptions of global transport and supply chains. Faced with the immediacy of domestic shortages in medical goods due to "just in time" business practices and less than ample emergency stockpiles, the first frantic response of some countries to the pandemic was to restrict and to otherwise distort trade in medical goods. India banned exports of respiratory masks.[41] The Indians also banned the export of 26 pharmaceutical ingredients and some of the products made by them.[42] The European Union announced emergency export restrictions on hospital supplies needed to fight the pandemic.[43] German authorities halted delivery of 240,000 medical masks to a Swiss buyer.[44]

At the same time, a presidential executive order in the United States required federal agencies in need of "essential drugs" and other medical supplies to "Buy American."[45] In addition, the US federal government contracted with the company that makes the first drug licensed for treatment of Covid-19 — remdesivir — to provide the bulk of its production, at least temporarily, exclusively to Americans.[46] By the spring of 2020, 75 governments had restricted exports of medicines and medical supplies.[47] As the year continued, dozens of additional trade restrictions of all kinds were applied to medical products worldwide as a pandemic protectionism infected more and more countries.[48]

A bewildered Simon Evenett lamented from Switzerland, "Now, beggar-thy-neighbour becomes sicken-thy-neighbor."[49] Restrictive trade measures prevent limited drugs and supplies from going to where they are most needed to conduct effective coordinated global combat against the global virus, especially in the poorest countries where the outbreak may ultimately be the worst.[50] It is perfectly understandable that national leaders will want to do all they can to make certain their own citizens have all of the medicines, medical supplies, and medical care they need, particularly during a pandemic. Yet, once again, on what moral basis do we favor people here over people there? What is more, ultimately, these leaders will not help their citizens by restricting trade in medicines and other medical products. Autarky is not the answer. Economic self-sufficiency is as illusory as ever. Measures restricting trade in medicines and medical supplies "hurt all countries, particularly the more fragile."[51]

Poorer countries, which must import much of the medical goods they need to fight Covid-19, will be hurt first, and maybe the most, from the scarcities and the higher prices resulting from such measures. For them, the consequence "could be deadly."[52] Wealthier countries, usually those imposing the restrictions, will likewise be harmed. World Bank economists Aaditya Mattoo and Michele Ruta have explained, "Prices (will) be higher than they need be, and supplies (will) be distributed neither efficiently nor equitably."[53] Nigerians and Indonesians, Bolivians and Ceylonese will suffer; but so too will Americans and Europeans, Australians and Canadians. Further, there is, equally, the timeless but too-often ignored objection to attempts at self-sufficiency. No one country, not even the wealthiest, will be able to make and to assure for itself all the vast variety of essential medicines and medical supplies it needs.

Martin Wolf of the *Financial Times* has reminded us that the case with medical export restrictions is much the same as with trade restrictions in general during the pandemic: "Remember that the problem (in the pandemic is) not with trade, but rather with a lack of supply. Export restrictions merely reallocate the shortages, by shifting them on to countries with the least capacity. A natural response to this experience is for every country to try to be self-sufficient in every product that might turn out to be relevant. …Yet businesses would then lose economies of scale, as global markets fragmented. Their capacity to invest in innovation would be reduced. Only the largest and most advanced economies could plausibly seek self-sufficiency in such a wide range of technologies. For all others, this would be a dead end."[54]

In general, WTO rules prohibit export restrictions. Significantly, export taxes are not forbidden by WTO rules (although they are not an option for the United States because they are barred by the US Constitution).[55] But, otherwise, "prohibitions or restrictions other than duties, taxes or other charges, whether made effective through quotas… export licenses or other measures…on the exportation or sale for export of any product" are inconsistent with WTO obligations.[56] This obligation, however, does not apply to "export prohibitions or restrictions temporarily applied to prevent or relieve critical shortages of foodstuffs or other products essential to the exporting" WTO member.[57]

All export restrictions, even when they are applied because of critical shortages, must, under WTO rules, be transparent through publication.[58] Also, they must not be discriminatory.[59] Importantly, any export restriction, even if it not eligible for the carve-out for measures relating to critical shortages, will be excused from the general WTO ban on such measures if it is necessary to protect public health or essential to address general or local short supply and if it is not applied "in a manner which would constitute arbitrary or unjustifiable discrimination between countries where the same conditions prevail, or a disguised restriction on international trade.[60] All of these legal terms are, of course, the topics of much trade debate, and are subject to clarification in WTO settlement of international trade disputes.

This said, the fact that many of the export restrictions imposed on medical goods during the pandemic are probably legal under international law does not, as Wolf has said, "make them wise."[61] Export restrictions raise prices. They create scarcity where it would not otherwise exist. They cause "disproportionate harm to developing nations that cannot otherwise compete in bidding wars."[62] As Jennifer Hillman, a leading American trade scholar and jurist, has explained, "[S]uch actions clearly work to the detriment of the world's ability to distribute…scarce medical resources to where they are needed most with the minimal amount of red tape. When one country imposes an export ban, others tend to follow, resulting in higher prices and pockets of scarcity outside of the silos created by the bans. Moreover, given the number of components that must cross borders in today's global supply chain manufacturing system, export bans may disrupt supply chains and delay the production of critical medical supplies or devices."[63]

In the new pandemic world, instead of restricting exports of medical goods, countries should be freeing up both exports and imports of those goods. At the top of the "to-do" list of new rules needed in this new world by the WTO is the pressing necessity for rules that eliminate all existing trade restrictions on medicines and medical supplies, and that require WTO members to refrain from enacting any more. Although restrictive national measures can be politically appealing, and although — depending on how they are applied — they may be legal under WTO rules, the reality is, they prevent medicines and other essential medical supplies from going to where they are most needed to conduct effective coordinated global combat against the global virus, especially in the poorest countries where the outbreak may ultimately be the worst. There may be plenty of a drug helpful in treating the virus in San Francisco but not nearly enough in South Sudan.

Another needed new WTO rule is an immediate elimination worldwide of all tariffs on imports of drugs and medical equipment. These essential goods are needed everywhere to confront the Covid-19 emergency. As with all goods, no one country can produce all these goods in the amounts they may eventually need. All countries — even the wealthiest countries — will need to import at least some of them. Tariffs rarely make any sense, and these border taxes on imports of life-saving goods may make the least sense of all. As Hillman has written, these increased taxes are passed along as increased prices to consumers and thus reduce access to essential goods. They can also contribute to creating shortages, with the same results. With respect to health products, "the fact that tariffs exist at all is puzzling in light of the importance of ensuring access to affordable medicines for poor people."[64] In addition, as Anabel Gonzalez, a former Costa Rican trade minister and senior WTO and World Bank official, has observed, "Eliminating such protectionist measures could also lower the cost of inputs like active ingredients and other chemical products, encouraging domestic investment and production."[65]

Some of the numerous WTO members that depend heavily on medical imports have sought to encourage multilateral actions to write new rules to achieve these ends. Looking outward instead of inward, New Zealand and Singapore committed in March 2020 to continue to keep their own medical supply chains open. Canada, Australia, Chile, Brunei, and Myanmar soon made similar commitments. In April 2020, New Zealand and Singapore entered into a bilateral agreement to eliminate tariffs, refrain from export restrictions, negotiate removal of non-tariff barriers, and further trade facilitation, on a long list of medical products. These conveners invited other countries to join them in the agreement.[66]

Encouragingly, that same month, Phil Hogan, then the European Union Trade Commissioner, suggested that the EU should consider negotiation of an international agreement to waive tariffs on medical goods permanently.[67] Several dozen additional WTO members expressed similar sentiments.[68] Former Commissioner Hogan predicted that, "If more countries pursue the track of self-sufficiency, it will increase competition for scarce resources, drive up prices and deepen international hostilities."[69] Yet, immobilized by their years of near inertia, the membership of the WTO as a whole made little progress thereafter toward concluding a multilateral agreement. In the United States especially, the political momentum was not toward medical multilateralism but toward achieving medical self-sufficiency.

Eliminating tariffs and other restrictions on trade in medical goods should be just the start in new WTO rulemaking on medical trade. In the new pandemic world in which we find ourselves, a world in which moving essential medicines and other medical goods quickly across borders is critical to fighting Covid-19 and will be equally critical to fighting any pandemics yet to come, still more must be done also to remove the red tape at the border that impedes the flow of trade. In 2013, in one of their few real successes since the creation of the WTO, the members of the WTO concluded an agreement on trade facilitation in Bali, Indonesia.[70] Still being implemented, this agreement cuts a lot of needless red tape at the border while modernizing trade and making it much more digital. Facilitating trade increases trade. Building on this agreement, WTO members should zero in on further facilitating trade in medical goods. As one example, China and the European Union have each created "green lanes" in their customs procedures to speed the inspection and release of medical goods.[71] This innovation should be emulated everywhere.

Other worthy ideas for new WTO rules include: promoting transparency in all national measures taken to fight the virus; waiving "buy local" requirements for medical goods, which inflate the prices of government purchases in much of the world; eliminating all the non-tariff barriers that hinder trade in medicines and medical equipment; adopting international standards to help ensure the safety and the quality of imported medical goods; giving the go-ahead to targeted subsidies for producing the new medicines urgently needed to stop Covid-19; reaffirming that WTO rules permit compulsory licensing of needed medicines by developing countries in dire circumstances such as these; and permitting health care workers to move more easily across borders to provide health services. In the United States, for example, about 1.5 million immigrants are employed as doctors, nurses, and pharmacists.[72] Where would other Americans have been without them in 2020?

All these new rules relating to trade in medicines and medical products should be combined into a WTO medical goods agreement. Ideally, such an agreement would be fully multilateral, including all 164 WTO members. If that is not at first achievable, then such an agreement could initially include some but not all WTO members, and WTO members could build toward making it fully multilateral over time. The key to the success of such an agreement would be making it enforceable, like all other WTO agreements, through WTO dispute settlement. As with other WTO agreements, WTO members would be free to choose not to comply with an obligation in such a medical goods agreement, but choosing not to comply would invite, as a "last resort," application of economic sanctions in the form of withdrawal of previously grant trade concessions by any WTO members harmed by that decision.[73]

The answer is not to break the links in global medical supply chains and attempt to replace them with an exclusive reliance on national production. As Shannon O'Neill of the Council on Foreign Relations and others have recommended, the links in supply chains should be strengthened by adding strategic redundancies and by stockpiling emergency reserves of essential products. In the structure of supply chains, "just-in-time" should yield to "just-in-case." During emergencies such as Covid-19, the flow of trade in medical and other essential goods must continue. For medical goods and for other essential products, supply chains linked to single sources or only a few sources on the far side of the world should be made more redundant by diversifying them to include more sources of supply from reliable and perhaps not so distant locations. Likewise, for those same essential products, inventories should be increased "just-in-case" of a crisis. These two changes will increase consumer prices somewhat; but they will also help secure ample supplies during times when they are most needed.

Many of these needed changes in medical supply management will not have to be mandated by governments; they will likely occur naturally as an outcome of altered market forces in the wake of the pandemic. Thus, governmental interventions should be kept to the bare minimum required to assure a sufficiency of supplies. With some products, however, targeted governmental actions may be needed to provide incentives for private companies to diversify their supply sources and increase their inventories. Again, and as others have suggested, governments should, in addition, supplement private efforts by increasing strategic public stockpiles of critical medicines and medical products as well as other essential products.[74] In the United States, for example, two former commissioners for the FDA have advised that maintenance of sufficient diagnostic capacity for testing during a crisis should be part of such a national stockpile.[75]

Former WTO Director-General Pascal Lamy has suggested that the "pre-Covid balance between efficiency and resilience will have to tilt to the side of resilience."[76] In the new pandemic world, to some extent, this must happen. Indeed, in numerous instances, this is already happening, and it is driven by market forces. But self-sufficiency in all that may be desperately needed during a health crisis remains impossible for all countries. Moreover, "The quest for resilience comes with risks of its own."[77] There is abundant reason for governmental actions to help prevent future disruptions in supply chains. There is no reason whatsoever for governmental actions that cut the links of supply chains. Doing so would only deny people everywhere the many and undeniable advantages of the international division of labor.[78] Without question, medical supply chains must be made more resilient. But restricting medical trade will not enhance resilience; it will undermine it, locally and globally.

Free Trade in Environmental Goods

Negotiations on freeing trade in environmental goods began as part of the negotiations on trade and the environment in the Doha Development Round. It was agreed in Doha that WTO members would negotiate multilaterally on "the reduction or, as appropriate, elimination of tariff and non-tariff barriers to environmental goods and services."[79] For more than a decade, these multilateral negotiations were unsuccessful. Then, at the annual World Economic Forum in Davos in January 2014, a group of 14 WTO members announced their intent to negotiate a plurilateral agreement in pursuit of global free trade in environmental goods. Formal negotiations were launched at the WTO in 2014. Eventually, 46 members of the WTO participated in these plurilateral negotiations, representing nearly 90 percent of global trade in environmental goods, which totals more than $1 trillion and has been growing rapidly.[80]

The Obama Administration in the United States was late in giving priority to this issue, but it did participate. Even so, the negotiations collapsed in December 2016, when trade negotiators failed to find common ground on which goods would be covered by the proposed agreement. The United States was on a political deadline, trying to conclude an eleventh-hour "trade and environment" agreement to help advance climate action in the last weeks before Donald Trump was inaugurated as President. China, which had appeared a hesitant party to the talks all along, made new last-minute requests others could not accept. Everyone involved promised they would conclude an agreement in 2017. But the new Trump Administration in the United States, bent on denying climate change and repealing domestic regulations protecting the environment, and more inclined to raise tariffs rather than lower them, displayed scant interest in continuing with the environmental goods talks. The environmental goods negotiations stalled in 2017 and have remained frozen ever since. After nearly two decades of trade negotiations, there is no agreement.

Because these are plurilateral negotiations, a consensus of all 164 WTO Members would not be needed to conclude an agreement at the next ministerial conference of the WTO. The aim of the subset of WTO members that have been engaged in the negotiations on environmental goods has been to get coverage of environmental goods sufficient to constitute a "critical mass" of all the trade in such goods. Although there is no WTO rule defining such a "critical mass" of trade, the general rule of thumb in past trade negotiations has pegged a "critical mass" at 90 percent so as to minimize the "free riders" among WTO members when the tariff cuts in a plurilateral agreement are extended on a "most-favored-nation' basis to benefit all WTO members, including those who have not yet signed the agreement. Negotiating countries are confident at this point that they have that "critical mass" of 90 percent coverage.

The highest hurdle to a WTO environmental goods agreement is reaching a consensus on which goods are in fact environmental goods. This uncertainty has been the main obstacle to success from the outset. Negotiators have not tried to define environmental goods; they have only tried to list them. The negotiations began with a list of 54 products previously agreed by the APEC countries of the Asia-Pacific Region.[81] The OECD has a broader list.[82] The environmental groups have even broader lists. So does the business community. Some interest groups have proffered lists that contained seemingly everything, including (literally) the kitchen sink.[83] The Chinese want the covered list to include bicycles, which they claim are environmental goods. This has been resisted by the European Union and by the United States, which have imposed anti-dumping duties on imports of Chinese-made bicycles and see no need for such imports to be duty-free.[84]

Another hurdle to reaching an agreement is the expressed hope of the negotiators that it will become a "living agreement" that can expand and evolve over time.[85] The joint statement in Davos in 2014 of the countries that began the plurilateral negotiations speaks of concluding "a future-oriented agreement able to address other issues in the sector and to respond to green growth and sustainable development."[86] One key to the success of such an open-ended agreement will be agreeing on a timely means of applying duty-free treatment to new environmental goods as they as they are produced. In a comparable situation, it took WTO negotiators nearly twenty years to agree on adding new IT goods to the list of goods for duty-free treatment in the WTO Information Technology Agreement — even though information technology was revolutionized several times over during the interim.[87] A repeat of this long impasse would render a WTO agreement on environmental goods increasingly irrelevant as changes in technology continued.

Generally, developing countries have either seemed indifferent to a WTO environmental goods agreement or have actively resisted it. This resistance seems to be driven by their apprehension of being overwhelmed by a flood of imports of environmental goods. This is ironic; for the principal beneficiaries of an environmental goods agreement will be developing countries. Of course, developed countries will profit by selling more environmental goods in developing countries. But developing countries can gain even more by having ready access to these goods in their pursuit of sustainable development. As the United States Chamber of Commerce has put it, "The business of providing sustainability solutions has reached its present scale thanks to growing international demand and expectations of considerable growth potential. Trade policies can play an important role in enabling (the) private sector to mobilize its resource and creativity to deliver innovations where they are most needed and where they can have the biggest environmental payoff." Eliminating tariffs on environmental goods will help make this happen.

Whatever the final list may be, the goods covered by an environmental goods agreement will include "important environment-related products…that can help achieve environmental and climate-protective goals, such as generating clean and renewable energy, improving energy and resource efficiency, controlling air pollution, managing waste, treating wastewater, monitoring the quality of the environment, and combatting noise pollution." As it is, tariffs on some environmental goods are as high as 35 percent.[88] Abolishing tariffs would lower the prices of environmental goods and would thereby hasten their spread worldwide. This can only be of benefit to developing countries at a time when so many of them are sorely lacking in much of what they need to help further their development and help make it sustainable.

An oft-heard objection to a sectoral agreement that would eliminate tariffs on environmental goods is that environmental goods should not be singled out for special treatment, and that all tariffs on all goods should be eliminated. Tim Worstall of *Forbes* has wondered what makes environmental goods special. He asked, while applauding the collapse of the environmental goods negotiations in 2016, "Why not all goods? …How about we just go with the idea that more trade makes us all richer and so we'll not have tariffs at all?"[89] This is the right goal, and the ultimate goal. But this view ignores the urgency of our climate and our ecological situation, which is what makes environmental goods special, and what makes their rapid spread worldwide essential. This attitude also commits the tempting mistake of making the perfect the enemy of the good. By this reasoning, no trade agreement in history should ever have been concluded.

A more legitimate objection is that an agreement for free trade in environmental goods should also free trade in environmental services. This was the original intent of WTO members as voiced in the Doha Declaration. This should likewise be their intent now. For, increasingly, environmental goods and environmental services are integrated. Indeed, in trade, services are increasingly embedded in goods. Because goods and services are increasingly intertwined, and because their delivery is therefore often integrated, their trade treatment should likewise often be integrated. One example is with wind power plants: freeing trade in environmental goods will boost international shipments of the makings of wind power plants, while freeing trade in environmental services will lift the current obstacles to providing the international services that are often needed to maintain those plants.[90] But the conclusion of a WTO environmental goods agreement should not await conclusion simultaneously of an agreement to free trade in environmental services. Instead, an environmental goods agreement should become a basis for an expanded agreement that would later include environmental services.

Disciplines on Fisheries Subsidies

Negotiations on fisheries subsidies also began during the Doha Development Round. Like other production subsidies, fisheries subsidies are covered by existing WTO subsidies rules. WTO members have, however, concluded that fisheries subsidies require special treatment in the form of additional disciplines. As part of the Doha Development Agenda, they have endeavored since 2001 to "clarify and improve WTO discipline on fisheries subsidies, taking into account the importance of this sector to developing countries."[91] WTO members have now struggled through 18 rounds of negotiations without achieving success.

These negotiations were given renewed impetus in 2015, when all the members of the United Nations (including all the members of the WTO) agreed in the Sustainable Development Goals for 2030 to "prohibit certain forms of fisheries subsidies which contribute to overcapacity and overfishing, eliminate subsidies that contribute to illegal, unreported, and unregulated fishing and refrain from introducing new such subsidies, recognizing that appropriate and effective special and differential treatment for developing and least developed countries should be an integral part of the World Trade Organization fisheries subsidies negotiation."[92]

Despite this added incentive, WTO members failed to conclude a WTO agreement on fisheries subsidies at the 11th Ministerial Conference in Buenos Aires, Argentina, in 2017. They pledged then to conclude an agreement by the next ministerial conference, which was expected to take place in Nur-Sultan, Kazakhstan, in June 2020. The conference was delayed due to the Covid-19 pandemic. In May 2020, continuation of the fisheries talks was delayed because of the preoccupation of many countries with the pandemic.[93] In September, the talks were resumed, and, in October, negotiators continued to seek a compromise consensus by the deadline of yearend 2020, as set out by the UN in the SDGs.

Throughout these many years of negotiations, the United States has always been fully engaged. According to the initial American proposal submitted, in concert with a number of allied countries, to the WTO in 2005, "The United States believes that a broad prohibition addressing all elements that contribute most directly to overcapacity and overfishing would be the most effective way to fulfill our mandate."[94] In contrast to some other ongoing WTO efforts, the Trump Administration has voiced support for the fisheries talks, stating that it continues "to support stronger disciplines and greater transparency in the WTO with respect to fisheries subsidies."[95] It continued to take part in the fisheries negotiations in the run-up to the November presidential election.

The matter of fisheries subsidies is not a minor issue. It is a major one. Worldwide, three billion people depend on fish and fish products for up to 15 percent of their daily protein and nutrition.[96] Many of them live in the poorest and least-developed countries. And at least 140 million people depend on fisheries for their livelihood.[97] The demand for fish has been growing with a growing — and increasingly prosperous — global population. We now eat more fish than ever before, an average of 20 kilograms — 44 pounds — per person every year.[98] We eat more fish than beef.[99]

Meanwhile, the global fish catch has been declining.[100] According to the Food and Agricultural Organization of the United Nations, fish stocks that are within biologically sustainable levels fell from 90 percent in 1974 to 65.8 in 2017.[101] Underfished stocks accounted for only 6.2 percent.[102] In its 2020 annual report on the status of fisheries and aquaculture, the FAO said that, although there have been some improvements in sustainable fisheries practices, the statistics indicate that the United Nations target of ending overfishing of marines fisheries by 2030 will not be achieved.[103] The authors of a study released in the Proceedings of the National Academy of Sciences examined 4,713 fisheries worldwide, accounting for 78 percent of the world's catch. They found that only a third of these fisheries are in good biological condition. Offering hope for change, these scientists also concluded that — if applied globally — modern fishery management plans can make nearly every fishery in the world healthy by 2050.[104]

In this ecological context, almost 38 percent of all the fish caught or farmed in the world is traded, with a total export value of $164 billion.[105] The impact of Covid-19 has, of course, "negatively impacted" fish trade.[106] By far the major producer and exporter of fish and fish products is China, with 14 percent.[107] China has ranked first since 2002.[108] Norway is second, and Vietnam is third.[109] The United States accounts for four percent of global fish exports.[110] The United States and the European Union lead in global fish imports, with China third.[111] Developing countries account for 49 percent of global fish imports.[112] Trade in fish is of significance in every part of the world.

This trade is driven in part by subsidies. As explained by Elizabeth Wilson of the Pew Charitable Trusts, "Fisheries subsidies are one of the key drivers behind this decline in fish stocks. Governments pay…each year in damaging types of fisheries subsidies, primarily to industrial fishers, to offset costs such as fuel, gear, and vessel construction. Although not all subsidies are harmful, many encourage fishing beyond sustainable biological limits by helping vessels go farther and fish for longer periods and with greater capacity than they would without this assistance. Today, in part driven by fisheries subsidies, global fishing capacity — the total capability of the world's fleets — is estimated at 250 percent of the level that would bring in the maximum sustainable catch."[113]

Most countries, regardless of their stage of development, subsidize their fisheries.[114] Although "overfishing is one of the greatest threats to ocean health, …for decades many governments have paid subsidies to their fishing fleets, helping them fish beyond levels that are biologically sustainable."[115] In 2018, fisheries subsidies totaled $35.4 billion worldwide. Of these total subsidies, 22 percent were for fuel subsidies, which permit fishing trawlers, largely from the wealthier countries, to range farther into the global commons of the high seas. China granted 21 percent of total global fisheries subsidies, the European Union 11 percent, the United States 10 percent, and South Korea nine percent.[116] The global total of fisheries subsidies is between 30 and 40 percent of the landed value generated by wild fisheries worldwide.[117]

The Global Ocean Commission has estimated that 60 percent of global fisheries subsidies directly encourage "unsustainable, destructive and even illegal fishing practices."[118] The Commission said in 2016 that high seas fishing fuel subsidies should be capped immediately and then phased out over five years, and suggested that the money saved should be put into a dedicated "Blue Fund" to achieve the Sustainable Development Goal of saving the ocean.[119] This reform is still more imperative now when, according to the OECD, "All aspects of fish supply chains are strongly affected by the COVID-19 pandemic, with jobs, incomes and food security at risk."[120]

Fearful of lost markets, many developing countries have resisted new disciplines of fisheries subsidies. They have done so even though about two-thirds of the subsidies are provided by developed countries as the United States, the European Union, South Korea, and Japan, which have recently been joined by China.[121] Oft-cited are the perceived risks of lost subsidies to small fishers in developing countries. An express target of the SDGs is to "provide access for small-scale artisanal fishers to marine resources and markets."[122]

Yet most of the subsidies go to large fishers through fuel and other support to huge corporate fishing fleets. Moreover, 2020 case studies commissioned by the International Institute for Sustainable Development in Canada show that new WTO trade disciplines on fisheries subsidies "could help local fishers while increasing global cash."[123] These studies indicate that, in addition to improving fishery sustainability, "reforming harmful fisheries subsidies could lead to higher yields for local fishers, which could help provide more stable jobs, raise fishers' incomes, reduce poverty, and improve food security in local communities."[124]

One of the missed opportunities for the United States in international trade in recent years has been its withdrawal under President Trump from the proposed Trans-Pacific Partnership. In addition to other trade reforms and liberalization, what has now been renamed the Comprehensive and Progressive Agreement for Trans-Pacific Partnership among the remaining eleven Pacific Rim countries "contains the first disciplines on fisheries subsidies in any free trade agreement."[125] These countries have recognized in the CPTPP that "the implementation of a fisheries management system that is designed to prevent overfishing and overcapacity and to promote the recovery of overfished stocks must include the control, reduction and eventual elimination of all subsidies that contribute to overfishing and overcapacity."[126] Ricardo Melendez-Ortiz has observed that this obligation in the CPTPP could demonstrate that fisheries subsidies can be disciplined by a "select group of countries, and, in part for that reason," should serve "as inspiration for the so-far unsuccessful multilateral talks."[127]

Investment Facilitation

As the OECD has explained, "Investment is central to growth and sustainable development. Under the right conditions, international investment can enhance the host economy's productive capacity and growth potential, drive job creation and improvements in living standards, allow the transfer of technology and know-how, and spur domestic investment, including through the creation of local supplier linkages."[128] Skeptics of economic globalization see foreign direct investment as nefarious and exploitative, leading to worker oppression and environmental destruction. To be sure, this is true of some irresponsible FDI. But, for the most part, the opposite is the case. For the most part, FDI leads to higher wages, better working conditions, and better environmental protections. And, without question, more foreign direct investment will be needed for the world to recover from the Covid-19 pandemic.

Foreign direct investment is a reflective mirror of trade. FDI and trade are opposite images of the same face of economic growth. There is a tendency to think of the two separately. But FDI and trade are mutually reinforcing. As the WTO Secretariat has explained, "Given that two-thirds of world exports are governed by...multinational firms, deciding where to invest is simultaneously deciding from where to trade."[129] More trade creates more FDI by making more markets receptive to FDI. Also, more FDI creates more trade by spreading technology, shifting relationships between importers and exporters, enhancing financial relationships, and shaping supply chains.[130] In the new world linked by global value chains, the links between trade and investment have become all the more significant to economic growth. What is more, these links have acquired still more significance in the new pandemic world, where the worldwide spread of new technologies that accompanies foreign direct investment has acquired added urgency.

Because of the pandemic, global foreign direct investment is projected to plunge 40 percent in 2020. Further decreases of 5 percent to

10 percent are forecast for 2021 before an expected upturn in 2022.[131] In these circumstances, countries have sought to provide incentives to spur investment to increase their national production in the health sector and in other sectors related to or impacted by the pandemic.[132] They have tried to maintain and enhance the links between their struggling small and medium-sized enterprises to global value chains.[133] The plummet in foreign direct investment during the pandemic has had virtually nothing to do with the absence of multilateral investment rules. But more and better international investment rules could help facilitate more foreign direct investment.

Like rules for competition, rules for foreign direct investment have evolved separately from trade rules. For decades, there have been efforts to establish multilateral rules for FDI comparable to the multilateral rules for trade. Thus far, those efforts have failed. Instead, international investment rules are found in nearly 3000 bilateral investment treaties and hundreds of other treaties containing investment provisions.[134] The investment rules in these treaties sometimes conflict, and generally they lack the coherence that is largely characteristic of WTO trade rules, and would help ease and speed the flow of FDI. On the one hand, the existing investment rules are often too weak in countering investment protectionism; while, on the other, they are often too vague in assuring host countries a sufficiency of "policy space" for legitimate regulation.

Shortly after the establishment of the WTO, as one of the "Singapore issues" presented in 1996, the European Union and others proposed the negotiation of comprehensive rules dealing with the link between trade and investment in the WTO. But the proposal for investment negotiations was rejected. Thus, as it is, there are only limited WTO rules on "trade-related investment measures."[135] These WTO rules mandate most-favored-nation treatment for FDI.[136] They also prevent quantitative restrictions on FDI.[137] They do not, however, do much more. New WTO rules that address the numerous connections between trade and investment are much needed. Much needed too are multilateral rules on investment, whether in the WTO or in some other global framework.

Although there is seemingly no political appetite at this time for negotiating more substantive investment rules in the WTO, there is an apparent desire to negotiate new procedural rules that would help facilitate foreign direct investment. In Buenos Aires in 2017, 70 WTO members announced their support for negotiations on a multilateral framework for investment facilitation.[138] In 2019, 98 WTO members announced their intent to try to conclude a multilateral agreement on "investment facilitation for development" by the time of the next WTO ministerial conference in Kazakhstan.[139] In September, 105 WTO members began "structured discussions" as a prelude to securing a consensus of all WTO members to commence formal negotiations.[140] These two-thirds of WTO members have encouraged the rest of the WTO to join in these "structured discussions." Perhaps due to the Trump Administration's oft-professed distaste for foreign direct investment by American companies, the United States is not yet a participant in these discussions.

The proposed WTO agreement on investment facilitation for development is widely viewed as a counterpart to the WTO Trade Facilitation Agreement, which is the only full-fledged multilateral trade agreement concluded by the WTO since its establishment in 1995.[141] The TFA, concluded in Bali in 2013, deals mostly with "the simplification, modernization and harmonization of export and import processes" to prevent delays and eliminate "red tape" in moving goods across borders.[142] The aim with investment facilitation is much the same as with trade facilitation. The stated intent is to "improve the transparency and predictability of investment measures; streamline and speed up administrative procedures and requirements; and enhance international cooperation, information sharing, the exchange of best practices, and relations with relevant stakeholders, including dispute prevention."[143] Thus, the WTO discussions on investment facilitation, like the TFA, are centered on cutting international "red tape" and eliminating bureaucratic overlap.

Because some of the developing countries remain apprehensive about negotiating multilateral rules on investment liberalization in the WTO, the WTO members working on investment facilitation have specifically said that these talks will exclude sensitive substantive issues such as easing market access and assuring investment protection.[144] However, as scholars from the International Institute for Sustainable Development in Canada have observed, "the distinction between investment facilitation on the one hand and market access and protection on the other is blurry at best, so that the distinction would be hard to implement. Indeed, some issues that are already being considered could lead to potential disciplines, such as mandatory time limits for government decisions on the admission of proposed investments, go directly to market access questions and the ability of governments to evaluate proposed investments effectively before making decisions."[145]

In practice, there will be real difficulty in drawing this line. By far the biggest hurdle in making a framework agreement is likely to be that of distinguishing between facilitating investment and assisting in market access and investment protection. Finding the right line between the two will be even more of a task at a time when FDI has declined and countries have turned inward — even as many of them are much in need of more foreign direct investment. Likely to make this line-drawing even more delicate is the fact that, while trade facilitation deals solely with what happens in crossing the border, investment facilitation reaches beyond the border to dig deeper into second-guessing domestic decision-making.[146]

Investment facilitation is a broader concept than trade facilitation and not as easily defined. It is sometimes confused with mere investment promotion. The OECD has explained that, while investment promotion is about making a country more enticing as a potential target for FDI, investment facilitation is about making it easier for investors to establish investments and then operate and expand them. For this to happen, there must be a domestic framework for investment that is transparent, predictable, and efficient.[147] UNCTAD suggests, further, that investment facilitation relates to all stages of foreign direct investment, beginning with the pre-establishment phase, continuing through investment installation, and to services provided throughout the lifespan of an investment project.[148]

Perhaps the leading academic advocate of a WTO framework agreement for trade facilitation has been Karl Sauvant of Columbia University. In terms of "concrete measures" to include in such an agreement, he and Matthew Stephenson of the Graduate Institute of International and Development Studies in Geneva have recommended provisions that would facilitate access to business visas, deliver project evaluation assistance for large-scale projects, create early grievance mechanisms to avoid legal disputes, increase the transparency of investment incentives, create databases of lists of local suppliers, require investor statements on corporate social responsibility, and facilitate coordination on investment policy and measures among domestic government agencies and between those agencies and the private sector.[149] For their part, the WTO members discussing the matter have identified an 81-item checklist of issues for further examination and possible inclusion in such a framework agreement.[150]

In particular, Sauvant has focused on capacity-building; he has rightly stressed the imperative of providing the necessary assistance to enable the full engagement of developing countries in negotiating and implementing a trade facilitation agreement.¹⁵¹ As with trade facilitation, investment facilitation is in no small part a matter of providing developing countries — and especially least-developed countries — with the assistance they will need to fulfill any new obligations. Technical assistance will be needed. So, too, will financial assistance. And, like the TFA, an agreement on investment facilitation should include different categories of obligations that developing countries can choose depending on their stage of development and their access to assistance in compliance.

Although these potential new WTO investment rules will be procedural in nature, they will be part of a framework agreement that, if WTO members wished, could be augmented over time to add substantive obligations. The current rules on trade-related investment measures could be relocated within the new framework, and they could be supplemented with new multilateral commitments on matters that would include ensuring market access and investment protection while also preserving the sovereign space of countries to regulate on the environment and on public health and safety. This will be an even more challenging act of line-drawing. Attitudes have been changing in developing countries as they have emerged economically and have become sources as well as hosts for FDI. But, unless and until all developing countries fully realize that more foreign direct investment is in their interest and is essential to their further development, a WTO framework agreement on investment will remain purely procedural. It will not address the substance of the further development that is needed now more than ever by developed and developing countries alike.

Digital Trade

The most significant new dimension of international trade in the 21st century is that so much of it is now digital. In the 20th century, trade was largely comprised of exchanges of physical goods. Today, trade links are increasingly digital. Trade now "is increasingly defined by flows of data and information."[152] The McKinsey Global Institute reports that, since 1990, "global flows of goods, foreign direct investment, and data have increased current global GDP by roughly 10 percent compared to what would have occurred in a world without any flows," adding up to a value equivalent to $7.8 trillion.[153] Of these varied global flows, "[d]ata flows account for $2.8 trillion of this effect, *exerting a larger impact on growth than traditional goods flows.*"[154]

The surge in global flows of data and information has fundamentally altered the ways the world economy works. The revolutionary impacts of these digital flows on trade are, of course, most apparent in the information and communications technology sector. But those impacts extend far beyond the ICT sector to include manufacturing, agriculture, mining, finance, insurance, and more. Digital flows of data and information enable the logistics of global supply chains. They provide the technical basis for the cost efficiencies of cloud computing. They facilitate 3D printing and further development of machine learning through heightened artificial intelligence. Digital flows further the "smart manufacturing" that uses data to add value to products (as with the computerized GPS positioning systems in automobiles). They also make it possible to link household and other basic mechanical systems to the Internet to enable the sending and receiving of data in the "Internet of Things." All of these new cutting-edge processes and technologies are possible only because of flows of digital data.

The McKinsey Global Institute also reports that "virtually every type of cross-border transaction now has a digital component."[155] About 12 percent of all global trade in goods is currently conducted by international e-commerce.[156] About half of global trade in services is digital.[157] International exchanges of virtual goods via the Internet are now commonplace.[158] Sensors, software, and other add-on "digital wrappers" enable goods shipments and encourage the mutual trust needed to engage in international transactions.[159] Container ships still sail. Cargo planes still fly. Trucks still cross borders. But digitalization is altering how all of this takes place, and, in doing so, it is adding both volume and value to international trade.

What is more, digitalization is not only changing *how* we trade.[160] It is also changing *who* trades. One major impact of these digital changes is that international trade is no longer the province principally of multinational corporations. Digitalization makes it easy to connect with anyone anywhere with only a few clicks on a computer. In the digital economy, "artisans, entrepreneurs, app developers, freelancers, small businesses, and even individuals can participate directly on digital platforms with global reach."[161] This diversifying and "democratizing" impact on participation in trade is widespread. Not all these firms and people are in New York or the Silicon Valley. Many of them — including many women and members of other disadvantaged and marginal groups — are in developing countries. In the most recent count, 361 million people worldwide participate in e-commerce.[162]

One aim of Goal 9 of the United Nations Sustainable Development Goals for 2030 is to "foster innovation."[163] Toward this end, the shift to a digital economy has increased economic growth by spurring improved efficiencies and technological innovations worldwide. In many economic sectors, these efficiencies and innovations have increased productivity, which is the key to generating economic growth.[164] The spread of the digital economy "is making itself felt in the ways knowledge, skills and expertise can be sourced from around the world, and in the ways in which production can be integrated, 24 hours a day, across time zones and borders."[165] Perhaps most significantly, the innovations of digitalization are "also rapidly spreading the very factors of production — technology, information, and ideas — that make economic advances possible."[166] According to the WTO, these digital "technological innovations have significantly reduced trade costs and transformed the way we communicate, consume, produce and trade."[167]

The shift to a digital economy is especially important to developing countries, which continue to suffer "within and across countries" from a "digital divide."[168] Ninety percent of the people in the world without Internet access are in developing countries.[169] Eighty-eight percent of North Americans, 85 percent of Japanese, and 84 percent of Europeans have Internet access. Sixty-five percent of the people of the Middle East and North Africa, 63 percent of Latin Americans and 54 percent of Chinese do. But only 34 percent of Indians, 33 percent of the inhabitants of the small Pacific island states, and 25 percent of sub-Saharan Africans do.[170] Most of the people in these developing countries remain outside the productive engine of the digital economy. New rules for digital trade must be accompanied by new measures that expand Internet access in those countries and in all the world.

If applied along with such measures, new rules that lower the barriers to digital trade can be of disproportionate benefit to developing countries. As the WTO has pointed out, "Many trade costs such as logistics and transactions costs or cumbersome customs procedures…are much higher in developing countries."[171] Thus, developing countries will benefit proportionately the most by the digitalization of these trade procedures. The WTO predicts that developing countries' share of world trade will increase from 46 percent in 2015 to 51 percent by 2030; but, if developing countries "catch up on the adoption of digital technologies," their share of global trade in 2030 will be 57 percent.[172] If, however, developing countries are left behind in the digital economy by the digital divide, then they will be marginalized in the global economy of the future.

Essential to framing the trade rules required to help secure more innovation by supporting and speeding the shift to a digital economy, is understanding the role of data in this historic shift. The source of the many innovations flowing from the digital economy is the free flow of data; and "underpinning digital trade is the movement of data."[173] The European Strategic Strategy Centre — the in-house think tank of the European Union — has explained, "Data is rapidly becoming the lifeblood of the global economy. It represents a new type of economic asset. Those who know how to use it have a decisive competitive advantage in this interconnected world, through raising performance, offering more user-centric products and services, fostering innovation — often leaving decades-old competitors behind."[174] Or, as Richard Waters of the *Financial Times* has pithily put it, "In the digital world, data is destiny."[175]

Being able to move data across borders is indispensable to digital trade. The free movement of data has become still more indispensable as more digital transactions have begun to rely on computer cloud services, which are oblivious to borders. Mark Wu of Harvard Law School has explained also that, as the digital economy transitions more and more toward the Internet of Things, artificial intelligence, virtual reality, autonomous vehicles, an even greater economic premium will be placed on the free movement of data.[176] "Beyond this economic impact," the World Economic Forum has added, "the free flow of data is, itself, a significant driver of innovation. It allows the sharing of ideas and information and the dissemination of knowledge as well as collaboration and cross-pollination among individuals and companies."[177]

Necessary also to framing rules for digital trade is comprehending that, in the digital economy, the product is often the data. As is frequently the case with Internet transactions, the data collected by the seller about the purchaser may be of more value than the money paid by the purchaser. Dan Ciurak and Maria Ptashkina of the Centre for International Governance Innovation in Canada have observed that in Internet transactions there is an implicit "barter exchange" of free Internet access for useful data; "in the case of consumer data, firms provide the 'free' service of use of their platforms in implicit exchange for the data such use generates."[178] In making the same point, Joshua Meltzer of the Brookings Institution has noted, "In a digital economy, …data can be used to produce digital goods and services, and can be a source of information that leads to further action," such as with data collection by a bank before authorizing a money transfer, or data collection by an insurer before assessing and insuring against a risk.[179] The success of myriad such economic actions, including countless actions that affect international trade, depends on the free flow of data.

Even before the pandemic, the trend toward more digital trade seemed likely to continue and to accelerate. In the new pandemic world, trade is becoming even more digital. Before the pandemic, 41 percent of interactions with customers by North American companies were digital; now 65 percent of customer interactions are digital.[180] In international trade, as in all else, Covid-19 has clearly shown the necessity for better digital capability and better connectivity. With the trend toward online commerce speeding up, David Malpass, president of the World Bank, anticipates that, "Faster advances in digital connectivity…should get a vital boost from the pandemic, which heightened the value of teleworking capabilities, digital information, and broad connectivity."[181] These advances in connectivity can be expected to help facilitate more digital trade.

Moreover, in the wake of the pandemic, the importance of intangible assets is increasing. The need for physical assets is decreasing as businesses realize that employees do not need to congregate in expensive office space to be productive. As Greg Ip of the *Wall Street Journal* has observed, "Value is increasingly derived from digital platforms, software and other intangible investments rather than physical assets and traditional relationships."[182] In this altered commercial landscape, the necessity for quick and effective communications is greater than ever before.[183] The businesses that are the most engaged in the digital economy are likely to lead the way in the economic recovery from the Covid-19 pandemic.

The Carlyle Group, a leading global private-equity firm, informs us that the pace of digitalization will accelerate in the new pandemic world; for "technology-enabled adaptation has opened the door to more sweeping changes in business models and strategies. …(and) tech-enabled digital platforms tend to outperform the broader market…."[184] Rana Foroohar of the *Financial Times* predicts that, of the new start-up enterprises that will emerge in the aftermath of the pandemic, "it's a fair bet that many will be highly digital. They are likely to hold a large chunk of value in intangible assets such as research and development, brands, content, data, patents or human capital, rather than in physical assets such as industrial machinery, factories or office space."[185] When these new enterprises engage in international trade, whether of goods or of services, they will be more likely to do so digitally.

Digital trade is not defined in the WTO trade rules. There is, moreover, no one recognized and accepted definition of digital trade. However, according to the OECD, "there is a growing consensus that it encompasses digitally-enabled transactions of trade in goods and services that can be digitally or physically delivered, and that involve consumers, firms, and governments. That is, while all forms of digital trade are enabled by digital technologies, not all digital trade is digitally delivered. For instance, digital trade also involves digitally enabled but physically delivered trade in goods and services such as the purchase of a book through an on-line marketplace, or booking a stay in an apartment through a matching application."[186]

Although there are no WTO rules written specifically for digital trade, there are WTO rules that apply to certain aspects of digital trade. As Ciuriak and Ptashkina have put it, numerous rules that apply to non-digital trade also apply "by default" to digital trade, even in the absence of specific rules on digital trade.[187] Moreover, "WTO rules are technologically neutral," which means that the mere fact that trade is conducted other than by means of a physical transaction should not change WTO obligations.[188] Yet there are many legal uncertainties about whether existing rules apply, which existing rules apply, and how existing rules apply. To some extent, the WTO Appellate Body has reduced these legal uncertainties in WTO dispute settlement.[189] But the fact remains, the WTO rules on goods trade date back to 1947, long before the information revolution, and the WTO rules on services trade date back to 1994, when the Internet was still an obscure novelty and "many of today's digital technologies and applications did not yet exist."[190]

Despite their technological neutrality, basic legal questions remain unanswered about the extent to which current WTO rules are relevant to digital trade. For example, is a product provided online a good or a service? To illustrate this dilemma, as economist Robert Staiger has done, "[I]s a blueprint for use in a 3D printer, when delivered from abroad, a traded good or a traded service?"[191] The answer matters in part because the national treatment obligation applies automatically to all trade in goods but applies to trade in services only if a specific trade concession has been made. Also, where commitments have been made that could apply to digital trade, do those obligations in fact apply to services such as cloud computing and search engines, which did not exist when those commitments were made in the 1990s? If they do not apply, then WTO members are free to impose any restrictions they may wish on the foreign digital delivery of those services.

Mindful of these limitations in the existing rules, WTO members have been trying to modernize the trade rules to deal with digital trade since 1998. They approved a temporary moratorium that year on the application of customs duties on electronic transactions, which has been renewed repeatedly.[192] But they have not yet made this moratorium permanent, and they have accomplished little else since then toward addressing the manifold commercial concerns of what has become an increasingly digital economy. The absence of specific rules on digital trade in the WTO trade rulebook is emblematic of the near paralysis of the WTO negotiating function thus far in this century.

The inability of the WTO to negotiate specific rules on digital trade was a major reason for the seeming indifference of so many in the international business community to the demise of the Doha round in Nairobi in 2015. Since then, commercial concerns relating to digital trade have continued to multiply and intensify while acquiring an array of geopolitical dimensions. The rise of digital trade has created digital trade rivalry, which is most evident in the commercial relations between and among the United States, the European Union, and China. This rivalry reveals in the new digital realm the profound differences between those who believe in open and closed societies, between those in the world who favor free individual choices about how to live, what to do, and what to think, and those who do not.

Broadly speaking, the European Union and the United States favor open and market-based approaches to digital trade while China does not. The EU and the US have agreed on certain principles for cross-border ICT services, including open networks, network access, and use; no governmental restrictions on cross-border flows of data and information; no discrimination in licensing; and no requirements of local infrastructure or local presence as a condition of delivering services.[193] The two differ, however, on the meaning of some of these principles. Most notably, the EU and the US differ on the sensitive issue of data privacy, with the EU favoring more privacy protections for consumers and other Internet users than does the US.[194] This difference prevents them from presenting an entirely united front on the need for free flows of data and information in their dealings with China.

For their part, the Chinese profess to believe in "Internet sovereignty"— the notion that each country has the sovereign right to control its domestic Internet space by limiting the free flow of data and information. As Mark Wu has pointed out, most countries think the Internet is subject to national laws, but "China is unique in its lack of respect for the idea of an open Internet."[195] On this philosophical basis, the Chinese defend their digital "Great Firewall," with which they routinely censor online content and online product delivery throughout China. In China's unopposed and omnipresent one-party state, this digital firewall, coupled with their recent intensifying of overall political surveillance of the Chinese people, discourages unwanted domestic dissent, and deters the introduction of unsanctioned and unsettling ideas from abroad. Continued popular support for the unchallenged reign of the Chinese Communist Party is thereby solidified.

The "Great Firewall" is also a tool employed for digital protectionism. The digital firewall denies Chinese consumers access to online content and to other goods and services accessible on the Internet from foreign suppliers. This gives an unfair trade advantage to Chinese domestic firms, which are, in effect, subsidized by the Chinese government in both Chinese and foreign markets. Digital protectionism may benefit these Chinese firms now, but this policy is shortsighted; it only seems to be in the economic self-interest of China. As with all other forms of economic nationalism, by denying these Chinese firms the benefits of foreign competition, this favoritism in the short term sets them up for failure in the long term. As always, the lack of competition diminishes the likelihood of innovation.

Despite these increasing geopolitical tensions, some of the basic issues relating to digital trade seem conducive to negotiated WTO solutions. Issues ripe for WTO resolution include: making the WTO moratorium on customs duties on digital products permanent; defining digital trade and basic terms for digital trade; authorizing electronic signatures to validate online transactions; authorizing cross-border paperless trading; facilitating additional digital trade through electronic means; providing protections for e-consumers equivalent to those for other consumers; and requiring the establishment of domestic legal and regulatory rules and frameworks for electronic commerce.

Yet, amid "widespread concerns...about the fracturing of the global economy into walled-off and possibly warring data realms," other digital trade issues appear far from resolution.[196] Foremost among these unresolved issues is the question of the free flow of data, which is central to the debate about digital trade among the United States, the European Union, China, and other members of the WTO. Essential to innovation, the free flow of data is also vulnerable to digital protectionism, as seen in

China and elsewhere. As Meltzer has explained, "Government intervention in the free flow of data can reduce the potential of the Internet for international trade. Some of these restrictions are for legitimate reasons such as protecting the privacy of data, Internet Protocol (IP) protection, ensuring cybersecurity or regulatory access to harmful contact such as child pornography. In other cases, restrictions on cross-border data flows are being imposed to provide domestic companies with a competitive advantage by redirecting Internet search or blocking access to foreign sites."[197]

Impediments to the free flow of data in the new digital economy also take the form of data localization requirements. Some governments force companies to use domestic servers to store data locally. They prohibit the transfer of data offshore. Other governments do not bar data transfer but do require that a copy of the data be stored domestically. These governments cite the need for personal data protection and for access to data for law enforcement as justifying these restrictions. Yet these restrictions can also function as the equivalent of domestic content requirements to benefit national firms while discriminating against foreign firms. Such digital protectionism, as Wu has noted, becomes especially costly and discriminatory "as data takes on increasing value with big data services and the growth of artificial intelligences."[198]

In addition, some governments require companies to disclose their software source code for review as a condition of doing business in their territory. They justify this requirement as necessary to prevent the possibility that imported digital technologies will undermine personal privacy or threaten national security. This disclosure requirement can be tantamount to a mandate to turn over proprietary trade secrets. Not surprisingly, foreign companies that are compelled to disclose their source codes are much concerned that their compliance with this requirement could lead to illegal technology transfer and the theft of their intellectual property rights.[199] This is a main concern of European and American companies in China.

Frustrated by their continuing inability to negotiate rules on digital trade within the WTO, the United States, the European Union, and other countries with a stake in the digital economy — developed and developing alike — have ventured outside the WTO legal framework to agree on digital trade rules in regional and other preferential trade agreements. About half of WTO members are now parties to non-WTO agreements that contain rules on digital trade.[200] These other agreements lack the advantages of multilateral agreements, in which a balance of mutual obligations can be secured based on a weighing of all global points of view. These other agreements also can reflect the "take-it-or-leave-it" typical of the approach of larger countries in negotiating with smaller ones. Yet the digital provisions in some of these other agreements offer templates for crafting digital trade rules within the WTO.

Notable are the rules on digital trade in what is now named the Comprehensive and Progressive Agreement for Trans-Pacific Partnership (CPTPP). Although President Trump pulled the United States out of the then Tran-Pacific Partnership in one of his first acts as President, the eleven other countries in the TPP retained the digital trade rules the United States had negotiated in their slightly revised agreement that they rechristened as the CPTPP. For example, the CPTPP requires participating countries to permit cross-border data flows, and it includes a general restriction on data localization. Exceptions to these requirements are limited to those that achieve legitimate public policy goals. In addition, the CPTPP prohibits forced transfer or disclosure of software source code.[201]

The recently revised North American Free Trade Agreement — now known in the US as the United States-Mexico-Canada Agreement (USMCA) — goes beyond the CPTPP in establishing rules for digital trade. The Internet was new and digital trade did not exist when the NAFTA was concluded in 1994. A new chapter on digital trade in the USMCA is more precise than some of the CPTPP rules in broadening the scope of the protections for digital trade. Exceptions to the free flow of data across borders are limited in the USMCA to those that are "necessary to" achieve legitimate public policy goals. There is no specific exception in the USMCA to the restriction on data localization. In contrast to the CPTPP, the financial services sector is clearly covered, there is a provision promoting open government data, and there is a prohibition of forced transfer or disclosure not only of software source code, but also of the algorithms that are the basic ingredients of digital commerce and communications.[202]

In January 2019, 76 WTO members announced the commencement of "negotiations on trade-related aspects of electronic commerce."[203] Although President Trump's priority has been the protection of traditional smokestack industries, his administration helped launch these negotiations on WTO digital trade rules. The European Union is also engaged in these negotiations. China is not. These 76 countries have said they seek the participation of "as many members as possible;" they have not said whether their goal is a multilateral agreement among all WTO members or only a plurilateral agreement among a subset of WTO members. Nor have they defined the scope of their negotiations. During the pandemic, the usual difficulties of negotiating trade agreements have been magnified. Virtual negotiations are less conducive to making trade deals than are face-to-face discussions around a negotiating table. Yet there is hope for consensus on at least some of the issues of digital trade. And, once there is a consensus on the easier issues, there will be a basis for building on that consensus to confront the harder ones and perhaps to bring China, at least in part, into the ambit of new WTO digital trade rules.

A start toward an early consensus by these 76 WTO members on some of the digital issues can be found in the provisions on digital trade in the CPTPP, the USMCA, and other regional and preferential trade agreements. By one recent count, there are 69 RTAs with either a chapter on electronic commerce or provisions on electronic commerce.[204] In particular, an appealing model for moving forward in the WTO is the Digital Economy Partnership Agreement (DEPA), which was concluded during the midst of the pandemic in June 2020 by Chile, New Zealand, and Singapore.[205] The three parties to DEPA are small countries that know well the economic value of freeing trade and shortening long distances. They are "well-known not just for their openness but for their creativity when it comes to trade."[206]

Appropriately, their conclusion of DEPA was conducted virtually. DEPA builds on some of what is already contained in the CPTPP, the USMCA, and other preferential and regional agreements on digital trade. For instance, DEPA is the first trade agreement to deal with digital identities (such as national business numbers), which are an important component of the digital economy.[207] DEPA includes rules on financial technology and artificial intelligence that are not in the CPTPP. In addition, DEPA establishes programs to foster the inclusion of women and indigenous peoples in the digital economy.[208] But what is most distinctive — and what is most conducive to emulation — in the DEPA is its unique structure.

Chile, New Zealand, and Singapore have agreed to the DEPA in its entirety. The three countries have, however, structured their tripartite agreement to contain a dozen subject-specific categories of matters relating to digital trade, which they have labeled "modules." As Deborah Elms of the Asian Trade Centre in Singapore has said, "These modules are meant to be building blocks. Countries could opt to dock directly into

DEPA, expanding the agreement with new Members. Or governments could decide to pick up and use modules, in whole or in part, in various settings. These include slotting them directly into other trade agreements or opting to align domestic policies to DEPA."[209]

WTO members could use this "modular" approach in negotiating rules for digital trade. Each digital issue or group of related issues could be placed in a distinct category. Each category could be treated separately, negotiated separately, and agreed separately. In addition, different levels of digital commitments could be agreed for each category. There could be "building blocks within a building block."[210] This would enable individual members of the WTO to agree to commitments in one or more "modular" categories but not in others. This would also enable WTO members to make different levels of commitments within each "module."

It may turn out to be a relatively simple matter to achieve global consensus on some of the most basic issues — such as, say, providing consumer protections against the "spam" of unsolicited messages. Unquestionably, issues such as free data flow, source code disclosure, and data privacy will not be easily resolved. Nor are there any ready answers about how best to climb "the lofty heights of grappling with principles and ethics for regulating complex frontier technologies such as artificial intelligence and digital identity."[211] But a consensus on the right answers in rules for digital trade is more likely to be reached with a flexible negotiating approach that permits WTO members to make some commitments without having to make, at the outset, all of the commitments that may be asked of them. And such a consensus is more likely to be reached as well with a flexible approach that permits WTO members also to agree to different levels of commitments within different categories of digital trade.

With the benefit of such a flexible approach, the 76 members of the WTO that have agreed to negotiate rules on "trade-related electronic commerce" may be able to conclude an initial and partial WTO digital trade agreement that could ultimately become fully multilateral and fully responsive to the evolving needs of the new digital economy.

Conclusion

These first five pieces of WTO reform will not be easy pieces to put in place. They are instead hard pieces. Agreements on free trade in environmental goods, fisheries subsidies, and investment have eluded consensus of WTO members for decades. Negotiating lines on these three WTO reforms have cemented through long years of frustrated negotiations. Agreements on free trade in medical goods and on digital trade present newer issues for WTO members. Some of the negotiating lines on these two issues have yet to form. Each of these proposed WTO reforms presents different negotiating challenges. But as hard as it will surely be to achieve consensus on these five reforms, these are nevertheless the five reforms now seem the ripest for resolution in June 2021 at the next WTO ministerial conference in Kazakhstan. Success in reaching an agreement in Nur-Sultan on all five of these pieces of WTO reform would do much to end the existential crisis of the WTO. Failure to reach an agreement on any of them would prolong and worsen that crisis, with unforeseeable but undoubtedly unfortunate consequences for all WTO members.

Endnotes

[1] Peter S. Goodman, "A Global Outbreak Is Fueling the Backlash to Globalization," *New York Times* (March 5, 2020).

[2] Goal 3, "Transforming Our World: The 2030 Agenda for Sustainable Development," A/RES/70/1 (September 25–27, 2015). *See* Targets 3.3 and 3.b under Goal 3.

[3] WTO, "Trade in Medical Goods in the Context of Tackling Covid-19," Information Note (April 3, 2020), 2.

[4] *Ibid.*

[5] *Ibid.* at 3.

[6] *Ibid.* at 4.

[7] *Ibid.*

[8] *Ibid.* at 3 (Table 1).

[9] *Ibid.* at 3.

[10] *Ibid.*

[11] WTO, ITC, and UNCTAD, "World Tariff Profiles 2020," at 225–226.

[12] *Ibid.* at 226.

[13] WTO, "Trade in Medical Goods in the Context of Tackling Covid-19," at 6.

[14] *Ibid.*

[15] https://www.wto.org/english/thewto_e/glossary_e/tariff_peaks_e.htm.

[16] *Ibid.* at 1.

[17] WTO, "Trade in Medical Goods in the Context of Tackling Covid-19," at 1.

[18] *Ibid.*

19 Simon J. Evenett, "Tackling Coronavirus: The Trade Policy Dimension," Global Trade Alert (March 11, 2020), 4.
20 *Ibid.*
21 WTO, "Trade in Medical Goods in the Context of Tackling Covid-19," at 7.
22 *Ibid.* at 6.
23 Chuin-Wei Yap, "Pandemic Lays Bare U.S. Reliance on China for Drugs," *Wall Street Journal* (August 5, 2020).
24 Denise Roland and Jared S. Hopkins, "FDA Cites Shortage of One Drug, Exposing Supply-Line Worry," *Wall Street Journal* (February 28, 2020).
25 "Growing U.S. Reliance on China's Biotech and Pharmaceutical Products," U.S.-China Economic and Security Review Commission (March 2020), 250.
26 Michael T. Osterholm and Mark Olshaker, "Chronicle of a Pandemic Foretold: Learning from the COVID-19 Failure — Before the Next Outbreak Arrives," *Foreign Affairs* (July/August 2020), 10, 13.
27 *Ibid.*
28 Karen M. Sutter, Andres B. Schwarzenberg, and Michael D. Sutherland, "COVID-19: China Supply Chains and Broader Trade Issues," Congressional Research Service, R46304 (April 6, 2020), 19.
29 Denise Roland and Jared S. Hopkins, "FDA Cites Shortage of One Drug, Exposing Supply-Line Worry," WTO, "World Statistical Report 2020," at 57.
30 *Ibid.*
31 Preetika Rana and Denise Roland, "Drugmakers Gain More Access to China, but at a Price," *Wall Street Journal* (November 27, 2018).
32 Chuin-Wei Yap, "Pandemic Lays Bare U.S. Reliance on China for Drugs."
33 Denise Roland and Jared S. Hopkins, "FDA Cites Shortage of One Drug, Exposing Supply-Line Worry."
34 *Ibid.*
35 Chuin-Wei Yap, "Pandemic Lays Bare U.S. Reliance on China for Drugs."
36 Karen M. Sutter, Andres B. Schwarzenberg, and Michael D. Sutherland, "COVID-19: China Supply Chains and Broader Trade Issues," at 20.
37 Yanzhong Huang, "The Coronavirus Outbreak Could Disrupt the U.S. Drug Supply," Council on Foreign Relations (March 5, 2020), at https://www.cfr.org/in-brief/coronavirus-disrupt-us-drug-supply-shortages-fda; *see also* Kritika Krishnakumar, "Active Pharmaceutical Ingredients Business in India Gains as Pharma Firms Diversify Raw Material Sourcing from China," *Indian Wire* (July 31, 2020).
38 "India's incentives for domestic API production could cut supply risk: Fitch," *Economic Times* (August 10, 2020), at https://health.economictimes.indiatimes.com/news/pharma/indias-incentives-for-domestic-api-production-could-cut-supply-risk-fitch/77459098.
39 WTO, "Trade in Medical Goods in the Context of Tackling Covid-19," at 4.
40 For an excellent in-depth analysis of this issue and its implications for managed trade, *see* Scott Lincicome, "The Government's Plan to Turn Kodak Into a

Pharmaceutical Company Sure Seems *Underdeveloped*," Cato (July 29, 2020), at https://www.cato.org/blog/governments-plan-turn-kodak-pharmaceutical-company-seems-underdeveloped. (emphasis in original)

[41] "Coronavirus outbreak: India bans exports of all kinds of respiratory masks; toll due to virus tops 200 in China," *First Post* (February 1, 2020).

[42] Simon J. Evenett, "Tackling Coronavirus: The Trade Policy Dimension," Global Trade Alert (March 11, 2020), 3.

[43] Chad P. Bown, "EU limits on medical gear exports put poor countries and Europeans at risk," Peterson Institute for International Economics (March 19, 2020), at https://www.piie.com/blogs/trade-and-investment-policy-watch/eu-limits-medical-gear-exports-put-poor-countries-and-europeans-at-risk.

[44] Simon J. Evenett, "Tackling Coronavirus: The Trade Policy Dimension," at 3.

[45] David Lim, "Trump signs 'Buy American' executive order for essential drugs," *Politico* (August 6, 2020).

[46] Maria Cheng, "Health experts slam US deal for large supply of the only drug licensed so far to treat COVID-19," *Associated Press* (July 1, 2020).

[47] Simon J. Evenett and L. Alan Winters, "Preparing for a Second Wave of Covid-19," Global Trade Alert (April 26, 2020), 3.

[48] Simon J. Evenett, "Tackling Coronavirus: The Trade Policy Dimension," at 3.

[49] *Ibid.* at 2.

[50] James Bacchus, "Governments Should Rely More on the WTO in the Fight Against the Coronavirus," Cato (April 3, 2020).

[51] Aaditya Mattoo and Michele Ruta, "Don't close borders against coronavirus," *Financial Times* (March 13, 2020).

[52] *Ibid.*

[53] *Ibid.*

[54] Martin Wolf, "The dangerous war on supply chains," *Financial Times* (June 23, 2020).

[55] Article I, Section 10, Clause 2, United States Constitution. *See* Boris I. Bittker and Brannon P. Denning, "The Import-Export Clause," *Mississippi Law Journal*, Volume 68 (1998), 521–564. Some WTO members, including China, have accepted limits on their right to impose export taxes as part of their accession agreements to membership in the WTO.

[56] Article XI (1), General Agreement on Tariffs and Trade.

[57] Article XI (2) (a), General Agreement on Tariffs and Trade.

[58] Article X, General Agreement on Tariffs and Trade.

[59] Article XIII, General Agreement on Tariffs and Trade.

[60] Article XX, General Agreement on Tariffs and Trade.

[61] Martin Wolf, "The dangerous war on supply chains."

[62] Richard Baldwin and Simon Evenett, "COVID-19 and Trade Policy: Why Turning Inward Won't Work," at https://voxeu.org/article/new-ebook-covid-19-and-trade-policy-why-turning-inward-wont-work.

[63] Jennifer Hillman, "Six Proactive Steps in a Smart Trade Approach to Fighting COVID-19," Think Global Health (March 20, 2020), at https://www.thinkglobalhealth.org/article/six-proactive-steps-smart-trade-approach-fighting-covid19.

[64] Matthias Helble and Benjamin Shepherd, "Trade in Health Products: Reducing Trade Barriers for Better Health," Asian Development Bank Institute, Working Paper Number 643 (January 2017), 6.

[65] Anabel Gonzalez, "A memo to trade ministers on how trade policy can help fight COVID-19," Peterson Institute for International Economics (March 23, 2020), at https://www.piie.com/blogs/trade-and-investment-policy-watch/memo-trade-ministers-how-trade-policy-can-help-fight-covid19.

[66] WTO, "DDG Wolf: Policy coordination needed to address pandemic challenges" (April 20, 2020), at https://www.wto.org/english/news_e/news20_e/ddgaw_20apr20_e.htm.

[67] *Ibid.*

[68] *Ibid.*

[69] Jacob M. Schlesinger, "How the Coronavirus Will Reshape World Trade."

[70] WTO Trade Facilitation Agreement, WT/L/940 (November 27, 2014).

[71] Anabel Gonzalez, "A memo to trade ministers on how trade policy can help fight COVID-19."

[72] Miriam Jordan and Annie Correal, "Foreign Doctors Could Help Fight Coronavirus. But U.S. Blocks Many," *New York Times* (April 3, 2020).

[73] Article 3.7 and Article 22.2, WTO Dispute Settlement Understanding.

[74] *See* Anshu Siripurapu, "The State of U.S. Strategic Stockpiles," Council on Foreign Relations (June 15, 2020), at https://www.cfr.org/backgrounder/state-us-strategic-stockpiles.

[75] Scott Gottlieb and Mark McClellan, "Covid Shows the Need for a Diagnostic Stockpile," *Wall Street Journal* (July 26, 2020).

[76] Jacob M. Schlesinger, "How the Coronavirus Will Reshape World Trade."

[77] Editorial, "Building resilience should not lead to trade barriers," *Financial Times* (June 12, 2020).

[78] *Ibid.*

[79] Paragraph 31(iii), Doha Declaration.

[80] WTO, "Environmental Goods Agreement (EGA)," at https://www.wto.org/english/tratop_e/envir_e/ega_arc_e.htm.

[81] APEC, "The APEC List of Environmental Goods," APEC Secretariat (November 2012), at https://apec.org/Publications/2012/11/The-APEC-List-of-Environmental-Goods.

[82] OECD Joint Working Party on Trade and Environment, "The Stringency of Environmental Regulations and Trade in Environmental Goods (November 19, 2014), Annex 1, 51.

[83] This was the suggestion of the National Association of Manufacturers in the United States. *See* Matt Roessing, "Greed is (an environmental) Good" (June 27,

[84] "Environmental Goods Agreement — why talks faltered," *Borderlex* (December 6, 2016), at https:///www.borderlex.eu/2016/12/06/environmental-goods-agreement-talks-faltered/.

[85] *See* James Bacchus, "Good news for green goods," World Economic Forum (February 3, 2014).

[86] "Joint Statement Regarding Trade in Environmental Goods" (January 24, 2014), at https://kr.usembassy.gov/p_econ_012414b/.

[87] WTO, "Information Technology Agreement," at https://www.wto.org/english/tratop_e/inftec_e.htm.

[88] For more details, *see* James Bacchus, "Ending tariffs on green goods will show free trade can fight climate change," *Guardian* (August 12, 2014).

[89] Tim Worstall, "How Excellent, WTO Talks on Environmental Goods Agreement Collapses," Forbes (December 4, 2016), at https://forbes.com/sites/timworstall/2016/12/04/how-excellent-wto-talks-on-environmental-goods-agreement-collapse.

[90] *See*, in part for a slightly different view, Bernhard Potter, "TTIP in Green: Free Trade for Ostensibly Eco-Goods," *Green European Journal* (June 24, 2016).

[91] Ministerial Declaration, Ministerial Conference, Fourth Session, Doha, Qatar, November 9–14, 2001, WT/MIN(01)DEC/1.

[92] Target 14.6, "Transforming Our World."

[93] "WTO fisheries talks suspended due to COVID preoccupations: document," *Reuters* (May 20, 2020).

[94] "Paper from Brazil, Chile, Colombia, Ecuador, Iceland, New Zealand, Pakistan, Peru and the United States to the Negotiating Group on Rules, Fisheries Subsidies," TN/RL/W/196 November 22, 2005).

[95] USTR, "2017 Trade Policy Agenda and 2016 Annual Report" (March 2017), 5.

[96] U. Rashid Sumaila, "Trade Policy Options for Sustainable Oceans and Fisheries," at 6. See generally "Fish to 2030: Prospects for Fisheries and Aquaculture," World Bank Report 83177-GLB (Washington: World Bank, 2013).

[97] *Ibid.*

[98] "Ocean Fishing: All the Fish in the Sea," *Economist* (May 27, 2017).

[99] Editorial, "The Marine World: Deep Trouble," *Economist* (May 27, 2017).

[100] U. Rashid Sumaila, "Trade Policy Options for Sustainable Oceans and Fisheries," at 10.

[101] FAO, "The State of World Fisheries and Aquaculture 2020: Sustainability in Action" (2020), 13.

[102] *Ibid.*

[103] *Ibid.*

[104] Christopher Costello et al., "Global fishery prospects under contrasting management regimes," Proceedings of the National Academy of Sciences (March 29,

2016); *see also* Editorial, "How to save the world's fisheries," *Washington Post* (March 29, 2016).

[105] FAO, "The State of World Fisheries and Aquaculture 2020," at 16.

[106] *Ibid.* at 18.

[107] *Ibid.* at 17.

[108] *Ibid.* at 18.

[109] *Ibid.* at 17.

[110] *Ibid.*

[111] *Ibid.*

[112] *Ibid.* at 18.

[113] Elizabeth Wilson, "Fishing Subsidies Are Speeding the Decline of Ocean Health" (July 19, 2018), at https://www.pertrusts.org/en/research-and-analysis/article/2018/07/19/fishing-subisides-are-speeding-the-decline-of-ocean-health.

[114] Basak Bayramoglu, Brian Copeland, Marco Fuguzza, and Jean-Francois Jacques, "Trade and Negotiations on Fisheries Subsidies" (October 21, 2019), at https://voxeu.org/article/trade-and-negotiations-fisheries-subsidies.

[115] Isabel Jarrett, "Fisheries Subsidies Reform Could Reduce Overfishing and Illegal Fishing Case Studies Find," Pew Charitable Trusts (July 22, 2020), at https://www.pertrusts.org/en/research-and-analysis/articles/2020/07/22/fisheries-subsidies-refomr-could-reduce-overfishing-and-illegal-fishing-case-studies-find.

[116] U. Rashid Sumaila, Daniel Skerritt, Anna Schuhbauer, Naazia Ebrahim, Yang Li, Hong Sik Kim, Tabitha Grace Mallory, Vicky W.L. Lam, and Daniel Pauly, "A global dataset on subsidies to the fisheries sector," *Marine Policy*, Volume 109 (November 19, 2019), 103695-104706.

[117] U. Rashid Sumaila, "Trade Policy Options for Sustainable Oceans and Fisheries," at 6.

[118] Global Ocean Commission, "The Future of Our Ocean: Next Steps and Priorities. Report 2016," 7, 23.

[119] *Ibid.*

[120] OECD, "Fisheries, aquaculture and COVID-19: Issues and Policy Responses" (June 4, 2020), 1.

[121] U. Rashid Sumaila, "Trade Policy Options for Sustainable Oceans and Fisheries," at 13.

[122] Target 14.b, "Transforming Our World."

[123] Isabel Jarrett, "Fisheries Subsidies Reform Could Reduce Overfishing and Illegal Fishing Case Studies Find."

[124] *Ibid.*

[125] Ricardo Melendez-Ortiz, "Additionality, Innovation and Systemic Implications of Environment, Fisheries and Labour in TPP: A Preliminary Review," (March 2016) (unpublished paper in possession of the author), 3.

[126] Article 20.16(5), Comprehensive and Progressive Agreement for Trans-Pacific Partnership.

[127] Ricardo Melendez-Ortiz, "Additionality, Innovation and System Implications of Environment, Fisheries and Labour in TPP: A Preliminary Review," at 4.

[128] Ana Novik and Alexandre de Crombrugghe, "Towards an International Framework for Investment Facilitation," OECD Investment Insights (April 2018), 1.

[129] WTO, "World Trade Report 2013: Factors shaping the future of world trade," 138, at https://www.wto.org/english/res_e/publications_e/wtr13_e.htm.

[130] *Ibid.* at 135, 141. *See* James Bacchus, *The Willing World*, at 110-111.

[131] UNCTAD, "World Investment Report 2020: International Production Beyond the Pandemic," at https://unctad.org/webflyer/world-investment-report-2020.

[132] *Ibid.* at 90.

[133] *Ibid.*

[134] https://investmentpolicy.unctad.org/international-investment-agreements/by-economy.

[135] WTO Agreement on Trade-Related Investment Measures.

[136] Article 2, WTO Agreement on Trade-Related Investment Measures.

[137] *Ibid.*

[138] "Joint Ministerial Statement on Investment Facilitation for Development," WT/MIN(17)/59 (December 13, 2017).

[139] *Ibid.* WT/L/1072/Rev.1 (November 22, 2019).

[140] WTO, "Structured discussion on investment facilitation for development move into negotiating mode" (September 25, 2020), at https://www.wto.org/english/news_e/news20_e/infac_25sep20_e.htm.

[141] WTO Agreement on Trade Facilitation, "Annex to the Protocol Amending the Marrakesh Agreement Establishing the World Trade Organization," WT/L/940 (November 28, 2014).

[142] WTO, "Trade facilitation," at https://www.wto.org/english/tratop_e/tradfa_e.htm.

[143] Paragraph 4, "Joint Ministerial Statement on Investment Facilitation for Development," WT/MIM(17)/59 (December 13, 2017).

[144] Sofia Balino and Nathalie Bernaconi-Osterwalder, "Investment Facilitation at the WTO: An Attempt to bring a controversial issues into an organization in crisis," International Institute for Sustainable Development (June 27, 2019).

[145] *Ibid.*

[146] *Ibid.*

[147] Ana Novik and Alexandre de Crombrugghe, "Towards and International Framework for Investment Facilitation," at 3.

[148] UNCTAD, "World Investment Report 2016: Investor Nationality: Policy Challenges," 117, at https://unctad.org/webflyer/world-investment-report-2016.

[149] Karl P. Sauvant and Matthew Stephenson, "Concrete measures for a Framework on Investment Facilitation for Development: Report," Expert Workshop on Opportunities and Challenges of Establishing an International

Framework on Investment Facilitation for Development in the WTO held at the WTO (December 12, 2019).

[150] Sofia Balino and Nathalie Bernasconi-Osterwalder, "Investment Facilitation at the WTO."

[151] Karl P. Sauvant, "Enabling the Full Participation of Developing Countries in Negotiating an Investment Facilitation Framework for Development," Columbia FDI Perspectives, Number 275 (April 6, 2020).

[152] McKinsey Global Institute, "Digital Globalization: The New Era of Global Flows" (March 2016), 1.

[153] *Ibid.* These number are for 2016.

[154] *Ibid.* (emphasis added)

[155] McKinsey Global Institute, "Digital Globalization," at 30.

[156] *Ibid.* at 7.

[157] *Ibid.*

[158] *Ibid.*

[159] *Ibid.*

[160] Daniel Griswold, "The Dynamic Gains from Free Digital Trade for the U.S. Economy," Testimony before the U.S. Congress Joint Economic Committee (September 12, 2017).

[161] McKinsey Global Institute, "Digital Globalization," at 7.

[162] *Ibid.* at 8. These numbers are as of 2016; the total is undoubtedly larger now.

[163] Goal 9, "Transforming Our World."

[164] World Bank, "World Development Report 2016: Digital Dividends" (Washington, D.C.: World Bank Group, 2016), 105–130.

[165] *Ibid.* at 19.

[166] *Ibid.*

[167] WTO, "World Trade Report 2018: The future of world trade: How digital technologies are transforming global commerce" (Geneva: WTO, 2018), 6.

[168] Mark Wu, "Digital Trade-Related Provisions in Regional Trade Agreements: Existing Models and Lessons for the Multilateral Trading System," Inter-American Development Bank and International Centre for Trade and Sustainable Development, RTA Exchange, Overview Paper (November 2017), 1.

[169] Joshua P. Meltzer, "The Internet and international data flows in the global economy," E15 Initiative, World Economic Forum and International Centre for Trade and Sustainable Development (May 27, 2016).

[170] Richard Webb, "The greatest network the world has ever seen: The global internet map," *New Scientist* (October 23, 2019). These are 2017 numbers.

[171] WTO, "World Trade Report 2018," at 9.

[172] *Ibid.* at 11.

[173] OECD, "The impact of digitalization on trade," at https://www.oecd.org/trade/topics/digital-trade/.

174 European Political Strategy Centre, "Enter the Data Economy: EU Policies for a Thriving Data Ecosystem," EPSC Strategic Notes, Issue 21 (January 11, 2017), 1 (emphasis in original).

175 Richard Waters, "They're Watching You," *Financial Times* (October 24, 2020).

176 Mark Wu, "Digital Trade-Related Provisions in Regional Trade Agreements," at 23.

177 Robert Pepper, John Garrity, and Connie LaSalle, "1.2 Cross-Border Data Flows, Digital Innovation, and Economic Growth," World Economic Forum (2016), at https://www.reports,weforum.org/global-information-technology-report-2016/1-2-cross-border-data-flows-digital-innovation-and-economic-growth/.

178 Dan Ciuriak and Maria Ptashkina, "The Digital Transformation and the Transformation of International Trade," Inter-American Development Bank and International Centre for Trade and Sustainable Development, RTA Exchange Issues Paper (January 2018), vi.

179 Joshua P. Meltzer, "Governing Digital Trade," World Trade Review, Volume 18, no. S1 (2019), s23-s48, s29.

180 David Ignatius, "After covid-19, it will be a different world," *Washington Post* (October 9, 2020).

181 World Bank, "Global Economic Outlook" (June 2020), xiv.

182 Greg Ip, "Pandemic Hastens Shift to Asset-Light Economy," *Wall Street Journal* (October 8, 2020).

183 Jason Thomas, "When the Future Arrives Early," Carlyle Group Global Insights (September 16, 2020), at https://www.carlyle.com/global-insights/when-the-future-arrives-early-thomas.

184 *Ibid.* at 14, 16.

185 Rana Foroohar, "Covid recovery will stem from digital business," *Financial Times* (October 4, 2020).

186 OECD, "The impact of digitalization on trade."

187 Dan Ciuriak and Maria Ptashkina, "The Digital Transformation and the Transformation of International Trade," at 1.

188 Dan Ciuriak, "The WTO in the Digital Age," Centre for International Governance Innovation (May 4, 2020), at https://www.cigionline.org/articles/wto-digital-age.

189 *See* Appellate Body Report, *China — Measures Affecting Trading Rights and Distribution Services for Certain Publications and Audiovisual Entertainment Products*, WT/DS363/AB/R (2009), para. 196; *see also* Panel Report, *United States — Measures Affecting the Cross-Border Supply of Gambling and Betting Services*, WT/DS285/R (2004).

190 Mark Wu, "Digital Trade-Related Provisions in Regional Trade Agreements," at 2.

191 WTO, "World Trade Report 2018," at 150.

192 WTO Work Programme on Electronic Commerce, Ministerial Decision of December 13, 2017, WT/MIN(17)/65, December 18, 2017.
193 European Commission, "European Union-United States Trade Principles for Information and Communication Technology Services" (2011), at https://www.trade.ec.europa.eu/doclib/docs/2011/april/tradoc_147780.pdf.
194 *See* EU General Data Protection Regulations, L119/1, 679, Article 45 (April 27, 2016).
195 Shannon Tiezzi, "China's 'Sovereign Internet,'" *The Diplomat* (June 24, 2014), at http://thediplomat.com/2014/06/china-sovereign-internet/.
196 Dan Ciuriak, "World Trade Organization 2.0: Reforming Multilateral Trade Rules for the Digital Age," Centre for International Governance Innovation (July 11, 2019), 3.
197 Joshua P. Meltzer, "A New Digital Trade Agenda," E15 Initiative, E15 Expert Group on the Digital Economy Overview Paper (Geneva: World Economic Forum and International Centre for Trade and Sustainable Development, August 2015), 4.
198 Mark Wu, "Digital Trade-Related Provisions in Regional Trade Agreements," at 24.
199 *Ibid.* at 25.
200 *Ibid.*
201 Chapter 14, Comprehensive and Progressive Agreement for Trans-Pacific Partnership.
202 Chapter 19, United States-Mexico-Canada Agreement.
203 "Joint Statement on Electronic Commerce," WT/L/1056 (January 25, 2019).
204 Mark Wu, "Digital Trade-Related Provisions in Regional Trade Agreements," at 6.
205 *See* Digital Economy Partnership Agreement, at https://www.mfat.govt.nz/assets/FTAs-agreed-not-signed/DEPA/DEPA-Chile-New-Zealand-Singapore-21-Jan-2020-for-release.pdf.
206 Stephanie Honey, "Digging DEPA: the Digital Economy Partnership Agreement," *Trade Works* (June 16, 2020), at https://www.tradeworks.org.nz/digging-depa-the-digital-economy-partnership-agreement/.
207 Module 7, DEPA.
208 Module 11, DEPA.
209 Deborah Elms, "Unpacking the Digital Economy Partnership Agreement (DEPA)," Asian Trade Centre, Singapore (January 2020), at http.//asiantradecentre.org/talkingtrade/unpacking-the-digital-economy-partnership-agreement-(DEPA).
210 Giridharan Ramasubramanian, "Building on the modular design of DEPA," East Asia Forum (July 10, 2020), at https://www.eastasiaforum.org/2020/07/10/building-on-the-modular-design-if-depa/.
211 Stephanie Honey, "Digging DEPA."

Chapter 4

Some But Not (Yet) All: Plurilateral Agreements and the Future of the World Trade Organization*

Introduction

Since its 1947 inception as the General Agreement on Tariffs and Trade (GATT), the World Trade Organization (WTO) has generally practiced an "all-or-nothing" approach to multilateral negotiations in which the "consensus" of all WTO members was for trade liberalization. Although this approach worked throughout the second half of the 20th century, its shortcomings were laid bare in the past two decades by the failure of the Doha Development Agenda and the inability of WTO members to achieve further broad, multilateral trade liberalization. Today, amid heightened animosity toward additional trade liberalization, the prospects for the traditional "consensus"-based approach seem dimmer than ever.

WTO members should not abandon their longstanding aim of liberalizing trade on a multilateral basis. But they would be wise to consider addressing some of the most pressing issues facing the world trading system through *plurilateral* agreements, through which a subset of WTO members agree on new trade commitments and then either extend the benefits to all other members on a most-favored-nation (MFN) basis

---

*This essay was previously published by the Cato Institute as James Bacchus, "The Future of the WTO: Multilateral or Plurilateral?," Cato Policy Analysis no. 947 (May 25, 2023).

or offer non-signatories the opportunity to choose to join the agreements in the future. This approach is not unprecedented. Plurilateral agreements have been a feature of the trading system for decades, and members are pursuing several plurilateral initiatives within the organization now. Although opposition to plurilateralism exists among some WTO members, it is largely misguided, in part because it has the effect of shifting new trade issues and disciplines outside the legal framework of the WTO.

Certainly, plurilateralism should not supplant multilateralism; nor is plurilateralism an appropriate means for resolving every issue on which deep divisions among WTO members exist. Yet, at a time when the traditional approach appears to be ineffective, the plurilateral alternative can spur willing members to address some complex issues, and, in the process, help restore the WTO's centrality in world trade.

Stepping Back from the Abyss of Irrelevance

In June 2022, the World Trade Organization stepped back from the abyss of irrelevance.[1] For only the second time since the establishment of the international institution in 1995, its 164 member countries were able to conclude a multilateral trade agreement — an agreement that is accepted and is binding on all WTO members. Indeed, they concluded several multilateral agreements: a waiver on COVID-19 vaccines, a set of new disciplines on fisheries subsidies, an agreement on food security, and an extension of a moratorium on tariffs on electronic commerce. These agreements are all noteworthy, and they are reassuring evidence that all the members of the WTO can, in fact, come together to get some things done some of the time.

Yet, each of these multilateral agreements is less than it could and should be. And the list is long of the topics of potential multilateral agreements that are much needed but were not able to make it onto the WTO agenda for the June ministerial conference. Despite the recent successes, at a time when the WTO has been pushed more and more to the periphery in world trade by the forces of economic nationalism, and when a shift toward retreat is prevailing almost everywhere over the commitment to international cooperation, the prospects for the WTO accomplishing much more toward further trade liberalization through "all-or-nothing" agreements that require a "consensus" of all 164 members of the organization are not encouraging.

The WTO should not set aside its commitment to multilateralism, which is much needed in trade as in many areas of global concern. A new approach, however, is needed to pursue trade multilateralism. As an alternative to seeking a consensus of 164 countries for every agreement, it makes practical sense on many issues for WTO members to move forward instead within the WTO legal framework through plurilateral agreements on such topics as digital trade and investment facilitation among some but not all the WTO membership. These plurilateral agreements should be open to any WTO member that wishes to join them. The aim should be to expand these plurilateral agreements over time into fully multilateral agreements that include all WTO members, which is legally permissible under the WTO treaty and has been done successfully in the past. For the WTO today, plurilateralism is the best path to multilateralism.

The Consensus Approach

Since its original formation by 23 countries in 1947 as the General Agreement on Tariffs and Trade (the GATT), the multilateral trading system that now covers about 98 percent of all world trade has progressed incrementally in freeing more trade worldwide largely through a series of multilateral "rounds" of negotiations that have included all the members of the system. The eighth of those rounds — the Uruguay Round — concluded in 1994 and led to the transformation of the GATT into the WTO in 1995. The ninth round — the Doha Development Round — began in 2001 in the immediate aftermath of the September 11 terrorist attacks and, after 14 years of disappointment after disappointment, in effect ended with the failure of WTO members to conclude it at the WTO ministerial conference in Nairobi, Kenya, in 2015.

Generally, the approach taken by the members of the system toward concluding new multilateral trade agreements has been by "consensus" in a "single undertaking." Nothing has been agreed until everything has been agreed to by everyone. Thus, any one negotiating country can, conceivably, block any and all agreement. Even so, for decades, this approach, while it sometimes took years to work, nevertheless did work. In the first decades after the creation of the GATT in the wake of World War II, it was possible to conclude such "all-or-nothing" multilateral trade agreements among all the members of the trading system that gradually advanced the world toward more trade liberalization.

The mutual advantages of multilateral agreements liberalizing trade are considerable. The most basic rules of the multilateral trading system are rules against trade discrimination. One of those rules is requires "most-favored-nation" (MFN) treatment, meaning that any trade advantage given by one WTO member to another WTO member — such as a tariff cut on a particular product — must be given also immediately and unconditionally to all other WTO members.[2] Thus, if country A makes a trade "concession" to country B to eliminate its tariffs on imports of widgets from country B, then that same concession must also be granted immediately and unconditionally to the entirety of the rest of the global alphabet of WTO members.

This has the effect of lowering the barriers to trade in widgets — not just between the first two countries — but among all 164 countries that comprise the WTO-based multilateral trading system. This in turn has the effect of increasing the overall global volume in widget trade. And this in consequence increases the overall global economic gains from widget trade. The advantage of multilateral trade agreements is, thus, that, through the operation of the rule of "most-favored-nation" treatment, they multiply the gains from trade and extend those gains worldwide. The gains can then be shared domestically in each country according to that country's own distributional and other designs. Hence, the understandable bias in the WTO system for multilateral trade agreements.

Likewise, the traditional bias in the system for reaching multilateral agreements by consensus is understandable. If a consensus were not required to conclude a new multilateral trade agreement — if, for example, WTO members employed the alternative provided in the WTO Agreement of deciding by a majority vote — then the new trade obligations in that agreement would be imposed on WTO members that may have abstained or voted against them.[3] This is contrary to the basic principles of international law. Moreover, this is hardly the way to free trade, advance the cause of multilateral cooperation, and restore the WTO to its rightful place at the center of world trade. Clearly, countries should be bound only by those treaty obligations to which they have agreed. Anything other than that would lead to the rapid demise of the multilateral trading system.

During the first decades of the trading system, there were fewer negotiating countries. The United States and its European and other allies accounted for a large share of global GDP and thus were able to steer the negotiations toward their trade-liberalizing ends. There were also fewer divisive issues. For the most part, the early negotiating rounds dealt with tariff cuts. But then, in the latter decades of the last century, more countries became part of the system, developing countries acquired a larger voice in the system, and the trade issues confronted by the system gradually extended beyond the mathematics of tariff cuts into the sensitive complexities of behind-the-border non-tariff trade discrimination, thus facilitating deeper economic integration. The Tokyo Round, concluded in 1979, first began to grapple with some of these non-tariff trade issues. The Uruguay Round, concluded in 1994, delved more deeply into them, producing a series of multilateral agreements on such non-traditional trade issues as trade-related health and safety concerns and the trade-related aspects of intellectual property rights.

Yet, as the effects of trade globalization and other forms of international economic integration began to be felt, there was a growing political backlash against trade liberalization. This was especially so in developed countries that had made few provisions for cushioning their negative effects on traditional manufacturing workers who were confronting increased foreign competition because of lower tariffs and other lower trade barriers. The impetus for freeing trade subsided in these developed countries and in other parts of the world, and it became ever more difficult to reach new multilateral liberalizing trade agreements.

The political possibility of concluding another major multilateral trade round by consensus of all 164 WTO members began to dim with the global financial crisis that began in 2008 and continued through 2011. It diminished further with the global retreat from international cooperation in trade and the embrace of a resurgent and spreading trade protectionism led by then-president Donald Trump of the United States starting in 2017. Now, there is continued resistance to further trade liberalization in many countries amid the confluence of COVID-19 and the economic consequences of the Russian invasion of Ukraine.

To be sure, several new multilateral agreements have been concluded since the turn of the century, among them a public health waiver relating to HIV-AIDS drugs in 2001, a trade facilitation agreement in 2013, a prohibition on agricultural export subsidies in 2015, and the new agreements concluded at the ministerial conference in Geneva in June. These are all hard-won achievements. These agreements, however, have all been limited in scope. There is no current likelihood or impetus for undertaking broader multilateral negotiations that would confront the full range of trade and trade-related issues that increasingly confront policymakers. And the list of these largely unaddressed issues is lengthening with every passing day as the global economy continues to evolve into increasing complexity.

As it is, any one WTO member — for any reason — can, under the consensus approach, veto the conclusion of any multilateral trade agreement, even if all the other 163 members agree on it. This, too, is not the way to advance trade liberalization and achieve other WTO goals. Recalcitrant countries, we have seen, are not above threatening to torpedo years, even decades, of multilateral negotiations if they do not get their way. The sad tale of the slow death of the Doha Development Round is abundant evidence that, in the current state of geopolitics, the consensus approach that worked in the previous century will not work in the imminent and foreseeable future of this one.

What, then, is the alternative?

The Plurilateral Option

It is widely lamented that the WTO is dysfunctional because it can no longer conclude multilateral agreements on the multiplying proliferation of trade and trade-related issues confronting the global economy. But, despite what many politicians and other policymakers seem to think, WTO members are not required by the WTO treaty to agree on new trade obligations *only* through multilateral agreements that include all 164 WTO members. Plurilateral agreements that cover less than "substantially all the trade" between and among some but not all WTO members are clearly permitted by the WTO Agreement.[4] (Such agreements are to be distinguished from free trade agreements that do cover "substantially all the trade" between and among the parties to them, which are also permitted, as an exception to the basic MFN obligation.)[5] These plurilateral agreements add new obligations and rights for the WTO members that are parties to them, but they "do not create either obligations or rights for Members that have not accepted them."[6]

No permission slip is needed by WTO members to negotiate a plurilateral trade agreement on any matter falling within the scope of the WTO Agreement. That agreement "places no constraint on how plurilateral negotiations are initiated and organized. ... There is no legal constraint on sub-sets of WTO Members discussing any aspect of trade policy among themselves and formulating policies to improve it."[7] With respect to plurilateral agreements on trade in services, new obligations can be added by modifying the existing WTO schedules of services commitments.[8] With respect to plurilateral agreements on trade in goods, new agreements can be added to an annex in the WTO Agreement where other plurilateral agreements have previously been placed.[9] But new plurilateral agreements on trade in goods can be added to this annex only "exclusively by consensus," and therein lies the political rub.[10]

Why block a consensus to add a new plurilateral agreement? Some WTO members may not wish for the trading system to venture into a new policy area that may facilitate even deeper international economic integration. Or some members may be apprehensive that, even though they are not parties to a new plurilateral agreement, it may nevertheless, in its effect, add to their obligations or subtract from their rights as a member. And some members are so firmly committed to the principle of multilateralism in the trading system that they do not wish to allow any departure from it through something less than a fully multilateral agreement, whether they support the policy goals of the proposed agreement or not. Then, too, the blocking of a consensus may, from time to time, be mainly an exercise in obstructionism for purely political reasons. Members have successfully negotiated and implemented these deals on both an MFN and non-MFN basis (Table 1). Twenty-one parties comprised of 48 WTO members have concluded the plurilateral Government Procurement Agreement, which provides for the mutual opening of government purchasing markets and has opened government purchases valued at $1.7 trillion annually.[11] Eighty-two WTO members representing 97 percent of world trade in information technology products have entered into the plurilateral WTO Information Technology Agreement.[12] In 2015, an additional 201 products valued at more than $1.3 trillion were added to the coverage of this agreement.

Table 1 WTO plurilateral agreements.

Agreement Name	Purpose	Year Effective	Number of WTO members	Coverage	MFN/Non-MFN
Trade in Civil Aircraft	Eliminate duties on all non-military aircraft and other covered products, and discipline government procurement and financial support for the civil aircraft sector.	1980	41	All civil aircraft; all civil aircraft engines and their parts; all other parts and components of civil aircraft; and ground flight simulators and their components.	Non-MFN
Government Procurement	Liberalize certain government procurement markets to international competition.	1981	46	Government procurement of goods and services specified by each party, and at or above a value specified by each party.	Non-MFN
Pharmaceuticals	Eliminate tariffs and other duties and charges on certain pharmaceutical products and their inputs.	1995	34	All finished pharmaceutical products and more than 7,000 active pharmaceutical ingredients (APIs) and chemical components.	MFN
Information Technology (ITA)	Eliminate tariffs on certain information technology products.	1997	82	High-technology products such as computers, telecommunications equipment, semiconductors, semiconductor manufacturing and testing equipment, software, scientific equipment, and their parts and components.	MFN

Table 1 (*Continued*)

Agreement Name	Purpose	Year Effective	Number of WTO members	Coverage	MFN/ Non-MFN
Information Technology Expansion (ITA 2)	Update and expand on the first ITA by eliminating tariffs on an additional 201 products, for which trade is valued at $1.3 trillion per year.	2015	52	Additions include new-generation semiconductors and semiconductor testing and packaging equipment; optical lenses; GPS navigation equipment; and modern medical equipment, such as MRI products.	MFN
Services Domestic Regulation	Set out common rules on best domestic regulatory approaches to facilitate trade in services.	2021	70	No additional services trade liberalization. Parties commit to enhanced transparency, cooperation, and efficiency when adopting and enforcing domestic regulations affecting the provision of services by foreign entities.	MFN

Sources: "Agreement on Trade in Civil Aircraft," World Trade Organization; "Agreement on Government Procurement," World Trade Organization; "The WTO's Pharma Agreement," World Trade Organization; "Information Technology Agreement," World Trade Organization; and "Services Domestic Regulation," Geneva Trade Platform.

Notes:
- Only agreements that are currently in force are included. Sectoral agreements negotiated during the Uruguay Round, other than the Pharmaceutical Agreement, are excluded from this list.

- Member states of the European Union are counted on an individual basis.
- All members of ITA 2 are members of the original ITA.
- Commitments reached as part of the negotiations on Services Domestic Regulation do not exist as a standalone agreement, but are incorporated into the signatories' liberalization schedules under the General Agreement on Trade in Services (GATS).

Option #1: "Critical mass" most-favored nation (MFN) plurilaterals

One way to minimize the chances that a proposed plurilateral agreement will be denied a consensus is to stipulate up-front that the benefits of the agreement will be extended to all WTO members, whether they have become parties to the agreement and undertaken its new obligations or not. The agreement is applied on an MFN basis. Thus, WTO members that have not signed the plurilateral agreement will be allowed to be free riders. Generally, the countries negotiating the agreement will be willing to do this if, altogether, they represent a "critical mass" of the global trade in the product or products that are covered by the agreement. What is a "critical mass"? The WTO Agreement does not say, nor does economics offer any definitive answer; however, as a rule of thumb in trade negotiations, a "critical mass" is generally thought to be 90 percent.

An example of a plurilateral agreement that has been applied on an MFN basis is the Information Technology Agreement, which was originally agreed in 1996, includes 82 WTO members, and provides for duty-free treatment of information technology products. The ITA covers 96 percent of world trade in these products, thus minimizing any potential concern about free riders.[13] Other plurilateral agreements concluded on an MFN basis since the establishment of the WTO in 1995 are two protocols to the General Agreement on Trade in Services: an agreement on basic telecommunications services and on financial services.[14] Inherited from the GATT and updated since the creation of the WTO is an agreement on trade in pharmaceutical products.[15]

Option #2: Non-critical-mass, Non-MFN plurilaterals

Where there is no "critical mass," and where the concessions in a plurilateral agreement would provide significant market access for free riders who are not parties to it if it were applied on an MFN basis, parties to the agreement may wish to deny its benefits to those WTO members that are unwilling to sign it and thereby accept its obligations. Economists, including many Cato Institute scholars, rightly contend that it makes perfect sense for any country to eliminate its trade barriers unilaterally, irrespective of whether its trading partners eliminate their own trade barriers. As a political matter, however, the lowering of a trade barrier is described in the WTO as a "concession," reflecting the reality that mercantilist "reciprocity" continues to drive most national trade policy. Thus, WTO members negotiating a plurilateral agreement will often seek a consensus of all WTO members to incorporate it into the WTO agreement on a "non-MFN" basis. Only those WTO members that have signed the agreement will be entitled to its benefits.

The Government Procurement Agreement is such a "non-MFN" agreement.[16] Agreed in 1979, it was incorporated into the WTO Agreement in 1994 and revised and updated in 2012.[17] The 48 WTO members that are parties to the GPA have agreed to open their markets for government purchases of goods and services to the other parties to the agreement. Other WTO members, though, are reluctant to do so. Government purchases often represent a sizeable share of the national economy and, in many countries, domestic political pressures make opening these purchases to foreign competition difficult. Other WTO members are free to join the GPA, but if they do so, they must refrain from trade discrimination against other parties to the agreement. Because the GPA is non-MFN, the parties to it continue to discriminate in their government purchases against the goods and services of WTO members that are not GPA parties.

Obstacles to Negotiating Plurilateral Agreements Inside the WTO

The expectation of some of the founders of the WTO in the 1990s was that the WTO would become a framework for numerous plurilateral agreements — MFN and non-MFN alike — that would gradually evolve into fully multilateral agreements. At first, this seemed to be happening with the conclusion of the Information Technology Agreement and the two protocols to the General Agreement on Trade in Services dealing with basic telecommunications services and financial services. The era of comprehensive "all or nothing" single undertakings in which nothing was agreed until everything was agreed by everyone on a whole array of trade concessions was thought to be over.

Then, when launching the Doha Development Round after the 9/11 terrorist attacks in 2001, WTO members, without evident reflection on the pros and cons of doing so, chose once more to embrace the traditional consensus approach. This choice ultimately doomed the round when, despite years of trying, developed and developing countries could not come together on a balance of mutual concessions on which all WTO members could agree. During the same period, efforts to conclude plurilateral agreements on environmental goods and services trade likewise failed.

Today, this impasse persists on many of the issues relating to the elimination of the remaining — and, recently, mounting — barriers to manufacturing and agricultural trade. Some of these longstanding issues can only be resolved multilaterally. For example, why would a few countries agree in a plurilateral agreement to eliminate their agricultural subsidies if other countries outside that agreement do not? There are, however, numerous old and new trade issues that can be addressed plurilaterally. Quite a few of them are more likely to be addressed successfully — at least in the near term — if they are addressed on a non-MFN basis. Cumulative success in addressing these issues plurilaterally could contribute to building the political momentum needed to set aside the lingering anguish in the trading system over the fate of the Doha round and return to the negotiating table on some of the long-intractable manufacturing and agricultural issues that were central to it.

Yet, today, it is doubtful that any new non-MFN plurilateral agreement such as the Government Procurement Agreement could be approved within the WTO by the required consensus of WTO members. The preference for the "first-best" choice of multilateral solutions is deep-seated in the WTO, particularly among developing countries that are apprehensive of what they perceive as the possibility of having new trade obligations imposed upon them indirectly through their acquiescence to the inclusion of more non-MFN plurilateral agreements in the WTO Agreement. If, for example, a subset of WTO members comprised of some of the largest developed countries in the world agreed on a technical standard relating to digital trade or a professional standard relating to trade in services, then how, as a practical matter, could other countries keep from embracing it? Among the developing countries, India and South Africa have been notably outspoken in opposing plurilateral agreements, portraying them as potential threats to the principles of non-discrimination and multilateralism that form the foundation of the WTO-based trading system.[18]

Opposition to Plurilateral Agreements Within the Framework of the WTO Is Misguided

Yet, on this matter, these developing countries have been outsmarting themselves. Their adamant opposition to plurilateral trade agreements has not prevented the conclusion of such agreements. Rather, it has pushed the negotiation and conclusion of plurilateral trade agreements outside the legal framework of the WTO. Frustrated by their inability to address the new trade issues of the 21st century inside the WTO, many WTO members have concluded that they have had no choice but to go outside the WTO to deal with them. Hundreds of free trade agreements and other preferential trade arrangements have been reached outside the WTO since the turn of the century. This has been a major factor in the shift of the WTO away from what was intended to be its central place in world trade. And, ironically, the members of the WTO that oppose plurilateral agreements are being put precisely in the situation they have feared: they are being surrounded by new rules for trade that they did not play a part in writing but need to embrace if they are going to continue to trade successfully in the new world economy.

Of course, the economic downside of the piling up of these bilateral and plurilateral agreements outside the WTO is also exactly what these same WTO members have feared: trade discrimination. In the absence of the application of the MFN principle, an agreement to give favored treatment to one trade partner is also an agreement not to give that same favored trade treatment to another trade partner. It is discrimination. If a non-MFN plurilateral agreement has been approved by consensus of the members of the WTO to be annexed into the WTO Agreement, then other WTO members are able to eliminate any discrimination against them simply by agreeing to join the agreement, which will afford them its rights in exchange for their agreement to comply with its obligations. But, if that non-MFN plurilateral agreement is concluded outside the legal framework of the WTO, then WTO members — as with, say, the Comprehensive and Progressive Trans-Pacific Trade Partnership — will have to apply for membership to eliminate the discrimination and attain the agreement's trade benefits. In the first case, *inside* the WTO, acceptance into the club upon expressing a willingness to abide by its terms is automatic. In the second case, *outside* the WTO, it is not. The current opposition of India and South Africa to concluding plurilateral agreements inside the WTO is simply leading to the conclusion of agreements outside the WTO of which India, South Africa, and other developing countries are not a part and in which they have no say.

There is abundant precedent for "multilateralizing" a WTO plurilateral agreement. In the Tokyo Round, which concluded in 1979, the contracting parties to the GATT concluded nine plurilateral GATT "codes" that applied only to those GATT signatories that agreed to be bound by them. Five of the GATT codes were later made fully multilateral by their incorporation in the WTO Agreement: the Agreement on Implementation of Article VI of the General Agreement on Tariffs and Trade 1994 (the anti-dumping agreement), the Agreement on Implementation of Article VII of the General Agreement on Tariffs and Trade 1994 (the customs valuation agreement), the Agreement on Subsidies and Countervailing Measures, the Agreement on Technical Barriers to Trade, and the Agreement on Import Licensing Procedures. Without the fifteen years of experience with the operation of these GATT codes, it is unlikely that a consensus on making them multilateral as part of the package of agreements reached in the Uruguay Round in 1994 could have been achieved. Learning by doing applies in trade as in much else, and this past experience provides evidence that the negotiation of plurilateral agreements can be a pathway toward multilateralism within the WTO trading system.

What, then, are the current opportunities for pursuing the plurilateral path toward multilateralism in the WTO?

The Plurilateral Opportunities

Encouragingly, a plurilateral negotiation was concluded successfully in 2021 on services domestic regulation. This is a notable achievement; apart from the early agreements on protocols on basic telecommunications services and financial services, little had been accomplished to liberalize services trade in the more than quarter of a century since the adoption of the General Agreement on Trade in Services in the Uruguay Round. Negotiations on services got nowhere during the long years leading to the failure of the Doha Development Round. In the aftermath of the collapse of that round, in 2017, 59 WTO members launched a Joint Statement Initiative aimed at "increasing transparency, predictability and efficiency of authorization procedures for service providers hoping to do business in foreign markets."[19] They sought "new disciplines to help services trade flow more easily and to reduce unintended trade restrictions resulting from licensing requirements and procedures, qualification requirements and procedures, and technical standards and other measures."[20]

In December of 2021, 67 WTO members adopted a declaration announcing the successful conclusion of their negotiations.[21] Since then, three more members have joined this group.[22] In furtherance of this declaration, new disciplines on trade in services are in the process of being incorporated as additional commitments in the GATS schedules of specific commitments of the 70 WTO members that have adopted this declaration. These new disciplines are contained in a Reference Paper on Services Domestic Regulation.[23] They "focus mainly on the transparency, predictability and effectiveness of procedures that businesses have to comply with to obtain authorization to supply their services. They have been designed to apply to all sectors where participants have undertaken commitments in their schedules for trade in services."[24]

India and South Africa have questioned the legality of this approach to adding new commitments to the GATS.[25] Others have defended this approach.[26] Because the benefits of this plurilateral declaration will be extended to all WTO members on an MFN basis — including India and South Africa — it seems doubtful that those two dissenting countries will challenge the structuring of these additional services concessions in WTO dispute settlement. (It is, in any event, exceedingly difficult to apply, say, a licensing standard, to the services suppliers from one country and a different licensing standard to those from other countries.) The parties to the declaration on domestic regulation of services are proceeding with talks on potential additional disciplines, including on certification procedures.[27] After decades of stalemate, this breakthrough shows the way forward for future progress on further liberalization in trade in services.

As with domestic regulation of services, on some other issues WTO members are already shifting toward the plurilateral path. Despite the recent modest successes at the ministerial conference in Geneva in June, there is still scant political support for trying again in a multilateral negotiation to address the longstanding divides over manufacturing, agriculture, and more that were the focus of the agenda of the Doha Development

Round. But, encouragingly, there is increasing interest by WTO members in addressing other and newer trade issues within the legal framework of the WTO in a plurilateral process. This interest is being displayed on a number of fronts both in formal negotiations and in discussions among various subsets of the WTO membership on specific trade topics that could lead to formal negotiations (Table 2). Procedurally, as with domestic services, most of these efforts have emerged from Joint Statement Initiatives — "JSIs" — announced by these assorted subsets of WTO members.[28] These current endeavors are opportunities for the WTO to build on the momentum emerging from the ministerial conference and make real progress toward restoring the role of the WTO at the center of world trade.

Table 2 Several plurilateral agreements and initiatives remain in progress; others have stalled.

Agreement Name	Type	Purpose	Year Initiated	Number of WTO Members	MFN/ Non-MFN	Current Status
Trade in Services (TiSA)	Agreement	Liberalize trade across different services sectors, in essence updating the General Agreement on Trade in Services.	2013	50	Non-MFN	Negotiations suspended indefinitely
Environmental Goods	Agreement	Reduce tariffs and liberalize trade in "green" goods.	2014	46	MFN	Negotiations suspended indefinitely
Investment Facilitation	Agreement	Facilitate foreign direct investment by improving the transparency of investment measures, streamlining and speeding up administrative procedures, and enhancing international cooperation.	2017	112	MFN (reportedly)	Text-based negotiations ongoing

Table 2 (*Continued*)

Agreement Name	Type	Purpose	Year Initiated	Number of WTO Members	MFN/Non-MFN	Current Status
Trade and Gender	Informal Working Group	Bolster efforts towards improving women's participation in international trade.	2017	127	N/A	Active
Micro, Small, and Medium-Sized Enterprises (MSMEs)	Informal Working Group	Identify ways the WTO could support the integration of MSMEs in international trade.	2017	91	N/A	Active
Electronic Commerce	Agreement	Agree common rules in areas including enabling electronic commerce, promoting openness and trust in e-commerce, cross-cutting issues, telecommunications and market access for e-commerce firms.	2017	86	TBD	Negotiations ongoing
Trade and Environmental Sustainability Structured Discussions (TESSD)	Discussions	Promote discussions on trade-related practices and measures that can promote environmental sustainability.	2020	57	N/A	Active
Plastics Pollution	Discussions	Identify how the WTO could contribute to efforts to reduce plastics pollution and promote more environmentally sustainable trade in plastics.	2020	62	N/A	Active

(*Continued*)

Table 2 (Continued)

Agreement Name	Type	Purpose	Year Initiated	Number of WTO Members	MFN/Non-MFN	Current Status
Fossil Fuel Subsidies Reform	Discussions	Increase dialogue and information-sharing at the WTO with the aim to limit and, eventually, phase out fossil fuel subsidies.	2021	42	N/A	Active

Sources: "Trade in Services Agreement," Office of the United States Trade Representative; "Environmental Goods Agreement (EGA)," World Trade Organization; "WTO Plurilaterals," Geneva Trade Platform.

Notes:
- Informal Working Groups are formed with the aim of presenting non-binding recommendations for action by WTO members. Discussions, meanwhile, are more informal arrangements with the aim of exploring potential avenues for action by the WTO and its members on the issues at hand.
- The Trade in Services Agreement (TiSA) was negotiated outside the WTO, but reportedly with the ultimate goal of incorporating it into the WTO framework.
- Member-states of the European Union are counted on an individual basis.
- GATS = General Agreement on Trade in Services.

Pharma Agreement

Surprisingly missing from the list of topics that are most mentioned as opportunities for plurilateral progress is the Agreement on Trade in Pharmaceutical Products, which was the only plurilateral agreement reached at the conclusion of the Uruguay Round in 1994.[29] The Pharma Agreement, as it is known, eliminates tariffs and other duties and charges on a sizeable number of pharmaceutical products and the substances used to produce them. Thirty-five WTO members are currently parties to this agreement. The scope of the product coverage of the agreement has been extended four times, most recently in 2010. Even so, it has not kept up with the growth and the diversity of the global trade in pharmaceuticals.

The parties to the agreement represent about two-thirds of all pharmaceutical trade, but, since the conclusion of the Uruguay Round, other WTO members have entered the pharmaceuticals market without also signing the Pharma Agreement. As a percentage of the burgeoning trade in pharmaceuticals, the coverage of the Pharma Agreement has shrunk. In 1994, the agreement accounted for about 90 percent of world trade in the covered products. At present, it accounts for only about 66 percent of that trade. Furthermore, the Pharma Agreement deals only with the tariffs on international trade in medicines and in what goes into making them. It does not address the tariffs on the growing trade in other medical goods.

Thus, tariff-free trade in medical goods other than medicines remains mostly an aspiration for the WTO. To their credit, four WTO members — Macao, China; Hong Kong, China; Singapore; and Iceland — have eliminated all duties on all medical products.[30] The other 160 WTO members have not. While most of the world continues to struggle to secure essential medicines and other medical goods at affordable prices to battle the ongoing COVID-19 pandemic (and perhaps prepare for future pandemics), most WTO members continue to apply tariffs that limit international trade in those products. Despite the labors of the like-minded Ottawa Group of WTO members, proposals to liberalize medical trade have not gotten far in the WTO, not least because of the puzzling opposition of the United States under the Biden administration.

To the list of initiatives that many of them are already undertaking, WTO members should add the need to eliminate all tariffs on medicines and other medical goods, which would do much to contribute to the health of people throughout the world. Practically speaking, this could be done in part by expanding both the membership and the scope of the Pharma Agreement as part of a broader effort to include a comprehensive agreement within the WTO on trade and health.[31] All WTO members should become parties to the Pharma Agreement, making it fully multilateral. And the scope of coverage of the agreement should be expanded to cover trade in all medicines and also trade in all other medical goods. This pandemic is not over. And this pandemic will not be the last one.

Environmental Goods Agreement

Also conspicuously missing from the agenda at the June, 2022, ministerial conference was the proposed Environmental Goods Agreement. For more than 20 years, WTO members have been pursuing freer trade in environmental goods. The aim is twofold: to increase trade and to speed the spread of new environmental technologies worldwide. These innovative goods can be helpful tools for confronting the many perils to the planet. They are especially needed in developing countries, which do not always have access to the advanced technologies of the developed countries. Global distribution of these environmental goods can best be accomplished through international trade. The lower the prices of these goods, the more will be sold, and the greater the volume will be in the trade in them. The border taxes we call tariffs add to the prices of goods and thus limit sales. The WTO members seeking to remove these impediments to trade are right in trying to do so.[32]

When the multilateral negotiations in the Doha Development Round collapsed, 46 members representing nearly 90 percent of all world trade in environmental goods began negotiations on what would be an MFN plurilateral agreement. Yet this group of negotiating countries has been unable so far to agree on what constitutes an "environmental good." All are agreed on including wind turbines, solar panels, and the like. But beyond this, an absence of agreement on the scope of what more should be included within the meaning of "environmental goods" has impeded success from the outset. In their long effort to reach agreement, the trade negotiators have not tried to define environmental goods; they have only tried to list them. There was hope that a list of goods would be agreed to in time for the June ministerial conference, but that did not happen, and the EGA did not make it to the agenda of the conference. Thus, the hopes were dashed — once again — for concluding this long-sought plurilateral agreement. Without question, these negotiations must move ahead, at last, to a mutually agreed conclusion.

Digital Trade

Trade is "increasingly defined by flows of data and information."[33] About 12 percent of all goods traded internationally are purchased online, and about half of global trade in services is digital. The McKinsey Global Institute reports that, since 1990, the global economy is 10 percent larger than it would have been without those increased data and information flows — an added global economic output equivalent to $7.8 trillion. Moreover, "Data flows account for $2.8 trillion of this effect, *exerting a larger impact on growth than traditional goods flows.*"[34] Yet, there are no specific WTO rules on digital trade.

Although digital trade is growing exponentially internationally, regulatory restrictions on international digital trade are increasing at the same pace, if not more rapidly. WTO rules are much needed to limit these restrictions on digital trade by drawing agreed lines that clarify which such restrictions are appropriate and which are not. If the members of the WTO can agree on rules for digital trade, then the abundant benefits of digital trade will spread more rapidly and more widely throughout the world. If they cannot agree on rules for digital trade, then the WTO will surely be relegated to the periphery of world trade; it will become increasingly irrelevant to the continuing advance of trade through digital connections of all kinds.

Eighty-six members of the WTO are currently negotiating on possible rules for digital trade pursuant to the announcement of a joint initiative on electronic commerce at the WTO ministerial conference in Buenos Aires in 2017. They are aiming for a "high standard outcome" that will put in place more than merely the bare rudiments of a legal framework for governing digital trade.[35] It is unclear at this time whether they intend for any agreement they reach to be MFN or non-MFN. A bracketed text still leaves much to be decided. Meanwhile, bilateral and small plurilateral digital trade agreements outside the legal framework of the WTO are proliferating. These include the Digital Economy Partnership Agreement among Chile, New Zealand, and Singapore,[36] which has a modular approach that is a model for how the 86 WTO members might best proceed in structuring a WTO agreement.[37] In the 21st century, a world trading system without rules on digital trade is not truly a world trading system.

Investment Facilitation

At the ministerial conference in Bueno Aires in 2017, a group that now consists of 111 WTO members, comprising both developed and developing countries, endorsed a joint statement agreeing to start "structured discussions with the aim of developing a multilateral framework on investment facilitation."[38] Examples of what an agreement on investment facilitation would contain include strengthened "electronic governance" such as a "single electronic window" that would publish investment documents and help streamline applications and admissions procedures for incoming investments, a national focal point for mediating and facilitating investor concerns with public authorities, voluntary standards of corporate social responsibility, and guarantees of transparency.[39]

Ideally, this new WTO framework on investment facilitation would accompany, and perhaps be an expansion of, the multilateral Trade Facilitation Agreement, which was concluded in Bali in 2013 and is being phased into full implementation.[40] It, too, could be phased in over time, and it could contain differing obligations for WTO members at different stages of development. Moreover, it could be accompanied by technical assistance. Should WTO members not be able to proceed multilaterally on this topic, then it should be the subject of a WTO plurilateral agreement that could evolve into a fully multilateral pact.

The proposed investment facilitation agreement does not cover the difficult issues of market access, investment protection, and investor–state dispute settlement that are most significant to stimulating the flow of foreign direct investment, especially to developing countries. Rather, it focuses on the "red tape" issues that frustrate foreign direct investment (FDI), mainly at the border. It could, though, help build the basis for addressing the tougher FDI issues later, once the investment facilitation agreement is in place. There are numerous issues relating to FDI that fall outside the scope of the WTO Agreement; but quite a few investment issues are "trade-related," as evidenced by the core commitment of MFN treatment included in the WTO Agreement on Trade-related Investment Measures.[41] Those WTO members wishing to add to the limited obligations in the TRIMS Agreement and can do so plurilaterally with the goal of extending the new obligations to more members, and eventually all members, over time.

Micro, Small, and Medium-Sized Enterprises (MSMEs)

Yet another focus of plurilateral initiative is micro, small, and medium-sized enterprises. According to the WTO, "Today, 95% of companies across the globe are MSMEs, accounting for 60% of the world's total employment." Large multinational corporations have the wherewithal and the in-house technical know-how to navigate international trade, but many smaller businesses do not. In Buenos Aires in 2017, 88 WTO members announced an initiative to explore ways to provide better support for the participation of MSMEs in international trade.[42] This group has now grown to include 94 WTO members, representing about 80 percent of global exports and 65 percent of global GDP.[43]

In 2020, the WTO members engaged in the "informal working group" of this JSI endorsed a package of recommendations for facilitating this participation.[44] Their approach is "a developmental one" that emphasizes that "helping MSMEs to trade supports economic development by bringing new opportunities and connections to businesses in developing economies."[45] Notably absent from this working group is the United States, although there are many thousands of American MSMEs that could benefit from the recommendations urged by this working group. At this point, the main objectives of the working group on MSMEs are trade facilitation, transparency and due process in domestic regulation, access to trade data, and access to trade finance. It is unclear whether this initiative will lead to a plurilateral agreement.

Gender Equity and Women in Trade

One more JSI launched in Buenos Aires in 2017 is an attempt to improve the participation and elevate the role of women in trade.[46] At the outset, 115 WTO members were engaged in this initiative; today, that number has increased to 127. Like the initiative on MSMEs, the initiative on women in trade is not now aimed at changes in WTO rules. Instead, it is centered on sharing experiences, best practices, and best methods and procedures for bringing women more fully into trade so that they can share more fully in the benefits of trade and the multilateral trading system. It seeks "inclusive trade policies" that "can contribute to advancing gender equality and women's economic empowerment, which has a positive effect on economic growth and helps to reduce poverty."[47]

A joint report by the WTO and the World Bank in 2020 shows how men and women are currently affected by trade differently.[48] The report "confirms that trade is largely beneficial to women, although many women continue to face discrimination and challenges." Furthermore, it "shows that women have unique opportunities to benefit from new trends in global trade, specifically the rise in services, global value chains, and the digital economy. However, for women to fully reap these trade gains, different public policies aimed at reducing discrimination toward women in trade policy, supporting women's capacity to engage in international trade and mitigating the risks from trade faced by women might be necessary."[49]

These new public policies must be a part of an overall endeavor to make trade more inclusive by sharing its benefits more widely. This is primarily a domestic challenge, but more can be done through the multilateral trading system to help facilitate such policies and ensure their success. Toward this end, in November 2021 the WTO members working on this matter issued a declaration affirming their commitment to a two-year plan for their continued work on this issue, looking ahead to the presentation of something more specific at the 13th WTO ministerial conference, for which the date and venue have not yet been set. They stressed in this declaration that "women constitute an economic force globally, that increasing their participation in the labour market to the same level as men's and ensuring full recognition of women's economic rights will raise Members' GDP; and that the WTO can provide a venue to engage on trade and gender to positively impact women's economic empowerment and to achieve sustainable economic growth."[50]

Trade and Environmental Sustainability

The Joint Statement Initiative that presents the greatest potential for significant change in the WTO trading system is the "structured discussions" on "trade and environmental sustainability" — or, in the inevitable acronym, "TESSD." Confronting the connections between trade and the environment was long on the back burner for the WTO, but pressures to do so have been increasing in recent years. In November 2020, 50 WTO members announced their intention to intensify work on issues at the nexus between trade and environmental sustainability. This has been gradually emerging as a major issue in world trade and will, unavoidably, move toward the center of the work of the WTO in the years to come.[51] At present, 74 WTO members are engaged in these structured discussions, accounting for 84 percent of all world trade.[52] The statements relating to these discussions do not expressly say so, but the work of this JSI could become a prelude to formal negotiations.

These discussions are centered on four issues relating to the links between trade and environmental sustainability: the relationship between trade and climate change, trade in environmental goods and services, a circular economy that recycles rather than wastes, and sustainable supply chains. The discussants have noted the plethora of "issues where trade, environmental and climate policies intersect, including on circular economy; natural disasters; climate change mitigation and adaptation; fossil fuel subsidies reform; plastic pollution; combatting illegal, unreported and unregulated fishing and ensuring legal and sustainable trade in wildlife; the conservation and sustainable use of biodiversity; sustainable oceans; facilitating access to green technology; sustainable tourism; sustainable agriculture as well as trade in environmental goods and services."[53] This is a lengthy list indeed, and it is a list that will surely grow longer over time. For now, two of these issues are the subjects of parallel initiatives by some of these same WTO members.

Plastics Pollution and Environmentally Sustainable Plastics Trade

In November 2020, in the same month when the structured discussions on trade and environmental sustainability were announced, a small group of seven WTO members announced the beginning of an Informal Dialogue on Plastics Pollution and Environmentally Sustainable Plastics Pollution.[54] At present, 72 WTO members are participating in this informal dialogue, representing more than 75 percent of global plastics waste.[55] The aim of this dialogue is to identify "how the WTO could contribute to efforts to reduce plastics pollution and promote the transition to more environmentally sustainable trade in plastics." Subjects of this dialogue include "improving transparency, monitoring trade trends, promoting best practices, strengthening policy coherence, identifying the scope for collective approaches, assessing capacity and technical assistance needs, and cooperating with other international processes and efforts."[56] These other international undertakings with which this subset of the WTO membership are cooperating include those of the United Nations, which approved in March of 2022 a plan to negotiate and conclude the first-ever global plastics pollution treaty over the next two years.[57] Those engaged in the WTO dialogue on plastics pollution have emphasized their desire to complement and not overlap this UN endeavor.

Fossil Fuel Subsidies Reform

Perhaps most controversially in the wider world, pursuant to a statement they issued in June in Geneva at the 12th ministerial conference, 46 WTO members have embarked upon a "high-level work plan" that will set up a "forum for dedicated discussions" on the "trade relevance" of fossil fuel subsidies in the multilateral trading system.[58] Notably, apart from Norway, the major producers of fossil fuels are not among these 46 members. In parallel with the work on subsidies by the TESSD, the 46 WTO members participating in these talks on fossil fuel subsidies reform are seeking "the rationalization and phase out of inefficient fossil fuel subsidies that encourage wasteful consumption along a clear timeline." They aim to "elaborate clear options" for attaining this goal by the time of the 13th WTO ministerial conference. As with the WTO discussions on plastics pollution, these talks in the WTO on fossil fuel subsidies are part of wider discussions at the international level involving a number of international institutions.[59]

The global stakes involved in the reform of fossil fuel subsidies were made clear in a presentation in the TESSD in March of 2022 by the International Institute for Sustainable Development. At a time when the members of the United Nations have committed in the Paris climate agreement to move away from the use of fossil fuels to reduce carbon dioxide and other greenhouse gas emissions, the calculation of annual global fossil fuel subsidies ranges from $345 billion (Organisation for Economic Co-operation and Development) to $440 billion (International Energy Agency) to $5.9 trillion (International Monetary Fund). These numbers vary so widely because of the different forms of direct and indirect subsidies that are included in the calculations. These subsidies can distort trade by reducing the market share of a competitor, displacing the imports from a competitor, and reducing the competitiveness of alternative fuels that are more climate friendly.[60] Distorting the market by subsidizing the production and consumption of fossil fuels at a time when the world has agreed to reduce its dependency on fossil fuels for energy is, as a matter of public policy, perverse. Whether the WTO can play a role in reforming these fossil fuel subsidies depends on the outcome of this informal dialogue.

Food, Energy, and Industrial Inputs

Additional opportunities abound for concluding new plurilateral agreements — both sectoral and topical — within the legal framework of the WTO. During a time of insecure supply chains and skyrocketing food and energy prices, particular opportunities are presented for negotiating plurilateral agreements related to food, energy, and industrial inputs. A plurilateral agreement could provide new disciplines for the dangerous imposition of food export restrictions. A plurilateral agreement could discipline energy export restrictions while also stimulating more sustainable energy practices and trade. A plurilateral agreement could remove tariffs and help harmonize standards on trade in many of the basic inputs that go into the making of industrial products. To date, none of these opportunities has been pursued seriously within the WTO. Now is the perfect time to pursue them.

Conclusion

These and perhaps other plurilateral initiatives yet to come can proceed toward the conclusion of plurilateral agreements within the WTO while the members of the WTO struggle simultaneously to turn the WTO back toward effective multilateralism. To some, this may seem a contradictory thought. However, in the current trade climate, the best way to return to multilateralism is to embrace plurilateral approaches that can produce plurilateral agreements that can be extended over time to become fully multilateral, applying to all 164 WTO members. Just as the modest multilateral successes at the June ministerial conference in Geneva have given the WTO trading system a jolt of optimism, so, too, can successes that result from these plurilateral initiatives now being pursued by various subsets of the WTO membership. In the WTO, success can build upon success, whether of a plurilateral or multilateral kind. New rules that apply to some can ultimately apply to all once all are willing to accept them. As in the past, the watchful experience of new rules by those who have not yet accepted them can help lead to their eventual acceptance. In the meantime, the WTO will no longer be as limited as it is now in what it can achieve toward further trade liberalization. The WTO can become what it was meant to be by those who founded it: an ongoing and overarching architecture for addressing new trade and trade-related issues as they arise for all WTO members that are willing to address them.

Endnotes

[1] James Bacchus, "WTO Steps Back from the Abyss of Irrelevance...but Crucial Issues Remain Unsolved," Cato at *Liberty* (blog), Cato Institute, June 17, 2022.

[2] General Agreement on Tariffs and Trade (hereafter GATT) art. I, October 30, 1947, 61 Stat. A-11, 55 U.N.T.S. 194.

[3] Marrakesh Agreement Establishing the World Trade Organization art. IX.1, April 15, 1994, 1867 U.N.T.S. 154 [hereinafter Marrakesh Agreement].

[4] Marrakesh Agreement art. II.3.

[5] Whatever that may mean. There is no WTO jurisprudence clarifying the meaning of the term "substantially all the trade." *See* GATT art. XXIV:8(b).

[6] Marrakesh Agreement art. II.3.

[7] Bernard Hoekman, L. Alan Winters, and Yohannes Ayele, "Delivering Plurilateral Trade Agreements within the World Trade Organization," United Kingdom Department of Trade, December 2021, p. 7.

[8] General Agreement on Trade in Services part III, April 15, 1994, Marrakesh Agreement Establishing the World Trade Organization, Annex 1B, 1869 U.N.T.S. 401.

[9] Marrakesh Agreement, Annex 4.

[10] Marrakesh Agreement art. X.9.

[11] Agreement on Government Procurement, amended March 30, 2012, Marrakesh Agreement Establishing the World Trade Organization, Annex 4(b), 1869 U.N.T.S. 401.

[12] World Trade Organization, Ministerial Declaration of December 13, 1996, WTO Doc. WT/MIN(96)/16, 36 ILM 383 (1997); and World Trade Organization, Ministerial Declaration of December 16, 2015, WTO Doc. WT/MIN(15)/25, 15-6657 WTO (December 16, 2015).

[13] Committee of Participants on the Expansion of Trade in Information Technology Products, *Status of Implementation, Note by the Secretariat*, WTO Doc. G/IT/1/Rev. 58 (March 25, 2022).

[14] World Trade Organization, Fourth Protocol to the General Agreement on Trade in Services, April 30, 1996, WTO Doc. S/L/20, 36 ILM 366 (1997); and World Trade Organization, Fifth Protocol to the General Agreement on Trade in Services, December 3, 1997, WTO Doc. S/L/45, 97-5441 WTO (1997).

[15] Committee on Market Access, Trade in Pharmaceutical Products: Communication from the European Union, WTO Doc. G/MA/W/102 (August 2, 2010).

[16] *Agreement on Government Procurement 2012 and Related WTO Legal Texts* (Geneva: World Trade Organization).

[17] Another plurilateral agreement included in Annex 4 to the WTO Agreement was the Agreement on Civil Aircraft. This agreement is still in force but has been supplanted by the Government Procurement Agreement and the WTO Agreement on Subsidies and Countervailing Measures.

[18] Iana Dreyer, "WTO 'Plurilateral' Agreements Brace for Moment of Truth," *Borderlex*, October 19, 2021.

[19] "Joint Initiative on Services Domestic Regulation," World Trade Organization; and World Trade Organization, Joint Ministerial Statement on Services Domestic Regulation, WTO Doc. WT/MIN(17)/61, 17-6900 WTO (December 13, 2017).

[20] Peter Ungphakorn, "Explainer: The 18 WTO Plurilaterals and 'Joint Statement Initiatives'," *Trade β Blog* (blog), January 3, 2022.

[21] World Trade Organization, Declaration on the Conclusion of Negotiations on Services Domestic Regulation, WTO Doc. WT/L/1129, 21-9081 WTO (December 2, 2021).

[22] "Georgia, Timor-Leste and United Arab Emirates Join Initiative on Services Domestic Regulation," World Trade Organization, June 13, 2022.

[23] World Trade Organization, Declaration on the Conclusion of Negotiations on Services Domestic Regulation Annex 1, WTO Doc. WT/L/1129, 21-9081 WTO (December 2, 2021).

[24] "Joint Initiative on Services Domestic Regulation," World Trade Organization.

[25] Iana Dreyer, "WTO 'Plurilateral' Agreements Brace for Moment of Truth," *Borderlex*, October 19, 2021. *See* General Council, The Legal Status of 'Joint Statement Initiatives and Their Negotiated Outcomes, WTO Doc. WT/GC/W/819 (February 19, 2021).

[26] *See* the views of two leading authorities on WTO law and negotiations: Gary Clyde Hufbauer, "Focused Trade Agreements Can Sustain the WTO in Time of Economic Nationalism," Peterson Institute for International Affairs, April 12, 2021; and Andrew Stoler, "'Joint Statement Initiatives' and Progress in the WTO System," Institute for International Trade, University of Adelaide, May 21, 2021.

[27] Gary Clyde Hufbauer, "Focused Trade Agreements Can Sustain the WTO in Time of Economic Nationalism," Peterson Institute for International Affairs, April 12, 2021; and Andrew Stoler, "'Joint Statement Initiatives' and Progress in the WTO System," Institute for International Trade, University of Adelaide, May 21, 2021. *See also* Council for Trade in Services, Procedures for the Certification of Rectifications or Improvements to Schedules of Specific Commitments, WTO Doc. S/L/84 (April 18, 2000).

[28] "Joint Initiatives," World Trade Organization.

[29] "The WTO's Pharma Agreement," World Trade Organization.

[30] "Trade in Medical Goods in the Context of Tackling COVID-19: Information Note," World Trade Organization, April 3, 2020, p. 6.

[31] James Bacchus, "Trade Is Good for Your Health: Freeing Trade in Medicines and Other Medical Goods during and beyond the COVID-19 Emergency," Cato Institute, Policy Analysis no. 918, June 30, 2021.

[32] James Bacchus and Inu Manak, "Free Trade in Environmental Goods Will Increase Access to Green Tech," Cato Institute Free Trade Bulletin no. 80, June 8, 2021.

[33] James Manyika et al., "Digital Globalization: The New Era of Global Flows," McKinsey Global Institute, February 24, 2016.
[34] *Ibid.*
[35] World Trade Organization, Joint Statement on Electronic Commerce, WTO Doc. WT/L/1056 (January 25, 2019).
[36] Digital Economy Partnership Agreement, June 12, 2020, New Zealand Foreign Affairs & Trade.
[37] James Bacchus, "The Digital Decide: How to Agree on WTO Rules for Digital Trade," Special Report, Centre for International Governance Innovation, August 2021.
[38] "WTO Ministerial: In Landmark Move, Country Coalitions Set to Advance on New Issues," *Bridges* Special Update, December 13, 2017, p. 2.
[39] "Brazil Circulates Proposal for WTO Investment Facilitation Deal," TRALAC, February 8, 2018).
[40] Protocol Amending the Marrakesh Agreement Establishing the World Trade Organization: Decision of November 27, 2014, November 28, 2021, Marrakesh Agreement Establishing the World Trade Organization, Annex 1A, 1869 U.N.T.S. 401.
[41] Agreement on Trade-Related Investment Measures, April 15, 1994, Marrakesh Agreement Establishing the World Trade Organization, Annex 1A, 1869 U.N.T.S. 401.
[42] World Trade Organization, Joint Ministerial Statement: Declaration on the Establishment of a WTO Informal Work Programme for MSMEs, WTO Doc. WT/MIN(17)/58, 17-6871 WTO (December 13, 2017).
[43] "Informal Working Group on Micro, Small and Medium-Sized Enterprises (MSMEs)," World Trade Organization.
[44] Informal Working Group on MSMEs, "Declaration on Micro, Small and Medium-Sized Enterprises (MSMEs), WTO Doc. INF/MSME/4, 20-9040 WTO (December 14, 2020).
[45] "Informal Working Group on Micro, Small and Medium-Sized Enterprises (MSMEs)," World Trade Organization.
[46] World Trade Organization, Joint Declaration on Trade and Women's Empowerment on the Occasion of the WTO Ministerial Conference in Buenos Aires in December 2017, WTO (December 2017).
[47] *Ibid.*
[48] *Women and Trade: The Role of Trade in Promoting Gender Equality* (Washington: The World Bank and World Trade Organization, 2020).
[49] *Ibid.*
[50] World Trade Organization, Joint Ministerial Declaration on the Advancement of Gender Equality and Women's Economic Empowerment Within Trade: 12th WTO Ministerial Conference, WTO Doc. WT/MIN(21)/4, 21-8524 WTO (December 2021).

[51] Committee on Trade and Environment, Communication on Trade and Environmental Sustainability: Communication from Australia; Canada; Chad; Chile; Costa Rica; European Union; the Gambia; Fiji; Iceland; Japan; Korea, Republic of; Liechtenstein; Maldives; Mexico; Moldova, Republic of; Montenegro; New Zealand; North Macedonia; Norway; Senegal; Switzerland; the Separate Customs Territory of Taiwan, Penghu, Kinmen and Matsu; and the United Kingdom, WTO Doc. WT/CTE/W/249, 20-8239 WTO (November 17, 2020).

[52] "Trade and Environmental Sustainability," World Trade Organization.

[53] World Trade Organization, Trade and Environmental Sustainability Structured Discussions (TESSD): Ministerial Statement on Trade and Environmental Sustainability, Revision, WTO Doc. WT/MIN(21)/6/Rev.2, 21-9322 WTO (December 14, 2021).

[54] "New Initiatives Launched to Intensify WTO Work on Trade and Environment," World Trade Organization, November 17, 2020.

[55] "Trade Ministers Present Early Results, Pledge to Advance Plastics Dialogue at MC12 Event," World Trade Organization, June 13, 2022.

[56] "Plastics Pollution and Environmentally Sustainable Plastics Trade," World Trade Organization.

[57] Sam Meredith, "'Most Important Climate Deal since Paris': UN Agrees Treaty to End Scourge of Plastic Pollution," *CNBC*, March 3, 2022.

[58] World Trade Organization, Ministerial Statement on Fossil Fuel Subsidies, WTO Doc. WT/Min(22)8, 22-4425 WTO (June 10, 2022).

[59] "Fossil Fuel Subsidy Reform (FFSR): Background Information for Press," World Trade Organization.

[60] Ieva Baršauskaitė, "Fossil Fuel Subsidies: Types, Measurement, Impacts and Reform Efforts," (presentation, Trade and Environmental Sustainability Structured Discussions (TESSD), World Trade Organization, Geneva, March 31, 2022).

Chapter 5

The High Price of Buying American: The Harms of Domestic Content Mandates[*]

Introduction

The high price to the American people from government "Buying American" initiatives is ignored in the vast array of subsidies included in the recent Inflation Reduction Act. So, too, are the repercussions of such discrimination in the trade relationships of the United States, including with a number of U.S. trading partners who are also U.S. allies. The reaction of these U.S. allies to the discriminatory features in the structure of tax credits for electric vehicles is just one example; there are others.

"Buy American" measures harm U.S. businesses, workers, consumers, and taxpayers. They also raise serious questions about whether these measures comply with the obligations of the United States under several international trade agreements that fall within the jurisdiction of the World Trade Organization (WTO). In implementing and applying these discriminatory measures, the United States may be in violation of WTO rules on trade in goods, on governmental subsidies, and on trade-related investment measures. The United States is unlikely to be able to prove it is entitled to an exception to these violations under WTO rules. Having

---

[*]This essay was previously published by the Cato Institute as James Bacchus, "The High Price of Buying American: The Harms of Domestic Content Mandates," Cato Policy Analysis no. 948 (June 6, 2023).

suffered significant economic losses through the years from "Buy American" requirements in public procurement, the United States would be wise to reconsider and not impose "Buy American" conditions on obtaining public support for private purchases in the wider marketplace.

The Inflation Reduction Act

The Inflation Reduction Act (IRA) narrowly approved by a Democratic Congress in 2022 and strongly supported by the administration of President Joe Biden is the most ambitious climate action taken to date by the United States. It is also replete with governmental subsidies that mark a shift by the United States away from market-based solutions and toward a more state-directed "industrial strategy" aimed at speeding the shift of U.S. industry and the U.S. economy away from reliance on carbon-emitting fossil fuel energy and toward the use of wind, solar, and other forms of renewable energy. Many of these new subsidies discriminate against the use of products from a number of the leading trading partners of the United States by conditioning the availability of the subsidies on the use of "domestic content" in the subsidized production.

These "Buy American" provisions raise serious legal issues under the international law of the World Trade Organization (WTO) and expose the United States to potential challenges in WTO dispute settlement. Initially, the concern of the European Union (EU), the United Kingdom (UK), Japan, South Korea, and other major U.S. trading partners (and allies) has centered on the discriminatory "Buy American" aspects of the IRA tax credits for purchases of electric vehicles (EVs). As implementation of the sweeping legislation proceeds, other subsidies it provides will provoke still more criticism from abroad. If not resolved, the United States will pay a high price economically for its misguided passion for "buying American," including the costs of a tit-for-tat "subsidies war" in trade that neither the United States nor its aggrieved trading partners can afford.

The high price to the American people from "buying American" is ignored in the vast array of subsidies included in the recent IRA. So, too, are the repercussions of such discrimination in the trade relationships of the United States, including with a number of U.S. trading partners who are also U.S. allies. The reaction of these U.S. allies to the discriminatory features in the structure of tax credits for electric vehicles is just one example. There are others. In addition to the economic damages caused to

U.S. businesses, workers, consumers, and taxpayers by these "Buy American" measures, they also raise serious questions about whether these measures comply with the obligations of the United States under several international trade agreements that fall within the jurisdiction of the WTO. In implementing and applying these discriminatory measures, the United States may be in violation of WTO rules on trade in goods, on governmental subsidies, and on trade-related investment measures. The United States is unlikely to be able to prove it is entitled to an exception to these violations under WTO rules. Having suffered significant economic losses through the years from "Buy American" requirements in government procurement, the United States would be wise to reconsider and not impose these conditions on obtaining public support for private purchases in the wider marketplace.

Discrimination in Tax Credits for Electric Vehicles

At a White House state dinner for visiting French President Emmanuel Macron, the main topic of conversation was not the quality of the wine or even the fact that the wine served was American and not French; it was the new U.S. consumer tax credits for purchases of electric vehicles. The discriminatory aspects of these tax credits threaten to launch a new trade conflict between the United States and some of its most important geopolitical allies at a time when the alliance of democratic countries must be solidified and strengthened, and not weakened by needless trade disputes.

President Joe Biden and his administration seek to increase manufacturing production in the United States while also achieving their ambitious decarbonization goals for addressing climate change. In accomplishing these aims, they also seek to weaken Russia and counter and constrain the geopolitical ambitions of China. Biden and his advisers — as well as many members of Congress in both parties and in both chambers — see limiting China's access to new and strategic technologies and constructing alternative supply chains as key means to their success in the pursuit of these aims. Cooperation and close collaboration with America's democratic allies are indispensable in the pursuit of those ends.

The centerpiece so far in the Biden administration's pursuit of these goals is the IRA, which has much more to do with forging a transition to renewable energy in the face of climate change than it does with fighting inflation. The IRA is central to the hopes of Biden and his Democratic Party of reducing U.S. carbon emissions 40 percent by 2030 — the promise they have made in climate negotiations with the wider world. The IRA is also replete with new governmental subsidies intended to accelerate climate action by incentivizing an economic shift from dependence on carbon-emitting fossil fuels to use of solar, wind, and other renewable energies that emit less or no carbon during operation. The "Buy American" features of these subsidies, which in many places limit access to the subsidies to production based on "domestic content," give rise to serious legal questions under international trade law and — quite predictably — are beginning to generate widespread negative reaction from U.S. trading partners, including U.S. allies whose products have been denied access to these subsidies in the IRA.

The IRA's "king's ransom" of subsidies range across numerous economic sectors, with subsidies "for clean energy, mostly via tax credits for projects ranging from solar farms to battery manufacturing to facilities that remove climate-warming carbon dioxide from the air."[1] The new law provides new subsidies for "critical minerals" produced only in the United States, including advanced manufacturing tax credits ($30 billion), "enhanced use" of Defense Production Act contracts ($500 million), and "innovative technology" loan guarantees. This leaves out major non-China producers of these minerals such as U.S. allies Australia and Canada. The IRA also boosts tax credits for the production of zero carbon energy (wind, solar, geothermal, hydropower) in the United States; but the biggest of these subsidies are limited to projects that meet two "Buy American" requirements:

- All of a project's iron and steel products must be produced in the United States.
- All of a project's manufactured products must contain set amounts of U.S. content.

Furthermore, projects that do not satisfy these local content requirements are disqualified from certain subsidies, in whole or in part.[2] The IRA also provides additional subsidies to U.S. shipbuilders who already benefit from the protectionism afforded by the U.S. Jones Act, which has the effect of hindering the development of offshore wind energy. Vessels that are capable of installing offshore wind turbines and that are also compliant with the restrictions of the Jones Act do not currently exist.[3]

Significantly, also among the $369 billion in new subsidies intended to address climate change by speeding a transition from fossil fuels to clean technology and renewable sources of energy, the IRA offers U.S. consumers tax credits of up to $7,500 for new purchases of electric vehicles assembled in North America, including in Mexico and Canada, which are parties with the United States to the United States–Mexico–Canada Agreement (USMCA, successor to the North American Free Trade Agreement). As the implementation of the IRA continues and accelerates, all of the discriminatory aspects of its various subsidies (summarized in Table 1) will draw more criticism worldwide. For now, it is the new tax credit scheme for the purchase of electric vehicles that has been the target of the most international contention.

Casting a pall on the French state dinner was the fact that, under the IRA, eligibility for half of the EV tax credit ($3,750) depends on where the electric vehicle is assembled, and eligibility for the other half depends on where the vehicle's battery materials are sourced. The IRA extends the tax credit for EV purchases only to those from countries that have a "free trade agreement" with the United States, such as the USMCA. Thus, it does not include such American allies as Japan, South Korea, the UK, or EU members such as France. These countries — like the United States — are WTO members; however, unlike Canada and Mexico, they do not have separate bilateral free trade agreements with the United States. Carmakers from these countries typically assemble their electric vehicles overseas with the hope of selling them worldwide, including in the United States.

Significantly, the IRA also includes strict new rules for sourcing and manufacturing batteries for EVs. Starting this year, at least 40 percent of the critical materials for batteries for electric vehicles must be sourced in the United States or in countries that have a "free trade agreement" with the United States. This 40 percent requirement will rise to 80 percent by 2026. EVs must also have batteries with at least 50 percent North American content by 2024 and 100 percent by 2028.[4] These stringent requirements have been introduced at a time when the United States is highly dependent on foreign production for these critical materials. Certain minerals — mainly lithium, cobalt, manganese, nickel, and graphite — "are essential to constructing the lithium-ion batteries used in electric vehicles."[5]

As it stands, China controls an estimated 60–80 percent of the chemical processing and refining of these critical battery materials, and it

Table 1. The Inflation Reduction Act prescribes numerous domestic content requirement rules in order to access.

Name/Purpose of Credit	Issue Area/Product	Local Content Rule	Role of Local Content Rule	Credit if Local Content Rule is Met
Clean Electricity Production Credit (CEPTC)	Electric Power	– 100% of iron and steel that is a component of the facility must be produced in the United States; and – At least 40% of manufactured products that are components of the facility are produced in the United States, increasing to 45% on January 1, 2025; 50% on January 1, 2026; and 55% on January 1, 2027. – For offshore wind, base rate for manufactured products is 20%, increasing to 27.5% on January 1, 2025; 35% on January 1, 2026; 45% on January 1, 2027; and 55% on January 1, 2028.	Condition for additional credit	10% additional to the base CEPTC dollar amount
Clean Energy Investment Tax Credit (CEITC)	Electric Power	– 100% of iron and steel that is a component of the facility must be produced in the United States; and – At least 40% of manufactured products that are components of the facility are produced in the United States, increasing to 45% on January 1, 2025; 50% on January 1, 2026; and 55% on January 1, 2027. – For offshore wind, base rate for manufactured products is 20%, increasing to 27.5% on January 1, 2025; 35% on January 1, 2026; 45% on January 1, 2027; and 55% on January 1, 2028.	Condition for additional credit	2–10% additional to the CEITC rate*

The High Price of Buying American 157

Advanced Manufacturing Credit	Manufacturing of Green Goods and Infrastructure	Items must be produced in the United States.	Condition for base credit
			Credits include: • 4 cents times the capacity of solar cells • 10% of the sales price of the offshore wind vessels • $35 times the capacity of battery cells • 10% of production costs for critical minerals
Clean Vehicle Credit (Critical Minerals)	Electric Vehicles	The following percentage of the value of applicable critical minerals in the EV's battery must be extracted or processed in the United States or any country with which the United States has a free trade agreement, or recycled in North America: • 40% if placed in service before January 1, 2024 • 50% if placed in service in 2024 • 60% if placed in service in 2025 • 70% if placed in service in 2026 • 80% if placed in service in 2027 or beyond.	Condition for base credit
			$3,750 per vehicle

(Continued)

Table 1. (Continued)

Name/Purpose of Credit	Issue Area/Product	Local Content Rule	Role of Local Content Rule	Credit if Local Content Rule is Met
		Final assembly of the vehicle must also take place in North America. For vehicles placed in service beginning in 2025, none of the applicable critical minerals contained in their battery can be extracted, processed or recycled by a "foreign entity of concern."		
Clean Vehicle Credit (Battery Components)	Electrics Vehicles	The following percentage of the value of the components of the EV's battery must be manufactured or assembled in North America: • 50% if placed in service before January 1, 2024 • 60% if placed in service in 2024 or 2025 • 70% if placed in service in 2026. • 80% if placed in service in 2027 • 90% if placed in service in 2028 • 100% if placed in service in 2029 or beyond Final assembly of the vehicle must also take place in North America. For vehicles placed in service beginning in 2025, none of their battery components can be manufactured or assembled in a "foreign entity of concern."	Condition for base credit	$3,750 per vehicle
Clean Fuel Production Credits	Transportation Fuel	Production must take place in the United States.	Condition for base credit	• 20¢-$1.00 per gallon* • 30¢-$1.75 per gallon for "sustainable fuel"*

Source: Inflation Reduction Act of 2022, Pub. L. no. 117-169, 136 Stat. 4392.

Note: *Upper bound is conditional on the taxpaying firm also meeting prevailing wage and apprenticeship requirements.

manufactures more than 75 percent of all EV batteries.[6] "Most of the mining for materials like lithium and cobalt isn't in China, but the country dominates the subsequent steps in the value chain."[7] The United States imports more than half of its use of each of these critical materials, including all its manganese and graphite and 76 percent of its cobalt. China's significant lead in this sector can be attributed to hefty Chinese EV subsidies through the years, which have facilitated the development of a strong global battery supply chain leading upstream to China.

The IRA provides that, beginning in 2024, no battery parts can be imported from a "foreign entity of concern," such as China or Russia. The same requirements will be extended to minerals in 2025. The question for the United States — and for its allies — is how best to build their own supply chains for these critical inputs into EV batteries *soon*, so as not to be largely dependent on China as a "middleman."

Further complicating matters for the United States is the perfectly foreseeable reaction of the excluded U.S. allies to the economic slight against them in the new U.S. law. While in Washington, President Macron pronounced the trade discrimination in the EV tax credits a "job killer" for Europe.[8] France and the other excluded U.S. allies and trading partners contend that these new U.S. requirements relating to electric vehicles may violate WTO rules.[9] The EU has warned that, if applied in their current form, these new U.S. EV measures could "trigger a harmful global subsidy race" for critical green technologies and their components and create "tensions that could lead to reciprocal or retaliatory measures."[10] Thus far, this trade discrimination by the United States has not led to any action in the WTO by the affected countries. Nor has it inspired reciprocal or retaliatory subsidies. Yet, these new U.S. EV requirements could well lead to both.

The American Response So Far to U.S. Allies' Concerns

President Joe Biden and his administration have struggled to articulate a credible response to the concern over the new discriminatory features of the EV tax credit, which is widely shared among America's friends and trading partners outside of North America. He must placate the slighted U.S. allies while also preserving his support within his own party in Congress. Having won the bare minimum of a majority in support of the

IRA in Congress with pledges of an industrial strategy that tilts the market-based American economy toward more governmental direction (ironically, in tacit emulation of authoritarian China), he is committed to following through on the trade and other economic distortions that will now result. Having lit the fire of protectionism with the discriminatory EV tax credits and the other massive subsidies in the IRA, he must be careful not to be burned.

The United States is striving to maintain a united economic front against the Russian government of President Vladimir Putin, whose unprovoked invasion of neighboring Ukraine has, thus far, inspired a cooperative effort by many Western and Asian democracies to arm and otherwise support the Ukrainians in their brave defense of their country. The Biden administration also seeks to unite these same democracies in a common response to what they perceive as significant and ongoing trade transgressions by China as well as increasingly ominous Chinese geopolitical actions. The last thing Joe Biden needs now is a messy trade split between the United States and the EU over EV tax credits. Yet, the discriminatory IRA measures threaten to drive a divide between the United States and the EU as well as the UK, Japan, and South Korea at the worst possible time for the conduct of American foreign policy.

During the French state visit, Biden told Macron that there could be "tweaks" to the law to smooth the way for French and other European EVs to be eligible for the tax credits.[11] The bilateral U.S.–EU Trade and Technology Council is supposed to figure out how to make these "tweaks."[12] The hope is that these technocrats from both sides of the Atlantic Ocean can somehow make this controversy disappear. The IRA passed in the Congress by only one vote after nearly two years of trying — and that was a Democratic Congress ostensibly supportive of Biden. Now there is a Republican House of Representatives. No one knows how either the Democrats or the Republicans in the new Congress would react to a proposal to change the law; and no one in the Biden administration wants to find out by asking.

This leaves Biden with only the possibility of an administrative solution that does not alter the intent of the statute. The problem is the language in the IRA extends the EV tax credit only to U.S. products and to products from countries with which the United States has a "free trade agreement." Only Congress can change a statute; the executive branch cannot do so. This is part of the separation of powers in the U.S.

Constitution. Biden has suggested, however, that administrative rule-making could somehow make this statutory requirement more flexible. He has said the IRA provision limiting the tax credits to nations with free trade agreements with the United States "was added by a member of the U.S. Congress who acknowledges that he just meant allies. He didn't mean literally free trade agreements. So, there's a lot we can work out."[13]

This jaw-dropping explanation says all too much about the current capabilities of the Congress in writing legislation. Not only can major legislation rarely be enacted, but even when it is enacted, it is often rife with drafting error. This is such a case. Nearly two years of work went into drafting the IRA. But a member of Congress who was in a sufficiently senior place to add this requirement evidently did not comprehend the implications of the wording they chose to use. What is perhaps more distressing, the congressional staff advising that member apparently did not notice the extent of the discrimination entailed in this wording, did not foresee its economic and geopolitical consequences, and did not warn the member that broader language should be used that would not discriminate against important U.S. allies and trusted trading partners. Given this sloppy legislating, there is little wonder that Biden decided not to mention this member of Congress by name.

To try to assuage the concerns of the victims of this trade discrimination, the Treasury Department, shortly before the new requirements took effect on January 1, issued a guidance that will allow some EV vehicles assembled outside North America to qualify for the tax credit through a separate commercial electric vehicle program if they are purchased for lease by businesses, not for resale.[14] Furthermore, the Treasury Department has noted that the phrase "free trade agreement" is not defined in the legislation and therefore could be interpreted to include other agreements that "reduce or eliminate trade barriers" in addition to "comprehensive" free trade agreements.[15] This signals that the Biden administration may adopt administratively an expansive definition of the undefined statutory phrase.[16]

As Kathleen Claussen has noted,

> When it comes to the more than 1,200 trade-related agreements that the United States maintains covering over 100 countries, they very often "reduce or eliminate trade barriers," just not all of them.... [T]hese mini-deals or trade executive agreements could still be

considered free trade agreements or at least "free-ing" agreements: they almost always make the exchange of goods and services easier. The United States has 107 such agreements with Japan and about 60 with the European Union, despite not having a comprehensive trade agreement with either partner. These agreements cover everything from avocados to zoning.[17]

It is unclear how much domestic pushback will be generated by these and potentially other concessions made by the Biden administration with the intent of placating U.S. allies that are victimized by this trade discrimination. Democratic Senator Joe Manchin of West Virginia, an author of the legislation and a pivotal force in the U.S. Senate, has criticized the commercial lease concession, maintaining that the interpretation by the Treasury Department "bends to the desire of the companies looking for loopholes and is clearly inconsistent with the intent of the law." This, he has said, "only serves to weaken our ability to become a more energy secure nation."[18] In the wake of the announcement of the Treaty guidance, Senator Manchin has introduced legislation in the new Congress that would delay the implementation of the tax credits for electric vehicles.[19] He has said he seeks legislation that "further clarifies the original intent of the law and prevents this dangerous interpretation from Treasury from moving forward."[20] He has also acknowledged, however, that when he was crafting the new requirements for the EV tax credits, he did not realize that the United States and EU do not have a free trade agreement and is open to "tweaks" on that requirement.[21]

Criticisms of these administrative actions may be forthcoming domestically from Democrats and Republicans alike. Reconciling the principles of free and open trade with the professed desire of the Biden administration and the congressional supporters of the IRA to lure much of the current foreign assembly and production of electric vehicles into North America and to source domestically as many inputs into EVs as possible, is a bit like trying to make a square of a circle economically. The American supporters of these discriminatory measures have their eyes on the ongoing and intensifying U.S. competition with China in this key high-tech sector; however, the U.S. ability to compete with China in the growing global EV market will be hindered if long-existing trade ties in the automotive sector between the United States and such allies as the EU, UK, Japan, and South Korea are damaged in the process.

The Economic Damage of Domestic Content Requirements

Why would the United States risk such controversy by engaging in such trade discrimination in the first place? It is because the Biden administration and congressional Democrats, along with a growing number of "Make America Great Again" congressional Republicans, see discriminatory "Buy American" provisions as advantageous because they think they either advance a decarbonizing transition or enhance U.S. economic competitiveness in domestic and foreign markets. In their eyes, domestic content requirements are essential to what they perceive as an eroded manufacturing base that has been victimized in recent decades by unfair foreign competition from China and elsewhere. They view these requirements as incentives for buying American-made products and as encouragements for both keeping production onshore and stimulating foreign direct investment in U.S.-based production. Buying American is seen as a way of lifting America anew to the dominant role in the world economy that it played in the first few decades following World War II.

President Biden and his administration make no apologies for their embrace of domestic content requirements and other forms of economic nationalism as part of their rediscovery of the supposed need for the United States to have a government-led industrial policy. As Deputy Secretary of Commerce Don Graves has expressed it, "For the first time in decades, we have a generational opportunity to lay claim to the competitive industries of the future, along with the good-paying jobs and economic security that will come with them. But it's going to require government, business, workers, and communities to work together in new and innovative ways, and it will require the private sector to consider national competitiveness and economic security as part of their corporate social responsibility."[22] Framed as an "industrial strategy," the aim of the Biden administration is, he has said, to "rebuild and invest in our industrial base, bolster our resilience to threats from adversaries and climate change, and chart a path to long-term growth."[23] Domestic content requirements are perceived as necessary to accomplishing this overall aim.

Yet, the economic reality is that domestic content requirements will not achieve these worthy aims. Instead, they will undermine them. A requirement to "Buy American" leads to less competition and thus to higher prices. This in turn leads ultimately to a global economy in which higher-priced American goods are priced out of markets; fewer American-made goods will be bought than would be bought through freer trade. Such a requirement also leads to less innovation. With competition limited, there is less of an incentive for domestic producers to keep up with their competition by innovating. Thus, burdened by domestic content requirements, protectionist legislation such as the subsidy provisions in the IRA will have the opposite effect of what the Congress and the Biden administration intend: they will create a domestic disincentive to engage in the extent of innovation that is necessary to make the transition to a cleaner and greener economy.

But the act of political representation is complicated by complexity. Try (as I did when I was a member of Congress) to explain these downsides of economic nationalism away from Washington and at a meeting with your skeptical congressional constituents back home. All of this is hard for a member of Congress to communicate to a constituent who equates buying American with an expression of patriotism. It is equally hard for a constituent to comprehend. Nevertheless, it is true. And there is an abundance of evidence dating back decades demonstrating that it is true.[24] Enhancing the competitiveness of American production in the U.S. economy and in the overall global economy is the right goal; but is not a goal that can be reached through the shortsighted and self-defeating devices of economic nationalism.

Deputy Secretary Graves has said that the ambition of the Biden administration is "to enable the private sector to do what it does best — innovate, scale, and compete."[25] But domestic content requirements are obstacles to doing this. Such requirements are always tempting as means of securing domestic support for legislation. A call to "Buy American" is always a guaranteed applause line in a political campaign for either party. However, domestic content requirements to "Buy American" distort trade while denying domestic producers and consumers alike the benefits of the competition, the lower prices, and the broader choices of more effective energy and environmental alternatives offered by being open to foreign trade and to foreign direct investment.[26] Domestic content requirements create a national economy that is smaller than it otherwise would be in the absence of such requirements.

The key to increased economic competitiveness is increased productivity: the making of more production while using fewer resources to do it. This requires an efficient allocation of resources. "Buy

American" provisions cause an inefficient allocation of domestic resources by artificially inflating production in a targeted industry independent of its competitiveness and at the expense of other industries and sectors. Because of this inefficient resource allocation, less technology transfer can occur and thus increases in productivity are inhibited. Downstream from final production, there are increased production costs because of increased prices for intermediate inputs of goods and services and potential supply bottlenecks that result in reduced competitiveness.

Likewise, internationally there are increased production costs of inputs of goods and services as well as inefficiencies in coordination in supply chain networks and thus fewer gains from trade and less overall new wealth. In today's economy, and despite the recent reorientation and retrenchment of some international supply chains, inputs into final production frequently cross borders many times before becoming part of end products. Government-imposed distortions to this process can diminish competitiveness domestically and worldwide. For consumers, there are increased prices of often lower quality goods. Moreover, where there are domestic content requirements, the latest technologies are not always available.

Initially, domestic content requirements may enable domestic producers to capture economies of scale and enter global markets; but, over the long term, they insulate firms from competition and thereby diminish the incentive for innovation. Because domestic content requirements seldom contain "sunset" provisions with an expiration date, they tend to remain in place for a long time, leaving in place the disincentive for innovation and thereby impeding productivity growth. Few beneficiaries of subsidies ever ask that their subsidies be withdrawn. What is more, at a time when innovation in addressing climate change and its multiplying effects is urgently needed, such disincentives for innovation are doubly deleterious. As the eminent Swiss trade scholar Thomas Cottier has observed: "From the point of view of decarbonization, a local content requirement does not make sense as it increases costs for hardware and installations. Imported and competitive products are likely to contribute to more rapid deployment of the technology."[27] Leading American trade scholar Robert Howse has added that "domestic content requirements and other discriminatory measures actually undermine environmental objectives, by shifting production to higher-cost jurisdictions, and therefore making clean energy, or clean energy technologies, more expensive than they need to be."[28]

The EU and the other affected U.S. allies could try to match the IRA subsidies with subsidies of their own. Some within the EU have urged doing precisely that, even at the risk of setting off a tit-for-tat "subsidies race" that would only add to the economic damage of the discriminatory dimensions of the IRA subsidies on both sides of the Atlantic Ocean while perhaps also spreading that trade-distorting race worldwide.[29] This is not merely a matter of the EV tax credits. France calculates that about $200 billion of the $369 billion in new IRA subsidies are inconsistent with U.S. WTO obligations.[30] Retaliation by the EU and others against these massive U.S. subsidies by endeavoring to match them would be enormously expensive. It is not clear that these U.S. allies and trading partners can afford such a "subsidy war." (Whether the United States can afford this level of largesse at the expense of American taxpayers is another question.) And what would Russia and China be doing while the United States and its allies squabble over tit-for-tat subsidies and other forms of trade discrimination? The energy and economic transition sought by the Biden administration will occur sooner and more successfully if the United States works closely with its allies and not against them.

WTO Rules Relating to Domestic Content Requirements

For these economic reasons, international trade rules have long imposed disciplines on the trade distortions caused by domestic content requirements. Among these legal disciplines, three WTO rules are especially relevant here. The first are the rules against discriminatory internal taxation and regulation in article III of the General Agreement on Tariffs and Trade (the GATT). The second is the rule prohibiting subsidies that are contingent upon the use of domestic content in article 3.1(b) of the Agreement on Subsidies and Countervailing Measures (the SCM Agreement). The third is the requirement in article 2.1 of the Agreement on Trade-Related Investment Measures (the TRIMS Agreement) that no trade-related investment measure shall be applied inconsistently with article III of the GATT.

Table 2. WTO jurists have previously found domestic content requirements to be in violation of the WTO

Case ID	Parties	Products Involved	Measures Contested	WTO Agreement Provisions at Issue*	Years Active
DS54, 55, 59, 64	Complainants: European Communities, Japan, United States; Respondent: Indonesia	Automobiles and auto parts	— "1993 Programme" providing tariff reductions or exemptions on imports of auto parts based on local content percentage. — "1996 Programme" providing benefits such as luxury tax exemption and tariff exemption to "qualifying" (based on local content) or Indonesian cars.	• TRIMS art. 2.1	1997–1998
DS139, 142	Complainants: Japan, European Communities; Respondent: Canada	Motor vehicles and parts	— Import duty exemptions for certain manufacturers, in conjunction with Canadian Value-Added (CVA) and production-to-sales ratio requirements.	• GATT III:4 • GATTS art. XVII	1999–2000
DS108 (Article 21.5)	Complainant: European Communities; Respondent: United States	All foreign goods affected by the U.S. measure	— FSC Repeal and Extraterritorial Income Exclusion Act of 2000 (the "ETI" Act).	• GATT art. III:4	2000–2002
DS146, 175	Complainants: United States, European Communities; Respondent: India	Automobiles and auto parts	— "Indigenization" (i.e., local content requirement) imposed on the automotive sector.	• GATT art. III:4	2000–2002

(Continued)

Table 2. (Continued)

Case ID	Parties	Products Involved	Measures Contested	WTO Agreement Provisions at Issue*	Years Active
DS267	Complainant: Brazil Respondent: United States	Upland cotton	— U.S. agricultural "domestic support" measures, export credit guarantees, and other measures alleged to be export and domestic content subsidies.	• ASCM art. 3.1(b) and 3.2	2003–2005
DS339, 340, 342	Complainants: United States, European Communities, Canada Respondent: China	Auto parts	— A 25 percent "charge" on certain imported auto parts.	• GATT III:4	2006–2009
DS412, 416	Complainants: Japan, European Union Respondent: Canada	Certain electricity generation equipment (for renewable energy) and the electricity generated	— Feed-in Tariff (FIT) program of the province of Ontario and the contracts implementing it.	• TRIMS art. 2.1 • GATT art. III:4	2011–2013

DS438, 444, 445	Complainants: European Union, United States, Japan Respondent: Argentina	Goods imported into Argentina	– Measures conditioning the importation of goods into Argentina (or the contention of other benefits), including requirements to reach a certain level of local content in domestic production.	• GATT art III:4	2013–2015
DS456	Complainant: United States Respondent: India	Solar cells and/or modules	– Domestic content requirements imposed by India on solar power developers selling electricity to the government.	• GATT art. III:4 • TRIMS art. 2.1 • GATT art. III:8 (government procurement derogation)	2014–2016

Source: WTO Dispute Settlement: One-Page Case Summaries, 1995–2020 (Geneva: World Trade Organization, 2021); and "WTO Case Law Index," WorldTradeLaw.net.

Note: European Communities was the official name of the European Union at the WTO until November 30, 2009.

*Only provisions raised in the context of local content restrictions.

The same measure can violate all three of these rules, which have been strictly applied by WTO panels and the WTO Appellate Body in dispute settlement, consistently with the instructions given to jurists by WTO Members in the Dispute Settlement Understanding, which is part of the WTO treaty.[31] The United States assembly and sourcing measures relating to EV tax credits are highly vulnerable to challenge in WTO dispute settlement under all three of these rules. So, too, are the discriminatory elements in other IRA subsidies provisions. Furthermore, no credible defense appears to be available to the United States under WTO rules to justify these violations.

First, there is GATT article III. The Appellate Body has stated, quoting article III:1, that, "The broad and fundamental purpose of Article III is to avoid protectionism in the application of internal tax and regulatory measures. More specifically, the purpose of Article III is to ensure that internal measures 'not be applied to imported or domestic products so as to afford protection to domestic production.'"[32] Article III:2, second sentence, provides that no WTO member "shall apply internal taxes or other internal charges to imported or domestic products in a manner contrary to the principles set forth in" article III:1.[33] For a violation of article III:2, second sentence, to be established, there must be a situation in which "directly competitive or substitutable" imported and domestic products are "not similarly taxed" through an "internal tax or other charge" that "is applied ... so as to afford protection to domestic production."[34] A pivotal question relating to a potential challenge in WTO dispute settlement to the electric vehicle tax credit in the IRA would be whether it "is applied ... so as to afford protection to domestic production." It seems obvious that protecting domestic production is indeed the purpose of the discriminatory structure of this tax credit.

Article III:4 of the GATT provides, in pertinent part, that, "The products of the territory of any contracting party imported into the territory of any other contracting party shall be accorded treatment no less favourable than that accorded to like products of national origin in respect of all laws, regulations and requirements affecting their internal sale, offering for sale, purchase, transportation, distribution or use."[35] This "national treatment" rule forbids discrimination in favor of local over foreign producers of like imported products. As the WTO Appellate Body has explained, "For a violation of Article III:4 to be established, three elements must be satisfied: that the imported and domestic products at issue are 'like products'; that the measure at issue is a 'law, regulation, or requirement affecting their internal sale, offering for sale, purchase, transportation, distribution, or use'; and that the imported products are accorded 'less favourable' treatment than that accorded to like domestic products."[36]

A key question relating to potential challenges to IRA subsidies in WTO dispute settlement under article III:4 would be whether these U.S. measures result in "less favourable" treatment. The test of whether treatment is "less favourable" to imported than to domestic like products focuses on the conditions of competition and whether there is an "effective equality of opportunities" in the marketplace.[37] Treatment is "less favourable" when there is a denial of equal competitive opportunities in the marketplace.[38] With respect to the EV taxing scheme, because of the price differentials that are created, the denial of tax credits for purchases of EVs to products from countries that do not have a "free trade agreement" with the United States and that do not meet the IRA's battery sourcing requirements constitutes a denial of an equal competitive opportunity to those products in the U.S. marketplace. A similar denial of equal competitive opportunities in the marketplace is likely to result from the discriminatory grant of other subsidies under the IRA.

Second, there is the SCM Agreement, which disciplines certain kinds of governmental subsidies. Some are inconsistent with the SCM Agreement if they have certain injurious trade effects.[39] Others are prohibited by the SCM Agreement simply because of how they are structured.[40] Article 3.1(b) of the SCM Agreement prohibits "subsidies contingent, whether solely or as one of several other conditions, upon the use of domestic over imported goods."[41] Such subsidies are illegal *per se* under this WTO rule, irrespective of any proof of injurious trade effects.[42] With such subsidies, trade injury is, as a matter of law, presumed. Subsidies are "contingent … upon the use of domestic over imported goods" if the use of domestic goods is "a condition, in the sense of a requirement, for receiving a subsidy."[43] Clearly, this is the case with respect to the assembly and battery sourcing requirements for eligibility for tax credits when purchasing an electric vehicle under the IRA. If a country from which a vehicle or a battery input or component is sourced does not have a "free trade agreement" with the United States, then the tax credit is unavailable for that purchase.

Until recently, the United States has been in the forefront among WTO members in opposing domestic content requirements such as those found in the IRA. Such requirements, of course, can result in discrimination against U.S. exports, just as they can result in discrimination against imports into the United States. Economically, domestic content requirements are a double-edged sword. Most recently, and perhaps most famously, the United States failed in 2018 to prove its claim under article 3.1(b) in the prolonged "Boeing–Airbus" civilian aircraft dispute that the European subsidies at issue there were prohibited import substitution subsidies.[44] Small wonder that U.S. trading partners are puzzled by the recent about-face in U.S. trade policy on domestic content requirements. For decades, market-oriented Americans have been telling them to refrain from granting trade-distortive governmental subsidies.

Third and lastly, there is article 2.1 of the TRIMS Agreement, which provides that "no Member shall apply any TRIM that is inconsistent with the provisions of Article III ... of GATT 1994."[45] The TRIMS Agreement essentially interprets and clarifies the provisions of GATT article III where trade-related investment measures are concerned.[46] TRIMS measures have been heavily scrutinized in WTO committees. As with import substitution subsidies under the SCM Agreement, the United States has, until recently, supported this strict scrutiny. For example, the United States has argued that what it sees as local content requirements related to China's cybersecurity measures restrict the ability of Chinese companies to procure the technology of their choice and reduces market access for foreign investors.[47] In addition, the United States has argued that localization measures in India's measures relating to pharmaceutical and medical devices; mining, oil, gas, and solar aspects of the energy industry; and the telecommunication, agriculture, and retail industries are in violation of the TRIMS Agreement.[48] Such measures imposed by other countries discriminate against U.S. goods and U.S. foreign direct investments.

Does the United States have a legal defense under WTO law to its own domestic content requirements in the IRA? Article XX of the GATT sets out "general exceptions" to GATT obligations.[49] Potentially relevant to claims of a GATT violation is article XX(g), which provides a general exception for measures "relating to the conservation of exhaustible natural resources if such measures are made effective in conjunction with restrictions on domestic production or consumption."[50] The Appellate Body has ruled that for a measure to be "related to" the conservation of exhaustible natural resources, there must be "a close and genuine relationship of ends and means" between that measure and the conservation objective of the WTO Member maintaining the measure.[51] With respect, for example, to the IRA tax credits for EV purchases, there appears to be such a means–end relationship; the means of the tax credits serve the end of conserving air and, indirectly, other exhaustible natural resources by mitigating climate change.

But that is not the conclusion of the inquiry into whether this "general exception" is justified under GATT article XX. Once it is established that a measure could be justified under article XX, the WTO member defending the measure must also prove that it is "not applied in a manner which would constitute a means of arbitrary or unjustifiable discrimination between countries where the same conditions prevail, or a disguised restriction on international trade...."[52] Here the United States is likely to fall short. With respect, for example, to the EV tax credits, how likely is it that the United states could prove that — for reasons relating to the conservation of exhaustible natural resources — its decision to discriminate by providing the tax credit for products from Canada and Mexico but not for those from the EU, UK, Japan, South Korea, and other countries is anything but "arbitrary and unjustifiable"? (Worth noting here is that while the "general exceptions" in GATT article XX apply to trade-related investment measures under the TRIMS Agreement,[53] it is unclear whether these exceptions apply to subsidies under the SCM Agreement.[54])

It may be suggested that any WTO violations in the IRA can be justified by the national security exception in article XXI of the GATT.[55] The United States continues to insist that the mere invocation of the national security exception in GATT article XXI is sufficient to excuse what would otherwise be a WTO violation. A series of WTO panels have, however, ruled consistently that this is not so. As I have explained and explored in a recent Cato policy analysis, acceptance by WTO jurists of the contemporary and bipartisan U.S. view that the WTO has no jurisdiction on such matters would open up a black hole of national security in which professed national security measures of all kinds could swallow up the entirety of all WTO obligations — something the United States itself warned against when the national security exception was written at the creation of the multilateral trading system in the immediate aftermath of World War II.[56] What is more, as with GATT article XX, it is unclear under WTO law whether a GATT article XXI defense is available for a violation of the SCM Agreement. Furthermore, it is equally unclear under WTO law whether the scope of the coverage of article XXI includes such competitiveness measures, whatever their broader and long-term national security implications.

What are the chances that disputes over the subsidies in the IRA will end up in WTO dispute settlement? The U.S. allies whose products are the subjects of this trade discrimination appear reluctant to go to the WTO for dispute settlement. While expressing their aggrievement, Japan, South Korea, and the UK seem, for now, to prefer to hold back while letting the EU take the lead on this issue. If, however, the EU did file a WTO complaint challenging the EV tax credit scheme or any of the other discriminatory aspects of the IRA, those other U.S. trading partners could be expected to join as co-complainants in the dispute. A proliferation of WTO dispute settlement could ensue.

Having recently resolved some long-lingering trade disputes with the United States, the EU, understandably, is hesitant to launch into more. The Europeans seem to prefer negotiation to litigation. With U.S. intransigence continuing to keep the WTO Appellate Body bereft of any judges, the EU is perhaps also, understandably, not optimistic about securing a resolution of the dispute from the WTO dispute settlement system. Should the EU (and other U.S. allies) bring a case and prevail before a WTO panel, the United States could prevent the adoption of the panel report by the WTO by filing an appeal to an Appellate Body which currently has no judges to hear an appeal. It could also simply announce that it will not comply with the adverse ruling, repeating what it did — to its discredit — after the adverse ruling over the Section 232 tariffs imposed on steel and aluminum imports by former President Donald Trump.[57] These potential outcomes, of course, have dimensions that extend far beyond the legality under WTO law of the U.S. EV tax credits and other IRA subsidies, including fundamental systemic issues about the fate of the WTO dispute settlement system and the WTO itself.

Conclusion

Article III:8(a) of the GATT provides that the provisions of article III — including the "national treatment" obligation in article III:4 — shall not apply to laws, regulations, or requirements relating to government procurement.[58] Relying on this exception, and apart from the limitations on it to which the United States has agreed in the plurilateral WTO Government Procurement Agreement,[59] the U.S. government has long been in the business of "buying American" in its public purchases.[60] The costs to American taxpayers and the American economy have been enormous. By one estimate, the United States would gain 300,000 jobs if it got rid of its domestic content rules in public purchases.[61] Buy American provisions are the equivalent of a 25 percent tariff on federal government purchases (and thus a 25 percent surtax on American taxpayers).[62] And even when jobs are supposedly "saved," the costs to taxpayers are often much larger than the incomes earned at "saved" jobs. The Peterson Institute for International Economics estimates that every job "saved" by buying American when making government purchases costs American taxpayers roughly $250,000.[63] With such harmful effects from "Buy American" requirements in public purchasing, why would we Americans want to impose such requirements on private purchasing as well?

Endnotes

[1] Janan Ganesh, "The West Will Rue Its Embrace of Protectionism," *Financial Times*, January 25, 2023; and Phred Dvorak, Jenny Strasburg, and Kim Mackreal, "U.S., Europe Tussle over Frenzy of Clean-Energy Subsidies," *Wall Street Journal*, January 26, 2023.

[2] Scott Lincicome, "…But We Won't Do That," *The Dispatch*, August 10, 2022.

[3] Colin Grabow, "The Jones Act Continues to Hamper the Development of Offshore Wind Energy," Cato at Liberty (blog), Cato Institute, May 19, 2021.

[4] Yuka Hayashi, "Biden Administration Pressed by Allied Nations to Revise EV Subsidy Program," *Wall Street Journal*, November 30, 2022.

[5] Joe Lancaster, "Good Luck Qualifying for New Tax Credits on Electric Cars," *Reason*, January 1, 2023.

[6] Jacky Wong, "EV Makers' Next Headache: Scarce Battery Chemicals, Made in China," *Wall Street Journal*, January 21, 2022.

[7] *Ibid*.

[8] Andrea Shalal and David Lawder, "Tax Credits for EU Electric Vehicles Dominate U.S. Trade Talks," *Reuters*, December 5, 2022.

[9] "U.S. Green Subsidies Take Effect amid Harsh Criticism," CGTN, January 2, 2023.

[10] Yuka Hayashi, "Biden Administration Pressed by Allied Nations to Revise EV Subsidy Program," *Wall Street Journal*, November 30, 2022.

[11] Andrea Shalal and David Lawder, "Tax Credits for EU Electric Vehicles Dominate U.S. Trade Talks," *Reuters*, December 5, 2022.

[12] *Ibid*.

[13] Doug Palmer, "Biden 'Confident' U.S. Can Address EU Concerns about IRA Subsidies," *Politico*, December 1, 2022.

[14] Yuka Hayashi, "U.S. Moves to Appease Allies on EV Subsidies," *Wall Street Journal*, December 29, 2022.

[15] *Ibid*.

16 Likewise, there is no definition of a "free trade agreement" in the Marrakesh Agreement Establishing the World Trade Organization. Article XXIV(8)(b) of the General Agreement on Tariffs and Trade speaks of a "free-trade area" and states that one "shall be understood to mean a group of two or more customs territories in which the duties and other restrictive regulations of commerce (except, where necessary, those permitted under articles XI, XII, XIII, XIV, XV and XX) are eliminated on substantially all the trade between the constituent territories in products originating in such territories." These terms have not, however, been clarified in WTO dispute settlement; nor is there any mention in the Marrakesh Agreement of a "free trade agreement" nor what would comprise one.

17 Kathleen Claussen, "What Is a Free Trade Agreement, Anyway?," International Economic Law and Policy Blog, WorldTradeLaw.net, January 3, 2023.

18 *Ibid.*

19 Matthew Daly, "Manchin Pushes to Delay Tax Credits for Electric Vehicles," *Associated Press*, January 26, 2023.

20 Steven Overly, "6 Big Trade Predictions for 2023," Politico, January 3, 2023.

21 Ari Natter, "Manchin Says He Didn't Know US, EU Lacked Free Trade Agreement," *Bloomberg*, January 19, 2023.

22 "Remarks by Deputy Secretary Don Graves at the Georgetown Business School Forum: Modern Industrial Strategy for U.S. Competitiveness, Equity, and Resilience," U.S. Department of Commerce, November 29, 2022.

23 *Ibid.*

24 *See*, for example, Scott Lincicome, "Ignoring the Recent (and Ignominius) History of 'Buy American,'" Cato at Liberty (blog), Cato Institute, July 10, 2010; Gary Clyde Hufbauer and Eujin Jung, "Buy American" and Similar Domestic Purchase Policies Impose High Costs on Taxpayers," Peterson Institute for International Economics, August 6, 2020; and Tori Smith, "'Buy American' Laws: A Costly Policy Mistake That Hurts Americans," The Heritage Foundation, May 18, 2017.

25 "Remarks by Deputy Secretary Don Graves at the Georgetown Business School Forum: Modern Industrial Strategy for U.S. Competitiveness, Equity, and Resilience," U.S. Department of Commerce, November 29, 2022.

26 *See* Gary Clyde Hufbauer et al., Local Content Requirements: A Global Problem *Policy* (Washington, D.C.: Peterson Institute of International Economics, September 2013).

27 Thomas Cottier, "Renewable Energy and WTO Law: More Policy Space or Enhanced Disciplines?," *Renewable Energy Law and Policy Review* Volume 5, Number 1 (2014): 40–51.

28 Rob Howse, "Securing Policy Space for Clean Energy under the SCM Agreement: Alternative Approaches," The E15 Initiative, p. 1.

29 Raf Casert, "EU Outlines Plan for Clean Tech Future Boosted by Subsidies," *Associated Press*, January 17, 2023; Kim Mackrael and Jenny Strasburg, "EU Seeks to Counter U.S. Clean-Tech Subsidies with New Funding," *Wall Street*

Journal, January 18, 2023; Katie Martin and Anne-Sylvaine Chassary, "Davos Delegates Praise Biden's 'Huge' Green Package, as Europe Voices Complaints," *Financial Times*, January 20, 2023.

[30] Alice Tidey, "EU Countries Say Action Needed against US Subsidies but Options Are Limited," *Euro News*, November 25, 2022.

[31] Understanding on Rules and Procedures Governing the Settlement of Disputes art. 3.2, April 15, 1994, Marrakesh Agreement Establishing the World Trade Organization, Annex 2, 1869 U.N.T.S. 401.

[32] Appellate Body Report, *Japan — Alcoholic Beverages II*, p. 16, WTO Doc. WT/DS8/AB/R; WT/DS10/AB/R; WT/DS11/AB/R (adopted November 1, 1996).

[33] General Agreement on Tariffs and Trade art. III:2, second sentence, October 30, 1947, 61 Stat. A-11, 55 U.N.T.S. 194.

[34] Appellate Body Report, *Japan — Alcoholic Beverages II*, p. 24, WTO Doc. WT/DS8/AB/R; WT/DS10/AB/R; WT/DS11/AB/R (adopted November 1, 1996).

[35] General Agreement on Tariffs and Trade art. III:4, October 30, 1947, 61 Stat. A-11, 55 U.N.T.S. 194.

[36] Appellate Body Report, Korea — Various Measures on Beef, ¶ 133, WTO Doc. WT/DS161/AB/R; WT/DS169/AB/R (adopted January 10, 2001).

[37] Panel Report, Japan — Film, ¶ 10.379, WTO Doc. WT/DS44/R (adopted April 22, 1998).

[38] Appellate Body Report, US — Gasoline, ¶ 6.10, WTO Doc. WT/DS2/AB/R (adopted May 20, 1996).

[39] Agreement on Subsidies and Countervailing Measures arts. 5 and 6, April 15, 1994, Marrakesh Agreement Establishing the World Trade Organization, Annex 1A, 1869 U.N.T.S. 401.

[40] *Ibid.* art. 3.

[41] *Ibid.* art. 3.1(b).

[42] *Ibid.* art. 3.2.

[43] Appellate Body Report, US — Tax Incentives, ¶ 5.7, WTO Doc. WT/DS487/AB/R (adopted September 4, 2017).

[44] Appellate Body Report, EC and Certain Member States — Large Civilian Aircraft, Recourse to Article 21.5 of the DSU by the United States, ¶ 5.77–5.81, WTO Doc. WT/DS316/RW/AB/R (adopted May 28, 2018).

[45] Agreement on Trade-Related Investment Measures art. 2.1, April 15, 1994, Marrakesh Agreement Establishing the World Trade Organization, Annex 1A, 1869 U.N.T.S. 401.

[46] Panel Report, EC — Bananas III, ¶ 7.185–7.186, WTO Doc. WT/DS27/R/ECU; WT/DS27/R/GTM; WT/DS27/R/HND; WT/DS27/R/MEX; WT/DS27/R/USA (adopted May 22, 1997).

[47] "Local Content Measures Scrutinized by WTO Members in Investment Committee," World Trade Organization, June 9, 2019.

[48] *Ibid.*

⁴⁹ General Agreement on Tariffs and Trade art. XX, October 30, 1947, 61 Stat. A-11, 55 U.N.T.S. 194.

⁵⁰ *Ibid.* art. XX(g).

⁵¹ Appellate Body Report, China — Rare Earths, ¶ 5.90, WTO Doc. WT/DS431/AB/R; WT/DS/432/AB/R; WT/DS433/AB/R (adopted August 7, 2014).

⁵² General Agreement on Tariffs and Trade art. XX, October 30, 1947, 61 Stat. A-11, 55 U.N.T.S. 194.

⁵³ Agreement on Subsidies and Countervailing Measures art. 3, April 15, 1994, Marrakesh Agreement Establishing the World Trade Organization, Annex 1A, 1869 U.N.T.S. 401.

⁵⁴ An open question in WTO jurisprudence, however, is whether article XX of the GATT can provide a defense to what would otherwise be an illegal subsidy under the SCM Agreement. The question turns on the extent to which the obligations in the SCM Agreement can be seen legally as elaborations of obligations relating to subsidies and to the application of countervailing duties under the GATT and therefore as a legal part of the GATT Agreement for the purposes of GATT article XX. The Appellate Body has touched on this unresolved legal issue obliquely, but to date this legal issue has not been raised squarely on appeal, and thus there is no definitive WTO ruling. *See* Appellate Body Report, *US — Shrimp (Thailand)*, WTO Doc. WT/DS343/AB/R; WT/DS345/AB/R (adopted July 16, 2008); Appellate Body Report, ¶ 229, *China — Publications and Audiovisual Products*, WTO Doc. WT/ DS363/AB/R (adopted January 19, 2010); Appellate Body Report, *China — Rare Earths*, ¶ 5.53–5.55, WTO Doc. WT/DS431/AB/R; WT/DS432/AB/R; WT/DS433/AB/R (adopted August 7, 2014); and Appellate Body Report, *Argentina — Footwear (EC)*, ¶ 97, WTO Doc. WT/ DS121/AB/R (adopted Jan. 12, 2000).

⁵⁵ General Agreement on Tariffs and Trade art. XXI, October 30, 1947, 61 Stat. A-11, 55 U.N.T.S. 194.

⁵⁶ James Bacchus, "The Black Hole of National Security: Striking the Right Balance for the National Security Exception in International Trade," Cato Institute Policy Analysis no. 936, November 9, 2022.

⁵⁷ James Bacchus, "Echoing Trump, Biden Embraces International Trade Lawlessness," Cato at Liberty (blog), Cato Institute, December 12, 2022.

⁵⁸ General Agreement on Tariffs and Trade art. III:8(a), October 30, 1947, 61 Stat. A-11, 55 U.N.T.S. 194.

⁵⁹ *Agreement on Government Procurement 2012 and Related WTO Legal Texts* (Geneva: World Trade Organization).

⁶⁰ The Buy American Act was passed by Congress in 1933 and signed into law by President Herbert Hoover on his last day in office.

⁶¹ "The Folly of Buying Local: Buy American Is an Economic-Policy Mistake," The Economist, January 28, 2021.

[62] Erika York, Alex Muresianu, and Alex Durante, "Taxes, Tariffs, and Industrial Policy: How the U.S. Tax Code Fails Manufacturing," Tax Foundation Fiscal Fact no. 788, March 17, 2022.

[63] Gary Clyde Hufbauer and Eujin Jung, "The High Taxpayer Cost of 'Saving' US Jobs through 'Made in America,'" Trade and Investment Policy Watch (blog), Peterson Institute for International Economics, August 5, 2020.

Chapter 6

Democrats and Trade: A Pro-Trade Policy for the Democratic Party*

Introduction

A narrative of popular discontent against open trade has taken hold, and politicians on both the left and the right have reacted by taking aim at trade agreements and proclaiming their support for economic nationalism. This is both bad policy and a misreading of the views of most Americans. Democrats should not fall into the trap of trying to compete with Donald Trump in skepticism about trade. Instead, Democrats should set out the positive case for trade liberalization and the rule of law in international trade.

To do so, they should look to the Constitution and reclaim the greater responsibility over trade for Congress envisioned there. Executive branch protectionism championed by President Trump has harmed the U.S. economy and worsened relationships with our allies. Congress needs to institute checks to make sure this does not happen again in the future. Democrats should also reengage in a constructive manner with U.S. trading partners in multilateral, bilateral, and regional settings. Working with allies, instead of against them, has its own rewards, and can also be used

---

*This essay was previously published by the Cato Institute as James Bacchus, "Democrats and Trade 2021: A Pro-Trade Policy for the Democratic Party," Cato Policy Analysis No. 900 (August 11, 2020).

as a basis for addressing the challenge of China's integration into the trading system. In this way, Democrats can develop a pro-trade policy that creates jobs and prosperity for Americans, and that also restores American leadership of the global economy.

A New Trade Opportunity for Democrats

Democrats hope to elect a Democratic president and a Democratic Congress. If they succeed, they will become responsible for, among much else, setting a new trade policy for the country, which has been in retreat from trade liberalization and from international trade cooperation under President Trump. Democrats have ample reasons to be pro-trade. Yet, at times, Democratic officeholders and candidates have seemed to echo Trump's espousal of trade protectionism. Even when Democrats have supported trade, they have sometimes seemed to apologize for it. They have not portrayed support for trade as the affirmative and progressive policy that it is.

If Democrats control the White House and Congress in 2021, they must return to their long and historic tradition of supporting trade and articulate why they support it instead of just saying that they oppose Trump's protectionist policies. They must do what virtually no one in national politics in either party has tried to do lately: they must remind all the American people why being for trade is in their best interest and why being against trade is not. Support for trade must be an essential part of any overall Democratic economic policy that aspires to restore and revitalize American prosperity.

But what should a pro-trade policy for Democrats in 2021 include? Being pro-trade is not as simple as saying "tariffs should be set at zero." There are complex constitutional, international relations, and governance questions to answer. As I set out below, the key elements of a Democratic trade policy should include the following: reclaim Congress's constitutional authority over trade policy; repeal Trump's unilateral tariffs; recommit to multilateralism; recommit to the rule of law in trade; support the modernization of the World Trade Organization (WTO); find a coherent approach to dealing with China; support bilateral and regional trade liberalizing efforts; and promote domestic actions that improve American competitiveness. Through implementation of these specific items, Democrats can rehabilitate U.S. trade policy, and, in doing so, they can reclaim U.S. leadership in the international trading system.

Reclaim Congress's Constitutional Authority over International Trade

In the United States, authority over trade is established in the Constitution, and Congress must reclaim that authority. Article I, Section 8, of the Constitution provides: "The Congress shall have Power To lay and collect ... Duties" and to "regulate Commerce with foreign Nations." Thus, it is Congress that has been entrusted with primary responsibility for international trade. Yet, for nearly a century now, the legislative branch has been slowly ceding its constitutional authority over trade to the executive branch, with the president and specific executive agencies being granted ever-increasing powers.

Some of this delegation has been for the good. Congress has neither the time nor the need to vote on approving every single tariff reduction on every product that may be negotiated as part of a trade agreement. For this reason, Congress has long since given presidents the power to negotiate trade agreements, along with congressional guidelines for negotiating them. This negotiating approach has helped the United States create a multilateral trading system based on trade liberalization and the rule of law. Under this negotiating approach, according to a study by the Bertelsmann Foundation, membership in this global system has boosted annual GDP by $87 billion in the 25 years since the establishment of the WTO — more than any other country.[1]

There has also, however, been congressional delegation that has given presidents the power to impose tariffs unilaterally. Although some of this delegation has made sense in principle, in practice it has given rise to abuse, especially during the Trump administration. Most notably, the legislation ceding congressional trade authority includes Section 232 of the Trade Expansion Act of 1962, which grants the president authority to restrict trade for national security reasons. It also includes Section 301 of the Trade Act of 1974, which gives the president authority to impose trade sanctions against what the executive branch deems to be unfair trade practices. These statutes are left over from the Cold War era and served a purpose when they were originally enacted, but they are now outdated and need to be rethought. They give the president sweeping powers to impose a whole range of restrictions on trade unilaterally, without consulting Congress and without requiring a congressional vote.

When presidents apply their discretion under these statutes reasonably and responsibly, that can be of value. But as with many other issues where he has pushed the outer limits of his legislated and constitutional powers, Trump has abused this delegated power over trade. He has seized on the broad discretion accorded to him as president under these long-ignored statutes to apply tariffs unilaterally — and often for dubious reasons — on imports from many of our leading trading partners without first seeking the consent of Congress. Actions taken under Section 301 have ostensibly been in response to assertions of unfair trade practices by the targeted countries. Actions taken under Section 232 have been justified on specious claims of national security. Most of these unilateral trade actions taken by the Trump administration are illegal under international trade law.

Reform is likewise needed to the process by which Congress delegates to a president the authority to negotiate trade agreements — the so-called "trade promotion authority." As a practical matter, some delegation is necessary to negotiate and conclude international trade agreements. If our negotiators had to go to Congress for approval before agreeing to cut every fraction of every tariff, no other country would ever agree to a trade deal with the United States.

Furthermore, as a practical matter in the modern world, there must be a congressional delegation of at least some unilateral trade authority in case of national emergency. At the same time, a president should not be given a blank check to pursue unilateral or other trade actions. Appropriately, in constructing trade promotion authority, Congress has sought to constrain trade negotiations by the executive branch. In 2021 and beyond, even more attention must be paid by Congress to striking the right balance by imposing negotiating constraints, irrespective of which party happens to hold the presidency.

A pro-trade policy should start by reclaiming Congress's largely abandoned constitutional authority over foreign commerce. Congressional Democrats should rein in legislatively what a president is allowed to do unilaterally to restrict trade. And this should not be a Democratic initiative alone. As many Republicans as possible should be recruited to join in achieving this restorative end through bipartisan legislative action. They, too, have sworn to uphold the Constitution.

Worthy of consideration is a bill introduced by Rep. Warren Davidson (R-OH) that would subject all trade actions by the executive branch to congressional approval.[2] Also deserving of consideration are a bipartisan bill introduced by Sen. Rob Portman (R-OH)[3] that would give the Department of Defense a more prominent role in assessing any potential national security threats posed by traded products, and a bipartisan bill introduced by Rep. Mike Gallagher (R-WI)[4] that would allow Congress to review and approve any executive branch action based on an alleged national security threat posed by a traded product before tariffs are implemented.[5] These additional legislative constraints would prevent presidents from continuing to use "national security" as an excuse to justify an array of trade restrictions that have little or nothing to do with protecting national security.

Two additional proposed bills to amend Section 232 were introduced in July 2019 by Rep. Joe Cunningham (D-SC) and Sen. Sheldon Whitehouse (D-RI). The Cunningham bill would give the Department of Defense a larger role in assessing national security threats and enable Congress to review and approve such actions.[6] Senator Whitehouse's bill would create a process by which U.S. businesses may request to be excluded from Section 232 import duties.[7]

With respect to Congressional delegations on trade liberalization, presidents must have the authority to negotiate trade agreements. Democrats should always support trade promotion authority — no matter who happens to be president. Any negotiating authority delegated to presidents must be accompanied by clear and specific instructions from Congress, and that authority must be limited to specific aims spelled out by Congress. Presidents must not be permitted by Congress to do whatever they wish on tariffs. By ending the open-endedness of statutes such as Section 301 and Section 232, and by modernizing trade promotion authority, Congress can go a long way toward reclaiming its constitutional authority over foreign commerce.

Repeal the Unilateral Tariffs Imposed by the Trump Administration

The president has claimed repeatedly that his unilateral tariffs under Section 301 are paid by the Chinese.[8] They are not. They are paid directly by importers and indirectly by Americans in the form of higher prices for much that they buy and make. An economic study published by the nonpartisan National Bureau of Economic Research (NBER) concluded that there has been a "complete pass-through of U.S. tariffs to import prices."[9] (Interestingly, according to their research, workers in heavily Republican counties have been the most negatively affected.)[10] The Trump tariffs on imported products have hurt American consumers by increasing the prices of retail goods and have harmed American manufacturers by increasing the prices of the inputs that go into making their final products. Another economic study published by NBER concluded that the Trump tariffs have "reduced real incomes (of Americans) by about $1.4 billion per month."[11] What is more, "Due to reduced foreign competition, domestic producer prices also increased."[12]

These tariffs under Sections 301 and 232 are hidden taxes. Because they are applied by the same percentage on products no matter who buys them, they are, like sales taxes, regressive taxes that fall most heavily on the middle class and on the poorest people. This is all the more reason why Democrats, who take pride in being champions of the poor, the workers, and the middle class, should oppose these tariffs and vote for their immediate repeal.

In addition, these taxes on imported products have prompted our trading partners to retaliate by imposing tariffs of their own on their imports of many U.S. products. This retaliation has hurt U.S. farmers, manufacturers, and other exporters, while adding even more to the costs that Americans are already paying because of protectionism. American taxpayers are, for example, paying billions of dollars in relief to farmers hurt by tariffs imposed on U.S. agricultural exports in retaliation against the Trump tariffs — farmers who would much rather sell their goods than be bailed out by taxpayers.[13]

A pro-trade policy must also support trade actions that are consistent with America's international treaty obligations and that do not circumvent or undermine them. It may be tempting to keep the Trump tariffs and try to use them as leverage to secure concessions from our trading partners in future trade deals — just as Trump has tried to do, largely unsuccessfully. But that would perpetuate the domestic economic damage caused by these tariffs while running counter to existing international treaty commitments in trade. Trump's tariffs are not only undermining the American economy, they are also undermining the American commitment to the rule of law in world trade, which is essential to continued and increased American prosperity.

The president's decision to use tariffs as leverage in seeking trade concessions from other countries is twice a mistake. First, the unilateral application by the United States of tariffs that are higher than those we have promised to levy in international trade agreements is illegal under international law and could lead to lawfully imposed economic sanctions by other countries on U.S. exports that could total billions of dollars in annual lost trade. Second, the assumption that the United States continues to have the economic leverage to bully other countries into submission on trade is founded on a world that no longer exists. The United States accounted for about half of the world's GDP in the halcyon days just after World War II, when the rest of the developed world was still devastated by the war and when what are now developing countries were not yet developing. Today, the United States accounts for a little less than one-fourth of the world's GDP.[14] A trade policy predicated on pushing other countries around is wrong. It also is inconsistent with what Americans are supposed to stand for. Further, it will not work. Eventually, other countries will push back and the American people will suffer the economic consequences.

When the United States approved the implementing legislation for the Uruguay Round trade agreements in 1994 and became a founding member of the WTO, it agreed to take all its trade disputes with other WTO members that fall within the scope of the treaty to the WTO for dispute settlement before taking any retaliatory trade action.[15] In many of the trade actions he has taken, Trump has ignored these treaty obligations.

One example stands out in the eyes of other WTO members: when enacting the implementing legislation for the Uruguay Round trade agreements in 1994, the United States stated its intention to refrain from using Section 301 unilaterally. For more than two decades, up until 2017, the United States remained true to this stated intent. No unilateral retaliatory actions were taken under Section 301. But without first going to the WTO, Trump cited Section 301 as the statutory authority for imposing tariffs on products imported from China. As the Chinese have alleged in a pending WTO dispute, these tariffs are in clear violation of U.S. obligations under the WTO treaty. (The retaliatory tariffs imposed by the Chinese on many U.S. exports to China may likewise be illegal.)

In addition, Trump has employed Section 232 as the statutory vehicle to justify the steel and aluminum tariffs applied to imports from many U.S. trading partners. The professed excuse for these metal tariffs is national security. Yet, what Trump poses as national security concerns are merely pretexts for protectionism.[16] It is doubtful that any trade-savvy American thinks that importing steel from our Canadian, Mexican, European, Japanese, and other friends and allies poses a threat to America's national security. The threat to our national security would be if we did not trade with our friends and allies.

This bogus national-security defense has put WTO jurists in a lose–lose position: either rule in favor of the United States and risk opening up a Pandora's Box of "anything goes" in the WTO when claiming a national security defense, or rule against the United States and risk that Trump will withdraw the United States from membership in the organization. The multilateral trading system thrived for more than 70 years without having to define what the national security defense means. Now, it is being compelled to answer a legal question that no one really wants answered.[17]

Trump and his trade negotiators have sometimes visibly and vocally — and sometimes surreptitiously — wielded the metals tariffs as cudgels in continuing trade negotiations. The president says, "I am a tariff man," and on numerous occasions has threatened to levy higher tariffs while attempting to bully other countries into bending to his will on other matters in trade negotiations.[18] To the extent that any such tariffs would exceed the bound rates pledged by the United States in the WTO, they would be illegal under the WTO treaty. Also, there is the question of whether bullying America's longtime allies and other trading partners by threatening illegal trade restrictions is in the long-term national interest of the United States.

The Trump administration has also, behind closed doors, intimidated a number of other countries into "voluntarily" accepting quotas on their exports of metals to the United States in exchange for being excused from the illegal U.S. tariffs. These export quotas are simply outlawed "voluntary export restraints" by another name. One of the aims of the Uruguay Round trade negotiations that led to the WTO treaty and to the establishment of the WTO was the abolition of the involuntary "voluntary export restraints" that were forced on small countries by the United States and other large countries in the 1970s and 1980s as a convenient device for protectionism. Voluntary export restraints are the trade form of a protection racket. They are rightly illegal under the WTO treaty, and the United States is acting inconsistently with its WTO obligations by insisting on them.[19]

What is more, these are all violations of international law and are subject to economic sanctions authorized by the WTO. The United States stands to lose an increasing number of pending WTO cases challenging these illegal trade actions and, unless they are thwarted by further manipulations by the United States of the dispute settlement process, are likely to reach judgment starting in 2021. Why should we care? In the aftermath of these legal losses, if these adverse rulings are adopted in dispute settlement, the complaining countries will be authorized by the WTO to impose lawful economic sanctions against the United States. These sanctions will consist of the withdrawal of previously granted trade concessions to the United States in what could add up to hundreds of billions of dollars in trade annually. These future trade losses would amount to far more than any conceivable gains the Trump administration may claim could result from its continued actions of circumventing and undermining the international treaty obligations that are upheld through the agreed legal framework of the WTO.

As part of a pro-trade policy for 2021, Democrats should disavow unilateral trade restrictions as illegal under international law where trade disputes fall within the scope of the WTO treaty. Democrats must work with willing Republicans to refrain from testing the outer limits of international obligations and return to a policy of restraint in international trade law and in international trade institutions.

Reaffirm the American Commitment to Multilateralism

Democrats must return to multilateralism in trade. They should reaffirm the longstanding bipartisan commitment of the United States to multilateral trade solutions and to the centrality of the multilateral WTO-based world trading system. Democrats should also recommit the United States to keeping all of its multilateral trade obligations while cooperating constructively with other WTO members to continue to strengthen the global trading system and free more trade worldwide.

Democrats are often supporters of multilateral solutions through international cooperation everywhere except in international trade. On climate change, on ocean preservation, on biodiversity, on hunger, on global health, on war and peace — on virtually every concern that transcends national borders, Democrats favor multilateral solutions. Now they must offer their support for multilateral cooperation toward solutions in trade as well.

Why cooperate? Because almost all the commercial and other economic issues that America faces flow across the artificial bounds of national borders. With each passing day, there are fewer public concerns that are not international in at least some respect. International cooperation is increasingly the only way to address these concerns effectively. Active engagement by the United States in international cooperation and its willing compliance with mutually agreed and mutually binding international rules are not obeisant sacrifices of our national sovereignty on the altar of some forbidding foreign suzerain. They are often the only ways in which we can make effective use of our national sovereignty.[20] In today's ever more globalized world, if we do not have ambitious, continuous, and effective international cooperation, then American national sovereignty will eventually become worthless because we will not be able to meet many of the challenges that will face us.

Why multilateralism? In trade, multilateralism is by far the best approach because it maximizes the mutual gains that can be derived from trade. At the core of the WTO-based world trading system is the international legal principle of "most-favored-nation" (MFN) treatment: a basic rule of non-discrimination that requires that any trade advantage granted by any one WTO member to any other WTO member must also be granted immediately and unconditionally to all other WTO members. The application of the MFN treatment obligation in multilateral trade negotiations under the auspices of the WTO multiplies the opportunities for mutual trade concessions that provide mutual trade benefits, and it maximizes the economic gains from trade agreements for all the countries that belong to the WTO.

However, the WTO treaty does not require that the further liberalization of trade occur only multilaterally. It offers additional practical means of moving forward on new trade issues as they arise through trade agreements that begin with adherence by some, but not all, WTO members and that can evolve to become fully multilateral agreements that include all WTO members. The use of this negotiating approach in the 1970s and 1980s led to the establishment of the WTO. It can be used now to overcome the long stalemate over many pressing and seemingly intractable trade issues that have long stymied global trade negotiators and that have caused the United States and other WTO members to look outside the legal framework of the WTO for trade solutions.

Why adhere to the MFN principle? Why not engage in trade discrimination by managing trade? The ever-present political temptation is for government to intercede in the market to manage trade. The temptation is to have the government dictate market outcomes — to substitute political judgment for the judgment of the marketplace. This is true in China. This is true in Europe and Japan, in India and Brazil. This is equally true in the United States, where Trump has demonstrated his abiding belief in managed trade. Lining up thousands of U.S. companies to beg government bureaucrats for exemptions from needless steel tariffs is statist (and some would say socialistic) managed trade.

Managed trade is contrary to the fundamentals of a free and open society. It violates the rights of those engaged in the free private enterprise that is the source of so much of American prosperity and that is indispensable to sustaining and enhancing American prosperity. Moreover, managed trade does not work. It distorts market decisions and, in so doing, it undermines the market innovations that are indispensable to attaining more prosperity, much less sharing in it. In contrast, free trade liberates the market by spreading innovations and by stimulating the domestic and foreign competition that inspires more innovations. Free trade makes possible more choices for individuals to decide for themselves how they will use their human freedoms in a free and open society.[21]

Managed trade encourages a transactional view of trade. But this type of approach does not create more trade. It mainly manipulates existing trade, moving it from place to place in contravention of the more productive efficiencies that would result from market-driven outcomes. A transactional approach also results in more trade discrimination. If, for example, China buys more soybeans from the United States while not increasing overall Chinese soybean consumption, then China will also be buying fewer soybeans from the European Union, Brazil, and its other trading partners — in violation of the core WTO most-favored-nation treatment obligation. American producers can equally be the victims of such illegal discrimination.

It is freer trade that creates more trade. By lowering barriers to trade everywhere, multilateral liberalization of trade boosts the volume of trade everywhere. Thus, the gains from trade are increased everywhere. Once trade barriers are lowered, each country can decide how best to distribute and make the most of its gains from trade domestically. In the United States, it is not in supporting free trade that we have erred; rather, it is in the failure to do all we should be doing to help more Americans share in the gains from trade. Instead of supporting managed trade, Democrats must support freer trade. Increasing and maximizing the gains from trade of the United States is essential to making it possible for all Americans to share in a more bountiful national prosperity.

In contrast to the current trade policies, the emphasis should not be on individual trade transactions; it should be on enhancing the prosperity of the American people by ensuring the survival and success of the WTO and other WTO-consistent bilateral and regional trading systems. For it is from such a systemic focus that the numbers and amounts of individual trade transactions can best be maximized. Above all else, what is needed in international trade is a mutually agreed and mutually upheld rule-based system that enables the freer flow of trade worldwide. As the core of a pro-trade policy, Democrats must support, strengthen, and ensure the continued global success of the WTO.

Renew the American Commitment to the Rule of Law in Trade

Democrats should work with other WTO members to find a multilateral solution to save the WTO's independent and impartial system for judging appeals in international trade disputes. By spreading misinformation and false accusations, stonewalling appointments to fill vacancies, and making draconian budget cuts, the Trump administration has eroded the credibility and possibly the existence of the WTO Appellate Body, which is the tribunal of final appeal in world trade. Because the Trump administration has refused to join in the required consensus of all WTO members to appoint new judges, the Appellate Body has been reduced to one judge; without the minimum of three required by the WTO treaty, the tribunal cannot accept any new appeals.

In its brief history of less than a quarter century, the WTO Appellate Body has become arguably the most significant and successful international legal tribunal in the history of the world. WTO rules have practical meaning only if they are upheld in ways that provide necessary security and predictability to the multilateral trading system.[22] Without the legal check of the Appellate Body, the risk of inconsistency in applying WTO rules rises. So, too, does the likelihood that countries that lose cases before WTO panels will appeal those rulings "into the void," to an Appellate Body that is no longer there, which in effect blocks enforcement of the rulings against them. The absence of an appellate process puts the fundamental integrity of WTO dispute settlement at risk and thus the continued flow of international trade that is channeled by the fair and effective functioning of the WTO-based trading system.

The framework of international rules that enable the freer flow of trade in the world will work only if the rules are followed and upheld through the international rule of law. As Americans were taught by Alexander Hamilton in the Federalist Papers, and as we have preached for decades to other countries throughout the world, the rule of law requires judges to be independent and impartial.[23] For this reason, WTO rules require both independence and impartiality from WTO judges. In rendering their decisions, these judges must not be influenced by any conflicting interests, including those of the 164 members that appointed them to serve the entire trading system.

No one would claim that WTO judges have ruled perfectly, just as no one would claim that about any other tribunal in the world. The act of exercising human judgment is, by its very nature, an act that falls short of perfection simply because it is a human act. Yet any errors the Appellate Body has made while judging hundreds of appeals do not support the unfounded U.S. charge of routine "overreaching" by the WTO appellate judges. The view, in the words of Trump's trade ambassador, Robert Lighthizer, and now widely accepted within the Washington Beltway, that members of the Appellate Body have a history of creating "new obligations out of whole cloth" has no basis in fact.[24]

Part of this fiction is comprised of "alternative facts" about the outcome of appeals in WTO trade disputes involving the United States. Trump has told the American people that the United States has lost "almost all the lawsuits" it has taken to the WTO.[25] According to one count, however, the United States has won 85.4 percent of the cases it has taken to the WTO, slightly more than the average for all WTO members.[26] On the other hand, the United States has lost 83.5 percent of the cases that have been brought against it in the WTO, slightly less than all other WTO members.[27]

Why these widely divergent percentages? One reason is that the United States and other WTO members do not take the geopolitical, commercial, and legal risk of bringing a WTO case unless they are highly confident that they have a winning case. Another reason is that the United States has lost a long string of frequently related WTO cases involving trade remedies because the United States has failed repeatedly to apply its antidumping, anti-subsidy, and other trade remedies consistently with WTO rules.

Trump and his trade advisers have condemned the Appellate Body but have been mute in explaining what they would prefer instead. Their silence on an explanation shows that what they really want is for WTO jurists always to rule as the United States wishes. They seek the rule of power and not the rule of law in the WTO.[28] Democrats must oppose Trump and his administration with respect to the WTO. They must see the facts as they truly are and commit to working with other members of the WTO to restore the full functioning of the WTO Appellate Body.[29]

Unquestionably, there is much in the WTO dispute settlement system that can be improved, but the improvements that are needed are largely not the changes sought by the Trump administration. Instead of perpetuating a trade policy that undermines the fairness and efficiency of the WTO dispute settlement system by crippling the Appellate Body, the rule of law in world trade should be reinforced by restoring the Appellate Body and strengthening it against future political assault.

Support the Modernization of the WTO

In addition to restoring the Appellate Body, Democrats should draw on the extensive experience of 25 years of working with the WTO and its dispute settlement process to update and improve the organization. Without question, the WTO dispute settlement system has been the most successful system ever devised for resolving international trade disputes, although it can certainly be improved in numerous respects. Moreover, improvements in dispute settlement must be only one item on an overall agenda for WTO reform that will help bring the WTO fully into the 21st century. In recommitting the United States to the centrality of the WTO in world trade, Democrats also must commit to more cooperation with other countries in updating the current multilateral trade rules and extending the existing multilateral trade framework. Instead of abandoning the WTO, which has taken more than 70 years to build, the United States must work with other countries to improve it in response to ever-new and ever-changing global trade realities.

Built up through round after round of global trade negotiations over the course of more than seven decades, the current scope of the WTO treaty is extensive and includes thousands of pages of rules and rulings that were agreed on and adopted by 164 members. The WTO rules apply to about 98 percent of all world commerce. There is, however, still need for negotiation and agreement on many longstanding issues of international trade. Trade-distorting agricultural subsidies that deny producers the benefits of their comparative advantages should be abolished. The remaining tariff obstacles to trade in manufactured goods should be eliminated. These and other important issues remain outstanding after the 15 years of multilateral trade negotiations in the Doha Development Round.

Since the conclusion of the WTO treaty, much has happened to transform world trade and the world economy. Although the WTO rules were written in the 20th century, most are still fit for the 21st century. But no small number of trade rules need updating and, in many aspects of contemporary commerce, new rules are very much needed. Democrats should support the negotiation of new and better WTO rules on digital trade, services trade, and intellectual property, all of which are areas of vast importance to American workers and businesses. New rules are needed to facilitate investment and to ensure free and fair competition. Better disciplines are required for trade-distorting subsidies, including new rules forbidding the favoring by WTO members of their state-owned enterprises. New rules also are needed to provide protections against forced transfers of technology, while encouraging the lawful spread to poorer developing countries of the new technologies they urgently need to confront environmental, health, and other global challenges. Rules are also needed to address product standards, technical regulations, and the proliferation of other non-tariff barriers that are increasingly substituted for tariffs and that pose protectionist obstacles to trade.

Ideally, these new and improved rules should be multilateral, applying to all WTO members from the beginning. Practically, though, it will doubtless be necessary to negotiate and agree on many of these needed updates through approaches within the WTO that include, at the outset, some but not all WTO members. This has often happened in the world trading system, and Democrats should lead in making it happen again. As was done in transforming the 1948–1994 General Agreement on Tariffs and Trade into the WTO, the better rules that result from these plurilateral negotiations can then be entered into force for member nations that have initially agreed to them and can afterwards be extended to eventually cover all WTO members once the worth of the new rules is demonstrated in the practice of the world marketplace.

Cordell Hull was a long-serving Democratic Congressman and Secretary of State in the Franklin Roosevelt administration who won the Nobel Peace Prize for his role in creating the United Nations. He wrote in his memoirs, "To be sure, no piece of social machinery, however well-constructed, can be effective unless there is back of it a will and a determination to make it work."[30] Missing in Trump's administration is the will and the determination to make the world trading system entrusted to the WTO work. The president and his trade team seem indifferent to whether the WTO-based trading system, in which Americans have invested more than seven decades of energy, ingenuity, and hope for a better and a more prosperous world, even survives. In the spirit of Hull, Democrats must make the multilateral trading system work by cooperating with our trading partners to modernize the WTO.

Seek Mutually Beneficial Trade Relations with China Under the Rule of Law

Crucial to maintaining and modernizing the multilateral trading system will be establishing and sustaining a mutually beneficial working and trading relationship between the United States and China. Achieving this goal is in the mutual interest of the United States, China, and the 162 other members of the WTO. For all his preoccupation with China, Trump has so far failed to achieve this goal and does not have a comprehensive strategy for achieving it. His "trade war" with China, comprised of mostly unilateral and illegal trade restrictions on imported goods from China, is a series of impulsive and improvisational salvos; it is not the implementation of a carefully considered overall strategy. The bilateral commercial conflict between the two major trading partners has harmed the economies of both while accomplishing almost nothing toward addressing the structural hurdles in China that frustrate its full compliance with its WTO obligations.

Democrats must have a strategy for China that encompasses all aspects of the complex American relationship with China. This includes American differences with China on human rights, global health, national security, and more. Yet, this strategy must proceed from an understanding that we live in a globalized world where both the United States and China can prosper the most only if the two countries find some way, despite their differences, of prospering together. We live, too, in a threatened world where such worldwide challenges as confronting pandemics, terrorism, cybersecurity, climate change, and biodiversity loss can be met only if the United States and China work together. In this world, part of the Democratic strategy for China must address American trade with China.

Unquestionably, there are genuine concerns about Chinese protectionist trade practices. These concerns must be addressed. We Americans have, however, always favored practical approaches that work. Trump's approach of using unilateral and illegal tariffs to intimidate China into changing its behavior has not worked. Democrats should abandon this approach and take a cooperative, constructive, and lawful approach to resolving legitimate concerns about Chinese trade practices.

Democrats should repeal the unilateral tariffs Trump has imposed on Chinese imports and refrain from imposing more. And, in concert with many other countries that have similar concerns about Chinese trade practices, they should refocus U.S. actions on using the legal remedies that are available in WTO dispute settlement and on negotiating more effective legal remedies where they do not yet exist. Only where a WTO remedy has been sought, and where China has chosen not to comply with a WTO ruling against it, should the United States impose economic sanctions on Chinese trade. And only where WTO rules do not exist — such as on many aspects of foreign direct investment — and where there are no bilateral or other treaty obligations, should the United States act unilaterally to counter discriminatory Chinese commercial practices.

As it now stands in the U.S.-China trade war, the tariffs imposed on more than $350 billion worth of Chinese goods imported into the United States are burdening the economies of both countries.[31] Caught in the vice of a no-win choice between fueling continued growth by priming the pump or, instead, tackling an ever-rising mountain of debt by limiting credit, the Chinese have already found that Trump's tariffs constrain their growth and complicate their economic decision-making. Now, with the additional and manifold economic and social pressures inflicted by the coronavirus pandemic, these constraints are even more confining. Meanwhile, in the United States, in 2018 American companies and consumers faced almost $69 billion in higher tariff costs.[32] Every month, these tariffs cost Americans an additional $3 billion in extra taxes and $1.4 billion in lost economic growth — revenues and growth that are sorely needed in the midst of the costly effects of the COVID-19 pandemic in the United States.[33]

The tangible result of all these tariffs has been an anomalous "managed trade" agreement between the United States and China, the so-called "phase one" deal that, amid the pandemic, seems less like a deal and more like wishful thinking. In contrast to the negotiating philosophy of both Republicans and Democrats in the past, the phase-one deal centers on achieving supposed guarantees of individual international trade transactions and not on altering the underlying trade arrangements that impede, and thus minimize, the flow of all international trade transactions. The Chinese commitments to make specific purchases of American agricultural and manufactured goods seemed unrealistic and unreachable even before the arrival of the pandemic. Now those commitments seem the stuff of fantasy.

Even if the Chinese commitments in the phase-one deal were realistic when they were made, and even if China had every intention of keeping those commitments, in the current circumstances China is probably incapable of keeping them. The deal contains a unilateral enforcement mechanism, but this mechanism seems better suited for closing markets than for opening them. Likely, the use of this mechanism would serve mainly as an excuse for ending the truce in the trade war and starting another round of tariffs and counter-tariffs between the two countries, thus adding more economic harm to both in addition to the extensive economic damage wreaked by the pandemic.

Contrary to the narrative offered by Trump and his trade negotiators, some WTO legal remedies for discriminatory Chinese trade actions do exist and are effective.[34] The Trump administration has simply chosen to ignore most of them and instead has tried to intimidate the Chinese with tariffs. These existing WTO legal remedies should be used by the United States. And, where WTO remedies do not yet exist, the United States should negotiate and agree on new remedies with other WTO members, including China. At the same time, Democrats should join with Republicans in applying a heightened scrutiny to Chinese investments in the United States and finding solutions to the very real threats of Chinese computer hacking, cyber theft, and commercial espionage that may fall outside the scope of the WTO treaty. These piratical practices, too, must be subjected to the international rule of law.

Further integrating China into the global trading system through full compliance with WTO rules is imperative. Since entering the WTO in 2001, the Chinese have made great progress in bringing their economy into compliance with most WTO rules. They have also, for the most part, complied with the WTO rulings rendered against them when they have lost cases in WTO dispute settlement. (In some respects, the Chinese have a better record of complying with adverse WTO rulings than the United States.) Overall, though, China continues to fall short of where it should be in fulfilling its trade obligations to the United States and other WTO members under the WTO treaty. China has benefited enormously from membership in the WTO, and it must do more to be fully deserving of that membership.

Full compliance by China with its WTO obligations will benefit the Chinese people more than anyone else. China should not be "contained."

Like any other country, it has every right to rise economically, to climb the ladder of comparative advantage and develop a more innovative, value-added economy driven by high-tech manufacturing. WTO rules do not prevent the economic rise of China, and Americans should welcome that. To be sure, America must do more domestically and internationally to compete with China economically, but it is neither right nor in America's interest to try to contain China economically. Through increased trade, investment, and other added economic ties between the two countries, increased Chinese prosperity can continue to help lift American prosperity, and vice versa. By far the greater concern for the United States should not be what will happen if China continues to rise economically; it should be what will happen if China does not rise.

The assault by the coronavirus has reminded us that it is imperative to maintain adequate local inventories of essential goods and materials, not least medical equipment and pharmaceuticals. Global supply chains come with productive efficiencies that can make needed goods more available and more affordable for everyone. Global supply chains also come with risks. Equally, the absence of diverse supply chains can pose risks. The solution is to minimize risks of all kinds. It is not to eliminate supply chains. In particular, a decoupling of the closely linked U.S. and Chinese economies, in part through a dismantling of the current supply chains that connect them, would deny to Americans and Chinese alike the continued and considerable gains in prosperity that will result from a substantial and mutually beneficial bilateral trade relationship.

For China, these gains would be enhanced through additional opening up and reform of the Chinese economy to make it more market oriented. Small and medium private enterprises "create 90 percent of the new jobs in China."[35] Private enterprise can be the source of sustained growth and offer a bright economic future for China. But the recent direction of Chinese economic policy has been toward consolidating more of the Chinese economy under ever tighter centralized state control, a trend heightened in China by the coronavirus pandemic. China can continue to rise only by continuing to open up its economy to the innovative productivity of a free market within an enabling framework of rules upheld by the rule of law.

Clearly, in its size and structure, China presents some unique challenges to the WTO-based trading system. But the challenges it presents are not altogether unique for the WTO. Nor are they entirely unanticipated under WTO rules.[36] To be sure, more and better rules must be negotiated to make certain that China participates fully and fairly in international trade. Yet WTO rules already exist that have not yet been used — and are waiting to be used — to discipline Chinese trade practices within the current WTO legal framework. For all its circumventions of WTO rules and criticisms of the organization, the Trump administration has not altogether ignored the remedy of WTO dispute settlement. It is, however, puzzling why more WTO cases have not been brought by the United States against China since its accession to the WTO in 2001, where legal remedies are already available.

A variety of discriminations in China's internationally controversial "Made in China 2025" program can be challenged successfully in the WTO under current rules. A case against the flagrant failures throughout China in the enforcement of intellectual property rights can be brought under existing WTO rules on intellectual property rights. China's failure to ensure the protection of the trade secrets of foreign companies can be the basis of a WTO complaint under an existing WTO intellectual property rule. Transfers of technology forced on foreigners by the Chinese government are inconsistent with an obligation in China's membership agreement in the WTO. Chinese requirements of domestic content in locally produced products are in violation of long-existing WTO rules. Likewise, many of the manufacturing and agricultural subsidies provided by the Chinese government to state-owned enterprises and other Chinese firms and entities are inconsistent with WTO current subsidies rules.[37] Conceivably, too, a systemic case could be brought against China on the basis that it has impeded the objectives of the WTO treaty and has nullified or impaired the benefits that other WTO members ought to be receiving under the treaty.[38]

Instead of taking illegal unilateral actions, Democrats must use these existing avenues in the WTO treaty for confronting many of the unfair Chinese trade practices. Currently, the administration contends that there is no legal recourse for the United States against China in the WTO, and it is using that fabricated excuse as justification for acting illegally outside the WTO. The United States must not go it alone in conducting trade relations with China. The European Union, Japan, Canada, and other WTO members share many of the same concerns as the United States about Chinese trade and would likely be willing allies in WTO negotiations and litigation. The United States should work closely with its allies and other trading partners instead of bullying them and insulting them. Multilateral actions are the best way to discipline unfair Chinese trade practices, ensure non-discriminatory treatment of our own goods and services, help provide more and better jobs for the American people, and help the Chinese people move more quickly toward creating the broader market economy that will bring them greater prosperity.

Support Bilateral and Regional Arrangements for Freer Trade

A Democratic policy that affirms the centrality of the WTO in expanding trade need not be a policy that relies on the WTO exclusively in expanding trade and the opportunities that can be derived from trade. Democrats should also support trade agreements with other countries whenever such agreements add to the volume of trade and to the commercial domain covered by the rules for trade. A free trade area between countries that belong to the WTO is permitted under WTO rules as an exception to the most-favored-nation treatment obligation that prohibits trade discrimination when it covers substantially all the trade between the area's members.[39] If poorly constructed, such agreements can impede or divert trade, but if they are well constructed they can be proving grounds for new approaches to trade that can be tried first bilaterally or regionally and then, once proven, be implemented globally.

Throughout the past quarter of a century, foremost among the free trade agreements of the United States has been the North American Free Trade Agreement (NAFTA) with our closest neighbors and major trading partners, Mexico and Canada. NAFTA created the world's largest free trade area, linking 470 million consumers in a $19 trillion market. Trade among the three countries has quadrupled under this treaty. Investment has multiplied fivefold. The U.S. Chamber of Commerce estimates that six million U.S. jobs depend on trade with Mexico and eight million jobs depend on trade with Canada. A narrow focus on bilateral trade deficits among the three countries can be misleading. For example, 40 percent of every dollar of the value of every good exported from Mexico to the United States is — in reality — the re-export back to the United States of something made in America by U.S. workers. For U.S. trade with Canada, the comparable figure is 25 percent. Workers and businesses in each of the three NAFTA countries are made more competitive worldwide through the integration of regional supply chains that create and sustain jobs throughout North America.[40]

After long assailing NAFTA, Trump has renegotiated it and rechristened it the United States-Mexico-Canada Agreement (USMCA). This new NAFTA is in many respects identical to the old one. In digital trade and a few other sectors, the new agreement incorporates long-needed improvements developed in the Trans-Pacific Partnership (TPP) — the regional trade agreement that Trump rejected in one of his first acts as president. Otherwise, however, the new provisions in the revised agreement fully justify the glaring omission of the words "free trade" in its new name. The new treaty is less of a free trade agreement and more of a managed trade agreement. All in all, the revised regional agreement could be called "NAFTA minus."

In particular, the new and esoteric rules of origin that impose stricter requirements of more domestic content in automobile production are classic examples of managed trade. These rules of origin replace market-based outcomes with the arbitrary dictates of politicians and bureaucrats. For U.S. consumers, the result will be fewer choices and higher-priced autos. For U.S. businesses, the result will be less global competitiveness. For U.S. workers, the result will be the short-term protection of some jobs in the U.S. auto industry at the expense of the long-term preservation and the innovative creation of many more jobs throughout the economy. These are always the costs of protectionism. This said, "NAFTA minus" is better than no NAFTA at all. And Democrats should, over time, endeavor to transform "NAFTA minus" into "NAFTA plus" by engaging in more negotiations with our friends and closest neighbors to the north and the south.

Democrats in Congress should take another look, too, at the Trans-Pacific Partnership, which was rejected by President Trump on his first day in office. With the United States on the sidelines, 11 other countries along the Pacific Rim have gone ahead to form the TPP without America, renaming it the Comprehensive and Progressive Agreement for Trans-Pacific Partnership (CPTPP). This partnership includes almost all the mutual trade commitments in the TPP agreement that was negotiated by Obama. A return by the United States to the treaty could be conditioned on agreement by the 11 other countries to implement about 20 provisions that were put on hold when Trump withdrew the United States, including intellectual property protections, safeguards against the illegal taking and trade of wildlife, and more.[41]

In the aftermath of rejecting the TPP, Trump has been trying to negotiate bilaterally many of the trade concessions that would have been secured in the TPP. Meanwhile, America's trading partners along the Pacific Rim, and especially those in Southeast Asia, are left to doubt our commercial and national commitment to the Pacific region as it becomes an ever-increasing part of the global economy and an ever more important factor in geopolitics. By becoming a part of the CPTPP, the United States can secure many trade benefits while also reassuring trans-Pacific allies and other trading partners that America has not retreated from that crucial crossroads of the world.

Democratic trade policy should also include support for other current and proposed trade arrangements, such as seeking broader trade liberalization with Japan. The Trump administration has signed a partial deal with Japan, but much work remains to be done. Democrats should move ahead with negotiations on a trade deal to eliminate the remaining tariff and non-tariff barriers to trade with the European Union, including on both agricultural and manufactured goods, and they should proceed with free trade negotiations with Brazil and Kenya, and perhaps with other Latin American and African countries. And Democrats should most certainly enhance America's commercial relations with the United Kingdom by early conclusion of a U.S.-UK free trade agreement. In all these endeavors, Democrats must insist on negotiating tactics that are firmly in support of U.S. trade interests but that do not descend into unseemly threats and bullying.

Moving forward, more attention will need to be given when negotiating and renegotiating all international trade agreements to a number of the so-called "trade and" issues that have met with mixed success in recent decades: "trade and labor," "trade and the environment," "trade and human rights," and more. Criticisms of WTO and other international trade rules and rulings on these "trade and" issues have often been incorrect or exaggerated, yet these are entirely legitimate concerns in 21st century world commerce.

The kinds of provisions to seek in trade agreements that would address these concerns could include those intended to improve working conditions and enhance environmental protections when making and trading goods. For instance, current trade agreements do not even mention climate change. Democrats could insist that current trade agreements and any new ones acknowledge the common global interest in pursuing trade in ways that are consistent with compliance with the Paris climate agreement and with accomplishment of the United Nations Sustainable Development Goals. As policy, such positions could help weave together

U.S. actions on several vital policy fronts into a consistent approach that could work affirmatively on all fronts. As a political tactic, such actions would also make it likely that more congressional Democrats would be willing to vote for trade agreements. The challenge, as always, would be in drawing the right lines that would promote trade while also taking seriously these other equally legitimate concerns.

Support Effective Domestic Actions to Enhance American Competitiveness

An increase in trade will produce the most prosperity for Americans — and for lower-income Americans even more than for those with the highest incomes — if it is accompanied by the many domestic initiatives that are needed to create more competitiveness. This approach alone will ensure that all Americans are empowered to compete in the new global economy. Only if Americans have the skills, the tools, and the enabling frameworks they need to compete will increased trade lead to a much broader sharing of the gains from trade and thus to a more widely shared prosperity. For this reason, a pro-trade policy must not be limited solely to trade policy. A commitment to achieving more openness in international trade must be one part of an overall strategy for legislation and governance that supports and secures the best from liberal, market-based capitalism while enabling the full flourishing of all Americans.

Openness is a prerequisite to competitiveness, but it does not guarantee it. Thus, in addition to openness, this comprehensive strategy must provide all Americans with an equal opportunity to achieve a personal competitiveness that can be maximized only if there is openness, because "openness alone does not lead to success. The competitiveness of economies in an integrated world [is determined by] how well they convert the potential created by access to global markets into opportunities for their ... people."[42] The opportunities offered by more trade will result in more freedom for all of us only if trade is accompanied by domestic actions that better enable all of us to make the most of more trade. An increased openness to more and freer trade internationally must be matched domestically by actions that open the way for more people everywhere to share in the gains from trade. Without such domestic actions, the gains derived from more and freer trade will be fewer, and those gains will be enjoyed by fewer people. All too often, in America and elsewhere, this is precisely what has happened so far in this century.[43]

During the past several decades, an increasing number of Democratic activists and members of the House and Senate have turned away from trade because they have mistakenly seen it as a cause of U.S. economic stagnation and anxiety. But domestic policy, not international trade policy, is largely to blame. Democrats should refrain from reflexively opposing trade and trade agreements. Instead, they should work to improve existing agreements and negotiate new ones in ways that address 21st century needs without descending into the false promise of protectionism. Simultaneously, they should focus on finding ways to reeducate, retrain, reemploy, and generally reengage American workers and communities that have been caught short by the relentless and disruptive march of technology and globalization. Democrats should do much more to help prepare the American people to compete in an increasingly integrated and technologically advanced global economy.

What are the needed domestic actions that would enhance American competitiveness in the trading world? The list is long. The alienation and distrust of Americans who feel abandoned by their elected representatives and the rest of their government has fueled the populist reaction against trade and globalization. The widespread failure of leadership — from both Democrats and Republicans — has contributed significantly to a misplaced opposition to free trade. But stopping trade will not restart job creation. Freeing trade will.[44]

Open economies are engines of growth. Closed economies decline and die. Competitiveness can only be maximized if there is openness.[45] The best path to competitiveness will vary from country to country, yet the basic ingredients of competitiveness are everywhere much the same. These ingredients include open trade and investment, supportive laws and institutions that enable open markets, and — to glue it all together — the rule of law. Equally essential are financial stability and fiscal solvency. What is more, the basic ingredients of competitiveness include maximizing the potential gains from trade and other economic endeavors — and thus the potential for the enjoyment of individual human freedom — by finding and combining the right mix of market and government actions.

The right line must be drawn everywhere between private and public, between markets and governments, between the necessity to preserve personal liberty and the necessity to empower it. In striving always to find this right line, we must provide: accessible lifelong education for both work and citizenship, beginning with essential and cost-saving investments in early childhood development; practical, skills-based training and other forms of transitional assistance, such as refundable tax credits for workers; modern and environmentally friendly roads, transit systems, water systems, bridges, seaports, airports, spaceports, communications, power grids, and all other kinds of infrastructure; a fair, limited, and broadly shared tax base; and strong protections for civil rights and worker rights. We must also do more to improve labor mobility; make health care more accessible and affordable; encourage basic scientific research and development; enable an economic atmosphere that supports individual and cooperative initiative, incentive, and enterprise; enforce antitrust laws that ensure ample market competition; and pursue other initiatives that help motivate new economic opportunities through an open economy in an open society.

We Americans cannot maximize our share of the future if we cling stubbornly to a past that no longer exists. One essential ingredient of sustaining and strengthening competitiveness is an openness to change. The embrace of freedom demands a willingness to undergo "the ordeal of change" for the sake of a better future.[46] For any individual, any enterprise, or any country to be competitive in shaping such a future, there must be a firm and unwavering understanding that, as Nobel Prize–winning economist Michael Spence put it, "Sustained growth and structural change go hand in hand."[47] To be successful in generating economic growth, free markets must be free, if need be, to reinvent the old and create the new.

The older sectors of our economy resist the creative destruction of capitalism.[48] They resist the idea of comparative advantage — the economic concept that we prosper most when we specialize in producing things that we produce relatively better than others. (Note the word "relatively" here, the oft-omitted core of this enduring concept.) As we have witnessed time and again, in trade policy and otherwise, those who derive power and profit from the status quo will seek to forestall change, even change for the better. The less-competitive parts of the economy will resist yielding to the arrival of the new, and they will often seek to survive by securing the subsidizing support and other favoritism of government through crony capitalism.

As Franklin Roosevelt said in 1932, "The same man who tells us that he does not want to see the government interfere with business ... is the first to go to the White House and ask the government for a prohibitive tariff on his product."⁴⁹ Entrenched economic interests that are no longer internationally competitive will do all they can to preserve their entrenchment while denying to themselves the incentivizing benefits of international competition and denying to others new opportunities resulting from new ideas, goods, and services that derive from increased trade and investment. All those engaged in the broader economy will pay the opportunity costs of this protectionism through higher costs, higher taxes, lost innovation, and lost job opportunities.

Conclusion

Whether or not Democrats win the presidency and control of the Congress in the next election, they should adopt a pro-trade agenda that centers on renewing support for trade as a policy that can benefit all Americans. They should restore the constitutional authority of Congress over international trade, and, at the same time, ensure the authority of the president to negotiate new trade agreements in accordance with the expressed will of Congress. To reset our currently fraught trading relationships, Democrats should immediately repeal all unilateral tariffs imposed on imports by the Trump administration under Sections 232 and 301. There must also be a new approach to trade with China, one that makes better use of existing rules and works with America's allies to develop new rules.

Democrats should also renew the United States' commitment to the rule of law in trade, including exclusive reliance on the WTO dispute settlement mechanism for resolving all trade disputes with other WTO members that fall within the scope of the WTO treaty, as well as support for the WTO's multilateral trading system. Democrats should disavow managed trade, support the basic WTO rules forbidding trade discrimination, and work with U.S. trading partners to restore the WTO Appellate Body as an independent and impartial tribunal for final appeals in WTO dispute settlement.

They should also work to reform the WTO by modernizing it as a fully 21st century international trade institution. This should be done, in part, by negotiating new and better WTO rules on digital trade, services trade, intellectual property protections, investment, competition, product standards and regulations, and more. Moreover, in addition to strengthening multilateral rules, Democrats should also negotiate new bilateral and regional trade agreements wherever needed to reduce trade barriers and serve as proving grounds for potentially new and improved global trade rules.

Lastly, to increase and distribute more widely the benefits of trade, Democrats must also undertake reform at home. Effective domestic actions to help all Americans make the most of the gains from trade by enhancing American competitiveness in the United States and in global markets are essential. Making it easier for Americans to innovate and compete at home and abroad is a crucial element to a continued and broadened American prosperity.

Endnotes

[1] Gabriel Felbermayr, Mario Larch, Yoto V. Yotov, and Erdal Yalcin, *The World Trade Organization at 25: Assessing the Economic Value of the Rules Based Global Trading System* (Gütersloh, Germany: Bertelsmann Stiftung, November 2019).

[2] Global Trade Accountability Act of 2019, H.R. 723, 116th Cong., January 23, 2019. An earlier version of this bill was introduced by Sen. Mike Lee (R-UT) in 2017 during the 115th Congress: *see* Global Trade Accountability Act of 2017, S. 277, 115th Cong., January 20, 2017.

[3] Trade Security Act of 2019, S. 365, 116th Cong., February 6, 2019. For the related House version of the bill, *see* Trade Security Act of 2019, H.R. 1008, 116th Cong., February 6, 2019.

[4] Bicameral Congressional Trade Authority Act of 2019, H.R. 940, 116th Cong, January 31, 2019. For the identical Senate version of the bill, *see* Bicameral Congressional Trade Authority Act of 2019, S. 287, 116th Cong., January 31, 2019.

[5] Both pieces of legislation were touted by Senate Finance Chairman Chuck Grassley in November 2019. *See* Chuck Grassley, "Grassley on 232 Tariff Reform," news release, November 5, 2019.

[6] Promoting Responsible and Free Trade Act of 2019, H.R. 3673, 116th Cong., July 10, 2019.

[7] American Business Tariff Relief Act of 2019, S. 2362, 116th Cong., July 31, 2019.

[8] Donald J. Trump (@realDonaldTrump), "For 10 months, China has been paying Tariffs to the USA of 25% on 50 Billion Dollars of High Tech, and 10% on 200 Billion Dollars of other goods. . . .," *Twitter*, May 5, 2019, 12:08 p.m., https://twitter.com/realDonaldTrump/status/1125069835044573186.

[9] Pablo D. Fajgelbaum, Pinelopi K. Goldberg, Patrick J. Kennedy, and Amit K. Khandelwal, "The Return to Protectionism," NBER Working Paper No. 25638, October 2019.

[10] Fajgelbaum, Goldberg, Kennedy, and Khandelwal, "The Return to Protectionism."

[11] Mary Amiti, Stephen J. Redding, and David Weinstein, "The Impact of the 2018 Trade War on U.S. Prices and Welfare," NBER Working Paper No. 25672, March 2019.

[12] Amiti, Redding, and Weinstein, "The Impact of the 2018 Trade War on U.S. Prices and Welfare."

[13] Alan Rappeport, "A $12 Billion Program to Help Farmers Stung by Trump's Trade War Has Aided Few," *New York Times*, November 19, 2018.

[14] This figure is without an adjustment for purchasing power parity. After adjustment, the figure for U.S. GDP is around 16 percent of world GDP. World Bank, Data, "GDP (current US$)," https://data.worldbank.org/indicator/NY.GDP.MKTP.CD.

[15] WTO Understanding on Rules and Procedures Governing the Settlement of Disputes, Article 23.1.

[16] Simon Lester and Huan Zhu, "Closing Pandora's Box: The Growing Abuse of the National Security Rationale for Restricting Trade," Cato Institute Policy Analysis no. 874, June 25, 2019.

[17] In the Russia — *Traffic in Transit* case, a WTO panel interpreted GATT Article XXI as a national security exception for the first time. That panel report was not appealed.

[18] Donald J. Trump (@realDonaldTrump), ". . . I am a Tariff Man. When people or countries come in to raid the great wealth of our Nation, I want them to pay for the privilege of doing so. . . ., Twitter, December 4, 2018, 10:03 a.m., https://twitter.com/realDonaldTrump/status/1069970500535902208.

[19] WTO Agreement on Safeguards, Article 11.1(b).

[20] Stewart Patrick, *The Sovereignty Wars: Reconciling America with the World* (Washington: Brookings Institution, 2018).

[21] James Bacchus, *Trade and Freedom* (London: Cameron May, 2004).

[22] WTO Understanding on Rules and Procedures Governing the Settlement of Disputes, Article 3.2.

[23] Alexander Hamilton, John Jay, and James Madison, *The Federalist* (New York: Modern Library, 1937). Originally in John Hamilton, *Federalist* no. 78 (1788), p. 502.

[24] Megan Cassella, "Lighthizer Launches His USMCA Charm Offensive," *Politico*, March 13, 2019.

[25] Donald Trump, interview by Lou Dobbs, *Fox Business*, October 25, 2017.

[26] Bryce Baschuk, "U.S. Keeps Winning WTO Cases, Despite Claim of Anti-U.S. Bias," *Bloomberg*, March 7, 2019; see also Simon Lester, "U.S. 'Wins' and 'Losses' in WTO Disputes," *International Economic Law and Policy Blog*, March 15, 2020.

[27] Baschuk, "U.S. Keeps Winning WTO Cases."

[28] *See* James Bacchus, "Might Unmakes Right: The American Assault on the Rule of Law in World Trade," Centre for International Governance Innovation, CIGI Papers no. 173, May 18, 2018.
[29] Bacchus, "Might Unmakes Right."
[30] Cordell Hull, *Memoirs of Cordell Hull* (New York: MacMillan, 1948).
[31] Chad P. Bown, "Phase One China Deal: Steep Tariffs Are the New Normal," Peterson Institute for International Economics, *Trade and Investment Policy Watch*, December 19, 2019.
[32] Fajgelbaum, Goldberg, Kennedy, and Khandelwal, "The Return to Protectionism."
[33] Mary Amiti, Stephen J. Redding, and David Weinstein, "The Impact of the 2018 Trade War on U.S. Prices and Welfare," Centre for Economic Policy Research, Discussion Paper DP 13564, March 2, 2019.
[34] For a detailed discussion of these available WTO remedies, *see* James Bacchus, Simon Lester, and Huan Zhu, "Disciplining China's Trade Practices at the WTO: How WTO Complaints Can Help Make China More Market Oriented," Cato Institute Policy Analysis no. 856, November 15, 2018.
[35] Keith Bradsher and Chris Buckley, "Facing Slowing Economic Growth, Chinese Premier Promises Relief for Business," *New York Times*, March 4, 2019.
[36] For a somewhat different view, *see* Mark Wu, "The 'China, Inc.' Challenge to Global Trade Governance," *Harvard International Law Journal* 57, no. 2 (Spring 2016), 261–324.
[37] For details, *see* Bacchus, Lester, and Zhu, "Disciplining China's Trade Practices at the WTO."
[38] "2018 Annual Report to Congress," U.S.-China Economic and Security Review Commission," November 2018; and *Multilateral Economic Institutions and U.S. Foreign Policy, Before the Subcommittee on Multilateral International Development, Multilateral Institutions, and International Economic, Energy, and Environmental Policy of the Senate Committee on Foreign Relations*, 115th Cong., 2nd Sess. (November 27, 2018) (testimony of Jennifer Hillman, Professor, Georgetown Law Center).
[39] General Agreement on Tariffs and Trade 1994, Article XXIV:8(b).
[40] See, for example, Carla A. Hills, "NAFTA's Economic Upsides: The View from the United States," *Foreign Affairs*, January/February 2014; and James Bacchus, interview by Paul Owens, "NAFTA at 20: U.S. Jobs Engine," *Orlando Sentinel*, January 7, 2014.
[41] Jeffrey J. Schott, "TPP Redux: Why the United States Is the Biggest Loser," Peterson Institute for International Economics, *Trade and Investment Policy Watch*, January 23, 2018.
[42] Global Agenda Councils on Competitiveness and Trade and FDI, *The Case for Trade and Competitiveness* (Geneva: World Economic Forum, 2015), p. 6.

⁴³ James Bacchus, *The Willing World: Shaping and Sharing a Sustainable Global Prosperity* (Cambridge: Cambridge University Press, 2018), pp. 84–90.
⁴⁴ Global Agenda Councils, *The Case for Trade and Competitiveness*, p. 4.
⁴⁵ Organisation for Economic Co-operation and Development, *Towards a More Open Trading System and Jobs Rich Growth* (Paris: OECD, 2012), p. 2.
⁴⁶ Eric Hoffer, *The Ordeal of Change* (New York: Harper and Row, 1952).
⁴⁷ Michael Spence, *The Next Convergence: The Future of Economic Growth in a Multispeed World* (New York: Farrar, Straus and Giroux, 2011), p. 67.
⁴⁸ Spence, *The Next Convergence*.
⁴⁹ "Speech to the Commonwealth Club of San Francisco," quoted in Edmund Fawcett, *Liberalism: The Life of an Idea* (Princeton: Princeton University Press, 2014), p. 270.

Chapter 7

The Black Hole of National Security: Striking the Right Balance for the National Security Exception in International Trade[*]

Introduction

Article XXI of the General Agreement on Tariffs and Trade (GATT) reserves for members of the World Trade Organization (WTO) the legal authority to restrict trade in goods to protect members' "essential" security interests. Similar exceptions to WTO trade obligations exist in other WTO agreements. For more than seven decades, WTO members exercised self-restraint in invoking these exceptions, doing so only for narrow purposes and in truly exceptional circumstances to avoid pushing the boundaries of the law too far and thereby upending the delicate balance between members' legitimate pursuit of their security interests and their obligations to reduce barriers to trade. Yet, trade restrictions justified on national security grounds have proliferated in recent years and are increasingly subject to litigation in WTO dispute settlement. As a result, the national security provisions contained within the WTO agreements, as well as fundamental questions about the nexus between trade and national security, are set to

---

[*]This essay was previously published by the Cato Institute as James Bacchus, "The Black Hole of National Security: Striking the Right Balance for the National Security Exception in International Trade," Cato Policy Analysis No. 936 (November 9, 2022).

be tested and clarified by WTO jurists — a less than ideal outcome that could lead to the further undermining of WTO dispute settlement and the rules-based international trading system more broadly.

This essay explains the origins of the national security exceptions in the GATT and the WTO agreements and the history of their invocation, summarizes recent litigation that has clarified these exceptions, discusses current developments and upcoming litigation that could prove pivotal to our understanding of the trade-security nexus and the future of the world trading system, and offers some concluding thoughts on the options available to WTO members for striking a balance between trade liberalization and the defense of national security.

The Russian Invasion of Ukraine

The Russian invasion of Ukraine has raised numerous questions about the efficacy of international law. One question involves the mounting number of trade sanctions that have been imposed on Russia in response to its egregious actions. How can a long-standing exception to the basic rule of non-discrimination in trade law — for measures taken for reasons of "national security" — be respected without permitting it to turn the world trading system into a black hole of an exception that becomes the new rule? And further: how can this be accomplished while maintaining the multilateralism that has long been the hallmark of that rule-based system, which is overseen by the WTO?

Even before Russia invaded Ukraine on February 24, 2022, the "national security" exception had been increasingly invoked in recent years, principally by the U.S. government under former president Donald Trump. International trade has been increasingly viewed in numerous countries not only as a mundane matter of buying and selling goods and services across international borders but also as a vital matter affecting national defense. Many factors have led to this change in perspective. First, more and more WTO members turned inward and away from further trade liberalization in the wake of the global financial crisis that began in 2008. Second, the final collapse of the Doha Development Round of WTO trade negotiations in Nairobi in 2015 further slowed liberalization. Third, commercial and security issues became increasingly blurred with the development of new technologies amid rising geopolitical competition between China and Russia on the one hand and the United States, the other NATO countries, Japan, and their global allies on the other.

With Russia's criminal aggression against Ukraine, this gradual trend has suddenly been accelerated by a spate of retaliatory trade sanctions imposed by NATO and other countries on a panoply of Russian goods and services, and all of the sanctions are claimed to be actions taken for reasons of national security.[1] Banning and otherwise putting imports of Russian products at a disadvantage in competition with imports of like traded products from other WTO members is inconsistent with the fundamental most-favored-nation obligation in the WTO treaty. The sanctions are therefore excused under international trade law only if they fit within the bounds of the national security exceptions in the treaty.

Member nations' increasing reliance on the WTO's national security exceptions marks a profound change for the WTO. For three quarters of a century, the world trading system flourished almost entirely without disputes over the nexus between trade and national security. Today, more than a dozen international disputes are pending in the WTO dispute settlement system in which the national security exception has been invoked, most of them challenging unilateral steel and aluminum tariffs applied by the former Trump administration for what it claimed were national security reasons.[2] In resolving these pending disputes by clarifying the meaning of the national security exception, WTO jurists must, of course, acknowledge the sovereign right generally of WTO members to make their own determinations about what is best for their national security. Yet, they must do so in a way that acknowledges and affirms the treaty obligation that such determinations must remain *exceptions*. These actions must not become the norm. If that happens, the very foundation of the multilateral trading system will be undermined, and international trade will plummet into a black hole in which the exceptions will become the rules.

The National Security Exceptions

Article XXI of the General Agreement on Tariffs and Trade (GATT), which relates to trade in goods and is part of the WTO treaty, provides in full:

Security Exceptions
Nothing in this Agreement shall be construed

(a) to require any contracting party to furnish any information the disclosure of which it considers contrary to its essential security interests; or

(b) *to prevent any contracting party from taking any action which it considers necessary for the protection of its essential security interests*
  (i) relating to fissionable materials or the materials from which they are derived;
  (ii) relating to the traffic in arms, ammunition and implements of war and to such traffic in other goods and materials as is carried on directly or indirectly for the purpose of supplying a military establishment;
  (iii) *taken in time of war or other emergency in international relations*; or
(c) to prevent any contracting party from taking any action in pursuance of its obligations under the United Nations Charter for the maintenance of international peace and security.[3]

Two largely identical provisions are found elsewhere in the WTO treaty: Article *XIVbis* of the General Agreement on Trade in Services (GATS), relating to services trade, and Article 73 of the Agreement on Trade-Related Aspects of Intellectual Property Rights (TRIPS Agreement), relating to the treatment of intellectual property. GATT Article XXI has been in force since the original agreement on the GATT in 1947. GATS Article *XIVbis* and TRIPS Article 73 were added in 1995 when the scope of the trading system was broadened to include services and intellectual property.[4] For the most part, until recently, all three of these treaty provisions have not been the subject of clarification in WTO dispute settlement. Members have invoked the exceptions — for example, in required member notifications or Trade Policy Reviews — but narrowly and not in ways that caused any major disagreements among members (such as during actual armed conflicts or to restrict trade in weapons and related technologies).

The exceptions offer affirmative defenses in WTO dispute settlement. A WTO member claiming the defense will do so in response to a legal complaint that the member's actions are inconsistent with its obligations under the WTO treaty. As with other exceptions to WTO obligations, the member claiming the defense has the burden of proving it is entitled to it. Thus, the defense has relevance only in the context of dispute settlement. Before it can be asserted, another member must first begin legal proceedings based on that member's contention that there is a treaty violation. Historically, members of the multilateral trading system have hesitated to initiate such legal actions in WTO dispute settlement in deference to the fundamental significance of questions of national security and national sovereignty.

The Origins of the Exception and Longstanding Practice

The modern debate over the intersection of trade and national security began during and immediately after World War II as the United States and its allies conceived and constructed the architecture of the postwar liberal international economic order. GATT Article XXI is one pillar of that architecture. In the United States, the internal debate at the time was about where to set the line between ensuring the opportunity for American goods to have more access to foreign markets while reserving an appropriate amount of discretion for necessary actions to safeguard American national security. This internal debate occurred in parallel with some of the first internal U.S. deliberations on what would soon become the Cold War with the Soviet Union.

Indeed, it was the United States that played by far the largest role in crafting the language that ultimately became Article XXI. Most of the 22 other original contracting parties to the GATT had no difficulty in accepting the text for the exception proposed by the United States. The historical record reflects that the negotiating parties, including the United States, assumed that the availability of the exception in any specific instance would be a question for determination under the terms of the new trade agreement. It is clear from the negotiating history that, at the time, the United States did not view the Article XXI exception as a mechanism to excuse all restrictions on trade that might be labeled by the country imposing them as national security measures.[5] Quite the opposite. As Daria Boklan and Amrita Bahri wrote in the *World Trade Review*:

> The drafting history of GATT Article XXI shows that most contracting parties engaged in GATT negotiations, including the U.S. negotiators, had never intended the security exception to be construed in a purely self-judging manner. On the contrary, they advocated that national security and trade liberalization should coexist in a balanced manner and national security should not be construed in a subjective manner so as to allow free flow of trade between members.[6]

The crux of the dilemma over the national security exception, then and now, was perhaps best expressed by one of the lead American negotiators on the GATT back in 1947, who said at the time: "It is really a question of a balance. We have got to have some exceptions. We cannot make it too tight, because we cannot prohibit measures *which are needed purely for security reasons*. On the other hand, we cannot make it so broad that, under the guise of security, countries will put on measures which really have a commercial purpose."[7] In other words, despite what the United States is insisting now, there is no blanket national security exception. The language of the exception in the treaty is meant to reflect a balancing of two potentially competing and conflicting interests: lowering barriers to trade and maintaining national security.

The balance that the GATT negotiators struck in crafting the national security exception for trade in goods remains today in the language of Article XXI. Unavoidably, determining how to strike that balance in particular instances includes an element of judgment that is left to independent and impartial WTO jurists. Yet, having even the most objective of trade jurists making judgments on matters ostensibly relating to national security is less than ideal. For that reason, the GATT contracting parties, and later the members of the WTO, long did all they could to make such judgments unnecessary. They attempted to resolve any trade-related national security questions through negotiations outside the trade dispute settlement process and by keeping express invocations of national security exceptions to a minimum.

Mutual restraint is too little valued as essential ballast for upholding the rule of law, domestically and internationally. Judicial restraint is much to be valued; but so, too, is restraint by those who would compel judges to make judgments — especially on the most difficult legal questions. It is best not to test the outer boundaries of any international agreement — not to pursue the extreme case. In making decisions about how far to go legally when trying to prevail in any one dispute, short-term political pressures should yield to long-term considerations about preserving the rule of law and the institutional system that strives to uphold it. It is tempting to want to prevail in the trade dispute at hand, but doing so by pushing rules to the outer bounds of their legal limits may not always be the best course overall and for the long term, including for the complainant in that dispute.

For many decades, mutual restraint was exercised on GATT Article XXI. The nexus between trade and national security did not become an issue in the world trading system largely because the members of the system refused to allow it to become one.[8] They understood that, with respect to the nuances of the terms of international agreements, some questions are better left unasked, for if they are not asked, they will never need to be answered. This was true for many years regarding the national security exception. Having struck a balance in the language of the exception, the members of the trading system did not want to test that balance. They were content to not know the answers to the unasked questions. It would have been best if this restraint had continued for another 75 years. But that did not happen. Instead, where that balance lies is now at the center of the global trade debate.

Recent WTO Dispute Settlement on the National Security Exception

The Trump steel and aluminum tariffs are mostly responsible for moving the national security exception to center stage in trade — an outcome that WTO members, including the United States, had spent decades trying to avoid. Those unilateral tariffs did not, however, give rise to the first WTO dispute leading to a judgment on the nature of the exception. Instead (and interestingly, given recent events) that first dispute was brought by Ukraine against Russia over Russian measures imposed between 2014 and 2018 that restricted Ukraine from using transit routes across Russia for traffic destined for markets in Central Asia. Ukraine claimed the Russian actions were inconsistent with Russian obligations under Article V of the GATT, which requires freedom of transit for traffic in traded goods.[9] Russia did not deny this or bother to address Ukraine's factual and legal claims. Instead, Russia simply claimed the shelter of the GATT exception for national security. In 2019, a WTO panel ruled in favor of Russia by acknowledging Russian entitlement to the national security defense based on the facts of that dispute.[10]

More important than the outcome of this dispute between Ukraine and Russia, however, was the way in which the panel reached its conclusions. Some of the unanswered questions about Article XXI were answered in the panel report. Others were not. In some respects, the answers the panel gave raised still more questions about other legal nuances of the exception. In the aftermath of this panel ruling, the contentious disputes about the meaning of Article XXI have by no means ended. Given the backload of similar disputes still winding their way through the WTO dispute settlement system, these disputes are only beginning. Yet, for the most part, the legal reasoning and legal rulings by the panel in the *Russia — Measures concerning Traffic in Transit (Russia — Traffic in Transit)* dispute provide a firm foundation for further clarification of Article XXI.

Perhaps the most important question that was resolved by the panel in the *Russia — Traffic in Transit* dispute was the threshold question of whether a WTO panel has the legal authority to judge a WTO trade dispute when the affirmative defense of the national security exception is invoked by a WTO member responding to a legal complaint by another member. Russia claimed that the national security exception is self-judging — that a WTO member cannot be second-guessed by WTO jurists when the member claims it is acting in defense of its national security. Therefore, Russia argued that only Russia could decide what was necessary to protect its own security interests, a decision the panel should, in Russia's view, accept.[11]

The United States, a third party to the dispute, agreed with Russia, despite what the U.S. GATT negotiators had said when the GATT was written about the need for a balance in the exception between national security and commercial interests.[12] In contrast to its original view, the bipartisan view of the United States in recent decades has been that such disputes are non-justiciable in the WTO because, the United States contends, WTO jurists do not have the authority to question trade restrictions when the country imposing them maintains that they are imposed for national security reasons; the mere invocation of the defense is sufficient to establish it. The four most recent American presidential administrations, two from each party, have agreed — the second Bush administration, the Obama administration, the Trump administration, and now the Biden administration.

For their part, Australia, Brazil, China, the European Union, Japan, and other third parties to the dispute between Ukraine and Russia disagreed.[13] They contended that the panel did have the legal authority to rule in the dispute, although they urged the panel to proceed carefully because such a sensitive systemic matter was at issue. As some of the third parties essentially did, one might ask the following question in response to the assertion that Article XXI is self-judging: If the national security exception is self-judging, then why bother to limit the circumstances in which it is available in the text of Article XXI? For that matter, if this exception is self-judging, why is Article XXI in the treaty at all? The customary rules of interpretation of public international law must be used when clarifying the obligations in the WTO agreement in WTO dispute settlement. This is required by the dispute settlement rules written by the WTO members as instructions for WTO jurists. These customary rules dictate that if a provision is included in a treaty, it must have a meaning, and that meaning must be accorded to it by those who are entrusted with clarifying it. In the WTO, those so entrusted are the WTO jurists.

The panel in the *Russia — Traffic in Transit* dispute decided that the Russian measures at issue were justified under Article XXI because of the fraught factual circumstances that existed at the time between Ukraine and Russia, and it determined that the measures were "taken in a time of war or other emergency in international relations." But the panel disagreed with Russia and the United States on the preliminary question of the justiciability of the dispute. The panel agreed with Ukraine and the third parties mentioned previously that it had the legal authority to decide the case.[14] While acknowledging that WTO members have very broad discretion in invoking Article XXI, the panel ruled that such invocations are nevertheless subject to review by WTO panels. Acknowledged implicitly in this ruling is that the balance struck in the text of Article XXI can only be upheld if such a measure (characterized as a national security measure by the member imposing it) can be reviewed in WTO dispute settlement. If this were not so, then, as Peter Van den Bossche and Werner Zdouc have expressed, Article XXI would be "prone to abuse without redress."[15]

WTO law is not self-contained; it is a part of broader public international law.[16] A basic principle of public international law is that international agreements must be carried out in good faith.[17] Indeed, it is "perhaps the most important principle, underpinning many international legal rules."[18] In addition to ruling that it had the authority to judge the case, the panel in the *Russia — Traffic in Transit* dispute reasoned that, while WTO members have much discretion in invoking the national security defense, that discretion is not without bounds. It has limits under the international legal requirement of good faith. The panel ruled that this principle of good faith mandates that Article XXI not be used as a means of circumventing WTO obligations.[19]

In relying on the good faith principle, the panel in the *Russia — Traffic in Transit* dispute was not embarking on new legal ground in the WTO. It was echoing previous statements by WTO jurists, including the WTO Appellate Body, which has declared the good faith principle to be:

> A general principle of law and a general principle of international law, [which] controls the exercise of rights by states. One application of this

general principle, the application widely known as the doctrine of *abus de droit*, prohibits the abusive exercise of a state's rights. . . . An abusive exercise by a Member of its own treaty right thus results in a breach of the treaty rights of the other members and, as well, a violation of the treaty obligation of the Member so acting.[20]

With this principle of good faith in fulfilling the terms of international agreements in mind, recall the most relevant language in Article XXI:

> Nothing in this Agreement shall be construed . . . (b) to prevent any contracting party from taking any action which it considers necessary for the protection of its essential security interests . . . (iii) taken in time of war or other emergency in international relations.[21]

Based on its close reading of this treaty language, the panel in the *Russia — Traffic in Transit* dispute concluded that the phrase "which it considers necessary" confirms that a WTO member has the sole discretion in "taking any action . . . for the protection of its security interests." Significantly, though, the panel ruled that this singular discretion under the introductory language of Article XXI(b) does not extend to the determination of the circumstances in the subparagraphs under (b).[22] Thus, it does not extend to a determination under subparagraph (iii) of whether such a measure is "taken in a time of war or other emergency in international relations." That is a question that can be judged; it is a question for a legal determination by a WTO panel when the issue is raised in WTO dispute settlement. In the *Russia — Traffic in Transit* dispute, the panel judged that the Russian action was justified; in another dispute involving different facts, another panel could reach another result.

Significantly, too, the panel in the *Russia — Traffic in Transit* dispute observed that "war is one example of the larger category of 'emergency in international relations,'" and that an emergency in international relations encompasses "all defense and military interests, as well as maintenance of law and public order interests." The panel emphasized that "political or economic differences between members are not sufficient, of themselves, to constitute an emergency in international relations for the purposes of subparagraph (iii) . . . unless they give rise to defense and military interests, or maintenance of law and public order interests."[23] In effect, then, the *Russia — Traffic in Transit* panel may have excluded political and economic differences from the scope of "essential security interests."

In addition, the panel ruled that there must be some nexus between the measure taken and the "essential security interest" that the member seeks to serve by applying it. One element of good faith is that the restrictive trade measure in dispute must not be an "implausible" means of protecting the security interest in question.[24] Not just any measure restricting trade can be employed to pursue an "essential security interest." The measure must help further the "essential security interest." (Thus, it appears that former president Trump and his administration were overreaching — to say the least — in contemplating trade restrictions on imports of automobiles from two of America's allies, Germany and Japan, for supposed reasons of national security. If Americans can trust these countries to stand with us in times of military conflict, if we can trust them to risk their very lives for us, then why can we not trust them to sell us automobiles?)[25]

With its rulings in the *Russia — Traffic in Transit* dispute, the panel did not, technically, establish precedents. There is no law of precedent in the WTO or in other public international law. Yet, in keeping with their obligation under the WTO Dispute Settlement Understanding to provide "security and predictability to the multilateral trading system," WTO jurists generally try to maintain consistency in clarification of WTO obligations.[26] If they did not, uncertainty about the meaning of trade rules — or worse, conflicting interpretations of them — would impede the flow of world trade. Products are more likely to be traded if WTO members have certainty about how their products will be treated by their trading partners. Minimizing uncertainty about the meaning of the rules to ease and speed the flow of trade, and thereby increase the volume of trade, was the motivation of WTO members in stressing the necessity for providing "security and predictability" in the world trading system through the dispute settlement rules in the WTO treaty.

Although the panel ruling in the *Russia — Traffic in Transit* dispute was not appealed to the WTO Appellate Body, the panel was chaired by a distinguished former member of the Appellate Body, Georges Abi-Saab, who is also one of the world's most prominent scholars on public international law — adding further credence to the ruling. Furthermore (and surely not coincidentally), the reasoning of the panel in that dispute is in many respects persuasive, and thus it seems likely that much the same line of reasoning will be followed by other WTO jurists in pending and forthcoming WTO disputes involving Article XXI. So far, this is what has occurred. In the one dispute since the *Russia — Traffic in Transit* ruling involving a national security defense assertion that was resolved in WTO dispute settlement, the WTO panel largely followed the reasoning of the previous panel.

In 2017, before *Russia — Traffic in Transit*, the government of Saudi Arabia cut off all contact between it and the citizens and firms of Qatar, which the Saudis claimed was harboring and supporting terrorists. Among other results, the "anti-sympathy" measures the Saudis imposed on Qatar prevented Qatari holders of intellectual property rights from having access to Saudi courts to protect those rights when they were abused by a Saudi company. In the *Saudi Arabia — Measures concerning the Protection of Intellectual Property Rights* dispute, Qatar claimed that this refusal of access, in effect, denied its IP right holders the due process and other protections they are accorded under the TRIPS Agreement. Saudi Arabia invoked the national security defense under Article 73 of the TRIPS Agreement.[27] The relevant language of TRIPS Article 73 is identical to the relevant language of GATT Article XXI, namely:

> Nothing in this Agreement shall be construed . . . (b) to prevent a Member from taking any action which it considers necessary for the protection of its essential security interests . . . (iii) taken in time of war or other emergency in international relations.[28]

In its ruling, which was rendered after that in the *Russia — Traffic in Transit* dispute, the panel in the dispute between Saudi Arabia and Qatar echoed the reasoning of that previous panel: it acknowledged the extent of the breadth of the discretion reserved in the TRIPS national security exception for a determination by a WTO member of what "it considers necessary for the protection of its security interests." The panel found that, because the Saudi measures had been taken during a time of severed relations between the two countries, they had been "taken in time of . . . emergency in international relations." The panel concluded, however, that the Saudis had not demonstrated that their refusal to apply criminal remedies to a Saudi company for violation of the IP rights of a Qatari company was plausible as a necessity to their "essential security interest" of protecting themselves from terrorism and extremism. It found "no rational or logical connection" between the two.[29] Thus, in the first rejection of an assertion of a national security defense by a member of the WTO, the panel ruled in favor of the claimant, Qatar.

As one reason for its ruling, the panel pointed to multiple third-party submissions in the dispute by WTO members whose rights were also affected by the challenged Saudi measure. Thus, the panel evidently found third-party arguments such as the following made by the European Union to be persuasive:

> When assessing the necessity of the measure, and particularly the existence of reasonably available alternatives, the Panel should ascertain whether the interests of third parties which may be affected were properly taken into consideration. Thus, the European Union would appreciate if Saudi Arabia could provide a plausible explanation of the reasons why "it considers necessary" to allow the systematic infringement of the intellectual property rights of EU right holders in order to protect its essential security interests.[30]

It can be expected that future panels will follow the same or similar reasoning when third-party rights are affected.

Notably, like the *Russia — Traffic in Transit* panel, the *Saudi — IP* panel rejected the argument that the matter of national security is non-justiciable by WTO jurists. The United States reiterated the argument it had made in the previous dispute that the panel had no legal authority to rule in the new dispute. However, of the 13 WTO members that filed third-party submissions, only Bahrain agreed with the United States. The *Saudi — IP* panel adopted the same line of reasoning on this threshold issue as did the previous panel, and it appears likely that future panels will do the same, no matter how ardently the United States may continue to contend this point (again, contrary to its original position).

The Trade Sanctions Against Russia

In the wake of the Russian invasion of Ukraine, numerous WTO members have imposed economic sanctions — including trade sanctions — against Russia. These range from higher tariffs to outright trade bans to a complete repeal of normal trade relations. These discriminatory trade sanctions are generally inconsistent with various WTO obligations, including the basic obligation of each WTO member to provide most-favored-nation treatment to like imported products of every other WTO member.[31] That raises the issue of whether the trade sanctions against Russia can be excused because they fall within the boundaries of the national security exception in the WTO treaty.

Yes, they can. Indeed, these sanctions seem tailor-made to fit within those legal boundaries. This is not a situation involving ostensibly ominous Mercedes-Benz automobile imports into the United States from America's longtime ally, Germany. This is not former president Trump's pretend prosperity and peace. This is a situation of grave global concern. With military conquest in mind, and in violation of the Charter of the United Nations, Russian troops have been sent into the neighboring country of Ukraine by Russian president Vladimir Putin.[32] They have engaged in scorched-earth warfare there against Ukrainian soldiers and civilians alike, and, despite recent Ukrainian successes in turning the Russians back, they remain there now, occupying cities, continuing their aggression, and reportedly engaging in war crimes.[33] The Russians have a large arsenal of nuclear weapons, and Putin has made increasingly bellicose threats to use them.[34]

Without question, these are circumstances in which any other country in the world could reasonably consider that trade and other economic sanctions are "necessary for the protection of its essential security interests." Without question, too, these are circumstances that constitute a "time of war or other emergency in international relations." So long as there is some legitimate nexus between the measure taken and the "essential security interest" that the member applying the trade sanction against Russia seeks to serve by applying it, that member should be able to meet the burden of proving its entitlement to the national security exception in WTO dispute settlement.

The very existence of GATT Article XXI (and its companions in the services and intellectual property agreements) is evidence that, in conceiving and writing the rules in the WTO treaty, member nations clearly contemplated that a situation such as the one the trading system faces now might occur and that trade sanctions against an errant member could be the result. The proliferation of trade sanctions against Russia is therefore not a harbinger of the breakup of the WTO-based multilateral trading system; rather, it is an event that fits within the legal framework of that system, highly regrettable for the system but nevertheless clearly foreseen in its construction. The Russian trade sanctions pose a new challenge for the WTO, but this challenge can be met within the legal framework of the existing trade dispute settlement system.[35]

Whether Russia will file any legal complaints against these trade sanctions in WTO dispute settlement is, at the time of writing, not yet known. Russia threatened at one point to withdraw from the WTO, but the Russian Foreign Ministry has since said that withdrawal is not being considered.[36] In June 2022, Russia threatened to respond to Lithuania's ban on the shipment of Russian goods by rail through Lithuania to the Russian Baltic city of Kaliningrad. The response Russia had in mind, though, appeared to be the imposition of retaliatory trade sanctions against Lithuanian products, and not legal action in WTO dispute settlement.[37] Regardless of what Russia may do in engaging in WTO dispute settlement, any WTO cases brought by Russia that challenge the current trade sanctions Russia faces will not be the next cases to clarify further the national security exception in WTO dispute settlement.

Striking the Right Balance on the National Security Exception

The next WTO cases to address the national security exception will be a series of pending cases against the United States. All the questions about the availability and scope of the national security exception will gain clarity when WTO panels render their rulings in the pending disputes against the United States arising from former president Trump's unilateral steel and aluminum tariffs. It is long past due for WTO panels to render these rulings. If they have been procrastinating in the hope that the geopolitical context would improve, that hope has been in vain.

These long-awaited panel rulings are a sword of Damocles hanging over the WTO: if the rulings are against the United States, it is not at all clear that the Biden administration will accept them. In such an event, Biden's trade team may be reduced to reiterating some of the dubious claims by the previous administration about the supposed misdeeds of WTO jurists, further poisoning the view of the WTO held by Congress and, thanks to much misinformation, widespread in the country as a whole. A refusal by the United States to comply with the rulings by removing the steel and aluminum tariffs would only further embolden all the destructive forces that seek to undermine trade multilateralism. The door would be opened anew to the rule of power instead of the rule of law in international trade.

In all likelihood, the United States — having emptied the bench of the Appellate Body of any judges because of its bipartisan frustration that the Appellate Body will not do its bidding in trade remedies and other cases — will nevertheless and hypocritically exercise its right to appeal any rulings against it. That will put these disputes into a legal abyss because the members of the WTO will be unable to adopt those panel rulings. The U.S. treaty violations will likely continue even if they have been found by WTO jurists not to be justified by a national security defense. This may be one reason why the Biden administration continues to be reluctant to engage seriously with other WTO members on appointing new members to the Appellate Body.

Should the United States refuse to comply with an adverse WTO panel ruling on national security, the stability and integrity of the WTO dispute settlement system will be further undermined. The United States will be the culprit. Yet, it was the United States that led the way in creating the system and, despite what a growing number of American politicians in both parties may think, the United States has as much interest in maintaining the success of the system as any other member of the WTO, if not more. Membership in the WTO system has boosted annual U.S. GDP by about $87 billion since the establishment of the WTO — more than for any other country.[38] Further undermining the WTO dispute settlement system will further undermine the institution as a whole. The WTO will be shunted still further from its rightful place at the center of world trade.

This raises the obvious and crucial question: How to prevent the potential undermining of the dispute settlement system and avoid the consequent marginalization of the WTO.

Clearly, the inclination of most members of the WTO is toward inertia — continuing to present claims of national security defenses on a case-by-case basis in dispute settlement. In the two cases brought against Russia and Saudi Arabia, WTO jurists have shown that they are capable of judging such cases and that they can reach the right result. Overall, their line of reasoning seems appropriate. Even so, as Simon Lester and Inu Manak have written, "To some extent, a Member's declaration that a measure is for national security purposes could be taken as a statement that it will not change the measure even in the face of a WTO DSB [Dispute Settlement Body] ruling against it. As a result, there may be limits to the effectiveness of litigation in this area."[39] The cumulative institutional cost to the WTO from resolving such disputes through litigation will be considerable.

Despite the sensitivities involved in such disputes, some WTO members may be inclined to accept adverse WTO judgments when their assertion of an exception for national security is declined by WTO jurists.

In their own national utilitarian calculation, they will conclude that the costs of not complying with such a judgment will outweigh the benefits. But this will likely be the exception. In most cases, a member facing an adverse judgment will likely ignore it or render it moot by appealing the decision to an Appellate Body that is not there because it has no appointed judges. If the United States (or China, the European Union, or some other large trading country) chooses not to comply with a WTO judgment against it when it claims a defense of national security, other WTO members will do the same. Assertions of national security defenses will continue to proliferate and a black hole created by the national security exception will beckon as more and more WTO obligations will be overridden by what is meant to be only an exception.

The alternative to litigation is negotiation. Conceivably, WTO members could come together to identify what they perceive as the balance contained in the national security exception. Lester and Manak have suggested that negotiations should establish an ongoing Committee on National Security as part of the institutional structure of the WTO "to address the growing challenges to the trade regime presented by national security measures." More specifically, they have noted: "One solution that is always available is to rebalance the obligations as between the parties involved in the conflict, in the form of compensation and suspension of concessions or other obligations as temporary measures." Toward this end, they point to the rebalancing that is permitted in the context of safeguard measures restricting imports, which (as their advocates generally neglect to mention) are applied in the absence of any allegation of an unfair trade practice.[40] Indeed, China and the European Union have treated the unilateral U.S. steel and aluminum tariffs as though they are safeguard measures and, on that basis, have, in response, "rebalanced" by imposing restrictions on U.S. imports.

Clearly, negotiation is the preferred approach to finding a solution that will be satisfactory for all WTO members. But how likely is negotiation? Russia is in limbo in the WTO, a *de facto* pariah, pointedly ignored by virtually all other WTO members in WTO councils.[41] The United States may also cling to its current insistence that the WTO has no say whatsoever whenever a WTO member invokes a national security defense. It is hard to imagine any circumstances in which the United States would then be willing to negotiate about the national security exception. And what of China? The Chinese government has joined with others as a third party in the two disputes and has thus far taken the position that the national security exception is not self-judging. Whether China will maintain its current position when it wishes to assert a national security defense remains to be seen.

One critical question that ought to be addressed through negotiation instead of further litigation is whether there is any circumstance besides actual war and other martial conflict that could conceivably be considered an "emergency in international relations." The ruling by the panel in the *Russia — Traffic in Transit* dispute that the scope of such emergencies includes "all defense and military interests, as well as maintenance of law and public order interests" omits all purely economic measures. This is the most cautious clarification of the national security exception, and there are good reasons to think it is the correct one.

Yet are these wholly non-commercial military situations truly the only kinds of emergencies in international relations that fall within the legal scope of the national security exception? Increasingly, the line between domestic economic and national security measures has been blurred in the 21st century global economy as continued technological advances have had important national security and commercial implications. Dispute settlement is less than ideal for discerning this line. But could negotiation help identify the right balance and add clarity to how the line is reflected in the national security exceptions in the WTO treaty — or will that task continue to be left to WTO jurists in further dispute settlement, with unforeseeable consequences? This is merely one of the many critical and complex questions that must be asked and answered by the WTO, ideally through negotiations.

Conclusion

It is far better to negotiate than to litigate. Indeed, it would have been far better to have negotiated on these and other important nuances of the national security exception some time ago when it first became apparent that, after decades of mutual restraint, WTO members were beginning to contemplate seriously the widespread use of such trade restrictions for the first time. Perhaps some of the current consternation could have then been avoided and the WTO members might not have found themselves caught in a geopolitical vise between the illegal Trump tariffs on one side and the legal trade sanctions against Russia on the other. Nor would they be squeezed as they are now by competing understandings of the limits imposed by the exceptions on actions taken by WTO members for what they see as national security reasons. But that opportunity was missed.

In 2015, two years before Donald Trump became president of the United States and began to set aside what had long been the U.S. policy of restraint on invoking the national security exception, another member of the WTO "requested that WTO members engage in negotiations on the scope of the rights and obligations under Article XXI of the GATT 1994 and Article XIV*bis* of the GATT and adopt by June 2016 a General Council decision on the interpretation of these provisions."[42] At the time, the other WTO members declined to engage in the requested negotiations. In yet another irony given the circumstances within the trading system today, the WTO member that made that request was Russia. Perhaps, belatedly, WTO members will now change their minds and negotiate.

Endnotes

[1] Michelle Toh et al., "The List of Global Sanctions on Russia for the War in Ukraine," *CNN Business*, February 28, 2022.

[2] Recent WTO disputes involving national security elements include eight complaints against the United States in *United States — Certain Measures on Steel and Aluminum Products*, filed in 2018 by China (DS544), India (DS547), the European Union (DS548), Norway (DS552), Russia (DS554), and Switzerland (DS556). Cases challenging the U.S. steel and aluminum tariffs brought by Canada (DS550) and Mexico (DS551) have been settled. In addition, there have been five complaints involving Qatar as a complainant or a respondent, two filed in 2019 (DS567 and DS576), one filed in 2018 (DS526), and two filed in 2017 (DS527 and DS528); four disputes between Russia and Ukraine, one filed in 2020 (DS499), one filed in 2019 (DS512), and two filed in 2017 (DS525 and DS532); and a complaint, filed in 2019, by South Korea against Japan (DS590). For a thoughtful exploration of the rationale of the United States in using Section 232 of the Trade Expansion Act of 1962 in applying the unilateral trade restrictions challenged in these pending WTO disputes, *see* Scott Lincicome and Inu Manak, "Protectionism or National Security? The Use and Abuse of Section 232," Cato Institute Policy Analysis No. 912, March 9, 2021.

[3] The General Agreement on Tariffs and Trade (GATT), Article XXI. (emphasis added)

[4] World Trade Organization (WTO), General Agreement on Trade in Services, Article 14bis; and WTO, Agreement on Trade-Related Aspects of Intellectual Property Rights, Article 73.

⁵ For a thorough and enlightening historical account of the negotiation and approval of GATT Article XXI, see Mona Pinchis-Paulsen, "Trade Multilateralism and U.S. National Security: The Making of the GATT Security Exceptions," *Michigan Journal of International Law* 41, no. 1 (2020): 109–193.

⁶ Daria Boklan and Amrita Bahri, "The First WTO's Ruling on National Security Exception: Balancing Interests or Opening Pandora's Box," *World Trade Review* 19 (2020): 132.

⁷ "Second Session of the Preparatory Committee of the United Nations Conference on Trade and Employment, Verbatim Report: Thirty-Third Meeting of Commission A, Held on Thursday, July 24, 1947, at 2.30 P.M. in the Palais de Nations, Geneva," United Nations Economic and Social Council, E/PC/T/A/PV/33, July 24, 1947, p. 21. (emphasis added)

⁸ Although national security was invoked on several occasions before 2019, no panel report on the topic was ever adopted.

⁹ The GATT, Article V. Ukraine also claimed the Russian measures were inconsistent with Article X of the GATT, which requires the transparency of rules and regulations, and with several provisions of the Russian accession agreement to membership in the WTO.

¹⁰ "*Russia—Measures concerning Traffic in Transit*," Report of the Panel, World Trade Organization, WT/DS512/R, April 5, 2019.

¹¹ *Ibid.* p. 38, para. 7.57.

¹² *Ibid.* Report of the Panel, Addendum, World Trade Organization, WT/DS512/R/Add. 1, April 5, 2019, pp. 106–110.

¹³ *Ibid.* Addendum, pp. 69–110.

¹⁴ *Ibid.* p. 51, para. 7.104.

¹⁵ Peter Van den Bossche and Werner Zdouc, *The Law and Policy of the World Trade Organization* (Cambridge, U.K.: Cambridge University Press, 2017), p. 620.

¹⁶ See "*United States—Standards for Reformulated and Conventional Gasoline*," Report of the Appellate Body, World Trade Organization, WT/DS52/AB/R, April 29, 1996.

¹⁷ The Latin phrase for this principle is *pacta sunt servanda*.

¹⁸ Malcolm N. Shaw, *International Law* (Cambridge: Cambridge University Press, 2003), p. 97.

¹⁹ "*Russia—Measures concerning Traffic in Transit*," p. 56, paras. 7.132–7.133.

²⁰ "*United States—Import Prohibition of Certain Shrimp and Shrimp Products*," Report of the Appellate Body, World Trade Organization, WT/DS58/AB/R, October 12, 1998, pp. 61–62, para. 158.

²¹ The GATT, Article XXI.

²² "*Russia—Measures concerning Traffic in Transit*," p. 50, para. 7.101.

²³ *Ibid.* p. 41, paras. 7.72 and 7.74–7.75.

²⁴ *Ibid.* p. 57, para. 7.138.

25 Paul Krugman, "Trump Is Abusing His Tariff Power, Too," *New York Times*, January 23, 2020.
26 Understanding on the Rules and Procedures Governing the Settlement of Disputes (DSU), Article 3.2.
27 "*Saudi Arabia—Measures concerning the Protection of Intellectual Property Rights*," Report of the Panel, World Trade Organization, WT/DS567/R, June 16, 2020.
28 The GATT, Article XXI.
29 "*Saudi Arabia—Measures concerning the Protection of Intellectual Property Rights*," p. 123, para. 7.292
30 *Ibid*. Report of the Panel, Addendum, World Trade Organization, WT/DS567/R/Add. 1, p. 64, para. 21.
31 The GATT, Article I.
32 Charter of the United Nations, Article 4.2. "All Members shall refrain in their international relations from the threat or use of force against the territorial integrity or political independence of any state, or in any other manner inconsistent with the Purposes of the United Nations."
33 Glenn Thrush, "Garland, Visiting Ukraine, Names Prosecutor to Investigate Russian War Crimes," *New York Times*, June 21, 2022.
34 David E. Sanger and William J. Broad, "Putin's Threats Highlight the Dangers of a New, Riskier Nuclear Era," *New York Times*, June 1, 2022.
35 For some interesting observations on these legal issues, *see* Mona Pinchis-Paulsen, "Characterizing War in a Trade Context," *Opinio Juris* (blog), March 10, 2022.
36 "Russia's Withdrawal from the WTO Not Being Considered," *Interfax*, June 16, 2022.
37 "Russia Vows to Respond to Lithuania's Ban on Goods Transit," *Associated Press*, June 21, 2022.
38 Gabriel Felbermayr, Yoto V. Yotov, and Erdal Yalcin, "The World Trade Organization at 25: Assessing the Economic Value of the Rules Based Global Trading System," Bertelsmann Stiftung, November 2019, p. 33.
39 Simon Lester and Inu Manak, "A Proposal for a Committee on National Security at the WTO," *Duke Journal of Comparative and International Law* 30 (2020): 272.
40 *Ibid*. pp. 269 and 272.
41 Sarah Anne Aarup and Ashleigh Furlong, "Russia Takes First Steps to Withdraw from WTO, WHO," *Politico*, May 18, 2022.
42 Van den Bossche and Zdouc, *Law and Policy of the World Trade Organization*, p. 622.

Chapter 8

Might Unmakes Right: The American Assault on the Rule of Law in World Trade*

Introduction

As Thucydides taught in his Melian Dialogue, there are always those who believe that might makes right. The human struggle has long been to prove that it does not. Our tool in this struggle is the rule of law. Through the rule of law, right becomes might. Long a champion of the international rule of law, the United States of America, under the leadership of President Donald Trump, has embraced the belief that might makes right, and is using its might to unmake right by assaulting the rule of law in world trade. Trump, and those who serve him, are taking illegal, unilateral actions and pursuing other trade policies that circumvent and threaten to undermine the rules-based world trading system. They are also engaged in a stealth war against the continued rule of law in the World Trade Organization (WTO) dispute settlement system through intimidation of those who serve at the apex of the system: the judges on the WTO Appellate Body. The other members of the WTO must not yield to the unilateral ultimatums of the Trump administration or to its actions of intimidation that threaten to halt WTO dispute settlement.

---

*This essay was previously published by the Centre for International Governance Innovation as James Bacchus, "Might Unmakes Right: The American Assault on the Rule of Law in World Trade," CIGI Papers No. 173 (May 2018).

In the near term, the other WTO members should circumvent the recalcitrance of the United States by using arbitration under article 25 of the WTO Dispute Settlement Understanding as an alternative form of WTO dispute settlement. In the long term, they should eliminate the possibility of intimidation of WTO judges by the United States, or by any other country, by removing the design flaw of the possibility of reappointment to a second term for any member of the WTO Appellate Body. At the same time, the Appellate Body should be recast as a full-time, standing tribunal of judges who will serve longer single terms and will have the resources sufficient to improve the performance of the WTO dispute settlement system. These changes in the WTO in the near term and in the long term will prevent might from unmaking right in world trade.

The Timeless Appeal of Might Makes Right

In 416 B.C., after nearly two decades of intermittent conflict, the Peloponnesian War between Athens and Sparta was going badly for the Athenians.[1] The moderate and the temperate no longer held sway in the unruly popular assembly in Athens. Reason had succumbed to the impulses of passion. An ancient form of populism prevailed. Alone, the Greek inhabitants of the tiny Aegean island of Melos had "stubbornly maintained their independence" and their neutrality, and had refused to join the Athenian-led league.[2] This "allowed them to enjoy the benefits of the Athenian Empire without bearing any of its burdens."[3] Today, we would say that Melos was a "free rider."

As recalled by Thucydides, the great historian of that long-ago conflict, those leading Athens, frustrated with their endless war and fed up with Melos, sent a military expedition to bring Melos forcibly into the Athenian empire. The Melians accused the invading Athenians of coming "to be judges in your own cause" and asked what would happen to them "if we prove to have right on our side and refuse to submit."[4] Bluntly, coldly, succinctly, the Athenians replied, "You know as well as I do that right, as the world goes, is only in question between equals in power, while *the strong do what they can and the weak suffer what they must.*"[5]

In other words, might makes right.

Firmly believing they were in the right, the Melians refused to submit. The Athenians then besieged Melos for a number of months. As Thucydides tells it, eventually the siege was "pressed vigorously," and "the Melians surrendered at discretion to the Athenians, who put to death all the grown men whom they took, and sold the women and children for slaves, and subsequently sent out five hundred colonists and settled the place themselves."[6] The Athenians did what they could to the Melians simply because they could. In the dispute between Athens and Melos, might, in the end, did make right.

Because of Thucydides, we still remember today, millennia later, what would be "an otherwise forgotten act of aggression."[7] No one has ever done more to explain why we need the international rule of law. What is known as his Melian Dialogue illustrates the danger of the arbitrary exercise of power in the absence of the rule of law. The timeless lesson it teaches is that, in the unending struggle between right and might, right can make might only if the strong are not the judges of their own cause and only if the strong and the weak are made "equals in power." This is only possible through the rule of law. The rule of law equalizes the strong and the weak by establishing and upholding rules that apply equally to all and that treat all equally before the law. The arbitrariness of power is thus replaced by the security and the predictability of impartial rules enforced by impartial judges.

The American Turn to Protectionism and Mercantilism

Today, the Athenian generals are once again invading Melos, and once again their aim is to prove that might makes right. This time, sadly, these invaders are from the United States of America. This time they are seeking to make might into right in the judicial rulings on the treaty obligations of WTO members in the internationally agreed rules of the WTO. Since its transformation from the General Agreement on Tariffs and Trade (GATT) into an international institution in 1995, the WTO has done much to establish the rule of law in international trade, and thus has done much also to accord reality to the cooperative global enterprise of establishing the international rule of law overall. These institutional achievements are due in no small part to the United States' steadfast support through the years for the mission and the work of the WTO. But now, American support for the WTO is much in doubt as one manifestation of the ascendancy of a plutocratic populist with protectionist inclinations to the presidency of the United States.

If there is one consistency among all the myriad inconsistencies in the distorted worldview of President Donald Trump, it is his opposition to free trade. Trump has long been a full-throated (if ill-informed) voice for protectionism. If there is another consistency in his generally erratic thinking, it is his disregard for global cooperation through multilateralism. He prefers confrontation to cooperation. Thus, he has long been an exponent of unilateralism — of the short-term view that the best choice for Americans is to abandon or ignore the international institutions that Americans have done so much to help create and, instead, go it alone in global affairs, sure in the knowledge that the economic and martial might of the United States can be used as leverage to get other countries in the world to do as the United States desires.

Given these personal predilections of the president of the United States, it should come as no surprise that, in his first 16 months in office, he has made no secret of his utter disdain for the WTO and for the architecture of international cooperation through multilateralism that created and sustains it. He has been increasingly vocal about his preference for one-on-one bilateral trade deals, in which the United States can often impose its will on smaller countries, over the multilateral regional and global deals that produce vastly more gains from trade for everyone and that have, in the past, been generally preferred by US presidents, Republican and Democrat alike. Global and other "mega" trade deals are equally and almost universally preferred by economists, trade advocates and, not least, all the 163 other countries that, like the United States, are members of the WTO.

In his tumultuous first 16 months in the White House, Trump has abandoned the Trans-Pacific Partnership, negotiated and signed by his predecessor with 11 other countries on the Pacific Rim. Finding the negotiations with the European Union on a proposed Trans-Atlantic Trade and Investment Partnership in impasse when he took office, he has left them in a frozen limbo. Following repeated campaign threats to unravel and perhaps even withdraw from the North American Free Trade Agreement (NAFTA) with Mexico and Canada, he has entered into trade negotiations with America's two closest neighbors, with the ostensible goal of modernizing NAFTA, but in which the US negotiating position seems to be largely "my way or the highway" with shrill, tweeted threats of a US pullout still heard. He has coerced South Korea into renegotiating the recent Korea-US Free Trade Agreement at a time when tensions remain high on the Korean Peninsula. In going alone, increasingly, Trump and those who serve him have left the United States standing alone in world trade — with not one new bilateral trade deal to show to his supporters as he approaches the half-way point of his first term as president.

In a presidency increasingly clouded by criminal investigations and hindered by instability in politics and in policy, President Trump's advocacy of protectionism in trade has been one of the few constants. Now he has moved from threats to actions, and these actions have displayed a deep and disturbing indifference on the part of the Trump administration to the constraints of the rules-based world trading system overseen by the WTO. In early March, the president employed a long-unused provision of the US Trade Expansion Act of 1962 — section 232 — to impose 25 percent tariffs on imports of steel and 10 percent tariffs on imports of aluminum.[8] In late March, he used a long-abandoned provision of the US Trade Act of 1974 — section 301 — to impose up to US$60 billion in tariffs on imports of about 100 products from China in retaliation for what the United States sees as costly widespread infringement in China of US intellectual property rights.[9] In the midst of taking these two actions, the president boasted that he was striking back at "free-trade globalists."[10]

In acting unilaterally under both section 232 and section 301, the Trump administration has not bothered to go first to the WTO to seek a remedy for the allegedly unfair actions of US trading partners it claims to be addressing. This is a violation by the United States of international trade law. Where the matters in dispute fall within the scope of the WTO treaty, taking unilateral action without first going to WTO dispute settlement for a legal ruling on whether there is a WTO violation is, in and of itself, a violation of the WTO treaty. Article 23.1 of the WTO Dispute Settlement Understanding (DSU) establishes mandatory jurisdiction for the WTO dispute settlement system for all treaty-related disputes between and among WTO members.[11] The WTO Appellate Body has explained, "Article 23.1 of the DSU imposes a general obligation to redress a violation of obligations or other nullification or impairment of benefits under the covered agreements only by recourse to the rules and procedures of the DSU, and *not through unilateral action*."[12]

The United States has not abandoned WTO dispute settlement altogether. The Trump administration continues to defend complaints made against the United States in the WTO, and it has also initiated a few complaints. In 2017, the United States filed a complaint against Canada relating to measures of the province of British Columbia governing the sale of wine in grocery stores.[13] In March 2018, while busy also imposing the unilateral trade restrictions under sections 232 and 301, the United States requested consultations with India on a range of Indian export subsidies.[14] Further, in its trade confrontation with China, the Trump administration has filed one WTO complaint, alleging that the Chinese are violating WTO intellectual property rules by failing to enforce the patent rights of foreign patent holders.[15] At the same time, the United States has refrained from initiating additional and broader WTO cases against Chinese intellectual property practices, instead preferring to pressure China with steep unilateral tariffs.[16] And, tellingly, the United States has not followed through to pursue a WTO complaint filed against Chinese aluminum subsidies by the Obama administration just one week before Trump's inauguration.[17] Instead, the president chose to levy the unilateral tariffs outside the legal framework of the WTO.

As president, Trump has increasingly recycled his campaign rhetoric that the WTO is "horrible" and has reiterated his campaign threat to withdraw the United States from membership in the WTO. It can only be hoped that this is merely a hollow threat. Even with so capricious a president and so self-destructive a presidency, a formal American pullout from the WTO would be an economically suicidal move. If President Trump does decide to pull the United States out of the WTO, then every other country in the world with which the United States does not have a free trade agreement will be free to discriminate against all American trade in goods and services in any way it chooses. The United States has free trade agreements with just 20 countries.[18] In contrast, US next-door neighbor Mexico has concluded free trade agreements with 45 countries.[19] Therefore, more than 140 members of the WTO will be given a free pass to discriminate against all US trade if the United States leaves the WTO.

Freedom from such trade discrimination is one vital benefit to the United States and to every other member of the WTO from having agreed in the WTO treaty to be bound by the foundational rule of most-favored-nation (MFN) treatment. The MFN obligation is at the heart of the WTO-based world trading system and can be traced back six centuries to 1417 as the fundamental tool for lowering barriers to international trade.[20] As a core of the GATT, this basic trade rule of non-discrimination has prohibited discrimination between and among the like traded products of other countries for the past 70 years, and has thereby lowered barriers to trade and helped lift the flow and the value of world trade by trillions of dollars annually throughout those seven decades.[21] The president's secretary of commerce, Wilbur Ross, has cast aspersions on the operation in the WTO of the MFN rule, calling it a "significant impediment to anything like a reciprocal agreement."[22] His knowledge of what would happen to US trade without the security blanket of the MFN rule outside the legal shelter of the WTO may be one reason for his preemptive criticism of the rule. Someone should explain to the current occupant of the White House, albeit belatedly, "This, Mr. President, is how MFN works."

At various times during his first 16 months in office, President Trump and assorted members of his new administration have threatened to withdraw from the WTO, ignore the WTO, go around the WTO and refuse to comply with adverse WTO rulings.[23] At home, these and his many other threats to disrupt trade and dismantle trade agreements have thrilled his economic nationalist political base. In Geneva, these threats have generated both dismay at the US renunciation of its long bipartisan tradition of supporting international trade rules and trade and other international institutions, and mystification at what, setting aside the rhetoric, the actual unfolding trade policy of the United States might be. A peculiar combination of US disregard and indifference to the WTO by President Trump has only added to the long-standing difficulties of the members of the WTO in concluding trade negotiations on almost anything. At the WTO Ministerial Conference in Buenos Aires, Argentina, more and more of those from other countries who are engaged in the work of the WTO were asking, "What does the United States want?" With the United States largely on the sidelines, very little of note was agreed in Buenos Aires.

On September 19, 2017, in his first speech to the United Nations, President Trump (in between threatening to destroy North Korea and casting doubt on the legal right of the United Nations to second-guess sovereign states) took time to rail against the WTO without directly mentioning it. "For too long," he said, "the American people were told that mammoth multinational trade deals, unaccountable international tribunals, and powerful global bureaucracies were the best way to promote their success. But as those promises flowed, millions of jobs vanished and thousands of factories disappeared."[24] The president cited no evidence, however, that global trade deals had caused the effect of the job losses in the United States, and he did not mention the US jobs gained from those trade deals. Nor did he zero in on precisely which "unaccountable international tribunals" and which "powerful global bureaucracies" he had in mind.

On October 25, 2017, during a televised interview on Fox Business by the virulently protectionist broadcaster Lou Dobbs, the president got more specific in his denunciations of the WTO and especially of WTO dispute settlement. "They have taken advantage of this country like you wouldn't believe," he complained. The United States, he went on, has lost "almost all the lawsuits" it has brought to the WTO "because we have fewer judges than other countries. It's set up as you can't win. In other words, the panels are set up so that we don't have majorities."[25] The president said he is persuaded that the WTO is "set up for the benefit of taking advantage of the United States."[26] Despite these criticisms, though, he did not say what he proposed for or wanted from the WTO.

Then, on November 10, 2017, at the annual Asia Pacific Economic Cooperation Forum meeting in Da Nang, Vietnam, President Trump unleashed in full to the assembled Asia-Pacific regional leaders his frustrations with multilateral trade agreements in general and with the WTO specifically. "We are not going to let the United States be taken advantage of anymore," he said. "I am always going to put America first, the same way that I expect all of you in this room to put your countries first....What we will no longer do is enter into large agreements that tie our hands, surrender our sovereignty and make meaningful enforcement practically impossible.... [I will] aggressively defend American sovereignty over trade policy....Simply put, we have not been treated fairly by the World Trade Organization."[27]

Trump may not have read — or even have heard of — the Melian Dialogue. It does not appear in his musings on the art of the deal.[28] But whether he knows it or not, he is channeling the edicts of the ancient Athenian generals on Melos. In trade, as in much else, he is saying that might makes right, and, in his recent unilateral trade actions outside the legal structure of the WTO, he is trying to prove it.

The Trade Views of the United States Trade Representative

In his attacks on the WTO-based world trading system, President Trump has the more subtle, but equally ardent, support of his hand-picked trade ambassador, United States Trade Representative (USTR) Robert Lighthizer. A highly intelligent and highly skilled trade lawyer, an experienced trade negotiator and a long-time trade counsel for the protectionist-minded in the US steel industry, Lighthizer lends a leaven of reflective trade philosophy to the uninformed bluster of the president. More subdued than the president he serves, he espouses, beneath a thin veneer of gratuitous pro-trade euphemism, a deeply felt belief in the virtues of protectionism and mercantilism that seems to animate almost all his actions on behalf of the Trump administration.

Lighthizer rightly denounces protectionism and mercantilism in other countries — notably China, which is touting free trade while turning more and more economically nationalist. Yet he advocates both protectionism and mercantilism for his own country in the guise of a Trumpian version of a misguided, short-sighted and inward-looking industrial policy. Lighthizer echoes the view, dating back to some of the ancient Greeks, that all of us in our country will be better off if we discriminate in favor of our own producers while limiting competition from imports from other, "foreign" countries.[29] He claims he is committed to "working with other members to improve the functioning of the WTO"[30] and, further, to increasing "the WTO's ability to promote free and fair trade."[31] But, whatever soothing reassurances he may offer about supposedly supporting the WTO, Lighthizer, on behalf of his president, is pursuing a protectionist and mercantilist agenda that, if it is fully implemented, and, if it is not resisted, could well destroy the WTO-based world trading system.

The USTR is not new to his views, which he has long professed. After nearly 25 years, Lighthizer remains unreconciled to the decision by the US Congress in 1994 to support inclusion of the establishment of a binding dispute settlement system as part of the WTO, when approving the Uruguay Round trade agreements.[32] As a former trade negotiator who had effectively wielded a unilateral club, he did not think it wise for the United States to relinquish its legal right to take unilateral trade actions in exchange for a binding WTO dispute settlement system in which trade rules and trade rulings could be enforced through economic sanctions in the form of the "last resort" of a loss of previously granted trade benefits.[33]

Moreover, Lighthizer did not believe then that it was a good idea for the United States to agree to be bound by the judgments of what would often be foreign judges, whom he feared would be biased against the United States and whose delegation of global legal authority, as he saw it, amounted to a surrender of a slice of American sovereignty. During the rowdy run-up to the congressional approval of the Uruguay Round trade agreements, he pushed unsuccessfully for the establishment of a domestic commission to review WTO decisions whenever the United

States lost a case. He would have required the United States to consider leaving the WTO if — in the view of this commission — the United States lost three cases it should not have lost in any period of five years.[34] He has given no reason now for anyone to think he has abandoned this view.

The USTR preferred then — and he looks "wistfully" back on now — the pre-WTO system of GATT dispute settlement, in which a GATT panel ruling was not binding unless all the countries that were contracting parties to the GATT agreed that it should be.[35] This meant that, for a ruling to be legally binding, the country that lost the legal ruling in the dispute had to agree to make it binding. This meant, as well, the preservation of more national control over disputed trade outcomes and, therefore, to Lighthizer's way of thinking, the preservation of more national sovereignty. In contrast, in WTO dispute settlement, a WTO panel ruling, as amended by the WTO Appellate Body, is binding unless every WTO member agrees that it should not be binding. This means that, for a ruling not to be binding, the country that won in the dispute has to agree to set its winning verdict aside.[36] Not surprisingly, after more than two decades, this has never happened.

During the Uruguay Round, decades of frustration with enforcing winning panel verdicts in the GATT led US trade negotiators to push hard for a binding dispute settlement system in the WTO. They sought rules that could be upheld. They wanted to be able to enforce international legal judgments against other countries that had violated WTO rules, backed by economic sanctions authorized by the WTO. But, unlike many at the time, Lighthizer realized that the United States would lose cases as well as win them in the WTO. He may also have foreseen that the United States would be most likely to lose WTO cases (including cases involving his steel clients) when defending the expansive and highly discretionary US anti-dumping and anti-subsidy trade remedies that would be indefensible under the new and binding trade remedies rules in the WTO Agreement.[37] What is more, based on his experience in the 1980s at the USTR in challenging Japan (the commercially insurgent "China" of the time) with singular trade threats, Lighthizer was very much inclined to stick with the old GATT system that left the United States free to go on the offense aggressively in trade by taking unilateral trade actions without any international legal constraint.

Since 1994, Ambassador Lighthizer's opposition to the basic legal underpinning of the WTO dispute settlement system has remained unrelenting. In January 2001, at a seminar on Capitol Hill, he voiced anew his long-held view that it was a "mistake" for the United States to agree to a binding system that infringed on US sovereignty instead of retaining its previous unilateral discretion to assert its sovereign will. He said then that WTO panels are often comprised of jurists who are "not qualified."[38] Shockingly, he then went so far as to say that he suspected that some WTO jurists "may be crooked, although I have no evidence of it."[39] In making such a serious ethical charge on what he admitted was no evidence whatsoever, he was a Trumpian before Trump's time. Even if the panels were "fair arbiters," he contended, they would still be "a threat to sovereignty," for "our laws are being threatened in a very serious way."[40]

In 2003, in a bit of trade irony, Lighthizer, perhaps the most fervent and outspoken critic of the WTO dispute settlement system, and someone who had professed that WTO jurists "may be crooked," was one of two candidates nominated by the United States to become one of the seven members of the WTO Appellate Body. When confronted with this irony at the time by a journalist, Lighthizer was reported as asking himself aloud, "Do you criticize the system and hope to kill it, or do you think it is worthwhile to go to Geneva and apply a strict constructionist's perspective, and add a certain credibility?"[41] He was not selected by the members of the WTO.

Five years later, invoking the economic nationalist spirit of one of America's foremost founding fathers, Alexander Hamilton, Lighthizer derided free traders in a fervent opinion column in *The New York Times*:

> Modern free traders embrace their ideal with a passion that makes Robespierre seem prudent. They allow no room for practicality, nuance or flexibility. They embrace unbridled free trade, even as it helps China become a superpower. They see only bright lines, even when it means bowing to the whims of anti-American bureaucrats at the World Trade Organization. They oppose any trade limitations, even if we must depend on foreign countries to feed ourselves or equip our military. They see nothing but dogma — no matter how many jobs are lost, how high the trade deficit rises or how low the dollar falls.[42]

By 2010, Lighthizer was telling the US-China Economic Security and Review Commission, "Trade policy discussions in the United States have increasingly been dominated by arcane disputations about whether various actions would be 'WTO-consistent' — treating this as a mantra of almost moral or religious significance....WTO commitments are not religious obligations."[43] He maintained it made little sense to have "an unthinking, simplistic and slavish dedication to the mantra of 'WTO-consistency.'"[44] Rather, he recommended that "where a trade relationship has become so unbalanced that the threat of retaliation pales in comparison to the potential benefits of derogation — it only makes sense that a sovereign nation would consider what options are in its own national interest (up to and including potential derogation from WTO stipulations)."[45] In other words, if you wish to do so, ignore the WTO.

The American Attempt to Unmake Right in the WTO

Little wonder that Lighthizer was appointed as the USTR by Trump. Now, thanks to President Trump, he is doing his best to turn back the clock in world trade to a time when the United States could employ its considerable leverage without the inconvenient constraint of WTO rules, and often did so. While taking reckless unilateral and other highly publicized trade actions outside of Geneva, at the same time, inside Geneva, Trump and his atavistic acolytes have been waging a "stealth war" against the WTO, cleverly disguised by Lighthizer and his lieutenants at the USTR as an arcane procedural challenge to the appointment and the reappointment of the members of the WTO Appellate Body. The European trade minister, Cecilia Malmström, speaks for a great many worried WTO members in warning that this procedural challenge by the United States risks "killing the WTO from the inside."[46] Continued success in this stealth war could turn out to be all the United States needs to topple the WTO.[47]

This stealth war was not started by Trump and Lighthizer. For the past 12 years, dating back to the second term of President George W. Bush and then continuing and gradually intensifying under the administration of President Barack Obama, the United States, through the USTR, has voiced concerns about some of the rulings and about some of what the United States perceives as the aggrandizing inclinations of the seven members of the WTO Appellate Body, the final tribunal of appeal in the WTO. The United States tried unsuccessfully to raise some of its concerns in the failed Doha Round of multilateral trade negotiations. They voiced their concerns from time to time within the councils of the WTO. Unfortunately, over time they succumbed to the temptation to apply inappropriate pressure outside the legal norms of the system, but, for the most part, they worked within it to try to resolve their professed concerns.

As he has done in so many instances, Trump has, in the WTO, seized on an inherited conflict and has made it immeasurably worse by making it his own. Trump, Lighthizer and other political appointees at the USTR have used the pretext of this preexisting and low-key controversy as a convenient cover for what has become their systematic assault against rules-based multilateralism and dispute settlement. Within the broader geopolitical context of the overall direction and disruption of Trump trade policy, this previously arcane internal debate largely among trade diplomats and trade legal theorists has been transformed and elevated by Lighthizer and his USTR colleagues since Trump's inauguration into a political wedge issue against the WTO as an international institution. They have eagerly enlisted in this stealth war against the WTO and escalated it to the point where it now poses an existential crisis for the WTO.

Substantively, as voiced, the concerns raised by the United States have, during most of the past 12 years, been mainly about the Appellate Body rulings in a long string of "zeroing" and other trade remedies disputes in which the United States has repeatedly ended up on the losing side.[48] Zeroing is a methodology used by US trade agencies to determine whether a foreign producer is dumping and to calculate the margin of dumping; WTO panels and the Appellate Body have consistently ruled that the use of zeroing does not result in the making of a fair comparison between the export price and the normal value of an imported product, as required by the WTO Anti-Dumping Agreement.[49] This series of WTO rulings has had the effect of limiting the latitude of US trade agencies in finding the existence of dumping and in levying high anti-dumping duties — not a result that has been welcomed by Lighthizer and other US trade lawyers for steel and other trade-sensitive and trade-exposed US industries.

Procedurally, as voiced, these US concerns, throughout the past 12 years and continuing now, have been mostly about what the United States has increasingly seen as a gradual expansion by the Appellate Body of the scope of its jurisdiction beyond what is mandated in the WTO treaty. In the deliberations of the WTO Dispute Settlement Body (DSB), the United States has, throughout those 12 years, from time to time, charged the Appellate Body with exceeding the bounds of its treaty mandate by either adding to or subtracting from the obligations in the WTO covered agreements in violation of the terms of the DSU.[50] In the view of the United States, these alleged procedural excesses of the Appellate Body are creating an unhealthy imbalance among the internal bodies within the WTO, an imbalance that could have serious substantive consequences.

The United States has been frustrated in addressing these substantive and procedural concerns by the rules-based reality of WTO dispute settlement — a reality the United States played a major role in shaping during the Uruguay Round of trade negotiations that led to the establishment of the WTO and WTO dispute settlement. When a panel report is appealed, the Appellate Body must hear the appeal.[51] It has no discretion not to do so. When a legal issue on appeal claims a violation of a WTO obligation, the Appellate Body must render a judgment clarifying the meaning of that obligation, and it must do so even when the trade negotiators who wrote it may have left its meaning less than crystal clear.[52] Again, the Appellate Body has no discretion not to do so.

The appellate judges can rule only on those legal issues that are appealed. They cannot wander from those legal issues into mere conjecture on others that have not been appealed. Their job is to answer the legal questions they have been asked — nothing more and nothing less. The frustration of the United States is found in the instructions the members of the WTO — including the United States — have given the Appellate Body on how it must answer legal questions when they are appealed. The members of the Appellate Body have been told by the WTO members in the dispute settlement rules that they must fulfill their mandate in strict accordance with the "customary rules of interpretation of public international law."[53] Although those customary rules exist independently of any treaty because of their status as customary international law, they find reflection in the Vienna Convention on the Law of Treaties[54] (the Vienna Convention). Article 31.1 of the Vienna Convention states the general rule of treaty interpretation: "A treaty shall be interpreted in good faith in accordance with the ordinary meaning to be given to the terms of the treaty in their context and in the light of its object and purpose."[55] These interpretive rules assume not only that treaty obligations have a meaning; they also assume that they have one meaning — a single meaning that must be clarified by the Appellate Body when a legal issue is appealed that requires a judgment on the meaning of an obligation.

From this requirement springs the bulk of the American accusations of "overreaching" and "gap filling" by the Appellate Body. But what the United States derides as overreaching and as gap filling is almost always only the Appellate Body doing its job for the members of the WTO according to its specific instructions in the WTO treaty. For instance, when the legal issue is, say, whether a fair comparison has been made between the export price and the normal value of a product when making a dumping determination in a process called zeroing, as is required by article 2.4 of the Anti-Dumping Agreement, then the Appellate Body has no choice but to decide what a fair comparison is, and then to apply that decision to the measure in question, given the facts as found by the panel in that appeal. No one argues for the infallibility of the Appellate Body in making legal judgments — least of all those who serve on it. The Appellate Body may be right or wrong in the eyes of others in any given judgment — like any other tribunal in the world. But the act of judging and applying the meaning of, in this example, a fair comparison is not overreaching or gap filling. It is simply the Appellate Body fulfilling its mandate by doing the job it is supposed to do.

In fulfilling their mandate, the seven members of the standing Appellate Body must use their own judgment. Under the dispute settlement rules, they "shall be unaffiliated with any government."[56] Furthermore, under those rules, Appellate Body members "shall not participate in the consideration of any disputes that would create direct or indirect conflict of interest."[57] The WTO Rules of Conduct reinforce these treaty requirements. As a "Governing Principle," the Rules of Conduct state, "Each person covered by these rules… shall be independent and impartial [and] shall avoid direct or indirect conflicts of interest."[58] The Rules of Conduct go on to say, "Pursuant to the Governing Principle, each covered person, shall be independent and impartial."[59] Furthermore, "such person shall not incur any benefit that would in any way interfere with, or which would give rise to, justifiable doubts as to the proper performance of that person's dispute settlement duties."[60] These Rules of Conduct explicitly apply to the members of the Appellate Body.[61] Indeed, the Appellate Body adopted these Rules of Conduct in 1995 even before the rest of the WTO did.

Significantly, the DSU provides that the members of the WTO, acting together in their dispute settlement role as the DSB, "shall appoint persons to serve on the Appellate Body for a four-year term, and each person may be reappointed once."[62] This is the institutional source and pivot of the current crisis involving the Appellate Body. As with virtually all decisions by the WTO, a decision on a reappointment of a member of the Appellate Body is made by consensus.[63] Apparently, the treaty drafters during the Uruguay Round negotiations that created the Appellate Body overlooked that this beckoning possibility of reappointment puts those members of the Appellate Body who have not yet been reappointed in the highly uncomfortable position of sitting in judgment on appeals involving countries whose support they need to help make the consensus that is required for their reappointment.[64]

Oversight or not, the possibility of reappointment for a member of the Appellate Body is a design flaw in the architecture of the WTO dispute settlement system.[65] Clearly, there is no right to reappointment for any member of the Appellate Body. Clearly as well, a decision on whether to approve a reappointment is a decision reserved for the members of the WTO, and solely for the members of the WTO. No one member of the Appellate Body has any role in this decision, nor does the Appellate Body as a whole. Should the members of the WTO be unable to reach a consensus on reappointment of a sitting member of the Appellate Body, then that member will not be reappointed. Moreover, because of the necessity for a consensus, any one country among the 164 that are members of the WTO — whether it be the United States or any other WTO member — can block the reappointment of a member of the Appellate Body.[66] Yet evidently unforeseen by the designers of the DSU was that this provides every WTO member with the potential of employing the leverage of its right to veto a reappointment as a tool for trying to influence the actions of those members of the Appellate Body desirous of reappointment.

For the first decade and more of WTO dispute settlement, the reappointment of members of the Appellate Body occurred entirely without controversy. Although members had no right to reappointment, no one member who sought reappointment was denied it. Despite the inevitable disappointments of some WTO members with Appellate Body legal judgments that went against them, not one member of the WTO interjected such disappointments into the reappointment process. This show of mutual self-restraint for the sake of the entire cooperative enterprise of the WTO contributed much to the establishment of the legitimacy and the credibility of the WTO dispute settlement system worldwide. But human nature is human nature. One who has a post will tend to want to keep it. One who has leverage will be tempted to use it. Under the cumulative domestic pressures of losing politically sensitive WTO trade disputes, the United States has yielded to this temptation and has, for the past 12 years, sought to exploit the all too human tension felt by sitting WTO judges between their devotion to responsibility and their desire for reappointment in the United States' accelerating stealth war against the WTO.

Since long before the Trump ascendancy, the United States has been trying to intimidate both aspiring judges who have been nominated for vacant seats on the Appellate Body and sitting judges on the Appellate Body who have been candidates for reappointment by attempting to pressure them into ruling the way the United States wants them to rule as the price for US consent to their appointment or reappointment. The first inklings of the US campaign of intimidation were heard during the second Bush administration at a time when the United States had become increasingly vocal in its complaints about adverse Appellate Body rulings in various trade remedies disputes. The first public confirmation of US intimidation occurred in 2011 during the Obama administration, when the USTR informed a sitting judge from the United States that, because of continued adverse Appellate Body rulings in trade remedies disputes, the United States would not support her for reappointment. She protested publicly, but she was not reappointed.

Emboldened by this experiment in judicial intimidation, during Obama's second term (from 2013 through 2016) the USTR broadened the sweep of its pressure tactics in Geneva to include sitting Appellate Body members from countries other than the United States, employing such tactics as requests for one-on-one *ex parte* meetings to discuss their candidacies for reappointment. The United States and any Appellate Body members who chose to participate in these *ex parte* meetings were, of course, both to blame for the harm these meetings threatened to the WTO dispute settlement system. Such *ex parte* meetings between Appellate Body members and individual WTO members pose possible legal conflicts in violation of the WTO Rules of Conduct and should be specifically prohibited by an amendment to the Appellate Body working procedures. Over time, other WTO members became aware of these dubious US tactics and were increasingly disturbed by them. However, to avoid embarrassing the United States and further risking the integrity of the world trading system, they chose not to say anything publicly about these US tactics, while working quietly and informally to fashion a reappointment process consistent with the rule of law and acceptable to all.[67]

Then, in 2016, the United States stoked the intensifying conflict by announcing that it would not support the reappointment of Appellate Body member Seung Wha Chang of South Korea. The United States maintained that Appellate Body divisions on which he had served had exceeded the bounds of their jurisdiction by overreaching in their judgments in some disputes during his tenure. An uproar ensued in the DSB, with many other WTO members protesting the US action. Nevertheless, while Obama was still president, the United States succeeded in preventing Chang's reappointment by blocking the required consensus. Other WTO members ultimately acquiesced because of the legal straitjacket of the consensus rule. This only encouraged the United States to persist in its bullying inside the councils of the WTO.

As the jurisprudence of the schoolyard teaches us, if not stopped, bullying only begets more bullying. The inauguration in January 2017 of a president unabashedly inclined toward bullying only intensified the US campaign of intimidation of WTO judges and, more broadly, of other members of the WTO. Eventually, the US pressure tactics were broadened to extend to stonewalling the appointment of any new Appellate Body members to fill the vacancies occurring on the seven-member tribunal. In the normal course of regular turnover, as some of the incumbent judges completed their allotted mandates, more vacancies opened on the Appellate Body. Seeing a chance in the second half of 2017 to link its long-standing grievances to the process of judicial reappointment, the United States decided to hold the Appellate Body hostage. These vacancies have not been filled.

Moreover, the United States opened a new front in its stealth war by contesting for the first time the long-standing practice — set out for more than 20 years in the Appellate Body Working Procedures following due consultations with the DSB — of having retiring judges complete their work as members of divisions on pending appeals when their mandate ends before the Appellate Body report is submitted.[68] Until the United States raised its objection in 2017, this practice had enjoyed the universal support of WTO members since the inception of the WTO as the most practical way of proceeding to the goal identified in the WTO treaty of a "positive solution" of pending trade disputes.[69] This US objection is not without merit. At the outset, the seven founding members of the Appellate Body sought consultations with the DSB on this issue to make certain that the practical extension of the service of a departed member to complete a pending appeal would not raise issues of legal jurisdiction.[70] Urged to do so by the DSB to facilitate the resolution of disputes, the Appellate Body adopted the working procedure permitting such temporary holdovers of judicial authority. But much has changed since then. Holdovers that, for many years, lasted only a few weeks are now, amid a proliferation of more complex and more prolonged disputes, lasting for months on end. This is a legitimate issue for due attention by the DSB.

This said, the way in which the United States has chosen to address this issue in the DSB is far from being legitimate. In late September 2017, when an appellate report was circulated that was signed by two judges whose terms had already expired and was therefore not signed by three sitting judges, the United States went so far as to suggest that this was grounds for reviving the old GATT practice of permitting any one member to veto a dispute settlement ruling.[71] Although this retro US gambit likely gladdened the heart of Lighthizer, there is no legal basis for this view in the DSU or elsewhere in the WTO treaty. It could conceivably be argued with some merit that an appellate report signed by fewer than three sitting members of the Appellate Body does not fulfill the requirement in article 17.1 of the DSU that each appeal be decided by "three persons."[72] Presumably, and logically, the three persons to whom this requirement applies must all be members of the Appellate Body. The DSU does not, however, permit a singular veto of an Appellate Body report by the United States or any other one member of the WTO. Under the so-called reverse consensus rule, "an Appellate Body report shall be adopted by the DSB and unconditionally accepted by the parties to the dispute unless the DSB decides by consensus not to adopt the Appellate Body report within 30 days following its circulation to the Members."[73]

This may or may not have been an idle threat. The United States has, in the past, been known from time to time to utter such sentiments in part to encourage other WTO members to pay more heed to US frustrations with the dispute settlement system. Ultimately, the United States agreed to join in the consensus to adopt that appellate report. The mere mention, though, of reviving the rejected GATT practice of dispute settlement by allowing just one WTO member among all the 164 WTO members to block the adoption of a WTO ruling "set off alarm bells in Geneva from trade officials who are already worried that the U.S. is trying to undermine the WTO's dispute settlement system."[74] Many WTO members saw flashbacks to the frustrating days before the creation of the binding WTO dispute settlement system, when a country that lost before a GATT panel could single-handedly block the implementation of a ruling against it. This happened in a number of major GATT disputes. Ironically, the American consternation with this less-than-binding GATT practice led the United States to lead the charge for a binding dispute settlement system in the Uruguay Round.

All the while, throughout Trump's first year, the United States continued to use the WTO dispute settlement system and take part in the sessions of the DSB. But the new administration of the United States seemed determined at the same time to paralyze the rules-based system. As their condition for getting on with the necessary task of supporting the continued resolution of international trade disputes by appointing new Appellate Body members, Lighthizer and other politically appointed and like-minded minions of Trump at the USTR demanded of other WTO members what they described as "reform" of the WTO dispute settlement process. But they refrained from saying what they meant by reform. Hence the increasingly widespread question asked by more and more WTO members: "What does the United States want?"

At year-end in 2017, three of the seven Appellate Body seats were open, leaving only four members, and there were fears that, if the stalemate on appointment continued, the Appellate Body would be reduced in 2018 to three members, just enough to comprise the division of three required by the DSU to hear an appeal.[75] If the appointments impasse continues beyond December 10, 2019, when two more members are due to complete their second terms, the Appellate Body will be reduced at that time to just one member and will be rendered incapable of forming a division. Meanwhile, as 2018 began, facing an avalanche of appeals and approaching appeals, including some with myriad legal complexities, the Appellate Body and WTO panels alike labored with inadequate financial and personnel resources, leading to a lengthening of the times taken to render judgments and diminishing the timely responsiveness of the system in resolving trade disputes. As the United States continued its intimidation and intransigence, there were growing fears that the work of the Appellate Body would be undermined and the entire WTO dispute settlement system would grind to a halt. All in all, it appeared to many that the United States, under the sway of Trump, was bent on using American might to unmake the right of the rule of law in world trade.

Making Right into Might Through the Rule of Law

In its ever-increasing pressure tactics in the WTO, the United States, as led by Trump and enabled by Lighthizer, seems to think that it has enough power to get its way, and that because it has this power, it is entitled to use it, whatever that may do to the supposedly equal power of every other member of the WTO. This goes against all the United States has long asserted and defended internationally.

The rule of power is the very opposite of the rule of law. With the rule of power, power alone is all that matters. The law is uncertain and arbitrary. The law means only what those with power say that it means for any one person on any one issue at any one time. With the rule of law, power is subdued. The law is certain and not arbitrary. The law is written and the rules are known, in advance. The law is written to apply to all equally, and all — in practice — in reality — are equal under the law and before the law. No one — no one — is beneath the concern of the law, and no one — no one — is above the law. Anything less than this cannot rightly be called the rule of law.

Through all the long centuries of experience since the sad events on Melos, four basic elements have been identified as a "core definition of the rule of law." First, the power of the state must not be exercised arbitrarily. There must be the rule of law and not the "rule of men." Second, the law must be applied to sovereign and citizens alike, with an independent institution such as a judiciary "to apply the law to specific cases." Third, "the law must apply to all persons equally, offering equal protection without prejudice or discrimination. Furthermore, for there to be the rule of law, the law must be of general application and consistent implementation; it must be capable of being obeyed."[76] Words in a statute book or in a judicial ruling are not enough. The words must have reality. What matters is not only what the law says but also, even more, what the law does. The rule of law is more than simply "law in words;" it is "law in action."[77] These four considerations, to my mind, apply as much to law between nations as to law within nations.

A tendency in some places is to speak of "rule by law" instead of the "rule of law." But the two are not the same. Rule by law is a means for imposing the power of the state. Not surprisingly, it is favored by authoritarian rulers in authoritarian states. The rule of law is a means of ensuring individual freedom, including freedom from the arbitrary say of the state. Compliance with the caprice of some potentate as expressed in law is not the rule of law. Where the law is subject to the whim of whoever happens to be wielding the power of the state at the time, there may, as a useful expedient of autocratic rule, be rule by law, but there is no rule of law. This distinction between rule by law and the rule of law applies equally to every country — to Russia, China, Turkey, Poland, Hungary, Venezuela and the Philippines — and also to the United States of America.

The truest test of whether there is the rule of law is whether there is an independent judiciary. As Anne Marie Slaughter has explained,

"The definition of an 'independent judiciary' is a judiciary that is not the handmaiden of State power, that answers to law rather than to the individuals who make it."[78] Those who advocate rule by law favor subordinating the judiciary to those who hold power in the executive branch of governance. In contrast, those who favor the rule of law understand that it can only exist if there is a strict separation of the judicial powers from the executive and the legislative powers of governance. Judges can be impartial in applying the rule of law only if they are independent, and judges can be independent only if they are free from all outside control and influence — including that of those who appointed them.

During the Enlightenment of the 18th century, Baron de Montesquieu of France was one of the first to see the need for an independent judiciary as being at the very core of the rule of law. "There is no liberty," he said, "if the power of judging be not separated from the legislative and executive powers."[79] In 1788, Alexander Hamilton — the American founding father whose views on trade are much admired by Lighthizer — quoted this assertion by Montesquieu approvingly in one of his contributions published in The Federalist Papers, the essays written in support of the ratification of the United States Constitution.[80] Today, in the institutional context of the WTO, the separation of powers is that between the WTO panelists and Appellate Body members fulfilling their mandates to the members of the WTO sitting as the DSB (the judicial branch) and all the rest of the endeavors of the members of the WTO sitting as the WTO General Council and overseeing the WTO Secretariat (the executive and legislative branches).

There is no lack of those in the world today who continue to believe, like the Athenian generals on Melos, that the strong, because they have power, should be able to use it as they choose — including by wielding power arbitrarily over the weak. All of human history through all of the centuries since the Peloponnesian War can be seen as a commentary on the events on Melos — as a struggle to curb and tame the worst in our nature by replacing the arbitrary exercise of power with the rule of law.[81] Might does not make right where there is the rule of law. In our pursuit of something worthy of being called human civilization, we can choose the arbitrary rule of might in all its manifestations, or we can choose the lawful rule of right through the rule of law. On this central issue, there can be no in between, and there can be no compromise. Anything less than the rule of law is only the rule of power as described long ago by Thucydides in the Melian Dialogue.

Not long ago, the United States was among the foremost in the world in understanding and in communicating all of this. The United States has long preached the need for the rule of law and for the international rule of law to the unpersuaded of the world. But, when Lighthizer and other appointees of the current US president invoke the rule of law now, their words ring hollow. Their words are betrayed by many of their actions. Under the sway of its wayward president, the United States is not only failing to speak up against authoritarian actions abroad,[82] it has succumbed to the lure of arbitrary executive actions on the outer edges of lawfulness at home.[83] The WTO is only one of a growing number of arenas — domestic and international alike — in which, under the mercurial auspices of Donald Trump, the executive branch of the federal government of the United States seems in sad retreat from the rule of law.

Defending Right Against Might in the WTO

Missing in the US assault on the WTO and especially on the WTO dispute settlement system is the strong support for the rule of law that results from taking the longer and more enlightened view of the self-interest of the United States. The shorter, myopic view is that the American self-interest lies in reserving the right to throw America's weight around unilaterally in world trade. The longer, better view is that the American self-interest lies in relinquishing the right to act unilaterally outside the bounds of law by supporting a binding dispute settlement system with the authority and the ability to uphold and enforce trade rules on which all the countries comprising the world trading system have agreed. The shorter view favors the rule of power. The longer view favors the rule of law. In taking the shorter view, the United States is turning back toward Melos.

The animus of President Trump and his administration against the WTO and against WTO jurists seems to be an end product of their visceral belief that the United States should never allow itself to be second-guessed by foreigners. Instead, they think the United States should cling to the solitary preserve of their perception of American sovereignty. Trump and his followers appear to believe that any national decision to defer to the judgment of an international tribunal or some other international institution is a subversion of national sovereignty. This helps explain why the president mentioned "sovereign" or "sovereignty" 16 times in his first speech to the United Nations.[84] In explaining Trump's new trade policy, the USTR put this concern this way in March 2017, soon after the president took office: "Ever since the United States won its independence, it has been a basic principle of our country that American citizens are subject only to laws and regulations made by the U.S. government — not rulings made by foreign governments or international bodies. This principle remains true today. Accordingly, the Trump administration will aggressively defend American sovereignty over matters of trade policy."[85]

John Bolton, President Trump's latest national security adviser and a former US ambassador to the United Nations, who seems to oppose the very idea of multilateral cooperation through the United Nations, has had high praise for Trump's condemnation of the WTO and, in particular, of WTO dispute settlement. It is not clear that Ambassador Bolton has ever read the GATT. Yet he assumes the trappings of a legal authority on trade in denouncing the "faulty decisions" of WTO jurists in the WTO's "faltering" dispute settlement system. He tells us, "Although technical, even arcane, the DSU is dear to the hearts of global governance advocates. The Trump administration is right to criticize its performance... The unspoken objective is to constrain the U.S., and to transfer authority from national governments to international bodies...The common theme is diminished American sovereignty, submitting the United States to authorities that ignore, outvote or frustrate its priorities....U.S. sovereignty is at stake."[86] In recruiting Bolton as his national security adviser, Trump is simply enlisting an echo. His own stress on the sanctity of national sovereignty has been equally insistent and equally strident. In such a singular stress on such a narrow view of the notion of sovereignty, Trump rejects the very foundation of the liberal international order, which is based on a sharing of national sovereignty through international cooperation.

Those now in the ascendancy in the United States cite their contorted view of national sovereignty as an excuse for employing America's considerable economic leverage to try to bully other countries into doing as the United States demands on trade. They impose illegal unilateral trade actions. They issue ultimatums. They threaten more unilateral actions. They tell other countries, in so many words, to take it or leave it. They see the rules of trade as tools they can choose to acknowledge or not, ignore or not, in the singular exercise of an American commercial realpolitik. Internationally, they answer to no one but themselves — not to their allies or their friends, not to the previous promises of their predecessors, not to the commitments of their predecessors as participants in international institutions, and not to their trading partners and to the rules and obligations of the global trading system that the United States long helped lead the world in creating. They are in the thrall of might makes right.

But bullying will get them only so far. Although still considerable, the economic leverage of the United States is not, relatively speaking, what it used to be. Other countries have growing economic leverage in a world in which the US share of global GDP has declined significantly since the first decades after the Second World War. The United States accounted then for about half of global GDP. Now it accounts for about one-fifth. Other developed countries have long since recovered from that global conflict and have continued to grow. Developing countries have emerged from poverty and grown as well. All the trading countries of the world have become not only inter-connected through a global division of labor and the fragmented production of global supply chains, they have also become interdependent, economically and in many other ways. The initial response from some countries to the economic bullying of Donald Trump and his cohorts may be a reluctant acquiescence. But, in time, the limits of this acquiescence will be reached, and other countries will in turn assert their own significant economic leverage against the United States. If there is not a return to multilateralism through the WTO, the results of such a mutual descent into unilateralism will be fateful for the rules-based world trading system.

One problem with the Trump administration's constricted view of sovereignty in the 21st century is that it will not work. Not for the United States. Not for any other country. And certainly not in world trade. This is a century in which economic and other concerns are increasingly global in nature and in which many of those concerns can therefore only be addressed through cooperative international action. The late John Jackson, the greatest of all trade law scholars, pointed out soon after the dawn of this century that "in the area of trade policy…and…in the real world of today's 'globalization,' there are innumerable instances of how actions by one state (particularly an economically powerful nation) can constrain and influence the internal affairs of other nations."[87] In such a world, a stubborn, insistent invocation of an insular sovereignty solves no problems, globally or — often — domestically. Cooperative international action is necessary, and such action is usually much more likely to succeed if the United States is actively engaged and is helping point the way toward a solution.

The WTO is one example of cooperative international action to solve a global problem — that of easing and increasing the flow of trade worldwide so that all in the world can have the opportunity to share in the gains from trade. Together, the 164 members of the WTO have rightly resolved that this problem can best be solved if they agree on rules for trade as part of a global framework enabling trade. And they have rightly realized that the rules on which they have agreed in the WTO treaty will not truly be effective as international laws unless they are upheld and enforced in accordance with the rule of law in a binding dispute settlement system. This is why we have the WTO, and this is why we have WTO jurists, including those on the WTO Appellate Body.

The WTO is a realization of what Jackson called "sovereignty-modern."[88] It is not a subversion of national sovereignty. It is an expression of their national sovereignty by each of the members of the WTO — including the United States of America. The WTO is a sharing of sovereignty resulting from 164 sovereign decisions to take the longer view of national self-interest. With the death of distance, the advance of transport, the ubiquity of instant communication, the emergence of digital trade and the arrival of global value chains that cross the globe back and forth many times over, it is simply not the case that, in the absence of the WTO, individual nation-states would, in the consoling sanctuaries of their sovereign territories, be able to achieve their national economic goals by acting alone. In the 21st century, almost every national issue is also international in its causes and in its effects. Joshua Meltzer has it right in saying that "growing interdependence and globalization has reduced the ability of states to achieve optimal policy outcomes acting alone."[89]

To maximize outcomes for the people of every trading country — including the United States — global rules for trade within an enabling global framework for trade are essential. The only alternative to acting alone is to design and to support the WTO — or something very much like it. In the absence of the WTO, we would soon have to reinvent it. Ironically, in the light of the recent US rhetoric, one reason why we would be engaged in this reinvention would be to preserve our national sovereignty and to make the most of it. Every nation-state in the 21st century faces the challenge of proving anew that the Westphalian system of nation-states established in the 17th century remains the best way to organize and to govern the world. In this globalized world in this 21st century, where so much of what happens that affects each of us seems to be out of our reach and beyond our control, it falls to nation-states to reaffirm their relevance by demonstrating their continued effectiveness. This aim can only be achieved if nation-states work cooperatively and in concert toward shared aspirations. Thus, the continued success of the WTO does not undermine national sovereignty; it reaffirms it. The WTO makes sovereign states stronger, not weaker. It proves that national independence is still possible in an interdependent world.[90]

A binding dispute settlement system in which the rules are upheld and enforced is imperative to providing the "security and predictability" WTO members seek through the enabling WTO framework.[91] WTO rules are the guiding rules for the daily conduct of WTO trade. Agreement on trade rules creates an atmosphere of certainty that helps advance the flow of trade. Awareness that trade rules can be enforced and that there will be an economic price to pay for not following them encourages trading countries to comply with the rules. As a result, almost all WTO members comply with almost all WTO trade rules almost all the time.[92] By far, this has been the biggest success to date of the WTO. Although they draw most of the public attention, international trade disputes are rare exceptions to the day-to-day conduct of world trade within the agreed rules. The media is endlessly fascinated by the prospect of trade wars; the WTO-based world trading system prevents trade wars every day — and has been doing so for 70 years. But, without a binding dispute settlement system in which all sovereign states are equal in power and equally subject to the rule of law, and without a continuing willingness by the United States and all other members of the WTO to keep their treaty commitments to resolve all their trade disputes in that system, the current security and predictability in world trade will vanish, with grave economic consequences for all the members of the WTO, not least the United States. We would be left with only might makes right, in a wary world of reduced trade gains and diminished economic possibilities.

But what of President Trump's trumpeting that the WTO and the WTO dispute settlement system are rigged against the United States? Here the president is indulging, as he often does, in the fabrication of alternative facts. He claims that the WTO is "set up for taking advantage of the United States," and that Americans "have not been treated fairly by the World Trade Organization."[93] This utterly unfounded assertion must surely amuse many other members of the WTO, who are long accustomed to the United States playing an outsized role in the doings of the WTO. The United States did at least as much as any other country to set up the WTO, and, by any credible and rational economic measure, the United States must be numbered among the major beneficiaries of the WTO. As what President Trump would quite rightly call a "huge" trading nation, the

United States benefits "hugely" from the fact that world trade flows more smoothly, more quickly, in greater volumes and in greater value because it is conducted within the enabling WTO rules framework.

Does the United States, as Trump alleges, lose almost all the lawsuits? Far from it. With an army of accomplished trade attorneys in the USTR, and with the frequent outside assistance of equally accomplished private attorneys, the United States is far better equipped than the vast majority of other WTO members to win WTO disputes. And it does win. Several similar studies have reached slightly different conclusions due to differing methodologies. They come, however, to the same conclusion: in WTO disputes, complainants mostly win, and respondents mostly lose. In this, the United States, the most frequent litigant in the WTO, has done somewhat better in both roles than the average. In data compiled by Bloomberg, the United States, as complainant, has won 86 percent of the time, slightly more than the WTO average, and the United States, as respondent, has lost 75 percent of the time, less than the WTO average of 84 percent. By comparison, since becoming a member of the WTO in 2001, China has won six of the nine cases it has brought and has lost all but one case when a case has been brought against it.[94] Yet, China remains a strong supporter of WTO dispute settlement (no doubt in part because China knows that, without the shelter of WTO rules against non-discrimination, Chinese trade would be singled out for discrimination all over the world).

The fact is, WTO members do not file a complaint in WTO dispute settlement unless they think they have a very good chance of winning. The political fallout back home from initiating a dispute and then losing it can be high. Often, as well, WTO members resort to WTO litigation only after years of trying unsuccessfully to resolve a dispute without litigation. Why do negotiations fail? Often, it is because the political cost of changing the offending measure is considerable. On occasion, a WTO member has even been known to suggest that another WTO member file a complaint against it so that it can lose in the WTO and, in losing, secure the political leverage back home to change what the member knows is an illegal measure. As Louise Johannesson and Petros Mavroidis have said, "WTO Members pick winners, and do not litigate ad nauseum."[95]

It should come as no surprise, then, that complainants usually prevail in WTO cases. But what really is a win? Is there a win only if the complainant prevails on all the legal claims it makes? What if the complainant prevails on more legal claims than not? What if it prevails on only one legal claim, but that verdict results in the alteration or withdrawal of the contested measure? This raises yet another question: can there be a win only if the contested measure is altered or withdrawn? And what about the nature of the legal claims? Are they all equal? Or are some claims more significant than others? Is winning a legal claim that there has been a denial of national treatment more significant than winning a claim that the respondent has not filed a required notification? Most members of the WTO would say "Yes." Like many others, the president of the United States likes to win. But when does he know he has won? It is not at all unusual in the WTO for both sides to claim victory.

What is more, the fact is that every WTO case is actually two cases. It is the discrete dispute over the unique facts of a particular instance of trade in a specific good or service, and it is the dispute over the legal principles that are the focus for resolving that discrete dispute. Thus, a win can be a win in the particular dispute before a WTO panel and the WTO Appellate Body, or it can be a win in the interpretation and the clarification of the legal principles brought to bear in that single dispute resolution. Often, in a given dispute, it will be both. But not always. A win in the dispute at hand involving trade in some specific widget is, of course, pleasing and beneficial. It is vital to the success of the trading system for WTO members to know and see that WTO obligations will be upheld. But a win on a legal principle may prove over time to be far more valuable to the prevailing WTO member and to WTO members as a whole.

Sometimes, as well, a complainant will be better off over the long term if it loses on a legal principle at issue in a dispute. In a natural desire to prevail in the immediate legal battle over the widget at hand, there will sometimes be a temptation to take a legal position on the meaning of a WTO obligation that, while it may be helpful in winning in that widget dispute, may not, in the eyes of an objective outside observer, serve the overall interest of the complaining WTO member in the long term. To be sure, WTO members are free to determine for themselves what is or is not in their national interest. But, take, for example, the United States. If the United States were to prevail in defending a sanitary or phytosanitary measure that was not based on scientific principles and that was maintained without sufficient scientific evidence, then what would happen next? Other WTO members would line up to apply trade restrictions on all kinds of US agricultural exports for equally phony scientific reasons.[96] Is that truly a win?

In toting up the wins and the losses of the United States in WTO dispute settlement, there is also, unavoidably, the sore subject of US trade remedies. As Rufus Yerxa, president of the National Foreign Trade Council and a former deputy director-general of the WTO, has explained about US losses in WTO dispute settlement, "Most of the...losses were a result of the United States refusing to change its anti-dumping methodology even after it lost cases, thereby incurring repeated rulings against them for continuing the same practice. If you take those cases out, the United States has a better record as a defendant than China or most others."[97] Behind the scenes of the American stealth war against the WTO, the issue of US discretion in the employment of trade remedies is — in my considered judgment based on several decades of legal and political immersion in these matters in the United States and worldwide as negotiator, legislator, lawyer, and judge — the true core of the grievance of much of the current leadership of the United States against the WTO and against WTO dispute settlement.

In brief, the Trump administration wants to retain the freedom to do whatever it wishes to do in applying trade remedies without the annoying constraints of WTO rules. The president supports a broad sway for applying anti-dumping and other trade remedies for one compelling reason: the businesses and workers that desire them are centered mostly in the Midwest political swing states that gave him his narrow presidential election, and he will need the support of those same voters in those same states to get re-elected. Lighthizer and other highly experienced trade attorneys he has assembled at the USTR take the same position for the same political reason. Also, their previous legal experience has been largely in the specialized trade silo of representing US steel companies and other US industries that want to use trade remedies more freely as a tool against their foreign competition.

Their problem is this: WTO rules on which the United States agreed long ago govern the application of all trade remedies, and a refusal to comply with these largely procedural rules can lead to losses in WTO dispute settlement and to the possibility of economic sanctions in the form of the loss of previously granted trade concessions that can in some cases add up to billions of dollars annually. "WTO jurists have engaged in an all-out assault on trade remedy measures," Lighthizer claimed back in 2007, when he was leading the charge for steel protectionism while still in private practice.[98] Since then, US trade remedies have suffered even more of a beating in the WTO. This is not due to any actions initiated by the WTO or by WTO jurists. The WTO cannot bring WTO cases. The WTO is only the members of the WTO acting together as something they have chosen to call the WTO in a pooling of their national sovereignty. Only members of the WTO can bring cases. When they do, the WTO jurists are required to rule on all the legal issues on which they must rule "to secure a positive solution to a dispute."[99] And the fact is that the United States often acts inconsistently with WTO rules in applying trade remedies. Thus, other WTO members have brought a series of cases against the United States, and, according to the calculation of Dan Ikenson of the Cato Institute, since 1995, and as of 2017, WTO jurists have found it necessary on 38 occasions to find aspects of US trade remedy measures inconsistent with WTO obligations.[100]

The disregard for the WTO treaty obligations of the United States that is sometimes shown by US agencies when applying trade remedies guarantees that, when those actions are challenged in the WTO, the United States will lose. What is it that keeps the United States from simply complying with the WTO rules? In part, it is the tacit assumption by many in the US government that the United States is somehow not bound by the strictures of the rules that apply to everyone else. Other countries must, of course, comply. The United States need not. Ikenson, a very astute American trade observer, rightly sees this US sentiment as Orwellian, harking back to the barnyard animals in *Animal Farm*: "Agreeing that 'all animals are equal,' then adding the famous caveat, 'but some are more equal than others' is what is meant by 'defending our national sovereignty.'"[101] Seemingly, in the current view of the United States, all members of the WTO are equal, except for the United States, which is more equal than others. This is not the rule of law. This is the rule of power.

What, then, of Trump's charge that the United States is "losing" in the WTO "because we have fewer judges than other countries"? This charge is an expression of either demagoguery or ignorance. Either the president knows the facts and is simply disregarding them for inflammatory political purposes or he is ignorant of the rules of the WTO dispute settlement system and how they work. Either way, the rule of law in world trade is jeopardized by the recklessness of such a charge, and, once again, the view of the current US president and his administration is revealed as merely a flexing of might as the would-be maker of right in world trade. In making this charge, President Trump seems to assume that all WTO jurists will always rule in favor of their own countries in WTO disputes. There is no evidence whatsoever in more than two decades of WTO dispute settlement to support this assumption — and plenty to refute it.

There are numerous instances where members of the Appellate Body have found it necessary to rule against their own countries because their own countries had not fulfilled their WTO treaty obligations in a particular dispute.[102]

The fact is that the number of judges of any one nationality is of absolutely no significance in WTO dispute settlement. WTO jurists — wherever they may happen to be from — serve the world trading system as a whole and not their own countries. The "independence" of jurists is mandatory under the dispute settlement rules.[103] The seven members of the Appellate Body, as already noted, "shall be unaffiliated with any government."[104] The WTO Rules of Conduct reinforce these treaty requirements by insisting on both the independence and the impartiality of all WTO jurists.[105] Indeed, at the WTO panel level, nationality is in fact a bar to being a panelist, which means that — unless the parties to a dispute agree otherwise (which rarely happens) — no one from any of the disputing parties or the third parties to a dispute will be eligible to serve on the panel.[106] Nationality is not a bar to judging a dispute on the WTO Appellate Body. If it were, Appellate Body members from the United States, the European Union, China, and Japan — which, as the largest trading countries, are parties or third parties in most WTO disputes — would rarely be permitted to judge an appeal in a dispute. Furthermore, the fact is that every new member of the Appellate Body leaves the cloak of nationality behind when crossing the threshold of the Appellate Body. Any one of the seven members of the Appellate Body who ever so much as uttered even the slightest hint of national bias would lose all credibility with the rest of the Appellate Body forever.

Apparently, President Trump wants WTO judges who are partial, not impartial, and who are, especially if they are Americans, dependable parrots of the American point of view at any given time, and not independent in their judgments. This attitude is not original with Trump. It originated in the two previous American administrations as the United States was put more and more on the defensive during the depths of the Great Recession about its errant application of a series of largely politically motivated trade remedies in WTO dispute settlement. The blame for this departure from the traditional American view that respect for the independence of the judiciary is central and indispensable to the rule of law must be put in part on Presidents Bush and Obama.

This acknowledged, it is Trump who has intensified the US attack on the independence and impartiality of WTO jurists to the point where it threatens the future of the world trading system. First, under Bush and Obama, the United States sought, through its tactics of intimidation, to impose its will on American judges — based evidently on the premise that, because they were American, they should be shills in the judicial deliberations of the Appellate Body for every argument made by the United States in every dispute. Emboldened by the lack of pushback from other WTO members against these tactics, next, under Obama, the United States sought to impose its will on Appellate Body members from other countries by blocking or threatening to block their reappointments. Now, under Trump, the United States is paralyzing the WTO appointment and reappointment process altogether by refusing to cooperate in any kind of process to replenish the thinning ranks of Appellate Body members.

Not only the United States, but also all the members of the WTO, afford far too much emphasis to nationality in the process of selecting Appellate Body members. Certainly, the seven members of the Appellate Body must be "broadly representative of membership in the WTO."[107] And it would be naïve for anyone — especially a former politician — to think that politics (diplomacy by its real name) never plays a role in the international selection of judges.[108] But the fact is that nationality is irrelevant to the actual work of the Appellate Body. Far more important in the selection process should be ensuring that those appointed to the Appellate Body are "persons of recognized authority, with demonstrated expertise in law, international trade and the subject matter of the covered agreements generally" — no matter where they may happen to be from.[109] (To my mind, this means, for future appointments, that Appellate Body members must, at a minimum, be lawyers.) Has the United States, as Trump claims, had "fewer judges than other countries" on the Appellate Body? In fact, more Americans have served on the Appellate Body than citizens of any other country (primarily due to the dissatisfaction of the United States with some of the Americans who have served).

In a letter provoked by the intimidating tactics of the United States even before Trump became president, all the 13 living former members of the Appellate Body at the time wrote to the DSB in May 2016:

> There must be no opening whatsoever to the prospect of political interference in what must remain impartial legal judgments in the WTO's rule-based system of adjudication. As our revered late colleague Julio Lacarte once said of any action that might call into question the impartiality and the independence of the Appellate Body, "This is a Rubicon

that must not be crossed." The unquestioned impartiality and independence of the Members of the Appellate Body has been central to the success of the WTO dispute settlement system, which has in turn been central to the overall success of the WTO. Undermining the impartial independence of the Appellate Body now would not only call into question for the first time the integrity of the Appellate Body; it would also put the future of the entire WTO trading system at risk.[110]

In explaining US actions, Ambassador Lighthizer has said, "We think the Appellate Body has not limited itself…to precisely what's in the agreement."[111] In this statement, Trump's trade ambassador has not expressed a novel view for the US government. A statement submitted by the Obama administration to the DSB in 2016 attempting to justify the administration's opposition to the reappointment of Seung Wha Chang offers detailed criticisms of a number of appellate reports as supposedly exemplifying a pattern of overreaching in rendering legal judgments by the Appellate Body.[112] The United States did not mention in this statement any of the zeroing disputes it had lost. With respect to the several disputes it did mention, the United States emphasized that "the US position on this issue is not one based on the results of those appeals in terms of whether a measure was found to be consistent or not."[113] The United States acknowledged that, in WTO dispute settlement, "there can always be legitimate disagreement over the results."[114] Instead, the United States insisted in its statement to the DSB that its "concerns with the adjudicative approach" of the Appellate Body are "systemic concerns."[115] Professedly for these reasons, the United States opposed the reappointment of Chang, explaining that "we do not think his service reflects the role assigned to the Appellate Body by WTO Members in the WTO agreements."[116]

Although only the three members of the Appellate Body sitting as a division "serve on any one case" and sign the Appellate Body report in that case, all seven of the members of the Appellate Body engage in an exchange of views in every case.[117] The purpose of the exchange of views in an appeal is to reach a broad consensus among the seven on the legal issues appealed that will inform the decision of the three on the division while ensuring — in the words of the DSU — "security and predictability" for the WTO trading system.[118] The aim of the exchange, for example, is to avoid having a basic trade principle such as "national treatment" be interpreted in one way by a division in one case and in another way by a division in another case.[119] Furthermore, any separate opinions expressed in an Appellate Body report by individuals "shall be anonymous."[120] With the Appellate Body speaking almost always by consensus, with all seven of the Appellate Body members working in some fashion on every appeal and with any dissents required to be anonymous, how confidently can the individual views of any one member of the Appellate Body be discerned and somehow distinguished from those of the other six?

With respect to the Chang reappointment in 2016, the United States said, "We have reviewed carefully his service on the divisions for the various appeals and conducted significant research and deliberation. Based on this careful review, we have concluded that his performance does not reflect the role assigned to the Appellate Body by Members of the DSU."[121] So far as this US assessment of Chang's performance was based on the recommendations and rulings he signed, and given how the Appellate Body is structured and works, this statement could as easily have been made by the United States about any of the members then serving on the Appellate Body. In their letter to the DSB, the Appellate Body members serving at the time noted this and added, "We are concerned about the tying of an Appellate Body Member's reappointment to interpretations in specific cases. The dispute settlement system depends upon WTO members trusting the independence and impartiality of Appellate Body Members. Linking the reappointment of a Member to specific cases could affect that trust."[122]

In other words, intimidation could possibly lead to accommodation and capitulation in rendering appellate judgments. Moreover, even the appearance of bowing to the will of the United States in an appeal could undermine the continuing credibility of the entire dispute settlement process and thus of the whole WTO. Given all that has already happened, going forward from here, when the Appellate Body rules in favor of the United States — as it often does — will it do so because the United States is correct on the legal merits or, instead, because some members of the Appellate Body desire the support of the United States for reappointment? Inevitably, this question will be asked. Due to the pressure tactics of the United States, some extent of institutional damage has already been done.

The 13 former Appellate Body members made much the same point, but more bluntly: "A decision on the reappointment of a Member of the Appellate Body should not be made on the basis of the decisions in which that Member participated as a part of the divisions in particular appeals, lest the impartiality, the independence, and the integrity of that one Member, and, by implication, of the entire Appellate Body, be called into question. Nor should either appointment or reappointment to the Appellate Body be determined on the basis of doctrinal preference, lest the Appellate Body become a creature of political favor, and be reduced to a mere political instrument."[123] South Korea was even more straightforward in its statement to the DSB: "This opposition is, to put it bluntly, an attempt to use reappointment as a tool to rein in Appellate Body Members for decisions they may make on the bench. Its message is loud and clear: 'If AB Members make decisions that do not conform to U.S. perspectives, they are not going to be reappointed.'"[124]

In its statement to the DSB about the Chang reappointment, the United States said as well, "We are concerned about the manner in which this member has served at oral hearings, including that the questions posed spent a considerable amount of time considering issues not on appeal or not focused on the resolution of the matter between the parties."[125] If loquaciousness were a cardinal sin in judges, we would have many fewer judges. Often, too, it may be necessary to ask questions that do not seem to be to the legal point to litigators but are nevertheless very helpful to judges in doing their job. Ninety percent of judging an appeal in a WTO dispute is deciding what judgments not to make so as not to pre-judge future disputes. Sometimes, this may lead to questions in an appellate oral hearing that may not seem legally relevant to those of whom the questions are asked. There is also this: the United States assumed that the questions asked by Chang were his own questions reflecting his own views of the legal issues in the dispute on appeal. This is an assumption. Who can say with any assurance that Chang was asking his own question and not asking a question of another Appellate Body member? And since when has the Socratic method of questioning that should be familiar to all legal advocates everywhere been a method that necessarily reveals the personal views of the one doing the questioning?

In its 2016 statement, the United States stressed that it was not contesting the outcomes of any disputes. Should the United States or any other WTO member ever want to contest a legal outcome, the 13 former Appellate Body members have pointed in their letter to the DSB to an alternative course provided in the WTO Agreement:

> Should WTO Members ever conclude that the Appellate Body has erred when clarifying a WTO obligation in WTO dispute settlement, the Marrakesh Agreement establishing the World Trade Organization spells

out the appropriate remedial act. Article IX:2 of the Marrakesh Agreement, on "DecisionMaking," provides, "The Ministerial Conference and the General Council shall have the exclusive authority to adopt interpretations of this Agreement and of the Multilateral Trade Agreements" by a "three-fourths majority of the Members." Any such legal interpretation would, of course, be binding in WTO dispute settlement. We observe that, to date, the Members of the WTO have not seen the need to take any such action.[126]

Of course, as these 13 jurists know, the path to approval of such an authoritative legal interpretation is far from an easy one. This is undoubtedly one reason why this path has yet to be taken. Nevertheless, this is an appropriate avenue set out by the members of the WTO in the WTO treaty. Whatever the merits of the concerns professed by the United States about the performance of the Appellate Body, engaging in tactics that threaten to shut down the whole WTO dispute settlement system is not the appropriate way to address these concerns. Instead of assaulting the continued rule of law, the United States should work within the rule of law. To be sure, before Trump became president, the United States tried and failed to forge a consensus on proposals to change the DSU to address its concerns. That failed, an effort should now be made to resolve the US concerns — where they are legitimate — within the DSB through improvements that do not require changing the DSU. Ideally, this should be done after consultations with the Appellate Body. If legitimate US concerns cannot be resolved in this way, and, if other WTO members agree, then the concerns should be resolved by revising the dispute settlement rules to provide added clarity to the instructions given to the Appellate Body for rendering appellate judgments. If the United States cannot find support for its positions among other WTO members — if other WTO members do not share the US view that the Appellate Body has been increasingly overreaching the bounds of its proper jurisdiction and engaging in inappropriate gap filling — then that speaks for itself as to the merits of the US concerns. It is inappropriate for the United States to use its professed dispute settlement concerns as an excuse to slow the WTO dispute settlement system toward a halt. It is even more inappropriate to do so if the underlying goal is to intimidate Appellate Body members into allowing the United States, in effect, to be the judge of its own cases. That would be the very opposite of the rule of law.

Options for Ending the Appointments Impasse for the Near Team

In every way they can find, the strong in power in the United States are doing what they can in the WTO to assert their ascendancy. Must the weak suffer what they must? As the campaign of US intimidation has intensified, increasingly, some of the most influential voices in world trade have protested. Pascal Lamy, a former director-general of the WTO and also a former European trade minister, has said that, of all Trump's scattered flurry of trade initiatives, the real risk is the destabilization of the WTO dispute settlement system. In Lamy's judgment, "This is the only manifestation so far of a clear danger for the (global trading) system."[127] Speaking of WTO dispute settlement, the current director-general of the WTO, Roberto Azevêdo, has cautioned, "If we compromise this pillar (of the trading system), we will be compromising the system as a whole. There is no doubt about that."[128]

Yet, so far, the increasingly firm opposition of what appears to be, at the least, almost all other WTO members to the pressure tactics of the United States has yielded no result in ending the WTO impasse over Appellate Body appointments. While some have suggested that there may be room for compromise if other WTO members agree to address what the United States has described as its systemic concerns,[129] other WTO members seem disinclined to negotiate on these concerns with the United States unless and until it removes its roadblock to the continued working of the WTO dispute settlement system. The media, when not ignoring the impasse, is mostly portraying it as an arcane political sideshow to Trump's more bombastic threats and actions on trade when, in truth, it should be center stage. When journalists do report on the impasse, they treat it mainly as a political tug of war between the United States and its trading partners without addressing the critical fundamental issue at stake. What is more, back in the United States, not one single member of either party in the House of Representatives or in the Senate has denounced this assault by their country on the rule of law in world trade.

For the near term, a number of respected WTO scholars and experienced WTO lawyers who are concerned about the future of the WTO dispute settlement system and of the WTO trading system have suggested various creative means, largely within the existing rules of the WTO trading system, that the 163 other WTO members might employ to circumvent and thereby to overcome the continued adamant opposition of the United

States to appointments and reappointments of Appellate Body members. One proposal, by Steve Charnovitz, a leading thinker on the knottier questions of international trade law, is that "the Appellate Body amend Rule 20 of the (appellate) Working Procedures to state that in the event of three or more expired terms in the Appellate Body membership, the Appellate Body will be unable to accept any new appeals."[130] WTO rules give the Appellate Body sole control of its working procedures.[131] Appellate "working procedures shall be drawn up by the Appellate Body in consultation with the Chairman of the DSB and the Director-General, and communicated to the Members for their information."[132] There is, however, no requirement that the Appellate Body consult with the DSB as a whole or that the DSB as a whole approve the appellate working procedures. Therefore, the United States does not have a veto over the working procedures.

Charnovitz contends,

> Although the Appellate Body does not have the right to formally take away the right to appeal, it does have the right to declare in advance that under extreme circumstances, the "completion of the appeal" will occur automatically on the same day that any new appeal is lodged. In other words, by removing itself from the dispute process for new cases, a disabled Appellate Body will step aside so that the panel decision can automatically be adopted by the WTO Dispute Settlement Body on a timely basis. For a depleted Appellate Body bench to continue processing new cases would necessarily cause huge delays, thus frustrating the Uruguay Round goals of a prompt dispute system.[133]

The United States may well be perfectly content, of course, for this to happen when the United States prevails before a panel. But the United States will not prevail before every panel. Like any other WTO member, it will want to preserve its right of appeal. Moreover, while on some of the most contentious current legal issues, the United States has been satisfied with simply a panel result, on others, it may prefer to have a result that has been vetted by the Appellate Body. Recall that every WTO case is really two cases, the immediate dispute and the legal principles involved, and the fact — decidedly contrary to the Trump telling — that the United States wins the vast majority of the cases it takes to the WTO. As Charnovitz puts it, "By limiting the potential damage to WTO dispute settlement in this way, the Appellate Body could, in effect, call the

Trump Administration's bluff."[134] Does the United States want to continue to be able to use the appellate process in WTO dispute settlement, or does it want to shut it down?

A second proposal, by Peter Jan Kuijper, a former principal legal adviser to the WTO, is that, to circumvent the US intransigence, the other members of the WTO resort to majority voting. He maintains that "recourse to majority voting is perfectly legal, once it is clear that consensus cannot be reached."[135] Just so, article IX:1 of the WTO Agreement provides that "where a decision cannot be arrived at by consensus, the matter at issue shall be decided by voting," and that "[d]ecisions of the Ministerial Conference and the General Council shall be taken by a majority of the votes cast, unless otherwise provided in this Agreement or in the relevant Multilateral Trade Agreements."[136] This option has rarely been used by the members of the WTO. They prefer always, if they can, to operate by the general rule of consensus. Yet, Kuijper advises, "This is no small matter, it is a true emergency. Times of emergency justify emergency measures, also in the law of international organizations."[137] He contends, "Direct appointment of AB members by the General Council applying majority vote, under the strict limitation that this is an exceptional one-off measure connected to the threat of malfunctioning of the Appellate Body, and accompanied by explicit openness to further discussions with the United States, seems to be the best possible option for action inside the WTO. Ideally, merely the threat of majority voting may create leverage to arrive at consensus."[138]

Kuijper also offers an alternative to majority voting, saying that "if WTO Members are so strongly opposed to majority voting as to shy away from action inside the WTO, they will have to seek a solution outside the WTO."[139] For guidance, he points us to the customary rule of international law on fundamental change of circumstances, reflected in article 62 of the Vienna Convention on the Law of Treaties.[140] Article 62 provides that a fundamental change of circumstances that has occurred with regard to those existing at the time of the conclusion of a treaty, and that was not foreseen by the parties, may not be invoked as a ground for terminating or withdrawing from a treaty or suspending the operation of a treaty unless: the existence of those circumstances constituted an essential basis of the consent of the parties to be bound by the treaty; the effect of the change is radically to transform the extent of obligations still to be performed under the treaty; the treaty does not establish a boundary; and the fundamental change is not the result of a breach by the party invoking it either of an obligation under the treaty or of any other international obligation owed to any other party under the treaty.[141]

On the basis of a change in circumstances, Kuijper argues that all the members of the WTO except the United States could negotiate and conclude outside the WTO a new treaty that would essentially duplicate the appellate provisions of the DSU or even the entirety of the DSU. "Then the sitting members of the Appellate Body would resign and be taken over as members of the Appellate Tribunal of the new treaty, to be joined by new selected members. On a voluntary basis, the Members of the Appellate Body Secretariat could leave the WTO as well and join the new Appellate Tribunal."[142] He adds, in another innovation, that "this new Tribunal could be opened up as an Appeals Tribunal from decisions of the dispute settlement mechanisms of regional FTA agreements."[143] The costs would be defrayed by member contributions which, he predicts, would be offset by declines in contributions to the WTO budget due to the WTO no longer having to pay for the Appellate Body or perhaps even for dispute settlement.[144] In sum, the WTO dispute settlement system could be recreated outside the legal framework of the WTO — while excluding the United States.

A third proposal — by Scott Andersen, Todd Friedbacher, Christian Lau, Nicolas Lockhart, Jan Yves Remy, and Iain Sandford — resembles Kuijper's proposal for a new dispute settlement treaty based on changed circumstances outside the WTO, but it has the practical virtue of, in effect, creating an identical parallel dispute settlement system within the WTO. These private practitioners of WTO law — who have also previously worked for governments and for the WTO itself — are steeped in knowledge of how the WTO dispute settlement system works. Confronted by this impasse, they point to article 25 of the DSU, a hitherto largely neglected legal provision that relates to arbitration.[145] Article 25.1 of the DSU expresses the agreed treaty view of the members of the WTO that "expeditious arbitration with the WTO as an alternative means of dispute settlement can facilitate the solution of certain disputes that concern issues that are clearly defined by both parties."[146] Article 25.2 provides, "Except as otherwise provided in this Understanding, resort to arbitration shall be subject to mutual agreement of the parties which shall agree on the procedures to be followed."[147] Other members may become parties to the arbitration with the agreement of the parties that have decided to arbitrate.[148] Arbitration awards shall be binding and notified to the DSB.[149] Furthermore, the usual DSU rules relating to the implementation of recommendations and rulings under article 21 of the DSU and to compensation and the suspension of concessions under article 22 of the DSU will apply.[150]

As Andersen and his colleagues see it, "Article 25 is drafted in terms that are sufficiently flexible to allow a process that replicates closely the essential features of the appellate process under Article 17 of the DSU."[151] Article 25 does not define arbitration. Therefore, arbitration can be defined as WTO members may choose to define it consistently with the provisions of Article 25, which say nothing about not duplicating the usual WTO dispute settlement procedures, including the procedures for appeals. The arbitration under Article 25 thus need not follow the familiar parameters of private arbitrations around the world but can mirror the more truly adjudicatory dimensions of WTO dispute settlement. What is more, under Article 25 (which, ironically, was first proposed by the United States during the Uruguay Round[152]), "arbitration...does not depend on any action by the DSB...and the binding character of an arbitration award does not depend on adoption or approval by the DSB. Instead, an award must simply be notified to the DSB and the relevant WTO Councils and Committees."[153] Thus, the United States could not block an arbitral award by refusing to join in a consensus to approve it. Much like Kuijper, Andersen and his colleagues envisage that the arbitrators could be "selected randomly from an agreed roster of individuals comprising current and previous Appellate Body members, with membership of the roster being broadly representative of WTO membership."[154] In their proposal, Andersen and his colleagues spell out in some detail how this alternative process of what they call "appeal-arbitration" would work in practice.[155]

There are legal quibbles aplenty, mainly about the first two of these proposals. The provisions of the WTO treaty are rarely without legal nuance, and there are legal nuances yet to be resolved. With the first proposal, the United States would likely argue that the singular authority of the Appellate Body to adopt its working procedures does not extend to, in effect, denying the legal right of appeal mandated by the DSU, even if the Appellate Body is unable to hear the appeal. With the second proposal, the United States would likely insist that the provisions of the DSU requiring a consensus trump (if you will) the provisions in Article IX:1 of the WTO Agreement allowing for majority voting. As Charnovitz, Kuijper and others have set out at some length, counter-arguments can be made to both of these potential US arguments.[156] With the third proposal, arbitration, it is more difficult to discern an argument on which the United States could base an objection. Where in Article 25 does it say that any one WTO member can object to any other WTO members having recourse to arbitration? And where does it forbid WTO members having recourse to arbitration to duplicate the existing WTO appellate procedures and employ whomever they choose as arbitrators? For these reasons, the third proposal may be the best way to proceed with the ongoing work of WTO dispute settlement within the existing WTO rules for the near term.

Reinforcing the Rule of Law in WTO Dispute Settlement for the Long Term

For the long term, more must be done. For the long term, the existing rules must be improved. The sturdiest frames in the enabling framework of WTO dispute settlement have been those raised by the rulings of the WTO Appellate Body. The Appellate Body has unique and unprecedented authority for an international legal tribunal. Yet, after the still short span of slightly more than two decades, its authority remains fragile, and it remains dependent on the continued willingness of all WTO members to comply with the rule of law and otherwise to uphold the rule of law. The continued success of the WTO requires that the Appellate Body continue to be true to its treaty mandate so that it will continue to have the strong support of the members of the WTO against those both within the WTO and without who would undermine its necessary judicial authority. Moreover, through further WTO rule making, the WTO must be strengthened to the task of continuing to serve its members while meeting the new challenges facing the world trading system in the 21st century.

The members of the WTO should make the standing WTO Appellate Body a full-time instead of a nominally part-time tribunal. Serving on the Appellate Body has never really been a part-time job. It is certainly not one now. The rules must be changed to acknowledge this. As full-time jurists, given the nature of their work, Appellate Body members need not necessarily be resident full time in Geneva. As it is now, they will need to be in Geneva only for hearings and deliberations. (A legal brief and a panel record and report can be read anywhere.) Moreover, as members of the highest court of world trade, the members of the Appellate Body should be given pay and benefits appropriate to their high standard of service on an international tribunal dealing with trillions of dollars in trade disputes. Currently, they make in a day with the WTO what they could make as international arbitrators in an hour. In addition, Appellate Body members and WTO panelists alike should be given the full extent of the financial, personnel and other resources they need to get the job done. In its first year, 1996, the Appellate Body was given a budget for its legal library for the entire year of just 50 Swiss francs.[157] Things have changed since then but, all considered, not all that much. The WTO is hardly the biggest financial drain among international institutions on the limited treasuries of WTO members. The time when the members of the WTO could afford to run a worldwide international dispute settlement system on the cheap has long since passed. In the end, as with so much else, with the international rule of law, in the long term, we are likely to get what we pay for.

"What remains essential," the 13 former members of the Appellate Body wrote in 2016 to the DSB, is "the unflinching independence of the Members of the Appellate Body in fulfilling their pledge to render impartially what they see as the right judgments in each dispute by upholding the trade rules on which all WTO Members have agreed."[158] Will precedes law. Law builds institutions. Will, then, must sustain both law and institutions. An indispensable part of the expression of such will is the ongoing exercise of restraint. Mutual self-restraint is the underpinning of the framework of law and of the institutions that make law and aim to uphold law through the rule of law. The ultimate test of the show of such self-restraint in a system dedicated to the resolution of international disputes is when a dispute is lost. A legal loss in any one dispute, or even in a series of disputes, should not lead a country to undermine the upholding of the rule of law that is the transcendent purpose of an international dispute settlement system, and that is in the long-term interest of every country. Real respect for the rule of law is shown by what you do not when you win, but when you lose.

It can be hoped that those entrusted, for now, with leading the American people will remember in time why the United States has long supported a rules-based world trading system and the rule of law in world trade. Perhaps this is too much to expect from Trump and those who pay obeisance to him. Yet America is bigger and better than those who may happen to govern it at any given time. In time, America will rediscover the better angels of its nature. When it does, it would be best for the WTO simply to remove the continuing temptation for the United States — or for any other WTO member — to engage in the tactics of intimidation to which the United States has descended lately. The possibility of reappointment for Appellate Body members should be eliminated. This one change in the dispute settlement rules would end this form of intimidation and would reinforce the essential independence and impartiality of the Appellate Body.

Two options for implementing this change in the current WTO rules seem most attractive. There could continue to be seven members of the Appellate Body, but with each appointed for a single seven-year term and with one of the seven rotating off the tribunal each year. Or, as an alternative, the size of the Appellate Body could be increased to nine members, with each one appointed for a single nine-year term and with one of the nine departing each year. The first option, by preserving the current number of seven judges, would do more to ensure the continued collegiality of the Appellate Body in working toward a desired consensus in each dispute. The second option, by adding two more judges, would do more to make the Appellate Body representative of the membership of the WTO, given that there are many more members of the WTO now than when it was established in 1995. Provisions could be made in the transition to retain the current members of the Appellate Body on new and revised terms.

With either of these two options for improving the existing WTO dispute settlement rules, the original design flaw permitting the possibility of the reappointment of a member of the Appellate Body would be eliminated. No longer could the United States or any other errant WTO member risk undermining the rule of law in world trade over Appellate Body appointments and reappointments because it had been lured by low political motives into forgetting the enduring lesson of Melos — that might must never be allowed to make right. No longer could might threaten to unmake right as it is doing now so sadly in WTO dispute settlement.

Endnotes

[1] John H. Finley Jr., *Thucydides* (Cambridge, MA: Harvard University Press, 1942) at 210.
[2] Donald Kagan, *The Peloponnesian War* (New York: Penguin Books, 2003) at 247–249.
[3] *Ibid.*
[4] Robert B. Strassler, ed., *The Landmark Thucydides* (New York: The Free Press, 1996) at 351.
[5] *Ibid* at 352. (emphasis added)
[6] *Ibid.*

[7] Finley, *supra* note 1 at 209.

[8] Jacob M. Schlesinger Jr., Peter Nicholas and Louise Radnofsky, "Trump to Impose Steep Aluminum and Steel Tariffs," *The Wall Street Journal* (March 2, 2018).

[9] Mark Landler and Alan Rappeport, "Trump Plans to slap tariffs and investment restrictions on China," *The New York Times* (March 22, 2018).

[10] Josh Dawsey and Damian Paletta, "Assailed for remarks on trade, Trump doubles down on claims about Canada," *Washington Post* (March 16, 2018).

[11] WTO, *Understanding on Rules and Procedures Governing the Settlement of Disputes*, 1869 UNTS 401, 33 ILM 1226 (1994), art. 23.1 [DSU], www.wto.org/english/tratop_e/dispu_e/dsu_e.htm.

[12] *United States — Certain EC Products* (2001), WTO Doc WT/DS165/ AB/R at para 111 (Appellate Body Report) (emphasis added). It should be noted that, while a member of the Appellate Body, I was the chair of the division in the appeal in that dispute. The Appellate Body has since reiterated and reinforced this ruling in *United States — Canada — Continued Suspension* (2008), WTO Doc. WT/DS231/AB/R at para 371 (Appellate Body Report).

[13] *Canada — Measures Governing the Sale of Wine in Grocery Stores* (second complaint), WT DS531.

[14] *India — Export Related Measures*, WT DS541.

[15] *China — Certain Measures Concerning the Protection of Intellectual Property Rights — Request for Consultations by the United States* (2018), WTO Doc. WT/DS542/1.

[16] See James Bacchus, "How the World Trade Organization Can Curb China's Intellectual Property Transgressions" (March 22, 2018) *Cato at Liberty* (blog), www.cato.org/blog/how-world-trade-organization-can-curb-chinas-intellectual-property-transgressions.

[17] *China — Subsidies to Producers of Primary Aluminum*, WT DS519.

[18] See Office of the United States Trade Representative, www.ustr.gov/trade-agreements.

[19] ProMexico, www.promexico.gob/my/en/mx/tradados-comerciales.

[20] *General Agreement on Tariffs and Trade*, April 15, 1994, 1867 UNTS 187, 33 ILM 1153, art. I:1 (entered into force January 1, 1995). John H Jackson, *World Trade and the Law of GATT* (New York: Bobbs-Merrill, 1969) at 245.

[21] See "The Case for Open Trade", WTO www.wto.org/english/thewto_e/whatis_e/tif_e/fact3_e.htm.

[22] Office of the Press Secretary, The White House, Press Release, "Press Briefing by Secretary of Commerce Wilbur Ross on an Executive Order on Trade against Violations and Abuses" (April 28, 2017).

[23] Editorial, *The New York Times* (February 27, 2017); Damian Paletta and Ana Swanson, "Trump suggests ignoring World Trade Organization in major policy shift," *Washington Post* (March 1, 2017); Shawn Donna and Demetri Sevastopulo,

"Trump team looks to bypass WTO dispute system," *Financial Times* (February 27, 2017); Alex Lawson, "Trump Will Not Comply With Adverse WTO Rulings" (March 1, 2017) *Law 360* (blog).

[24] "Remarks of President Trump to the 72nd Session of the United Nations General Assembly" (Address delivered at the United Nations, New York, September 19, 2017), The White House www.whitehouse.gov/briefings-statements/remarks-president-trump-72nd-session-united-nationsgeneral-assembly/.

[25] Interview of President Trump by Lou Dobbs (October 25, 2017) on *Fox Business*.

[26] *Ibid.*

[27] Ashley Parker and David Nakamura, "At summit, Trump return to tough stance on trade," *Washington Post* (November 11, 2017); John Wagner and David Lynch, "On Trump's trade trip to Asia, nations keep his one-on-one dance card empty" *Washington Post* (November 15, 2017).

[28] Donald Trump, *The Art of the Deal* (New York: Random House, 2004).

[29] James Romm, "Greeks and Their Gifts," *The Wall Street Journal* (May 23, 2015).

[30] Bryce Baschuk, "U.S. Pledges Work to 'Improve' WTO Rather Than Destroy It," *Inside US Trade* (June 9, 2017).

[31] Eduardo Porter, "Trump's Endgame Could Be the Undoing of Global Rules," *The New York Times* (October 31, 2017).

[32] It should be acknowledged that, while a Member of Congress, I was one of the six original co-sponsors of the implementing legislation for the Uruguay Round trade agreements and, thus, have long been on the opposite side of Ambassador Lighthizer in the debate over whether the national interest of the United States is best served by participating in the WTO dispute settlement system.

[33] DSU, *supra* note 11, art. 3.7.

[34] Shawn Donnan, "Fears for free trade as Trump fires first shots to kneecap WTO," *Financial Times* (November 9, 2017).

[35] *Ibid.*

[36] DSU, *supra* note 11, art. 16.4.

[37] WTO, *Agreement on the Implementation of Article VI of GATT 1994*, 1868 UNTS 201 [*Anti-dumping Agreement*]; WTO, *Agreement on Subsidies and Countervailing Measures*, 1869 UNTS 14.

[38] Greg Rushford, "Bob Lighthizer, WTO Jurist?" (October 2003) *The Rushford Report*, www.rushfordreport.com/2003/10_2003 Publius.htm.

[39] *Ibid.*

[40] *Ibid.*

[41] *Ibid.*

[42] Robert E. Lighthizer, "Grand Old Protectionists," *The New York Times* (March 6, 2008).

[43] Robert E. Lighthizer, "Evaluating China's Role in the World Trade Organization Over the Past Decade" (Testimony before the U.S.-China Economic and Security

Review Commission, June 9, 2010) at 33, www.uscc.gov/sites/default/files/6.9. 10Lighthizer.pdf.

[44] *Ibid.* at 35.

[45] *Ibid.* at 33.

[46] Eduardo Porter, "Trump's Endgame Could Be the Undoing of Global Rules," *The New York Times* (October 31, 2017).

[47] Gregory Shaffer, Manfred Elsig, and Mark Pollack, "Trump is fighting an open war on trade. His stealth war on trade may be even more important," *Washington Post* (September 27, 2017).

[48] *See United States — Zeroing* (EC) (2006), WTO Doc. WT/DS294/AB/R (Appellate Body Report); *United States — Zeroing (Japan)* (2007), WTO Doc. WT/DS322/AB/R (Appellate Body Report); *United States — Zeroing (Japan)* (2007), WTO Doc WT/DS/322/21 (Article 21.3(c) Arbitration Report); *United States — Zeroing (Japan)* (2009), WTO Doc WT/DS322/ RW (Article 21.5 Panel Report); *United States — Zeroing* (EC) (2009), WTO Doc WT/DS294/ AB/RW (Article 21.5 Appellate Body Report); and *United States — Zeroing* (2011), WTO Doc WT/DS402/R (Panel Report). The initial dispute in which the Appellate Body ruled against the use of zeroing methodology in determinations of the existence of dumping and of dumping margins was *European Communities — Bed Linen* (2001), WTO Doc WT/DS141/AB/R (Appellate Body Report), in which the United States was not a party to the dispute. It should be noted that I was one of the members of the division of the Appellate Body in that appeal.

[49] *See Anti-dumping Agreement, supra* note 37, art. 2.4.

[50] DSU, *supra* note 11, arts. 3.2, 19.2.

[51] *Ibid.* art. 17.1.

[52] *Ibid.* art. 17.12.

[53] *Ibid.* art. 3.2

[54] *Vienna Convention on the Law of Treaties*, May 23, 1969, 1155 UNTS 331, 8 ILM 679 (entered into force January 27, 1980) [Vienna Convention].

[55] *Ibid.* art. 31.1.

[56] DSU, *supra* note 11, art. 17.3.

[57] *Ibid.*

[58] WTO, *Rules of conduct for the understanding on rules and procedures governing the settlement of disputes* (1995), WTO Doc WT/DSB/RC/1, art. II.1 [Rules of Conduct].

[59] *Ibid.* art. III.2.

[60] *Ibid.*

[61] *Ibid.* art. IV.1.

[62] DSU, *supra* note 11, art. 17.2.

[63] *Agreement Establishing the World Trade Organization* (1994), 1867 UNTS 154, 33 ILM 1144, art. IX.1, n. 1 [WTO Agreement].

⁶⁴ *Ibid.* art. IX.1. The late Julio Lacarte Muro, who chaired the dispute settlement negotiations during the Uruguay Round, was the principal author of the DSU and was also a founding member and the first chair of the Appellate Body, lamented to me on numerous occasions that this was indeed an oversight.

⁶⁵ I owe the phrase "design flaw" to my friend and CIGI colleague, Hugo Perezcano Díaz.

⁶⁶ *WTO Agreement, supra* note 63, n. 1.

⁶⁷ I rely here, in part, on my personal knowledge of these events. Among numerous accounts, most of them in the trade press, *see, e.g.* "Pressure on U.S. Mounts as it maintains link between Appellate Body seats, WTO reform", *Inside US Trade* (September 15, 2017); Alex Lawson, "WTO Dispute Roundup: Appellate Body Impasse Persists" (September 29, 2017) *Law 360* (blog); "Dispute Unsettlement", *The Economist* (September 23, 2017); Alex Lawson, "WTO Members Clash Over Appellate Body Reappointment" (May 23, 2016) *Law 360* (blog) [Lawson, "WTO Members Clash"].

⁶⁸ Shawn Donnan, "WTO chief warns of risks to world peace," *Financial Times* (October 1, 2017); *see* WTO, *Working Procedures for Appellate Review* (2010), WTO Doc WT/AB/WP/6, Rule 15 [*Working Procedures*].

⁶⁹ *DSU, supra* note 11, art. 3.7.

⁷⁰ This is based on my personal recollections as a participant in those discussions with the DSB at the time.

⁷¹ Bryce Baschuk, "U.S. Claims Right to Veto any Errant WTO Dispute Rulings", *International Trade Daily* (September 29, 2017).

⁷² *DSU, supra* note 11, art. 17.1.

⁷³ *Ibid.* art. 17.14.

⁷⁴ Baschuk, *supra* note 71.

⁷⁵ *DSU, supra* note 11, art. 17.1.

⁷⁶ Simon Chesterman, "An International Rule of Law?" (2008) 56 *American Journal of Comparative Law*, 331 at 342.

⁷⁷ This description in this paragraph paraphrases the classic definition in Roscoe Pound, "Law in Books and Law in Action" (1910) 44 Am L Rev 12; *see also* AW Bradley & KD Ewing, *Constitutional and Administrative Law*, 12th ed. (New York: Longman, 1997) at 105.

⁷⁸ Anne-Marie Slaughter, "International Law in a World of Liberal States" (1995) 6 *European Journal of International Law* 503 at 511, n. 18.

⁷⁹ Baron de Montesquieu, "The Spirit of the Laws" (1748), as quoted in Alexander Hamilton, *The Federalist Papers, Number 78* (1788).

⁸⁰ *Ibid.*

⁸¹ I first explored this point in James Bacchus, "The Rule of Law: Reflections on Thucydides and the World Trade Organization" Winter/Spring 2000 Vanderbilt Magazine 16. I have made it many times since on numerous platforms and in numerous other appearances worldwide. For a broader discussion of this point,

see James Bacchus, *The Willing World: Shaping and Sharing a Sustainable Global Prosperity* (Cambridge, UK: Cambridge University Press, 2018) ch. 4.

[82] Declan Walsh, "As Strongmen Steamroll Their Opponents, U.S. Is Silent", *The New York Times* (February 1, 2018).

[83] *See, e.g.* Bob Dreyfus, "Trump's All-Out Attack on the Rule of Law," *The Nation* (February 1, 2018); Yascha Mounk, "Donald Trump Just Asked Congress to End the Rule of Law," *Slate* (January 30, 2018); Jeffrey Toobin, "Donald Trump and the Rule of Law," *The New Yorker* (January 6, 2018).

[84] Philip Zelikow, "The Logic Hole at the Center of Trump's U.N. Speech," *Foreign Policy* (September 20, 2017).

[85] "New USTR agenda dismisses WTO dispute settlement authority, says U.S. to stress 'sovereignty'," *Inside US Trade* (March 1, 2017).

[86] John Bolton, "Trump, Trade and American Sovereignty," *The Wall Street Journal* (March 7, 2017).

[87] John H. Jackson, *Sovereignty, the WTO, and Changing Fundamentals of International Law* (Cambridge, UK: Cambridge University Press, 2006) at 69.

[88] *Ibid* at 61.

[89] Joshua Meltzer, "State Sovereignty and the Legitimacy of the WTO" (2014) 26:4 *University of Pennsylvania Journal of International Law* 693 at 702.

[90] I have made this same point in "A Few Thoughts on Legitimacy, Democracy, and the WTO" (2004) 7:3 *Journal of International Economic Law* 667 at 670.

[91] *DSU, supra* note 11, art. 3.2.

[92] Here, of course, I echo the famous dictum of Louis Henkin half a century ago that "[a]lmost all nations observe almost all principles of international law and almost all of their obligations almost all of the time." Louis Henkin, *How Nations Behave: Law and Foreign Policy* (New York: Frederick A Praeger, 1968) at 42.

[93] Parker & Nakamura, *supra* note 27.

[94] Andrew Mayeda, "Trump's No Fan of WTO, but U.S. Lawyers Often Win There," *Bloomberg* (March 29, 2017).

[95] Louise Johannesson & Petros C Mavroidis, "The WTO Dispute Settlement System 1995–2016: A Data Set and Its Descriptive Statistics" (2016) European University Institute Working Papers RSCAS 2016/72 at 24.

[96] WTO, *Agreement on the Application of Sanitary and Phytosanitary Measures*, April 15, 1994, 1867 UNTS 493, art. 2.2 (entered into force 1 January 1995), www.wto.org/english/tratop_e/sps_e/spsagr_e.htm.

[97] Robert Farley, "Trump Wrong About WTO Record" (October 27, 2017) *FactCheck* (blog).

[98] Council on Foreign Relations, "Is the WTO Dispute Settlement System Fair?" (February 26, 2007), www.cfr.org/article/wto-disputesettlement-system-fair.

[99] *DSU, supra* note 11, art. 3.7.

[100] Dan Ikenson, "US Trade Laws and the Sovereignty Canard," *Forbes* (March 9, 2017).

101 *Ibid.*
102 While a member of the WTO Appellate Body, I found it necessary to do so on a number of occasions myself.
103 *DSU, supra* note 11, art. 8.2.
104 *Ibid.* art. 17.3.
105 *Rules of Conduct, supra* note 58, arts. II.1, III.2, IV.1.
106 *DSU, supra* note 11, art. 8.3.
107 *Ibid.* art. 17.3.
108 I am, I confess, a former member of the Congress of the United States.
109 *DSU, supra* note 11, art. 17.3.
110 Letter from 13 former Appellate Body members to Ambassador Xavier Carim, chairman of the DSB (May 31, 2016) [May 31, Letter], http://worldtradelaw.typepad.com/files/abletter.pdf. I was one of the 13 former Appellate Body members who signed the letter.
111 Interview of Ambassador Robert Lighthizer by John J Hamre, "U.S. Trade Policy Priorities" (September 18, 2017) at the Center for Strategic and International Studies, https://www.csis.org/analysis/us-tradepolicy-priorities-robert-lighthizer-united-states-trade-representative.
112 Statement by the United States to the DSB (May 22, 2016) [May 22, US Statement]. The four appellate reports referenced by the United States were *Argentina — Financial Services* (2016), WTO Doc. WT/DS453/AB/R (Appellate Body Report); *India — Agricultural Products* (2015), WTO Doc. WT/DS430/AB/R (Appellate Body Report); *European Communities and Certain Member States — Large Civil Aircraft* (2014), WTO Doc. WT/DS347/AB/R (Appellate Body Report); and *United States — Countervailing and Anti-Dumping Measures (China)* (2014), WTO Doc. WT/DS449/AB/R (Appellate Body Report).
113 May 22 US Statement, *supra* note 112.
114 *Ibid.*
115 *Ibid.*
116 *Ibid.*
117 *DSU, supra* note 11, art. 17.1; *Working Procedures, supra* note 68, Rule 4.
118 *Ibid.* art. 3.2.
119 *Ibid.*
120 *Ibid.* art. 17.11.
121 May 22. US Statement, *supra* note 112.
122 Quoted in Lawson, "WTO Members Clash," *supra* note 67.
123 May 31. Letter, *supra* note 110.
124 Lawson, "WTO Members Clash," *supra* note 67.
125 May 22. US Statement, *supra* note 112.
126 May 31. Letter, *supra* note 110.
127 Tom Miles, "WTO Is Most Worrying Target of Trump's Trade Talk: Lamy," *Reuters* (November 14, 2017).

128 Donnan, *supra* note 68.

129 Robert McDougall, "Standoff on WTO tribunal is more about the scope of intergovernmental adjudication than Trump unilateralism" (January 12, 2018) International Centre for Trade and Sustainable Development.

130 Steve Charnovitz, "How to Save WTO Dispute Settlement from the Trump Administration" (November 3, 2017) *International Economic Law and Policy* (blog) [emphasis in original].

131 *DSU, supra* note 11, art. 17.9.

132 *Ibid.*

133 Charnovitz, *supra* note 130.

134 *Ibid.*

135 Peter Jan Kuijper, "Guest Post from Peter Jan Kuijper on the US Attack on the Appellate Body" (November 15, 2017) *International Economic Law and Policy Blog* (blog).

136 *WTO Agreement, supra* note 63, art. IX:1.

137 Kuijper, *supra* note 135.

138 *Ibid.*

139 *Ibid.*

140 *Vienna Convention, supra* note 54, art. 62.

141 *Ibid.*

142 Kuijper, *supra* note 135.

143 *Ibid.*

144 *Ibid.*

145 *DSU, supra* note 11, art. 25.

146 *Ibid*, art. 25.1.

147 *Ibid*, art. 25.2.

148 *Ibid*, art. 25.3.

149 *Ibid.*

150 *Ibid*, arts. 21, 22.

151 Scott Andersen et al., "Using Arbitration under Article 25 of the DSU to Ensure the Availability of Appeals" (2017) Center for Trade and Economic Integration Working Papers CTEI-2017-17 at 1.

152 GATT, *Improved Dispute Settlement: Elements for Consideration: Discussion Paper Prepared by United States Delegation*, GATT Doc. No. MTN.GNG/NG13/W/6 (June 25, 1987) at 2.

153 Andersen et al., *supra* note 151 at 2.

154 *Ibid.* at 5.

155 *Ibid.* at 4–8.

156 See the illuminating exchange of views among scholars and practitioners on the *International Economic Law and Policy Blog.*

157 This is a personal recollection.

158 May 31, Letter, *supra* note 110.

Chapter 9

The Digital Decide: How to Agree on WTO Rules for Digital Trade*

Introduction

The new Digital Economy Partnership Agreement (DEPA) among Chile, New Zealand and Singapore may be a model for how members of the World Trade Organization (WTO) should proceed in agreeing on global rules for digital trade. The modular approach used in this first ever "digital only" trade agreement may help the 86 WTO members negotiating on e-commerce resolve some of the seemingly intractable digital trade issues that stand in the way of a WTO agreement. For more than two decades, WTO members have been unable to negotiate specific rules for digital trade to include in the WTO treaty. Permitting negotiating countries to select among different digital commitments they are willing to assume at this time while establishing a WTO legal framework in which they can add to their commitments over time — as modelled in the structure of the DEPA — could enable WTO negotiators to make a breakthrough in current negotiations and conclude a basic agreement by the convening of the Twelfth WTO Ministerial Conference in Geneva, Switzerland, in late November 2021. The digital commitments made in this basic agreement could then be broadened and deepened thereafter to bring the WTO more fully into the 21st century by setting out, for the first time, global rules for

---

*This essay was previously published by the Centre for International Governance Innovation as James Bacchus, "The Digital Decide: How to Agree on WTO Rules for Digital Trade," Special Report (August 16, 2021).

digital trade. Agreement on digital trade rules could also prove anew that the members of the WTO are not only able to negotiate but they are also able to conclude negotiations successfully. In the absence of such proof, the WTO is at much risk of being sidelined in the global economy as global commerce becomes ever more digital.

The Digital Economy Partnership Agreement

Although it received little attention at the time, a new agreement that took effect on January 7, 2021, among three trade-minded countries may signal the way forward for successfully negotiating new global rules on digital trade. On that date, the DEPA among Chile, New Zealand and Singapore entered into force (Falak, 2021). As the world's first "digital only" trade agreement, the DEPA was signed in June 2020, fittingly in a virtual ceremony. At a time when a sizeable subset of the 164 member countries of the WTO are negotiating on what they hope will ultimately become multilateral rules for conducting digital trade (International Institute for Sustainable Development, 2021), this accord among these three ambitious WTO members features a novel approach to making commitments on digital trade. If embraced by the WTO, this approach could be the key to unlocking agreements on many needed WTO digital trade rules, and it could also help begin to build toward an eventual consensus on some of the most divisive issues that pose the biggest obstacles to a WTO digital trade agreement.

The novel approach in the DEPA is a "modular" approach that permits countries to pick and choose which specific legal commitments on digital trade they are willing to assume immediately while refraining for the present from assuming other potential commitments that are not currently politically attainable. The "modules" in the DEPA are structured so that they can be adopted and then slotted into other trade agreements in addition to the DEPA, which could have the effect of extending the reach of the broad range of potential digital trade commitments set out in the DEPA harmoniously. In this way, the DEPA puts in place a set of legal building blocks that can be stacked up in different combinations by different countries while establishing a basic framework for the incremental construction of a global legal architecture to promote digital trade.

New leadership at the WTO aspires to revitalize and modernize the WTO to make it more fit for purpose in the 21st century. Agreement by the WTO for the first time on rules for digital trade must be a central part of these reforms since, by far, the most significant new dimension of international trade in the 21st century is that so much of it is now digital. Indeed, trade "is increasingly defined by flows of data and information" (McKinsey Global Institute, 2016: 1). About 12 percent of all goods traded internationally are purchased online (*Ibid.*, 7), and about half of global trade in services is digital (*Ibid.*). The McKinsey Global Institute reports that, since 1990, the global economy is 10 percent larger than it would have been without those increased data and information flows — an added global economic output equivalent to $7.8 trillion[1] (*Ibid.*, 1). Moreover, "Data flows account for $2.8 trillion of this effect, exerting a larger impact on growth than traditional goods flows" (*Ibid.*, emphasis added).

Adding to the pressing need for rules on digital trade is the persistence of the coronavirus disease 2019 (COVID-19) pandemic. Even before the pandemic, the trend toward more digital trade seemed likely to continue and to accelerate. Now, spurred by the need for more global connectivity during the pandemic, trade is becoming even more digital. In the pre-COVID-19 world, for example, 41 percent of the interactions between customers and North American companies were digital (Ignatius, 2020). In the new pandemic world of more virtual and other digital connections, 65 percent of customer interactions are digital (*Ibid.*). As the Organisation for Economic Co-operation and Development (OECD) has pointed out, "The current crisis has accelerated the digital transformation and underscored its importance for mitigating the economic slowdown, sustaining wellbeing, and speeding up recovery" (OECD, 2020: 2).

Although digital trade is growing exponentially internationally, the "regulatory restrictions on international digital trade are growing equally, if not more, rapidly" (Lovelock, 2020). WTO rules are much needed to limit these restrictions on digital trade by drawing agreed lines that clarify which restrictions are appropriate and which are not. If WTO members can agree on rules for digital trade, then the abundant benefits of digital trade will spread more rapidly and more widely throughout the world. If they cannot agree on rules for digital trade, then the WTO will surely be relegated to the periphery of world trade; it will become increasingly irrelevant to the continuing advance of trade through digital connections of all kinds.

The 86 WTO members that are negotiating on possible rules for e-commerce and the facilitation of digital trade must bridge the geographical and geopolitical "digital divide" by producing a "digital decide" that will serve all WTO members while helping ensure the continued centrality of the WTO-based multilateral system to world trade. They must prove anew that they can, in fact, succeed through trade negotiations by concluding at least some rules to liberalize more digital trade by the time of the next WTO Ministerial Conference, which, because of the COVID-19 pandemic, has been delayed and relocated and will be held in Geneva, Switzerland, in late 2021. Employing the new modular approach chosen by Chile, New Zealand, and Singapore in the DEPA can help them accomplish this goal.

WTO Actions Thus Far to Address Digital Trade

Despite the scope and the speed of the global digital economic transformation, there are no specific WTO rules that apply to international digital trade. Although the internet was invented in 1983,[2] and commercial internet service providers began to emerge in the late 1980s,[3] the World Wide Web was not created until 1990,[4] and it was not commonly used commercially until the mid-1990s.[5] Thus, digital trade barely existed during the Uruguay Round[6] of multilateral trade negotiations, which began in 1986 and concluded with the Marrakesh Agreement[7] of 1994 that established the WTO in 1995. Digital trade was, therefore, not on the trade agenda several decades ago. As Mark Wu (2017) has written, WTO rules date back to when the internet was still an obscure novelty and "many of today's digital technologies and applications did not yet exist."

Mindful of the absence of specific WTO digital trade rules, WTO members have been trying to modernize WTO rules to deal with digital trade since shortly after the WTO was established. At the First WTO Ministerial Conference, held in Singapore in 1996, members agreed on a temporary moratorium[8] on the application of customs duties for electronic transmissions of digital products and services (which does not prevent internal taxes, fees or charges on content transmitted electronically). This action was taken by consensus of WTO members to prevent the rapid spread of digital trade from being slowed by increased costs resulting from a feared outpouring of border tariffs. At the next Ministerial Conference, held in Geneva in 1998, this temporary moratorium was renewed. Accompanied by much debate, the moratorium has been renewed repeatedly at each successive Ministerial Conference since.

Yet, after all this time, WTO members have still not been able to reach a consensus that would make this moratorium permanent.

Also in Geneva in 1998, WTO members adopted a declaration on global e-commerce,[9] which called on the WTO General Council to set up a work program to examine all trade-related issues of e-commerce. At the time, this work program was intended to be exploratory; it did not launch formal negotiations. Because of the inherently cross-cutting nature of issues relating to e-commerce, the work program was divided among four different WTO councils: those on goods, services, intellectual property (IP) and development. In June 2001, the General Council held the first of a series of "dedicated discussions"[10] on the work program in e-commerce.

At that time, the council identified seven issues for deliberation by the members that ranged across a number of the existing trade agreements in the WTO portfolio:

- the classification of digital products as goods or services;
- issues concerning developing and least developed countries (LDCs);
- the revenue implications of e-commerce, especially for developing countries;
- the relationship between e-commerce and traditional forms of commerce (to assess short-term disadvantages for developing countries);
- the impact on developing countries of a continued moratorium on customs duties;
- competition-related issues, including constraints on e-commerce due to concentration of market power; and
- jurisdictional challenges for e-commerce disputes.

Of these seven issues, the two most significant and controversial at the time were the classification of digital products as goods or services and the continued moratorium on customs duties.

Despite many subsequent discussions — "dedicated" and otherwise — in the 16 years that followed, WTO members accomplished little within the WTO toward addressing the mounting and manifold commercial concerns of what was rapidly becoming an increasingly digital global economy. The WTO Secretariat, in an understatement, described the work of the WTO members on e-commerce as "unfinished."[11] The inability of WTO members even to agree to negotiate specific rules on digital trade was a major reason for the seeming indifference of so many in the international business community to the demise of the multilateral Doha Development Round in Nairobi, Kenya, in 2015. Much that was important to them in the new global economy — including multiplying digital trade concerns — was not on the Doha negotiating agenda. The continued absence of specific rules on digital trade in the WTO trade rulebook is emblematic of the near paralysis of the WTO negotiating function thus far in this century.

Real progress did not seem possible until 2017 when, at the 11th WTO Ministerial Conference in Buenos Aires, Argentina, 71 WTO members — led by the United States, the European Union and Japan — issued a Joint Statement on Electronic Commerce.[12] In this statement, these 71 countries announced that they would "initiate exploratory work together toward future WTO negotiations on trade-related aspects of electronic commerce."[13] At the World Economic Forum in Davos, Switzerland, on January 25, 2019, 76 WTO members issued another Joint Statement, which announced their intention to "commence WTO negotiations on trade-related aspects of electronic commerce."[14]

The 76 countries joining in the second statement said they sought "to achieve a high standard outcome that builds on existing WTO agreements and frameworks with the participation of as many WTO Members as possible."[15] They added that, in the beginning of these negotiations, they recognized and would "take into account the unique opportunities and challenges faced by Members, including developing countries and LDCs, as well as by micro, small and medium sized enterprises, in relation to electronic commerce."[16] Lastly, these countries pledged to "continue to encourage all WTO Members to participate in order to further enhance the benefits of electronic commerce for businesses, consumers and the global economy."[17] A notable new participant in the second announcement was China, which, evidently, had noted the progress of the talks and had concluded that it could not afford to remain on the sidelines.

Since then, numerous negotiations have occurred, including virtual sessions during the COVID-19 pandemic. Co-conveners Australia, Japan and Singapore have structured the virtual sessions to include both large and small groups, with many of the group meetings focusing on individual issues relating to digital trade. As these virtual sessions have continued throughout 2020 and 2021, the negotiators have reported progress in these small groups on such digital trade issues as e-signatures and authentication, paperless trading, customs duties on electronic transmissions, open government data, open internet access, consumer protections and source code.

In December 2020, the 86 negotiating countries agreed on a consolidated negotiating text[18] for a proposed WTO agreement on digital trade. Topics in the consolidated text included enabling e-commerce, transparency and e-commerce, trust and e-commerce, cross-cutting issues, market access, telecommunications, and scope and general provisions. Although the 90 pages of this text are replete with bracketed language, which denotes that no agreement has yet been reached on most of the major issues, the negotiations' co-convenors have stated nonetheless that they are on pace to deliver on their goal of "successful progress" by the time of the upcoming WTO Ministerial Conference in late 2021 (WTO, 2021a).

At this writing, there has been no indication of any intention to depart from the traditional WTO approach of an "all or nothing" agreement, in which WTO members must agree to all the commitments in the agreement as a condition to becoming a party to it. The number of countries participating in the e-commerce negotiations has grown to 86 WTO members, accounting for 90 percent of world trade (Ministry of Economy, Trade and Industry, 2020) — a "critical mass" of trade that is sufficient to support the goal of a plurilateral WTO agreement with benefits that would be applied by the negotiating parties on a non-discriminatory "most-favored-nation" basis to include all the "free riders" that do not sign the agreement.

Importantly, these non-participating WTO members that will become free riders — all of them developing countries and LDCs — would therefore appear to have no incentive to join the new agreement. However, an incentive can be provided in that becoming a party to the agreement would give them access to much-needed financial and technical assistance to help them ramp up their own participation in digital trade. Furthermore, the initial "down payment" of digital trade commitments by those WTO members that do choose at the start to be parties to a new WTO agreement will be more substantial if they are permitted at the outset to select from among different digital commitments and among different levels of those commitments.

With a critical mass of countries engaged, with the co-conveners pushing hard, with a new and ambitious WTO Director-General in place, with the United States turning more toward multilateralism under a new administration, with China as well as all the other major trading countries at the table, and with the commercial demands for global digital trade rules intensifying, the negotiating countries hope that the limited success they anticipate by the time of the year-end gathering in Geneva will lead to more substantial success beyond that meeting, including on the most difficult issues of digital trade. They hope for as much of a down payment as they can get on digital trade, and they hope the extent of that down payment at the end of 2021 will inspire greater commitments in 2022 and beyond. The fulfillment of this hope could eventually lead to a WTO digital trade agreement that is fully multilateral in fact, if not yet in law.

The Modular Approach of the DEPA

As they strive to turn this hope into reality, the 86 WTO members engaged in negotiations on digital trade should look to the DEPA as their model in structuring a new WTO digital trade agreement. Not only is the DEPA the first stand-alone international agreement that deals exclusively with digital trade, but it is also innovative in the modular approach it employs in framing the new digital trade obligations it contains. In the array of options that the DEPA itself offers and, equally, in the various ways that it aspires to emulation elsewhere, this innovative framing is a promising architectural template for digital trade and is much deserving of multilateral attention by the WTO.

In addition to offering a menu of possible commitments that can be chosen by the parties to it, the DEPA also invites those who are not parties to the new agreement to select from the DEPA menu. It is not meant to be an isolated accord; instead, it is intended to be an agreement that will "coexist" in legal parallel with other existing international trade agreements while providing portable and variable commitments that can be included in those other agreements. The DEPA was negotiated by Chile, New Zealand, and Singapore with the belief that its individual provisions could end up being cut, pasted, and tailored for inclusion in other international agreements, potentially including a WTO agreement. The aim of these three WTO members is to use the DEPA as a foundation and a funnel for building, over time, not merely a critical mass of digitally trading countries but also a critical mass of ambitious and largely matching digital trade obligations that can move closer and closer, over time, to being fully multilateral.

The three parties to the DEPA are relatively small countries that are nevertheless major players in world trade. They are heavily engaged in and heavily dependent on trade. They know the immense economic value of freeing trade and shortening long distances, and they are well-known not just for being open and creative in trade. Chile, New Zealand, and Singapore are also frequent leaders on cutting-edge issues in the deliberative councils of the WTO. How these three WTO members have chosen to structure the legal commitments in their new digital trade agreement can show the way forward for all the 86 WTO members engaged in the Joint Statement Initiative on multilateral rules for e-commerce.

The DEPA features several substantive innovations that add to the sum of what has previously been achieved and is already contained relating to digital trade in a growing proliferation of bilateral and regional trade agreements (RTAs) concluded outside the legal framework of the WTO. For instance, the DEPA is the first trade agreement in the world to deal with digital identities (such as national business numbers), which are an important component of the digital economy.[19] It also includes rules on financial technology (fintech) and artificial intelligence (AI).[20] Moreover, it establishes innovative programs to foster the inclusion of women and Indigenous peoples in the digital economy.[21] These substantive DEPA innovations are noteworthy in their own right.

But what is most distinctive about the DEPA — and what is most conducive to emulation by the WTO — is its distinctive structure. Chile, New Zealand, and Singapore have each agreed to the DEPA in its entirety. These three countries have, however, structured their agreement to contain separate subject-specific categories for different topics relating to digital trade. They call these categories "modules." The DEPA is open to accession by other countries, and, as other countries join, they can choose to accept the different levels of commitments contained in each of these modules. Through this structure, the DEPA affords countries additional choices. Conceivably, other countries could join the agreement as a whole; or they could incorporate individual modules of the agreement either within their domestic law or in separate trade agreements.

Furthermore, the innovative modular design of the DEPA allows negotiators in other arenas to pick and choose among the separate DEPA modules while borrowing from them. Because these modules are separate and distinct, they are each whole unto themselves. The goal of the DEPA participants is to encourage international multiplication of these modules in a variety of legal contexts in which different countries can select different initial levels of commitment that match their current levels of political and technical comfort in taking on different kinds of digital trade commitments. As Giridharan Ramasubramanian of the Australian National University has explained, the DEPA modules "cover discrete components within a broader issue area. This modular structure allows policy negotiators to elaborate on the specific characteristics of a component and segment it from other components while ensuring that they all fit within the wider framework of an agreement. It also allows specific parts of an agreement to be transferred to various other contexts."[22]

Regarding this novel feature of the DEPA, Debra Elms of the Asian Trade Centre in Singapore (2020) has similarly explained that "these modules are meant to be building blocks. Countries could opt to dock directly onto the DEPA, expanding the agreement with new members. Or governments could decide to pick up and use modules, in whole or in part, in various settings. These include slotting them directly into other trade agreements or opting to align domestic policies to DEPA." Thus, she adds, "the DEPA represents a promising start to creating harmonized frameworks for the digital economy. It contains flexibility to allow members to adapt the rules to local conditions, when clearly warranted, and should provide conditions for greater adoption of the modules by other members" (*Ibid.*).

The DEPA modules subject to some or all of this picking and choosing in this innovative trade design are:

- initial provisions and general definitions (module 1);
- business and trade facilitation (module 2);
- treatment of digital products and related issues (module 3);
- data issues (module 4);
- wider trust environment (module 5);
- business and consumer trust (module 6);
- digital identities (module 7);
- emerging trends and technologies (module 8);
- innovation and the digital economy (module 9);
- small and medium enterprises cooperation (module 10);
- digital inclusion (module 11);
- joint committee and contact points (module 12);
- transparency (module 13);
- dispute settlement (module 14);
- exceptions (module 15); and
- final provisions (module 16).

Already, the provisions of the DEPA have been largely replicated in another "digital only" deal, the Singapore-Australia Digital Economy

Agreement (SADEA),[23] which was signed in August 2020 and entered into force in December 2020. The SADEA mostly borrows the DEPA's modular approach. It is intended as a modernization of an existing bilateral trade agreement between Singapore and Australia, two close trading partners. Thus, it is more akin to a conventional free trade agreement than is the DEPA. At the same time, the SADEA goes beyond the DEPA in providing for more liberalization of digital trade on electronic authentication and signatures (article 9), submarine telecommunications cable systems (article 22), location of computing facilities for financial services (article 25), source code (article 28), and standards and conformity assessment for digital trade (article 30). As part of the SADEA, Singapore and Australia have also signed a series of memoranda of understanding on areas including e-invoicing, e-certification, personal data protection and digital identity.

Already, too, the DEPA is drawing even wider notice as other countries consider joining the new agreement. Canada has begun public negotiations on joining the DEPA (Global Affairs Canada, 2021), and South Korea is also seeking to join (Yonhap, 2021). In this, they will be joined soon by still more WTO members. Yet with two of the leading advocates of these two new stand-alone digital trade agreements — Singapore and Australia — serving as two of the co-conveners of the WTO negotiations, they can be expected to encourage the 86 WTO members negotiating on possible WTO rules for digital trade to consider using something akin to the DEPA modular approach.

In contrast to other plurilateral and multilateral WTO agreements, which generally are "all or nothing" in their commitments, individual WTO members could be given the option in a new WTO digital framework of agreeing to digital commitments in one or more modular categories but not in others. Also, as has frequently been the case with other WTO agreements, WTO members could be afforded the option of acceding to different categories and levels of commitments at different times by agreement on transitional periods for implementation for different countries and for different categories of countries based on their stage of development. Also, where a consensus can be reached, some of the categories of new digital commitments could be made multilateral from the outset while others could instead start as plurilateral, with the ambition of evolving them into fully multilateral WTO commitments over time as more WTO members see their usefulness and decide to embrace them.

The WTO negotiations have produced a consolidated negotiating text[24] on digital trade, dated December 14, 2020. This text is very much a work in progress. Mostly, as of this writing, it is replete with bracketed language and suggested alternatives on which the negotiators have not yet agreed. With a few exceptions, the individual submissions containing recommendations by the participating WTO members to other participants remain restricted (although they are referenced in the draft text). Chairing the negotiations is Permanent Representative to the WTO and Ambassador George Mina of Australia, a seasoned, insightful trade diplomat well acquainted with the intricacies of complex digital trade issues and with the esoteric nuances of WTO negotiations. The approach thus far in the negotiations has been to build step by step toward a consensus on all those digital trade issues on which it is thought a consensus can be reached at this time. Notably, at this point, the scope of the coverage in the consolidated negotiating text is roughly the same as that of the modular categories in the DEPA.

The consolidated negotiating text is divided into sections on:

- facilitating electronic and other digital transactions and their logistics (including such basic matters as electronic signatures, electronic payment services, paperless trading, customs procedures and enhanced trade facilitation);
- openness (transparency) in e-commerce (including non-discrimination and liability, flow of information, customs duties on electronic transmissions, and access to internet and data);
- trust in e-commerce (consumer protection, privacy and business source codes);
- cross-cutting issues (including domestic regulation, cooperation, capacity building and cybersecurity);
- telecommunications (including network equipment and products and updating the WTO Reference Paper on Telecommunications Services);
- market access (including both goods and services); and
- scope and general provisions (including definitions, principles, general exceptions and a security exception).

On numerous issues, the draft text contains several alternatives drawn from the various and differing submissions of the participants. In February

2021, the negotiating countries celebrated their first success in achieving consensus when they finalized an agreed text on treatment of unsolicited commercial messages (spam) (WTO, 2021b). Of course, this was surely the easiest of all digital trade issues on which to reach consensus. Who in the world likes to receive spam? In contrast, the bulk of the issues in the negotiations remain, as of this writing, short of resolution (and, in many cases, distantly so.)

The step-by-step approach taken by the WTO negotiators is, no doubt, the proper approach. The negotiators, however, need a structure to this approach that will help maximize the negotiated results while also establishing a firm core of rules on which additional commitments can be made in the years to come. This structure should be a flexible, modular framework much like the DEPA, which, because it will be put in place by the WTO, will be able to accomplish the goals of the DEPA more quickly and more extensively in many more countries worldwide. This WTO structure could range widely from the easiest issues to resolve, such as spam, to the very hardest to resolve, such as those relating to the cross-border flow of data. Employing this structure would permit different initial outcomes on each issue in different countries while laying the foundation for further incremental progress in supporting digital trade in the future.

General Rules in a WTO Digital Trade Agreement

Before erecting this flexible, modular structure, though, the 86 negotiating members of the WTO should, ideally, agree to include in their new agreement some new general rules that are needed to help maximize the flow of digital trade. First, they should decide what precisely they are negotiating about, and how specifically the existing WTO rules apply to digital trade; they should first define what they mean by "digital trade." In addition, they should eliminate the lingering global market uncertainty about whether customs duties will be imposed on digital transactions; they should make the WTO moratorium on such taxation permanent. Moreover, they should eliminate some of the current uncertainties in digital trade by clarifying the ways in which a number of existing WTO rules apply to digital trade; otherwise, digital trade will be constrained because many of those uncertainties will be left to resolution in the outcomes of future contentious international trade disputes.

Defining the scope of digital trade

Digital trade is not defined in the current WTO trade rules. Any consideration of WTO rules to govern digital trade should begin by defining it. Only then can WTO members know the scope of what will be covered by the new rules. What is more, the continuing and accelerating technological evolution of digital trade, which involves the ever more varied dimensions of constantly transforming international commerce, suggests that digital trade should be defined in broad terms that will encompass its ever-widening scope, not only now but also in the future.

Separate and apart from this current omission in the WTO rules is that worldwide, there is no one recognized and accepted definition of digital trade. Globally, the terms "digital trade" and "e-commerce" are often used interchangeably. Helpfully, but without the force of law, the OECD (2011: 72) describes an e-commerce transaction as "the sale or purchase of goods or services, conducted over computer networks by methods specifically designed for the purpose of receiving or placing of orders. The goods or services are ordered by those methods, but the payment and the ultimate delivery of the goods or services do not have to be conducted online. An e-commerce transaction can be between enterprises, households, individuals, governments, and other public or private organisations."

The WTO work program on e-commerce defines it ("without prejudice" to the outcome of the WTO digital trade negotiations) as "the production, distribution, marketing, sale or delivery of goods and services by electronic means."[25] The identical phrasing — still in brackets — is used to define "[digital trade/e-commerce]" in Annex 1(2)1 of the WTO consolidated negotiating text. Thus, in defining the scope of the potential new rules as they have done in their work program, these 86 WTO members seem to have taken sides in the long-running debate over whether e-commerce is comprised of only those transactions where the end product or service delivered is digital, or whether e-commerce also includes every part of the global value chain of that end product or service. In effect, the WTO negotiators appear to have embraced much of the second broader view in their negotiations.

To make way for the innovations of the future, these WTO members should consider going further by emulating the scope of coverage in the DEPA. The DEPA does not define digital trade as such; however, module 1, article 1.1.1 of the DEPA defines the scope of that agreement broadly as covering "measures adopted or maintained by a Party that affect trade in the digital economy." The DEPA makes exceptions in module 1, article 1.1.2 for services made in the exercise of governmental authority, electronic payments through delivery of financial services, government procurement, and — apart from open government data — "information held or processed by or on behalf of a Party, or measures related to that information, including measures related to its collection." This DEPA approach is arguably more expansive than the one being considered by the WTO negotiators.

Not surprisingly, the broader the definition of digital trade, the more controversy there will be, and the more contentious the negotiations are likely to be. Yet the WTO members negotiating on digital trade should cross the Rubicon on this central threshold question. Clearly confirming their embrace of an expansive definition of digital trade would help erase remaining uncertainties and help reduce the number of future disputes over this issue in WTO dispute settlement.

Making the Moratorium on Tariffs on Digital Trade Permanent

Since the temporary moratorium on customs duties on electronic transmissions of goods and services was first introduced in Singapore in 1996, the challenge facing those that wish to make it permanent has been the reluctance of some of the developing countries to join in a consensus to do so. While most countries, developed and developing alike, see the assurance of no tariffs as a means of advancing trade, some developing countries are apprehensive of the tariff losses due to the moratorium.

Some developing countries see the customs duties moratorium as benefiting only developed countries. Of course, the growth of digital trade is of great importance to developed countries, but the shift to a digital economy is especially important to developing countries, which continue to suffer "within and across countries" from a "digital divide" (Wu, 2017: 1). Ninety percent of the people in the world without internet access are in developing countries (Meltzer, 2016). Eighty eight percent of North Americans, 85 percent of the Japanese and 84 percent of Europeans have internet access (Webb, 2019). So do 65 percent of the people in the Middle East and North Africa, 63 percent of Latin Americans and 54 percent of the Chinese (*Ibid.*). But only 34 percent of Indians, 33 percent of the inhabitants of the small Pacific Island states and 25 percent of Sub-Saharan Africans can get online to connect with the wider world (*Ibid.*). Most of the people in these developing countries remain outside the productive engine of the digital economy.

If applied along with measures that enhance digital access, new rules that lower the barriers to digital trade can be of disproportionate benefit to developing countries by narrowing the digital divide. As the WTO (2018: 9) has pointed out, "Many trade costs such as logistics and transactions costs or cumbersome customs procedures…are much higher in developing countries." Thus, developing countries will benefit proportionately the most by the digitalization of these trade procedures. The WTO predicts that developing countries' share of world trade will increase from 46 percent in 2015 to 51 percent by 2030 (*Ibid.*, 3), but if developing countries "catch up on the adoption of digital technologies" (*Ibid.*, 11), their share of global trade in 2030 will be 57 percent (*Ibid.*). If, however, developing countries are left behind in the digital economy by the digital divide, then they will be largely bypassed in the global economy of the future.

In March 2020, India and South Africa circulated a communication[26] to all WTO members in which they set out what they perceived as the harmful impacts of the moratorium on customs duties on developing countries, including losses of tariff revenue, constraints on industrialization and what they saw as the negative local consequences of the use of digital technologies such as 3D printing in manufacturing. The two countries argued that the moratorium was "equivalent to developing countries giving the digitally advanced countries duty-free access to [their] markets."[27] They cited a research paper published by the United Nations Conference on Trade and Development (UNCTAD), which concluded that in 2017 alone, the potential tariff revenue loss to developing countries because of the moratorium was $10 billion (Banga, 2019: 17). UNCTAD researcher Rashmi Banga calculated that removing the moratorium could increase policy space for developing countries to enable them to regulate imports by electronic transmissions and thus generate annual tariff revenue of as much as 40 times more than that in developed countries (*Ibid.*, 19).

In reply to this communication by India and South Africa, a communication[28] circulated to all WTO members in June 2020 by a diverse group of likeminded countries (comprised of Australia, Canada, Chile, China, Colombia, Hong Kong, Iceland, New Zealand, Norway, the Republic of Korea, Singapore, Switzerland, Thailand and Uruguay) highlighted a 2019 paper by the OECD, which concluded that the studies cited by India

The Digital Decide: How to Agree on WTO Rules for Digital Trade 303

and South Africa "overestimate the revenue implications" of the moratorium (Andrenelli and López González, 2019: 6). According to the OECD, "the opportunity cost of the Moratorium in terms of foregone government revenue is likely to be low," and "the overall benefits" of duty-free electronic transmissions "outweigh the potential forgone government revenues" due to the moratorium (*Ibid.*).

Similarly, a study by the European Centre for International Political Economy (ECIPE) in 2019 concluded that developing countries and LDCs would lose more in GDP than they would gain in tariff revenues with the withdrawal of the WTO moratorium (Makiyama and Narayanan, 2019). According to this study, the annual GDP losses of China, India, Indonesia and South Africa alone would total $10.6 billion and, furthermore, each of those four countries would lose vastly more than it gained by ending the duty moratorium. For example, for Indonesia, the losses would be 160 times the gains (*Ibid.*, 2). Overall, the ECIPE research showed that "if countries ceased to uphold the moratorium and levied import duties on digital goods and services, they would suffer negative economic consequences in the form of higher prices and reduced consumption, which would in turn slow GDP growth and shrink tax revenues" (*Ibid.*). At the same time, "the payoff in tariff revenues would ultimately be minimal relative to the scale of economic damage that would result from import duties on electronic transmissions" (*Ibid.*).

According to a worldwide group of 40 tech-minded think tanks called the Global Trade & Innovation Policy Alliance (2020), the developing countries that are calling for an end to the moratorium are

> often ignoring the larger net negative effect digital tariffs would have on global trade, innovation and competitiveness, domestic output, and productivity.... Keeping the moratorium in place fosters certainty and predictability for both domestic digital economic activity and global production networks and supply chains. It is unclear whether it's even technically feasible to administer a fair, predictable, and efficient system to identify and collect digital duties. Either way, any effort to collect customs on every digital transaction would disrupt the seamless global flow of information and data via software, digital content, and any number of other Internet-based processes, which would inevitably impact broader economic output as well as the levels of global productivity and innovation. (*Ibid.*, 7)

Opportunity costs such as these in digital trade are often overlooked in public policy debates of all kinds and, in particular, this is so of those that relate to trade. These costs must not be overlooked here. In module 3, article 3.2 of the DEPA, the DEPA parties have barred customs duties on electronic transmissions, including content transmitted electronically, without adding any time limit. Section B.3.2 of the WTO draft text includes three alternatives with essentially the same effect. At a minimum, when writing new rules specifically designed for digital trade, WTO members should at least — and at last — eliminate the trade-constraining uncertainties about the imposition of customs duties on electronic transactions by making the WTO moratorium on such customs duties permanent.

Clarifying the application of existing wto rules to digital trade

There is no need for WTO members to start with a blank slate in drafting digital trade rules in the current negotiations; despite the absence of specific WTO rules on digital trade, some existing WTO rules in WTO agreements relate to certain aspects of digital trade and thus already apply to digital transactions. As Dan Ciuriak and Maria Ptashkina (2018: 1) have put it, numerous rules that apply to non-digital trade also apply "by default" to digital trade, even in the absence of specific rules on digital trade. Yet many legal uncertainties remain about whether existing rules apply, which existing rules apply and how these existing rules apply. Ideally, these uncertainties should be eliminated when devising new rules.

For example, there is a threshold question that must be asked and answered in every individual case: Is a particular product that is traded online a good or a service? To illustrate, as economist Robert Staiger has done, it may be asked: "Is a blueprint for use in a 3D printer, when delivered from abroad, a traded good or a traded service?" (WTO, 2018: 150). The answer to this question matters, in part, because the national treatment obligation, which forbids discrimination in favor of domestic over foreign producers of like products, applies automatically to all trade in goods, but it applies to trade in services only when a WTO member has explicitly agreed to it.[29] This is the most significant distinction between WTO rules on trade in goods and WTO rules on trade in services.

There is no economic or legal logic for making this distinction; it is simply a consequence of a political compromise made during the Uruguay

Round that made it possible to achieve a consensus on including services trade within the scope of the trade rules. No consensus could be reached then to apply the national treatment rule automatically to all trade in services; instead, WTO members agreed to limit the application of national treatment in services trade to those sectors inscribed in a member's schedule, which leaves out much services trade. As a result, if a particular traded product is deemed a service instead of a good, WTO members are often legally free to discriminate against foreign suppliers of that service. Hence, there are domestic pressures in many places to define as the delivery of services digital trade that also has aspects of the delivery of goods.

Under the existing WTO rules, digital transactions will sometimes give rise to issues under the General Agreement on Tariffs and Trade (GATT)[30] relating to trade in goods; however, for the most part, digital transactions will fall within the scope of the General Agreement on Trade in Services (GATS).[31] The GATS rules are technologically neutral, which "means that GATS disciplines apply to services supplied electronically and that the supply of a service across borders includes all means of delivery, including electronic delivery…. As a result, trade restrictions, as well as domestic regulations affecting electronic trade in services, are subject to the GATS" (WTO, 2018: 152). Add to this the broad scope of the GATS, which applies to all "measures by Members affecting trade in services."[32] This includes "any service in any sector except services supplied in the exercise of governmental authority"[33] and "any measure by a Member, whether in the form of a law, regulation, rule, procedure, decision, administrative action, or any other form."[34]

Beginning with the supply of services in the famous bananas dispute[35] in the 1990s, WTO panels and the WTO Appellate Body have rendered a long series of rulings and recommendations that have confirmed the broad scope of the "measures affecting trade in services" that fall within the coverage of article I.1 of the GATS. Likewise, WTO panels and the WTO Appellate Body have discerned broad scope in the meaning of whether a national measure is one "affecting" trade in services under article I.1 of the GATS, beginning with the *Canada — Autos* dispute.[36] Taken together, all this provides ample legal room for concluding that many digital services are currently covered by the GATS.

Also relevant to the conduct of digital trade are two sets of added obligations under the GATS: the Annex on Telecommunications,[37] which applies to all WTO members, and the Reference Paper on Regulatory Principles on Basic Telecommunications,[38] which applies to the 103 WTO members that have incorporated it into their WTO schedules of GATS commitments. Also clearly relevant to digital trade among the existing WTO rules are provisions of the GATS Annex on Financial Services,[39] which states that WTO members will not "prevent transfers of information or the processing of financial information, including transfers by electronic means"; the plurilateral Information Technology Agreement[40] among 82 WTO members, which reduces tariffs worldwide on information and communications technology (ICT) products; the Agreement on Technical Barriers to Trade (TBT Agreement),[41] which applies to governmental standards and regulations for ICT and electronic products and has "a range of implications for digital trade, including in areas such as standards for broadband networks, regulations on encryption, privacy, and data storage" (Meltzer, 2019); the Agreement on Trade-Related Aspects of Intellectual Property Rights,[42] which "sets out intellectual property rights protections for technologies that enable e-commerce, such as computers, software, routers, networks, switches, and user interfaces" (Ismail, 2020: 6) and thus arguably applies in the digital arena; and the Agreement on Trade Facilitation,[43] which speeds the flow of trade through "the simplification, modernization and harmonization of export and import processes"[44] and thus has a major impact on digital trade. The WTO consolidated negotiating text on digital trade does not answer the legal questions about how these existing rules apply to digital trade or, for the most part, even try to answer them.

Ideally, the 86 WTO members negotiating on digital trade should try to answer at least some of these questions in the new rules in a digital trade agreement. If these questions are not answered there, they will ultimately be sought in litigation in WTO dispute settlement. Negotiation is always preferable to litigation in clarifying rules and their application. Litigation should be a last resort. What is more, if WTO members decide to leave these unresolved legal issues to litigation, then, between now and then, the current legal uncertainties and, thus, the current economic uncertainties in conducting digital trade will continue.

Modular Obligations in a WTO Digital Trade Agreement

Apart from negotiating general rules defining digital trade, making permanent the moratorium on customs duties on digital trade and answering some of the questions about the application of some existing rules to digital trade, WTO members should structure the remainder of the potential obligations in a WTO digital trade agreement as optional obligations in the same modular format as the DEPA and by drawing on the substantive obligations in the DEPA. The agreement should include the "low-hanging fruit": individual modules containing strong obligations on a list of basic commercial obligations that are necessary to facilitate digital trade and are, in most instances, largely uncontroversial. The agreement should also include the "fruit at the top of the digital tree": individual modules with initially weaker but potentially ascending obligations on the much more difficult issues in digital trade, which, although highly controversial, cannot be ignored.

Within each of these modules, WTO members should be given options to accept a range of new digital obligations incrementally and over different periods of time. At the start, this approach would produce an array of piecemeal obligations in an arrangement that political scientists would call "asymmetrical." But, over time, with the benefits of mutual experience and accruing habits of cooperation in dealing with digital trade rules, this initial arrangement could be expected to become more symmetrical; the multi-colored tapestry at the beginning of the WTO digital trade agreement could blend gradually into one color. What began as a collage of piecemeal plurilateralism could eventually grow into a genuine multilateralism.

One risk of attempting to conclude a WTO digital trade agreement among so many countries is that the result could be a "lowest common denominator" agreement. Such a result would not achieve much globally for digital trade, and it could conceivably have the unintended effect of undermining the DEPA and other ambitious bilateral and regional digital trade initiatives. The best way to prevent such a result is to build the broadest and highest possible base of new obligations on which all the participants can agree at the outset while also putting in place an agreed architectural foundation of rules on which WTO members can erect higher beams through progressively higher commitments on the hardest issues over time.

The hardest issues in digital trade involve opening closed economies to a freer flow of more digital data. The DEPA enables this opening to be accomplished selectively and incrementally. As Wendy Cutler and Joshua P. Meltzer (2021) have written of the DEPA, "This approach opens the door for new entrants to sign up for parts of the agreement as a first step, while putting off the more difficult areas until they are ready. If the U.S. and its close partners are serious about promoting a model for the digital economy based on the values of openness and inclusiveness, allowing countries to join certain parts without waiting until they are ready to commit to everything is an innovative way to encourage countries to gravitate to this model over time."

Models in other non-WTO agreements

In addition to the DEPA, a helpful place where WTO negotiators should look for the basis of a consensus on the digital trade issues that seem to be capable of early resolution is in the proliferation of digital chapters and other digital provisions in the host of bilateral, regional and other preferential trade arrangements that have been agreed outside the WTO since the turn of the century. Frustrated by their inability to negotiate rules on digital trade within the WTO, the United States, the European Union and other countries with a huge stake in the digital economy — developed and developing alike — have ventured outside the WTO legal framework to agree on digital trade rules. By one count, there are 69 RTAs with either a chapter on e-commerce or provisions on e-commerce (Wu, 2017: 2). About half of the 164 WTO members are now parties to non-WTO agreements that contain rules on digital trade (*Ibid.*, 7).

These non-WTO agreements lack the inherent advantages of multilateral agreements, in which a balance of mutual obligations can be secured based on weighing all global points of view. The RTAs also lack the global coverage that comes with multilateral agreements and apply only in those countries that are parties to these less-than-multilateral agreements. Multilateral agreements lower barriers to trade globally; other agreements do not. As well, these bilateral agreements and RTAs can also be unbalanced in their effects, including digitally; they can reflect the "take-it-or-leave-it" approach typical of the larger countries in negotiating with smaller ones.

What is more, as with all non-multilateral trade agreements, a commitment by the parties to a bilateral agreement or an RTA to discriminate in favor of the digital products of other parties to that agreement is, by definition, a commitment to discriminate against the digital products of all those countries that are not parties to that agreement. Such bilateral or regional discrimination is permissible under long-standing WTO rules as an exception to the basic legal obligation of most-favored-nation treatment only if that agreement meets the requirements of article XXIV.8(a)(i) of the GATT,[45] including the elimination of the "duties and other restrictive regulations of commerce" on "substantially all the trade" between and among the parties to the non-WTO trade agreement.

To the extent that a digital-only agreement such as the DEPA covers matters that fall within the scope of the existing WTO rules, any trade discrimination within it is vulnerable to a potential challenge in WTO dispute settlement for not covering "substantially all the trade" between and among its parties. This is, however, true also of many RTAs, yet such challenges have not previously been made. The WTO jurisprudence offers little guidance in foreseeing the outcome of such a dispute, which is best avoided, of course, by making the DEPA rules multilateral.

As it stands, the digital provisions in some of these non-WTO agreements besides the DEPA offer templates for crafting digital trade rules within the WTO. The language about various aspects of digital trade has increasingly been shared across these agreements so that the makings of a potential global consensus on some of the less contentious issues are already in place. Plus, some of these agreements have now been in force long enough to offer the benefit of useful experience with their implementation and application. Learning by doing on a bilateral and regional basis can inform negotiations on a global basis. In short, although the WTO has so far been unsuccessful in negotiating specific multilateral rules on digital trade throughout the digital age, there is, nevertheless, no need now for WTO members to begin from the very beginning on global digital governance.

In addition to the DEPA, several of these many other non-WTO agreements can be especially helpful to the WTO negotiators. Notable, for example, are the rules on digital trade in what is now named the Comprehensive and Progressive Agreement for Trans-Pacific Partnership (CPTPP).[46] Although, in one of his first acts as president, former US President Donald Trump pulled the United States out of what was then the Trans-Pacific Partnership; the 11 remaining member countries in the Pacific Basin regional agreement retained the digital trade rules the United States had negotiated in the slightly revised agreement they rechristened as the CPTPP. In several respects, the DEPA builds on the innovations on digital trade in chapter 14 of the CPTPP.

The Canada-United States-Mexico Agreement (CUSMA)[47] — a 2020 update of the North American Free Trade Agreement (NAFTA) — is more recent than the CPTPP, and it adds to the template of the CPTPP in establishing rules for digital trade among those three North American countries. Both the internet and digital trade were new when the original NAFTA was concluded in 1994. Chapter 19 on digital trade, which is new in CUSMA, is more precise in some places than the CPTPP in broadening the scope of protections for digital trade. The United States is also a party to the US-Japan Digital Trade Agreement[48] of 2020, which parallels CUSMA and includes prohibitions on customs duties, data localization and other protectionist measures that restrict trade in digital products.

Patrick Leblond (2020) has suggested that a "good harbinger" of what he worries will be the "lowest common denominator" rules that could emerge from the WTO digital trade negotiations, could be the digital chapter in the new Regional Comprehensive Economic Partnership (RCEP),[49] a regional agreement signed by Australia, China, Japan, New Zealand, the Republic of Korea, and the 10 member states of the Association of Southeast Asian Nations (Brunei, Cambodia, Indonesia, Laos, Malaysia, Myanmar, the Philippines, Singapore, Thailand and Vietnam) in November 2020. As he has written, "This is because [this new agreement] showcases what China, the RCEP's dominant member state, is willing to accept in terms of e-commerce/digital trade provisions" (*Ibid.*).

Chapter 12 of the RCEP, on e-commerce, differs in some respects from the digital trade provisions in the CPTPP, to which some RCEP members are also parties. In contrast, however, to CUSMA, which adds to the digital obligations in the CPTPP, some of the digital provisions in the CPTPP are missing in the RCEP, and other RCEP provisions do not go as far as those in the CPTPP in liberalizing digital trade. In addition, as Leblond (*Ibid.*) has noted, "The RCEP and the CPTPP diverge on provisions covering the location of computing facilities, cross-border transfer of information by electronic means, source code and dispute settlement. In all these cases, the RCEP's chapter 12 is much weaker than the CPTPP's chapter 14, to the point of rendering the provisions meaningless in terms of liberalizing cross-border digital trade and data flows. The RCEP's language is such that it allows member states to impose whatever national regulatory restrictions they wish, as long as they are applied in a non-discriminatory way (are applied equally to domestic and foreign businesses)."

The presence of China at the negotiating table is clearly visible in these less ambitious RCEP provisions. China is also present now in the

WTO negotiations on digital trade. One question in avoiding agreement on the lowest common denominator in the WTO negotiations is: How far will China be willing to go toward global governance of digital trade under the aegis of the WTO? Another question — the central negotiating question — is: How should a legal framework for WTO rules on digital trade be structured to secure the maximum in commitments from China and other developing countries while also accomplishing the maximum attainable now in liberalizing digital trade? In sum, in confronting the complex technical and geopolitical dimensions of the digital divide in writing new digital rules for world trade, what, for the WTO members, should be the "digital decide"?

The Low-Hanging Fruit of Digital Trade

Despite the many brackets and blank spaces in the current consolidated text of a proposed WTO digital trade agreement, some of the pressing commercial issues relating to digital trade seem conducive to a negotiated WTO solution in the near term. Many of these issues involve the establishment of the foundational legal infrastructure needed to facilitate the day-to-day commerce of digital trade. On these issues, there seems to be common ground on which a framework of rules on digital trade can be based in the WTO. This low-hanging fruit of digital trade issues that should be addressed by the WTO in separate modules, offering a range of additional commitments over varying lengths of time, includes a long list of topics that are mostly the same as those of the DEPA modules. The WTO digital modules of possibly low-hanging fruit should include, but not be limited to, the following:

- **Facilitation of digital trade through electronic transaction frameworks:** Whatever else may be in other modules, in a WTO digital trade agreement, there should be a module committing countries to facilitate additional trade through electronic means. An unqualified obligation to "maintain a legal framework governing domestic electronic transactions consistent with the principles of the UNCITRAL [United Nations Commission on International Trade Law] Model Law on Electronic Commerce" of 1996 — perhaps "taking into account, as appropriate, other relevant international standards" — is in section A.1(1) of the WTO consolidated negotiating text. Module 2, article 2.3

of the DEPA provides that these rules and frameworks should be consistent with the UNCITRAL Model Law on Electronic Commerce[50] or the United Nations Convention on the Use of Electronic Communications in International Contracts[51] of 2005, which promotes the validity and the enforceability of electronically exchanged communications and provides for even-handedness in the conduct of cross-border digital transactions.

- **Transparency:** The transparency of all measures relating to digital trade may well be required by article X of the GATT (for trade in goods) and by article III of the GATS (for trade in services). Nevertheless, it makes sense to include in a WTO digital trade agreement a module that specifically requires transparency in digital trade. Different versions of a requirement of transparency — allowing for temporary exceptions for "emergency situations" — are currently bracketed in section D.1(1)1 of the WTO draft text. Module 13, article 13 of the DEPA and article 14 of the SADEA offer useful language to include in a WTO module on transparency in digital trade.
- **Non-discriminatory treatment of digital products:** Equal treatment of digital products is necessary to increase the amount of digital trade through competition while also enhancing consumer choices based on quality and on price. Section B.1.2 of the WTO draft text echoes article III.4 of the GATT in mandating no less favorable treatment for imported than for domestic like digital products (while excepting government subsidies). Similarly, module 3, article 3.3.1 of the DEPA provides, "No Party shall accord less favorable treatment to digital products created, produced, published, contracted for, commissioned or first made available on commercial terms in the territory of another Party, or to digital products of which the author, performer, producer, developer or owner is a person of another Party, than it accords to other like digital products."
- **Enforcement of domestic laws on online consumer protection:** Digital trade requires trust, and trust requires consumer protections against fraud and other forms of commercial digital abuse. There must be a module containing domestic protections for online consumers that are equivalent to those provided to other consumers. Module 6, articles 6.3.3 and 6.3.4 of the DEPA mandate, respectively, that each DEPA party shall adopt or maintain laws or regulations "to proscribe fraudulent, misleading or deceptive conduct that causes harm, or is likely to cause harm, to consumers engaged in online commercial

activities," and to "(a) require, at the time of delivery, goods and services provided to be of acceptable and satisfactory quality, consistent with the supplier's claims regarding the quality of the goods and services; and (b) provide consumers with appropriate redress when they are not." Section C.1(1) of the WTO draft text includes a range of suggested options for ensuring online consumer protection.

- **Electronic signatures, electronic invoicing and payments, and paperless trading:** To make digital trade possible, there must be mutual recognition of electronic signatures to verify and to validate online transactions, assurance of the interoperability and security of electronic invoicing and payments, and sanction for cross-border trading through paperless transactions. In the WTO draft text, section A.1(1) authorizes electronic signatures, section A.1(4) electronic invoicing, section A.1(5) electronic payments and section A.2(1) paperless trading. Likewise, in the DEPA, module 2, article 2.2 provides for paperless trading, article 2.5 allows electronic invoicing and article 2.7 permits electronic payments. Article 9 of the SADEA provides for electronic signatures, article 10 for electronic invoicing, article 11 for electronic payments and article 12 for paperless trading.
- **Logistics services and express shipments:** As the current WTO text explains in section A.2(6), logistics services are important to "the development of cross border electronic commerce and even the economic development at large." The language in that provision in the current text sets out a range of specific commitments on improvements in logistics services. Commitments on logistics services are also in module 2, article 2.4 of the DEPA. In addition, while maintaining appropriate customs control, expedited customs procedures should be made available for express shipments, which have proven critical in delivering medical goods during the COVID-19 pandemic. Module 2, article 2.6.2 of the DEPA provides for "expedited customs procedures for express shipments while maintaining appropriate customs control and selection." In similar language, so does article 13 of the SADEA.
- **Cooperation on cybersecurity:** The WTO consolidated negotiating text recognizes in alternative bracketed versions of section D.2(1) the threats that cybercrime and fraud pose to cybersecurity and thus to digital trade. Several versions of section D.2(3) contemplate capacity building and cooperation in countering these threats; another,

however, counsels that, in these efforts, WTO members "should respect internet sovereignty." Section D.2(3), proposed by the United States and the United Kingdom, calls for employing risk-based over regulatory-based approaches in addressing cybersecurity threats. In the DEPA, module 5, articles 5.1.1 and 5.1.2 set out the "shared vision" of the DEPA parties for furthering digital trade by ensuring cybersecurity. They "recognise the importance of" national capacity building, cooperation under existing collaborative mechanisms for online safety and security, and workforce development in cybersecurity. But, like the WTO draft text, the DEPA does not include any "hard" legal obligations, nor does article 34 of the SADEA, which also deals with cybersecurity.

- **Interoperability of data protection regimes:** A module is needed to increase the efficiency and efficacy of national data protection schemes by making them work in concert. In section A.2(5) of the WTO draft text, WTO negotiators contemplate interoperability between national single window systems, including the exchange of data through single window systems by authorized private entities. The SADEA is the first agreement calling for interoperability of national data protection regimes. Article 19.7 of the SADEA states, "Each Party shall encourage the development of mechanisms to promote compatibility between these different regimes. These mechanisms may include the recognition of regulatory outcomes, whether accorded autonomously or by mutual arrangement, or broader international frameworks."
- **Unsolicited commercial electronic messages (spam):** The worldwide clutter of spam undermines the efficiency of digital trade while increasing the likelihood that digital trade will be conducted in fraudulent ways. Already, WTO negotiators have agreed to regulate spam, which is addressed in section C.1(2) of the draft WTO text. In module 6, article 6.2 of the DEPA, the parties have agreed to regulate unsolicited commercial electronic messages by requiring the consent of recipients to receive it, requiring spam suppliers to enable recipients to opt out of receiving it and otherwise minimizing it. A like obligation is in article 19 of the SADEA.
- **Data innovation:** New in the DEPA and the SADEA is a provision that underscores the significance of being digital by encouraging collaborative cross-border projects that share practices relating to data innovation. Such collaboration can spread innovation and add to

digital trade. In module 9, article 9.4.3 of the DEPA, the DEPA parties agree that, "to promote data-driven innovation," they shall "endeavour to collaborate on data-sharing projects and mechanisms, and proof of concepts for new uses of data, including data sandboxes" (in which data, including personal information, is shared among businesses in accordance with applicable laws and regulations). A similar obligation is in article 26 of the SADEA. To further innovation in ICT, the European Union has suggested that the WTO agreement include updates in the WTO Reference Paper on Telecommunications Services, which are in section E.1 of the WTO draft text.

- **Open government data:** As explained by the parties to the DEPA in module 9, article 9.5.1, "facilitating public access to and use of government information may foster economic and social development, competitiveness and innovation." For this reason, the DEPA parties have committed, in module 9, article 9.5.2 of the DEPA, to "endeavour to ensure" that any government information, including data, that is made available to the public "is made available as open data," and, in module 9, article 9.5.3 to "expand access to and use of open data, with a view to enhancing and generating business opportunities." Like obligations are in article 27 of the SADEA. Bracketed language on open government data — replete with many options — is in section B.4(1) of the WTO draft text.
- **Cryptography:** One form of forced technology transfer is a requirement that a manufacturer or a supplier of an ICT product either transfer or provide access to proprietary information relating to the encryption of that product as a condition of manufacture, sale, distribution, import or use in a market. Such requirements undermine IP rights and impede digital trade. Detailed provisions prohibiting such requirements as conditions of market access and use are in section C.3(2) of the WTO draft text. Similar provisions are also in article 3.4 of the DEPA and article 7 of the SADEA.
- **Digital identities:** A digital identity is the entire compilation of information that exists about an individual or an organization in digital form. A digital identity is thus comprised of multiple characteristics, or data attributes, such as username and password; date of birth; Social Security number; online search history, including electronic transactions; medical history; and purchasing history — any or all of which may be linked to one or more digital identifiers, such as an email address, a URL or a domain name. Principal concerns with

digital identities are privacy and security. In part because identity theft is rampant online, digital identity authentication and validation measures are critical to ensuring online security. In module 7, articles 7.1.1 and 7.1.1(c) of the DEPA, the parties to that agreement commit that "each Party shall endeavor to promote the interoperability between their respective regimes for digital identities," including through establishment of best practices, technical interoperability, common standards and "broader international frameworks." A similar obligation to facilitate the compatibility of parties' respective digital identity regimes is in article 29 of the SADEA. At present, there is no language on digital identities in the WTO draft text.

- **AI:** Machine learning is an intrinsic part of innovation in the digital technologies that are employed to conduct digital trade. Advances in digital trade are often made possible by advances in machine learning, which is often called AI. In module 8, article 8.2.2 of the DEPA, the DEPA parties "recognise the economic and social importance of developing ethical and governance frameworks for the trusted, safe and responsible use of AI technologies." In the same article, the parties "further acknowledge the benefits of developing mutual understanding and ultimately ensuring that such frameworks are internationally aligned, in order to facilitate, as far as possible, the adoption and use of AI technologies across the Parties' respective jurisdictions." Toward this end, in article 8.2.3, the parties affirm that they "shall endeavour to promote the adoption of ethical and governance frameworks that support the trusted, safe and responsible use of AI technologies." Similar commitments are found in article 31 of the SADEA. There is nothing on AI in the WTO draft text.

- **Fintech cooperation:** Globally, a rapidly growing component of digital commerce is "fintech" — computer programs and other technologies used to support or enable online banking and financial services in competition with the traditional means of delivering those services. Digital trade is increased if these technologies and the regulations that apply to them are compatible. In module 8, article 8.1 of the DEPA, the parties agree to promote cooperation within the fintech industry consistent with national laws and regulations. A parallel provision is in article 32 of the SADEA. There is no comparable provision in the WTO draft text.

- **Small and medium enterprises:** As noted in module 10, article 10.1 of the DEPA, the role of small and medium enterprises (SMEs) "in maintaining dynamism and enhancing competitiveness in the digital economy" is "fundamental." Thus, the DEPA parties have agreed in module 10, article 10.2 to seek "more robust cooperation between the Parties to enhance trade and investment opportunities for SMEs in the digital economy." This will be done by exchanging information and best practices and by encouraging SMEs to participate in platforms that can help them "link with international suppliers, buyers and other potential business partners." Toward this end, per module 10, article 10.4, the parties are to start by convening a "Digital SME Dialogue" to promote awareness and collaboration. Similar language is in article 36 of the SADEA. In section A.2.4, the WTO draft text acknowledges that, through digital trade, "micro, small and medium-sized enterprises ... have acquired unprecedented opportunities of direct access to international markets"; however, there are no specific obligations relating to SMEs in the draft.

- **Prudential measures:** Some of the WTO members negotiating on digital trade have stressed the importance of reserving in a WTO digital trade agreement the right to apply prudential measures with respect to digital financial services. Annex 1(8) of the WTO draft text provides that nothing in the proposed digital trade agreement "shall prevent a [party/member] from adopting or maintaining measures for prudential reasons, including for the protection of investors, depositor, policyholders or persons to whom a fiduciary duty is owed by a financial service supplier, or to ensure the integrity and stability of the [party's/ member's] financial system." Nearly identical language is in article 2(a) of the GATS Annex on Financial Services. Similar language is also in module 15, article 15.4 of the DEPA.
- **Digital inclusion:** Although digital trade has made it possible for many millions of people worldwide to link up to the global economy and to share in its bounty, many more millions are still not connected and are thus denied the opportunity to benefit from digital trade. Mindful of the persistence of the digital divide, especially in developing countries, the parties to the DEPA, in module 11, article 11.3, have agreed to "cooperate on matters relating to digital inclusion, including participation of women, rural populations, low socioeconomic groups and Indigenous Peoples in the digital economy." The DEPA parties envisage, in module 11, article 11.1.4, that cooperation "relating to digital inclusion may be carried out through the coordination, as appropriate, of the Parties' respective agencies, enterprises, labour

unions, civil society, academic institutions and non-governmental organisations, among others." At present, there is no similar provision in the WTO draft text.
- **Dispute settlement:** A WTO digital trade agreement will begin as a plurilateral agreement with the expectation that, over time, it will become fully multilateral. Like other plurilateral WTO agreements, the digital trade agreement should be subject to binding WTO dispute settlement. In the absence of a dispute settlement system, disputes arising under the agreement would go unresolved and, if a dispute settlement system is not binding, then rulings against a party could go unenforced, thereby undermining the agreement. Module 14, article 14 of the DEPA creates a dispute settlement system, but it is limited in scope by article 14A.1 to issues relating to non-discriminatory treatment of digital products, ICT products that use cryptography, cross-border transfer of information by electronic means and location of computer facilities.

A cautionary example of what WTO members should not do on dispute settlement in digital trade is the RCEP. As Leblond (2020) has pointed out, "even with respect to the non-discrimination provisions (in the RCEP), a member state could get away with discriminating against specific foreign firms since the RCEP's dispute settlement mechanism does not apply to chapter 12. If the RCEP's member states cannot resolve a dispute on their own through consultation, then it moves to the RCEP Joint Committee (ministerial level) for further discussion but without the power to impose any decision." Reminiscent of the early days of the GATT, this could lead to a lot of talk and perhaps even, from time to time, some progress, but in the absence of binding rulings, it is unlikely to lead to genuine and effective dispute resolution, which will be required to ensure and enhance the flow of digital trade. A WTO digital trade agreement should refer disputes to binding WTO dispute settlement — without the qualifications in the dispute settlement provisions of the RCEP.

Financial and Technical Assistance

Not even this low-hanging fruit in digital trade can be picked if WTO members do not have the capacity and the capability to pick it. The reality is that many of them do not. Clearly, financial and technical assistance from developed countries is needed by developing countries — and especially by the LDCs. Agreement to commitments by developing countries in some of these modules for the low-hanging fruit of digital trade should be conditioned on the provision of financial and technical assistance by developed countries, ideally through international institutions that focus on development.

A similar approach has been previously taken multilaterally by the members of the WTO in the Trade Facilitation Agreement (TFA),[52] which was concluded at the WTO Ministerial Conference in Bali, Indonesia, in 2013, and entered into force in 2017. The innovative TFA is "the first WTO agreement in which ... WTO members can determine their own implementation schedules and in which progress in implementation is explicitly linked to technical and financial capacity. In addition, the Agreement states that assistance and support should be provided to help them achieve that capacity."[53] Significantly, "A Trade Facilitation Agreement Facility (TFAF) was created at the request of developing and least-developed countries to help ensure that they receive the assistance needed to reap the full benefits of the TFA and to support the ultimate goal of full implementation of the new agreement by all WTO members."[54]

Agreement on the TFA was the first time the acceptance of additional WTO obligations was specifically linked to technical assistance and capacity building. Technical assistance and capacity building are needed equally — if not more — by developing countries if new WTO rules on digital trade are to begin to eliminate the digital divide. In return for WTO commitments by developing countries to assume new obligations to liberalize digital trade, developed countries should agree to provide sufficient financial and other support for technical assistance and for capacity building. In the current WTO digital negotiations, criteria should be agreed for establishing where such help may be needed by developing countries (Bacchus and Manak, 2021). (The LDCs and many other developing countries need it; China, for one, does not.) As with the TFA on digital trade, the WTO should work in concert with other international institutions to make certain the needed help is forthcoming.

The Fruit at the Top of the Digital Trade Tree

Ideally, in a WTO digital trade agreement, there should be modules, too, for picking the fruit at the top of the digital trade tree modules for each of the intractable issues relating to the international transfer of data, freedom in the flow and location of data, protections against mandatory technology transfer, safeguards on the use of personal data, competition policies, and the assurance of appropriate domestic policy space and the protection of national security in the national treatment of data. Also needed is a module that addresses how global standards will be established and employed in digital trade.

The expectation of the negotiators should be that the modules for some of these issues on which consensus is harder to reach will be filled over time and, perhaps, a lengthy period of time. A WTO digital trade agreement will be only a beginning, but it can be the basis for establishing a global framework for what — it can be hoped — will one day become a global consensus on these most difficult issues. With mutual effort, it can also be, from the outset, more than merely the lowest common denominator on digital trade.

Cross-Border Data Flows

Essential to framing the trade rules required to help secure more innovation by supporting and speeding the shift to a digital economy, is understanding the role of data in this historic shift. The source of the many innovations flowing from the digital economy is the free flow of data, and "underpinning digital trade is the movement of data."[55] The European Political Strategy Centre — the in-house "think tank" of the European Union — has explained that "data is rapidly becoming the lifeblood of the global economy. It represents a key new type of economic asset."[56] Or, as Richard Waters (2020) of the *Financial Times* has pithily put it, "In the digital world, data is destiny."

Being able to move data across borders is indispensable to digital trade. Wu (2017), formerly of Harvard Law School and now an adviser to the United States Trade Representative, has explained that, as the digital economy transitions more and more toward the Internet of Things, AI, virtual reality and autonomous vehicles, an even greater economic premium will be placed on the free movement of data. "Beyond this economic impact," the World Economic Forum has added, "the free flow of data is, itself, a significant driver of innovation. It allows the sharing of ideas and information and the dissemination of knowledge as well as collaboration and crosspollination among individuals and companies"

(Pepper, Garrity and LaSalle, 2016). The success of myriad economic actions, including innumerable digital actions that affect international trade, depends on the free flow of data.

Moreover, amid the pandemic, the importance of intangible assets is increasing. The need for physical assets is decreasing as businesses everywhere realize that their employees need not congregate in expensive office space to be productive (Haag, 2021). As Greg Ip (2020) of *The Wall Street Journal* has observed, "Value is increasingly derived from digital platforms, software and other intangible investments rather than physical assets and traditional relationships." In this altered commercial landscape, "the future arrives early" (Thomas, 2020), and the necessity for quick and effective communications is greater than ever before, which shifts more and more of day-to-day business online. The businesses that are the most engaged in the digital economy are most likely to lead the way in the economic recovery from the COVID-19 pandemic.

Section B.2(1)5 of the WTO draft text includes several versions of a proposed prohibition on restrictions on the flow of information through the free flow of data. The most liberal is the version submitted by the European Union, which states specifically that cross-border data flows shall not be restricted by requiring the localization of computing facilities, network elements or data; prohibiting data storage or processing elsewhere; or making the cross-border transfer of data contingent on some form of localization. Module 4, article 4.3.2 of the DEPA states that each party to the agreement "shall allow the cross-border transfer of information by electronic means, including personal information," when it is done to conduct business. Likewise, chapter 14, article 14.11.2 of the CPTPP provides in similar terms for the cross-border transfer of information by electronic means. Chapter 19, article 19.11.1 of CUSMA includes identical language.

Data Localization

Data localization is a requirement that the data generated in a country be stored on a server or other storage device located within that country. Ostensibly taken for security reasons, data localization measures are often imposed for protectionist reasons that can impede the free flow of digital trade. This is an increasing concern for large global companies that deal with data worldwide. Module 4, article 4.4 of the DEPA, article 24.1 of the SADEA, article 14.13 of the CPTPP and article 19.12 of CUSMA all include a general restriction on data localization. Article 25.2 of the SADEA includes a specific restriction on data localization of computing facilities for financial services.

In stark contrast are the data localization provisions in the RCEP. Article 12.14.1 of the RCEP — perhaps influenced by the participation of China — recognizes that "each Party may have its own measures regarding the use or location of computing facilities, including requirements that seek to ensure the security and confidentiality of communications." Moreover, article 12.14.3(b) of the RCEP states that no party to the agreement is prevented from taking "any measure that it considers necessary for the protection of its essential security interests" (*Ibid.*). What is more, "Such measures shall not be disputed by other Parties" (*Ibid.*). The combined effect of these two provisions makes data localization requirements relating to computer facilities self-judging under the RCEP — perhaps a sign of the preference of China, and certainly an unwelcome outcome that should be avoided in a WTO digital trade agreement.

Section B.2(2)5 of the WTO draft text offers two alternatives that have been submitted so far that prohibit the use or location of computing facilities in a WTO member's territory as a condition for conducting business in that territory. More submissions may be forthcoming. It is important to put an end to mandatory data localization measures. Yet it is not at all clear that WTO negotiators will be able to reach a consensus on an outright prohibition on data localization requirements at the outset of a WTO digital trade agreement. China, in particular, may prove willing to agree at this time to quite a few other digital trade obligations — but not this one.

Thus, this is one of the issues on which the WTO negotiators may benefit in concluding a digital trade agreement from taking a modular approach, which will prevent the absence of a consensus on one issue from holding up the entire agreement. The cumulative refusal of traders and investors from other countries to comply with data localization requirements could help, over time, to alter the commercial circumstances, and could thereby impose an escalating economic price on the continued insistence on such requirements, which could, in turn, change the political atmosphere of future WTO negotiations on this divisive issue in digital trade.

Permitted Limits on Cross-Border Data Flows

As advantageous as the free flow of data surely is, data cannot be expected to cross borders entirely without limits. There must be some room for discretionary domestic decision making where other public policy goals are at stake. Inevitably, discerning the appropriate scope of such domestic latitude becomes a line-drawing exercise in international rulemaking. What is needed is an identification of the right "in between" separating too much from too little scope for domestic actions that constrain data flows. Thus far, negotiating countries have fallen short in clearly identifying that right dividing line in other digital trade agreements in allowing for restrictions based on "legitimate public policy objectives," general exceptions and national security exceptions. WTO negotiators must strive for more clarification.

Legitimate public policy objectives

Module 4, article 4.3.3 of the DEPA specifies that nothing in that agreement "shall prevent a Party from adopting or maintaining measures inconsistent with [the general obligation to prevent the cross-border transfer of information by electronic means] to achieve a legitimate public policy objective, provided that the measure (a) is not applied in a manner which would constitute a means of arbitrary or unjustifiable discrimination or a disguised restriction on trade; and (b) does not impose restrictions on transfers of information greater than are required to achieve the objective." Identical language is in article 14.11.3 of the CPTPP. Illustrating the diverging views of the United States and China on the proper scope of such an exception, such restrictions on the free flow of data across borders are allowed, in article 19.11.2 of CUSMA, only for those measures "necessary to" achieve legitimate public policy objectives while, in article 12.15(a) of the RCEP, they are all allowed for "any measure" limiting cross-border transfer of information by electronic means that a party itself "considers necessary" to achieve a legitimate public policy objective. A legitimate public policy objective is not defined in the DEPA, the CPTPP, CUSMA or the RCEP.

The WTO consolidated negotiating text offers four varying alternatives in section B.2(1)6 that limit the cross-border flow of data as a legitimate public policy objective. These alternatives largely track the language in the previous non-WTO agreements on digital trade. Notably, the first of the four current alternatives adds a proportionality standard in that the allowance of a restriction to achieve a legitimate public policy objective is available only to a measure that "does not impose restrictions of information greater than are [necessary/required] to achieve the objective." Similarly, section B.2(2)6 of the WTO draft text states that parties to the proposed WTO digital trade agreement cannot be prevented from adopting or maintaining measures contrary to the prohibition on data localization in order to pursue a legitimate public policy objective, so long as these measures are not "applied in a manner which would constitute a means of arbitrary or unjustifiable discrimination or a disguised restriction on trade" and do not "impose restrictions on transfers of information greater than are required to achieve the objective."

Like the digital trade provisions in other agreements, the WTO agreement does not define a legitimate public policy objective. This creates the potential for an open-ended exception. The WTO negotiators may wish to look to the non-exclusive list of "legitimate objectives" of technical regulations set out in article 2.2 of the WTO TBT Agreement, which may provide a starting point in defining a legitimate public policy objective for the purposes of a WTO digital trade agreement. Without a definition, much that is otherwise established in a WTO agreement to free cross-border data flows may be undone in application.

General exceptions

The 86 WTO members engaged in negotiations on digital trade are contemplating including "general exceptions" to digital trade obligations in Annex 1(6) of the WTO draft text. One submitted alternative is simply to incorporate by reference article XX of the GATT[57] and article XIV of the GATS,[58] mutatis mutandis. Some of the WTO members participating in the digital negotiations have suggested supplementing these traditional provisions with additional exceptions, including exceptions that would safeguard "cyberspace sovereignty" and achieve "other legitimate public policy objectives." At this writing, an open question is whether any of these proposed additional exceptions will end up in the final WTO text.

Elsewhere, article 3 of the SADEA incorporates article XX of the GATT and article XIV of the GATS, mutatis mutandis. In contrast, module 15, article 15.1.3 of the DEPA incorporates article XIV of the GATS mutatis mutandis while making no mention of article XX of the GATT. (Interestingly, article 15.1.4 of the DEPA also makes an exception for "measures necessary to protect national treasures or specific sites of historical or archaeological value, or to support creative arts of national value.") Article 29.1.3 of the CPTPP also incorporates by reference article XIV of the GATS but not article XX of the GATT for the purposes of chapter 14 on digital commerce. Under article 32.1 of CUSMA, only article XIV of the GATS is incorporated for the purposes of chapter 19 on digital trade. In the RCEP, article 17.12.1 incorporates article XX of the GATT, and article 17.12.2 incorporates article XIV of the GATS, both mutatis mutandis.

The best decision would probably be to incorporate both article XX of the GATT and article XIV of the GATS, mutatis mutandis. Although some exceptions to digital trade obligations are necessary as a matter of public policy, the risk is that if there are too many exceptions, and if they are too broad, then the exceptions will have the effect of erasing those obligations altogether. Thus, here is one example of where caution is needed in drawing the right line "in between" that will provide appropriate exceptions while also ensuring the overall efficacy of the obligations. This is the challenge that must be confronted by the WTO negotiators in crafting options to include in a module in a WTO digital trade agreement on general exceptions to digital trade obligations.

National security

Exceptions from trade obligations for reasons of national security are already among the most divisive issues in the WTO-based trading system. Some countries contend that their national security decisions are beyond the jurisdiction of the WTO and cannot be second-guessed by the WTO. Other countries rightly point to the existence of article XXI in the GATT[59] and article XIV bis in the GATS,[60] both dealing with national security, and insist that those two treaty provisions must have meaning and must be given effect. The little jurisprudence[61] there is, so far, in WTO dispute settlement strongly supports the latter view. For nearly seven decades, up until recently — first under the GATT and then under the WTO — countries engaged in the mutual restraint of avoiding confrontations on this issue in dispute settlement, but now the national security issue faces the WTO-based trading system squarely, including in digital trade.

The wide gulf among WTO members on this issue is reflected in the current negotiations over the appropriate scope of a national security exception to proposed digital trade obligations. At present, three bracketed alternatives are in Annex 1(7) of the WTO consolidated negotiation text.

Two of these alternatives illustrate the extent of the current gulf. Alternative 1 in Annex 1(7) would incorporate GATS article XIV bis, for services, and GATT article XXI, for goods, *mutatis mutandis* in a WTO digital trade agreement, without further qualification. This incorporation would include three conditions in GATS article XIV *bis* 1(b) and in GATT article XXI(b) that limit recourse to the national security exception by providing that the security interests asserted must be related to the supply of services as carried out directly or indirectly for the purpose of provisioning a military establishment, related to fissionable and fusionable materials or the materials from which they are derived, or taken in time of war or other emergency in international relations. In addition, it would include the identical language in GATS article XIV bis 1(c) and GATT article XXI(c), providing that nothing in the rules "shall be construed...to prevent any Member from taking any action in pursuance of its obligations under the United Nations Charter for the maintenance of international peace and security."

In sharp contrast, Alternative 2 would enlarge the scope of the security exception by removing the three conditions in GATS article XIV bis 1(b) that limit the circumstances in which a WTO member may take "any action which it considers necessary for the protection of its essential security interests." It would also omit the language in article XIV bis 1(c) dealing with the maintenance of international peace and security. If this alternative becomes part of the final text of a WTO digital trade agreement, then any measure that limits the cross-border flow of data and digital trade would be permitted if a party to the agreement asserts that "it considers" that the measure is necessary to protect its national security. In the absence of conditions akin to those in both GATT article XX and GATS article XIV bis, the phrase "it considers" makes the assertion of a national security interest essentially self-judging.

Module 15, article 15.2 of the DEPA poses concerns similar to these two alternatives in the WTO draft text by providing, "Nothing in this Agreement shall be construed to: (a) require a Party to furnish or allow access to any information the disclosure of which it determines to be contrary to its essential security interests; or (b) preclude a Party from applying measures that it considers necessary for the fulfillment of its obligations with respect to the maintenance or restoration of international peace or security, or the protection of its own essential security interests." It attaches no conditions, thus rendering the assertion of a national security interest likewise self-judging. The DEPA echoes identical language in article 29.2 of the CPTPP and in article 32.2 of CUSMA.

There is similar language in article 17.13 of the RCEP — but with conditions. In a variation and elaboration on the GATT and GATS conditions, article 17.13(B)(i)–(iv) requires that the action taken by a party "which it considers necessary" for the protection of an essential security interest must be "(i) relating to fissionable and fusionable materials or the materials from which they are derived; (ii) relating to the traffic in arms, ammunition and implements of war and to such traffic in other goods and materials, or relating to the supply of services, as carried on directly or indirectly for the purpose of supplying or provisioning a military establishment; (iii) taken so as to protect critical public infrastructures including communications, power, and water infrastructures; [or] (iv) taken in time of national emergency or war or other emergency in international relations." RCEP article 17.13(c) provides that nothing in the agreement shall be construed "to prevent any Party from taking any action in pursuance of its obligations under the United Nations Charter for the maintenance of international peace and security" (italics in original).

Finding the right line "in between" will be even more difficult for the WTO negotiators on an exception for national security than on general exceptions and exceptions for legitimate public policy objectives. This issue is the fruit at the very top of the digital trade tree. Nevertheless, taking a modular approach here, too, could be helpful in setting out different options that may be acceptable to different WTO members at this time — in the hope that another time may yet come that will be more conducive to achieving a broader consensus.

Source code

Source code is a collection of digital code that is written in a language that can be read by human computer programmers and is used by them to specify the actions to be performed by a computer. One form of forced technology transfer is the requirement that source code be disclosed or transferred as a condition for market access. Such a requirement limits digital trade by putting traders at risk of losing their IP. For this reason, section C.3(1)2 of the WTO draft text provides that no member of the proposed digital trade agreement "shall require the transfer of, or access to, source code of software...as a condition for the import, distribution, sale or use of such software, or of products containing such software, in its territory." One alternative in the draft text would extend this prohibition to the algorithms expressed in the source code — to the defined sequence of digital steps set out in it. Similar language is in article 28 of the SADEA and in article 14.17 of the CPTPP, which prohibit forced transfer or disclosure of software source code as a condition to use or trade. Going further, article 19.16 of CUSMA includes a prohibition on the forced transfer or disclosure not only of software source code, but also of the algorithms that are the basic ingredients of digital commerce and communications.

In striking contrast, the RCEP contains no restriction whatsoever on requiring the transfer of software source code as a condition for market access. Nor does it contain any provision relating to source code at all. This leaves the parties to the RCEP free — if they are not constrained by other digital trade commitments in other agreements — to impose any source code transfer requirements they may wish. This also illustrates the polar extremes that currently prevail among WTO members in confronting this issue. Other WTO negotiators are highly unlikely to agree to such a formulation if it is submitted by China in the WTO talks, but the remaining division on this issue is another example of why they may be more likely to conclude a WTO digital trade agreement if they take the modular approach.

Privacy (personal information protection)

One decidedly unresolved issue in digital trade is the extent to which personal information should be protected. Preventing a consensus on this issue are the differing positions of the European Union, the United States and China. In broad terms, the European Union and the United States favor the free flow of data across borders while, for the most part, China seeks digital rules that permit governments to restrict data flows in exercise of what China describes as "digital sovereignty." However, the European Union and the United States have taken different approaches to personal privacy protections on the internet. The European Union favors strong protections that preserve the privacy of personal information. While not opposed to privacy protections, the United States has not yet gone so far as the European Union in supporting them. These different approaches to personal privacy have prevented the two of them from presenting an entirely united front on their general mutual desire for free flows of data and information in their dealings with China and its touted "Great Firewall" against digital and other free flows of information.

These differences are reflected in the WTO negotiations on digital trade and will make it hard for negotiators to agree on the contents of a module providing for the protection of personal information. As of this writing, section C.2 of the WTO draft text relating to "privacy" is filled with bracketed submissions from numerous WTO members. In Alternative 2, section C.2(3), the European Union has proposed language describing the protection of personal data and privacy as a "fundamental right." In Alternative 2, section C.2(4), the European Union has also suggested language stating that "nothing in the agreed disciplines and commitments shall affect the protection of personal data and privacy afforded by the [parties'/members'] respective safeguards." The European Union has proposed identical language in Alternative 4, section B.2(1)6 of the WTO draft text.

WTO members may not be able to reach a consensus on the language proposed by the European Union. All the same, it could be included as one option in a module on personal information protection in a WTO digital trade agreement. What is more, there are a number of issues relating to privacy protection on which a consensus could be reached: a recognition of the economic and social benefits of protecting personal information and of the contribution it makes to building consumer trust in digital trade; a commitment to create and maintain legal frameworks and safeguards for protecting personal data and privacy; a commitment to take OECD guidelines[62] on privacy protection into account and, in doing so, a commitment to require the consent of individuals for cross-border transfer and processing of their personal data; and more. At the outset, China, and perhaps some others among the 86 negotiating countries, will be unlikely to agree to such commitments, but most WTO members engaged in the digital negotiations will be likely to agree.

In trying to find the right line "in between" on digital privacy, other agreements offer a variety of approaches for consideration. Many of the submissions currently bracketed in the WTO draft text are found in module 4, article 4.2 of the DEPA, which does not go as far as the European Union does in declaring digital privacy a "fundamental right," but also does not include any language permitting digital restrictions to "digital sovereignty." In protecting personal digital information, the DEPA emphasizes cooperation and the construction of compatible and interoperable data systems. Article 17 of the SADEA contains similar provisions, including recommending use of the Asia-Pacific Economic Cooperation (APEC) Cross-Border Privacy Rules (CBPR) System,[63] a government-backed data privacy certification that private companies can join to demonstrate their compliance with internationally recognized data privacy protections.

In the CPTPP, article 14.8.2 states that "each Party shall adopt or maintain a legal framework that provides for the protection of the personal information of the users of electronic commerce. In the development of its legal framework for the protection of personal information, each Party should take into account principles and guidelines of relevant international bodies." Article 14.8.3 adds that "each Party shall endeavour to adopt non-discriminatory practices in protecting users of electronic commerce from personal information protection violations occurring within its jurisdiction." Similarly, articles 19.8.2 and 32.8.2 of CUSMA require that CUSMA parties adopt or maintain a legal framework that provides for the protection of the personal information of the users of digital trade. CUSMA goes beyond the language in the CPTPP by mentioning by name in article 32.8.2 both the APEC CBPR and the OECD guidelines as "principles and guidelines of relevant international bodies" to shape a legal framework for protecting personal information. Article 19.8.3 of CUSMA adds an element of proportionality by stating that the parties "recognize the importance of…ensuring that any restrictions on cross-border flows of personal information are necessary and proportionate to the risks presented."

Competition policies

Much needed in a WTO digital trade agreement is a module containing a commitment to cross-border cooperation in the development and enforcement of competition rules. Competition policy (in the United States, antitrust policy) is not generally viewed as an international trade issue; however, it has a major impact on digital trade. By cooperating, countries can become better prepared for potential anti-competitive practices across borders. In addition, harmonized substantive and procedural rules on competition can help reduce costs and thus prices. With WTO rules on competition in digital trade would come increased legal certainty and decreased risks of inconsistent regulations and divergent findings by different competition authorities.

In section B.4(4)1 of the WTO draft text, WTO negotiators recognize that "some characteristics of digital trade, such as platform-based business models, multi-sided markets, network effect and economies of scale, may pose additional challenges on competition policy." With this in mind, the draft text would include a commitment to "endeavour to...develop adequate approaches to promoting and protecting competition in digital market[s]" and "strengthen collaboration mechanisms for cooperating to identify and mitigate market distortions arising from abuses of market dominance."

In module 8, article 8.4 of the DEPA, the parties recognize that they "can benefit by sharing their experiences in enforcing competition law and in developing and implementing competition policies to address the challenges that arise from the digital economy." Accordingly, the parties undertake to exchange information and experiences in developing competition policies for digital trade, share best practices, build capacity through training and exchanges of officials, and cooperate on enforcement. In addition to these undertakings, article 16.1(d) of the SADEA adds that there will also be "any other form of technical cooperation agreed by the Parties."

Of course, these are soft obligations that go not much beyond "best efforts." Considerably more than these best efforts will be needed to adapt WTO digital and other trade rules to the new challenges of ensuring fair competition in the 21st century. This said, though, the current language in the WTO draft text may be about as far as WTO members may be willing to go at the outset in a module on competition policies.

Digital standards

Amid "widespread concerns...about the fracturing of the global economy into walled-off and possibly warring data realms" (Ciuriak, 2019: 3), seemingly irresolvable divisions over central issues relating to the free flow of data appear far from resolution. In the face of these divisions, Patrick Leblond and Susan Ariel Aaronson (2019: 1) have contended that Canada, the European Union, Japan and the United States should — separate and apart from the WTO e-commerce negotiations — "develop a single data area that would be managed by an international data standards board.

The envisioned single data area would allow for all types of personal and non-personal data to flow freely across borders while ensuring that individuals, consumers, workers, firms and governments are protected from potential harm arising from activities such as the collection, processing, use, storage or purchase/sale of data."

One reason the authors think a new international standard-setting arrangement outside the WTO is necessary, is because the WTO negotiations include "China and Russia, two countries that have, to a large extent, walled off their digital realm with very different standards of data protection than Canada or other Western countries. As a result, it is highly unlikely that the WTO process will produce anything (if it does at all) close to what is found in the CPTPP and CUSMA. As such, should there ever be a WTO agreement on trade-related aspects of e-commerce, it would likely be a superficial accord based on general principles with emphasis on the 'legitimate public policy objective' general exception" (*Ibid.*, 9). The authors perceive their proposed separate arrangement as "an alternative to China's Digital Silk Road" (*Ibid.*, 10), which is part of China's Belt and Road Initiative on infrastructure and, as they see it, features "very different standards for governing data than what individuals and businesses can expect in liberal democracies" (*Ibid.*). As they see it, because of this international push by the Chinese government, the possibility looms that, in the absence of a non-Chinese alternative, a Chinese standard that is inconsistent with the norms of human rights and with other aspects of human freedom could come to dominate global cyberspace.

There is merit to their proposal. Admittedly, if this approach is taken, it could move the world toward rival technical digital standards, which could slow the acceleration of global digital trade and could reinforce the current trend toward digital line-drawing between China and its environs, and the rest of the trading world. Yet, if this approach is not taken, fundamental values of human freedom that are vital to all in the world could be put further at risk. Unquestionably, the world would be best served by having a single digital standard, but, alas, geopolitical forces are not currently trending toward such unity. Nor should the currently insurmountable geopolitical hurdles to such a single standard — one that would serve human freedom and not suppress it — be allowed to stand in the way of all that currently can be accomplished multilaterally on digital trade, and of all that currently can be done to create a legal framework for attaining global digital unity on some future brighter day.

As in all public policy making — and particularly in international policy making — second-best solutions are often the only solutions that can be achieved within a given context, and the perfect must not be permitted to be the enemy of the good.

Furthermore, as Leblond and Aaronson (2019) have stated, the WTO is not qualified to develop technical data protection standards, nor should it try. Rather, the inclination of the WTO on digital standards should be the same as that taken in the WTO TBT Agreement: that of relying on other relevant standard-setting organizations that are qualified to do so. The digital board they propose could be one of them. Without doubt, WTO negotiations would stumble to a standstill if the 86 negotiating countries tried to agree on the precise technical terms of data protection standards. Instead, separate plurilateral efforts by the WTO members that Leblond and Aaronson have listed — and others — to set out the arcane details of internationally agreed technical standards could proceed simultaneously and not inconsistently with the WTO negotiations on e-commerce.

But a word of advice here to those engaged in any such undertaking: to be recognized by the WTO, these plurilateral efforts should be structured so that the separate arrangement will qualify as a source of "relevant international standards" within the meaning of article 2.4 of the TBT Agreement. As the WTO Appellate Body ruled in the appeal in the *US — Tuna II* dispute, "a required element of the definition of an 'international' standard for the purposes of the TBT Agreement is the approval of the standard by an 'international standardizing body,' that is, a body that has recognized activities in standardization and whose membership is open to the relevant bodies of at least all Members."[64] With respect to the requirement in Annex 1.4 of the TBT Agreement that the membership in an international standardizing body must be "open to the relevant bodies of at least all Members," the Appellate Body noted in that appeal that "the term 'open' is defined as 'accessible or available without hindrance', 'not confined or limited to a few; generally accessible or available.'"[65] Thus, a body will be open if membership to the body is not restricted. It will not be open if membership is a priori limited to the relevant bodies of only some WTO members.

Conclusion

It should be a relatively simple matter for the 86 WTO members negotiating on a WTO digital trade agreement to achieve a consensus on some of the most basic issues, such as has already been done with spam. Indeed, much of the low-hanging fruit of digital trade seems ripe to be picked. In contrast, though, much of the fruit at the top of the digital tree seems to be beyond our current grasp. This is why a modular approach to a WTO digital trade agreement would be best. It would enable WTO members to agree on what they can agree on now while offering options for incremental agreement on the harder issues on which they cannot currently agree. A consensus on the most that can be achieved now is more likely to be reached with a flexible approach that permits WTO members to agree to different levels of commitments at different times within different modular categories of digital trade.

With the benefit of such a flexible approach, the members of the WTO that are working diligently to negotiate rules on "trade-related electronic commerce" may be able to conclude an initial plurilateral WTO digital trade agreement that could help spur more digital trade now and that could ultimately become more fully multilateral and more fully responsive to the evolving needs of the new digital economy. Failure to conclude a digital trade agreement by the time of the upcoming WTO Ministerial Conference in Geneva should not be considered an option if WTO members hope to sustain the credibility of the WTO and to maintain the centrality of the WTO to world trade.

Endnotes

[1] All figures in US dollars.
[2] *See* www.usg.edu/galileo/skills/unit07/internet07_02.phtml.
[3] *See* https://en.wikipedia.org/wiki/History_of_the_Internet.
[4] *Ibid.*
[5] *Ibid.*
[6] *See* https://en.wikipedia.org/wiki/Uruguay_Round.
[7] *See* www.wto.org/english/docs_e/legal_e/04-wto_e.htm.
[8] *See* www.wto.org/english/thewto_e/minist_e/mc11_e/briefing_notes_e/bfecom_e.htm.
[9] *Ibid.*
[10] *See* www.wto.org/english/tratop_e/ecom_e/ecom_briefnote_e.htm.
[11] *Ibid.*
[12] WTO, Ministerial Conference, Joint Statement on Electronic Commerce, 11th sess, WTO Doc. WT/MIN (17)/60, WTO https://ustr.gov/sites/default/files/files/Press/Releases/Joint%20Statement%20on%20Electronic%20Commerce.pdf.

[13] *Ibid.*
[14] WTO, Joint Statement on Electronic Commerce, WTO Doc. WT/L/1056, WTO https://docs.wto.org/dol2fe/Pages/SS/directdoc.aspx?filename=q:/WT/L/1056.pdf&Open=True.
[15] *Ibid.*
[16] *Ibid.*
[17] *Ibid.*
[18] WTO, *WTO Electronic Commerce Negotiations: Consolidated Negotiating Text — December 2020*, WTO Doc. INF/ECOM/62/Rev. 1 [*WTO Consolidated Negotiating Text*].
[19] *See* www.mfat.govt.nz/kr/trade/free-trade-agreements/free-trade-agreements-in-force/digital-economy-partnership-agreement-depa/depa-text-and-resources/.
[20] *See* www.mti.gov.sg/Improving-Trade/Digital-Economy-Agreements/The-Digital-Economy-Partnership-Agreement.
[21] *See* www.mfat.govt.nz/assets/Trade-agreements/DEPA/DEPA-at-a-Glance-factsheet.pdf.
[22] *See* www.sice.oas.org/trade/DEPA/DEPA_index_e.asp.
[23] *Singapore-Australia Digital Economy Agreement*, August 6, 2020 (entered into force December 8, 2020), *Ministry of Trade and Industry Singapore* www.mti.gov.sg/Improving-Trade/Digital-Economy-Agreements/The-Singapore-Australia-Digital-Economy-Agreement.
[24] *WTO Consolidated Negotiating Text, supra* note 18.
[25] *See* www.wto.org/english/tratop_e/ecom_e/ecom_e.htm.
[26] WTO, General Council, *Work Programme on Electronic Commerce: The E-Commerce Moratorium: Scope and Impact, Communication from India and South Africa*, WTO Doc. WT/GC/W/798, WTO https://docs.wto.org/dol2fe/Pages/SS/directdoc.aspx?filename=q:/WT/GC/W798.pdf&Open=True.
[27] *Ibid.*
[28] WTO, General Council, *Work Programme on Electronic Commerce: Broadening and Deepening the Discussions on the Moratorium on Imposing Customs Duties on Electronic Transmissions, Communication from Australia, Canada, Chile, Colombia, Hong Kong, China, Iceland, Republic of Korea, New Zealand, Norway, Singapore, Switzerland, Thailand and Uruguay*, WTO Doc. WT/GC/W/799/Rev.1, WTO https://docs.wto.org/dol2fe/Pages/SS/directdoc.aspx?filename=q:/WT/GC/W799R1.pdf&Open=True.
[29] *See* www.wto.org/english/res_e/publications_e/ai17_e/gats_art17_jur.pdf.
[30] *See General Agreement on Tariffs and Trade*, October 30, 1947, 58 UNTS 187 (entered into force January 1, 1948), WTO www.wto.org/english/docs_e/legal_e/06-gatt_e.htm.
[31] *See General Agreement on Trade in Services*, April 15, 1994, 1869 UNTS 183, 33 ILM 1167 (1994) (entered into force 1 January 1995), WTO www.wto.org/english/tratop_e/serv_e/gatsintr_e.htm.

[32] *Ibid.*
[33] *Ibid.*
[34] *Ibid.*
[35] *European Communities — Regime for the Importation, Sale and Distribution of Bananas (Complaint by Ecuador et al.)* (2012), WTO Doc. WT/DS27, WTO www.wto.org/english/tratop_e/dispu_e/cases_e/ds27_e.htm.
[36] *Canada — Certain Measures Affecting the Automotive Industry (Complaint by Japan)*, WTO Doc. WT/DS139, WTO www.wto.org/english/tratop_e/dispu_e/cases_e/ds139_e.htm.
[37] *See* www.wto.org/english/tratop_e/serv_e/12-tel_e.htm.
[38] *See* www.wto.org/english/tratop_e/serv_e/telecom_e/tel23_e.htm.
[39] *See* www.wto.org/english/tratop_e/serv_e/10-anfin_e.htm.
[40] WTO, *Information Technology Agreement*, December 13, 1996 (entered into force 1 July 1997), WTO www.wto.org/english/tratop_e/inftec_e/inftec_e.htm.
[41] *Agreement on Technical Barriers to Trade*, April 15, 1994 (entered into force January 1, 1995), WTO www.wto.org/english/tratop_e/tbt_e/tbt_e.htm.
[42] *Agreement on Trade-Related Aspects of Intellectual Property Rights*, April 15, 1994 (entered into force January 1, 1995), WTO www.wto.org/english/tratop_e/trips_e/trips_e.htm.
[43] *Agreement on Trade Facilitation* (entered into force February 22, 2017) [*Trade Facilitation Agreement*], WTO www.wto.org/english/tratop_e/tradfa_e/tradfa_e.htm.
[44] *Ibid.*
[45] *See* www.wto.org/english/tratop_e/region_e/region_art24_e.htm.
[46] *Comprehensive and Progressive Agreement for Trans-Pacific Partnership*, March 8, 2018 (entered into force December 30, 2019), *New Zealand Foreign Affairs & Trade*, www.mfat.govt.nz/en/trade/free-trade-agreements/free-trade-agreements-in-force/comprehensive-and-progressive-agreement-fortrans-pacific-partnership-cptpp/.
[47] *Canada-United States-Mexico Agreement*, November 30, 2018 (entered into force July 1, 2020), *Office of the United States Trade Representative*, https://ustr.gov/trade-agreements/free-trade-agreements/united-states-mexico-canada-agreement/agreement-between.
[48] *Agreement between the United States of America and Japan Concerning Digital Trade Agreement*, October 7, 2019 (entered into force January 1, 2020), *Office of the United States Trade Representative*, https://ustr.gov/countries-regions/japan-korea-apec/japan/us-japan-trade-agreement-negotiations/us-japan-digital-trade-agreement-text.
[49] *Regional Comprehensive Economic Partnership Agreement*, November 15, 2020 (not yet entered into force), *Regional Comprehensive Economic Partnership Agreement*, https://rcepsec.org/legal-text/.

[50] *See* https://uncitral.un.org/en/texts/ecommerce/modellaw/electronic_commerce.
[51] *United Nations Convention on the Use of Electronic Communications in International Contracts*, November 23, 2005 (entered into force March 1, 2013), UNCITRAL, https://uncitral.un.org/en/texts/ecommerce/conventions/electronic_communications.
[52] *Trade Facilitation Agreement, supra* note 43.
[53] *See* www.wto.org/english/tratop_e/tradfa_e/tradfa_introduction_e.htm.
[54] *Ibid*.
[55] *See* www.oecd.org/trade/topics/digital-trade/.
[56] *See* https://euagenda.eu/publications/enter-the-data-economy-eu-policies-for-a-thriving-data-ecosystem.
[57] *See* www.wto.org/english/res_e/booksp_e/gatt_ai_e/art20_e.pdf.
[58] *See* www.wto.org/english/res_e/publications_e/ai17_e/gats_art14_jur.pdf.
[59] *See* www.wto.org/english/res_e/booksp_e/gatt_ai_e/art21_e.pdf.
[60] *See* www.wto.org/english/res_e/publications_e/ai17_e/gats_art14_bis_oth.pdf.
[61] *Russia — Measures Concerning Traffic in Transit (Complaint by Ukraine)* (2019), WTO Doc. WT/DS512, WTO www.wto.org/english/tratop_e/dispu_e/cases_e/ds512_e.htm.
[62] *See* www.oecd.org/digital/ieconomy/oecdguidelinesontheprotectionofprivacy-andtransborderflowsofpersonaldata.htm.
[63] *See* www.apec.org/About-Us/About-APEC/Fact-Sheets/What-is-the-Cross-Border-Privacy-Rules-System.
[64] *United States — Measures Concerning the Importation, Marketing and Sale of Tuna (Complaint by Mexico)* (2019), WTO Doc. WT/DS381, WTO www.wto.org/english/tratop_e/dispu_e/cases_e/ds381_e.htm.
[65] *Ibid*.

Chapter 10

TRIPS-Past to TRIPS-Plus: Upholding the Balance Between Exclusivity and Access*

Introduction

A deadly global pandemic and other unique circumstances have combined to present the World Trade Organization (WTO) with an opportunity to modernize its rules for the trade-related aspects of intellectual property (IP) rights. There is the need to turn the "TRIPS-past" of WTO IP rules agreed in 1995 into the "TRIPS-plus" of improved rules more fit to purpose for the 21st century. New rules are needed to help spark new innovations of all kinds and the rapid spread of those innovations worldwide, including rules relating to intangible assets and especially to digital expressions of IP. New rules that have been made in regional and other trade agreements outside the WTO must be imported into the WTO and applied multilaterally among all WTO members. Differing cultures and differing histories give the 164 WTO members differing attitudes toward the protection of IP rights, which presents challenges in making new rules. Yet the WTO members have by consensus struck a balance in the existing WTO rules between exclusivity and access to new knowledge that has served all WTO members well. To continue to serve them well, this

---

*This essay was previously published by the Centre for International Governance Innovation as James Bacchus, "TRIPS-Past to TRIPS-Plus: Upholding the Balance Between Exclusivity and Access," CIGI Papers No. 254 (June 2021).

negotiated balance must be properly located and properly understood by both developed countries and developing countries, and it must be fulfilled and sustained in modernizing IP trade rules. Much more emphasis must be given by the developed countries to providing technology transfer and technical assistance and other capacity building for the developing countries. At the same time, the developing countries must do much more to comply with the legal requirement in the WTO rules that IP rights be enforced. In updating the WTO IP rules, both the developed countries and the developing countries must be ever mindful of the vital provisions in the current rules that permit case-by-case decisions for WTO members in drawing the line between upholding IP rights and allowing policy space for domestic actions conducive to social and economic welfare. In all respects, special allowances must be made and additional assistance must be provided to the least-developed countries of the world so that they can share in the global bounty from innovation.

In Search of the Balance

The coronavirus disease 2019 (COVID-19) pandemic has brought to the fore once more the debate within the WTO over the balance between exclusive ownership of new knowledge and broad public access to it in the WTO Agreement on Trade-Related Aspects of Intellectual Property Rights — commonly called the TRIPS Agreement.[1] Continuing questions over the extent to which the TRIPS Agreement protects the exclusivity of IP rights in COVID-19 vaccines (Farge and Nebehay 2020) — even during the lethal course of a global health emergency in which global access to those vaccines is urgently needed — underscore how much uncertainty remains about where the line of this balance is in this multilateral trade agreement, and also how much doubt still exists about whether that line is in the right place.

The inauguration of Joe Biden as president of the United States promises a re-engagement by the United States in the WTO, and thus WTO members are offered a new opportunity to confront mutual trade challenges old and new on a multilateral basis. With the WTO in crisis in the wake of long years of failed trade negotiations and of recent years of willful destruction by the nihilistic presidency of Donald Trump in the United States, WTO members must now "think anew, and act anew" (Lincoln [1862] 1953) on numerous policy fronts relating to international trade.

One of these necessary policy fronts is the trade-related aspects of IP rights, where the best place to begin is with a full realization of the negotiated balance between exclusivity and access in the TRIPS Agreement.

Beginning with what has long been an elusive comprehension of this balance is a prerequisite to a much-needed modernization of this multilateral trade agreement. Without a clear comprehension by all the members of the WTO of the meaning of the balance they have established in the text of the TRIPS Agreement, and of the justification for it, there will be little hope of transforming the TRIPS-past of an outdated accord on the nexus of trade and IP rights that was written nearly three decades ago into the TRIPS-plus of an updated agreement that can best serve the new world of the 21st century — a world where that nexus has been greatly altered by time, technology and the transformation of trade.

Behind the Balance

Generally, the debate over the balance between exclusivity and access in the TRIPS Agreement is characterized as a commercial confrontation between the developed countries, which have a huge economic stake in having their IP rights protected in world trade, and the developing countries, which, despite their recent climb up the economic ladder, still, for the most part, do not. For the developed countries, there are millions of jobs and billions of dollars at risk if IP rights are not upheld worldwide. For many developing countries, in the near term, jobs and dollars are at risk if they enforce IP rights by ridding their economies of the vast illegal proceeds of counterfeiting and piracy. Yet counterfeiting and piracy hurt developing countries as well as developed countries, in part by undermining the growth of their own creative sectors. And compliance with the TRIPS Agreement has helped developing countries enjoy greater inflows of foreign direct investment, technology transfer and IP-sensitive imports. The common view of this ongoing confrontation often overlooks the stake that developing countries have in protecting IP rights both now and in the longer term. A balanced updating of the TRIPS Agreement can potentially benefit all WTO members by incentivizing innovation and technology transfer in an inclusive, market-oriented manner, appropriate to anticipated conditions in the global economy for decades to come.

Linked inextricably to this commercial confrontation, of course, and often highlighted in media reports and policy discussions, is a geopolitical contest among the United States, the European Union, China, Japan and other leading economic powers for access to and control over the new technologies that will shape the rest of the 21st century. The trade and other disputes between and among these competing countries over the legal rights to the new knowledge that drives automation, delivers digitalization and lifts all kinds of high technologies higher, are not only disputes about jobs and profits. They are equally disputes over acquiring, leveraging and using political power to chart the course of the rest of this century, whether for good or ill.

Yet, at its core, the debate over how to treat IP rights within the WTO is part of a larger, longstanding global and geopolitical debate over the merits of property rights, dating back to long before the expression of the contrasting views offered first by Adam Smith and later by Karl Marx during the first century of the Industrial Revolution. Within this larger historical debate over the worth of property rights, is a more specific debate over the worth of IP rights, the justifications for those rights and the appropriate limits of those rights. The debate within the WTO is one aspect of this more specific debate. It is focused on how IP rights relate to trade, not only in vaccines and in other medicines, but in all individual creations that can serve the public good, in commerce and in many other aspects of society, worldwide. The late Harold Demsetz, an American economist steeped in the nuances of property rights, pointed out decades ago that a clear definition of property rights is needed for a market to function, including with respect to intangible intellectual assets (Hubbard, 2019).

IP rights are limited property rights. They give individuals exclusive rights for a limited time to the creations of their own minds. These rights can be rights to inventions (patents); literary and artistic works (copyrights); and commercial symbols, names and images (trademarks). They can be rights to industrial designs, trade secrets and geographical indications. IP rights are varied in their nature and thus are varied, too, in their trade and other societal effects. Different protections afforded to different IP rights in different countries can have enormous implications for the dissemination and distribution of wealth and welfare in the global economy. If we unduly weaken protection for IP, then we need to ask ourselves: Where will the next innovation, the next new technology, the next life-saving medicine come from? Likewise, if writers, artists, musicians and others who adorn human civilization are deprived of any legal entitlement to their creations, will society continue to be blessed as much by their creative works?

IP rights are exceptions to free trade. They exist because they are incentives for innovation, which is the main source for long-term economic growth and enhancements in the quality of human life. The exclusivity of IP rights sparks innovation "by enabling innovators to capture enough of the economic gains from their own innovative activity to justify their taking considerable risks" (Ezell and Cory 2019). The new knowledge from the innovations inspired by IP rights spills over to inspire other innovations. The widespread protection of IP rights promotes the diffusion, domestically and internationally, of innovative technologies and new know-how.

From the early acknowledgment of IP rights in the Italian city-states of the Renaissance, to their development in Great Britain during the emergence of market-based capitalism, to their enshrinement in the United States Constitution, and to their international recognition beginning in the 19th century and continuing today, there have always been disputes over where exclusive IP rights stop and unlimited public access begins. In the 21st century, as global economic growth has become increasingly knowledge-based, and as competition for knowledge has matched competition for commodities and natural resources, these disputes have multiplied and intensified.

Today, with the rise of digital trade and other forms of trading in knowledge, an ever-growing portion of the value of traded goods and services is in the IP that is embedded and associated with them. IP is foremost among the intangible assets that are assuming more commercial significance in the new pandemic world.[2] Trade rules that did not address and protect IP rights would not reflect the true realities of international trade in the 21st century. Furthermore, trade rules that do not keep up now with the new developments in IP rights in the digital age will reflect those realities even less. IP protections belong in the WTO, and new rules are needed to help secure those protections.

Even so, because IP rights are exceptions to free trade, the multilateral decision to protect them as a part of the WTO treaty was a legal landmark in both trade law and in broader public international law. Mindful of this exceptional circumstance, when they drafted and established the TRIPS Agreement as part of the new WTO in 1995, WTO members asked themselves: Just how far does the exclusive ownership right of an individual to the financial and other benefits of their own creation extend? Just when and where does that right stop? And precisely when, and under what circumstances, must a property right in an intellectual creation be subordinated to a wider concept of what is in the overall public interest? Their answers to these questions are in the text of the TRIPS Agreement. And today, more than a quarter of a century later, WTO members continue to plumb their answers to these questions as they ponder the ongoing meaning of the balance represented in the TRIPS Agreement while adjusting to the new pandemic world.

Even though they have all signed on the dotted line of the TRIPS Agreement, and therefore have committed to the multilateral obligations in the agreement, the ways in which WTO members read their answers to these questions are not all the same. There are geographical variations in how these treaty obligations are perceived, and thus in the domestic protections provided for IP rights. These geographical variations are, in part, a consequence of the variations in the cultural inheritances of the West and East of the world on the concept of IP rights — a situation that must be faced squarely before TRIPS-past can become TRIPS-plus.

The protection of individual rights in IP is a creation of the West. IP rights can be justified as natural rights arising from John Locke's notion[3] that individuals have the right to the fruits of their own labor. In addition, or in the alternative, they can be justified as positive rights created by the state for the benefit of the general well-being. The justification of IP rights as positive rights can be accomplished by means of a utilitarian calculation resulting from Jeremy Bentham's belief[4] that public policy should be founded on utility — that it should be based on what provides the greatest happiness to the greatest number of people. Theoretical discussion has long continued in the West over whether IP rights are based in natural law, positive law or both. (Bentham thought natural law was "nonsense on stilts";[5] others think Bentham's utilitarianism inimical to the very idea of individual rights.[6]) But there is wide agreement in the West that these individual rights exist, that they are limited in time and that they must be protected for as long as they exist.

There is no comparable intellectual source for the concept of IP rights in the East; it is not a part of Asian history and tradition.[7] For example, in the Confucian tradition, the Chinese have long conflated the interest of the individual with the interest of the state. The role of the individual in this tradition is to further "the collective well being of society."[8] Accordingly, the traditional Chinese view of IP rights is that rights in creative works are not based in nature but, instead, derive from the state and are intended for the benefit of the state, not for the benefit of any particular individual.⁹ In this view, all works, creative and non-creative alike, belong to the people as manifested in the state. This ancient view was reinforced for the first 40 years that followed the Chinese Communist Revolution in 1949, until after the death of Mao Zedong and the subsequent "reform and opening up" under Deng Xiaoping.¹⁰

These conflicting intellectual antecedents clash every day in the WTO in deliberations over the interpretation and implementation of the TRIPS Agreement. To be sure, China and the numerous other developing countries that are members of the WTO have agreed to the TRIPS Agreement. They did so either when the WTO was established in 1995 or (as in the case of China in 2001) upon their later date of accession. All of them are also members of WIPO, a UN agency. Thus, legally, they are all adherents to the protection of IP rights, wherever the concept may have originated. The concept of IP rights may have begun in the West but, for some time now, it has, as a legal concept, been accepted globally.

Despite all this, many of the developing countries continue to have cultural as well as economic reservations about the protection of individual IP. Because of their legal obligations, they generally express their reservations about the protection of IP rights in procedural terms, citing the undeniable difficulties that those countries in the early stages of development have in summoning the resources to enforce IP rights. Yet, even so, much of their lingering hesitation about the protection of IP rights can be traced to the fact of the Western intellectual sources of those rights, which express a kind and a degree of individualism that many in the East still find it hard to embrace, even after decades of economic globalization.

This tacit reservation about the justification for IP rights among many WTO members — not only in the East but across much of the developing Global South — adds to the tensions within the WTO over the scope and the pace of recognizing and upholding such rights. It adds also to the divisions within the WTO over whether, nearly three decades later, the negotiated balance reflected in the text of the TRIPS Agreement between the individual right to a limited ownership interest in intellectual creations and the collective societal right to have early and widespread access to those creations, is still the right balance. These regional tensions have been heightened amid the life-or-death stakes of a global pandemic.

The Balance in the Text

The balance between exclusivity and access that has been agreed by all the members of the WTO on the trade-related aspects of IP property rights is given legal expression in articles 7 and 8 of the TRIPS Agreement,[11] as negotiated in the Uruguay Round of multilateral trade negotiations that established the WTO. As to the "objectives" of the TRIPS Agreement, article 7 provides: "The protection and enforcement of intellectual property rights should contribute to the promotion of technological innovation and to the transfer and dissemination of technology, to the mutual advantage of producers and users of technological knowledge and in a manner conducive to social and economic welfare, and to a balance of rights and obligations."[12]

In addition, as to the "principles" underlying the TRIPS Agreement, article 8, paragraph 1 states: "Members may, in formulating or amending their laws and regulations, adopt measures necessary to protect public health and nutrition, and to promote the public interest in sectors of vital importance to their socio-economic and technological development, provided that such measures are consistent with the provisions of this Agreement."[13] Further, article 8, paragraph 2 elaborates: "Appropriate measures, provided that they are consistent with the provisions of this Agreement, may be needed to prevent the abuse of intellectual property rights by right holders or the resort to practices which unreasonably restrain trade or adversely affect the international transfer of technology."[14]

Of relevance in clarifying the meaning of the balance described in these two TRIPS obligations are certain passages in the preamble of the agreement.[15] In the first words of the preamble, the members of the WTO have voiced their common desire, in their effort "to reduce distortions and impediments to international trade," to take "into account the need to promote effective and adequate protection of intellectual property rights, and to ensure that measures and procedures to enforce intellectual property rights do not themselves become barriers to legitimate trade."[16] They have gone on in the preamble to recognize that "intellectual property rights are private rights," and to acknowledge "the underlying public policy objectives of national systems for the protection of intellectual property, including developmental and technological objectives."[17]

Articles 7 and 8 are not general exceptions to the obligations to protect IP rights in the TRIPS Agreement. They are not textual equivalents to article XX of the General Agreement on Tariffs and Trade[18] and article XIV of the General Agreement on Trade in Services.[19] These TRIPS provisions are not there to excuse a failure to comply with what would otherwise be TRIPS obligations in certain circumstances, although that can often be their effective result. Instead, as the WTO panel in the *Australia — Tobacco Plain Packaging* dispute put it in 2018, "Articles 7 and 8, together with the preamble of the TRIPS Agreement, set out general goals and principles underlying the TRIPS Agreement, which are to be borne in mind when specific provisions of the Agreement are being interpreted in their context and in light of the object and purpose of the Agreement."[20] The panel there added that article 7, specifically, "reflects the intention of establishing and maintaining a balance between the societal objectives mentioned therein."[21]

In the same dispute, the panel stated that article 8.1 "makes clear that the provisions of the TRIPS Agreement are not intended to prevent the adoption, by Members, of laws and regulations pursuing certain legitimate objectives, specifically, measures 'necessary to protect public health and nutrition' and 'promote the public interest in sectors of vital importance to their socioeconomic and technological development', provided that such measures are consistent with the provisions of the Agreement."[22] The panel then went on to say, "Specifically, the principles reflected in Article 8.1 express the intention of drafters of the TRIPS Agreement to preserve the ability for WTO Members to pursue certain legitimate societal interests, at the same time as it confirms their recognition that certain measures adopted by WTO Members for such purposes may have an impact on IP rights, and requires that such measures be 'consistent with the provisions of the [TRIPS] Agreement.'"[23]

The language in the preamble to the TRIPS Agreement can be used by a treaty interpreter to help confirm the object and purpose of the agreement when clarifying its specific obligations. With this in mind, the panel in the *Australia — Tobacco Plain Packaging* dispute noted that "the first recital of the preamble to the TRIPS Agreement expresses a key objective of the TRIPS Agreement, namely to 'reduce distortions and impediments to international trade' and takes into account the need, on one hand, 'to promote effective and adequate protection of intellectual property rights' and, on the other, 'to ensure that measures and procedures to enforce intellectual property rights do not themselves become barriers to legitimate trade.'"[24]

Taken together, these provisions in the TRIPS Agreement evidence a consensus among the WTO members that insufficient protection of IP rights will lead to trade distortions, such as counterfeiting and piracy, that will impede development by inhibiting the creation and the spread of new knowledge. Therefore, the WTO members have concluded, minimum standards of IP protection are needed in WTO rules. At the same time, these provisions evidence a consensus that the overzealous protection of IP rights could unduly limit the discretion of WTO members in doing what they may conclude must be done in their own domestic economies to promote social and economic welfare. Thus, WTO members have sought to secure in the TRIPS Agreement both appropriate IP protections and appropriate policy space for individual WTO members to limit those protections domestically whenever they can demonstrate that such limitations are justified.

Locating the Line of the Balance

This is the line of the balance that has been struck between exclusivity and access in the TRIPS Agreement. But where precisely is this line in any given instance? In WTO dispute settlement, the line of the balance has been located, as with other negotiated lines in the WTO treaty, on a case-by-case basis. Going forward, this gradual accumulation of case-by-case clarification through dispute settlement will continue. Locating this line and other negotiated lines in the covered agreements of the WTO treaty to help reach a positive solution to international trade disputes is the purpose of the clarification of WTO dispute settlement. But in negotiations and in other deliberations, WTO members frequently disagree on where the line of the balance is in the TRIPS Agreement, and this explains much about why they have been unable to make progress on addressing TRIPS-plus concerns on both sides of the line.

In the still brief history of the WTO, the question of where this line is to be found has famously centered on the topic of compulsory licensing of medicines by the developing countries during times of health crisis. A compulsory license[25] is a legal authorization asserted by a government or granted by a government to a third party to produce a patented process or product without the express consent of the patentholder. Such a license overrides what is otherwise the patentholder's exclusive right to keep others from using its patented inventions. A compulsory license is a right to use patented information for processing or production; it is not a waiver of IP rights. The holder of the patent still retains rights over the patent, including the right to be paid compensation for copies of the product made under the compulsory license.

Compulsory licensing was a highly controversial issue for the WTO during the height of the HIV/ AIDS crisis at the turn of the century. After years of sometimes contentious debate, in the Doha Ministerial Declaration of November 2001, WTO members issued a Declaration on the TRIPS Agreement and Public Health,[26] which affirmed that WTO IP protections do not and should not prevent national measures taken to protect public health by the promotion of access to new medicines and the creation of new medicines. WTO members confirmed in this 2001 declaration that each WTO member "has the right to grant compulsory licenses and the freedom to determine the grounds upon which such licenses are granted."[27] In August 2003, WTO members followed up on their 2001 declaration by adopting a waiver that allows poorer countries that do not have the capacity to make pharmaceutical products — and thus cannot benefit from compulsory licensing — to import cheaper generic drugs from countries where those drugs are patent protected.[28] This waiver was transformed into an amendment to the TRIPS Agreement in 2017 styled as article 31bis.[29]

Arguably, as a legal matter, the identical results could have been achieved simply by reference to the texts of articles 7 and 8, which provide broad legal authority for domestic actions for such domestic purposes. Notably, in the 2001 declaration, WTO members emphasized that "in applying the customary rules of interpretation of public international law, each provision of the TRIPS Agreement shall be read in the light of the object and purpose of the Agreement as expressed, in particular, in its objectives and principles."[30] These objectives are expressed in article 7, and these principles are stated in article 8. These two articles must be read in the context of the object and purpose of the agreement as set out in its preamble. Therein lies the line of the balance. To adhere to this line, and to extend it into the future, developed and developing countries alike must begin to see it in its proper light and give a living and evolving reality to it.

Fulfilling and Sustaining the Balance

Toward this end, the developed countries must understand more clearly the legal nature of the negotiated balance reflected in the TRIPS Agreement. The balance between exclusivity and access put in the language of the TRIPS Agreement is not something that applies only in exceptional circumstances. It applies all the time. It is a central part of the bargain that is reflected in the agreement. Every obligation in the TRIPS Agreement must always be read with the objectives in article 7, the principles in article 8 and the related language in the preamble much in mind if the balance in the agreement is to be upheld. These two articles are immediate and relevant context that pervades the entirety of the agreement. The relevant language in the preamble reinforces this context by elucidating the object and purpose of the agreement.

Establishing such a negotiated balance is not new in IP law. Although the TRIPS Agreement itself is novel in bringing IP rights within the ambit of international trade law, the balance between exclusivity and access with respect to IP rights is not novel to the TRIPS Agreement. Indeed, this balance is intrinsic to the very nature of IP rights, in which a balance is evidenced by the facts that the scope of IP rights is defined, and the duration of IP rights is limited. Thus, the developed countries must understand that, when the developing countries assert their sovereign rights with reference to the general language in articles 7 and 8, they are not necessarily undermining the bargain in the TRIPS Agreement; it may well be that they are acting fully in accordance with it. Whether or not they are, in any given instance, acting consistently with the import of this balance, will depend on the facts of each specific case.

At the same time, the developing countries must realize that their WTO obligation to protect IP rights is not some post-colonial neo-imperialistic imposition that undermines their sovereignty and postpones their further development. Quite the opposite. The protection of IP rights is, in fact, a necessary means to their further development in a world in which the creation of more wealth depends more than ever on the creation of knowledge. There is a tendency in the developing countries (and in some non-commercial enclaves in the developed countries) to view the profits to right holders from the protection of IP rights as contrived, excessive and unearned "rents" rather than as legitimate earnings from investments made in creating knowledge. To be sure, such earnings can be excessive if they are not limited appropriately in scope and duration. But this tendency often betrays a lingering underlying cultural skepticism about the legitimacy of IP rights themselves — a skepticism that, if allowed to prevail, will impede the further economic advancement of the developing countries in the new pandemic world.

The developing countries must understand that upholding IP rights is not of interest only to the United States and the other advanced economies, which have, to date, led the way in knowledge-based enterprise. It is equally of interest to the developing countries. One of them, China, is closing in on the developed countries in the global flows of goods, services, finance and data, which depend for their success on the protection of IP rights. Other developing countries are likewise catching up in these IP-fueled flows. The evidence clearly shows that, when developing countries protect IP rights, they gain in economic growth (Cavazos Cepeda, Lippoldt and Senft, 2010). As shown by the Global Innovation Index of the World Economic Forum, countries that uphold IP rights "have more creative outputs ... even at varying levels of development" (Ezell and Cory, 2019). This is especially so when firms and individuals in developing countries are connected to global value chains. The capacity for creative innovation is not limited only to people in the developed world, and yet much of that capacity will remain untapped if developing countries do not protect IP rights.

All the members of the WTO — developed and developing countries alike — must comprehend completely that the new pandemic world presents new circumstances that demand that the text of the TRIPS Agreement be revisited to make certain that the agreement is up to date and that it truly fulfills the bargain it represents. It is widely assumed that this will involve additional difficult concessions at the negotiating table by both developed and developing countries. In fact, as difficult as it may be to achieve politically, the needed modernization of the TRIPS Agreement can be comprised entirely of reforms that will benefit all the countries that are members of the WTO; the wealth and the welfare of all of them can be enhanced if the original bargain in the agreement is entirely fulfilled to fit the global economy of the 21st century.

To realize fully the balance set out in the TRIPS Agreement, developed countries must keep their original promises made in 1995. Foremost among these is their promise in article 66 of the agreement to engage in "technical cooperation" with the 46 least-developed country members of the WTO, which are on the UN list of the poorest countries in the world.[31] Article 66, paragraph 2 states that "developed country Members shall provide incentives to enterprises and institutions in their territories for the purpose of promoting and encouraging technology transfer to least-developed country Members in order to enable them to create a sound and viable technological base."[32] This is a mandatory obligation that is enforceable in WTO dispute settlement.

The preamble to the agreement recognizes the "special needs" of the least-developed countries.[33] The presence of article 66, paragraph 2 was an important reason why the least-developed countries agreed to join other WTO members in the TRIPS Agreement. Yet the developed countries have not been meeting their end of this key part of the bargain in the TRIPS Agreement (Fox, 2019). Although technology transfer has been flowing more swiftly where developing countries have complied with the TRIPS Agreement, developed countries have fallen far short in providing incentives for technology transfer to their enterprises and institutions. Many developed countries have not even bothered to submit required annual reports of their attempts at compliance with this mandatory obligation. If developed countries continue to ignore or artfully evade this mandatory obligation, then they should be challenged in WTO dispute settlement.

If this happens, then WTO jurists should take a broad view of what constitutes technology transfer. As David M. Fox has observed in a thoughtful examination of the meaning of technology transfer, in the modern world, technology includes more than machinery and equipment; it also includes knowledge and skills, human resource development and domestic capacity building (*Ibid.*). Much of all of this happens every day in the normal course of the buy-and-sell of international commerce, but it does not happen automatically, and the developed countries must put incentives in place to help make it happen more often. At the same time, it is vital to build the capacity in developing countries — especially in the least-developed countries — to absorb and benefit from new imported technologies. This requires investments in human capital, human connectivity, better business conditions and, not least, the rule of law.

Substantial technology transfers are already occurring through the mediation of markets, most noticeably in those places where IP rights are upheld in accordance with the TRIPS Agreement (Park and Lippoldt, 2008). When IP right holders can be assured that their rights will be protected locally, they are more likely to share their technology by means of licensing, investing or engaging in research and development locally. Foreign direct investment includes not only hardware and software, but also, importantly, the tacit knowledge and the learning by doing that are critical to true development. These kinds of transfers have tended to vary in relation to the stringency of local compliance by developing countries with their legal obligations under the TRIPS Agreement (*Ibid.*). In updating the TRIPS Agreement, the aim should be to create an enabling atmosphere in which these market-based transfers of technology will be maximized (Branstetter, Fisman and Foley, 2005).

To achieve the full measure of the balance in the TRIPS Agreement, developing countries must also fulfill their treaty obligations. One obligation many developing countries have not met nearly to the extent they should is to enforce IP rights in accordance with the terms of the TRIPS Agreement. Most WTO obligations are negative obligations: they are legal obligations to not do something (for example, to not discriminate). The TRIPS Agreement is one of the few WTO agreements that contains positive obligations: it includes affirmative legal obligations to do something, namely, to protect IP rights. These affirmative obligations are in part III of the TRIPS Agreement, "Enforcement of Intellectual Property Rights," which is comprised of articles 41 through 48.[34]

Under part III of the TRIPS Agreement, it is not sufficient that a legal means for right holders to enforce their IP rights is written into the laws of a WTO member. Under article 42 of the agreement, that means must genuinely be "available to right holders" through "fair and equitable procedures."[35] As the Appellate Body of the WTO stressed with respect to the enforcement procedures under article 42 in *United States — Section 211 Omnibus Appropriations Act* in 2001, "making something available means making it 'obtainable,' putting it 'within one's reach' and 'at one's disposal' in a way that has sufficient force or efficacy"; therefore, "the ordinary meaning of the term 'make available' suggests that 'right holders' are entitled under Article 42 to have access to civil judicial procedures that are effective in bringing about the enforcement of their rights covered by the Agreement."[36] Thus, the enforcement of IP rights is not optional for WTO members under the TRIPS Agreement; it is mandatory as part of the bargain struck between exclusivity and access in the balance in the agreement. It is an affirmative legal obligation that requires that the words in laws be matched by actions that give those laws real meaning.

In addition to the enforcement of their own obligations under the TRIPS Agreement, the developing countries must also be able to assert their own rights under the agreement in their IP-related trade with other countries. As a practical matter, this means they must have the legal and technical means to participate successfully in WTO dispute settlement. Since the establishment of the WTO in 1995, numerous developing countries have acquired significant expertise in the conduct of dispute settlement — a level of expertise that matches or exceeds that of the developed countries. But many of the developing countries remain without such expertise and without the dispute settlement experience that helps hone it. More financial and other support by the developed countries must be provided for the current efforts to provide access to this expertise for these often least-developed countries.

What is more, to make the balance in the TRIPS Agreement work in the new pandemic world, all the members of the WTO must be willing to make and keep more promises by updating and adding to their obligations in the TRIPS Agreement. The balance between exclusivity and access in the agreement can only be fulfilled and sustained if it is practically fit for purpose for this new world. This means that the TRIPS Agreement must be revised to account for all the technological and other changes in IP since it entered into force in 1995 — a goal primarily of the developed countries. Moreover, this means also that the TRIPS Agreement must be further revised to address issues that are of special concern mostly to the developing countries.

Most immediately, as the newly elected WTO Director-General, Ngozi Okonjo-Iweala, has said, the balance in the TRIPS Agreement must be reflected in how the members of the WTO respond to the simultaneous urgency of developing new COVID-19 vaccines and providing them quickly to all the billions of people who are waiting for life-saving doses throughout the world. The compounding complexities of the global challenges of confronting COVID-19 and its multiplying mutations are beyond even those of confronting the HIV/AIDS crisis, and, as she has said, there is need for "a third way, in which we can license manufacturing to countries so that you can have adequate supplies while still making sure that intellectual property issues are taken care of" (Okonjo-Iweala, quoted in Josephs 2021). This "third way" may not require an amendment to the text of the TRIPS Agreement; however, as events unfold, it could involve a formal legal interpretation of the agreement or some other form of multilateral action by the members of the WTO.

As it is, the multilateral actions that have been undertaken outside the WTO to fight the COVID-19 pandemic pose no legal difficulties under the trade rules in the TRIPS Agreement. The unprecedented global collaboration to accelerate the development, production and equitable access to COVID-19 tests, treatments and vaccines under the auspices of the Access to COVID-19 Tools (ACT) Accelerator[37] is perfectly consistent with the TRIPS Agreement. Likewise, COVAX, the vaccines pillar under the ACT-Accelerator, is equally consistent with the WTO trade rules.[38] These global endeavors in no way infringe on IP rights. Nor would the voluntary pooling of patent rights and data to COVID-19 vaccines infringe IP rights if done with the participation and/or permission of the patent right holders.

In addition, the new international IP agreements concluded since the writing of the TRIPS Agreement in the early 1990s must be incorporated by reference into the TRIPS Agreement so that they can be enforceable in WTO dispute settlement. The TRIPS Agreement was written before the rise of the internet, and much has happened relating to IP in the nearly three decades since. The agreement incorporates by reference several longstanding international IP conventions, including on patents and copyrights.[39] Incorporating these IP conventions into the TRIPS Agreement has had the legal effect of making them fully enforceable for the first time through the WTO dispute settlement system. The same must be instituted now for the new international IP conventions.

In addition to the IP conventions that are already included, two treaties adopted in 1996 by WIPO should be incorporated by reference into the TRIPS Agreement. Commonly described together as the "Internet Treaties," one of these two WIPO agreements provides added protections for copyrights in response to advances in information technology, including the protection of IP rights in computer programs and in databases.[40] The other WIPO agreement updates protections of the rights of performers and producers of phonograms for the digital age.[41] Incorporating these two Internet Treaties into the WTO rules would make them, too, fully enforceable. Still another WIPO convention that should likewise be incorporated by reference into the TRIPS Agreement is the Marrakesh Treaty to Facilitate Access to Published Works for Persons Who Are Blind, Visually Impaired or Otherwise Print Disabled, which was adopted in 2013.[42]

Giving more reality to the balance in the TRIPS Agreement by modernizing the agreement must also include making multilateral many of the advances made in recent years in protecting IP rights in bilateral and regional trade arrangements. Because of the ongoing standoff between the developed countries and the developing countries on extending and modernizing IP protections inside the legal framework of the WTO, those who have sought modernization have gone outside the WTO. As Henning Grosse Ruse-Khan (2018) of the University of Cambridge has observed, international IP law has, since the entry into force of the TRIPS

Agreement, "primarily developed via a network of bilateral and regional agreements. These range from international investment and free trade agreements (IIAs, FTAs), via treaties on development cooperation, to comprehensive regional integration accords."

These non-multilateral, non-WTO and non-WIPO agreements often have IP chapters that provide IP protections over and above those provided in the TRIPS Agreement. This non-multilateral approach can be beneficial, as with, for example, the added protections for trade secrets in the "new NAFTA (North American Free Trade Agreement)," the Canada-United States-Mexico Agreement (CUSMA).[43] But this non-multilateral approach can also place smaller and poorer countries in an unequal bargaining position when they are negotiating with larger and wealthier countries. In a typical bilateral trade negotiation between a developing and a developed country, the developing country has no choice but to agree to TRIPS-plus protections if it wants to secure more access for its most significant exports to the domestic market of the developed country.

Moreover, this non-multilateral approach can also have the gradual effect of undermining on a piecemeal basis the policy flexibilities that have been afforded to developing countries under articles 7 and 8 of the multilateral TRIPS Agreement. By refusing to negotiate TRIPS-plus IP protections within the WTO, the developing countries have left the developed countries with the option only of going outside the WTO to modernize international IP protections. The TRIPS-plus obligations that have been negotiated in these non-WTO agreements are not constrained by the overarching presence of articles 7 and 8. Thus, ironically, the reluctance of the developing countries to negotiate further on IP rights in the WTO threatens to undermine the local discretions they have been assured in the TRIPS Agreement.

It is, therefore, much in the interest of the developing countries, in the short term and the long term, to centralize the making of international rules on the trade-related aspects of IP once more within the WTO. This would not be a concession to the developed countries; it would be a profession of their long-term self-interest by the developing countries. Moving many of the additional IP protections in these bilateral and regional agreements into the multilateral legal framework of the WTO would have the dual benefit of enhancing IP protections generally while also making certain that these additional protections were subject to the balance between exclusivity and access that has been agreed in the TRIPS Agreement.

Also worthy of consideration for multilateral expression in the TRIPS Agreement are the nuances on the balance between exclusivity and access described in one of the agreements concluded outside the WTO, the Regional Comprehensive Economic Partnership (RCEP),[44] a new trade arrangement among China, Japan, South Korea and a dozen other Asian and Pacific countries signed on November 15, 2020. In addition to echoing the wording about the needed balance in article 7 of the TRIPS Agreement, the RCEP underscores "the need to maintain an appropriate balance between the rights of intellectual property right holders and the legitimate interests of users and the public interest."[45]

RCEP parties must adopt appropriate measures "to prevent the abuse of intellectual property rights by right holders or the resort to practices which unreasonably restrain trade or adversely affect the international transfer of technology."[46] At the same time, these RCEP procedures must be applied in such a manner as to avoid the creation of barriers to legitimate trade and to provide for safeguards against their abuse. Most significantly for the new pandemic world, a party to the RCEP "may, in formulating or amending its laws and regulations, adopt measures necessary to protect public health and nutrition and to promote the public sectors of vital importance to its socioeconomic and technological development."[47]

Because of the urgent need to promote innovation worldwide, other international IP concerns addressed to varying extents in the ongoing proliferation of non-WTO agreements are also deserving of attention in a modernized TRIPS Agreement. Foremost among them is the pressing need to protect IP rights related to new technologies and to new methods of transmission in ways that facilitate trade. In particular, this should include the explosion of the digital trade that barely existed when the TRIPS Agreement was negotiated and agreed.[48] In their current WTO discussions of the pressing need for specific WTO rules that address digital trade, WTO members must keep much in mind the creative role of IP rights to digital trade.

In the wake of the COVID-19 pandemic, the importance of intangible assets is increasing. As Greg Ip (2020) of the *Wall Street Journal* has observed, "value is increasingly derived from digital platforms, software and other intangible investments rather than physical assets and traditional relationships." Jason Thomas, head of global research at The Carlyle Group, a leading global private-equity firm, informs us that the pace of digitalization will accelerate in the new pandemic world:

"technology-enabled adaptation has opened the door to more sweeping changes in business models and strategies (Thomas, 2020a) [and] tech-enabled digital platforms tend to outperform the broader market" (Thomas, 2020b).

Rana Foroohar (2020) of the *Financial Times* predicts that, of the new start-up enterprises that will emerge in the aftermath of the pandemic, "it's a fair bet that many will be highly digital. They are likely to hold a large chunk of value in intangible assets such as research and development, brands, content, data, patents or human capital, rather than in physical assets such as industrial machinery, factories or office space." When these new enterprises engage in international trade, whether of goods or of services, they will be more likely to do so digitally. IP will become even more of a trade issue than it is now.

Some of the basics of what should be included in a modernized TRIPS Agreement relating to the link between IP and digital trade through electronic commerce — on transparency, customs duties, online consumer protection, online personal information and more — are in chapter 12 of the RCEP.[49] Similar provisions are found in chapter 19 of CUSMA[50] and chapter 14 of the Comprehensive and Progressive Agreement for Trans-Pacific Partnership.[51] The continued economic advance of developed and developing countries alike requires a seamlessness in the treatment of digital trade to maximize the flow of digital trade. This seamlessness can only be achieved if the rules for digital trade are multilateral rules within the WTO.

Also, there is need for a negotiated compromise on an appropriate balance between exclusivity and access for protections of new pharmaceutical products, including the biological drugs — the biologics — that are made from living organisms or that contain components of living organisms. WTO members must make certain, of course, that the legal lines they draw between exclusivity and access in such new protections will indeed foster innovation and will not simply create undue global rents for the IP right holders.[52] Getting the balance between exclusivity and access right on the biologics that may increasingly typify medicines is especially significant.

At the same time, there is equal need for providing more international protections in the TRIPS Agreement for the traditional knowledge that has been passed down for generations as the heritage of Indigenous communities, often in developing countries where there are inadequate domestic rights to such knowledge.[53] And, more broadly, at a time when biodiversity is imperiled worldwide, WTO members must forge a stronger consensus on the line dividing where animal, plant and other natural resources can be patented and where they cannot. Those who create knowledge should be able to enjoy a limited right to the exclusive ownership of that knowledge; however, knowledge is not created by those who merely misappropriate traditional knowledge for commercial profits.[54]

A pioneering feature of the RCEP is that it includes — for the first time in any trade agreement — provisions to protect genetic resources, traditional knowledge and folklore. Section G of chapter 11 of the RCEP, on IP, specifies that, subject to their international obligations, parties to the RCEP "may establish appropriate measures to protect genetic resources, traditional knowledge, and folklore."[55] In particular, in patent examinations, "relevant publicly available documented information related to traditional knowledge associated with genetic resources may be taken into account."[56] Similar provision should be made by the members of the WTO in a TRIPS-plus agreement.

In addition, a modernized TRIPS Agreement should emulate the novel WTO Trade Facilitation Agreement (TFA)[57] in doing much more to help provide many of the developing countries with the capacity to meet their obligations to protect IP rights. Conceivably, like the TFA, a modernized TRIPS Agreement could allow the developing countries — particularly the least-developed countries — to determine when they will implement specific new obligations in the agreement, and to identify obligations they will only be able to implement upon the receipt of technical assistance and support for capacity building. The developing countries — especially the least-developed countries — cannot be expected to assume a whole slew of new IP obligations if developed countries do not provide them with sufficient technical support and adequate capacity-building and financial assistance to be able to fulfill those obligations.

The details of what the members of the WTO decide to include in fully realizing the balance in the TRIPS Agreement should be informed by the common commitment they expressed when creating the WTO to sustainable development. The first paragraph in the preamble on the first page of the WTO treaty proclaims that "trade and economic endeavour" should be conducted while "allowing for the optimal use of the world's resources in accordance with the objective of sustainable development, seeking both to protect and preserve the environment and to enhance the means for doing so."[58] The WTO Appellate Body has explained that this language in the preamble "gives colour, texture and shading to the rights and obligations of Members under the WTO Agreement."[59]

The objective of sustainable development is reflected in the Sustainable Development Goals (SDGs) of the United Nations for 2030.[60] These global goals were agreed in 2015 by all the members of the United Nations — including all the members of the WTO. Goal 9 of the 17 SDGs is, in part, to "foster innovation." This global goal cannot be achieved without the incentives provided by the protection of IP. At the same time, the SDGs also aim to end poverty and hunger, ensure health and education, promote sustainable and inclusive economic growth, and achieve much more on many fronts by the end of this decade. Implicit in the "integrated and indivisible" nature of these global goals is the assumption that achieving them all will depend on balancing them all through concerted international cooperation. With this global balancing in mind, WTO members can contribute most to achieving the goal of fostering innovation by upholding the balance between exclusivity and access in the WTO rules on the protection of IP rights.

Conclusion

The new pandemic world requires new innovations of all kinds, not least in new medicines to help prevent and cure new diseases. The protection of IP rights provides incentives for these new innovations. Multilateral incentives for innovations can be much more productive than bilateral and regional incentives because of the global reach of multilateral incentives and the global protections of the WTO rules against discrimination. In trade, more multilateral incentives for needed innovations will not be agreed unless and until all members of the WTO first agree on the meaning of the balance they have struck between exclusivity and access to new knowledge in the TRIPS Agreement and work together to realize that balance fully in their ongoing implementation of that agreement. Only once they have done this, will they be able to transform TRIPS-past into TRIPS-plus by fostering innovation and fulfilling their overall commitment to the objective of sustainable development, which is reflected in the UN SDGs.

Endnotes

[1] www.wto.org/english/tratop_e/trips_e/trips_e.htm.
[2] World Intellectual Property Organization (WIPO) (2017, chapter 1).
[3] https://oll.libertyfund.org/page/john-locke-two-treatises1689#lf0057_head_018.
[4] https://en.wikisource.org/wiki/An_Introduction_to_the_Principles_of_Morals_and_Legislation/Chapter_I.
[5] https://iep.utm.edu/bentham/.
[6] Himmelfarb (1990).
[7] Fowler, Charoenpot and Chernkwanma (2017).
[8] http://factsanddetails.com/china/cat3/sub9/entry-5561.html.
[9] *JIPEL* Blog (2014).
[10] Lu et al. (2019).
[11] WTO, *Agreement on Trade-Related Aspects of Intellectual Property Rights* (unamended), Annex 1C of the *Marrakesh Agreement Establishing the World Trade Organization*, April 15, 1994, 1867 UNTS 154, 33 ILM 1144 (1994) (entered into force January 1, 1995) [*TRIPS Agreement*], WTO www.wto.org/english/docs_e/legal_e/27-trips_01_e.htm.
[12] *Ibid*, art. 7.
[13] *Ibid*, art. 8 at para 1.
[14] *Ibid*, art. 8 at para 2.
[15] *Ibid*, preamble.
[16] *Ibid*.
[17] *Ibid*.
[18] *General Agreement on Tariffs and Trade*, October 30, 1947, 58 UNTS 187, art. XX (entered into force January 1, 1948), www.wto.org/english/docs_e/legal_e/gatt47_02_e.htm#articleXX.
[19] General Agreement on Trade in Services, Annex 1B of the *Marrakesh Agreement Establishing the World Trade Organization*, April 15, 1994, 1867 UNTS 154, 33 ILM 1144 (1994) (entered into force January 1, 1995), www.wto.org/english/docs_e/legal_e/26-gats_01_e.htm.
[20] WTO, *WTO Analytical Index, TRIPS Agreement — Article 8 (Jurisprudence)* [WTO Analytical Index, Article 8], www.wto.org/english/res_e/publications_e/ai17_e/trips_art8_jur.pdf.
[21] WTO, *WTO Analytical Index, TRIPS Agreement — Article 7 (Jurisprudence)* [WTO Analytical Index, Article 7], www.wto.org/english/res_e/publications_e/ai17_e/trips_art7_jur.pdf.
[22] *WTO Analytical Index*, Article 8, *supra* note 20.
[23] *Ibid*.
[24] WTO, *WTO Analytical Index, TRIPS Agreement — Preamble (Jurisprudence)*, www.wto.org/english/res_e/publications_e/ai17_e/trips_preamble_jur.pdf.

25 *See* www.wto.org/english/tratop_e/trips_e/public_health_faq_e.htm.
26 WTO, *Declaration on the TRIPS Agreement and Public Health* (adopted on November 14, 2001), WTO Doc WT/MIN(01)DEC/2 [Public Health], www.wto.org/english/thewto_e/minist_e/min01_e/mindecl_trips_e.htm.
27 *Ibid.*
28 WTO, General Council, *Implementation of paragraph 6 of the Doha Declaration on the TRIPS Agreement and public health* (Decision of the General Council of August 30, 2003), WT/L/540, www.wto.org/english/tratop_e/trips_e/implem_para6_e.htm.
29 *TRIPS Agreement, supra* note 11, art. 31bis.
30 *Public Health, supra* note 26 at para 5a.
31 *See* www.un.org/development/desa/dpad/least-developed-countrycategory.html.
32 *TRIPS Agreement, supra* note 11, art. 6 at para 2.
33 *Ibid.* preamble.
34 *Ibid.* arts. 41–48.
35 *Ibid.* art. 42.
36 WTO, *United States — Section 211 Omnibus Appropriations Act of 1998*, WT/DS176/AB/R, at para 215 (emphasis in original), www.wto.org/english/tratop_e/dispu_e/cases_e/ds176_e.htm.
37 *See* www.who.int/initiatives/act-accelerator/about.
38 *See* www.who.int/initiatives/act-accelerator/covax.
39 WTO, *WTO Analytical Index, TRIPS Agreement — Article 1 (Jurisprudence)*, www.wto.org/english/res_e/publications_e/ai17_e/trips_art1_jur.pdf.
40 *WIPO Copyright Treaty*, December 20, 1996, 36 ILM 65 (entered into force March 6, 2002), www.wipo.int/edocs/lexdocs/treaties/en/wct/trt_wct_001en.pdf.
41 *WIPO Performances and Phonograms Treaty*, December 20, 1996, 36 ILM 76 (entered into force May 20, 2002), www.wipo.int/edocs/pubdocs/en/wipo_pub_227.pdf.
42 *Marrakesh Treaty to Facilitate Access to Published Works for Persons Who Are Blind, Visually Impaired or Otherwise Print Disabled*, June 27, 2013 (entered into force September 29, 2016), www.wipo.int/treaties/en/ip/marrakesh.
43 de Beer (2020).
44 https://rcepsec.org/.
45 *Regional Comprehensive Economic Partnership Agreement*, November 15, 2020, sec. A, art. 11.1 at para 1c (not yet entered into force) [RCEP], http://rcepsec.org/wp-content/uploads/2020/11/Chapter-11.pdf.
46 *Ibid.* art. 11.4 at para 2.
47 *Ibid.* art. 11.4 at para 1.
48 www.oecd.org/trade/topics/digital-trade/.

⁴⁹ *RCEP, supra* note 45, chap. 12, http://rcepsec.org/wp-content/uploads/2020/11/Chapter-12.pdf.

⁵⁰ *Canada-United States-Mexico Agreement*, December 10, 2019 (entered into force July 1, 2020), www.international.gc.ca/tradecommerce/trade-agreements-accords-commerciaux/agr-acc/cusmaaceum/text-exte/toc-tdm.aspx?lang=eng.

⁵¹ *Comprehensive and Progressive Agreement for Trans-Pacific Partnership*, March 8, 2018, c. 14 (entered into force December 30, 2018), www.mfat.govt.nz/assets/Trade-agreements/CPTPP/CPTPP-TextEnglish.pdf.

⁵² Ciuriak (2017).

⁵³ www.wipo.int/pressroom/en/briefs/tk_ip.html.

⁵⁴ Nayak (2019).

⁵⁵ *RCEP, supra* note 45, c. 11, http://rcepsec.org/wp-content/uploads/2020/11/Chapter-11.pdf.

⁵⁶ *Ibid.*

⁵⁷ www.wto.org/english/tratop_e/tradfa_e/tradfa_e.htm.

⁵⁸ Marrakesh Agreement Establishing the World Trade Organization, April 15, 1994, 1867 UNTS 154, 33 ILM 1144 (1994) (entered into force January 1, 1995) (emphasis added), www.wto.org/english/docs_e/legal_e/04-wto_e.htm.

⁵⁹ WTO, Appellate Body, *United States — Import Prohibition of Certain Shrimp and Shrimp Products*, WTO Doc WT/DS58/AB/R, October 12, 1998 at para 155, https://docs.wto.org/dol2fe/Pages/SS/directdoc.aspx?filename=Q:/WT/DS/58ABR.pdf&Open=True.

⁶⁰ https://sdgs.un.org/2030agenda.

Chapter 11

A Common Gauge: Harmonization and International Law[*]

A favorite book of mine is *Speak, Memory*, the classic memoir by the Russian émigré, Vladimir Nabokov.[1] In one chapter, he tells of how, in the years shortly before the Bolshevik Revolution, his aristocratic family would flee every year from the snows of tsarist Russia to the sunny beaches of southern France. They traveled on the "then great and glorious" Nord-Express, the railway that connected St. Petersburg and Paris. To be more precise about that rail connection, and quoting the author, "I would have said: directly with Paris, had passengers not been obliged to change from one train to a superficially similar one at the Russo-German border..., where the ample and lazy sixty-and-a-half inch gauge was replaced by the fifty-six-and-a-half inch standard of Europe . . . ."[2]

I still recall being struck, when first reading Nabokov's book many years ago, by the spectacle, in August of 1909, of young Vladimir, his extended family, their entourage of servants, and their vast assemblage of baggage, all being unloaded with considerable labor from one train and being taken in a long procession across the border and put on another train just like it — except for the "gauge" of width between the wheels and the rails of the two stretches of train tracks.

---

[*] This essay was previously published as James Bacchus, "A Common Gauge: Harmonization and International Law," *Boston College International and Comparative Law Review*, Volume 37, No. 1 (2014), 1–18.

Even then, my interests tended more to the geopolitical than to the literary. So, for me, the question prompted by this passage all those years ago was not what it taught me about Nabokov's vivid writing style; rather, it was: what does the fact that the railways of Russia and Europe were not connected by a common gauge teach us about all the many historical misconnections between Russia and Europe?

Back then, I was immersed in the study of history in preparation for what I foresaw as a life spent as a history professor. I had no inkling then that mine would instead be a life spent in the law. And much of my study of history at the time was not of Russia, or Europe, but of the political and economic emergence of the United States of America.

Inspired to inquiry by my reading of Nabokov, I learned from further reading that the history of the United States may likewise have been influenced by the lack of a common gauge on the country's railways. Before the Civil War, the railways of the North used one gauge and the railways of the South used another. So, there was little commerce by rail between North and South. In this way as in other ways, the two were less than connected. Not until after the war was a common gauge embraced to connect America's railways — and thus help connect and reunite America.

The eminent economic historian George V. Hilton has told the tale. For two decades following the war, freight from one region to the other was — like the Nabokovs' baggage — still laboriously unloaded and loaded from one car to another in the border states where railroads of different gauges met. Then, in one single day, on May 31, 1886, in a massive effort months in the making, the spikes were pulled on thousands of miles of track across the South, and the rails of the South were moved in by three inches to match the narrower gauge of the North.[3]

The newly driven spikes set a common gauge for the whole country and helped spark a period of rapid regional economic development that historians have labeled the "New South." This common gauge bound the North and the South together economically in ways that did not exist in the antebellum era. It is perhaps not too much to say that the commercial harmonization of a common railway gauge in the later years of the 19th century helped ease the needed transit toward the eventual communal harmony between North and South that emerged in the later years of the 20th century and is now largely assumed — despite some continuing sectional differences — in the basic unity of America in the 21st century.

The trade of commerce thrives on a common gauge. As my fellow travelers who serve as the Secretariat of the World Trade Organization have said succinctly in their most recent World Trade Report, there is "a general finding in the literature that harmonization increases . . . trade."[4] A common standard helps maximize trade. The flow of commerce grows where there is only one standard to follow, only one regulation to meet, only one gauge to use. Where there are many, the flow of commerce is less than it could be. Competing standards slow the flow of trade.

Thus, the history of commerce can be seen in many ways as the search for a common gauge. The Northern railway gauge adopted by the South in 1886 was identical to the British gauge. The gauge adopted by the early British railways was based on the width of medieval British wagon roads. The width of those roads can be traced to the width of the roads that united the Roman Empire.

The same can be said of untold numbers of other goods and services that are traded and provided in what has become more and more a truly global economy. The commercial need for a common gauge has spurred a long-lasting and continuing effort to secure common standards. From these common standards have emerged the international rules that we call "international law." The commercial need for common standards and for other common ways of doing business internationally creates the international rules that are the most common kind of international law.

Indeed, it can be said with some assurance that the need for a common gauge in international commerce had much to do with the emergence of modern international law in the industrial age. As Mark Mazower recounts in his book, *Governing the World*, one of the world's very first international organizations was the International Telegraph Union, which was established in 1865.[5] The ITU was established, he explains, for a compelling commercial reason — "in order to overcome the delays that had been caused by the need to print out telegraph messages on one side of the border to walk them across to the other side."[6]

From these origins as an International Telegraph Union developed, over time, today's International Telecommunications Union, the specialized agency of the United Nations responsible for issues relating to information and communication technologies. Representatives of 193 member countries and 700 other affiliates work together writing global rules on these matters in a shiny spire overlooking the lake of Geneva just up the street from where I used to work at the WTO.[7]

Nor was the International Telegraph Union the only new international institution that emerged in the late 19th century to meet the needs of an industrializing economy in a shrinking world. Mazower explains that, among many other internationalizing initiatives, there were institutions established to make international rules to speed international postal delivery, to unify weights and measures, and to set one universal time. Safety-minded British engineers desirous of setting one standard size for screws and bolts, Mazower reminds us, "laid the foundation" for today's International Standards Organization.[8] Broadening from its beginnings in mechanical engineering, the ISO now has members in 164 countries and 3,368 technical bodies that have published more than 19,500 international standards for products covering virtually every kind of manufacturing and technology.[9]

ISO rules are far from the only common standards that have been agreed by standard-setting organizations in recent decades. The Codex Alimentarius Commission sets standards for food safety. The International Office of Epizootics sets standards for animal health. The International Plant Protection Convention sets standards for plant health. Regional and global standards of all kinds abound around the world, and they bind the world more tightly together in a global economy that is increasingly connected and increasingly one.

The logic of a common gauge can be limned by looking again into the division of labor in the pin factory described by Adam Smith in *The Wealth of Nations*. "Trade" is, of course, simply another name for "the division of labor."[10] All trade is a division of tasks in making goods and providing services. What distinguishes our economy in the 21st century from Smith's economy in the 18th century is that the trade in tasks today has led to ever more elaborate subdivisions of the division of labor in ever more complex supply chains that increasingly include the entire world.

Production now is truly global, and, increasingly, much of international trade consists of trade in the intermediate goods that serve as inputs into the final finished goods that are ultimately sold to consumers. As Gary Hufbauer and Jeffrey Schott of the Peterson Institute for International Economics have recently summed it up, "A large share of 21st century trade requires integrated global supply chains that move intermediate and finished goods around the world. Intermediate goods account for 60 percent of global commerce, and about 30 percent of total trade is conducted between affiliates of the same multinational corporation."[11] National borders are relevant to these global supply chains only because we choose to believe that national borders exist.

Nationality still denominates trade, and thus it still defines trade law and dictates how we choose up sides in trade disputes. We still pretend that products are "from" somewhere. We say they are "from" one country or another, and we engage in trade disputes over "our" products and "their" products as a result. Yet, with the ascendancy of global supply chains, value may be added to products in many places, and the most value may not be added where a product is supposedly "from." Political economy today is all about "value added" in global supply chains that are best seen as global value chains. With these global value chains, products are no longer "from" anywhere. They are "from" everywhere, and they are traded everywhere through the workings of the chain.

Smith taught us that the "division of labor" that is "trade" is limited only by the extent of the marketplace. With our successes over the past half century in lowering tariffs and other barriers to trade, with the willingness by emerging countries in the past two decades to open up their economies wider to the wider world, with the revolutionary rise of new information and communications technologies, and with all the new advances in travel and transit that can move people and goods with unprecedented speed around the planet, the extent of the marketplace for thousands upon thousands of goods and services has become worldwide. Through global trade, this international division of labor has given us unprecedented global prosperity.

Now, consider this. The division of labor through global value chains divides up the tasks of making these goods and providing these services. If these tasks can be made identical — if these parts of the global value chain can be made interchangeable — then how much more prosperous can the world become? What would Eli Whitney or Cyrus McCormick or Henry Leland or Henry Ford tell us about the potential of interchangeable parts for mass production and widespread prosperity? Or, for that matter, Bi Sheng, who first employed the concept of interchangeable parts by using moveable type a thousand years ago in China?

The benefits of a common gauge globally can be many. Lower costs. Higher efficiency. More productivity. Enhanced quality. Greater reliability. More consumer choices made more widely available by an international division of labor increased by the interchangeable parts that can arise from common global standards. For example: why have one set of specifications for an industrial fastener in one country and another set of specifications for the same fastener serving the same purpose in another? Cannot those two countries agree on what is needed in one of Adam Smith's famous pins to be sufficient to help hold a building up? Cannot all countries agree? If they do agree, can't they have identical or mutually recognized certification and testing procedures for that pin? Won't that agreement on a common standard for making pins ease and thereby increase the international trade in pins and thereby add to our overall prosperity?

The World Economic Forum, in collaboration with Bain & Company and the World Bank, has recently released a significant study of supply chain barriers to international trade entitled "Enabling Trade: Valuing Growth Opportunities."[12] Their conclusion: "Reducing supply chain barriers to trade could increase GDP up to [six] times more than removing tariffs," and, overall, it "could increase GDP by nearly 5% and trade by 15%."[13] Supply chain trade barriers take many forms. Red tape in border administration. Lack of transportation and communications infrastructure. And more. One common thread, though, to all the worldwide complaints about supply chain barriers to trade is always the needless costs arising from the endless duplications occasioned by the conflicts in competing regulations and the absence of common standards.

Traditionally, professors of international law and practitioners of international diplomacy have tended not to focus much on such mundane matters as the making of common commercial standards. Henry Kissinger himself supposedly once said — perhaps apocryphally — that he had little interest in learning about trade in butter. From this I conclude that he would likewise have little interest in trade in pins. After all, how could such a trivial matter as mere commerce have any consequence at all relevant to the weighty legal and diplomatic tasks of war and peace?

Lately this has been changing. This has been changing, not least because of the unfolding work of the World Trade Organization. The WTO's dull dealings with the mundane matter of commerce in butter, pins, and the like are increasingly the most prolific source of additional international law. The WTO Appellate Body and other jurists in WTO dispute settlement have produced more international law in the past two decades than the International Court of Justice in the Hague has produced in the entire past century. The proliferation of WTO rules and WTO rulings has added enormously in just a few years to the growing body of overall international law. Moreover, increasingly, WTO rules and WTO rulings are extending far beyond the traditional confines of butter and pins and into almost every corner of global concern.

To be sure, traditional trade issues such as tariffs and customs continue to be an important part of international trade law. (I say this as someone who spent several months some years ago striving in a judgment in a WTO appeal to isolate once and for all the timeless definition of an "ordinary customs duty" — and concluded — I think correctly — by not offering any definition at all.) This said, international trade law has long since ceased to be mainly about the tariffs levied and the customs procedures applied down at the port. Too, even at the port, containerization has helped open the way to the harmonization of common standards.

Indeed, trade law has never been solely about tariffs and customs. For example, Article III:4 of the General Agreement on Tariffs and Trade, which sets out the fundamental non-discrimination principle of "national treatment" for foreign products when competing with like domestic products in the domestic marketplace, has, from the very beginning, since 1947, applied to all internal "laws, regulations and requirements affecting [the] internal sale, offering for sale, purchase, transportation, distribution or use" of traded products.[14] This certainly includes standards set out by internal regulations. And, as successive rounds of global trade negotiations have reduced tariffs, the persistence of distinctive and disparate national standards in internal regulations for traded goods and services has risen as a divisive trade issue.

According to the OECD, today about 80 percent of all world trade — directly or indirectly — involves standards.[15] Out there among all those ever-extending and ever-subdividing value chains of global commerce, we are increasingly seeing evidence that standards can not only serve to bind the world together; they can also be used to help keep the world apart. Countries that have made tariff concessions with one hand are becoming ever more creative in taking them back with the other hand by applying discriminatory regulations. Constrained by international law from raising tariffs, they are erecting new barriers to trade in the form of domestic standards. Even as international standards continue to multiply through the work of the ITU, the ISO, and numerous other international standard-setting organizations, national — and sometimes regional — sanitary and phytosanitary measures, technical regulations, and other standards of vast variety are increasingly employed as a form of what rightly has been called "regulatory protectionism."

Sallie James and Bill Watson of the Cato Institute have published a perceptive paper on "regulatory protectionism," which they define as "the use of regulatory policy to discriminate against foreign firms in a way that is not necessary to achieve a legitimate objective."[16] As they point out, drawing the right line as a matter of international law between legitimate regulatory measures that serve a legitimate public purpose and protectionist measures that serve the purpose mainly of insulating and advantaging national producers is moving to the forefront in the shaping of a new global trade agenda for the 21st century.[17]

As we saw in the second half of the 20th century, with the success of the GATT and with the eventual establishment of the WTO, trade can help bring and bind the world together. So too can the law of trade. What is more, I believe (admittedly a bit idealistically) that the success of the international rule of law in trade can, by example, help bring and bind the world together by inspiring the increased success of the international rule of law outside the realm of trade. As it is, already, the centrality of standards to so many regulatory concerns that affect trade shows us, as do so many other aspects of the emerging new agenda of trade, that the reach of trade law extends already to many of those other realms.

Is your food safe? Will your phone make the call? Can you breathe the air? Can you drink the water? Do the lights work? Will the "pins" break and the building fall down? Will your "telegraph" in the form of a digital text message get from here to there, and will the person there be permitted to read it? These are all already questions relating to trade law, or soon will be. Further, they all can involve "regulatory protectionism."

In truth, "regulatory protectionism" is nothing new. It has been happening ever since we first began to find success in lowering tariffs decades ago. Having put aside history to study law, I first encountered the emerging issue of standards as a non-tariff barrier to trade when I arrived as a political appointee in the Office of the United States Trade Representative in 1979 and expressed the evidently novel desire — for a political appointee — to learn the substance of trade law. I was handed a then brand-new international trade agreement that I was told was the "standards code."

I have long since realized that I was given this assignment as a newcomer to trade because standards then were still on the periphery of trade concerns. The standards code was concluded by the Contracting Parties to the GATT during the Tokyo Round of global trade negotiations as a way of beginning to confront the emergence of standards as obstacles to trade. It bound only those countries that signed it, and it was not truly enforceable even against them. It was, alas, largely ignored. Yet the standards code was nevertheless an essential start toward defining and disciplining "regulatory protectionism."

A dozen years later, while a Member of Congress, I helped enact the implementing legislation for the Uruguay Round trade agreements that created the WTO. Among the many new trade agreements we approved then were two that built on the experience of the standards code — the WTO Agreement on the Application of Sanitary and Phytosanitary Measures and the WTO Agreement on Technical Barriers to Trade. The SPS Agreement deals with measures relating to human, animal, and plant life, health, and safety.[18] The TBT Agreement deals with other standards and regulatory measures of all kinds that affect trade.[19]

Unlike the standards code, the SPS Agreement and the TBT Agreement are automatically binding on all WTO Members and are fully enforceable in WTO dispute settlement. As WTO Members agreed in establishing the WTO, dispute settlement decisions by the WTO are enforceable in that they are backed by the ultimate "last resort" of economic sanctions against countries that choose not to comply with WTO rulings on the obligations in WTO rules. Given this potential price for non-compliance, WTO Members almost always choose to comply with WTO rulings.

Eight years as a judge in WTO dispute settlement gave me ample opportunity to acquaint myself with both the SPS Agreement and the TBT Agreement, and I have continued to delve into their legal depths in the years since I left the WTO. Today, I am far from alone in focusing more and more of my attention on these two successors to the standards code. For standards are no longer at the periphery of the trade debate; with the continuing evolution of a fully global economy connected by the endless intricacies of global value chains, and with the concurrent rise of "regulatory protectionism," standards are now at the very center of the trade debate.

Research by the World Bank and the United Nations Conference on Trade and Development has shown that technical barriers affect about 30 percent of international trade, and that SPS measures affect about 15 percent of international trade, including more than 60 percent of trade in agricultural products.[20] Furthermore, this research has shown that the use of non-tariff measures as barriers to trade is rising.[21]

So, it should come as no surprise that, within the WTO, an increasing number of international trade disputes involving standards and related issues are arising under the SPS Agreement, the TBT Agreement, and the GATT. In particular, and importantly, in a series of landmark rulings this year, my successors on the WTO Appellate Body have clarified the meaning and the interrelationship of some of the most basic provisions of the TBT Agreement involving technical regulations relating to the domestic sale of tuna, beef, and clove cigarettes.

These subjects may seem more than mundane to some, but, as might be mentioned to Secretary Kissinger, some of the landmark rulings of the Supreme Court of the United States interpreting the scope of the Commerce Clause of the U.S. Constitution during the New Deal in the 1930s involved the mundane subject of butter.[22] In like manner, the latest rulings of the Appellate Body on the TBT Agreement will ultimately reach in their implications into virtually every aspect of the global economy.

Meanwhile, outside WTO dispute settlement, the worldwide debate is intensifying about where and how to draw the right line between legitimate regulation and "regulatory protectionism." In bilateral relations between countries such as China and the United States, in regional groups such as APEC, in regional negotiations such as those on proposed trans-Pacific and trans-Atlantic trade agreements, and, of course, in the marathon Doha Round of global trade negotiations and other global deliberations by the Members of the WTO, the issue of standards is at the center of the debate.

At this center, the debate over standards is defined fundamentally by the fact that economics and politics are hard to connect. Economics knows no borders. Politics is defined by borders. The politicians find it hard to respond to the borderless economics of global value chains. In the increasing debate over common standards, perhaps more than in any other aspect of the current trade debate, the baggage of both economics and politics is piled up, separately, beside the railway tracks, awaiting a connection that can best come from global agreement on global rules.

The two scholars at the Cato Institute have suggested that the most important rule we need is one we already have. In their work on "regulatory protectionism," they have argued that the connection that should be used to link economics and politics where a proposed standard is concerned is the extent of the restriction that standard would impose on trade. Say Sallie James and Bill Watson, "Requiring agencies to consider and evaluate the impact of a proposed regulation on international trade could limit the incidence of protectionism."[23]

The particular focus of their study is the United States, which, I should perhaps point out, was the losing party in all three of the recent landmark disputes over technical regulations in the WTO, on tuna, beef, and clove cigarettes. (In full disclosure, I should note, too, that I was among the legal counsel advising Mexico as the prevailing party in the tuna and beef disputes, and Brazil as an interested third party in the clove cigarette dispute.) James and Watson advise that, "Prior to implementing a new regulation, federal agencies should be required to evaluate the possibility that less trade-restrictive alternatives could meet regulatory goals as effectively as their preferred proposal."[24] They say, "New limits should be placed on the discretion of administrative agencies to ensure that regulations meet WTO requirements. In addition to scientific risk assessment and cost-benefit analysis, agencies should consider whether proposed rules are more trade restrictive than necessary to meet their stated goals. Meeting this WTO requirement would prevent almost all regulatory protectionism."[25]

I agree. In addition, and although the Cato scholars confined their comments in their paper to regulations applied by the United States, I am confident they would agree with me that every other Member of the WTO should do the same. The United States is certainly not alone in being accused of "regulatory protectionism." Think, for example, of the charges that have been made by their trading partners about China's strategic industries initiative or Europe's data privacy directive or Russia's whole array of restrictive measures resembling Matryoshka nesting dolls. There is no lack of examples of measures that have been applied by almost every Member of the WTO that might be subject to the charge of "regulatory protectionism."

Moreover, and as James and Watson acknowledge, the obligation to act in a way that imposes the least possible restriction on trade consistent with a legitimate regulatory purpose is already an obligation to which every Member of the WTO has agreed by signing the WTO treaty, and by which every Member of the WTO is therefore already bound. The SPS Agreement and the TBT Agreement are both part of the WTO treaty, and I refer you in the treaty to Article 5.6 and Footnote 3 of the SPS Agreement and to Article 2.2 of the TBT Agreement, which spell out this obligation in no uncertain terms.[26]

Article 5.6 of the SPS Agreement states, "Members shall ensure that [SPS] measures are not more trade restrictive than required to achieve their appropriate level of sanitary or phytosanitary protection, taking into account technical and economic feasibility."[27] Footnote 3 to this provision explains that "a measure is not more trade-restrictive than required unless there is another measure, reasonably available taking into account technical and economic feasibility, that achieves the appropriate level of sanitary or phytosanitary protection and is significantly less restrictive to trade."[28] Similarly, Article 2.2 of the TBT Agreement provides that "technical regulations shall not be more trade-restrictive than necessary to fulfill a legitimate objective; taking account of the risks non-fulfillment would create."[29]

Whether any specific measure applied by any WTO Member is inconsistent with these treaty obligations is a question to be resolved, as we like to say in the WTO, "on a case-by-case basis." Having judged more than a few WTO disputes, I can assure you: every case is indeed different. The facts always matter. The point is, these obligations already exist. Better by far to comply with these obligations than to have them quoted against you in an appeal in WTO dispute settlement.

All this said, we should not by any means leave the making of connections where standards are concerned solely to the judges in WTO dispute settlement. The clarification of rules in dispute settlement can only go so far, and, though some obligations already exist, others must be established. This can only be done through international negotiations that improve existing rules and that agree on the new rules needed to ensure appropriate domestic space for legitimate regulation while fighting back against "regulatory protectionism." Through further rulemaking, we must build on the successes so far of the SPS and TBT agreements, and of the whole host of global standard-setting organizations. In the WTO and elsewhere, we must focus as a high priority on finding a common gauge through the harmonization of standards.

Harmonization is not required by the WTO treaty, but it is encouraged. The words of the WTO treaty have been agreed by all the countries that are Members of the WTO, and those words voice their shared goals. Both the SPS Agreement (in Article 3.1) and the TBT Agreement (in Article 2.6) speak of the aim of harmonizing regulatory measures "on as wide a basis as possible."[30] Importantly, too, both agreements also establish (in Article 3.3 of the SPS Agreement and in Article 2.5 of the TBT Agreement) a rebuttable presumption legally that compliance with a relevant international standard is consistent with the WTO treaty for purposes of WTO dispute settlement.[31]

Standardization can also be achieved de facto through mutual recognition. Short of full harmonization, both the SPS Agreement (in Article 4.1) and the TBT Agreement (in Article 2.7) encourage WTO Members to accept the differing standards of other WTO Members as "equivalent" to their own if it can be shown that they accomplish the same purposes.[32] The SPS Agreement, in addition, encourages (in Article 4.2) the negotiation of mutual recognition agreements on the equivalency of specified SPS measures.[33]

The way forward toward standardization through mutual recognition or harmonization is easier with some issues than others. Where one country requires that the vehicle identification number for an automobile be stamped on one end of a windshield and another country requires that the VIN number be stamped on the other end of the windshield, the opportunity for a compromise that will facilitate trade is obvious. Where one country has one regulatory view of genetically-modified food and another country has an entirely different view, the negotiations will be a bit more complicated. Still, negotiations are needed if agreement on international rules can safeguard legitimate domestic interests while also increasing the flow of international trade and investment.

In working toward harmonization, Members of the WTO should look first to the words on which they have already agreed in the SPS and TBT agreements in the WTO treaty, and to how some of those words have been clarified in WTO dispute settlement. They should look first also to the WTO itself as a forum for their further negotiations on standards. As a practical matter, they may need, initially, to take partial approaches, but they should aim to act multilaterally, and their shared goal should be to write new rules that will, ultimately, and ideally, apply standards globally.

It is encouraging that the issue of standards has been addressed in a number of recently concluded bilateral trade agreements, and that it is now drawing considerable attention on the negotiating table in current and contemplated regional negotiations. "WTO-plus" obligations on standards issues have been included in recent free trade agreements negotiating by the United States with a number of other WTO Members. The United States and the handful of other WTO Members engaged in negotiations on a Trans-Pacific Partnership are focusing as a cross-cutting issue on reducing regional divergences in standards through "regulatory coherence." Likewise, the United States and the member states of the European Union are anticipating that many of the benefits anticipated from their proposed Trans-Atlantic Trade and Investment Partnership would result from mutual recognition and from some harmonization of standards.

I applaud these efforts. If I were still a member of the Congress of the United States, I would be supporting these initiatives, and I would surely vote for them. But why pursue these initiatives outside the multilateral framework of the WTO? Every single country engaged in these regional negotiations is a Member of the WTO. If they wish to improve on current WTO obligations on standards, they can do so much more effectively within the framework of the WTO treaty.

I share in the widespread frustration with the seemingly endless impasse in the Doha round of multilateral trade negotiations under the auspices of the WTO. Under the negotiating approach chosen by the Members of the WTO in launching the round more than a decade ago, nothing can be agreed until everything is agreed by "consensus" of every one of the more than 150 countries engaged in the negotiations. So far, this has not been possible. We shall perhaps see at the WTO Ministerial Conference in Bali at yearend if anything can be achieved from the Doha round.

But the decision to make the Doha round a "single undertaking" — requiring a consensus on everything before there can be an agreement on anything — was a choice made by the Members of the WTO. They could have made another choice under the existing rules in the WTO treaty. They could still do so in going forward. The WTO treaty also permits WTO Members to conclude WTO agreements among some but not all WTO Members when a self-selected subset of WTO Members is willing to accept new obligations without waiting for all other WTO Members to agree to do so. This approach has been followed successfully by Members of the WTO on information technology and on government procurement. It has been followed successfully on financial services and on basic telecommunications services. Significantly, it is being tried now by the United States, the European Union, and other WTO Members as a way of enhancing existing WTO commitments on trade in services.

To me, this is the way forward for the WTO, and, importantly, this is a way that can be pursued without first getting agreement among all the WTO Members, because it does not require any change whatsoever in current WTO rules. Those WTO Members wishing to make additional concessions and be bound by additional obligations can go ahead now and do so. All other WTO Members are then free to make those same new concessions and to benefit from those same new obligations should they choose to do so later.

The shared hope in taking this alternative approach to writing global rules is that, once a "critical mass" of WTO Members accounting for a sufficiently sizeable share of global trade have "acceded" to membership in such a "plurilateral" agreement, the economic pressures encouraging other WTO Members to sign that agreement will intensify, and that, in time, the "plurilateral" agreement will become fully "multilateral." In fact, this is precisely what happened with the standards code I was handed decades ago at USTR, and with the similar GATT codes on subsidies and anti-dumping duties that were concluded in the Tokyo Round. Eventually, they became fully multilateral agreements that bind all WTO Members as part of the WTO treaty.

The professed hope of all those so busy now negotiating regional agreements outside the framework of the WTO is that the regional standards they are negotiating will, with time, and with the accumulating pressure of economic necessity, become fully global. This could happen. This is, after all, what happened over time with the International Telegraph Union and with other standard-setting efforts that began with only a limited number of countries. The risk, however, of these current efforts outside the WTO is that "regulatory protectionism" could become regional as well as national. If not applied carefully, regional and other partial efforts to harmonize standards outside the WTO may succeed only in raising new barriers to trade with those who are not part of those less-than-global understandings. Instead of building blocks, these regional efforts outside the WTO could become stumbling blocks to global harmonization.

The danger is that these regional efforts of integrating could become regional ways of discriminating unfairly. They could become exclusive, and not inclusive. Instead of bringing the world closer together, they could pull some parts of the world farther apart. This is in part because, as these regional agreements are currently contemplated, additional countries can join the negotiations only with the permission of the countries that are already engaged in them. Just the other day, for example, the United States announced that it will allow Japan to join in the negotiations on a Trans-Pacific Partnership. If the TPP negotiations were being conducted within the framework of the WTO, Japan would not need U.S. permission or permission from other negotiating countries. Japan would have an automatic right to participate if it wished to do so. So too would China and every other Member of the WTO.

The best forum by far for seeking global standards is the global forum of the WTO. The WTO is inclusive, not exclusive. WTO rules can only be building blocks. All those who are willing to accept and abide by WTO rules have the right to share, if they choose, in the bountiful benefits of WTO rules-based trading system. On standards and on numerous other issues of global concern in the 21st century, "plurilateral" agreements negotiated within the WTO can become, over time, fully "multilateral" as more and more WTO Members come to realize the economic importance of embracing the common gauge of new obligations.

I fear that, in reciting so many words from the WTO treaty, I risk sounding in these thoughts too much like a lawyer. So, I return, in conclusion, to the young Vladimir Nabokov, shivering with his family and their servants in the chill alongside the mismatched tracks at the Russo-German border, awaiting a railway connection in 1909. We know from his memoir that he never forgot that childhood experience.

As Nabokov wrote long afterwards, "We live not only in a world of thoughts, but also in a world of things. Words without experience are meaningless."[34] The things of life can shape our thoughts. The exchange of commerce can lead to other human exchanges. The relationships created by trading things can help establish and support other human relationships. The experience of mere commerce can have a meaning beyond things — if we find the right words.

Where standards are concerned, we must learn from the long experience of history, and we must employ this experience to write the right words as the right rules of international law. Many of the right words are already there in the WTO treaty. More are needed. The right words can help us create a meaning relating to things, and also a meaning beyond things, for a world awaiting the right connections. With the right words, we can further and facilitate the making for the world of common standards that can help us maximize global prosperity. With the right words, we can make a common gauge.

Endnotes

[1] *See generally* Vladimir Nabokov, *Speak, Memory: An Autobiography Revisited* (revised ed. 1960).
[2] *Ibid.* at 141.
[3] George V. Hilton, *American Narrow Gauge Railroads* 36 (1990).
[4] WTO Secretariat, World Trade Report (2012) *Trade and Public Policies: A Closer Look at Non-Tariff Measures in the 21st Century*, 10, (2012), at http://www.wto.org/english/res_e/booksp_e/anrep_e/world_trade_report12_e.pdf.
[5] Mark Mazower, *Governing the World: The History of an Idea* 102 (2012).
[6] *Ibid.*
[7] International Telecommunications Union, *About ITU*, at http://www.itu.int/en/about/Pages/default.aspx (last visited November 11, 2013).
[8] Mazower, *supra* note 5, at 102.
[9] International Standards Organization, *About ISO*, at http://www.iso.org/iso/home/about.htm.

[10] Adam Smith, *An Inquiry into the Nature and Causes of the Wealth of Nations* 5 (London and New York: Penguin Books, 1982) (1776).
[11] Gary Hufbauer & Jeffrey Scott, *Payoff from the World Trade Agenda 2013*, April 2013 Peterson Inst. for Int'l Econ. 11.
[12] World Economic Forum, *Enabling Trade: Valuing Growth Opportunities* (2013), at www3.weforum.org/docs/WEF_SCT_EnablingTrade_Report_2013.pdf.
[13] *Ibid.* at 4.
[14] General Agreement on Tariffs and Trade, art. III:4, October 30, 1947, 61 Stat. A-11, 55 U.N.T.S. 194.
[15] Org. for Economic Co-operation and Development, *Regulatory Reform and International Standardisation*, at XX, TD/TC/WP(98)36FINAL (January 29, 1999).
[16] K. William Watson & Sallie James, *Regulatory Protectionism: A Hidden Threat to Free Trade*, 723 Cato Institute, Policy Analysis 1, (2013), 2.
[17] *Ibid.*
[18] Agreement on the Application of Sanitary and Phytosanitary Measures, April 15, 1994, 1867 U.N.T.S. 493 [hereinafter SPS Agreement].
[19] Agreement on Technical Barriers to Trade, April 15, 1994, 1868 U.N.T.S. 120 [hereinafter TBT Agreement].
[20] U.N. Conference on Trade and Development, New York and Geneva, 2013, *A Preliminary Analysis on Newly Collected Data on Non-tariff Measures*, at iii, UNCTAD/ITCD/TAB/54.
[21] *Ibid.*
[22] Cloverleaf Butter Co. v. Patterson, 315 U.S. 148 (1942).
[23] Watson and James, *supra* note 16, at 19.
[24] *Ibid.* at 1.
[25] *Ibid.* at 3.
[26] SPS Agreement, *supra* note 18, art. 5.6; TBT Agreement, *supra* note 19, art. 2.2.
[27] *Ibid.* art. 5.6.
[28] *Ibid.* art. 5.6 n.3.
[29] TBT Agreement, *supra* note 19, art. 2.2.
[30] SPS Agreement, *supra* note 18, art. 3.1; TBT Agreement, *supra* note 19, art. 2.6.
[31] *Ibid.* art. 3.3; TBT Agreement, *supra* note 19, art. 2.5.
[32] *Ibid.* art. 4.1; TBT Agreement, *supra* note 19, art. 2.7.
[33] *Ibid.* art. 4.2.
[34] Vladimir Nabokov, *Lolita* 178 (2nd ed. 1989).

Chapter 12

Appellators: The Quest for the Meaning of And/Or*

It may have been my good friend Andy Stoler who, in referring to the seven Members of the Appellate Body of the World Trade Organization, first used the word "Appellators." Old GATT hand that he is, Andy did so with a wry smile. Like many another seasoned trade negotiator, he combines an enduring idealism with an endearing irreverence. This is undoubtedly the best way to survive, as Andy has survived, through several decades of the sheer tedium of trade negotiations. So, he meant it as a joke.

So did I when I told Debra Steger on the day when she and I first met, in 1995, that I was honored to be one of the first seven "Appellators" of the Appellate Body of the WTO. Debra, of course, was newly named at the time as the first director of the Appellate Body Secretariat. She appeared to me to be taken somewhat aback at my use of the word "Appellator." High-minded Canadians such as Debra rightly rue the errant excesses from time to time, rhetorical and otherwise, of their coarser neighbors to the south. After all, everyone in Geneva knows that the Members of the Appellate Body do not have titles.

Of course, Debra did not know me at the time. So, she did not know that, like Andy, I was joking. Later, she learned, as others have learned,

---

*This essay appeared previously as James Bacchus, "Appellators: The Quest for the Meaning of *And/Or*," *World Trade Review*, Volume 4, Number 3 (2005), 499–523. It was expanded from remarks made at the annual luncheon of the Advisory Centre on WTO Law in Bellevue, Switzerland, on June 1, 2005.

either to ignore my jokes, or to pretend to laugh at them. And yet, joke though it was for both Andy and me, the appellation of "Appellator" nevertheless can be seen as fitting for the seven Members of the quasi-judicial tribunal that has been adorned by the Members of the WTO with the decidedly less than felicitous name of the "Appellate Body."

Andy will perhaps admit, from his current refuge in Australia, to coining the word "Appellator." No one will admit to coining the phrase "Appellate Body" as the name for the international trade tribunal that serves the Members of the WTO as the quasi-court of last resort in WTO dispute settlement. In an act of fact-gathering that would be forbidden to me if I remained an "Appellator," I have tried my best to identify the culprit. Thus far, I have failed to coax anyone into confessing to concocting a name that is, shall we say, less than appealing.

A Uruguayan told me it was the Europeans. A European told me it was the Canadians. A Canadian told me it was the Americans. An American told me it was the Uruguayans. To help me find this elusive fact, I am starting to think that I should "seek" counsel from non-parties to this dispute through solicitation of *amicus curiae* briefs. I have not yet decided if thinking I "should" means that I "shall."[1]

In any event, I confess that, when the name "Appellate Body" was chosen by the negotiating countries that became the original Members of the WTO, I barely noticed. I was too busy elsewhere at the time. As a Member then of the Congress of the United States, I was busy at the time trying to pass the implementing legislation for the Uruguay Round trade agreements so that I could get out of Washington. My goal at the time was to become a former Member of the Congress.

I did not know then that I would soon also become an "Appellator."

Now, after eight eventful years of service to the Members of the WTO, I am content today to be a former "Appellator." I am content in part because, as a *former* "Appellator," I am free for the first time to speak publicly about some of the aspects of the important task of the Appellate Body in WTO dispute settlement.

The task of the "Appellators" is the task of treaty interpretation. In the fulfillment of this task, names must be noticed. For the "names" we call "words" are the basic tools of treaty interpretation.

Whatever we may call them, and however we may view them, in the first decade since the establishment of the WTO, the Members of the Appellate Body have helped make the Appellate Body an international tribunal of historic global achievement through the successful fulfillment of this task. Largely, the Members of the WTO seem satisfied with the ways in which the Members of the Appellate Body have done so. To be sure, there are, occasionally, criticisms of some of the rulings of the Appellate Body by some Members of the WTO when Appellate Body reports are adopted by the Members of the WTO in their guise as the Dispute Settlement Body. But these criticisms are usually, and predictably, voiced by those whose claims have not prevailed in a particular dispute, and these criticisms often are voiced largely for obligatory diplomatic and political reasons.

Significant evidence of the overall satisfaction of the Members of the WTO with the work of the Appellate Body in the first decade of the WTO is the fact that, in the ongoing process of "DSU review," negotiators for the Members of the WTO have simply assumed that, in the decades to come, there will continue to be an Appellate Body, and that it will continue to fulfill essentially the same task. Indeed, pending proposals such as the one to accord "remand" powers to the Appellate Body would only add to the discretionary authority of the "Appellators" in fulfilling that task. Sometimes the most important statements are unstated assumptions.

Sometimes the most important proposals are those that are not made, and, to date, no Member of the WTO has proposed abolishing the Appellate Body, or substantially diminishing the responsibilities of the Appellate Body in WTO dispute settlement. In my judgment, this evidence is sufficient to meet the burden of proof in asserting a *prima facie* case of the overall success of the Appellate Body.

In the wider world, the overall verdict seems much the same. Few in the wider world would quarrel with the conclusion that the Appellate Body has, in the first decade of the WTO, very quickly become an efficient forum and an effective force for upholding international trade law, and, as a result, for upholding the international rule of law. And few would quarrel with the conclusion that it has done so in an unprecedented and an unwavering way. One observer for the *New York Times*, for example, has characterized the Appellate Body as both "impartial and unflinching."[2] And, according to Professor John Jackson, perhaps the preeminent scholar in the world on the WTO and on WTO law, "The Appellate Body has brought a sense of rigor and deep analysis that goes well beyond the jurisprudence that developed during the more than three decades of the GATT, and indeed, may go beyond the record of any international law tribunal known to history."[3]

Even so, there are occasional criticisms of the ways in which the Appellate Body fulfills its task of treaty interpretation for the Members of the WTO. From time to time, from place to place, and from case to case, the Appellate Body is alleged to have engaged variously in inappropriate forms of quasi-judicial activism. It is said to have engaged in "lawmaking," in "gap filling," in "overreaching." It is said to have indulged in treatymaking instead of treaty-interpreting. It is accused, as a consequence, of having either added to, or subtracted from, the obligations of WTO Members in contravention of the express terms of the WTO treaty.[4]

With respect to some of these criticisms, we should simply consider the source. A lawyer who has convinced his country to spend several years, and who has convinced his client to spend several million dollars, in a losing case, is unlikely, when he loses, to admit that his was, from the beginning, a losing case. That lawyer is more likely to blame those who have judged the case for supposedly "overreaching." And some of the more self-serving in such circumstances have yielded to the temptation to do so after squandering the time and the money of others in WTO dispute settlement.

Similarly, some of these criticisms are made by certain "non-governmental organizations" and by certain other interest groups that oppose the whole enterprise of the WTO. So they do not hesitate to distort and to deceive when describing the outcomes of WTO dispute settlement. This is merely one of their ways of exploiting the global paranoias about "globalization." With respect to their criticisms as well, we should simply consider the source.

But others who voice these criticisms of WTO dispute settlement, both within the WTO and without, have better intentions. Some of them truly support the WTO dispute settlement system. And some of those who do support it, and who do criticize it, are only echoing the ill-founded and self-serving criticisms of others. Especially if they are busy serving in elected office, they may not yet have taken the time to read the dispute settlement rulings they are criticizing, or to think through the unintended consequences of simply echoing such criticisms. For the sake of the future of the WTO dispute settlement system, these well-intentioned critics deserve a reply.

The current Members of the Appellate Body are constrained by the WTO Rules of Conduct from offering a reply.[5] Fortunately, as a *former* Member of the Appellate Body, I am not.

As a former "Appellator," I continue to be bound by the WTO Rules of Conduct. I cannot therefore delve into the details of the reasonings or the rulings in any of the sixty appeals that were addressed by the Appellate Body during my eight years of service in Geneva. I am not free under those rules either to explain or to defend the specifics of past decisions. I am not free either to add to, or to subtract from, what I have already said, along with my former colleagues, in reporting those decisions to the Members of the WTO. Thus, this will not be an essay either to explain or to justify what was decided in, say, the appeal in *Argentina — Footwear*, on the issue of "unforeseen developments."[6] Much as I might wish to do so in reply to some of the more ill-founded criticisms of the Appellate Body, I am not free under the rules to engage in such an indulgence. What we said together as the Appellate Body at the time must suffice.

But I am free to offer a more general reply to some of the critics of those decisions by explaining, more fully than I was free to explain while I still served on the Appellate Body, precisely how the Members of the Appellate Body have approached the fulfillment of their task of treaty interpretation.

In defining this task, the old GATT hands among us will rush to recite the words of the WTO Understanding on Rules and Procedures Governing the Settlement of Disputes.[7] It is through the Dispute Settlement Understanding — the "DSU" — that the Members of the WTO established the WTO dispute settlement system, and, along with it, the Appellate Body, as a central achievement of the Uruguay Round. It is the DSU that both defines and delineates the task of the "Appellators" as treaty interpreters.

The DSU, of course, is an understanding among *all* of the Members of the WTO. They have all signed it. They are all bound by it. They have all agreed on it. Presumably, they all agree *with* it. It is the Members of the WTO speaking and acting through the DSU — and not the Appellate Body — that guides and governs the work of WTO dispute settlement. This clearly includes the parts of that work that require treaty interpretation.

In the DSU, we are told that "the dispute settlement system is a central element in providing security and predictability to the multilateral trading system."[8] In the DSU, we are told also that "[t]he aim of the dispute settlement mechanism is to secure a positive solution to a dispute."[9] In the DSU, we are told as well that the dispute settlement system, in pursuing this aim, "serves to preserve the rights and obligations of Members" of the

WTO "under the covered agreements" of the WTO treaty, "and to clarify the existing provisions of those agreements in accordance with customary rules of interpretation of public international law."[10]

Thus, when a dispute arises under the covered agreements among the Members of the WTO, when a panel is established in response to a request by one of the parties to that dispute, when the panel submits a written report to the Members of the WTO sitting together as the Dispute Settlement Body, when "issues of law covered in the panel report and legal interpretations developed by the panel" are raised by one or more of the parties to the dispute through the exercise of their automatic right of appeal to the Appellate Body, and when the Appellate Body convenes for the maximum of 90 days allowed under the DSU to "address" each of the issues raised" on appeal in appellate proceedings, there are clear instructions from the Members of the WTO as to the approach that must be used by the Members of the Appellate Body in fulfilling their required task under the DSU by "clarifying" the "existing provisions" of the "covered agreements" that are pertinent to those legal issues raised in that dispute.[11]

Those instructions are: The Appellate Body must fulfill its task of treaty interpretation "in accordance with the customary rules of interpretation of public international law." It must do so because the Members of the WTO have told it to do so.

And what are those "customary rules of interpretation of public international law"? They are the customary rules that are given expression in the Vienna Convention on the Law of Treaties.[12] The customary rules are, it must be emphasized, *given expression* in this international Convention. They exist *independently* of this Convention as customary rules of international law, as evidenced by state practice and by shared perceptions of the law worldwide. Thus, it does not matter for purposes of international law if, for example, one deliberative body of one state that is a Member of the WTO has not yet ratified the Convention. The customary rules are customary rules all the same.[13]

Foremost among the customary rules of treaty interpretation is one that is given expression in Article 31 of the Vienna Convention. Importantly, Article 31(1) provides: "A treaty shall be interpreted in good faith in accordance with the ordinary meaning to be given to the terms of the treaty in their context and in the light of its object and purpose."[14]

In the very first appeal in WTO dispute settlement, *United States — Reformulated Gasoline*, in 1996, the Appellate Body stated that Article 31 of the Vienna Convention "has attained the status of a rule of customary or general international law."[15] In the second appeal in WTO dispute settlement, *Japan — Alcohol*, in that same year, the Appellate Body described Article 31(1) of the Vienna Convention as a "fundamental" rule of treaty interpretation.[16] This "fundamental" rule is a rule that establishes a *textual* approach to the interpretation of a treaty. As the International Court of Justice has put it in describing this interpretative approach generally, and as the Appellate Body has agreed, "interpretation must be based above all on the text of the treaty."[17] This is no less so when this approach is used to interpret the text of the WTO treaty.

No Member of the WTO has ever disputed any of this before the Appellate Body in WTO dispute settlement.

Thus, the task of the Appellate Body, as defined by the Members of the WTO, is to assist the Members of the WTO by finding the meaning of the terms in the text of the WTO treaty. The quest of the "Appellators" is for the meaning of words.

Why words?

To answer this question, we might begin by asking what other approaches the Members of the WTO could conceivably have instructed the Appellate Body to employ instead when "clarifying" the "existing obligations" of the WTO treaty in WTO dispute settlement?

Some have suggested that the negotiating history of the WTO treaty would be a useful resource for the Appellate Body in determining the meaning of the text of the treaty when addressing legal issues raised on appeal in WTO dispute settlement. So, in some cases, it would. But our experience thus far in WTO dispute settlement teaches us that there is very little preparatory work that can rightly be described as "negotiating history" of the Uruguay Round agreements for the purpose of resolving trade disputes.

Some have suggested that the Appellate Body should interpret the text of the WTO treaty in a way that makes economic sense. But there are no such instructions from the Members of the WTO to the Appellate Body in the DSU. The Members of the Appellate Body are instructed by the Members of the WTO to assist them in their efforts to uphold the existing rules on which the Members of the WTO have agreed. The Members of the WTO — and not the Members of the Appellate Body — must decide whether those rules make economic sense.

Some have suggested that the Appellate Body should embrace expediency by making pragmatic, "political" decisions. But the DSU says that an appeal "shall be limited to issues of law," and the Members of the WTO have instructed the Members of the Appellate Body not once, but twice, in the WTO Rules of Conduct, to be both "independent and impartial" when addressing issues of law in an appeal.[18] It necessarily follows from this that the Appellate Body must never make political decisions, and I have never once heard even one national or other political consideration uttered by anyone in the deliberations of the Appellate Body.

Some have suggested as well that the Appellate Body should engage in purposive treaty interpretation by making "teleological" decisions according to what the Members of the Appellate Body themselves think *ought* to be the meaning of the text of the WTO treaty based on what *they* see personally, and according to their own individual preferences and predilections, as the treaty's purpose. But if the Appellate Body took that approach, then it surely *would* be "overreaching." (I trust that none of you will tell my former colleagues in the Congress that I actually used the word "teleological" in public.)

So, in fulfilling its task of treaty interpretation, and in thereby fulfilling its responsibilities to the Members of the WTO, the Appellate Body is left with the words of the treaty, and with the clear mandate of the Members of the WTO to use a textual approach to treaty interpretation that focuses above all on the words of the treaty.

The Members of the WTO have given the Appellate Body absolutely no discretion as to whether to use this approach to treaty interpretation. Furthermore, the Members of the WTO have given the Members of the Appellate Body absolutely no discretion as to when to use this approach. Those who see "overreaching" in some of the rulings of the Appellate Body tend to overlook this lack of "quasi-judicial" discretion in treaty interpretation in WTO dispute settlement. They tend also to overlook other limits on the discretion of the Appellate Body.

Under the terms of the DSU, the Appellate Body does not choose which disputes are resolved in WTO dispute settlement.[19] The Appellate Body does not choose which panel reports are appealed in WTO dispute settlement.[20] The Appellate Body does not choose which legal issues are appealed in those panel reports.[21] Nor does the Appellate Body have the authority under the DSU to refuse to "address" a legal issue when it is appealed.[22]

Thus, as I read the DSU, the Appellate Body is not free under the DSU to avoid making a legal judgment by seeking sanctuary in *non liquet*. It is not free simply to say that the text of the WTO treaty does not permit the

Appellate Body to decide a case one way or another. The purpose of the dispute settlement system is the settlement of disputes. A refusal by the Appellate Body to rule on a legal issue raised on appeal in dispute settlement would not help "secure a positive solution to a dispute."

Those who see "overreaching" tend also to overlook some other basic facts about the dispute settlement system. There is no such thing as "ripeness" in WTO dispute settlement. There is no such thing as a "political question." There is no such thing as a "writ of certiorari" in which the Appellate Body would have the discretion as to whether to accept, or not accept, a particular appeal. If even one WTO Member decides that it is "fruitful" to bring a case, and to raise a legal issue in that case, then that WTO Member has an exclusive and absolute right to do so under the DSU.[23] The Members of the WTO have made dispute settlement an "automatic" system, and discretion in the system on such matters is left entirely to the Members of the WTO, individually and collectively, in what rightly is, and must remain, a "Member-driven" organization.

And have any of the critics noticed that the Appellate Body has never once recommended *how* the Members of the WTO should implement the recommendations in an Appellate Body report in order to resolve a particular dispute? Unquestionably, the "Appellators" have been given the discretion by the Members of the WTO, in Article 19.1 of the DSU, to "suggest ways in which the Member concerned could implement the recommendations."[24] Frequently, and increasingly, they have been asked to do so. Yet, thus far, they have chosen not to make any such suggestions. Thus far, they have chosen to leave the specifics of implementation to the WTO Members that are parties to the disputes.

Furthermore, have those who have accused the Appellate Body of "overreaching" noticed also that, time and again, the Appellate Body has trimmed the legal reasoning of panels and tempered the legal rulings of panels when the reasoning or the rulings were not needed to reach a "positive solution" in a particular dispute? Literally hundreds of pages of panel reports have been erased by the Appellate Body on appeal for that reason. Did the critics notice, for example, that many of the rulings by the panel on legal issues were simply erased by the Appellate Body in the Appellate Body report in *United States — Steel Safeguards*?[25]

Given all this, I would submit that a considerably better case can be made, based on the first decade of WTO dispute settlement, that the Appellate Body has been a paragon of quasi-judicial restraint than that it has indulged in any quasi-judicial "overreaching." In keeping with the clear mandate of the DSU, the "aim" of the "Appellators" is to assist the parties in achieving a "positive solution" to a dispute. Their aim is not to tell disputing Members precisely how to resolve a dispute, or to answer every conceivable question that might be asked about a legal issue when that issue is raised on appeal in a dispute. Their aim is to rule only on those aspects of a legal issue on which they must rule to help the parties resolve that particular dispute. It is to say only what must be said about a legal issue in that specific case, and to leave what remains to be "clarified" about that issue to future negotiations and to future dispute settlement, on a case-by-case basis.

I recall in one of our early appeals in our very first year, *Japan — Alcohol*, someone saying around the table soon after the notice of appeal was filed, "This is a chance for the Appellate Body to write the definitive treatise on the meaning of national treatment." And I recall my close friend and colleague Julio Lacarte-Muro, the wise man that he is, saying very quickly in reply, "No, this is our chance to address the legal issues raised in this one dispute." This has always been the approach of the "Appellators" to fulfilling their task, and this, I submit, is the very opposite of "overreaching."

The Appellate Body considers and concludes much in every appeal, but much of what the Appellate Body considers and concludes in any one appeal does not end up as reasoning in the pages of the Appellate Body report for that appeal. It is left for the future, and for further consideration by future divisions of the Appellate Body as they reach their conclusions on legal issues raised on appeal in the unforeseen circumstances of future cases. This is part of what the Appellate Body means when it refers, as it often does, to the need to engage in treaty interpretation on a "case-by-case basis."

Frustrated by the pace of this incremental accumulation of jurisprudence on a "case-by-case basis," some of the critics of WTO dispute settlement want *more* from the Appellate Body, and not less. They want a definitive treatise. They want more words. They want more reasoning. They want more explanation. They echo what Lord Byron once said about the metaphysics of his friend Samuel Taylor Coleridge: "I wish he would explain his explanation."[26] But the "Appellators" explain by employing only as many words as they think they need to fulfill their appointed task under the DSU.

Most of the criticisms of the Appellate Body, though, seem, to me, to come down to the Appellate Body's fundamental approach to treaty interpretation and, thus, to the way in which the "Appellators" see words.[27] In these criticisms, the critics of the Appellate Body remind me, not of Byron and Coleridge, but rather of the maiden aunt of the French writer Stendhal who "mistrusted the written word as an agent of progress and a malign influence on young minds, all the more so because [the youthful Stendhal] was so avid a reader."[28]

In agreeing on the DSU, the Members of the WTO have placed their trust in the written word. In their instructions in the DSU, they have told the Members of the Appellate Body to place their trust likewise in the written word. In considering how the "Appellators" see words, we must begin by understanding that, like the Members of the WTO, they trust words, and they are therefore avid readers of words. They see words as having a meaning.

What makes humanity unique as a species on our small planet is our capacity for giving expression to our experience of existence rather than merely reacting to it.[29] We do this best with language. We do this best with words. With words, we communicate. With words, we express meaning. Our words must have meaning if we are to be able to give meaning to our experience of the world in communicating and in thereby living with others.

Increasingly, ours is a world of images, and not of words. Increasingly, ours is a post-modern, media-drenched world that is in dire danger of becoming post-meaning. We may see images, but the words we see and hear along with those images may have no real meaning. In such a world, we must cling to the notion that words do, and must, have a meaning.

Among those who cling to this notion are the Members of the Appellate Body. They do so in part because they know that, whereas images appeal only to emotion, words can appeal to both reason and emotion. Therefore, those who seek a more reasonable world must trust more in words, and less in images. The Members of the Appellate Body are among those who seek a more reasonable world. As heirs to the Enlightenment, they believe that, used wisely, words can help create a more reasonable world. They believe that words can serve the cause of reason, and that reason can serve the cause of justice. Words matter. So words must have a meaning.

The Members of the Appellate Body trust in words also, and not least, because the Members of the WTO have clearly told them to do so. The Members of the WTO likewise believe in the significance of words as essential tools for making a more reasonable world. They too believe that words must have a meaning. The thousands of words of the WTO treaty that resulted from their long years of hard negotiations are evidence of their belief.

With words, we make meaning. With words, we make life. With words, we make the world. With words, we make the future. And with words, we must make that part of our life, our world, and our future that finds expression in the multilateral trading system that serves the 148 countries and other customs territories that are the Members of the WTO in almost all of world trade every day.

My colleague for six years on the Appellate Body, Florentino Feliciano, is fond of reciting a favorite observation of another avid reader of words, Oliver Wendell Holmes, Jr., the famous American jurist. Justice Holmes said, "A word is not a crystal, transparent and unchanging; it is the skin of a living thought and may vary greatly in color and content according to the circumstances and the time in which it is used."[30]

If we assume that words have a meaning, then the task of the Appellate Body in treaty interpretation, as ordained by the Members of the WTO in the DSU, is to discern the meaning of the words of the WTO treaty by probing beyond their skin and into the depths of the living thought they name and represent. It is to take the potential meaning of the written words on the abstract pages of the treaty text and find their living meaning in the specific context of a concrete dispute.

If anything, in their focus on the living thoughts of words, the Members of the Appellate Body might best be described as "literalists," or, as we would say in the United States of America, "strict constructionists," in their approach to treaty interpretation. They are of the view that the Members of the WTO meant what they said when putting words into the WTO treaty — even if some Members of the WTO sometimes seem to have second thoughts about those words in the press of a particular dispute. At bottom, many of the criticisms of the "Appellators" are really criticisms, not of expansiveness, but of a literal and "strict construction." Like a character in one of Stendhal's books, the Appellate Body is thought by many of its critics to have, in its avid reading of the "covered agreements" of the WTO treaty, "the defect of calling things somewhat too readily by their own names."[31]

The passion of the "Appellators" for the precise meaning of words may sometimes seem to some to be almost obsessive. In my own experience, perhaps the most telling example of this passion in a particular dispute involved one difficult legal issue raised in the appeal in the *United*

States — Line Pipe dispute.³² In order to decide, in that dispute, whether the competent authorities of the United States had, or had not, fulfilled one of their obligations under the WTO Agreement in Safeguards when making a determination to apply a safeguard measure on imports of line pipe from Korea, it was necessary for the Appellate Body to find the living meaning of "*and/or*."

What do the words "*and*" and "*or*," when made into one word by connection through a right slash, really mean? Do they mean *either* "and" *or* "or"? Do they mean *both* "and" *and* "or"? Do they mean either and both? Or do they mean something else entirely? Finding the answer to this question about this curious conjunction consumed several reams of paper in appellate submissions, several hours of argument by the parties in an oral hearing, and several days of deliberations by the division in the appeal on its own and in a broader exchange of views around the round table of the Appellate Body.

The quest for the meaning of "and/or" in that one dispute is typical of the painstaking process that is pursued by the Appellate Body in its quest for the meaning of words in every dispute. Some may think this trivial. Others may think this extreme. The Members of the Appellate Body think this is necessary to fulfilling their task. Thus, to such lengths the Appellate Body will go in its trust in the written word. To such lengths it will go in its passion to find the meaning of words, and to be true in so doing to its obligations to the Members of the WTO under the DSU.

But often, the Appellate Body will go first to the dictionary. Indeed, so often has the Appellate Body gone to the Shorter Oxford English Dictionary to seek the meaning of words that some have suggested that the Members of the Appellate Body may see the Shorter Oxford English Dictionary as one of the "covered agreements" of the WTO treaty. This is not so. The Appellate Body itself has noted the limitations of relying on dictionary definitions.³³

But where better to go first to find a clue to the "ordinary meaning" of a word in the text of a treaty than to a dictionary? If the word is defined in the text of the treaty, or if the word has a specialized meaning that is revealed by the text of the treaty, then there may be no need to go to a dictionary to discern its "ordinary meaning." But what if it is not? What if, as is true so often in WTO dispute settlement, there is only the word itself, staring up at the treaty interpreter from the previously uninterpreted pages of the treaty?

Those who suggest that the Appellate Body should shun dictionaries when seeking the "ordinary meaning" of the words of the WTO treaty are really arguing for one of two possible alternatives. They are arguing that the words of the treaty should mean whatever any one Member of the WTO happens to say that they mean in the circumstances of a specific dispute. Or they are arguing that the words of the treaty should mean what the Members of the Appellate Body, as individuals, happen to think that the words ought to mean when considering how best to resolve a specific dispute.

The first argument leads to a WTO in which anything goes. It leads to a multilateral trading system that is anything but "rule based." It leads to a system that is anything but stable, secure, and predictable. The second argument leads to a WTO dispute settlement system in which the rules mean whatever particular individual "quasi judges" choose to say that they mean at a particular time. It leads to treaty interpretation that *is* purposive, that *is* "teleological," and that therefore truly *is* "overreaching." It is much better, in my view, to continue to turn, when necessary, to the dictionary.

Judge Richard A. Posner, who serves on the United States Court of Appeals for the Seventh Circuit, writes widely on the problems of jurisprudence. According to Judge Posner, "The alternative to purposive interpretation is to attempt to ascertain the deal embodied in the statute and enforce that deal. But since the deal is likely to be under the table, how is the court to determine its terms?"[34] I hope this is not the attitude of all federal judges in the United States when construing laws enacted by the Congress of the United States. I know this is not the attitude of the Members of the Appellate Body when construing the WTO treaty.

In the WTO, the "deal" is in the words of the treaty. The "deal" is the careful balance of rights and obligations of all WTO Members that was agreed in negotiating and concluding the treaty, and that is expressed in the words of the treaty and *only* in the words of the treaty. Therefore, the "deal" that can be enforced by WTO Members in WTO dispute settlement is only in the words. This is why the Members of the WTO have instructed the Members of the Appellate Body to trust in those words.

It is true that there are numerous definitions of some of those words in the dictionary. It is certainly true also that dictionary definitions are not always sufficient to discern the "ordinary meaning" of some of those words. Clearly, we should not look only to the dictionary to find "ordinary meaning." But this does not mean that the use of dictionary definitions by the Appellate Body as a tool of treaty interpretation is an arbitrary and artificial artifice.

Quite the contrary. Resort by the Appellate Body to dictionary definitions is part of how the Appellate Body follows its instructions from the Members of the WTO to trust in the meaning of words. It is *not* doing so that would be arbitrary and artificial. It is *not* doing so that would justly be criticized as "purposive interpretation." What would the critics say if the Appellate Body never opened a dictionary?

With respect to the meaning of many of the words in the WTO treaty, it is possible to discern the "ordinary meaning" of the word as used in the text of the treaty without going much beyond the word itself in the text of the treaty, and thus without venturing too far into the remoter reaches of "context" and "object and purpose." Whether there is need for reliance on a dictionary or not, the "ordinary meaning" of a word can often be discerned primarily from scrutiny of the word itself as used in the treaty text. The meaning of every other word is not as elusive as the meaning of "and/or." The meaning may only seem to be elusive at the time to a WTO Member on the defensive in dispute settlement. To every other Member engaged in that dispute, and perhaps also to the Appellate Body, the "ordinary meaning" of the word may be obvious.

Where a word in the text of the WTO treaty lends itself to more than one possible meaning — such as where there is more than one dictionary definition that may possibly be appropriate — the Members of the Appellate Body do precisely what the Members of the WTO have told them to do. They follow the interpretive approach set out in the customary rules of treaty interpretation that find their reflection in Article 31(1) of the Vienna Convention. They "clarify" the "ordinary meaning" of the word by considering "the terms of the treaty in their context and in the light of its object and purpose."

They look first as "context" to the words immediately adjacent to the word in question. They look next to other words in the same treaty provision. They look then, if need be, to other relevant provisions in the same agreement, and then, if need be, to other relevant provisions in other agreements that are part of the treaty. They look also to the "object and purpose" of the treaty as expressed in the other words of the treaty. In this way, they endeavor to discern the meaning of the word that was intended by the Members of the WTO in concluding the WTO treaty.

One of the most thoughtful and constructive critics of the work of WTO dispute settlement, Professor Donald McRae, has suggested that the

Appellate Body should rely more on context in discerning "ordinary meaning," should justify the relevance of the context on which it relies in any particular case, should seek more evidence of the intent of the framers of the treaty to understanding context, and, furthermore, should "find a way to incorporate intent into its justification of its interpretative approaches when evidence of that intent can be found."[35]

This is well-intended advice. This is also exactly what the Appellate Body has tried its best to do all along. Professor McRae seems to be among those who would usually prefer to see *more* reasoning, and not less, in the reports of the Appellate Body. But *more* is sometimes *less* in treaty interpretation. The Appellate Body is ever mindful that the words of sentences that are included in appellate reasoning in one case have a way of taking on a life of their own in later cases.

As the American Supreme Court Justice Benjamin Cardozo once said, "The sentence of today will make the right and wrong of tomorrow."[36] Thus, the "Appellators" are reluctant to include sentences as explanations for their reasoning on "ordinary meaning" unless such sentences seem absolutely necessary to the discharge of their duties to the Members of the WTO. They do not want the words of an unnecessary sentence needlessly to decide an unforeseen future case.

It is for this reason that examples of *obiter dicta* are rare in Appellate Body reports. Justice Cardozo may have felt free to indulge in such judicial liberties. The Appellate Body feels less so. The reports of the Appellate Body are therefore more sparing and more Spartan in the use of reasoning. When the "Appellators" allow themselves the indulgence of a bit of *obiter* in a particular report, it is worth reading very carefully.

It is also for this reason that the Appellate Body opines as little as possible in any given appeal on the question of the intent of the framers of the WTO treaty. For there is inherent difficulty to discerning the intent of the Members of the WTO from the text of the WTO treaty. There is, to be sure, some express evidence of intent in the treaty. There is the Marrakesh Declaration.[37] There is the preamble to the Marrakesh Agreement establishing the WTO.[38] There is some prefatory language to some of the "covered agreements."[39] There is the occasional additional explanation scattered throughout the treaty text.

But the treaty text is generally even more sparing of explanation than are Appellate Body reports. Where, to cite only one of many possible examples, is the prefatory language revealing the intent of the WTO Members in agreeing on the WTO Agreement on Subsidies and

Countervailing Measures?⁴⁰ And what, pray tell, was the intent of the WTO Members in agreeing in particular on, say, Item (k) of Annex I of that Agreement as part of an "Illustrative List of Export Subsidies"? Where are we to go to find the "object and purpose" of this Item of this important Agreement?⁴¹ And how are we to see and state the "object and purpose" of this Agreement as a whole? Are the Members of the WTO — who have chosen, for whatever reason, not to give vivid voice to their "object and purpose" in concluding this Agreement — eager for the Members of the Appellate Body to do so in their stead?

Should "context" be viewed more broadly by the "Appellators" in the effort to discern "ordinary meaning" in treaty interpretation? I, for one, have always been reluctant to view "context" too broadly, and so too have been all of those who have served alongside me on the Appellate Body. The more broadly we view "context," the more, it seems to me, we risk adding to, or subtracting from, the obligations in the WTO treaty. The more broadly we view "context" — the farther we venture from the adjacent words and the adjacent provisions in the treaty text — the farther we range into the unknown and uncharted territory of "object and purpose" — the more likely we are to identify our own preferred "object and purpose" as an individual treaty interpreter as the supposed "object and purpose" of the treaty makers. This, too, would be "overreaching."

Questions about the intent of the Members of the WTO, questions about their "object and purpose" as revealed in the text of the WTO treaty, are more easily asked and answered in the abstract than they are in the crucible of WTO dispute settlement around the round table of the Appellate Body. Here, too, the danger that would be posed by a practice by the Appellate Body of trying to read expressions of intent into the treaty when they are not clearly there, would be the danger of a "teleological," purposive interpretation contrary to the clearly expressed intent of the WTO Members as it relates to the interpretation of the WTO treaty.

Thus, on this issue, as on so many others, I agree with my esteemed former colleague Claus Dieter Ehlermann, who has concluded that "a method of interpretation that puts the emphasis on the ordinary meaning of the terms of the treaty is more faithful to the intention of the parties of the treaty."⁴² And my distinct impression is that, whatever their occasional criticisms in occasional cases, the Members of the WTO agree as well. If not, why would they have told the Appellate Body to use the textual approach when interpreting the meaning of the words in their treaty?

And what can be used to express the meaning of words but other words? When shorn of the surrounding rhetoric, some of the criticisms of the approach of the Appellate Body to treaty interpretation seem to me to consist essentially of a concern that the "Appellators" use words to describe other words. But what other choice do they have?

My dear friend and former colleague on the Appellate Body Said El-Naggar, who was both a lawyer and an economist, once suggested, in jest, that the reasoning in one of our reports might be improved if it took the form in part of mathematical formulas. (At least I think he was in jest.) Said observed that mathematical formulas are, by their very nature, more precise than words. I suppose they are. Still, as Said would remind us if he were here, the "covered agreements" are comprised of words, and not of mathematical formulas. And we must use other words to interpret the words of those agreements.

Is the use by the Appellate Body of words to describe other words "gap filling"? Is it "lawmaking"? Is it implying obligations where none exist? Is it "overreaching"? Not at all. It is simply the "clarification" by description of obligations where they already exist. It is the necessary stuff of treaty interpretation. It is the inevitable result of an approach to treaty interpretation that trusts in words, and that relies on words, and not on mathematical formulas.

As Said's distinguished successor, my former colleague on the Appellate Body Georges Abi-Saab, once expressed it to me, the task of the Appellate Body is to take a rule of general application and apply it to a particular situation. It is to take the law and apply it to the facts of a particular case. What could be simpler? But, oh, what could be more complex? For, unavoidably, applying a general rule to a specific dispute requires us to know the meaning of the general rule. And, inevitably, to attain such knowledge, we must give some serious thought to the meaning of words, and we must be able to articulate our conclusions from that thought in other words.

It may have been sufficient for Gertrude Stein to say that "a rose is a rose is a rose."[43] But she did not serve on the Appellate Body of the WTO. It is just not enough in WTO dispute settlement to say only that a "like product" is a "like product" is a "like product." This is especially so with a concept such as a "like product" that is an "accordion" that can vary in meaning from case to case.[44] And it is just not valid criticism to say that the Appellate Body is "gap filling" or "law-making" or "overreaching" merely because it does more than that in "addressing" a legal issue on appeal.

For only by doing more than that can the Appellate Body do its job for the Members of the WTO. Only by using other words can the Appellate Body assist the Members of the WTO in "clarifying" the existing words of the WTO treaty that express the treaty obligations of WTO Members, and thereby assist them in settling a trade dispute with a "positive solution." A description of a word is only a description. It is only a "clarification" of an obligation. But an obligation by any other name is still an obligation.

Must the "Appellators" be careful about the other words they choose to use in describing treaty obligations? Of course they must. They must, as they always do, labor through many drafts of a report in search of just the right words. For, as that intrepid treaty interpreter, Mark Twain, reminded us some time ago, the difference between the right word and the almost right word is the difference between lightning and the lightning bug.[45]

Does the Appellate Body always choose to use the right words? Of course not. In the thousands of pages of Appellate Body reports that have now accumulated, and that have been chosen along the way by the Appellate Body through the workings of consensus, there are a few words that even I might choose to change. Sometimes the choice of words in expressing a consensus does not allow for all of the ideal preferences of all of those joining in that consensus. Certainly, every Member of the WTO knows that.

Do the words used by the Appellate Body evidence a bias by the Appellate Body toward trade liberalization? Not at all. The WTO is not a free trade organization, and the WTO treaty is not a free trade agreement. In their work for the Members of the WTO, the Members of the Appellate Body favor trade liberalization only to the extent that the words the Members of the WTO have chosen to put into the WTO treaty require trade liberalization. Here, too, the "Appellators" are true to the words of the treaty.

Does the Appellate Body always reach the right decision as a result of its approach to treaty interpretation? In the many appeals in which I participated, there are no ultimate decisions that I would change. But I do not claim infallibility for the Appellate Body. Like all human institutions, the Appellate Body is limited in its decision-making by the burden of human frailty. Like any of us, the "Appellators" can only do their best while bearing this burden.

Have the Members of the Appellate Body gone beyond the words on certain issues relating to certain of the procedures followed in dispute settlement? Of course they have. They have done so necessarily on procedural issues such as allocating the burden of proof and "completing the legal analysis" in order to assist WTO Members in resolving disputes. The Members of the WTO expect the Appellate Body to do so on numerous issues relating to some of the procedural necessities that are distinct from substantive obligations.

Is there, inevitably, an element of personal judgment that enters into the making of such decisions? Of course there is. This is so of the decision-making of any deliberative body anywhere in the world, whether "quasi-judicial" or otherwise. And the Members of the WTO certainly know and assume this. This is why they have required in the DSU that "[t]he Appellate Body shall comprise persons of recognized authority, with demonstrated expertise in law, international trade and the subject matter of the covered agreements generally."[46] The Members of the WTO have chosen the Members of the Appellate Body in part for their judgment, in the hope that, within the bounds of the DSU, they will use it.

And have the Members of the Appellate Body generally exercised their judgment well in fulfilling their task in treaty interpretation? In answer, I will merely point out that, thus far, WTO Members have never once chosen to exercise the "exclusive authority" they clearly have under Article IX(2) of the WTO Agreement to "adopt an interpretation" of any of the "covered agreements" by altering a single word or amending a single decision of the Appellate Body.[47] This says much about how little credibility there is to criticisms that the Appellate Body has engaged in "overreaching."

In considering the continuing quest of the Appellate Body for the meaning of words, the Members of the WTO and the critics of WTO dispute settlement alike might do well to remember this. One Member's example of alleged "overreaching" is usually another Member's example of clear "ordinary meaning." One Member's controversial judgment is another Member's fundamental justice. In fulfilling its responsibilities to all of the Members of the WTO, the Members of the Appellate Body do not have the choice of avoiding criticism. They have only a choice of critics.

Is the quest of the Appellate Body for the meaning of "and/or" and for the meaning of so many other words in WTO dispute settlement a quixotic quest? With their pens as lances, are the "Appellators" only tilting at the windmills of words? I think not. I trust not. I hope not. On this, we await, not the verdict of the critics, but the verdict of time.

In the meantime, I recommend caution in making broad generalizations based on the limited experience thus far with WTO dispute settlement. National tallies of so-called "wins" and "losses" in WTO dispute settlement do not always reflect the relative significance of different legal issues or the realities of the immediate outcomes of cases in dispute settlement, nor do they reflect the broader consequences of those outcomes for WTO Members over the longer term. For example, the Member that opposes a ruling in one dispute will often rely on that ruling in the next.

Furthermore, a narrow focus on the outcomes of a few cases involving trade remedies, as a result of domestic political pressures, can cause WTO Members to overlook the considerable advantages of the much broader reach of international trade law under the WTO treaty, and the very value of having a rule-based system that upholds the international rule of law in world trade. As important as they are, there is much more to the WTO trading system than trade remedies. And, even with trade remedies, it is best to take a broader and longer view. The Member that applies a trade remedy one day will have a trade remedy applied against it the next, and the very same rules and rulings will apply.

I recommend also remembering that the experience of the WTO dispute settlement system thus far really is, for the longer term, a limited experience with only a few cases. Although there have been several hundred cases thus far in WTO dispute settlement, those cases are merely the beginning of the ever-unfolding interpretation of the WTO treaty. There are, for example, entire agreements that are part of the WTO treaty that have been interpreted by the Appellate Body only once, or twice, or not at all.

To offer just one illustration: Some critics have noted that the Appellate Body has not, to date, upheld the application of any safeguard measure that has been challenged in WTO dispute settlement, and from this they somehow generalize that the Appellate Body never will. But how many such safeguards cases have there been all told? The answer is "six."[48] This hardly exhausts the endless possibilities of the many provisions of the WTO Agreement on Safeguards.

Would these same critics have suggested that Justice John Marshall and his colleagues on the Supreme Court of the United States had exhausted all of the endless possibilities of the Interstate Commerce Clause of the United States Constitution in their first real construction of the clause in *Gibbons v. Ogden* in 1824?[49] How many times has that one clause been interpreted by that court in all the years since? With safeguards in the WTO, we have one whole agreement awaiting further interpretation, and not one clause. Again, we await the verdict of time.

And, while we wait, what do I think the Members of the WTO should do in the current multilateral trade negotiations to ease the concerns of the critics by advancing the quest of the "Appellators" for the meaning of words? What should they do to strengthen the rule-based trading system by providing the Members of the Appellate Body with additional guidance and with additional resources in fulfilling their task of treaty interpretation in future WTO dispute settlement?

In my view, the Members of the WTO should continue to place their trust in the written word.

They should, first of all, conclude their current negotiations successfully by agreeing on new rules and on any needed revisions of existing rules. Far better to negotiate than to litigate. Far better to have the Members of the WTO resolve trade issues through negotiations leading to new rulemaking than to have those issues resolved by panelists and by the Appellate Body through the "clarification" of existing rules in WTO dispute settlement. As it is, there is a dangerous unbalance in the WTO between a largely effective system for upholding existing rules and a largely ineffective system for making new rules. Dispute settlement is central to the success of the WTO, but dispute settlement alone cannot ensure the success of the WTO. A house unbalanced cannot stand.

Beyond this, there is much else that should also be done by the Members of the WTO in the Doha Development Round to further treaty interpretation in future dispute settlement. There is need for more prefatory and other language that truly explains the intent of WTO Members in their treaty-making. There is need for more — and for more precise — definitions of the words that WTO Members choose to use in their treaty-making. There is need for a more considered effort by WTO Members to resist the understandable urge of negotiators to gloss over their continuing differences by using general language that may facilitate treaty negotiation but may complicate particular treaty interpretation. There is need as well to revisit some of the current language in the WTO treaty that is the source of ongoing controversy in treaty interpretation — such as, for example, Article 17.6 of the Anti-Dumping Agreement, relating to the standard of review in disputes involving anti-dumping measures.[50]

There is need generally for WTO Members to be more mindful in all their treaty negotiations of the likelihood that many of the results of their negotiations will be subjected later to the scrutiny of treaty interpreters in

WTO dispute settlement. Unless and until WTO members decide otherwise, the textual approach described in the Vienna Convention will continue to be used in such treaty interpretation. The textual approach presumes that the words of the treaty have a meaning. So WTO Members must make certain that the words they choose to include in the treaty have a meaning on which all WTO Members have agreed.

Toward this end, there is need also — and frankly — to have the results of the current round of negotiations reviewed by lawyers as to their legal wording and their legal implications before approval by consensus by the Members of the WTO. Some old GATT hands will resist this. But this is one of the best ways the Members of the WTO could facilitate treaty interpretation. The truth is that, like it or not, the rule of law in a rule-based trading system requires a role for lawyers.[51] The only question is, will the lawyers play their role sooner — in negotiations — or later — in dispute settlement?

Perhaps most of all, there is need for agreement by the Members of the WTO on a common and official negotiating history of the Doha Development Round. A negotiating history on which all of the Members of the WTO agreed would be an invaluable tool to panelists and to the Appellate Body as preparatory work that could be consulted, when appropriate, as a supplementary means of interpretation under Article 32 of the Vienna Convention in fulfilling the task of treaty interpretation.[52] The absence of an agreed negotiating history of the Uruguay Round has contributed to the complexity of many of the challenges currently faced in dispute settlement.

My hope is that, over time, too, the Members of the WTO will develop sufficient "subsequent practice" within the meaning of Article 31 (3) (b) of the Vienna Convention to give panels and the Appellate Body more guidance as to the "ordinary meaning" of some of the words in the WTO treaty.[53] As the work of the Members of the WTO continues, there will be more occasions when a "concordant, common and consistent" sequence of acts or pronouncements by the Members of the WTO will be sufficient to establish a discernible pattern implying their agreement on the appropriate interpretation of some of the words of the treaty.[54] On such "subsequent practice," panels and the Appellate Body will undoubtedly rely.

In the meantime, the work of the WTO dispute settlement system continues. There are already about thirty thousand pages of reports from dispute settlement that "clarify" about thirty thousand pages of obligations in the WTO treaty. Many questions about the meanings of the words in the WTO treaty have been answered through the adoption of panel and Appellate Body reports by WTO Members during the first decade of WTO dispute settlement. But many more questions are yet to be answered. Over time, many of the most difficult of these unanswered questions are likely to arise in dispute settlement, and to demand even more skill and even more sagacity from panels and from the Appellate Body in the continuing quest for the meaning of the words of the WTO treaty.

A few of these unanswered questions come readily to mind.

I will ask them. I will not answer them.

What is "effective action" to enforce intellectual property rights under the first paragraph of Article 41 of the WTO Agreement on Trade-related Aspects of Intellectual Property Rights, and what are "fair and equitable" procedures concerning the enforcement of intellectual property rights under the second paragraph of that same Article?[55]

What, precisely, constitutes "substantially all the trade" between two or more customs territories sufficient to satisfy the definition of a "free trade area" for purposes of Article XXIV (8) (b) of the WTO General Agreement on Tariffs and Trade 1994?[56]

What are "scientific principles" and "sufficient scientific evidence" under Article 2 (2) of the WTO Agreement on the Application of Sanitary and Phytosanitary Measures, and what, for that matter, is the meaning of the word "scientific" as used by the Members of the WTO in that Agreement?[57]

What are "ordinary customs duties" under Article II (1) (b) of the GATT?[58] What are "public morals" under Article XX (a) of the GATT?[59] What are "essential security interests" under Article XXI of the GATT?[60]

What does Article XV (4) of the GATT mean in stating that "contracting parties shall not, by exchange action, frustrate the intent of the provisions of this Agreement...."?[61] And what, in this provision, is the meaning of the word "frustrate"?

What, precisely, is "special and differential treatment" for developing countries, and what, for that matter, is a "developing country"?[62]

What is required by the statement in Article 3.10 of the Dispute Settlement Understanding that "[i]t is understood that ... all Members will engage in these procedures in good faith in an effort to resolve the dispute", and what, for that matter, is "good faith"?[63]

What is the meaning of all of these names we call words in the WTO treaty?

In contemplating these and other questions that have yet to be answered in WTO dispute settlement, I am content even more to be a former Member of the Appellate Body.

For these and other difficult questions about the WTO treaty will not be answered by me.

They will be answered by the Members of the WTO *and/or* by those who will serve them, in the years to come, as "Appellators."

Endnotes

[1] *See United States — Import Prohibition of Certain Shrimp and Shrimp Products*, WT/DS58/AB/R (November 6, 1998).

[2] Michael W. Weinstein, "Economic Scene: Should Clinton embrace the China trade deal? Some say yes," *New York Times* (September 9, 1999), at C2.

[3] John Jackson, "Perceptions About the WTO Trade Institutions," Keynote Address, Inaugural Ceremony for the Advisory Centre for WTO Law, Geneva, Switzerland (October 5, 2001).

[4] Article 3.2, Understanding on Rules and Procedures Governing the Settlement of Disputes (the "Dispute Settlement Understanding" or the "DSU").

[5] *See* WTO Rules of Conduct.

[6] *See Argentina — Safeguard Measures on Imports of Footwear*, WT/DS 121/AB/R (January 12, 2000).

[7] *See* especially, for these purposes, Articles 3 and 17 of the DSU.

[8] Article 3.2, DSU.

[9] Article 3.7, DSU.

[10] Article 3.2, DSU.

[11] Articles 3 and 17, DSU.

[12] Vienna Convention on the Law of Treaties, *opened for signature* May 23, 1969, 1155 UNTS 331 ("Vienna Convention").

[13] *See*, e.g., *European Communities — Export Subsidies on Sugar*, WT/DS 265/AB/R (May 19, 2005), para. 167; *United States — Subsidies on Upland Cotton*, WT/DS 267)/AB/R (March 27, 2005); *United States — Continued Dumping and Subsidy Offset Act of 2000*, WT/DS 217/AB/R (January 27, 2003), paras. 276, 281.

[14] Article 31(1), Vienna Convention.

[15] *United States — Standards for Reformulated and Conventional Gasoline*, WT/DS 52/AB/R (May 20, 1996), p. 160 ("*United States — Reformulated Gasoline*").

[16] *Japan — Taxes on Alcoholic Beverages*, WT/DS/AB/R, WT/DS/10/AB/R, WT/DS 11/AB/R (November 1, 1996), p. 9 ("*Japan-Alcohol*").

[17] International Court of Justice, *Territorial Dispute (Libyan Arab Jamahiriya/Chad) Judgment*, (1994), ICJ Reports, p. 6 at 20; *Japan-Alcohol*, p. 10.

[18] WTO Rules of Conduct, Articles II and III(2).

[19] Article 3.7, DSU, provides: "Before bringing a case, a Member shall exercise its judgment as to whether action under these procedures would be fruitful."

[20] Article 16.4, DSU.

[21] Articles 17.4 and 17.6, DSU.

[22] Article 17.12, DSU.

[23] Article 3.7, DSU.

[24] Article 19.1, DSU.

[25] *United States — Definitive Safeguard Measures on Imports of Certain Steel Products*, WT/DS 248/AB/R, WT/DS 249/AB/R, WT/DS 251/AB/R, WT/DS 252/AB/R, WT/DS 254/AB/R (December 10, 2003) ("*United States — Steel Safeguards*").

[26] George Gordon, Lord Byron, *Don Juan*, "Dedication," Line 16.

[27] On this, I agree with Professor Donald McRae. *See* Donald McRae, "1995–2004, Ten Years and 63 Cases Later: The Contribution of the Appellate Body to the Development of International Trade Law," presentation at conference on "The WTO at 10: The Role of the Dispute Settlement System," March 13, 2005, in Stresa, Italy.

[28] Jonathan Keates, *Stendhal* (New York: Carroll & Graf, 1997), 9 [1994].

[29] This is a paraphrase and embellishment from Walker Percy, *The Message in the Bottle: How Queer Man Is, How Queer Language Is, and What One Has to Do With the Other* (New York: Farrar, Giroux and Strauss, 1990) [1954], 153–154.

[30] Oliver Wendell Holmes, Jr., *Towne v. Eisner*, 245 U.S. 418, 425 (1918).

[31] Keates, *Stendhal, supra*, at 396.

[32] *United States — Definitive Safeguard Measures on Imports of Circular Welded Carbon Quality Line Pipe from Korca*, WT/DS 202/AB/R (March 8, 2002), paras. 140–177 (*United States — Line Pipe*).

[33] *See United States –Continued Dumping and Subsidy Offset Act of 2000*, WT/DS 217/AB/R (January 27, 2003), para. 248, stating that "dictionaries are important guides to, not dispositive statements of, definitions of words appearing in agreements and legal documents." *See also United States — Final Counteracting Duty Determination with Respect to Certain Softwood Lumber from Canada*, WT/DS 257/AB/R/ (February 17, 2004), paras. 58–59.

[34] Richard A. Posner, *The Problems of Jurisprudence* (Cambridge, Massachusetts: Harvard University Press, 1993), 277 [1990].

[35] *See* Donald McRae, *supra*, note 27.

[36] Benjamin N. Cardozo, *The Nature of the Judicial Process* (New Haven and London: Yale University Press, 1949), 21 [1921].

[37] Merrakesh Declaration of April 15, 1994.
[38] Preamble, Merrakesh Agreement Establishing the World Trade Organization, *done at* Merrakesh, Morocco, April 15, 1994 (the "WTO Agreement").
[39] *See*, for example, the WTO Agreement on Agriculture.
[40] WTO Agreement on Subsidies and Countervailing Measures.
[41] Annex I, Item (k), WTO Agreement on Subsidies and Countervailing Measures.
[42] Claus-Dieter Ehlermann, "Reflections on the Appellate Body of the WTO," *Journal of International Economic Law*, Volume 6, Number 3 (September 2003), 695, 699.
[43] Gertrude Stein, "Sacred Emily," *Geography and Plays* (Boston: Four Seas Co., 1922), 178–188, reprinted by University of Nebraska Press (1993), 178.
[44] *See Japan-Alcohol*, p. 21 ("The concept of 'likeness' is a relative one that evokes the image of an accordion.")
[45] Mark Twain, Letter to George Bainton (October 15, 1888) ("The difference between the almost right word and the right word is really a large matter — it's the difference between the lightning bug and the lightning.")
[46] Article 17.3, DSU.
[47] Article IX(2) of the WTO Agreement.
[48] The six cases are: *Korea — Definitive Safeguard Measure on Imports of Certain Daily Products*, WT/DS 98/AB/R (January 12, 2000); *Argentina — Safeguard Measures on Imports of Footwear*, WT/DS 121/AB/R (January 12, 2000); *United States — Definitive Safeguard Measures on Imports of Wheat Gluten from the European Communities*, WT/DS 166/AB/R (January 19, 2001); *United States — Safeguard Measures on Imports of Fresh, Chilled or Frozen Lamb Meat from New Zealand and Australia*, WT/DS 177/AB/R, WT/DS 178/AB/R (May 16, 2001); *United States — Definitive Safeguard Measures on Imports of Circular Welded Carbon Quality Line Pipe from Korea*, WT/DS 202/AB/R (March 8, 2002); *United States — Definitive Safeguard Measures on Imports of Certain Steel Products*, WT/DS 248/AB/R (December 10, 2003).
[49] *Gibbons v. Ogden*, 9 Wheat, 1, 6 L. Ed. 23 (1824).
[50] Article 17.6, Anti-Dumping Agreement.
[51] *See* Debra P. Steger, "The Rule of Law or the Rule of Lawyers?," in Debra. P. Steger, *Peace Through Trade: Building the World Trade Organization* (London: Cameron May, 2004), 257.
[52] Article 32 of the Vienna Convention.
[53] Article 31(3)(b) of the Vienna Convention.
[54] *See Japan-Alcohol*, pages 11–12, citing especially Ian Sinclair, *The Vienna Convention on the Law of Treaties* (2nd Ed., 1984), 137.
[55] Article 41 of the WTO Agreement on Trade-related Aspects of Intellectual Property Rights.
[56] Article XXIV(8)(b) of the GATT 1994.

[57] Article 2(2) of the WTO Agreement on the Application of Sanitary and Phytosanitary Measures.
[58] Article II(1)(b) of the GATT 1994.
[59] Article XX(a) of the GATT 1994.
[60] Article XXI of the GATT 1994.
[61] Article XV(4) of the GATT 1994.
[62] These phrases appear many places in the covered agreements of the WTO treaty, but they are nowhere defined in the treaty.
[63] Article 3.10, DSU.

Chapter 13

The Garden*

In the center of our national capital is the garden of our national memory. On the day before I took the oath for the first time as a Member of the Congress of the United States of America, I walked along the forking paths of that garden. Along those green and winding paths in Washington, D.C. are memorials to all that we, as Americans, choose to cherish, to all we claim to serve, to all we hope to preserve. In that garden are marble monuments that remind us of all that we, as Americans, are supposed to remember, and all that we, as Americans, are supposed to be. To the American people, the Mall in the middle of our capital city is "sacred space."[1]

On that bright, cold January morning, I followed the paths of our national garden from green lawn to green lawn, from flower bed to flower bed, from reflecting pool to reflecting pool, and from memorial to memorial. Along a last paved path in the garden, around a last green turn, I arrived at last at the solemn majesty of the Jefferson Memorial. America's memorial to Thomas Jefferson stands all alone as a "shrine to freedom"[2] in a corner of the garden on the south bank of the capital's Tidal Basin. The white marble of the memorial forms an open, circular, neoclassical colonnade. In the center of the memorial is a bronze statue of the author of the American Declaration of Independence[3] — the "Founding Father" whose words inspired us in 1776, and whose words can still inspire us today. Nineteen feet high, the statue faces out from the colonnade toward

---

*This essay was previously published as James Bacchus, "The Garden," *Fordham International Law Journal*, Volume 28 (2004), 308–352.

the far end of the garden, and toward the shining White House that has long been home to Jefferson's successors.

Above the statue is a shining circular dome. Carved on the interior of the walls that surround and support the dome, are inscriptions of some of Jefferson's noble words about human rights. On that memorable morning, I emerged from the green of the garden, climbed up the white steps, walked between the white columns, and went into the memorial. I stopped, looked up, and read some of the noblest of those words: "I have sworn upon the altar of God, eternal hostility against every form of tyranny over the mind of man."[4] I read those words silently. Then, I read them aloud. And, as I stood there reading those words, as I stood there reflecting on those words, as I stood there reaffirming my own commitment to the spirit of those words amid the garden of our national memory, I noticed for the first time that I was not alone in the memorial.

Others were there as well. Others, too, had followed the forking paths of the garden to pay homage to the memory of Mr. Jefferson. Others, too, had made the pilgrimage through the garden to see his statue and read his noble words. Those other pilgrims were all around me. They were talking among themselves as they, too, pondered the meaning of the words carved into the marble of the memorial. As they, too, read those words aloud, I realized that their pilgrimage, unlike mine, was from afar.

For not a single one of them was speaking English.

As I stood there beneath the sheltering dome of the memorial, I heard Jefferson's words about human rights translated into many languages: Chinese, French, German, Japanese, Spanish. I heard a jumble of languages from all over the world. I heard what seemed to me that morning to be almost every language in the world *except English.*

I may very well have been the only American in the Jefferson Memorial that morning.

Although some who were there with me may have been Americans who happened to be speaking another language, it seems likely that most, if not all, of them must have come from afar to stroll through America's national garden. They must have been foreigners who had come to visit an American shrine that has long symbolized the American commitment to freedom. They must have come from around the world to visit the Jefferson memorial, and to read, in a number of languages, his noble words about the human rights that form the foundation of freedom.

I still heard their voices as I raised my hand and took the oath of office the next day.

That was in January, 1991. Some years later, and some time after I chose to leave the Congress, I found myself in the center of another national capital, in another national garden of memory. Far from Washington D.C. (and farther still from my abandoned political career), I sat in the back seat of a taxi in a traffic jam in the Plaza de Mayo, a place that has long served as the symbolic center of Buenos Aires, Argentina. From the window of the taxi, I saw what was causing the traffic jam. I happened to be passing by the plaza on a Thursday afternoon at 3:30. Every Thursday afternoon at 3:30 in Buenos Aires, the mothers of the "disappeared"[5] march in support of an honest reckoning with Argentina's national memory.[6] They march in support of human rights in the Plaza de Mayo.

On this Thursday afternoon, the mothers of the "disappeared" were marching in the plaza, as they always did. There were perhaps two dozen of them. They marched around the small pyramid in the center of the plaza, in front of the pink presidential palace.[7] They wore white handkerchiefs tied around their heads.[8] They carried placards adorned with faded photographs. They did not say a word.

The mothers of Argentina began marching there silently many Thursdays ago.[9] They did so in a display of courage during the torturous time when a military *junta* ruled Argentina, from 1976 to 1983.[10] Their courage was born of despair. They began meeting together, and then marching together, because they did not know the fate of their children who had "disappeared" during the "Dirty War" waged by the *junta* against various guerrilla groups in Argentina. They grew weary of meeting together in the waiting rooms of police stations, and so they began marching together in the Plaza de Mayo.

The very word "disappearance" speaks volumes to advocates of human rights. At least one leading human rights advocate maintains that, of all the many crimes against humanity, the most evil and most poignant of modern examples is causing a "disappearance" — a process by which a citizen suspected of harboring subversive sentiments is kidnapped, detained, and tortured for some time before finally being killed, all within a secret police or military operation which is utterly unlawful but none the less agreed in outline by the government.[11]

This "most evil" and "most poignant" of crimes against humanity has cruel consequences: "For the victims, and for their society, disappearance at the hands of police or military forces amounts to the most complete abnegation of human rights imaginable: arbitrary arrest, detention without trial, inhumane and degrading treatment and torture, followed by murder and secret disposal of the body. For friends and relations, the continuing horror of not knowing any details of the victim's fate adds a special layer of cruelty, driving them either to despair or to the courage displayed by the Mothers of the Plaza del Mayo...."[12]

So it was in Argentina under military rule. During those dark days of Argentina's history, more than ten thousand citizens of Argentina "disappeared."[13] They simply vanished. The death squads of the military dictatorship came and took them away during the dead and the dark of the night.[14] There was a sudden and fateful knock on the door — and then they were gone. They became prisoners without names in cells without numbers.[15]

Torture was commonplace then in Argentina, and it was often the first destination of those who were taken away. In a special section of the Navy Mechanics School in Buenos Aires, and in other dark corners of the country, were torture chambers that were the sordid scenes of unspeakable crimes.[16] Many of those who were tortured in those secret chambers were taken away afterwards, dropped from airplanes over the sea, or buried in mass graves.[17] They "disappeared" forever.

It has been said that the weekly demonstrations of the mothers of the "disappeared" in the Plaza de Mayo "on behalf of their lost children did more than anything else to expose the wickedness of the Argentinian *junta*."[18] Now, all these years later, democracy has been restored in Argentina.[19] Today, the people of Argentina are trying their best to sustain their democracy and to secure their hard-won freedoms.[20] The Argentines are trying their best to create a new prosperity through the exercise of their democratic freedoms, and to come to terms with those dark days of their past.[21] More than most, the people of Argentina know the necessity of giving primacy always to respect for human rights.

But, all these years later, the fate of many of the "disappeared" of Argentina is still unknown.[22] So the mothers of the "disappeared" continue to march once a week in the Plaza de Mayo.[23] The names of the "disappeared" are on the handkerchiefs they wear.[24] The faces of the "disappeared" are on the placards they carry. The mothers still march every Thursday afternoon at 3:30 in the garden of Argentina's national memory.[25] They march in a silent showing of public outrage. They march in dutiful display of their refusal to forget. They march in memory of what happened, and in the hope that, by marching, they can help keep it from happening ever again.

Watching them march from the window of my taxi on that one Thursday afternoon, I recalled something a friend of mine from Argentina told me once about what it had been like growing up under a military dictatorship during that grim time in his Nation's history. He knew that, in my youth, I had served in the administration of U.S. President Jimmy Carter during the years when the military ruled Argentina. President Carter was — and is — a champion of human rights. My friend from Argentina told me, "Every time President Carter gave a speech in favor of human rights, fewer people would disappear in Argentina." He added, "Even today, that remains for me the best evidence I have ever seen of the vast potential of America as a force for human rights in the world."

In the eyes of my Argentine friend, this vast potential has often been fulfilled. In his eyes, the ghost of Jefferson marches in silence alongside the mothers of the disappeared. In his eyes, too, there was a time when all Americans marched alongside them in the Plaza de Mayo. In his eyes, we Americans were true — when Jimmy Carter was President — to Thomas Jefferson's noble words about human rights. We knew then that Jefferson's words are not words only for Americans. They are words for all the world. We were worthy then of all the marble monuments in our national garden.

But are we, in the eyes of others throughout the world, still worthy of the monuments in our gardens today? Are we still true to Jefferson's noble words? Are we still fulfilling the vast potential of America as a force for freedom in the world by marching alongside all those throughout the world who are seeking to secure basic human rights?

The day after I watched the mothers of the "disappeared" march in the Plaza de Mayo, I boarded an airplane for the long flight home from Argentina. Next to me on the plane was a young Argentine couple. They were reading a magazine. They spoke heatedly in Spanish — one of the many languages I had heard all those years ago on that bright January morning at the Jefferson Memorial. They pointed angrily at one appalling photograph in the magazine.

It was a photograph that has become all too familiar lately to all Americans and to all the rest of the world. It was a photograph of an Iraqi prisoner of war in the prison near Baghdad called Abu Ghraib.[26] The prisoner stands on a wooden box, his legs bare, his arms outstretched, his hands connected to electrical wires, his torso shrouded by a dark cape, his head completely covered by a black hood.[27] He seems to be beseeching his captors for compassion. He seems to be pleading for pity. He is a portrait of utter and complete vulnerability. He is a statue of another kind.

What could I possibly have said to that couple from Argentina to make that appalling photograph go away? I do not speak Spanish. But even if I did, what could I possibly have said to them? That photograph — and all the many others like it that have been "leaked" to the media from behind the prison walls at Abu Ghraib — tells the rest of the world something about America that words alone — however noble — can never erase. I gazed at the photograph for a moment. I listened to the angry words. Then, silently, I turned my head. I looked the other way. Framed by the clouds floating outside, my reflection in the window of the airplane seemed to rebuke me for my silence.

Arriving home from Argentina, I chanced to read the anonymous comment of one of my fellow Americans in the column that serves as a forum for airing public complaints in my hometown newspaper. The column is called "Ticked Off." The comment I read in the column that day was offered in response to the photographs and other media revelations of American actions at Abu Ghraib. In the view of this one red-white-and-blue American patriot who happens to live in my hometown: "When I see 3,000 Islamist terrorists jump from the 130th floor from any building in New York City to their death, I'll shed a tear for those Iraqis who were abused by our soldiers in Baghdad. I think those soldiers who operated under direct orders of superiors deserve a Silver Star and commendations — certainly not courts-martial."[28]

If this were only an isolated view, then perhaps it could be overlooked. If this were only an exceptional expression of venom and vengefulness, then perhaps it could be ignored. Sadly, it is not. Sadly, this view is widespread among Americans, and, sadder still, it is still spreading throughout America.[29] Because this view is not isolated, because it is not exceptional, because it is still spreading, because it seems to me to be becoming more and more an accepted view in America even though several years have passed since the shock of the tragic events of September 11, 2001, I can no longer look the other way.

And I can no longer remain silent.

Consider these excerpts from a report of the International Committee of the Red Cross on the "Treatment During Arrest" of the Iraqi prisoners in Abu Ghraib.[30] The report speaks of arrests in the dead and in the dark of night. It speaks of a fateful and unexpected knock on the door. It explains: "In almost all instances .... arresting authorities provided no information about who they were, where their base was located, nor did they explain the cause of arrest. Similarly, they rarely informed the arrestee or his family where he was being taken and for how long, resulting in the de facto *'disappearance'* of the arrestee.... [M]any [families] were left without news for months, often fearing that their relatives unaccounted for were dead."[31]

The italics are not in the report of the Red Cross. The italics are mine. The italics are added because the mind cannot help but pause in this passage on the word "*disappearance.*" The eye lingers there as the mind conjures the terrible images in the photographs from Abu Ghraib: the hoods, the capes, the dogs, the prods, the lights, the sleepless nights. All the horror we have seen and heard about Abu Ghraib are contained in this one solitary word, "disappearance." It does not go away. It scars. It sears. It shivers. It stays.

We Americans must begin to come to terms with the staying power of this word. We must begin to realize just how much of what we most cherish about America may have "disappeared" because of the atrocities at Abu Ghraib. We must begin to understand the consequences of the photographs from Abu Ghraib — and the consequences of the policies those photographs represent — for ourselves as well as for others.[32] We must begin to see the indelible reality of the photographs of Abu Ghraib, for America and for the rest of the world.[33]

Those photographs fuel the hate of those who hate us.[34] They confirm the fear of those who fear us.[35] They undermine the support of those who support us.[36] Like the word "disappearance" in the report of the Red Cross, the images in the photographs from Abu Ghraib will not go away. They, too, will stay. Long after many Americans may have forgotten them, they, too, will linger. They will linger in the eyes of the world. So, we Americans cannot turn silently away. We must continue to make our way through the garden. And we must see the path before us clearly, for there are thorns in our path. They are the thorns of torture, the thorns of Abu Ghraib. We must remove those thorns because, if we do not, if they remain, we will take the wrong path as a Nation, and we will lose our way through the garden.

Many of those who would profess to lead us along the winding paths of the garden do not seem to see the damage done to America by Abu Ghraib.[37] They do not seem to see the italics of the word "disappearance." They do not seem to see how the images of torture linger. They do not see the thorns.

The Chairman of the Joint Chiefs of Staff, General Richard B. Myers, sits in his spacious office in the Pentagon. News of the photographs from Abu Ghraib reaches his desk. The Chairman does not choose to have the photographs sent to other top decision-makers in the government of the United States because "the impact of the photos [is] not appreciated."[38] He does not see the thorns.

The Secretary of Defense offers his view of the events at Abu Ghraib when he is asked about the atrocities there in an interview with a radio station in Phoenix, Arizona. "I have not seen anything thus far," he insists, "that says that the people abused were abused in the process of interrogating them or for interrogation purposes."[39] The Secretary chooses not to seize the chance to denounce torture.[40] He does not see the thorns.

Soon after the media revelations about Abu Ghraib, soon after the photographs from Abu Ghraib are shown to all the world, the President of the United States holds a rare press conference in Washington, D.C.[41] "Three times, journalists gave the President chances to condemn the use of torture, distancing himself and the [n]ation unequivocally from such practices. He didn't."[42] The President does not choose to foreswear forever the use of torture.[43] He does not see the thorns.

In the familiar way of Washington, following criticism, all three of these would-be leaders later "clarify their remarks." Later, the Chairman of the Joint Chiefs of Staff sees the significance of the photographs of Abu Ghraib.[44] Later, the principal spokesman for the Secretary of Defense admits, "He misspoke, pure and simple. But he corrected himself."[45] Later, the President states, "I will never order torture."[46] He adds, "The values of this country are such that torture is not a part of our soul, and our being."[47]

With the last remark, I would certainly agree. But how sincere are we to suppose all of this belated backing and filling by our current leaders to be? In my experience, what people mean most, is evidenced best by what they say and do first. As someone who has been, at various times, both a politician and a press aide to a politician, I know that political truth is often truer to the genuine views of politicians *before* it is politically corrected.

The scrubbed and sobered second thoughts of those who profess to lead America in our "war on terror" are less revealing of their real views than are their initial answers and actions in their occasional unscripted moments. What the President said belatedly in condemnation of torture is surely true of our values, but recent events lead to the conclusion that it is considerably less true of our recent actions, which do not reflect our values, and which certainly are not true to the Jeffersonian ideal of human rights that inspires those values.

Ample supporting evidence for this conclusion is found in almost everything that those in the current administration in the United States have said and done while they have sought to lead America. They have not only placed the thorns of torture along the paths of the American garden. Through their actions, and through their inactions, they have refused at every turn in the path to see them.

For example, only a few weeks after the world first saw the photographs from Abu Ghraib, the U.S. State Department released its annual report on human rights.[48] Dating back to the idealistic days of President Carter, this report details every year of the ongoing efforts of the United States to promote human rights and democracy in more than one hundred countries.[49] The latest annual report criticizes a number of countries — including allies of the United States in the "war on terror" — for engaging in torture and other human rights violations.[50] The United States of America is not among them.[51] The report does not so much as mention Abu Ghraib.[52] If this report is to be believed, the U.S. State Department, too, does not see the thorns.

Given such seeming blindness among those who would lead us, it is not surprising to learn that many other Americans appear to agree with them. A national poll of American attitudes on the appropriateness of various techniques of interrogating captive terrorists shows, reassuringly, that sixty-three percent of those polled think torture is never acceptable, but, disturbingly, slightly more than one-third of those polled say torture is legitimate in some cases.[53] Moreover, and most disturbingly, despite widespread objection among those polled to electric shocks, exposure, forced immersion, sexual humiliation, starvation, and other so-called interrogation "techniques" used against the inmates at Abu Ghraib, according to the poll, "only a third of Americans would define what happened at Abu Ghraib as torture."[54] Perhaps in part because of the blindness of our leaders, these Americans also do not see the thorns.

What would Jefferson say? Would he say, like so many Americans, that torture is not torture if we choose not to call it torture? Would he say that anything goes in the "war on terror"? Would he also not see the thorns? Or would he say that we Americans have strayed from the right path because we have not tended our garden?

Anyone who has ever visited his home at Monticello knows that Jefferson valued gardens. There are long and winding paths through the garden he made of his grounds there. Today, he would enjoy walking along the winding path of the garden in Washington that leads to his statue in the Jefferson Memorial. More than anyone, he would understand why the garden there is much more than merely another garden for America.

Jefferson, a lifelong student of the natural world, was fond of saying, "There is not a sprig of grass that grows uninteresting to me."[55] He once told a friend, "No occupation is so delightful to me as the culture of the earth, and no culture comparable to that of the garden."[56] For nearly fifty years, he kept a journal that he called his "Garden Book," in which he kept a lifelong record and loving description of "my native woods and fields [sic]".[57] In it he also recorded how, over the course of his long life, he gradually transformed his rustic mountaintop at Monticello into one of America's premier gardens.

He did so with a plan in mind. Like other 18th century exponents of the philosophical view called Enlightenment, Jefferson believed that "the economy of nature" established a rational order in the world.[58] Thus, he sought a "universal intelligibility" in his view of his surroundings.[59] From his studies of aesthetics, from his readings in the theories of the landscaping of English gardens, and from his tours (with John Adams) of some of the most famous English gardens of his time, he concluded that a garden could be a reflection of intelligibility. It could be a manifestation of the mind of those who made it.[60]

But the right kind of garden was needed. A natural garden was needed in a natural arrangement with sheltering trees, blowing waters — and winding paths. And the paths needed to wind in the right way. The right paths through the garden were needed. It was important to choose the right paths through the garden because the course the paths followed through the garden revealed the deepest beliefs of those who chose them.

It was equally important to tend the garden. A garden requires cultivation. To make the right kind of garden requires the right kind of gardener. To keep the right kind of garden requires the right kind of gardening. The fate of a garden depends on the care and the nourishment we give it. With the right kind of cultivation, a garden will last, it will flourish, it will flower into all that its makers hoped it would one day be. But without the right kind of cultivation, a garden will fill with thorns.

Jefferson tried to choose the right paths for his garden at Monticello. He tried to cultivate a garden that would flourish, one that would be filled with flowers. He would advise us to do the same for our garden of national memory along the Mall and around the Tidal Basin in Washington, D.C. He would have us choose paths for our national garden that would be true to our deepest beliefs, and he would have us tend our garden in ways that would make it flourish, would help fill it with flowers, and would keep it from filling with thorns.

We need not wonder what Jefferson would say about the thorns our current leaders refuse to see in the American garden. On that bright January morning years ago when I made my way through the garden to the Jefferson Memorial, I stopped afterwards in the gift shop kindly provided by the National Park Service in the basement below the Memorial. I bought a book there entitled *Thomas Jefferson: His Life and Words*.[61] I kept it as a souvenir of my pilgrimage to the Jefferson Memorial. I kept it on my desk all the while I was in the Congress. I keep it on my desk to this day. It is a slim volume containing some of Jefferson's most stirring statements.

On page fifteen of this book, filled with felicitous quotations, are these words of Jefferson: "The god who gave us life, gave us liberty at the same time; the hand of force may destroy, but can not disjoin them."[62] These noble words of Jefferson are from his rhetorical dress rehearsal of sorts for the Declaration of Independence, a manifesto he wrote in 1774 entitled *A Summary View of the Rights of British America*.[63] These bold words, written in protest to the King of England in 1774, helped inspire Jefferson's selection two years later as the principal draftsman of the *Declaration*.[64] They express his view at that time of the basic human rights of "British America." What is more, they express his view also of the basic human rights at all times of *everyone everywhere*. Life and liberty cannot be separated.

I am no pacifist. Not long after my visit to the Jefferson Memorial in 1991, I cast my first substantive vote as a Member of Congress. It was a vote in favor of the Congressional resolution that authorized the President of the United States to take military action in what became the Persian Gulf War.[65] It was a vote to engage as part of a coalition of nations in an act of collective security in response to a clear act of aggression in violation of international law by the murderous regime of Saddam Hussein of Iraq.[66] It was a vote to go to war.

In those same circumstances, I would cast that vote again today. I would vote for any military action necessary to defend America, and I would certainly not require us first to get the permission of others before defending ourselves. One of our human rights is our right to defend ourselves. Sometimes we must go to war to do that. Yet, that said, we Americans must look beyond our understandable outrage at the unspeakable evils of terrorism. We must see beyond the superficial political rhetoric that is used by those who seek to cloud our sight. We must pause and peruse the photographs from Abu Ghraib, and we must ask ourselves: what are we defending when we go to war to defend America?

What was it that I swore to uphold when I first took the oath as a Member of Congress on the day after my visit to the Jefferson Memorial? In our "war on terror," we Americans are defending our homes, our families, our borders. But are we not also supposed to be defending something more? Are we not also supposed to be defending the American heritage that we celebrate in all of those shining marble memorials in our national garden? Are we not also supposed to be defending the validity of Jefferson's noble words about human rights that are carved into the Jefferson Memorial?

Whatever else we may do as Americans, we must tend our garden. Whatever else we may be defending as Americans, we must defend the truth of Jefferson's words. Just as those words are carved into the Jefferson Memorial, so too must they be carved into all we say and all we do as Americans. For his words about human rights give expression to what has always been the best part of America. They give voice to the revolutionary idea that we all have human rights. They give voice to the breathtaking, world-shaking, freedom-making idea that human rights are universal.[67]

The Jeffersonian belief in the universality of human rights is the seed of the American garden. It is the audacious assumption on which America was founded. It has been, from the beginning, the most basic American belief. It has been the essential, the quintessential belief that we Americans have always professed, and that has always beckoned from America to the rest of the world. It is the reason why so many visitors from other countries have long made the pilgrimage from afar to the Jefferson Memorial. They come to share in the "radical thought" of his "magic words."[68]

Jefferson certainly believed that we must defend ourselves.[69] He would be among the first to acknowledge that the "hand of force" must be used from time to time.[70] He not only wrote the Declaration of Independence, he also signed it.[71] Later, he favored aggressive action against the pirates of Tripoli who were the "seafaring terrorists" of his time.[72] He would surely support our efforts in our time to maintain our independence in the aftermath of terrorist attacks through our "war on terror." Jefferson would, however, caution us now, as he did then, to remember always that although the "hand of force" may destroy both life and liberty, the "hand of force" can never "disjoin them."[73]

Perhaps the most radical aspect of the Jeffersonian vision of human rights is its universal application.[74] In this vision that has long been the bedrock American belief, the use of force can never erase the God-given right of every human being to be treated with humanity. The least of us is entitled to the same humane treatment as the rest of us. This is also true of the worst of us. There are no exceptions to the universality of human rights. If there were exceptions, then human rights would not truly be universal.

As Jefferson wrote so memorably in the Declaration of Independence, the rights of life, liberty, and the pursuit of happiness are "among" the rights with which we have each been "endowed" by our Creator, and these "certain" rights that are "among" our rights are "unalienable."[75] They are God-given rights that belong to each and every one of us. They are rights that can never be taken away. They are natural rights that are founded on the ultimate sovereignty of every individual. Jefferson lived his long life believing this. He went to his grave believing this. Two years before his death, he wrote, "Nothing then is unchangeable but the inherent and unalienable rights of man."[76]

This is the American idea. This is the American birthright. This is the indispensable American belief. This is what truly makes us "Americans." Not our flag. Not our patriotic anthems. Not our red-white-and-blue rhetoric. Not our economic power. And certainly not our martial might. But this, and this alone: this fundamental belief in the dignity and the worth of every single individual human being; this basic belief in human rights; this enduring belief that human rights are universal; this abiding belief that human rights are immutable and unalienable; this unwavering belief that the rights we each have as human beings do not change, and they cannot be taken away. Without this belief, America is no longer America. Without it, we are no longer Americans. Without it, we will surely lose our way along the meandering paths of the garden, and we will decline and fall as a nation among the thorns we will fail to see.

There are many good reasons to oppose torture, any one of which is reason enough to condemn what was done by Americans at Abu Ghraib in betrayal of the basic American belief in the universality of human rights.

There is, first of all, a purely practical reason. Torture does not work. As a means of interrogation, torture does not produce reliable information.[77]

There are literally centuries of accumulated evidence of the unreliability of torture as a means of eliciting the truth.[78] Prisoners will say absolutely anything while under torture in the desperate hope of making the torture stop.[79] Even in the medieval days of the Spanish Inquisition, this was widely known. At least formally, a confession to an inquisitor had to be voluntary.[80] The rules governing the Inquisition required that a confession made under torture "must be repeated the next day without torture, 'voluntarily.'"[81]

Another reason to oppose torture is because torture is counterproductive. We might be tempted to ask: Why not engage in torture? Have our opponents not "tortured" us with their reign of terror? But simple logic suggests that, if we torture others, they will, when they get the chance, also torture us. Even Hitler and his Nazis generally understood this. It was not a respect for human rights that caused them largely to refrain from torturing prisoners of war. It was logic. As Democratic Senator Joe Biden of Delaware — a supporter of the American military action in Iraq — explained to the Attorney General of the United States in a recent Congressional hearing, "There's a reason why we sign these treaties . . . so when Americans are captured they are not tortured. That's the reason, in case anybody forgets it."[82]

Another reason to oppose torture is because torture is against the law.[83] It is against American law, and it is against international law.[84] In addition to prohibitions against the use of torture in U.S. statutes, there are also prohibitions against torture in "these treaties" to which Senator Biden rightly referred.[85] The law prohibits torture, and thus the rule of law requires us to oppose torture. And is not ours a nation that respects and upholds the rule of law? Is not ours a nation that knows that the rights of individual human beings can rightly be restricted only through the due process of the rule of law? Is not ours a nation that understands that, without the rule of law, there can be no freedom to enjoy any of our human rights?

Is not ours a government of laws, and not of men?

Jefferson believed it ought to be. Indeed, he believed it had to be. Jefferson told us that ours must be a nation that upholds the rule of law if we hope to hold on to our basic belief in human rights. He saw the rule of law as our sole salvation from "tyranny over the mind of man."[86] On pages twenty-one and twenty-two of the book I bought as a souvenir in the gift shop at the Jefferson Memorial are words that tell us in no uncertain terms what Jefferson thought about the difference between a government of laws and a government of men.[87]

"It would be a dangerous delusion," Jefferson said, "were a confidence in the men of our choice to silence our fears for the safety of our rights: that confidence is everywhere the parent of despotism — free government is founded on jealousy, and not in confidence; it is jealousy and not confidence which prescribes limited constitutions.... In questions of power, then, let no more be heard of confidence in man, but bind him down from mischief by the chains of the Constitution."[88] Amid the mischief of the misadventures of our current leaders, these words — from Jefferson's draft of the Kentucky Resolutions of 1798 — deserve our continued resolution as Americans today.

Our current leaders would doubtless insist to us in soothing "sound bites" that they support the rule of law. But there is little in what they have said and done in the aftermath of Abu Ghraib to indicate that they truly agree with Jefferson about the indispensability of the rule of law. Their first inclination is to say that there is no law.[89] Their next recourse is to say that, even if there is law, the law does not apply.[90] Their last resort is to say that, even if there is law, and even if the law applies, it does not apply to us.[91] Why not? Because we are Americans, of course, and because the true belief of our current leaders seems to be that, in our dealings with the rest of the world, we Americans are above the law.[92]

There is no lack of American laws that condemn torture. In 1991, Congress enacted the Torture Victim Protection Act, which allows victims of torture, or the families of those who are killed by extrajudicial means, to sue their torturers in American courts, regardless of their citizenship, and regardless of where the crime occurred.[93] In 1994, Congress enacted a federal antitorture statute, which defines "torture" and establishes severe penalties for anyone who commits an act of torture outside the United States.[94] As a Member of Congress at the time, I voted for both of these laws. (The Library of Congress provides a convenient list of all Congressional votes on a website it calls "Thomas," in honor of the founder of the library, Thomas Jefferson.[95])

In addition, American law has long acknowledged that our leaders can be held accountable under the law for acts of torture committed by those under their command. The Supreme Court of the United States has stated that those with "command responsibility" can be held "individually responsible" for war crimes committed by their subordinates, not only when they directly ordered those crimes, but also when they knew or they should have known that their subordinates were committing those crimes, and failed to take necessary and reasonable steps to prevent or punish them.[96]

That ruling, in 1946, was in a case relating to the military tribunal convened to consider atrocities committed by Japanese troops under the command of General Tomoyuki Yamashita in the Philippines during World War II.[97] But why would not the same reasoning apply to troops under American command?

Clearly, the war crimes for which there should be such "command responsibility" would include torture. Torture is without doubt a crime against humanity under various international laws requiring humanitarian treatment and the protection of human rights. And, for the most part, these various international laws that outlaw torture as a crime against humanity have long been embraced and endorsed by the United States.

Like every other member of the United Nations, the United States of America has signed the Universal Declaration of Human Rights, which was adopted by the General Assembly of the United Nations in 1948.[98] In echo of Jefferson's ringing phrase in the American Declaration of Independence, Article 3 of this Universal Declaration proclaims: "Everyone has the right to life, liberty and security of person."[99] Further, Article 5 of this Universal Declaration provides: "No one shall be subjected to torture or to cruel, inhuman or degrading treatment or punishment."[100]

In addition to the Universal Declaration of Human Rights, the member States of the United Nations have also adopted the International Covenant on Civil and Political Rights.[101] This global Covenant was concluded in 1966 and entered into force in 1976.[102] It was ratified by the United States in 1992.[103] Echoing the Universal Declaration, and also expanding on it, Article 7 of the Covenant provides: "No one shall be subjected to torture or to cruel, inhuman or degrading treatment or punishment. In particular, no one shall be subjected without his free consent to medical or scientific experimentation."[104]

The International Criminal Tribunal for the Former Yugoslavia — which has been supported in its work by the United States — has said in no uncertain terms that "the prohibition of torture is an absolute value from which nobody must deviate."[105] Closer to home, the United States Court of Appeals for the Second Circuit has said that "deliberate torture perpetrated under color of official authority violates universally accepted norms of the international law of human rights, regardless of the nationality of the parties. . . . Among the rights universally proclaimed by all [n]ations is the right to be free of physical torture. Indeed, for purposes of civil liability, the torturer has become like the pirate and the slave trader before him *hostis humanis generis*, an enemy of all mankind."[106]

In addition to the international law that is found in treaties and other international conventions, there is also "customary international law," which draws on treaty law as one source but exists independently of treaty law as a matter of generally established and generally accepted international custom.[107] Determining whether a particular practice among States has acquired the legal status of international custom, can be difficult, but every State — including the United States — has long agreed that there is such a thing as "customary international law." The Statute of the International Court of Justice — approved by the United States and other members of the United Nations — reflects this shared international understanding in identifying custom as one of the sources of international law.[108]

Under customary international law, there are certain rules that are so "accepted and recognized by the international community of States as a whole" that they are considered to be rules "from which no derogation is permitted."[109] These rules of customary international law are, in the Latin phrasing of international lawyers, *jus cogens*.[110] They are universal and peremptory norms from which there can be no legal departure. Such rules give rise, in yet another lawyers' Latin phrasing, to duties that are *erga omnes*.[111] They give rise to universal duties that are owed to everyone everywhere. Under international law, these universal duties are binding on all States — whether or not those States have ratified the treaties that impose them.[112] Traditionally, the United States, like other countries, has supported these customary legal concepts.[113]

The rule against torture is *jus cogens*. In the words of at least one human rights advocate, and in an expression of the view of many more around the world, "[t]here can be no doubt that the rule against torture has evolved into a *jus cogens* prohibition which every [s]tate has a duty owed to the international community to outlaw and to punish."[114] I share this view. So, too, I think, would Thomas Jefferson.

This view is justified by a variety of international agreements. Most notably, the notion that the right not to be tortured is a basic human right is supported by the Convention Against Torture and Other Cruel, Inhuman and Degrading Treatment or Punishment, which was adopted by the General Assembly of the United Nations in 1984 and entered into force in 1987.[115] At last count, 137 of the States that are members of the United Nations are parties to this Convention.[116] One of them is the United States of America.[117]

The 1984 Convention Against Torture clarifies that under international law, every country has an obligation to prevent torture, and torture is never justified. Article 2(1) of the torture convention provides: "Each State Party shall take effective legislative, administrative, judicial or other measures to prevent acts of torture in any territory under its jurisdiction."[118] Article 2(2) of the torture convention provides: "No exceptional circumstances whatsoever, whether a state of war or a threat of war, internal political instability or any other public emergency, may be invoked as a justification of torture."[119] The United States ratified the Convention Against Torture in 1994.[120] As is permitted under international law, the American ratification was subject to a number of express reservations, but none of those reservations relate to these absolute obligations of Article 2 of the torture convention.[121]

In addition to this international convention against torture, there are the four Geneva Conventions.[122] The Geneva Conventions have their antecedents in the 19th century, were negotiated in their current form following World War II, and were concluded in 1949.[123] The four conventions cover, respectively, the treatment of the wounded and sick on land, the treatment of the wounded and sick at sea, the treatment of prisoners of war, and the treatment of civilians in time of war.[124] The Geneva Conventions have been ratified by nearly two hundred States.[125] All of the member States of the United Nations have ratified them — including the United States of America.[126] Indeed, the United States has been a party to the Geneva Conventions since 1955.[127]

Moreover, U.S. domestic law requires compliance with the important provisions of the four Geneva Conventions. The War Crimes Act of 1996, as amended, grants jurisdiction to federal district courts in the United States over certain violations of the Geneva Conventions by or against a member of the armed forces of the United States or a citizen of the United States either "inside or outside of the United States."[128] It makes grave breaches of the Geneva Conventions — including torture — war crimes that are punishable by penalties up to and including life imprisonment or the death penalty.[129] The war crimes covered by the statute include those falling under "common Article 3" of the Geneva Conventions.[130] Common Article 3 — so-called because it is identical in all four Geneva Conventions — specifically prohibits a number of different kinds of inhumane treatment.[131] Article 3 includes prohibitions of hostage-taking, extra-judicial executions, murder, mutilation, "cruel treatment," and "outrages upon personal dignity."[132] It also includes a ban on torture.[133]

The most recent international agreement that addresses the issue of torture is the Rome Statute of the International Criminal Court ("ICC"), which was adopted in 1998 at the United Nations Conference in Rome, Italy.[134] The Rome Statute created a permanent ICC.[135] This new international court has jurisdiction over genocide, the crime of aggression, war crimes, and crimes against humanity.[136] Under the Rome Statute, "crimes against humanity" specifically include "torture."[137] Our previous leaders in the United States signed the Rome Statute.[138] In an act that is decidedly dubious under international law, our current leaders have purported to "un-sign" it.[139] They have professed to erase America's signature from this international treaty.[140]

This is typical of the attitude of our current leaders to all of the national and international laws that condemn the use of torture. Time and again, they have acted in ways that suggest that they would prefer to erase the letter of the law. Time and again, they have interpreted the law in ways that suggest that law must yield to necessity in the face of the threat of unprecedented terror. Time and again, they have implied that the rule of law must submit to the rule of expediency in the aftermath of the tragic events of September 11, 2001.

Because of "leaks" to the press, we have been able to read confidential memos prepared by lawyers in the current administration that attempt to provide legal justification for the use of torture in interrogating suspected terrorists.[141] As Professor Allison Marston Danner of Vanderbilt University Law School has pointed out, "[w]hat is most disturbing" about what we have been able to read because of these leaks "is . . . the fact that lawyers from the Department of Justice, as well as the Department of Defense, have signed off on memos that represent 'how to' guides to circumventing U.S. laws and the Constitution."[142] In these memos, lawyers for our current leaders focus not on ways to follow the law, but on ways to evade the law. They suggest that the President's "inherent constitutional authority to manage a military campaign" overrides all of the domestic laws and the international conventions that prohibit the use of torture.[143] They go so far as to suggest that, in the "war on terrorism," torture "may be justified."[144]

In early August 2002, Jay S. Bybee, head of the Office of Legal Counsel in the Department of Justice, advised Alberto R. Gonzales, Counsel to the President in the White House: "Certain acts may be cruel, inhuman, or degrading, but still not produce pain and suffering of the requisite intensity to fall within [a legal] proscription against torture....

We conclude that for an act to constitute torture ... it must inflict pain that is difficult to endure. Physical pain amounting to torture must be equivalent in intensity to the pain accompanying serious physical injury, such as organ failure, impairment of bodily function, or even death."[145] President Bush later appointed Bybee to the United States Court of Appeals for the Ninth Circuit.[146]

Gonzales, the President's counsel, advises him that the "nature of the new war" on terror "renders obsolete Geneva's strict limitations on questioning of enemy wounded" and renders some of the other provisions of the Geneva Conventions "quaint."[147] The Secretary of Defense argues that the Geneva Conventions do not "precisely apply" to today's "set of facts."[148] We do not know if the President of the United States agrees with this conclusion. We do know that he has not said otherwise.

As our current leaders search for rationalizations to conclude that existing international law is "quaint" and "obsolete" for dealing with prisoners in the "war on terror," much of the rest of the world continues to work to strengthen the international law against torture. In December 2002, after a decade of negotiation, the General Assembly of the United Nations adopted an "Optional Protocol" to the U.N. Convention Against Torture.[149] This "Optional Protocol" will allow independent national and international experts to make regular visits to places of detention within the States that are parties to the Convention in order to assess the treatment of the wounded, and to make recommendations for improving their treatment.[150] There were only four votes against the "Optional Protocol" in the General Assembly. Those votes were cast by the Marshall Islands, Nigeria, Palau — and the United States of America.[151]

This is not surprising. At almost every turn, those who lead America today have cast the vote of America, in the United Nations and in numerous other international endeavors, against international law, and especially against global efforts to extend the current reach of international law.[152] They have rescinded America's previous signature of the Kyoto Accord on global climate change.[153] They have renounced the treaty on anti-ballistic missiles.[154] They have refused to seek ratification of a treaty banning land mines.[155] They have opposed a proposed treaty regulating international trade in small arms.[156] They have hindered enforcement of a treaty banning biological weapons.[157] And they have tried repeatedly to exempt American troops from prosecution by the new ICC.[158] The laws against torture are only some among the many current and proposed international laws that our current leaders would rather not apply to America and to Americans. At almost every turn, they have shown contempt for international law, contempt for the international rule of law, and contempt for the very concept of international cooperation that is essential to making international law and to upholding the international rule of law.

Their contempt has consequences.

There are many sources in many of the cultural and philosophical traditions throughout the world for the belief that there are human rights, and for the belief also that human rights are universal. But few in the world would deny that all of the many international laws that require humane treatment and respect for human rights can be seen at least in part as having been sown by the seeds of Thomas Jefferson's noble words.[159] All of those laws are efforts to heed Jefferson's admonition to rely in the unrelenting fight against tyranny on the government of laws and not of men. They are the flourishing of his revolutionary belief in basic human rights.

The international laws that affirm human rights and that require humane treatment are flowers that have long flourished in the American garden. If we choose to undermine international law, and if we choose to undermine the international rule of law, then we trample on those flowers. If we trample on the flowers, they will die, the thorns will grow, and we will lose our way along the winding paths of the garden.

We can pretend that torture is not torture if we refuse to call it "torture." The report of the Red Cross said specifically that some of the incidents that occurred at Abu Ghraib "were tantamount to torture."[160] The current leaders of the United States of America stubbornly insist otherwise.[161] The legal memos that have been "leaked" to the world give the narrowest possible definitions of torture and other prohibited acts of inhumane treatment.[162] The international investigation ordered by the Department of the Army speaks of the commitment of "egregious acts and grave breaches of international law" at Abu Ghraib, but stops short of using the word "torture."[163] The Secretary of Defense explains at a press conference, "[m]y impression is that what has been charged thus far is abuse, which I believe technically is different from torture, and therefore I'm not going to address the 'torture' word."[164] And, of course, at every turn, every effort is made to portray whatever it was that happened at Abu Ghraib — whether it was "torture" or not — as the aberrational acts of an errant few, and not as the predictable outcome in the field of a pronounced policy of contempt at the highest levels of the current administration for the laws that are supposed to safeguard human rights against such "abuse."[165]

We lawyers can — as lawyers often do — quibble about definitions. We can debate about the fine distinctions in the definitions in the national and international laws on humane treatment and human rights. We can quarrel about where to draw the fine lines in the law between humane and inhumane treatment. We can argue about the fine lines that can be drawn be ween inhumane treatment and abuse, and between abuse and torture. We can if we choose — and as the lawyers who serve our current leaders largely choose to do — look for ways to evade the law instead of looking for ways to obey it. We can refuse to address the "torture" word. But the thorns remain, and the thorns are all the more visible when we trample on the flowers. Our refusal to see the thorns does not remove them.

The various definitions of "torture" in American law and in the international laws that ban torture are very much the same.[166] In lawyerly fashion, we can read those definitions. If we are American lawyers, we can choose to rely on how our elected representatives in the Congress of the United States have defined "torture" in American law.[167] Here then is how one U.S. statute defines "torture." It says: "'torture' means an act committed by a person acting under the color of law specifically intended to inflict severe physical or mental pain or suffering (other than pain or suffering incidental to lawful sanctions) upon another person within his custody or physical control."[168]

The same U.S. statute goes on to define "severe mental pain or suffering" as "the prolonged mental harm caused by or resulting from — (A) the intentional infliction or threatened infliction of severe physical pain or suffering; (B) the administration or application, or threatened administration or application, of mind-altering substances or other procedures calculated to disrupt profoundly the senses or the personality; (C) the threat of imminent death; or (D) the threat that another person will imminently be subjected to death, severe physical pain or suffering, or the administration or application of mind-altering substances or other procedures calculated to disrupt profoundly the senses or personality."[169]

Tell me. Do any or all of the "enhanced interrogation techniques" that have been approved by our current leaders fall within this definition? What about so-called "water boarding" — when an inmate is strapped down, forcibly immersed under water, made to struggle for breath, and made to believe he will be drowned? What about prolonged placement in painful "stress positions?" What about extended "sleep deprivation?"

What about the "physical coercion" of old-fashioned beatings? Are these what we define as "torture"? Or is the Honorable Judge Bybee of the Ninth Circuit correct in his conclusion that, to amount to "torture," the pain must be "equivalent in intensity" to that of "organ failure, impairment of bodily function, or even death?"[170]

We lawyers can quarrel all we like over whether the hoods and the other humiliations at Abu Ghraib fall within this U.S. statutory definition or any of the other similar definitions of "torture" in American and international law. But recall the photographs from Abu Ghraib, recall especially the photograph I saw from Abu Ghraib in that magazine on my flight home from Argentina, and judge for yourself. Is the image in that photograph an image of human humiliation sufficient to meet the definition of "torture" I have recited from duly enacted American law? Moreover, is there not something more that ought to concern us over and above our quibbles about legal definitions? No matter how we may define "torture" according to law, must we not also define our actions according to some moral standard of right and wrong?

The internal report of U.S. Army Major Gen. Antonio M. Taguba on the abuses in the prison at Abu Ghraib was made public after the media released the photographs of that abuse.[171] The Taguba Report describes incidents of "sadistic, blatant, and wanton criminal abuses . . . inflicted on several detainees ... [that were] systemic and illegal."[172] These incidents included, among other atrocities, physical abuse, videotaping and photographing both male and female prisoners in the nude, posing and photographing prisoners in various sexually explicit positions, forcing a female prisoner to have sex with a male prison guard, using nuzzled military dogs to frighten and intimidate prisoners, and much more.[173] Separate and apart from the question of whether all of this is legal, is the moral question of whether it is right or wrong.

Still another reason to oppose torture is because torture, whether it is legal or not, is simply immoral.[174] Beyond law is morality. Beyond the quibbling questions of lawyers is the simple question of right and wrong. Others may contend otherwise in our all too relativistic, "postmodern" world.[175] Others may quarrel with the contention of Jefferson and other Enlightenment thinkers that there can be such a thing as a "universal intelligibility" in the world.[176] Others may contend that a "new paradigm" in our post-"9/11" world has somehow altered the previous dictates of both law and morality in ways that must alter also our traditional notions of right and wrong.[177] But I remain with Jefferson. I continue to cling to the belief that there are such absolutes as right and wrong — whatever the circumstances. And the torture of another human being is just plain wrong.

Missing from the memos of the lawyers in the current administration was a simple admonition: "But this would be wrong." Whatever distinctions we may try to make legally, it is simply wrong morally to submit another human being to the atrocities that were committed by Americans, and in the name of Americans, in the prison at Abu Ghraib. The lines that matter are not drawn only by law and by lawyers. No legal memorandum, no matter how persuasive the distinctions it makes, can change the dictates of morality. Over and above what the law may require of us looms our knowledge of what is required of us by the simple fact of our humanity.[178] Over and above the bounds of the law is the moral imperative imposed by our mutual humanity with others.[179]

Does this moral imperative have exceptions? Should it matter who the "others" are? Should it matter if they are "prisoners of war" or not? Should it matter if they are "terrorists" or not? Should it matter if they are torturers or not? The "war on terror" raises these questions in challenge to this moral imperative. Regardless of what the law may say in answer to these questions, what does morality say? Is there one morality where some of us are concerned, and another morality for some "others?"

Jefferson did not think so. "I know but one code of morality for man," he said, "whether acting singly or collectively.[180] We American have always agreed with him. For all our confessed shortcomings, for all our admitted failings, for all our poor choices from time to time along the paths of our garden, we Americans have always professed an allegiance to one code of morality for all.[181] Furthermore, we have always aspired to treat all "others" according to one code of morality, whoever they were, wherever they were from, and whatever they may have done in violation of law or morality.[182] Do we still pledge our allegiance to these noble words about morality by Mr. Jefferson?

During the darkest days of the "disappearances" in Argentina, the writer V.S. Naipaul, who would later be awarded the Nobel Prize, traveled to Argentina to see for himself why so many uncivilized things were happening in such a civilized country.[183] He interviewed Argentines on both sides of the "Dirty War."[184] He interviewed those who supported the military *junta*, and he interviewed those who opposed it.[185] He soon discovered that many of those he interviewed on both sides of the "Dirty War" made the same distinction.[186]

Whatever their political sentiments, many of those he interviewed in Argentina made a distinction between what Naipaul described as "good torture" and "bad torture."[187] As he explained their shared view, "Torture was going to continue; but there was good torture and bad torture. Bad torture was what was done by the enemies of the people; good torture was what, when their turn came, the enemies of the people got from the protectors of the people."[188] In other words, "It was 'all right' to torture an 'evildoer'; it was another thing to torture 'a man who's trying to serve the country.'"[189]

The moral courage of the mothers of the "disappeared" has long since defeated such sentiments in Argentina. But what about America? Do we Americans no longer agree with Jefferson that there is only one morality for everyone? Do we believe today in "good torture" and "bad torture?"[190] Have we concluded since September 11, 2001, that there is more than one code of morality, and that it is permissible to apply a different standard of right and wrong to our actions against "evildoers" because of the extent of the evil of their deeds? It seems so. In the action of our current leaders in America, it certainly seems so.

A senior general in the United States Army who investigated the abusive treatment of prisoners at Abu Ghraib tells a hearing of the U.S. Senate that the Central Intelligence Agency — in violation of the Geneva Conventions — may not have registered perhaps as many as 100 detainees in U.S. military facilities.[191] He acknowledges that he has failed in his efforts to obtain documents from the CIA about these unregistered detainees.[192] They are known as "ghost detainees."[193] They are prisoners without names in cells without numbers. They have "disappeared."[194]

In his annual State of the Union Address to the Congress of the United States and to the people of the United States, the President of the United States seems to boast of extra-judicial killings.[195] In a stilling, chilling moment in his speech, he reports that "more than 3,000 suspected terrorists have been arrested in many countries. Many others have met a different fate."[196] Within his familiar smirk, the President adds, "Let's put it this way — they are no longer a problem for the United States and our friends and allies."[197]

They have *disappeared*.

Yes, there is evil in the world. Evil must be acknowledged. Evildoers must be opposed. Evildoers must often be opposed with force. The evildoers who have declared war on America by inflicting terror on Americans and on many others around the world must be opposed with all the will we can muster, with all the strength we can summon, and with all the force we can apply to secure a victory in our "war on terror." But there is not one code of morality that is owed to evildoers and another that is owed to the rest of us.[198] There is, as Jefferson said, only one code of morality, and, because there is only one code of morality, there is no such thing as "good torture" and "bad torture."[199] There is only torture. And torture is always "bad." It is always wrong. If we choose to believe otherwise, then what has long been special about America, about Americans, and about the American garden, will disappear.

The final reason to oppose torture is because torture is "un-American."[200] A garden where the thorns of torture grow is not truly an "American" garden. We Americans may choose to engage in a collective act of national self-denial.[201] We may say, like our President, that the atrocities that were photographed at Abu Ghraib were "disgraceful conduct by a few American troops, who dishonored our country and disregarded our values."[202] We may say, like him, that the photographs "do not represent America."[203] We may say, like him, that this is not "the America I know."[204] But the images in the photographs from Abu Ghraib say otherwise. The torturers in those photographs are *Americans*.

We Americans may choose to say, with Thucydides, that "war is a stern teacher."[205] We may choose to say with that ancient chronicler of the Peloponnesian War among the Greeks that war is a violent and a terrible teacher. The Sicilian expedition from 415 B.C. to 413 B.C. began with the sails of a vast armada of Athenian ships filled with a hopeful wind. It ended with thousands of defeated Athenians dying one by one of unquenchable thirst, parched by an unforgiving sun while trapped in the stone quarries of Syracuse.[206] War, for them, was truly a stern teacher. But we are not ancient Athenians. The torturers in those photographs are *Americans*.

We Americans may also choose to invoke the ancient Old Testament adage of an eye for an eye.[207] We may ask about the abuse at Abu Ghraib, like our Secretary of Defense: "Does it rank up there with chopping someone's head off on television? It doesn't. It doesn't."[208] No, it doesn't. Of course it doesn't. But is this really the measure of America? Is this really the standard for Americans? Does every beheading deserve, if not another, then at least some other, perhaps less hideous, form of inhumane abuse? Does the fact that Saddam Hussein's torture chambers were far worse than ours make ours any less appalling? Again, the torturers in those photographs are *Americans*.

We Americans may choose as well to observe that we live in a world where there is a difference between "ought" and "is." We may choose to point out that ours is a less than perfect world, and that, in our less than perfect world, it is only to be expected that we might occasionally fall short of our highest ideals. We might even note the undeniable historical fact that Jefferson himself, the most eloquent exponent of our ideals, the author of all those noble words, fell short of living up to them. Not far from the winding paths of his garden at Monticello were the cabins of his slaves on Mulberry Row.[209] But again, the torturers in those photographs are *Americans*.

This is supposed to make a difference. This is supposed to make all the difference. As one commentator has put it, "These were, after all, Americans."[210] Americans are not supposed to be torturers. Americans are not supposed to cause "disappearances." The fact that those in charge of the prison at Abu Ghraib are Americans is supposed to make all the difference, because we Americans have always claimed to think that we are different, and, for all the shades of gray of our current day, for all the ways that the America of today differs from the America of Jefferson's day, we still do.

But the truth is we Americans are *not* different. We are just like everyone else in the world. We share the same DNA. We share the same frail and fallible human nature. We share the same fond hope of immortality, and the same fatal fear of an ever-approaching mortality. We share the same mortal fate as all the others of our striving, struggling species. The only thing that makes us different as Americans — the only thing that has ever made us different — is the American ideal of universal human rights that is given its most eloquent expression in the noble words of Thomas Jefferson.

Those of us who are so fortunate as to be able to call ourselves "Americans" have come, we and our forebears, from all over the world. We have come together to live together today, and we have also come together to try to achieve something together tomorrow. We are trying to achieve something together tomorrow, not only for America, but for all the world. What is it we hope to achieve? What is the historic contribution we Americans hope to make to humanity? What is the contribution we hope to make to the future of the world? The answer, now as always, is found in the words of Jefferson.

"The disease of liberty is catching," he said, and we Americans have long hoped to contribute to the future of the world by helping infect all the world with the emancipating malady of liberty.[211] In yet another of Jefferson's metaphors about freedom, he said, during the early days of the American experiment with freedom, "This ball of liberty ... is now so well in motion that it will roll round the globe."[212] Perhaps foremost among America's "Founding Fathers," he foresaw that a worldwide spread of liberty through the American example of liberty, and through the continuing American commitment to liberty, would become America's foremost contribution to the future of the world.

Jefferson still lives for Americans — he is more to us than merely a marble statue in a memorial on the Mall — because he still speaks for what Americans still see as this historic global mission of our country. The American idea is nothing more nor less than the contagious idea of the human opportunities and the human possibilities that are created through the free and liberating exercise of human rights. The American idea is the idea of a liberty that emancipates as it rolls ever onward around the globe. This is an idea that belongs by birth to Americans, but it is also an idea that belongs by equal birthright to everyone else. It is the idea of a universal liberty for all the world that is forever opposed to "every form of tyranny over the mind of man."[213]

Is not torture the worst form of such tyranny? And is not torture therefore the worst form of "anti-Americanism"? What does it say to us about "Americanism" — what does it say to us about all our patriotic pretensions as a nation — when we read that, in between other forms of "abuse," the inmates at Abu Ghraib were made to stand and sing "The Star-Spangled Banner" in the nude?[214] And, above all, what does it say about America, and about "Americanism," to all the rest of the world?

There can be no compromising with terrorism. There can be no compromising with terrorists. There can be no relenting in our "war on terror." But if we embrace a policy that justifies the use of torture, if we defend a policy that rationalizes the use of torture, if we reduce ourselves to engaging in torture, then the "war on terror" will be lost, because the terrorists will have won. They will have won, because they will have caused us to abandon the defining American idea of universal human rights that is the only thing about America that makes Americans different. They will have won the ultimate victory. For it is this very idea that they are most determined to defeat and to destroy with all their terror.

One of his earliest biographers wrote, "If Jefferson was wrong, America is wrong. If America is right, Jefferson was right."[215] Jefferson was right. And America has been right when America has followed

Jefferson. America will be right again only when America returns to the Jeffersonian ideal of universal human rights. Jefferson's noble words about human rights must continue to guide us through the American garden. His words are the only reliable map along the garden's winding paths. They are the only way we can see clearly enough to remove the thorns that impede us.

In our "war on terror," we must be true to the true idea of America that Jefferson's words represent. In all our dealings with the terrorists, we must remember his words, and we must hold ourselves to the higher standard of those words. We must hold ourselves always to the higher standard that service to the emancipating idea of America always demands of all Americans. In service to this higher standard, we must act always as Jefferson would urge us to act.

We must defeat our enemies. We must deny their cause. We must never deny their humanity.

As it is, the thorns are multiplying as we wander onto the wrong path of the garden. As embattled countries often do, we can seek the "last refuge" of a rhetorical patriotism.[216] But this will not lead us back to the right path, and this will not help us see or remove the thorns. We are not exonerated by all the euphemisms of our current leaders about the torture at Abu Ghraib. We are not excused by all their attempts at excuses. Nor are we spared by the ever-shorter attention span of the American people. The photographs from Abu Ghraib may have disappeared from the front pages of the American press, but the images from those photographs have not disappeared from the minds of the rest of the world. What is disappearing from the minds of the rest of the world is the Jeffersonian idea of America as an exemplar and an exponent of universal human rights.

Jefferson's passion for gardens was shared by the greatest of Argentine writers (and one of the greatest of all writers), Jorge Luis Borges. In his early poems, Borges celebrated the beauties of the gardens of Buenos Aires in the peaceful decades long before the "Dirty War."[217] In the celebrated short stories he wrote later in life, Borges, like Jefferson, often relied on metaphors.[218] In his own way, in his short stories and in his other fables, he, like Jefferson, tried to create new worlds with his words.[219] One of his most famous metaphorical fables is entitled *The Garden of Forking Paths*.[220]

The Garden of Forking Paths is a tale within a tale of a scholarly and learned politician who abandons politics and public life "in order to compose a book and a maze."[221] It turns out that "the book and the maze were one and the same thing."[222] The book and the maze he builds in what remains of his life take the form of a labyrinth that is a "garden of forking paths."[223] The forking paths of the garden in Borges' tale contain "all possible outcomes" in all the "various futures" that human choices might make.[224] The garden is forever "incomplete."[225] It is forever in the making. It is forever unfolding in new forks on new paths that result from new human choices. It is a garden that reveals the consequence of human choices.

The American garden is such a garden. It is likewise a garden of forking paths. It offers all possible outcomes. It offers all possible choices. It unfolds along paths that are created by our choices. It reveals the consequences of our choices.

Late in life, in his retirement at Monticello, the aged Jefferson spent part of most mornings working in his garden. He aligned the rows of flowers with a measuring line, and he clipped away excess buds and leaves with his pruning knife.[226] Jefferson tended his garden. He chose his own paths through his garden. So must we all. We must choose our own paths through the garden, and we must understand that we become the choices we make. Like Borges' story of *The Garden of Forking Paths*, our story of our American garden is a story of our success as gardeners. It is a story of the paths we choose, and thus it is a story that has alternative endings.

Freedom is about making choices. Freedom is about choosing our own paths. Freedom is truly freedom only if there are alternative endings. The ending we make to the American story will depend on the choices we make from now on as Americans among the forking paths of our garden.

Why are we Americans not choosing the path of public outrage in response to the photographs from Abu Ghraib? Why are we not marching in protest, like the mothers of the "disappeared" in Argentina, in the garden of our national memory? Why are we not choosing to use our freedom as Americans to make an ending to our story that will be true to the basic idea of what America is supposed to be?

Every choice we make becomes a new path in the garden. That new path can lead us to flowers, or it can lead us to thorns. The essential American idea of universal human rights is "disappearing" now amid the thorns in the garden. But it need not be that way. If we choose the right path, if we tend the garden, if we are true to Thomas Jefferson's words, we can yet see a new flowering of the hopes that were first sown there by Jefferson and by the other freedom-loving Americans who first planted the seed and first cultivated our garden.

On my next visit to Washington, I will walk again in the garden of our national memory. I will make another pilgrimage to the Jefferson Memorial. I will read once again the carved inscriptions of Jefferson's noble words. My hope is that, on that next visit, I will also hear once again the voices of other pilgrims from many other places, come from afar to pay their respects to Jefferson, and to read his words in their own languages. My hope is that, on that next visit, the Jefferson Memorial in the American garden will remain what it has always been — a symbol of the hope held by all the world for a future when everyone throughout the world will have a full flourishing of human rights.

Jefferson would urge us to remember always that the fate of a garden depends on the diligence of the gardeners. Some say that we Americans only pretend to be gardeners for human rights.[227] They say that we do not support human rights at all.[228] They point to the photographs from Abu Ghraib, and they say that all our noble words are only words.[229] But what do we say? What will we choose to cultivate? What path will we choose to take from here through the garden?

Endnotes

[1] Joseph J. Ellis, *American Sphinx: The Character of Thomas Jefferson* 10 (1996).
[2] *Ibid.* at 8 (quoting President Franklin Delano Roosevelt's speech on April 13, 1943 dedicating the Jefferson Memorial on the Tidal Basin).
[3] The Declaration of Independence (U.S. 1776), at http://www.law.indiana.edu/uslawdocs/declaration.html (last visited November 8, 2004).
[4] Letter from Thomas Jefferson to Dr. Benjamin Rush (September 23, 1800), in Thomas Jefferson, *Thomas Jefferson: Writings* 1082 (Merrill D. Peterson Ed., 1984).
[5] Lisa Avery, "A Return to Life: The Right to Identity and the Right to Identify Argentina's 'Living Disappeared'," 27 *Harvard Women's Law Journal* 235, 239 (2004) ("From these abductions [in the early days of the Argentine *Junta*], a new word came into common usage: *desaparecidos*, the 'disappeareds." *Desaparecido* was the word used by the *junta* to deny the kidnapping, torture, and slaying of thousands of Argentines.").
[6] Maria-Victoria Castro, "La mujer Argentina que soy yo [The Argentinean Woman That I Am]," 9 *Cardozo Women's Law Journal*, 321, 336 (2003).
[7] Avery, *supra* note 5, at 247. Every Thursday, the *Madres* gather to participate in the "ritual circling of the Pyramid of Mayo monument [which] grew out of pressure from the police to circulate because the regime prohibited public assembly; the Madres walked counterclockwise to show their defiance." *Id.*

[8] *Asociación Madres de Plaza de Mayo, Historia de las Madres de Paza de Mayo*, at http://www.madres.org (last visited November 20, 2004) ("*Y, bueno, elprimer dia, en esa marcha a Lujdn, usamos el pafiuelo blanco que no era otra cosa, nada mds ni nada menos, que un pafial de nuestros hijos.*" ["And well, the first day, on that march to Lujan, we used the white handkerchief that wasn't much more or much less than our children's diapers."]).

[9] Avery, *supra* note 5, at 247 ("Fourteen women assembled in the main square of Buenos Aires on April 30, 1977, for the first of many silent demonstrations.").

[10] *Ibid.*

[11] Geoffrey Robertson, *Crimes Against Humanity: The Struggle for Global Justice* 245 (1999).

[12] *Ibid.*

[13] Thomas C. Wright, "Human Rights in Latin America: History and Projections for the Twenty-First Century," 30 *CAL. W. INT'L L J.* 303, 311 (2000) ("The harvest of the dirty war was nearly 10,000 people disappeared according to the official inquiry conducted after the restoration of civilian government, but according to human rights groups the figure was some 30,000.").

[14] Avery, *supra* note 5, at 236 ("The military regime practiced a method of repression likened to Hitler's *Nacht und Nebel Erlass* (Night and Fog Decree), in which subversive citizens were made to disappear without a trace. Men, women, and children from all social classes were abducted, as were the elderly, the infirm, and the disabled. Thousands of people went missing, 'never to be seen again.'").

[15] Jacobo Timerman, *Prisoner Without a Name, Cell Without a Number* (Toby Talbot trans., 1980).

[16] Avery, *supra* note 5, at 241; *see also* Wright, *supra* note 13, at 311 ("The armed forces [during the Dirty War] set up some 340 secret detention centers across the country, most of them equipped for torture; one of the favored methods of killing leftists was dropping them, still alive, into the ocean from airplanes. Pregnant women prisoners were often held until they gave birth, then were killed and their babies given to childless military couples.").

[17] Laura Oren, "Righting Child Custody Wrongs: The Children of the 'Disappeared' in Argentina," 14 *Harvard Human Rights Journal* 123, 124 (2001) ("These victims were kidnapped, tortured, and killed; their fate was hidden from their families and the world by burying their bodies in mass graves or throwing them into the sea.").

[18] Robertson, *supra* note 11, at 245.

[19] Janet Koven Levit, "The Constitutionalization of Human Rights in Argentina: Problem or Promise," 37 *Columbia Journal of Transnational Law* 281, 288-92 (1999).

[20] *Ibid.*

[21] *Ibid. See generally* Avery, *supra* note 5.

[22] Avery, *supra* note 5.

²³ "The Mothers of the Plaza De Mayo," at http://lacc.fiu.edu/events-outreach/fulbright/argentina-web/BackgroundMadreshtm (last visited November 1, 2004).
²⁴ *Ibid.*
²⁵ Marguerite Guzman Bouvard, *Revolutionizing Motherhood: The Mothers of the Plaza De Mayo* 2 (1994); *see also Asociacidn Madres de Plaza de Mayo, supra* note 8.
²⁶ *See* Seymour M. Hersh, *Torture at Abu Ghraib*, New Yorker, May 10, 2004, at 42.
²⁷ *Ibid.*
²⁸ *Ticked Off* Orlando Sentinel, May 25, 2004.
²⁹ Elisabeth Bumiller, "White House Letter; Filmmaker Leans Right, Oval Office Swings Open," *New York Times*, September 8, 2003, at A19 ("That was also the day that Mr. Bush flew to New York to see Ground Zero, where he came face to face with the chanting of rescue workers demanding revenge. He said 'I was lifted up by a wave of vengeance and testosterone and anger.., it made your head spin.'"); *see also* Jane Moore, *We Must Root Out the Terror Sympathisers*, SUN (N.Y.), September 8, 2004 ("Forget the 'human rights' of those who commit atrocities on the scale of 9/11 ... the terrorist cells 'sleeping' in various countries have to be flushed out and dealt with. In short, it is time for zero tolerance. Then, only then, will the world even start to feel a safer place.'); Brian Suntken, "We're Called to Forgiveness Not Revenge," *Charlotte Observer*, September 6, 2004 ("Three years after the horrific events of September 11, our [n]ation is still breathing revenge and retribution.").
³⁰ Int'l Comm. Of The Red Cross, Report of The Int'l Comm. Of The Red Cross (Icrc) on The Treatment By The Coalition Forces Of Prisoners Of War And Other Persons Protected by The Geneva Conventions in Iraq During Arrest, Internment, and Interrogation (February 2004) [Hereinafter Report of The Int'l Comm. Of The Red Cross].
³¹ *Ibid.* (emphasis added).
³² Susan Sontag, "Regarding the Torture of Others," *New York Times*, May 23, 2004, at 25, at http://donswaim.com/nytimes.sontag.html ("[T]he photographs are us. That is, they are representative of the fundamental corruptions of any foreign occupation together with the Bush administration's distinctive policies."); *see also* Myriam Marquez, "Not Who Americans Are as a People," *Orlando Sentinel*, May 2, 2004, at G3 ("This is not who we are as a people. Because if it is, we are doomed to lose the war on terror, no matter how much anyone tries to excuse what happened at Abu Ghraib as necessary to break down Iraqi detainees for interrogation.").
³³ "Donald Rumsfeld Should Go," *New York Times*, May 7, 2004, at A30 ("The United States has been humiliated to a point where government officials could not release this year's international human rights report this week for fear of being scoffed at by the rest of the world. The reputation of its brave soldiers has been tarred, and the job of its diplomats made immeasurably harder......").

34 Reuel Marc Gerecht, "Who's Afraid of Abu Ghraib?," *Weekly Standard*, May 24, 2004, at http://www.weeklystandard.com/content/public/articles/000/000/004/096uutti.asp ("'[T]he humiliating scenes of abused Iraqi prisoners' and the war in general 'have turned that country [Iraq] into a model to be feared and avoided in the eyes of many in the Middle East, and a tool in the hands of governments reluctant to change.'").

35 *Ibid.*

36 Roger Cohen et al., "Challenging the Rest of the World with a New Order," *New York Times*, October 12, 2004, at A1 ("[N]ations like Pakistan, Jordan, Egypt and Saudi Arabia, [are] important allies whose leaders are sometimes supportive, but ... many people [there] believe Mr. Bush has ignited a war against Islam. Their reliability is uncertain.").

37 *Ibid.* ("It is a characterization of Mr. Bush's foreign policy style often heard around the world: bullying, unreceptive, brazen. The result, critics of this administration contend, has been a disastrous loss of international support, damage to American credibility, the sullying of America's image and a devastating war that has already taken more than 1,000 American lives."); *see also* "Abu Ghraib, Unresolved," *New York Times*, October 28, 2004, at A28 ("When the Abu Ghraib prison scandal first broke, the Bush administration struck a pose of righteous indignation. It assured the world that... the United States would never condone the atrocities... that it would punish those responsible for any abuse ... and that it was committed to the Geneva Convention and the rights of prisoners. None of this appears to be true."); Roger Cohen et al., *supra* note 36 ("The result ...has been a disastrous loss of international support, damage to American credibility, the sullying of America's image and a devastating war that has already taken more than 1,000 American lives.").

38 Eric Schmitt, "Abuse Panel Says Rules on Inmates Need Overhaul," *New York Times*, August 25, 2004, at A1. See "Rumsfeld Testifies Before House Armed Services Committee," *Washington Post*, May 7, 2004, at www.washingtonpost.com/ac2/wp-dyn/A9251-2004May7? [hereinafter *Rumsfeld Testifies*]. General Myers testified that he knew for months that the photos existed, but he had not seen them. *See Rumsfeld Testifies, supra.*

39 Eric Schmitt, "Rumsfeld Mischaracterizes Findings of 2 Studies on U.S. Abuse at Iraqi Interrogations," *New York Times*, August 28, 2004, at A6 [hereinafter Schmitt, *Rumsfeld Mischaracterizes Findings*].

40 *Ibid.*

41 *See* Press Release, Int'l Media Center, President Bush Holds Conference Following G8 Summit (June 10, 2004), at www.whitehouse.gov/news/releases/2004/06/ [hereinafter President Bush Holds Conference].

42 John Harwood, "New Values Debate Over Prisoner Abuse Could Hurt Bush," *Wall Street Journal*, June 23, 2004, at A4.

43 *Ibid.; see also* President Bush Holds Conference, *supra* note 41.

44 *Rumsfeld Testifies, supra* note 38 ("This situation ... is nothing less than tragic. The Iraqi people try to build a free and open society. And I regret that they saw such a flagrant violation of the very principles that are the cornerstone of such a society.").
45 Schmitt, *Rumsfeld Mischaracterizes Findings, supra* note 39, at 6.
46 Harwood, *supra* note 42, at 4.
47 *Ibid.*
48 U.S. State Department, Supporting Human Rights and Democracy. The U.S. Record 2003–2004 (2004), at www.state.gov/g/drl/rls/shrd/2003/ (last visited November 20, 2004).
49 *Ibid.*
50 *Ibid.*
51 *Ibid.*
52 *Ibid.*
53 Richard Morin and Claudia Deane, "Americans Split on How to Interrogate," *Washington Post*, May 28, 2004, at A20.
54 *Ibid.*
55 David McCullough, *John Adams* 357 (2001).
56 Letter From Thomas Jefferson to Charles Willson Peale (August 20, 1811), in Thomas Jefferson, *Thomas Jefferson: Writings* 1249 (Merrill D. Peterson Ed., 1984).
57 Andrew Burstein, *The Inner Jefferson: Portrait of a Grieving Optimist* 21 (1995). *See The Garden and Farm Books of Thomas Jefferson* 191 (Robert C. Baron, Ed., 1987).
58 Daniel J. Boorstin, *The Lost World of Thomas Jefferson* 41–53 (1948).
59 Karl Lehmann, *Thomas Jefferson: American Humanist* 156–76 (1947).
60 *See generally* McCullough, *supra* note 55, at 356–62; Willard Sterne Randall, *Thomas Jefferson: A Life* 418–25 (1993).
61 Thomas Jefferson, *Thomas Jefferson: His Life and Words* (Nick Beilenson Ed., 1986) [Hereinafter Jefferson: His Life and Words].
62 *Ibid.* at 15.
63 Thomas Jefferson, *A Summary View of the Rights of British America* (1774), at http://libertyonline.hypermall.com/Jefferson/Summary-Body.html (last visited November 7, 2004).
64 MSN Encarta Encyclopedia, Declaration Of Independence, at http://encarta.msn.com/encyclopedia_761559234/Declarationofindependence.html (last visited November 7, 2004).
65 Persian Gulf Resolution, H.R.J. Res. 658, 101st Cong. (1991), S.Con.Res. 147, 101st Cong. (1991).
66 *Ibid.*
67 The Declaration of Independence para. 2 (U.S. 1776) ("We hold these truths to be self-evident, that all men are created equal, that they are endowed by their

Creator with certain unalienable Rights, that among these are Life, Liberty and the pursuit of Happiness.").

[68] Ellis, *supra* note 1, at 10-11.

[69] Letter from Thomas Jefferson to William Smith (November 13, 1787), in Thomas Jefferson, Thomas Jefferson: Writings 911 (Merrill D. Peterson Ed., 1984) ("The tree of liberty must be refreshed from time to time with the blood of patriots & tyrants.").

[70] Jefferson, *A Summary View of the Rights of British America*, *supra* note 63.

[71] The Declaration of Independence (U.S. 1776).

[72] Ellis, *supra* note 1, at 75–76.

[73] Jefferson, *A Summary View of the Rights of British America*, *supra* note 63.

[74] The Declaration of Independence (U.S. 1776); *see also* MSN Encarta Encyclopedia, *supra* note 64.

[75] The Declaration of Independence (U.S. 1776).

[76] Letter from Thomas Jefferson to Major John Cartwright (June 5, 1824), in Thomas Jefferson, *Thomas Jefferson: Writings* 1490, 1494 (Merrill D. Peterson Ed., 1984).

[77] Amnesty International USA, "Stop Torture: Talking Points: How To Respond To Those Advocating The Use Of Torture," at http://www.amnestyusa.org/stoptorture/talking-points.html (last visited November 7, 2004).

[78] Peter Brooks, *Troubling Confessions: Speaking Guilt in Law and Literature* 154–55 (2000) (discussing the use of torture during the Spanish Inquisition including the Inquisitors' procedures for overcoming the unreliability of confessions made under pain of torture).

[79] Amnesty International USA, *supra* note 77.

[80] Brooks, *supra* note 78.

[81] *Ibid.*

[82] "A Memo Too Far: Torture," *Economist*, June 12, 2004, at 29.

[83] *See* U.S. Const. amend. VIII (prohibiting "cruel and unusual punishment"); *see also Universal Declaration of Human Rights*, G.A. Res. 217A (III), 3rd Sess., art. 5, U.N. Doc. A/RES/3/217 (1948) (stating that "No one shall be subject to torture.").

[84] *See* U.S. Const. amend. VIII; *see also Universal Declaration of Human Rights*, *supra* note 83.

[85] "A Memo Too Far: Torture" *supra* note 82.

[86] Letter from Thomas Jefferson to Benjamin Rush (September 23, 1800), in Thomas Jefferson, *Thomas Jefferson: Writings* 1082 (Merrill D. Peterson Ed., 1984).

[87] *Jefferson: His Life and Words*, *supra* note 61, at 21–22.

[88] *Ibid. See Draft of Kentucky Resolutions*, *reprinted in* Thomas Jefferson, Thomas Jefferson: Writings 449, 454–55 (Merrill D. Peterson Ed., 1984).

[89] *See, e.g.*, Bruce Zagaris, *Human Rights, Counter-Terrorism, War and Detention Policy: U.S. and British Detention Policies Continue to Unravel and Draw*

Litigation and Criticism, 20(8) Int'l Enforcement L. Rep. 338, § 5 (discussing White House memoranda that attempted to find loopholes in international law prohibiting torture).

⁹⁰ *Ibid.* (discussing the initiation of a "Common Plan" to violate the Geneva Conventions).

⁹¹ *Ibid.* (discussing how international laws and U.S. laws against torture were to be narrowly interpreted by the U.S. government).

⁹² *Ibid.*

⁹³ Torture Victim Protection Act of 1991, 28 U.S.C. § 1350 (1992) (giving the district courts original jurisdiction of any civil action by a non-U.S. citizen for a tort in violation of either an international law or a treaty of the United States).

⁹⁴ 18 U.S.C. §§ 2340, 2340A, 2340B (1994).

⁹⁵ Library of Congress, Thomas: Legislative Information on The Internet, at http://thomas.loc.gov (last visited October 24, 2004).

⁹⁶ Yamashita v. Styer, 327 U.S. 1, 15–16 (1946); *see also* Allison Marston Danner and Jenny S. Martinez, "Commanders Can Be Held Liable for Actions of Their Subordinates," *Miami Herald*, August 31, 2004.

⁹⁷ *Yamashita*, 327 U.S. at 15–16.

⁹⁸ *See generally Universal Declaration of Human Rights, supra* note 83.

⁹⁹ *Ibid.* at art. 3.

¹⁰⁰ *Ibid.* at art. 5.

¹⁰¹ *International Covenant on Civil and Political Rights*, G.A. Res. 2200A (XXI), U.N. Gaor, 21st Sess., Supp. No. 16, at 52, U.N. Doc. A/6316 (1966).

¹⁰² *Ibid.*

¹⁰³ Office of the U.N. High Commissioner for Human Rights, Status of Ratifications of the Principal International Human Rights Treaties, at http://www.unhchr.ch/pdf/report.pdf.

¹⁰⁴ *International Covenant on Civil and Political Rights, supra* note 101, art. 7.

¹⁰⁵ Prosecutor v. Anton Furundzija, Case IT-95-17/1-T, [1988] Int'l Crim. Trib. for Fmr. Yugoslavia (Trial Chamber II), 154, *reprinted in* [1999] 38 I.L.M. 317, 349, 154.

¹⁰⁶ Filartiga v. Pefia-Irala, 630 F.2d 876, 878, 890 (2d Cir. 1980).

¹⁰⁷ Barry E. Carter et al., *International Law* 120–24 (4th ed. 2003); *see also* Thefreedicrionary.Com (2004), at http://encyclopedia.thefreedictionary.com/custom+(law) (last visited November 8, 2004) (defining *customary international law* as "the Law of Nations or the legal norms that have developed through the customary exchanges between [s]tates over time, whether based on diplomacy or aggression").

¹⁰⁸ Statute of The International Court of Justice art. 38(1)(b), at http://www.icj-cij.org/icjwww/ibasicdocuments/ibasictext/ibasicstatute.htm (last visited October 25, 2004).

¹⁰⁹ Vienna Convention on the Law of Treaties, May 22, 1969, art. 53, 8 I.L.M. 679 (entered into force January 27, 1980).

[110] Barry E. Carter et al., *International Law* 107-9 (4th ed.); *see also* thefreedictionary.com (2004), at http://encyclopedia.thefreedictionary.com/jus%20cogens (last visited November 8, 2004) (defining *jus cogens* as "a peremptory norm ... a fundamental principle of international law considered to have acceptance among the international community of [s]tates as a whole. Unlike customary law that has traditionally required consent and allows the alteration of its obligations between [s]tates through treaties, peremptory norms cannot be violated by any [s]tate.").

[111] *See generally* Olivia Lopes Pegna, "Counter-claims and Obligations Erga Omnes Before the International Court of Justice," 9 *European Journal of International Law* 724 (1998), at http://www.ejil.org/journal/Vol9/No4/090724.pdf (last visited November 8, 2004).

[112] *See, e.g.*, Frederic L. Kirgis, "Treaties as Binding International Obligation," American Society of International Law (May 1997), at http://www.asil.org/insights/insight9.htm (last visited November 8, 2004).

[113] *Ibid.*

[114] Robertson, *supra* note 11, at 98.

[115] Convention Against Torture and Other Cruel, Inhuman or Degrading Treatment, G.A. Res. 39/46, U.N. GAOR, 39th Sess., Supp. No. 51, at 197, U.N. Doc. A/ 39/51 (1984), *opened for signature* December 10, 1984, 1465 U.N.T.S. 85 (entered into force June 26, 1987) [hereinafter Convention Against Torture].

[116] Office of the U.N. High Commissioner for Human Rights, Status of Ratification of the Convention Against Torture, at http://www.ohchr.org/english/law/catratify.htm [hereinafter Status Of Ratification of the Convention Against Torture].

[117] *Ibid.*

[118] Convention Against Torture, *supra* note 115, art. 2(1).

[119] *Ibid.* at art. 2(2).

[120] Status of Ratification of the Convention Against Torture, *supra* note 116.

[121] Office of The U.N. High Commissioner for Human Rights, Declarations and Reservations of the Convention Against Torture, at http://www.unhchr.ch/html/menu2/6/cat/treaties/convention-reserv.htm (last visited Nov. 21, 2004) [hereinafter Declarations And Reservations Of The Convention Against Torture].

[122] Convention for the Amelioration of the Condition of the Wounded and Sick in Armed Forces in the Field, August 12, 1949, 6 U.S.T. 3114, 75 U.N.T.S. 31; Convention for the Amelioration of the Condition of the Wounded, Sick, and Shipwrecked Members of Armed Forces at Sea, August 12, 1949, 6 U.S.T. 3217, 75 U.N.T.S. 85; Convention Relative to Treatment of Prisoners of War, August 12, 1949, 6 U.S.T. 3316, 75 U.N.T.S. 135; and Convention Relative to the Protection of Civilian Persons in Time of War, August 12, 1949, 6 U.S.T. 3516, 75 U.N.T.S. 287 [hereinafter Geneva Conventions].

[123] Francois Bugnion, "The International Committee of the Red Cross and the Development of International Humanitarian Law," 5 *Chicago Journal of International Law* 191, 193–94 (2004).

[124] Geneva Conventions, *supra* note 122.

[125] Int'l Comm. of The Red Cross, States Party to The Geneva Conventions and Their Additional Protocols, at http://www.icrc.org/Web/eng/siteengO.nsf/htmlall/partygc/$File/Conventions%20de%2GenSve%20et%2OProtocoles%20additionnels%20ENG-logo.pdf (noting that 192 States are parties to the Geneva Conventions).

[126] *Ibid.* (noting that all 191 members of the United Nations are parties to the Geneva Conventions).

[127] *Ibid.* (noting that the United States ratified the Geneva Conventions on August 2, 1955).

[128] War Crimes Act of 1996, 18 U.S.C. § 2441 (2004) (entered into force November 26, 1997)

[129] 18 U.S.C. § 2441 (a).

[130] Geneva Conventions, *supra* note 122, art. 3; *see also* 18 U.S.C. § 2441 (c) (3) (2004).

[131] Geneva Conventions, *supra* note 122, art. 3.

[132] *Ibid.* at art. 3(1).

[133] *Ibid.* at art. 3(1)(a).

[134] Rome Statute of the International Criminal Court, U.N. Doc. A/ CONF.183/9, *opened for signature* July 17, 1998, 2187 U.N.T.S. 3 (entered into force July 1, 2002) [hereinafter Rome Statute].

[135] *Ibid.* at art. 1.

[136] *Ibid.* at art. 5.

[137] *Ibid.* at art. 7.

[138] Jess Bravin, "U.S. to Pull Out of World Court on War Crimes," *Wall Street Journal*, May 6, 2002, at A4 (noting that the Clinton Administration signed the Rome Statute on December 31, 2000).

[139] *Ibid.* (noting that "international law generally requires that a country not undercut a treaty it has signed, even if it hasn't been ratified"); *see also* Ratification Status of the Rome Statute, at http://www.isc-icc.org/signedlist.html (last visited November 8, 2004) (noting that on May 6, 2002, the U.S. government informed the U.N. Secretary General that the United States "does not intend to be bound by its signature to the Rome Statute and that it has no intention to ratify.").

[140] Rome Statute, *supra* note 134, art. 7.

[141] "Legalizing Torture," *Washington Post*, June 9, 2004, at A20.

[142] Allison Marston Danner, "Administration's Position 'Appalling,'" *Miami Herald*, June 11, 2004.

[143] Dana Priest and R. Jeffrey Smith, "Memo Offered Justification for Use of Torture: Justice Dept. Gave Advice in 2002," *Washington Post*, June 8, 2004, at A1 (quoting a report by lawyers of the Department of Defense in March 2003).

[144] *Ibid.* (quoting a memorandum to the President by the Department of Justice in August 2002).
[145] Seymour M. Hersh, "Chain of Command: The Road From 9/11 To Abu Ghraib 4-5 (2004)." This memorandum was "leaked" to *Newsweek* in May 2004.
[146] Kathleen Clark and Julie Mertus, "Torturing the Law: The Justice Department's Legal Contortions on Interrogation," *Washington Post*, June 20, 2004, at B3.
[147] Anthony Lewis, "Making Torture Legal," *New York Review of Books*, July 15, 2004, at 4 (quoting a memorandum to the President by White House Counsel Alberto R. Gonzales on January 25, 2002).
[148] Fareed Zakaria, "The Price of Arrogance," *Newsweek*, May 17, 2004, at 39 (quoting Secretary of Defense Donald Rumsfeld).
[149] Optional Protocol to the Convention Against Torture and Other Cruel, Inhuman or Degrading Treatment or Punishment, December 18, 2002, G.A. Res. 57/199, U.N. GAOR, 57th Sess., 42 I.L.M. 26 (2003) (entered into force February 4, 2003) [hereinafter Optional Protocol to the Convention Against Torture].
[150] *Ibid.* at arts. 1, 11.
[151] The Optional Protocol to the Convention Against Torture was adopted by 127 votes to 4 with 42 abstentions. *See* Optional Protocol to the Convention Against Torture, *supra* note 149.
[152] Diane F. Orentlicher, "Unilateral Multilateralism: United States Policy Towards the International Criminal Court," 36 *Cornell International Law Journal* 415, 415–16 (2004) (discussing not only the U.S. refusal to support the International Criminal Court ("ICC"); but *see also* the Bush administration's focus on unilateralism as opposed to international law); *see also* Anne K. Heindel, "The Counterproductive Bush Administration Policy Toward the International Criminal Court," 2 *Seattle Journal for Social Justice* 345 (2004) (highlighting the Bush Adminstration's efforts to prevent the ICC's effective operation).
[153] Richard W. Thackeray, "Struggling for Air: The Kyoto Protocol, Citizens' Suits Under the Clean Air Act, and the United States' Options for Addressing Global Climate Change," 14 *Indiana International and Comparative Law Review* 855, 856–57 (2004) (noting the Bush Administration's reversal of the Clinton Administration's support of the Kyoto Protocol).
[154] Nina Tannenwald, "Law Versus Power on the High Frontier: The Case for a Rule Based Regime for Outer Space," 29 *Yale Journal of International Law* 363, 366–67 (2004) (stating that the Bush Administration pulled out of the Anti-Ballistic Missile Treaty as a move to remove constraints on its power).
[155] Randall H. Cook, "Dynamic Content: The Strategic Contingency of International Law," 14 *Duke Journal of Comparative and International Law* 89, 118–21 (2004) (commenting on the Bush Administration's lack of support for land mine initiatives in the context of rejecting international law that presents constraints on the United States).

156 Jeremy Ostrander, "Changing Direction on Non-Nuclear Arms Control? American Exceptionalism, Power, and Constancy," 21 *Berkeley Journal of International Law* 495, 508 (2003) (stating that the Bush Administration refused to sign the treaty based on its support of legitimate small arms trading).
157 *Ibid.* at 512–16 (discussing the Bush Administration's continual actions against the efforts of the international community to ban biological weapons using the argument that the drafted proposals were not realistic).
158 Orentlicher, *supra* note 152; *see also* Heindel, *supra* note 152.
159 The Declaration of Independence (U.S. 1776); *see also supra* note 75 and accompanying text.
160 Report of the International Commission of the Red Cross, *supra* note 30.
161 Sontag, *supra* note 32 (citing Secretary of Defense Donald Rumsfeld's response to Abu Ghraib and claims of torture).
162 Mike Allen and Dana Priest, "Memo on Torture Brings Focus to Bush," *Washington Post*, June 9, 2004, at A3 (citing a memorandum from the Justice Department Office of Legal Counsel to White House Counsel Alberto R. Gonzales, which stated that torturing suspected al Qaeda members abroad "may be justified").
163 Art. 15-6 Investigation of the 800th Military Police Brigade, Conclusion (February 26, 2004), at http://www.globalsecurity.org/intell/library/reports/2004/800-mp-bde.htm (last visited October 28, 2004) [hereinafter The Taguba Report]. The Taguba Report was issued on February 26, 2004, but was not made publicly available until after the photographs from Abu Ghraib were aired by CBS on 60 Minutes II on April 28, 2004. *See Compare 60 Minutes* (CBS television broadcast, April 28, 2004), *with Testimony on Mistreatment of Iraqi Prisoners: Hearing Before the Senate Committee on Armed Services*, 108th Cong. (2nd Sess. May 11, 2004) (Major General Taguba's testimony before the Senate Committee on Armed Services came only after the media made his report public.)
164 Sontag, *supra* note 32.
165 *See, e.g.*, Press Release, State Department, U.S. Human Rights Advocacy Not Stalled by Abu Ghraib, Powell Says (July 2, 2004) (deflecting the question of whether the occurrences at Abu Ghraib were torture, U.S. Secretary of State Colin Powell suggests that it was rather the misconduct of a few).
166 *Compare* 18 U.S.C. § 2340(1) (1994) (defining torture as an "act . . . specifically intended to inflict severe physical or mental pain or suffering") *with* Convention against Torture, *supra* note 115 (defining torture as "any act by which severe pain or suffering, whether physical or mental, is inflicted").
167 18 U.S.C. § 2340(1) (1994).
168 *Ibid.*
169 18 U.S.C. § 2340(2) (1994).
170 Allen and Priest, *supra* note 162, at A3 (citing the memo from the Justice Department Office of Legal Counsel composed by then Assistant Attorney

General now 9th Circuit judge, Jay S. Bybee, to White House Counsel Alberto R. Gonzales).

[171] *See supra* note 163.

[172] The Taguba Report, *supra* note 163, at Pt. I, 5 (2004).

[173] *Ibid.*

[174] Marcy Strauss, "Torture," 48 *New York Law School Law Review* 201, 253 (2004) (presenting the arguments for the immorality of torture).

[175] *See generally* Zygmunt Bauman, *Postmodern Ethics* (1993) (discussing postmodern ethics and morality).

[176] *See generally* Rex R. Perschbacher and Debra Lyn Basset, "The End of Law," 84 *B.U. L. Rev.* 1, 10–13 (2004) (analyzing the detachment of morality from law).

[177] William C. Bradford, "The Duty to Defend Them: A Natural Law Justification for the Bush Doctrine of Preventive War," 79 *Notre Dame Law Review* 1365, 1435–37 (2004) (examining how September 11th has allowed for a stronger preference of the sovereign to treat law in a manner consistent with asserting its will).

[178] Letter from Thomas Jefferson to Thomas Law (June 13, 1814), in *Jefferson: Writings*, *supra* note 4, at 1335–36.

[179] Thomas Jefferson, "Opinion on the French Treaties" (April 28, 1793), in Thomas Jefferson, *Thomas Jefferson: Writings* 423 (Merrill D. Peterson Ed., 1984); *see also* Duncan Kelly, "*Revisiting the Rights of Man: George Jellinek on Rights and the State*," 22 *Law and History Review* 493, 513–16 (2004) (discussing the origin and formation of law in the context of our common human bonds).

[180] Letter from Thomas Jefferson to James Madison (August 28, 1789), at http://www.founding.com/library/lbody.cfm?id=160&parent=57.

[181] George Washington, Farewell Address (1796), at www.yale.edu/lawweb/avalon.washing.htm (last visited November 6, 2004).

[182] Letter from Thomas Jefferson to Thomas Law (June 13, 1814), in Thomas Jefferson, *Thomas Jefferson: Writings* 1335–36 (Merrill D. Peterson Ed., 1984).

[183] V.S. Naipaul, "Two Worlds, "Nobel Lecture (December 7, 2001), at http://www.literature-awards.com/nobelprize-winners/naipaul_nobellecture.htm.

[184] V.S. Naipaul, *Argentine Terror: A Memoir*, N.Y. Rev. Of Books, October 11, 1979, at http://www.nybooks.com/articles/7671.

[185] V.S. Naipaul, "Argentina: Living with Cruelty," *New York Review of Books*, January 30, 1992, at http://www.nybooks.com/articles/3024.

[186] Naipaul, *Argentine Terror: A Memoir*, *supra* note 184 (noting that Peronist trade union men and high-ranking military officials acknowledged a dichotomy between "good" and "bad" torture).

[187] *Ibid.*

[188] V.S. Naipaul, "Argentina and the Ghost of Eva Peron, 1972–1991," in *The Writing and the World: Essays* 405 (Pankaj Mishra Ed., 2002).

[189] *Ibid.* at 395.

[190] Naipaul, *Argentine Terror: A Memoir*, *supra* note 184.

191 Bradley Graham and Josh White, "General Cites Hidden Detainees: Senators Told CIA May have avoided Registering Up to 100," *Washington Post*, September 10, 2004, at A24.
192 *Ibid.*
193 *Ibid.*
194 *Ibid.*
195 George W. Bush, State of the Union Address (January 28, 2003), at http://whitehouse.gov/news/releases/2003/01/print/20030128-19.html (last visited October 25, 2004).
196 *Ibid.*
197 *Ibid.*
198 Letter from Thomas Jefferson to James Madison, *supra* note 180.
199 Naipaul, *Argentine Terror: A Memoir*, *supra* note 184.
200 Christopher E. Smith, "The Bill of Rights After September 11th: Principles or Pragmatism," 42 *Duquesne Law Review* 259, 282–83 (2004).
201 Timothy Noah, "The Right's Abu Ghraib Denial: Is the Liberal Outrage Really Worse Than the Torture?" (May 11, 2004), at http://slate.msn.com/id/2100373.
202 Dana Milbank, "Bush Seeks to Reassure Nation on Iraq: President Talks of Razing Abu Ghraib Prison to Mark 'New Beginning,'" *Washington Post*, May 25, 2004, at Al.
203 Mark Danner, "Torture and Truth," *New York Review of Books*, June 10, 2004, at 47.
204 Frank Rich, "It Was the Porn That Made Them Do It," *New York Times*, May 30, 2004.
205 Thucydides, *History of The Peloponnesian War* 242 (Rex Warner trans., 1972) (431–404 BC).
206 *Ibid.* at 536–37.
207 *Exodus* 21:24 (King James Version).
208 John J. Lumpkin, "Rumsfeld Says Abu Ghraib Abuses Do Not Compare with Terrorist Atrocities," *New York Times*, September 10, 2004, at http://www.nctimes.com/articles/2004/09/11/military/1833_339_10_04.
209 "Monticello: The Home of Thomas Jefferson, To Labour for Another," at http://www.monticello.org/jefferson/dayinlife/plantation/home.html (last visited November 23, 2004).
210 *Danner, supra* note 203, at 46.
211 Letter from Thomas Jefferson to Marquis de Lafayette (December 26, 1820), at http://www.constitution.org/tj/jeff15.txt (last visited October 24, 2004).
212 Letter from Thomas Jefferson to Tench Coxe (June 1, 1795), at http://www.loc.gov/exhibits/jefferson/181.html (last visited October 24, 2004).
213 Letter from Thomas Jefferson to Dr. Benjamin Rush (September 23, 1800), in Thomas Jefferson, *Thomas Jefferson: Writings* 1082 (Merrill D. Peterson Ed., 1984).

[214] Kate Zernike and David Rohde, "Forced Nudity of Iraqi Prisoners is Seen as a Pervasive Pattern, not Isolated Incidents," *New York Times*, June 8, 2004, at A14.

[215] Ellis, *supra* note 1, at 3 (quoting James Parton (1874)).

[216] Samuel Johnson warned us, "Patriotism is the last refuge of a scoundrel." James Boswell, *The Life of Samuel Johnson* 543 (Alfred A. Knopf, 1992) (1791).

[217] Edwin Williamson, *Borges: A Life* (2004). The publisher's comment states that the book charts the evolution of Borges' political ideas, from his early days as a cultural nationalist through to his support for Argentine military *juntas* during the Dirty War of the 1970s.

[218] *Borges, Jorge Luis 1899–1986*, at http://www.biography.com/search/printable.jsp?aid=9220057 (last visited November 3, 2004) (stating that metaphors dominate Borges' poetry and short stories).

[219] "Jorge Luis Borges," at http://www.penguin.co.uk/nf/Author/AuthorPage/0,,0_1000004468,00.html (last visited November 3, 2004) (quoting Mario Vargas Llosa's tribute to Borges, "His is a world of clear, pure, and at the same time unusual ideas ... expressed in words of great directness and restraint...").

[220] Jorge Luis Borges, "The Garden of Forking Paths," *in Labyrinths: Selected Stories and Other Writings* 19 (Donald A. Yates and James E. Irby eds., 1964).

[221] *Ibid*. at 24.

[222] *Ibid*. at 25.

[223] *Ibid*. at 23.

[224] *Ibid*. at 26.

[225] *Ibid*. at 28.

[226] Ellis, *supra* note 1, at 231.

[227] "Tending the Garden of Liberty," *Hartford Courant*, July 4, 2004, at C2.

[228] Gary Younge, "Annan Rebukes Law-Breaking Nations," *Guardian* (London), September 22, 2004, at 4.

[229] "U.S. Election: In the In-Tray: Challenges for Next Four Years," *Independent* (London), November 3, 2004, at 10.

Chapter 14

Turning to Tacitus*

Tacitus?

Who was Tacitus?

It was a cold December day in 1967. It was my first final exam in my very first semester as a student at Vanderbilt University. And it was all I could do to keep from shivering in the wintry confines of Neely Auditorium as I stared at the first question I had been asked to answer in the university's effort to confirm my mastery of the mysteries of "Western Civilization" in History 101.

The question seemed to stare back at me from the single page of questions that I held in my shaking hand on that distant day — daring me for an answer. Even now, all these many years later, the question still stares back at me, and it still demands an answer, as I recall what my middle-aged memory remembers reading on that page:

What did Tacitus say about the Germanic tribes, and how did what he said about the Germanic tribes reveal how he viewed the Roman Empire?

I may not remember the question word for word. But this, give or take a word or two, was the question I was asked to answer. And I confess that the sheer recollection of this single question still makes me shiver and shake. For the cruel truth of my plight on that cold day was this. I knew who the Germans were. I knew who the Romans were. I knew that, in antiquity, the Germans had tribes and the Romans had an empire.

But I had never heard of Tacitus.

---

*This essay was previously published as James Bacchus, "Turning to Tacitus," *Vanderbilt Law Review*, Volume 37, Issue 3 (2004), 631–646.

Therefore, I would, I feared, fail my final exam in "Western Civ." I would fail a required course, I would forfeit my scholarship, and I would be flushed, as a result, from the elite gene pool of academe into the teeming cesspool of real life.

In my panic, I did what generations of undergraduates have undoubtedly done in such desperate circumstances. I faked it. I feigned the knowledge I did not possess. I wrote everything I knew about the Germanic tribes. I wrote everything I knew about the Roman Empire. I wrote feverishly. I wrote frantically. I wrote exhaustively on page after page in my "blue book."

And, every few pages or so, in what I hoped was a neutral and innocuous, but, nevertheless, a seemingly knowing and knowledgeable, way, I slowed from the fervor of my panicked pace, and I wrote — as clearly and as confidently as I could — the word "Tacitus."

Then, the exam over, I fled. I fled out of Neely, across the campus, and all the way to my dorm room, in search of Tacitus. And there I found him. There he was, right where, in my ignorance, I had imagined he might be, right where I had suspected he might be, hiding in the imposing pages of the hefty textbook that we all simply called "Hexter."

"Hexter" was a bulky, buff-colored tome entitled *The Traditions of the Western World*.[1] We freshmen at Vanderbilt all called our "Western Civ" textbook "Hexter" because the "General Editor" of the book was someone somewhere named "J. H. Hexter" whose name was emblazoned boldly on the cover of the book. My copy of "Hexter" contained 917 pages of excerpts in small print from the rich intellectual tradition of Western civilization (complete with my compulsive underlining and my cryptic marginal notes). The voluminous array of readings in "Hexter" ranged across the centuries, from Plato and Aristotle, to Shakespeare and Voltaire, to Tocqueville and Lincoln, to Plutarch and Cicero, and, yes, alas, to Tacitus.

Breathless from my flight across the campus, I pulled my volume of "Hexter" down from the bookshelf in my dorm room. There, on page 129, was an excerpt from *Germania*, an essay on "The Origins, Land, and Peoples of the Germans" written late in the first century A.D. In the caption that preceded the excerpt that began on that page, general editor Hexter and his contributing editorial colleagues asked their undergraduate readers: "What Can Citizens of a Highly Civilized State Learn from the Study of a Primitive People"?[2] The author of *Germania* was a Roman historian named Tacitus.

Still breathing heavily, my heart still beating rapidly, I noticed that, on the previous page, was a selection from an essay by another ancient Roman, Cicero, which addressed a number of issues "Concerning the Laws." I knew much about Cicero's concerns about the laws. I had read those pages from Cicero in "Hexter" several times. My underlining of the most pertinent passages in those pages was my proof of it. But I had not turned to the next page.

I had not turned to Tacitus.

I soon learned why. I soon discovered that, a few days before, after the last lecture of the semester, and after the last class of my discussion section of "Western Civ," one final reading assignment had been posted for all to see on the bulletin board in Neely Auditorium. That final assignment was to turn to Tacitus. Like countless generations of other hapless freshmen, I had somehow missed the last assignment.

As it turned out, somehow I also missed making a failing grade that semester in "Western Civ." As we used to say, I "pulled a B." Maybe all my artful, arduous faking and feigning paid off. Maybe I had been so clever in filling my "blue book" that the grader of my exam did not realize that I had never heard of Tacitus. Or maybe others in my class missed the last assignment, too, and the final exam was graded on a curve. Maybe. I suppose I will never know.

I do know, though, that, for all my fears, I returned for another semester of "Western Civ." I "pulled an A" that next semester (after making certain I read the last assignment); I became a history major; I earned my degree from Vanderbilt; and, a few years later, I was still pondering the many mysteries of Western civilization while studying for a graduate degree in history at Yale University.

One of my professors there was J. H. Hexter.

I soon realized that the late J. H. "Jack" Hexter was not nearly as thick as his textbook. In fact, he was one of the brightest men I have ever met. His field was Tudor-Stuart English history, and I met him while taking his famed seminar on the emergence of modern Britain under the Tudor and Stuart monarchs during the 16th and 17th centuries. But Jack Hexter's real field was freedom.

Professor Hexter was a tireless and fearless advocate for academic, intellectual, and many other kinds of freedom. In his weekly seminar, he taught us about Pym and Hampden, about Milton and Colonel Harrison. He taught us, too, that those and other great heroes of the struggle for freedom in Tudor-Stuart England were the heirs to many others who had preceded them, dating all the way back to the degradations of a dim antiquity.

Until then, I had perhaps been in danger of becoming what professional historians sometimes describe as a "presentist." With a passion — then — for politics, I had been so concerned with the present that I had a hard time seeing the human reality of the past. My studies until then had been largely of the recent past of my own native region in my own native country. The past was very much alive in the stormy present of the U.S. South of my youth.

Professor Hexter was not unconcerned with the present. Indeed, many years later, while he was still with us, and still teaching, and while I was a Member of the Congress of the United States, I was able to help him enact into federal law his idea for the "Troops to Teachers" program — a federal program to encourage former soldiers to become teachers. Jack Hexter simply understood that we cannot do all we should for freedom today if we do not know what others tried to do for freedom yesterday.

With his emphasis on the ancient origins of freedom, and with his stress also on the long and ongoing struggle for freedom, Professor Hexter inspired me to turn finally to the assignment I had missed during my first semester as a freshmen in "Western Civ" at Vanderbilt. His book of readings was still waiting on my bookshelf. I took it down once more, and I turned to Tacitus.

I read the few pages of excerpts from *Germania* that Hexter had included in the book. Then I found and read the rest of *Germania*. Then I read *Agricola*. And the *Annals*. And the *Histories*. And the *Dialogue on Orators*. I not only read the assignment. I went considerably beyond it. I read all of Tacitus.

In saying that I read all of Tacitus, I am saying that I read all that remains of Tacitus. For only a fraction of what he wrote remains, and that fraction remains fortuitously, almost by historical accident. One historian has put it this way:

"Of Tacitus we would know almost nothing if it were not for the 9th century copyists; and the only manuscript to contain the first six books of his 'Annals,' the Mediceus prior in the Laurentian Library in Florence, was probably copied at Fulda in the 9th century and sent to Corvey, where it was found towards the end of the 15th century. All our manuscripts of his 'minor' works, the Dialogue on Orators, the Germania and Agricola, are based on a 9th or 10th century text, now lost, which a monk of Hersfeld offered for sale to the humanist Il Poggio in 1425."[3]

Fortuitous indeed. Further, in saying that I read all of Tacitus, I am not saying that I read all that remains of Tacitus in *the original Latin* of his few fortuitously remaining manuscripts. Other than the few Latin phrases that are the familiar commonplaces of most U.S. lawyers and jurists, I profess to know no Latin. I am still learning English. So, I read all that remains of Tacitus in various translations into English. I can, thus, only report secondhand that many who have known Latin have, through the centuries, praised the balance and the brevity of his grand and eloquent Latin style.

In reading Tacitus, I began to understand for the first time the enduring wisdom of my Vanderbilt professors in asking me the question I was asked — but could not answer — on my final exam in "Western Civ" all those years ago. In undertaking the assignment that I had missed as a freshman, I began, too, to understand what might be the real answer, the right answer, to that unanswered question. The answer could be found by turning to Tacitus.

Tacitus had much to teach me — he has much to teach all of us — about the struggle for human freedom — both yesterday and today. The many who have taken the time to turn to Tacitus since he was so fortuitously rediscovered during the Renaissance have found, again and again, that he has much to teach all of us about the fragility of freedom, and about the frailty of humanity, which must somehow preserve it.

Lost and forgotten for many centuries, what remains of Tacitus was found by the humanists just in time to have a major impact on the humanistic view of human freedom in the Age of Reason. In Tudor-Stuart times, Jack Hexter's freedom-loving Englishmen, for example, were known to give lectures, ostensibly on Tacitus, that were, in truth, veiled criticisms and daring diatribes aimed at the oppressions of both church and state. Archbishop Laud was not amused.[4] Later, over in France, Madame Roland read Tacitus while she was imprisoned in the Conciergerie and awaiting her execution by the radical Jacobins during the French Revolution.[5] Edward Gibbon, that other historian of Rome, said that Tacitus was one of his "old and familiar companions."[6] Thomas Jefferson, a fair writer himself, said, "Tacitus I consider the finest writer in the world without exception."[7]

Who was Tacitus to have such an impact on these and so many others so many centuries after his death? The truth is, we really do not know.

We know very little about him. We know that his last two names were Cornelius Tacitus, but we do not know the first of his three Roman names. Perhaps it was Gaius. Or perhaps it was Publius. We know that he was born in 55 or 56 A.D., but we do not know when he died. Perhaps it was in 117 A.D. Or perhaps it was in 120 A.D. In many respects, Tacitus himself remains one of the mysteries of Western civilization.

We do know that Tacitus was a noted Roman orator, and that he was also a senator, consul, and governor of some renown in the late first century of our era. We think also that he may have taken to writing history as a way of handling what we might nowadays call a "mid-life crisis." Tacitus survived, in mid-life, the terror caused by the tyranny of the Emperor Domitian, and his very survival may have helped inspire him afterwards to write the history of how it happened that so few of the lofty ideals of the Roman Republic survived the bloody realities of the early years of the Roman Empire.

He may also have been inspired to write by *how* he survived. For Tacitus had not only survived the tyranny of Domitian. He had, in his own mind, been complicit in that tyranny. In the last lines of his first known work, a brief biography of his father-in-law, the *Agricola*, Tacitus acknowledges that, while he sat in the Roman senate, he failed to speak out against the tyranny of Domitian, and, further, and worse, that he joined in the condemnation of Domitian's senatorial victims. He confesses that "we senators... watched in shame... and stained ourselves with ... innocent blood."[8]

This may be the source of the timeless edge in what we read when we turn to Tacitus. He was a Roman aristocrat who longed for a lost world. He lamented the loss of the Roman Republic all the while he strived to serve the Roman Empire. He lived in a time when the Romans had lost much of the personal and political freedom that some of them, a few of them, had once had, and he was persuaded that, in his fear, and in the passivity that had been prompted by his fear, he had helped give that freedom away.

Thus, perhaps, the heavy-heartedness of his histories. Thus, perhaps, his seeming pessimism in telling his sad tale of all the shortcomings of human nature as manifested in the eventful first century of the Roman Empire. Thus, perhaps, his droll digressions, his snide and sometimes sneering asides, his apparent afterthoughts that still sparkle with world-weary wisdom centuries later. Thus, perhaps, the guilt in his pen that gives the edge to his prose, and, thus, perhaps, its resounding contemporary ring.

Why do the observations of Tacitus still have a contemporary ring after nearly two thousand years? It is because of their basic timelessness. Tacitus seemed to be writing about Rome. He was really writing about human nature. Because human nature does not change, because it remains fixed over time, because it remains the same through the centuries, the terse observations of Tacitus about human nature are timeless. They still seem to us, long centuries later, to have the ring of contemporary truth.

Many of these observations are, thus, still often cited. They are still often quoted in the contemporary fray. Heard this one? "Nothing succeeds like success."[9] How about this one? "Patriotism comes second to private profits."[10] Or have you happened to hear this one lately? "They make a desert, and they call it peace."[11]

Others among his acerbic asides likewise have a contemporary ring that still resonates today. The first century of the Roman Empire was, he said, a time of a "rising tide of flattery"[12] when "slavish obedience was the way to succeed, both politically and financially."[13] Moreover, "the more distinguished men were, the greater their urgency and insincerity."[14]

Ring a bell?

During that time of "slavish passivity,"[15] those who presumed to lead Rome relied on "borrowed eloquence"[16] to multiply "hostages to fortune."[17] They tried to "use antique terms to veil new sorts of villainy."[18] Some "had every asset except goodness."[19]

Sound familiar?

In that dark time, there were "world-wide convulsions."[20] Those who had "an instinctive love of power" had made that instinct a "dominant and uncontrollable force."[21] "But in the pursuit of an empire there was no mean between the summit and the abyss."[22]

Does this remind you at all of recent events?

Tacitus found little solace in the reactions of the "slavish" majority to the tribulations of Rome. When confronted with harsh tribulations, he said, civilization subsides. "Men's minds, once unbalanced, are ready to believe anything."[23] In such disturbed times, "crowds habitually find scapegoats, however unjustifiable."[24] Further, "in disturbed times uncivilized communities trust and prefer leaders who take risks."[25]

In such times, said Tacitus, "opportunists can always turn national disasters to advantage."[26] His histories were about how this had happened in Rome. In Rome, "existing resources were squandered as though the material for many more years of wastefulness were now accessible."[27] There were "imaginary treasures" in the expectation of great wealth from such great profligacy.[28] In the midst of this "national impoverishment,"[29] there was also an impoverishment of the national spirit. Patriotism, for many, did, indeed, truly come "second to private profits."[30] Worst of all, "terror had paralyzed human sympathy. The rising surge of brutality drove compassion away."[31]

Paralysis by terror? Did Tacitus, perchance, watch CNN?

Tacitus was an orator. His histories were recitations. In the custom of his time, they were written to be read aloud.[32] They were "designed to be declaimed"[33] in performances before audiences of aristocrats who assembled to hear them on ancient leisured evenings. In his *Dialogue on Orators*, Tacitus attributed the decline of eloquence in oratory to the suppression of freedom under the empire. His histories were intended in part as evidence that there could still be freedom-loving eloquence in such recitations.

Tacitus was also a moralist. His histories were not only recitations. They were exhortations. His oratory was meant not only to tell a story. It was meant as moral instruction. It was intended to inspire moral action in response to the eloquence of his exhortations. Like life itself, the histories of Tacitus were morality plays in which the principal plot was the never-ending struggle in human life between vice and virtue. In the Rome of his time, Tacitus was exhorting the Romans to choose, not vice, but virtue.

When Tacitus wrote his histories, the tyrannical reign of Domitian was over. There had been an easing of despotism under Nerva, Trajan, and Hadrian. Under the shrewder Caesars who succeeded Domitian, there was, once more, the pretense of the traditional republican virtues in the midst of autocratic rule. And yet the results of the terror remained. There were "virtues that were fictitious and vices that promised to return."[34]

Again and again, the Romans had chosen vice over virtue. The result was a Roman world that preached virtue but practiced vice. It was a world where vice ruled, and where it ruled in part because those who ruled were able to make vice seem to be virtue. They were able to do so in large part because those they ruled — the Roman patricians for whom Tacitus recited his eloquent histories — were willing to pretend that vice was virtue. They were willing to pretend that appearance was reality.

Tacitus understood how vice can be made to seem to be virtue. He knew the difference between appearance and reality. He saw through the veil of appeasing appearance that concealed the hypocritical reality of the exercise of raw political power in the Roman Empire. Most of all, he perceived how the citizens of Rome — he no less than others — had been complacent and even complicit in the making of their own subjugation.

In distinguishing vice from virtue, Tacitus was, as the late Oxford historian Sir Ronald Syme once put it, "ever alert for the contrast of name and substance."[35] Tacitus acknowledged that there was, in Syme's British phrasing and spelling, "the nominal sovranty of law."[36] All the same, he knew that, whatever the appearance, in reality, "sovranty" — sovereignty — in the Roman Empire had been ceded to one man, and thereby to those who, through the force of their arms, through the force of their martial and financial might, kept that one man in power. In the view of Tacitus, as Syme expressed it, in the Rome of his time, "Names did not matter much."[37]

The Romans of the early empire yearned for security in a world threatened by terror. To escape the threat of terror, they had chosen appearance over reality. They had chosen the illusion of security over the potential of what little they had once possessed of freedom. They had succumbed to the vice of fear because they were no longer willing to pay the high price for the virtue of freedom. And, of all that aggrieved Tacitus — the moralist — this aggrieved him by far the most.

Tacitus seems to have been a pessimist. But here, too, there was a difference between appearance and reality. What distinguished Tacitus from the other aggrieved Roman aristocrats of his time, from those others who longed for republican days, from those others who lamented the loss of freedom-loving republican ways, was that Tacitus alone had the courage to voice his grievances by writing his histories. His histories are evidence that, pessimist though he may have been, Tacitus nevertheless was still enough of an optimist to believe in the possibility that things might one day be different.

In the very first paragraph of the earliest manuscript that remains of his histories, Tacitus asserted his abiding belief that "an outstanding personality can still triumph over that blind antipathy to virtue which is a defect of all states, small and great alike."[38] This decidedly optimistic statement was made in the context of his fond memoir of his late father-in-law, Agricola. But Tacitus might have said this about himself, and he might have said this about others, in all states, and in all times. Despite the terror he had somehow survived, despite the vice he still beheld all around him, *despite all*, Tacitus still dared to believe that just one person could make a difference for the triumph of virtue.

In the assignment I missed in "Western Civ" at Vanderbilt in 1967, Professor Hexter said of Tacitus, "His writings reveal the fondness of the

Roman aristocrat for the Republic, and a distaste for the increasingly autocratic government of the emperors."[39] The Jack Hexter who taught me later would probably, with further reflection, agree with me that this is something of an understatement. More than a "distaste" for autocratic government, the writings of Tacitus reveal a profound distrust for the oppressive one-man rule of autocratic government. More, his writings reveal, too, a profound belief that, despite the evidence of history, which supports a paining pessimism, there is, nevertheless, reason remaining for optimism about the future, as evidenced by the efforts of those "outstanding personalities" who, despite all, still strive for the triumph of virtue.

One of the foremost English translators of Tacitus, the historian Michael Grant, has put it this way: "Human fate often looks black to Tacitus. So does human nature. Yet he is far from sceptical about the potentialities of the human spirit. Even in times of civil war and tyrannical government, he is able to point to human actions of extraordinary virtue, bravery, and pertinacity. Indeed he is a humanist, and one whose contribution to our western tradition of humanism has been immense and singularly inspiring."[40]

Tacitus watched forlornly as freedom was sacrificed to the false hope of security in an authoritarian state. He was no democrat. He was a Roman aristocrat. For him, freedom was aristocratic freedom, with all that the antiquated elitism of that phrase implies. Further, Tacitus definitely had his doubts about whether the possession of personal freedom, even by Roman aristocrats, was compatible with the practical necessities of governing a "global" state such as Rome. Thus, while he hoped for benevolence, he was largely reconciled to what he reluctantly concluded was the need in his time for some kind of imperial monarchy.

And yet there is, all the same, something about Tacitus that seems to suggest nevertheless that, for a suffering humanity, it might one day, some day, somehow, be otherwise. For all his elitism, for all his aristocratic disdain for the destructive emotionalism of the Roman mob, there is, in the histories of Tacitus, a redeeming undertone of what Grant has described as "the Stoic interpretation of the Roman Empire as the vehicle of human brotherhood."[41] This undertone in Tacitus implies and embraces a *universal* humanity as a corollary and as a consequence of a *universal* human nature. And it is this contemporary undertone of universalism that still resonates for us so loudly today.

Sir Ronald Syme spent many years researching and writing the two-volume biography that is widely considered the definitive work on Tacitus.[42]

Syme said afterwards, "It is good fortune and a privilege if one can consort for so many years with an historian who knew the worst, discovered few reasons for ease or hope or confidence, and nevertheless believed in human dignity and freedom of speech."[43] Tacitus knew the worst; yet he believed in the possibility of the best. Even as others sought a false security, even as others submitted to the seeming inevitability of autocratic rule in the face of the threat of terror, Tacitus still held fast to his underlying belief in the possibility that virtue would ultimately triumph through the fulfillment of human freedom.

All these years later, Professor Hexter's heavy tome on *The Traditions of The Western World* still sits on my bookshelf. "Middle-aged and well-meaning," as Tacitus might say,[44] I take down the book from the shelf, and I take up the assignment I left unfinished long ago. I turn, anew, to Tacitus, and I ask myself the question that, for all of my feigning, I left unanswered on my final exam in "Western Civ" in 1967: What was Tacitus trying to say to his fellow Romans in what he wrote about the Germans nearly two thousand years ago?

In the several pages of excerpts from *Germania* that begin on page 129 of my aging copy of "Hexter," Tacitus paints a highly favorable portrait of the German tribes that pressed the borders and challenged the rule of the Roman Empire. The Germans were a primitive people. They were, in the eyes of the Romans, mere barbarians. But Tacitus portrayed them, in the fastness of their forests, and in all their primitive and barbarian ways, as freedom-loving, and as free.[45]

In *Germania*, Tacitus described a people who shared in the exercise of their freedom at all times, and who shared also in the defense of their freedom at all costs. He observed that the power of the German kings was not "absolute or arbitrary."[46] Further, on major affairs, the German kings consulted with "the whole community."[47] "As for the leaders," Tacitus reported, "it is their example rather than their authority that wins them special admiration."[48]

In these and other remarks in *Germania*, Tacitus was denouncing the Romans of the empire as much as he was describing the Germans of the forests. Implicitly, but unmistakably, in describing the Germans, Tacitus contrasted their virtues with the vices of his own countrymen. In his eyes, the Germans, with all their virtues, resembled the Romans of the old republic during the glorious days before the dissolutions and the degeneracies of the empire, and, in his eyes, the Romans of his own time, with all their vices, had much to learn from the barbarians in the forests.

Tacitus especially envied the "complete liberty" of the Germans, which he saw as the source of many of their virtues.[49] In his admiring account of the Germanic tribes, Tacitus seemed to envy in them, in particular, the sheer freedom of their primitive and barbaric ways. He seemed to see in them a bit of the "noble savage." There is just a hint of Jean-Jacques Rousseau, just a whiff of romanticism, in the freedom-loving life he saw the Germans as leading in their "state of nature" in the primeval forests on the other side of the Danube and the Rhine rivers. This may very well have influenced how he portrayed them in *Germania*.

But now is not then. Whatever the "state of nature" may have been long ago in those pristine German forests, we have, all these centuries later, long since passed beyond the primeval. Now, on this side of the forest, on this side of the river, on this side of a wishful romanticism, there is the sobering realism of civilization, and there is as well the sobering challenge of trying our best to find a way to live together within civilization. Now, if we are fortunate, there is also the reassuring reality of the rule of law.

Did Tacitus understand the need for the reality of the rule of law? He must have. After all, Tacitus was, as an orator, also a lawyer. And there is reason to believe he was quite a good lawyer. His friend and contemporary, Pliny the Younger, heard Tacitus argue in the rhetorical arena of the Roman courts, and called him the greatest legal orator of his time.[50] Tacitus was certainly no stranger to the law.

Nor am I. And I have long since concluded that the rule of law is the surest safeguard of freedom in a civilized society. Indeed, I see the rule of law as an indispensable prerequisite to freedom and civilization. This said, what, then, do I, as a lawyer, and as a sometime jurist, make of the professed verdict of that optimistic pessimist, that romantic realist, that renowned lawyer, Tacitus, who said, "The more corrupt the republic, the more numerous its laws"?[51] What did Tacitus really mean to say by saying this?

This cryptic and oft-quoted assertion that there is a connection between corruption and law is not found in *Germania*, one of his early works, but in the *Annals*, his last known work. There, Tacitus told the sad tale of the decline of Roman freedom under the early principate, from Augustus onwards. Under the principate that soon became the Roman Empire, the *form* of the law was often observed, but the spirit of the law was often lost. The law said one thing; the law meant another. And, increasingly, this was so. The volume of the laws proliferated while the virtues of republicanism declined into the vices of despotism. Under the Roman Empire, the laws became more numerous as the laws became more meaningless.

What Tacitus said must be read in this context. Tacitus did not mean to imply that we should live without laws. He did not mean to say that with fewer laws, we would have more freedom. He did not mean to suggest that we should go back across the rivers and return to the forests. He meant only to say that the law must mean what it says. He meant only to remind us that we must have the reality as well as the appearance of laws, because he believed that, to be free, we must have laws, however numerous, that have real meaning.

In the *Annals*, Tacitus maintained that "the origins of law" were in the advent of civilization.[52] He praised "the rule of law" under the famous "Twelve Tables" of law that were enacted at the foundation of the Roman Republic.[53] The Twelve Tables, he said, were "the last equitable legislation. For subsequent laws, other than those directed against specific current offences, were forcible creations of class-warfare, designed to grant unconstitutional powers or banish leading citizens, or fulfill some other deplorable purpose."[54]

Today, unlike Tacitus, we have the benefit of a longer and broader view. We have the benefit of an extended experience of the world in which the "rule of law" has, fortunately, and, frequently, been something more than appearance, and something other than pretense. I would agree with Tacitus that the effort to establish the rule of law began with the beginnings of civilization. But I would also contend that neither freedom nor civilization can be sustained without it. Without the rule of law, there will be no freedom, and thus there will be no ultimate triumph of virtue.

Law is not words alone. Law is the will behind the words. Law is what we are willing to do to make the words of the law mean what they say. Law is also what we are willing to let others do that would leave the words of the law without real meaning. We can salute the flag. We can shed a tear as it passes in the parade. We can call ourselves "patriots." But all our pledges of patriotism will not make us patriots if we permit others to corrupt the law by emptying it of all meaning. Far more important than any legislative "Patriot Act" are all the patriotic acts we must take to make the law mean what it says by making certain that we preserve the freedom that makes the rule of law possible.

Tacitus knew this. He had learned this the hard way. Tacitus understood that the rule of law is not the mere pretense — the mere appearance — the mere semblance — of law. But do we? Tacitus understood that law can be corrupted when there is too much power in too few hands. But, again, do we? Tacitus understood that law will fail, and that vice will triumph over virtue, if we trade our freedom to those who hold power over us in exchange for their promise of our security. But, once more, do we?

What do we learn when, finally, we turn to Tacitus? Here, in our advancing age, it is true that "the few of us that survive are no longer what we once were."[55] Even so, we may be tempted, like some who opposed the oppressive rule in Rome, to see ourselves as "the last of the free."[56] If so, what, then, are we willing to do to preserve our freedom? What are we willing to sacrifice to save Rome?

Will we simply salute and shed a tear? Will it be said of us, as Tacitus said of the Romans during the time of the first treason trials, "Everyone refused. Their excuses were different, but they were all afraid."?[57] And will it be said of us, as Tacitus said of the Gauls who were defeated by the Romans, "Their valour perished with their freedom"?[58]

There is a price for valor, even as there is a price for freedom. The price for standing up for freedom is often high. Sometimes it is the ultimate price, and, yes, sometimes those who are willing to stand up and pay the ultimate price of freedom are forgotten. But sometimes they are not. Sometimes they are remembered ever afterwards. Tacitus tells us that, in a parade in Rome, in the days of the empire, "The effigies of twenty highly distinguished families ... headed the procession. But Cassius and Brutus were the most gloriously conspicuous — precisely because their statues were not to be seen."[59]

Like valor, and like freedom, terror has its price. The desire for security against terror is shared by all, and there can be no doubt that some limits on our freedom, as the price of opposing terror, must be accepted by all. But there are those who, in the name of opposing terror, really oppose freedom. There are those who, in the guise of opponents of terror, would manipulate our laws to eviscerate our freedoms. Subtle, soothing, but potentially insidious, this, too, is a form of terror. And terror, in all its guises, must be opposed.

In the face of terror today, what will we do? Will we be content to watch the passing parade? Or are we willing to take the risk of becoming unseen statues? Do we still believe sufficiently in anything to be willing to stand up for it, and to fight for it? Are we willing to think for ourselves — even at the risk that thinking for ourselves might actually inspire us to do something for ourselves and for others? Are we prepared to do whatever it takes to choose reality over appearance, and virtue over vice? Will we, in the end, have the courage to refuse to trade our freedom for a false security? Our laws will mean nothing if there are not still those among us who are willing to make certain that they do mean something and that they mean what they say. The rule of law will become the misrule of lawlessness if we allow our desire for security to prevail over our need for freedom. The worst terror will come only if we succumb to the worst fears that are caused by terror.

What is the answer to the unanswered question I was asked on my final exam in "Western Civ" at Vanderbilt in 1967? What was Tacitus trying to tell the Romans in what he wrote about the Germans? The answer is in one short sentence from *Germania* that Professor Hexter included in his textbook. It was the belief of the abiding Germans, said Tacitus, that, in battle, "To throw away one's shield is the supreme disgrace."[60] Tacitus was telling the Romans not to throw away their shields. And, if he were here with us today, he would surely tell us, embattled as we are, to hold fast to our shields, and to stand and fight for our freedom. This is the lesson we learn by turning to Tacitus.

Endnotes

[1] *The Traditions of the Western World* (J. H. Hexter et al. eds., 1967) [hereinafter Hexter].
[2] Tacitus, *Germania*, in Hexter, *supra* note 1, at 129.
[3] Philippe Wolf, *The Awakening of Europe* 75 (Anne Carter trans., 1968).
[4] Anthony Grafton, *The Footnote: A Curious History* 144–145 (2003) (quoting Ronald Mellor, *Tacitus: The Classical Heritage* 118–121 (1995)).
[5] Michael Grant IV, *Translator's Introduction*, in Tacitus, *The Annals of Imperial Rome* 7, 24 (Michael Grant IV trans., Penguin Books 1996) [109 A.D.] [hereinafter *The Annals*].
[6] Edward Gibbon, *Memoirs of My Life* 146 (Funk & Wagnalls 1969) [1796].
[7] Michael Grant, *Readings in The Classical Historians* 461 (1992).
[8] Tacitus, *The Agricola* and *The Germania* 97 (Harold Mattingly and S.A. Handford trans. (Penguin Books, 1970) [98 A.D.] [hereinafter *Agricola and Germania*].
[9] Tacitus, *The Histories* 190 (Kenneth Wellesley III trans., Penguin Books 1995) (circa 100–110 A. D.) [hereinafter The Histories]. *The Histories* is an account of the Roman civil wars of 68–69 A.D.
[10] *The Annals*, *supra* note 5, at 207 (1996) (circa 110–120 A.D.). What remains of *The Annals* is an account of the early Roman Empire from the last years of Augustus to the tumultuous years of Nero.

[11] Tacitus, *Agricola*, in *Agricola and Germania*, supra note 8, at 81, where this frequently-quoted excerpt from the supposed speech of an opponent of Rome named Calgacus is translated as "[they create a *desolation* and call it peace."
[12] *The Annals*, supra note 5, at 31.
[13] *Ibid.* at 32.
[14] *Ibid.* at 35.
[15] *Ibid.* at 388.
[16] *Ibid.* at 285.
[17] *Ibid.* at 114.
[18] *Ibid.* at 166.
[19] *Ibid.* at 306.
[20] *The Histories*, supra note 9, at 175.
[21] *Ibid.* at 103.
[22] *Ibid.* at 125.
[23] *The Annals*, supra note 5, at 48.
[24] *Ibid.* at 55.
[25] *Ibid.* at 65.
[26] *Ibid.* at 196.
[27] *Ibid.* at 382.
[28] *Ibid.* at 383.
[29] *Ibid.*
[30] *Ibid.* at 207.
[31] *Ibid.* at 209.
[32] This custom began in the time of the Greek historian Herodotus, in the fifth century B.C., and was continued by Tacitus and others in the Roman era. Michael Grant IV, "Translator's Introduction," *The Annals*, supra note 5, at 11.
[33] Harold Mattingly, *Introduction*, in *Agricola and Germania*, supra note 8, at 9, 12.
[34] *The Histories*, supra note 9, at 64.
[35] Sir Ronald Syme, *The Roman Revolution* 324 (Oxford University Press, 1960) (1939).
[36] *Ibid.* at 516.
[37] *Ibid.*
[38] *Agricola And Germania*, supra note 8, at 51.
[39] Hexter, supra note 1, at 129.
[40] Michael Grant, *The Annals*, supra note 10, at 23.
[41] *Ibid.* at 15.
[42] *See generally* Sir Ronald Syme, *Tacitus* (1958).
[43] Sir Ronald Syme, quoted online at http://www.ancienttimes.net/cgiancient-times/ikonboardltopic.cgi?forum=47&topic=11.
[44] *The Annals*, supra note 5, at 224.
[45] Generally, the Tacitean portrait of the Germanic tribes still holds up after two millennia. *See* Herwig Wolfram, *The Roman Empire and Germanic Peoples* 3–4, 12, 15–16 (Thomas Dunlap trans., 1997).

[46] Hexter, *supra* note 1, at 131.
[47] *Ibid.*
[48] *Ibid.*
[49] *Agricola And Germania*, *supra* note 8, at 119.
[50] Pliny The Younger, *Letters* 93 (Loeb Classical Library 1924) (1915).
[51] This is a common translation. Another translation of this passage is, "Corruption reached its climax, and legislation abounded." *The Annals*, *supra* note 5, at 133.
[52] *Ibid.* at 132.
[53] *Ibid.*
[54] *Ibid.*
[55] *Agricola and Germania*, *supra* note 8, at 53.
[56] *Ibid.* at 80.
[57] *The Annals*, *supra* note 5, at 91.
[58] *Agricola And Germania*, *supra* note 8, at 62.
[59] *The Annals*, *supra* note 5, at 156.
[60] Hexter, *supra* note 1, at 131.

Index

A

Aaronson, Susan Ariel, 331, 333
Abi-Saab, Georges, 43
Abu Ghraib, 415–419, 422–423, 425, 431, 433–441
active pharmaceutical ingredient, 76
Adams, John, 420
a disguised restriction on international trade, 81
a free trade agreement, 202
Agreement on Import Licensing Procedures, 132
Agreement on Subsidies and Countervailing Measures (the SCM Agreement), 166
Agreement on Technical Barriers to Trade (TBT Agreement), 132, 306
Agreement on Trade Facilitation, 306
Agreement on Trade in Pharmaceutical Products, 136
Agreement on Trade-Related Aspects of Intellectual Property Rights (TRIPS Agreement), 216, 306
Agreement on Trade-Related Investment Measures (the TRIMS Agreement), 166

Agricola, 460, 463
agricultural export subsidies, 123, 130, 194
aircraft subsidies, 41
American idea, 423, 438
a national security, 43
Anderson, Scott, 275–276
Annals, 466–467
Annex on Telecommunications, 305
"anti-coercion" countermeasures, 51
Anti-Dumping Agreement, 249, 379, 404
anti-dumping duties, 15
Appellate Body, 17–18, 53, 55–57, 74, 101, 170, 172, 174, 192–194, 207, 221, 223, 227–229, 235–236, 239, 244–252, 254, 256, 260, 263, 266–279, 305, 333, 353, 360, 370, 373–374, 383–404, 406
arbitrary or unjustifiable discrimination, 81
arbitration, 275, 276
Argentina, 42, 89, 241, 413–416, 433–435, 440
artificial intelligence (AI), 106, 295, 316
Asian Trade Centre, 296

473

Asia-Pacific Economic Cooperation Forum (APEC), 86, 242, 374
Athens, 236
Australia, 51–52, 82, 154, 220, 292, 297, 302, 310, 384
Australia — Tobacco Plain Packaging dispute, 347
Autarky, 79
Azevedo, Roberto, 272

B
Baghdad, 415
Bahrain, 225
Bahri, Amrita, 217
Bain & Company, 370
Bali, 140, 319
Bange, Rashmi, 302
Barfield, Claude, 47
basic telecommunications services, 378
Belgium, 75
Bertelsmann Foundation, 7, 183
Bhagwati, Jagdish, 12
Biden, 23–35, 38–39, 41–42, 44–46, 48–50, 52–55, 58, 152, 154, 161, 163, 424
Biden, Joe, 17, 153, 159–160, 340
bilateral investment treaties, 93
biodiversity, 143, 189, 196, 359
Bi, Sheng, 369
Boehm, Eric, 46
Boklan, Daria, 217
Bolshevik Revolution, 365
Bolton, John, 258
Borges, Jorge Luis, 439–440
Bown, Chad P., 41
Brazil, 9, 42, 190–191, 203, 220, 374
Brookings Institution, 99
Brunei, 82, 310
Buenos Aires, 93, 139–141, 241, 292, 413
Bush, George W., 28, 246, 266–267
Business Roundtable, 7

buy American requirements, 26, 34–35, 38, 53, 79, 151–154, 163–164, 174–175
Bybee, Jay S., 429, 433
Byron, (George Gordon) Lord, 392–393

C
Cambodia, 310
Canada, 35–36, 41–42, 76, 78, 82, 91, 94, 99, 154–155, 173, 200–201, 238–239, 297, 302, 332
Canada — Autos dispute, 305
Canada-United States-Mexico Agreement (CUSMA), 309, 356
Cardozo, Benjamin, 398
Carlyle Group, 100, 357
Carter, Jimmy, 415, 419
Cato Institute, 35, 49, 129, 265, 371, 374
Center for Disease Research and Policy, 77
Central Intelligence Agency, 435
Centre for International Governance Innovation, 99
Chang, Seung Wha, 251–252
Charnovitz, Steve, 273, 276
Charter of the United Nations, 226
child labor, 33
Chile, 29, 82, 106, 139, 287–288, 290, 294–295, 302
China, 9, 13–15, 27, 29, 32, 37–38, 41–42, 45–51, 54, 56, 73, 75–78, 83, 85, 90–91, 102–103, 105–106, 153–155, 159–160, 162–163, 166, 172, 182, 187, 190–191, 196–200, 207, 214, 220, 229, 240, 243, 262, 264, 292–293, 302–303, 310, 322, 328–329, 332, 342, 351, 357, 369, 374, 379
Chinese Communist Party, 103
circular economy, 142–143
Ciuriak, Dan, 99, 101, 331, 304

Civil War, 366
Claussen, Kathleen, 161
climate change, 14, 37, 39, 85, 143, 153, 155, 165, 173, 189, 196, 203, 430
Codex Alimentarius Commission, 368
Coleridge, Samuel Taylor, 392–393
Colombia, 302
Commerce Clause, 374
comparative advantage, 12–13, 35, 199, 206
competition policy, 93, 103, 330
competitiveness, 204–206, 208
compulsory licensing, 348–349
concessions, 122, 129, 189–190, 202
Confucian tradition, 344
consensus, 119–122, 124, 128, 131
Constitution, 31, 80, 161, 183–184, 256, 343, 374, 403, 425
Convention Against Torture, 427–428
Cottier, Thomas, 165
Council on Foreign Relations, 84
countervailing duties, 15
COVAX, 354
Covid-19, 36–37, 40, 47, 51, 54, 73, 75–77, 79, 82–84, 89–90, 92, 100, 123, 137, 197, 289–290, 292, 340, 354–355, 357
COVID-19 vaccines, 120
creative destruction, 206
critical mass, 128, 378
"critical mass" of trade, 86
critical materials, 155
critical minerals, 154
cross-border data flows, 104, 320–322
Cunningham, Joe, 185
customary international law, 427
customary rules of interpretation, 18, 220, 248, 388
Cutler, Wendy, 307

cybersecurity, 313–314
Cyrus McCormick, 369

D

Danner, Alison Marston, 429
data localization requirements, 104, 321–322, 324
data privacy, 102, 107, 375
data protection, 314
Davidson, Warren, 184
Declaration of Independence, 411, 426
Declaration on the TRIPS Agreement and Public Health, 349
Defense Production Act, 154
democracy, 52, 58
Democratic Party, 181
Demsetz, Harold, 342
Deng, Xiaping, 345
developing countries, 87, 90, 95–98, 123, 138, 140, 195, 259, 291–292, 302–303, 319, 340–341, 345, 350–351, 353–354, 356, 359
Dialogue on Orators, 462
digital divide, 98
Digital Economy Partnership Agreement (DEPA), 98–99, 102, 104, 106, 139, 287–288, 290, 294–296, 298–301, 304, 307, 309, 311–318, 321, 323, 326, 331
digital identities, 315–316
digital privacy, 329
digital protectionism, 103–104
digital trade, 14, 54, 74, 96, 98–108, 121, 130, 138–139, 195, 202, 260, 287–291, 293, 297–301, 304–313, 317–318, 323–325, 327, 329–334, 343, 357–358
discrimination, 4, 16, 131, 141, 159, 161, 163, 166, 171, 174, 190–191, 201, 207, 240, 308
dispute settlement, 14–15, 17, 42–43, 45–46, 57, 74, 101, 133, 140, 152, 170–171, 173–174, 187–188, 192,

194, 197, 200, 207, 214–216,
218–219, 221–222, 226–228, 230,
235, 239, 242–245, 247–250,
253–254, 260–262, 264–266,
268–269, 272–273, 275–276,
278–279, 306, 310, 318, 348,
352–353, 354, 373–374, 376, 384,
386–387, 389, 391–392, 395–396,
399, 401, 403–406
Dispute Settlement Body (DSB), 228, 247, 385, 388
Dispute Settlement Understanding (DSU), 170, 387, 393, 406
division of labor, 85, 259, 368–369
Dobbs, Lou, 241
Doha Declaration, 88
Doha Development Agenda, 88, 119
Doha Development Round, 73, 85, 88, 121, 124, 130, 132–133, 138, 194, 214, 292, 404–405
Doha Ministerial Declaration, 349
domestic content requirements, 34–35, 53, 104, 152, 154, 163–166, 171–172
Dominican Republic–Central America Free Trade Agreement, 29
Domitian, 460, 462
Drezner, Daniel, 13

E

economic nationalism, 73, 120, 163–164, 181
economic nationalists, 38
economic sanctions, 186, 188–189, 197, 225–226, 243–244, 264, 373
Ehlermann, Claus-Dieter, 399
electric vehicles (EVs), 35, 152–153, 155, 159, 162, 171
Electronic signatures, 313
Elms, Deborah, 106
Elms, Debra, 296

El-Nagger, Said, 400
enlightenment, 393, 420, 433
environmental goods, 12, 54, 74, 85–88, 108, 138
Environmental Goods Agreement, 137
environmental goods and services, 14
environmental standards, 12
erga omnes, 427
European Centre for International Political Economy (ECIPE), 303
European Political Strategy Centre, 320
European Strategic Strategy Centre, 99
European Union (EU), 41–43, 49, 51, 56, 76, 78–79, 83, 90–91, 93, 99, 102, 104–105, 152, 191, 200, 203, 220, 225, 229, 292, 308, 328–329, 342, 377–378
Evenett, Simon, 76, 79
EV tax credit, 155, 159–160, 162, 170, 173–174
export quotas, 188
export restrictions, 80–81, 145
export taxes, 80
exports, 28, 53, 79, 90, 171, 187–188

F

Federalist Papers, 192, 256
Feliciano, Florentino, 394
financial services, 301, 316, 378
financial technology (fintech), 295
Fintech, 316
fisheries subsidies, 54, 74, 88–92, 108, 120
folklore, 359
Food and Agricultural Organization, 89
food security, 120
forced labor, 33

Ford, Henry, 369
foreign direct investment, 92–95, 140, 163–164, 197, 341
Foroohar, Rana, 100, 358
fossil fuels, 144, 155
fossil fuel subsidies, 143–144
Fox, David. M., 352
France, 155, 166
free flow of data, 103–104
free market fundamentalism, 5
free rider, 86, 293
free trade, 4–5, 25–27, 29, 88, 107–108, 122, 191, 238, 243, 343, 401
free trade agreement, 32, 131, 155, 160–162, 171
Friedbacher, Todd, 275
FTAs, 356

G

Gallagher, Mike, 185
GATS Annex on Financial Services, 306
GATT codes, 132
Gender Equity, 141
General Agreement on Tariffs and Trade (GATT), 26, 34, 51, 56, 119, 121, 166, 170, 172, 174, 195, 213, 215–218, 224, 226, 231, 244, 237, 305, 312, 324, 326–327, 347, 371, 385, 405–406
General Agreement on Trade in Services (GATS), 128–129, 132, 216, 305–306, 312, 324, 326–327, 347
generic drugs, 77
genetic resources, 359
Geneva Conventions, 428, 435
Georges Abi-Saab, 223, 400
Germania, 456, 458, 469
Germany, 75, 223, 226
Gibbon, Edward, 459

globalization, 33, 92, 205, 345, 386
Global Ocean Commission, 91
Global Trade & Innovation Policy Alliance, 303
global value chains, 92–93, 260, 369, 374
Goal 3, 75
Goal 9, 98, 360
Gonzales, Alberto R., 429
Gonzalez, Anabel, 82
good faith, 221–223
Goodman, Peter S., 74
goods, 54
Gould, Noah C., 44
Government Procurement Agreement, 125, 129–130, 153, 174, 301, 378
Grant, Michael, 464
Graves, Don, 163–164
Great Firewall, 103
green technology, 143
Greg Ip, 321, 357
Griswold, Daniel, 7
Grundhoefur, Seara, 41

H

Hamilton, Alexander, 192, 245, 256
harmonization, 365–367, 371, 376–377, 379
Hawley, John, 5
Henry Ford, 369
Henry Leland, 369
Hexter, J.H., 456–459, 463–465, 469
Hillman, Jennifer, 41, 81–82
Hilton, George V., 366
Hitler, Adolf, 424
Hogan, Phil, 82
Holmes, Oliver Wendell Jr., 394
Hong Kong, 76, 137, 302
Howse, Robert, 165
Hufabuer, Gary, 44, 47, 368
Hull, Cordell, 195–196

human rights, 50, 196, 412–413, 415, 419, 422–424, 426, 431–432, 438–439, 441
hunger, 189
Hussein, Saddam, 436

I

Iceland, 76, 137, 302
Ikenson, Dan, 265
imports, 28, 32, 43, 86, 90, 172, 215, 229, 243
India, 9, 42, 78–79, 130–133, 172, 190, 240, 302–303
Indigenous communities, 358
Indonesia, 83, 303, 310, 319
Indo-Pacific economic framework, 49
industrial policy, 37–38, 46, 163, 243
Inflation Reduction Act (IRA), 40, 151, 152, 154
Information Technology Agreement, 125, 128–129, 306, 378
innovation, 164–165, 340–341, 343, 360
intangible assets, 100, 339
intellectual property, 14, 46, 104, 123, 195, 200, 224, 239–240, 339, 346, 406
intellectual property rights, 11
International Court of Justice, 370, 389, 427
International Covenant on Civil and Political Rights, 426
International Criminal Tribunal for the Former Yugoslavia, 426
International Energy Agency, 144
International Institute for Sustainable Development, 91, 94, 144, 288
international law, 9–10, 122, 186, 189, 214, 221, 223, 343, 349, 365, 367, 370–371, 380, 421, 424, 427, 430–431

International Monetary Fund, 144
International Office of Epizootics, 368
International Plant Protection Convention, 368
international rule of law, 56
International Standards Organization, 368
International Telecommunications Union, 367
International Telegraph Union, 367, 379
international trade, 2, 6, 26, 33, 97, 100, 104, 140, 183, 192, 204, 213–214, 227, 289, 340
international trade agreements, 186
Internet sovereignty, 102
Internet Treaties, 355
Interstate Commerce Clause, 403
investment facilitation, 14, 74, 92, 94–96, 121, 139–140
investment protectionism, 93
Ip, Greg, 100
ISO, 371
ITU, 371

J

Jackson, John, 259–260, 385
James, Sallie, 371, 374–375
Japan, 42, 44, 49, 56, 91, 152, 155, 160, 162, 173–174, 190, 200, 203, 214, 220, 223, 244, 292, 310, 342, 357, 379
Japan — Alcohol, 389, 392
Jefferson Memorial, 411–412, 420–422, 424, 441
Jefferson, Thomas, 411–412, 415, 419–425, 427, 431, 433, 435–441, 459
Jeremy, Bentham, 344
Johannesson, Louise, 262
Joint Statement Initiative, 132, 295

Index 479

Joint Statement on Electronic Commerce, 292
Jones Act, 154
jus cogens, 427
"Just-in-time" manufacturing, 75

K

Kazakhstan, 54, 74, 89, 94, 108
Kentucky Resolutions of 1798, 425
Kenya, 121, 203, 292
Kissinger, Henry, 370, 374
Korea-US Free Trade Agreement, 238
Kuijper, Peter Jan, 274–276
Kyoto, 430

L

Lacarte-Muro, Julio, 392
Lamy, Pascal, 54, 84, 272
Laos, 310
Lau, Christian, 275
least developed countries (LDCs), 9, 89, 96, 291, 340, 351–352, 354, 359
Leblond, Patrick, 310, 331, 333
Leland, Henry, 369
Lester, Simon, 26, 228–229
Lighthizer, 27, 42, 47, 243–247, 253–254, 257, 264, 268
Lighthizer, Robert, 24, 53, 193, 242
like products, 170
Lincicome, Scott, 35, 37
Lithuania, 51–52, 227
local content requirements, 154
Locke, John, 344
Lockhart, Nicolas, 275
logistics services, 313

M

Macao, 76, 137
Macron, Emmanuel, 153, 159–160

Malaysia, 310
Malmström, Cecilia, 246
Malpass, David, 100
managed trade, 34, 36, 43, 190–191, 202, 207
Manak, Inu, 9, 228–229, 319
Manchin, Joe, 162
manufactured goods, 28, 194, 197
Mao, Zedong, 345
Marshall Islands, 430
Marshall, John, 403
Marx, Karl, 342
Mattoo, Aaditya, 80
Mavroidis, Petros, 262
Mazower, Mark, 367
McCormick, Cyrus, 369
McKinsey Global Institute, 96–97, 138, 289
McRae, Donald, 397–398
medical goods, 74, 79, 81, 83, 108, 137
medical products, 78
Melendez-Ortiz, Ricardo, 92
Melian Dialogue, 235, 237, 256
Melos, 236
Meltzer, Joshua P., 99, 104, 260, 301, 306–307
mercantilism, 237, 243
Mexico, 36, 42, 155, 173, 201, 238, 374
Micro, Small, and Medium-Sized Enterprises (MSMEs), 140–141
Mina, George, 298
Montesquieu, Baron de, 256
Monticello, 420, 440
"most-favored-nation" (MFN) treatment, 52, 93, 119, 122, 190–191, 201, 215, 225, 240, 309
mothers of the "disappeared", 413, 414, 415
multilateral agreements, 120, 124

multilateralism, 121, 125, 145, 182, 189–190, 214, 227, 238, 247, 259, 293
mutual recognition agreements, 376
Myanmar, 82, 310
Myers, Richard B., 418

N
Nabokov, Vladimir, 365–366, 380
Naipaul, V.S., 434–435
Nairobi, 102, 121, 214, 292
National Academy of Sciences, 90
National Association of Home Builders, 40
National Bureau of Economic Research (NBER), 185
National Foreign Trade Council, 264
national security, 42, 44, 187–188, 196, 213–215, 217–219, 225, 230–231, 325, 327
national security defense, 221
national security exception, 173, 213–215, 218–219, 226–227, 229–230, 326
national treatment, 101, 170, 174, 305
NATO, 42, 214–215
Nazis, 424
negotiating history, 389
New Deal, 374
New Zealand, 82, 106, 139, 287–288, 290, 294–295, 302, 310
Nigeria, 430
non-discrimination, 34
North American Free Trade Agreement (NAFTA), 29, 36, 105, 155, 201, 238, 309, 356
North Korea, 241
Norway, 42, 76, 90, 144, 302

O
Obama, Barack, 246, 251–252, 266–267
ocean preservation, 189
oceans, 143
Ogden, Gibbons v., 403
Okonjo-Iweali, Ngozi, 354
Old Testament, 436
O'Neill, Shannon, 84
openness, 204–206, 308
Organisation for Economic Co-operation and Development (OECD), 13, 86, 91–92, 95, 101, 144, 289, 302–303, 329–330, 371
Ottawa Group, 25, 137

P
Pacific Island states, 301
Palau, 430
Paris climate agreement, 203
Peloponnesian War, 236, 256, 436
Peterson Institute for International Economics, 7, 175, 368
Pew Charitable Trusts, 90
pharmaceutical, 76, 77, 136–137
Philippines, 310, 426
plastics pollution, 143–144
Plastics Trade, 143
Plaza de Mayo, 413, 415
Pliny the Younger, 466
plurilateral agreements, 119–121, 124–125, 128–132, 136, 138, 140, 145
plurilateralism, 120–121
policy space, 10, 93
Portman, Rob, 184
Posner, Richard A., 396
precedent, 16, 223
prison labor, 51
productivity, 12, 164–165
protectionism, 2, 23–24, 29, 33, 35, 37, 57, 123, 154, 160, 170, 182, 186–188, 205, 237–239, 243, 264
Ptashkina, Maria, 99, 101, 304
public morals, 51
Putin, Vladimir, 160, 226

Index   481

Q
Qatar, 224
quantitative restrictions, 93

R
race to the bottom, 12, 13
Ramasubramainian, Giridharan, 295
reciprocity, 129
Reference Paper on Regulatory Principles on Basic Telecommunications, 305
Reference Paper on Services Domestic Regulation, 133
Regional Comprehensive Economic Partnership (RCEP), 32, 49, 310, 318, 322, 325, 327–328, 357–359
regional trade agreements (RTAs), 295, 308–309
regulatory protectionism, 371–372, 374–375, 379
Remy, Jan Yves, 275
renewable energies, 153–154
Republic of Korea, 310
reverse consensus rule, 253
Ricardo, David, 12
Roman Empire, 367, 456, 460–464, 467
Roman Republic, 460
Rome Statute, 429
Roosevelt, Franklin, 195, 206
Ross, Wilbur, 240
Rousseau, Jean-Jacques, 466
rule by law, 255–256
rule of law, 57, 181, 183, 186, 192–194, 198–199, 207, 227, 235, 237, 255–257, 265, 271, 277–278, 385, 403, 425, 431, 466–467, 469
rules of origin, 202
Ruse-Khan, Henning Grosse, 355
Russia, 42, 153, 159, 166, 214, 219–221, 225, 227–229, 231–332, 366

Russia — Traffic in Transit dispute, 220–223, 230
Russ, Kadee, 41
Ruta, Michele, 80

S
safeguard measures, 229
Sanders, Bernie, 30
Sandford, Iain, 275
"sanitary and phytosanitary" measures, 11
Saudi Arabia, 224, 228
Sauvant, Karl, 95
Schott, Jeffrey, 368
SCM Agreement, 171–173
section 232 tariffs, 26, 41, 44, 174, 183–187, 207, 239–240
section 301 tariffs, 26, 45, 183–187, 207, 239–240
self-sufficiency, 84
services domestic regulation, 132
Seung Wha Chang, 268
short supply, 80
Sicilian expedition, 436
Singapore, 76, 82, 106, 137, 139, 287–288, 290, 292, 294–297, 301–302, 310
Singapore-Australia Digital Economy Agreement (SADEA), 296, 312–316, 321–322, 324, 328, 330–331
Singapore issues, 93
single undertaking, 121, 378
Slaughter, Anne-Marie, 255
small and medium enterprises (SMEs), 316–317
Smith, Adam, 12, 37, 342, 368–369
softwood lumber, 40
solar energy, 44
source code, 104–105, 107, 310, 327–328
South Africa, 130, 132–133, 302–303

South Korea, 42, 90–91, 152, 155, 160, 162, 173–174, 238, 270, 297, 357
South Sudan, 81
sovereignty, 6–7, 190, 217, 242–245, 257, 260–261, 265, 314, 350
Soviet Union, 217
Spanish Inquisition, 424
special and differential treatment, 9, 406
Spence, Michael, 206
SPS Agreement, 375, 376
Staiger, Robert, 101, 304
standards, 372, 374, 376–377
state-owned enterprises, 195, 200
state trading enterprises, 6
steel and aluminum tariffs, 41–42, 44
Steger, Debra, 383
Stein, Gerturde, 400
Stendhal (Marie-Henri Beyle), 393–394
Stephenson, Matthew, 95
Stoler, Andy, 383
subsidies, 34, 37–38, 40, 44, 46, 83, 88, 90–91, 144, 151–155, 159–160, 165–166, 171–172, 200, 378
Summit for Democracy, 52
supply chain, 40, 75, 79, 81, 84–85, 91, 97, 142, 153, 165, 199, 201, 259, 369–370
Supreme Court of the United States, 374, 425
sustainable agriculture, 143
sustainable development goals (SDGs), 88, 91, 359–360
sustainable tourism, 143
Switzerland, 42, 75–76, 302
Syme, Ronald, 463–464

T

Tacitus, 455–457, 459–469
Taguba, Antonio M., 433
Taguba Report, 433

Tai, Katherine, 24–26, 31, 36, 39, 41–42, 46, 48, 50, 53–55, 57, 59
Taiwan, 51
tariff, 4, 6, 25–26, 34, 37, 39–41, 44–46, 54, 75–76, 81–82, 85, 87, 123, 136–138, 175, 182–186, 188, 191, 198, 229–230, 370
tariff peak, 76
tariffs on electronic commerce, 120
TBT Agreement, 333, 374–376
technical regulations, 11, 195, 373
technology transfer requirements, 46, 104, 165, 327, 340–341, 351–352
Thailand, 302, 310
The Development Dimension, 9
The Garden of Forking Paths, 439–440
the ordeal of change, 206
Thomas, Jason, 357–358
Thucydides, 235–237, 256, 436
Tokyo Round, 123, 132, 372
Toomey, Patrick J., 24–25
torture, 414, 417–419, 423–424, 426, 428–430, 432, 434–436, 438–439
trade, 2, 8
trade and climate change, 142
Trade and Environmental Sustainability, 142
trade facilitation, 83, 94–95, 123
Trade Facilitation Agreement (TFA), 96, 140, 319
trade in environmental goods and services, 142–143
trade in goods, 11, 101, 125, 153, 304–305, 312
trade in services, 11, 101, 125, 130, 133, 304, 312, 378
trade in wildlife, 143
trade liberalization, 145, 181–183, 185, 214, 401
trade promotion authority, 31, 184–185
trade-related investment measures, 93, 96, 151, 153

Index 483

trade secrets, 200
traditional knowledge, 358–359
Trans-Atlantic Trade and Investment Partnership, 238, 377
Trans-Pacific Partnership (TPP), 27, 29, 48, 91, 105, 131, 202–203, 238, 309, 358, 377, 379
Treaty of Westphalia, 3
TRIMS Agreement, 172–173
TRIPS Agreement, 224, 341, 343–346, 348–360
Trump, Donald, 4, 7–8, 14, 16–17, 23–24, 27, 34–35, 38–39, 41–42, 45–47, 49–50, 52–54, 58, 85, 123, 174, 181–182, 184–186, 188, 190, 193, 197–198, 202, 214, 223, 226, 231, 235, 238–239, 241–242, 245–247, 251, 254, 257, 259, 261–262, 265–266, 271–273, 278, 309, 340
Trump tariffs, 45
Trump trade war, 46
Tudor-Stuart England, 457
Turkey, 42
Twain, (Samuel Clemens) Mark, 401
Twelve Tables, 467

U

Ukraine, 123, 160, 214–215, 219, 221, 225
UNCITRAL, 311–312
unilateralism, 50, 238, 259
unilateral tariffs, 182, 185, 197
uniliteral actions, 46
United Kingdom, 44, 152, 203, 314
United Nations, 3, 88–89, 143–144, 241, 258, 360, 367, 426–427, 430
United Nations Charter, 326–327
United Nations Conference on Trade and Development, 373
United Nations Conference on Trade and Development (UNCTAD), 95, 302

United Nations Sustainable Development Goals, 75, 98, 203
United States, 1, 3, 7–8, 10, 12, 15–18, 29, 31, 42, 44, 46, 53, 56, 75–78, 83–84, 89–91, 102, 104, 122–123, 137, 141, 151–155, 159, 161, 163, 166, 170, 172–173, 183, 187–188, 190, 193, 196–197, 199–200, 203, 217–220, 226–229, 231, 235–237, 239–240, 242–245, 248, 251–252, 254, 257, 259, 264–265, 272, 292–293, 308, 314, 328, 340, 342, 366, 374, 377–378, 411, 419, 426, 428, 430
United States Chamber of Commerce, 87
United States Constitution, 10
United States — Line Pipe dispute, 394
United States-Mexico-Canada Agreement (USMCA), 36, 105, 155, 202
United States — Reformulated Gasoline, 388
United States — Steel Safeguards, 391
Universal Declaration of Human Rights, 426
Uruguay, 302
Uruguay round, 42, 121, 123, 132, 136, 187–188, 243–244, 248–249, 253, 276, 290, 346, 372, 384, 387, 389, 405
Uruguay Round Trade Agreements, 29
U.S. Chamber of Commerce, 201
US-China Economic Security and Review Commission, 245
U.S.-China trade, 197
U.S.–EU Trade and Technology Council, 160
US Food and Drug Administration, 78

US-Japan Digital Trade Agreement, 310
US — Tuna II dispute, 333
utilitarianism, 344
Uyghur Forced Labor Prevention Act, 50, 51
Uyghurs, 50

V

Van den Bossche, Peter, 221
Vienna Convention on the Law of Treaties, 248, 274, 388–389, 405
Vietnam, 90, 242, 310
voluntary export restraints, 42, 188

W

war, 197
War Crimes Act of 1996, 428
war on terror, 418–419, 422, 430, 434, 436, 438–439
Warren, Elizabeth, 30
Waters, Richard, 99, 320
Watson, Bill, 371, 374–375
Whitehouse, Sheldon, 185
Whitney, Eli, 369
wildlife, 202
Wilson, Elizabeth, 90
Wolf, Martin, 80
women in trade, 141
worker rights, 50
World Bank, 13, 80, 100, 370, 373
World Economic Forum, 85, 99, 292, 320, 351, 370
World Trade Organization (WTO), 1–3, 23, 52, 73, 78, 89, 119–120, 151–152, 182, 213, 235, 242, 261, 287, 339, 366, 370, 383
Worstall, Tim, 87
WTO agreement, 5–6, 132, 274
WTO Agreement on Safeguards, 42, 395, 403
WTO Agreement on Subsidies and Countervailing Measures, 398
WTO Agreement on Technical Barriers to Trade, 373
WTO Agreement on the Application of Sanitary and Phytosanitary Measures, 373, 406
WTO Agreement on Trade-Related Aspects of Intellectual Property Rights, 340
WTO Agreement on Trade-Related Investment Measures, 140
WTO Anti-Dumping Agreement, 247
WTO Dispute Settlement Body, 273
WTO Dispute Settlement Understanding, 236, 239
WTO Information Technology Agreement, 86
WTO Reference Paper on Telecommunications Services, 315
WTO Rules of Conduct, 249, 251, 266, 386–387, 390
WTO Trade Facilitation Agreement (TFA), 359
Wu, Mark, 99, 102, 104, 290, 301, 308, 320

X

Xi Jinping, 38, 48
Xinjiang, 51
Xinjiang Province, 50

Y

Yamashita, Tomoyuki, 426
Yellen, Janet, 40
Yerxa, Rufus, 264

Z

Zdouc, Werner, 221
zeroing, 247, 249

Printed in the United States
by Baker & Taylor Publisher Services